Test prep when you need it
Take a practice test to gauge your readiness. MyMathLab generates a personalized Study Plan with links to interactive tutorial exercises for those skills you need to review.

Study Plan

Click a chapter below to start practicing, or follow these steps to create a personalized study plan.

① Take a sample test or an assigned test or quiz. Then return to this page.
② Practice the topics you need to study(🖉).
③ To prove mastery(🏆), take another sample test or an assigned test or quiz.

▸ Course Calendar
Legend 🖨 ?
▸ Learn More

Show All 🖉 Show What I Need to Study

➡ Jump to where I worked last

Book Contents for Topics I Need to Study		Correct	Worked	Available Exercises	Time Spent
⊖ Ch 2: Matrices	🖉			32	
⊕ 2.1 Solving Systems of Linear Equations, I	🖉			6	
⊕ 2.2 Solving Systems of Linear Equations, II	🖉			6	
⊕ 2.3 Arithmetic Operations on Matrices	🖉			9	
⊕ 2.4 The Inverse of a Matrix	🖉			2	
⊕ 2.5 The Gauss-Jordan Method for Calculating Inverses	🖉			5	
⊕ 2.6 Input-Output Analysis	🖉			4	
Total: All Chapters		0	0	32	

▸ Show results that created this study plan

This course is based on Goldstein: Finite Mathematics and Its Applications, 9e
Copyright 2008 Pearson Education

Pearson
Tutor Center

Tutors when you need them
MyMathLab users have access to tutoring from the Pearson Math Tutor Center.*
The Tutor Center is staffed by qualified math instructors who provide one-on-one tutoring via toll-free phone, email, and real-time Internet sessions. For more details, visit **www.pearsontutorservices.com**

Proven
Since 2001, more than 3.3 million students at more than 1,800 colleges have used MyMathLab and MathXL. MyMathLab and MathXL provide you with a personalized, interactive learning environment where you can learn at your own pace, measure your progress, and improve your success in this course.

Student Purchasing Options
Talk to your instructor about using MyMathLab or MathXL for this course.

* Pearson Tutor Services are provided by Pearson Higher Education, a division of Pearson Education, for US and Canadian post-secondary students.
Pearson's offer of tutoring service is subject to change without notice.

Finite Mathematics & Its Applications

CUSTOM EDITION FOR WESTERN MICHIGAN UNIVERSITY

Larry J. Goldstein
David I. Schneider
Martha J. Siegel

Taken From:
Finite Mathematics & Its Applications, Tenth Edition
by Larry J. Goldstein, David I. Schneider, and Martha J. Siegel

Custom Publishing

New York   Boston   San Francisco
London   Toronto   Sydney   Tokyo   Singapore   Madrid
Mexico City   Munich   Paris   Cape Town   Hong Kong   Montreal

Cover Art: Courtesy of Art Explosion

Taken from:

Finite Mathematics & Its Applications, Tenth Edition
by Larry J. Goldstein, David I. Schneider, and Martha J. Siegel
Copyright © 2010, 2007, 2004, 2001, 1998, 1995, 1991, 1988, 1984, 1980 by Pearson Education, Inc.
Published by Prentice Hall
Upper Saddle River, New Jersey 07458

This special edition published in cooperation with Pearson Custom Publishing.

Printed in the United States of America

10 9 8 7 6 5 4 3

2009361207

WH

Pearson
Custom Publishing
is a division of

www.pearsonhighered.com

ISBN 10: 0-558-36888-3
ISBN 13: 978-0-558-36888-3

CONTENTS

The book divides naturally into four parts. The first part consists of linear mathematics: linear equations, matrices, and linear programming (Chapters 1-4); the second part is devoted to probability and statistics (Chapters 5-7); the third part covers topics utilizing the ideas of the other parts (Chapters 8-10); and the fourth part explores key topics from discrete mathematics that are sometimes covered in the modern finite mathematics curriculum (Chapters 11-12).

11 Difference Equations and Mathematical Models 525

This work is the tenth edition of our text for the traditional finite mathematics course taught to first- and second-year college students, especially those majoring in business and the social and biological sciences. Finite mathematics courses exhibit tremendous diversity with respect to both content and approach. Therefore, in developing this book, we incorporated a wide range of topics from which an instructor may design a curriculum, as well as a high degree of flexibility in the order in which the topics may be presented. For the mathematics of finance, we even allow for flexibility in the approach of the presentation.

The Series

This text is part of a series consisting of three texts: *Finite Mathematics & Its Applications*, *Calculus & Its Applications*, and *Brief Calculus & Its Applications*. All three titles are available for purchase in three formats: printed text, eBook and as an eBook within the MyMathLab online course.

Topics Included

This edition has more material than can be covered in most one-semester courses. Therefore, the instructor can structure the course to the students' needs and interests. The book divides naturally into four parts. The first part consists of linear mathematics: linear equations, matrices, and linear programming (Chapters 1–4); the second part is devoted to probability and statistics (Chapters 5–7); the third part covers topics utilizing the ideas of the other parts (Chapters 8–10); and the fourth part explores key topics from discrete mathematics that are sometimes included in the modern finite mathematics curriculum (Chapters 11 and 12). We prefer to begin with linear mathematics since it makes for a smooth transition from high school mathematics and leads quickly to interesting applications, especially linear programming. Our preference notwithstanding, the instructor may begin this book with Chapter 5 (Sets and Counting) and then do either the linear mathematics or the probability and statistics.

Minimal Prerequisites

Because of great variation in student preparation, we keep formal prerequisites to a minimum. We assume only a first year of high school algebra. Furthermore, we review, as needed, those topics that are typically weak spots for students.

Trusted Features

In this edition, we attempt to maintain our popular student-oriented approach throughout and, in particular, by the following features:

Relevant and Varied Applications

We provide realistic applications that illustrate the uses of finite mathematics in other disciplines. The reader may survey the variety of applications by referring to the Index of Applications. Wherever possible, we attempt to use applications to motivate the mathematics. For example, the concept of linear programming is introduced in Chapter 3 via a discussion of production options for a factory with labor limitations.

Plentiful Examples

We include 353 worked examples, many more than is customary. Furthermore, we include computational details to enhance comprehension by students whose basic skills are weak.

Exercises to Meet All Student Needs

The 3171 exercises comprise about one-quarter of the book, the most important part of the text in our opinion. The exercises at the ends of the sections are usually arranged in the order in which the text proceeds, so that homework assignments may be made easily after only part of a section is discussed. Interesting applications and more challenging problems tend to be located near the ends of the exercise sets. Supplementary exercises at the end of each chapter amplify the other exercise sets and provide cumulative exercises that require skills acquired from earlier chapters. Answers to the odd-numbered exercises are included at the back of the book.

Exercises from Professional Exams

We have included questions similar to those found on CPA and GMAT exams to further illustrate the relevance of the material in the course. These multiple-choice questions are identified with the notation **PE**. Examples of this can be found in Chapter 1, pages 34–35.

Practice Problems

The Practice Problems are a popular and useful feature of the book. They are carefully selected exercises located at the end of each section, just before the exercise set. Complete solutions follow the exercise set. The Practice Problems often focus on points that are potentially confusing or are likely to be overlooked. We recommend that the reader seriously attempt to do the practice problems and study their solutions before moving on to the exercises.

Use of Technology

Although the use of technology is optional for this text, many of the topics can be enhanced with graphing calculators, spreadsheets, and mathematical software. Whenever relevant, we explicitly show the student how to use graphing calculators and spreadsheets effectively to assist in understanding the fundamental concepts of the course. In addition, the text contains appendices on the fundamentals of using graphing calculators and spreadsheets. The powerful mathematical software Explorations in Finite Mathematics is available for download from the Pearson website (www.pearsoned.com/goldstein). Many sections contain specially designed technology exercises intended to be solved with one of these technologies.

In our discussions of graphing calculators, we specifically refer to the TI-83/84 Plus calculators and the TI-89 since these are the most popular graphing calculators. Therefore, most students will have a book customized to their calculator. Students with other graphing calculators can consult their guidebooks to learn how to make adjustments. Had the calculator material been written generically, *every* student would have to make adjustments. For the same reasons, the discussions of electronic spreadsheets refer to Microsoft Excel.

End-of-Chapter Study Aids

Near the end of each chapter is a set of questions labeled Review of Fundamental Concepts that help the student recall the key ideas of the chapter and focus on the relevance of these concepts. Each chapter also contains a detailed summary of the important definitions and results from the chapter. Finally, each chapter has a sample test that can be used by the student to help determine if he or she has mastered the important concepts of the chapter.

Chapter Projects

Each chapter has an extended project that can be used as an in-class or out-of-class group project, or special assignment. These projects develop interesting applications or enhance key concepts of the chapters. For example, the Chapter 2 project, entitled "Population Dynamics," focuses on how logging directly affects the spotted owl population. This environmental application is one that will have relevance for students.

New to This Edition

Among the changes in this edition, the following are the most significant.

1. *Additional Exercises and Updated Data* We have added 217 new exercises and have updated the real-world data appearing in 55 exercises and examples.

2. *Algebra Comments* The steps performed when solving linear equations and inequalities are explained with brief comments.

3. *Transition Diagrams* The discussion of Markov processes has been enhanced by the use of transition diagrams.

4. *Financial Computations* The computations for compound interest, annuities, and mortgages in Chapter 10 (The Mathematics of Finance) are carried out with formulas rather than with tables.

5. *TVM Solver* The use of the TI-83/84 Plus' TVM Solver financial calculator is explained.

6. *More About Mortgages* A discussion of interest-only and adjustable-rate mortgages has been added to Section 10.4 (Personal Financial Decisions). This topic is especially relevant due to the role these mortgages played in precipitating the foreclosure crisis.

7. *Excel Upgrade* Although the use of spreadsheets is optional, many students are familiar with Excel and use it to enhance their understanding of the topics presented in the textbook. The discussion of Excel has been expanded to include Excel 2007.

Program Supplements

For Students

Student's Solutions Manual (ISBN: 0-321-59898-9)
Fully worked solutions to odd-numbered exercises

DVD Lecture Videos (ISBN: 0-321-57734-5)
A comprehensive set of topical videos, in which examples for each topic are worked out by an instructor. The videos provide excellent support for students who require additional assistance, for distance learning and self-paced programs, or for students who missed class.

For Instructors

Instructor's Edition (ISBN: 0-321-60013-4)
This version of the text includes answers to all exercises presented in the book.

Instructor Resource Center
All instructor resources can be downloaded from www.pearsonhighered.com/irc. This is a password-protected site that requires instructors to set up an account or, alternatively, instructor resources can be ordered from your Pearson Higher Education sales representative. Instructors may use their instructor's log-in from MyMathLab to access the Instructor Resource Center.

Instructor's Solutions Manual (ISBN: 0-321-59897-0)
Fully worked solutions to every textbook exercise.

TestGen®
TestGen (www.pearsonhighered.com/testgen) enables instructors to build, edit, print, and administer tests using a computerized bank of questions developed to cover all of the text objectives. TestGen is algorithmically based, allowing instructors to create multiple but equivalent versions of the same question or test with the click of a button. Instructors can also modify test bank questions or add new ones. Tests can be printed or administered online. The software and testbank are available for download from Pearson Education's online catalog.

PowerPoint Lecture Slides
Fully editable and printable slides that follow the textbook. Use during lecture or post to a Web site in an online course. For download from the Instructor Resource Center and available within MyMathLab.

MyMathLab® Online Course (access code required)
MyMathLab is a series of text-specific, easily customizable online courses for Pearson Education's textbooks in mathematics and statistics. Powered by CourseCompass™ (our online teaching and learning environment) and MathXL® (our online homework, tutorial, and assessment system), MyMathLab gives you the tools you need to deliver all or a portion of your course online, whether students are in a lab setting or working from home. MyMathLab provides a rich and flexible set of course materials, featuring free-response exercises that are algorithmically generated for unlimited practice and mastery. Students can also use online tools, such as video lectures, animations, and a multimedia textbook, to independently improve their understanding and performance. Instructors can use MyMathLab's homework and test managers to select and assign online exercises correlated to the textbook, and they can also create and assign their own online exercises and import TestGen tests for added flexibility. MyMathLab's online gradebook—designed specifically for mathematics and statistics—automatically tracks students' homework and test results and gives the instructor control over how to calculate final grades. Instructors can also add offline (paper-and-pencil) grades to the gradebook. MyMathLab also includes access to the **Pearson Tutor Center** (www.pearsontutorservices.com). The Tutor Center is staffed by qualified mathematics instructors who provide textbook-specific tutoring for students via toll-free phone, fax, email, and interactive Web sessions. MyMathLab is available to qualified adopters. For more information, visit our website at www.mymathlab.com or contact your sales representative.

MathXL® Online Course (access code required)
MathXL® is a powerful online homework, tutorial, and assessment system that accompanies Pearson Education's textbooks in mathematics or statistics. With MathXL, instructors can create, edit, and assign online homework and tests using algorithmically generated exercises correlated to the textbook's objectives. They can also create and assign their own online exercises and import TestGen tests for added flexibility. All student work is tracked in MathXL's online gradebook. Students can take chapter tests in MathXL and receive personalized study plans based on their test results. The study plan diagnoses weaknesses and links students directly to tutorial exercises for the objectives they need to study and retest. Students can also access supplemental animations and video clips directly from selected exercises. MathXL is available to qualified adopters. For more information, visit our website at www.mathxl.com, or contact your Pearson sales representative.

Explorations in Finite Mathematics
Built from the ground up by David Schneider (University of Maryland), *Explorations in Finite Mathematics*, which runs on both Macintosh and PC computers, enhances the understanding of many topics covered in the text through the visualization of said topics. Part One of this software covers linear mathematics topics involving linear equations, linear inequalities, and matrices. Students will be able to perform routines such as Gauss–Jordan elimination, matrix operations and inversions, the simplex method, and Markov chains. Part Two contains routines for Venn diagrams, computation of combinations, permutations and factorials, statistical analysis of data, financial calculations and much more. *Explorations in Finite Mathematics* is available for download from the Website www.pearsoned.com/goldstein.

Acknowledgments

While writing this book, we have received assistance from many persons. And our heartfelt thanks go out to them all. Especially, we should like to thank the following reviewers, who took the time and energy to share their ideas, preferences, and often their enthusiasm, with us.

Reviewers of the Tenth Edition

Michelle DeDeo, *University of North Florida*

Helen M. Doerr, *Syracuse University*

Russell E. Goodman, *Central College*

Barry J. Griffiths, *University of Central Florida*

Klara Grodzinsky, *Georgia Institute of Technology*

Phillip Miller, *Indiana University Southeast*

Erika Miller, *Towson University*

Rennie Mirollo, *Boston College*

Reviewers of Earlier Editions

Josephine Battaglia, *Pennsylvania State University*

Karl A. Beres, *Ripon College*

Larry G. Blaine, *Plymouth State University*

William D. Blair, *Northern Illinois University*

Brenda Bloomgarden, *Chesapeake College*

Paul Boisvert, *Robert Morris College*

Bart Braden, *Northern Kentucky University*

Stephen H. Brown, *Auburn University*

Robert Carmignani, *University of Missouri*

Eric Chandler, *Randolph-Macon College*

James P. Coughlin, *Towson University*

Sam Councilman, *California State University, Long Beach*

D.R. Dunninger, *Michigan State University*

Karen J. Edwards, *Paul Smith's College*

Theodore Faticoni, *Fordham University*

Gary W. Frick, *The College of Southern Maryland*

Robert Gusalnick, *University of South Carolina*

Juan Gatica, *University of Iowa*

Ruthanne Harre, *Missouri Valley College*

Eric Heinz, *Catonsville Community College*

Russell Hendel, *Towson University*

Thomas J. Hill, *University of Oklahoma, Norman*

James F. Hurley, *University of Connecticut*

Ralph James, *California State University at Stanislaus*

Donald A. Jones, *Oregon State University*

Karla Karstens, *University of Vermont*

Philip Kutzko, *University of Iowa*

Peter Majumdar, *Indiana-Purdue University at Fort Wayne*

Manoug Manougian, *University of South Florida*

Joan McCarter, *Arizona State University*

Jeanette L. McGillicuddy, *River College*

Michael McLane, *Purdue University*

Carl D. Meyer, Jr., *North Carolina State University*

Juan Migliore, *University of Notre Dame*

Charles J. Miller, *Foothill Community College*

Donald E. Myers, *University of Arizona, Tempe*

Richard O'Malley, *University of Wisconsin at Milwaukee*

Roger Osborn, *University of Texas, Austin*

Hiram Paley, *Univeristy of Illinois, Urbana-Champaign*

Mary Pearce, *Austin Community College*

Richard Pellerin, *Northern Virginia Community College*

Dennis Pence, *Western Michigan University*

Richard Porter, *Northeastern University*

William Ramaley, *Fort Lewis College*

Henry J. Ricardo, *Medgar Evers College of the City University of New York*

Arthur Rosenthal, *Salem State College*

Linda Schultz, *McHenry County College*

Elisabeth Schuster, *DeVry Institute of Technology*

Randy Schwartz, *Schoolcraft College*

Joseph Stampfli, *Indiana University*

Phil Steitz, *Beloit College*

Robin G. Symonds, *Indiana University at Kokomo*

Martin C. Tangora, *University of Illinois, Chicago*

Elizabeth Teles, *Montgomery College*

James C. Thorpe, *University of Missouri, St. Louis*

David C. Vella, *Skidmore College*

Tan Vovan, *Suffolk University*

Hugh Walters, *Contra Costa College*

Chungkuang Wang, *Fashion Institute of Technology*

Frank Warner, *University of Pennsylvania*

Rebecca Wells, *Henderson Community College*

Peter Williams, *California State University at San Bernardino*

Cynthia Wilson, *Life College*

We also thank the many people at Pearson who have contributed to the success of this book. We appreciate the efforts of the production, art, manufacturing, marketing, and sales departments. We are grateful to Anthony Gagliardi, Damon Demas, Paul Lorczak, Helen Doerr, and Haizhang Zhang for their careful creation and thorough checking of solutions to exercises. Our sincere thanks to Erica O'Leary for her assistance throughout the revision of the book and Peter Rosenbaum for his assistance with the finance chapter. Production editor Bob Walters did a fantastic job keeping the book on schedule. The authors wish to extend special thanks to our editors Christine O'Brien and Chuck Synovec, and our typesetter Dennis Kletzing. Christine and Chuck's help in planning and executing this new edition was greatly appreciated. Dennis' considerable skills and congenial manner made for an uncomplicated and pleasant production process.

If you have comments or suggestions, we would like to hear from you. We hope that you enjoy using this book as much as we have enjoyed writing it.

Larry J. Goldstein
larrygoldstein@comcast.net

David I. Schneider
dis@math.umd.edu

Martha J. Siegel
msiegel@towson.edu

LINEAR EQUATIONS AND STRAIGHT LINES

Many applications considered later in this text involve linear equations and their geometric counterparts—straight lines. So let us begin by studying the basic facts about these two important notions.

1.1 Coordinate Systems and Graphs

Often we can display numerical data by using a **Cartesian coordinate system** on either a line or a plane. We construct a Cartesian coordinate system on a line by choosing an arbitrary point O (the **origin**) on the line and a unit of distance along the line. We then assign to each point on the line a number that reflects its directed distance from the origin. Positive numbers refer to points on the right of the origin, negative numbers to points on the left. In Fig. 1 we have drawn a Cartesian coordinate system on the line and have labeled a number of points with their corresponding numbers. Each point on the line corresponds to a number (positive, negative, or zero).

Figure 1

1

A Cartesian coordinate system may be used to numerically describe points on a line. In a similar fashion, we can construct a Cartesian coordinate system to numerically locate points on a plane. Each point of the plane is identified by a pair of numbers (a, b). To reach the point (a, b), begin at the origin, move a units in the x-direction (to the right if a is positive, to the left if a is negative), and then move b units in the y direction (up if b is positive, down if b is negative). The numbers a and b are called, respectively, the **x-** and **y-coordinates** of the point.

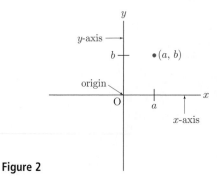

Figure 2

EXAMPLE 1

Plotting points Plot the following points.

(a) $(2, 1)$ (b) $(-1, 3)$ (c) $(-2, -1)$ (d) $(0, -3)$

Solution (a)

(b)

(c)

(d)

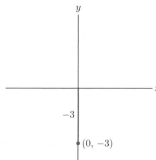

Now Try Exercise 1

In many applications one encounters equations expressing relationships between variables x and y. To any equation in x and y one can associate a certain collection of points in the plane. Namely, the point (a, b) belongs to the collection provided that the equation is satisfied when we substitute a for each occurrence of x and substitute b for each occurrence of y. This collection of points is usually a curve of some sort and is called the **graph of the equation**.

EXAMPLE 2

Solution of an equation Are the following points on the graph of the equation $8x - 4y = 4$?

(a) $(3, 5)$ **(b)** $(5, 17)$

Solution **(a)** Substitute 3 for each occurrence of x and 5 for each occurrence of y in the equation.

$$8x - 4y = 4$$
$$8 \cdot 3 - 4 \cdot 5 = 4$$
$$24 - 20 = 4$$
$$4 = 4$$

Since the equation is satisfied, the point $(3, 5)$ is on the graph of the equation.

(b) Replace x by 5 and y by 17 in the equation.

$$8x - 4y = 4$$
$$8 \cdot 5 - 4 \cdot 17 = 4$$
$$40 - 68 = 4$$
$$-28 = 4$$

The equation is not satisfied, so the point $(5, 17)$ is *not* on the graph of the equation.

Now Try Exercises 11 and 13

EXAMPLE 3

Graph of an equation Sketch the graph of the equation $y = 2x - 1$.

Solution First find some points on the graph by choosing various values for x and determining the corresponding values for y:

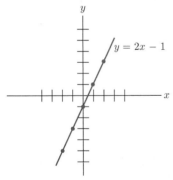

x	y
-2	$2 \cdot (-2) - 1 = -5$
-1	$2 \cdot (-1) - 1 = -3$
0	$2 \cdot 0 - 1 = -1$
1	$2 \cdot 1 - 1 = 1$
2	$2 \cdot 2 - 1 = 3$

Figure 3

Now Try Exercise 27

Thus the points $(-2, -5)$, $(-1, -3)$, $(0, -1)$, $(1, 1)$, and $(2, 3)$ are all on the graph. Plot these points (Fig. 3). It appears that the points lie on a straight line. By taking more values for x and plotting the corresponding points, it is easy to become convinced that the graph of $y = 2x - 1$ is indeed a straight line.

EXAMPLE 4

Graph of an equation Sketch the graph of the equation $x = 3$.

Solution It is clear that the x-coordinate of any point on the graph must be 3. The y-coordinate can be anything. So some points on the graph are $(3, 0)$, $(3, 5)$, $(3, -4)$, $(3, -2)$. Again the graph is a straight line (Fig. 4 on the next page).

Now Try Exercise 29

EXAMPLE 5

Graph of an equation Sketch the graph of the equation $x = a$, where a is any given number.

Figure 4

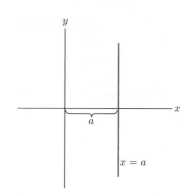

Figure 5

Solution   The x-coordinate of any point on the graph must be a. Reasoning as in Example 4, the graph is a vertical line a units away from the y-axis (Fig. 5). (Of course, if a is negative, then the line lies to the left of the y-axis.) ▪

Now Try Exercise 33

The equations in Examples 2 to 5 are all special cases of the general equation

$$cx + dy = e,$$

corresponding to particular choices of the constants c, d, and e. Any such equation is called a **linear equation in general form** (in the two variables x and y). A linear equation also can be put into standard form.

> **DEFINITION** The **standard form** of a linear equation is obtained by solving for y if y appears and for x if y does not appear. In the former case the standard form looks like
>
> $$y = mx + b \quad (m, b \text{ constants}),$$
>
> whereas in the latter it looks like
>
> $$x = a \quad (a \text{ constant}).$$

EXAMPLE 6

Standard form of a linear equation   Find the standard form of the following equations.

(a) $8x - 4y = 4$ (b) $2x + 3y = 3$ (c) $2x = 6$

Solution   (a) Since y appears, we obtain the standard form by solving for y in terms of x:

$$8x - 4y = 4$$
$$-4y = -8x + 4 \quad \text{Subtract } 8x \text{ from both sides.}$$
$$y = 2x - 1 \quad \text{Divide both sides by } -4.$$

Thus the standard form of $8x - 4y = 4$ is $y = 2x - 1$—that is, $y = mx + b$ with $m = 2$, $b = -1$.

(b) Again y occurs, so we solve for y:

$$2x + 3y = 3$$
$$3y = -2x + 3 \quad \text{Subtract } 2x \text{ from both sides.}$$
$$y = -\tfrac{2}{3}x + 1 \quad \text{Divide both sides by } 3.$$

So the standard form is $y = -(2/3)x + 1$. Here $m = -2/3$ and $b = 1$.

(c) Here y does not occur, so we solve for x:

$$2x = 6$$

$$x = 3 \quad \text{Divide both sides by 2.}$$

Now Try Exercise 19
Thus the standard form of $2x = 6$ is $x = 3$—that is, $x = a$, where a is 3.   ∎

We have seen that any linear equation has one of the two standard forms $y = mx + b$ and $x = a$. From Example 5, the graph of $x = a$ is a vertical line, a units from the y-axis. What can be said about the graph of $y = mx + b$? In Example 3, we saw that the graph is a straight line in the special case $y = 2x - 1$. Actually, the graph of $y = mx + b$ is always a straight line. To sketch the graph, we need only locate two points. Two convenient points to locate are the **intercepts**, the points where the line crosses the x- and y-axes. When x is 0, $y = m \cdot 0 + b = b$. Thus $(0, b)$ is on the graph of $y = mx + b$ and is the y-intercept of the line. The x-intercept is found as follows: A point on the x-axis has y-coordinate 0. So the x-coordinate of the x-intercept can be found by setting $y = 0$—that is, $mx + b = 0$—and solving this equation for x.

EXAMPLE 7

Graph of a linear equation   Sketch the graph of the equation $y = 2x - 1$.

Solution   Here $m = 2$, $b = -1$. The y-intercept is $(0, b) = (0, -1)$. To find the x-intercept, we must solve $2x - 1 = 0$. But then $2x = 1$ and $x = 1/2$. So the x-intercept is $(1/2, 0)$. Plot the two points $(0, -1)$ and $(1/2, 0)$, and draw the straight line through them

Now Try Exercise 23
(Fig. 6).   ∎

NOTE ▶   The line in Example 7 had different x- and y-intercepts. Two other circumstances can occur, however. First, the two intercepts may be the same, as in $y = 3x$. Second, there may be no x-intercept, as in $y = 1$. In both of these circumstances, we must plot some point other than an intercept in order to graph the line.   ∎

To summarize,

Figure 6

To graph the equation $y = mx + b$,

1. Plot the y-intercept $(0, b)$.

2. Plot some other point. [The most convenient choice is often the x-intercept $(x, 0)$, where x is determined by setting $y = 0$ and solving for x.]

3. Draw a line through the two points.

The next example gives an application of linear equations.

EXAMPLE 8

Linear depreciation   For tax purposes, businesses must keep track of the current values of each of their assets. A common mathematical model is to assume that the current value y is related to the age x of the asset by a linear equation. A moving company buys a 40-foot van with a useful lifetime of 5 years. After x months of use, the value y of the van is estimated by the linear equation

$$y = 25{,}000 - 400x.$$

(a) Sketch the graph of this linear equation.

(b) What is the value of the van after 5 years?

(c) When will the value of the van be \$15,000?

(d) What economic interpretation can be given to the y-intercept of the graph?

Solution **(a)** The y-intercept is $(0, 25{,}000)$. To find the x-intercept, set $y = 0$ and solve for x.

$$0 = 25{,}000 - 400x \qquad \text{Set } y = 0.$$
$$400x = 25{,}000 \qquad \text{Add } 400x \text{ to both sides.}$$
$$x = 62.5 \qquad \text{Divide both sides by 400.}$$

The x-intercept is $(62.5, 0)$. The graph of the linear equation is sketched in Fig. 7. Note how the value decreases as the age of the van increases. The value of the van reaches 0 after 62.5 months. Note also that we have sketched only the portion of the graph that has physical meaning, namely the portion for x between 0 and 62.5.

(b) After 5 years (or 60 months), the value of the van is

$$y = 25{,}000 - 400(60) = 25{,}000 - 24{,}000 = 1000.$$

Since the useful life of the van is 5 years, this value represents the *salvage value* of the van.

(c) Set the value of y to 15,000 and solve for x.

$$15{,}000 = 25{,}000 - 400x \qquad \text{Set } y = 15{,}000.$$
$$400x + 15{,}000 = 25{,}000 \qquad \text{Add } 400x \text{ to both sides.}$$
$$400x = 10{,}000 \qquad \text{Subtract } 15{,}000 \text{ from both sides.}$$
$$x = 25 \qquad \text{Divide both sides by 400.}$$

The value of the van will be \$15,000 after 25 months.

(d) The y-intercept corresponds to the value of the van at $x = 0$ months, that is, the initial value of the van, \$25,000. ∎

Figure 7

Now Try Exercise 41

INCORPORATING TECHNOLOGY

GC[1]   Appendices B and D show how to obtain a graph of a linear equation of the form $y = mx + b$, find coordinates of points on the line, and determine intercepts.

Vertical lines can be drawn on a TI-83/84 Plus with the Vertical command from the DRAW menu. To draw the vertical line $x = k$, go to the home screen, press 2nd [DRAW] **4** to display the word **Vertical**, type in the value of k, and press ENTER. With the TI-89, the vertical line $x = k$ can be drawn by entering **LineVert k** into the home screen. (The word **LineVert** either can be typed into the entry line or selected from the CATALOG menu.) ∎

Practice Problems 1.1

1. Plot the point $(500, 200)$.

2. Is the point $(4, -7)$ on the graph of the linear equation $2x - 3y = 1$? Is the point $(5, 3)$?

3. Graph the linear equation $5x + y = 10$.

4. Graph the straight line $y = 3x$.

---

[1]GC is an abbreviation for "Graphing Calculator." Throughout this text we discuss specifics of using TI-83/84 Plus and TI-89 calculators. Additional details are provided in Appendices B and D. For the specifics of using other calculators, consult the guidebook that comes with the calculator.

EXERCISES 1.1

In Exercises 1–8, plot the given point.

1. $(2, 3)$ **2.** $(-1, 4)$

3. $(0, -2)$ **4.** $(2, 0)$

5. $(-2, 1)$ **6.** $\left(-1, -\frac{5}{2}\right)$

7. $(-20, 40)$ **8.** $(25, 30)$

9. PE[2] In Fig. 8, the point P has coordinates

     (a) $(5, 3)$ **(b)** $(-3, 5)$ **(c)** $(-5, 3)$

     (d) $(3, -5)$ **(e)** $(5, -3)$

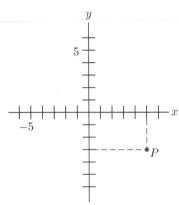

Figure 8

10. PE In Fig. 9, the point P has coordinates

     (a) $(-4, 5)$ **(b)** $(5, -4)$ **(c)** $(10, -8)$

     (d) $(-8, 10)$ **(e)** $(4, 5)$

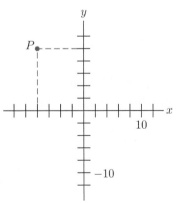

Figure 9

In Exercises 11–14, determine if the point is on the graph of the equation $-2x + \frac{1}{3}y = -1$.

11. $(1, 3)$ **12.** $(2, 6)$ **13.** $\left(\frac{1}{2}, 3\right)$ **14.** $\left(\frac{1}{3}, -1\right)$

In Exercises 15–18, each linear equation is in the standard form $y = mx + b$. Identify m and b.

15. $y = 5x + 8$ **16.** $y = -2x - 6$

17. $y = 3$ **18.** $y = \frac{2}{3}x$

In Exercises 19–22, put the linear equations into standard form.

19. $14x + 7y = 21$ **20.** $x - y = 3$

21. $3x = 5$ **22.** $-\frac{1}{2}x + \frac{2}{3}y = 10$

In Exercises 23–26, find the x-intercept and the y-intercept of each line.

23. $y = -4x + 8$ **24.** $y = 5$

25. $x = 7$ **26.** $y = -8x$

In Exercises 27–34, graph the given linear equation.

27. $y = \frac{1}{3}x - 1$ **28.** $y = 2x$ **29.** $y = \frac{5}{2}$

30. $x = 0$ **31.** $3x + 4y = 24$ **32.** $x + y = 3$

33. $x = -\frac{5}{2}$ **34.** $\frac{1}{2}x - \frac{1}{3}y = -1$

35. Which of the following equations describe the same line as the equation $2x + 3y = 6$?

     (a) $4x + 6y = 12$ **(b)** $y = -\frac{2}{3}x + 2$

     (c) $x = 3 - \frac{3}{2}y$ **(d)** $6 - 2x - y = 0$

     (e) $y = 2 - \frac{2}{3}x$ **(f)** $x + y = 1$

36. Which of the following equations describe the same line as the equation $\frac{1}{2}x - 5y = 1$?

     (a) $2x - \frac{1}{5}y = 1$ **(b)** $x = 5y + 2$

     (c) $2 - 5x + 10y = 0$ **(d)** $y = .1(x - 2)$

     (e) $10y - x = -2$ **(f)** $1 + .5x = 2 + 5y$

37. Each of the lines L_1, L_2, and L_3 in Fig. 10 is the graph of one of the equations (a), (b), and (c). Match each of the equations with its corresponding line.

     (a) $x + y = 3$ **(b)** $2x - y = -2$ **(c)** $x = 3y + 3$

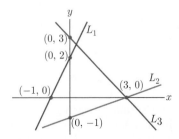

Figure 10

---

[2]Exercises denoted PE are similar to questions appearing in professional exams such as GMAT and CPA exams.

38. Which of the following equations is graphed in Fig. 11?

(a) $x + y = 3$ (b) $y = x - 1$ (c) $2y = x + 3$

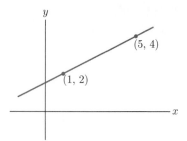

Figure 11

39. Heating Water The temperature of water in a heating tea kettle rises according to the equation $y = 30x + 72$, where y is the temperature (in degrees Fahrenheit) x minutes after the kettle was put on the burner.

(a) What physical interpretation can be given to the y-intercept of the graph?

(b) What will the temperature of the water be after 3 minutes?

(c) After how many minutes will the water be at its boiling point of $212°$?

40. Deforestation The amount of tropical rainforest area in Central America has been decreasing steadily in recent years. The amount y (in thousands of square miles) x years after 1969 is estimated by the linear equation $y = \left(-\frac{25}{8}\right)x + 130$.

(a) Sketch the graph of this linear equation.

(b) What interpretation can be given to the y-intercept of the graph?

(c) When were there 80,000 square miles of tropical rain forests?

(d) Approximately how large was the tropical rainforest in the year 2007?

41. Cigarette Consumption The worldwide consumption of cigarettes has been increasing steadily in recent years. The number of trillions of cigarettes, y, purchased x years after 1960, is estimated by the linear equation $y = .075x + 2.5$.

(a) Sketch the graph of this linear equation.

(b) What interpretation can be given to the y-intercept of the graph?

(c) When were there 4 trillion cigarettes sold?

(d) If this trend continues, how many cigarettes will be sold in the year 2020?

42. Ecotourism Income In a certain developing country, ecotourism income has been increasing in recent years. The income y (in thousands of dollars) x years after 2000 can be modeled by $y = 1.15x + 14$.

(a) Sketch the graph of this linear equation.

(b) What interpretation can be given to the y-intercept of this graph?

(c) When was there $20,000 in ecotourism income?

(d) If this trend continues, how much ecotourism income will there be in 2016?

43. Insurance Rates Yearly car insurance rates have been increasing steadily in the last few years. The rate y (in dollars) for a small car x years after 1997 can be modeled by $y = 60x + 678$.

(a) Sketch the graph of this linear equation.

(b) What interpretation can be given to the y-intercept of this graph?

(c) What was the yearly rate in 2000?

(d) If this trend continues, when will the yearly rate be $1578?

44. College Freshmen The percent of college freshmen who enter college intending to major in general biology has increased steadily in recent years.[3] The percent, y, who entered college x years after 2000 intending to major in general biology is approximated by the linear equation $y = .15x + 3.85$.

(a) What interpretation can be given to the y-intercept of the graph of the equation?

(b) Approximately what percent of college freshmen entering in 2005 intended to major in general biology?

(c) In what year did approximately 4.9% of entering college freshmen intend to major in general biology?

45. College Freshmen The percent of college freshmen who smoke has decreased steadily in recent years[3]. The percent, y, who smoked x years after 2000 is approximated by the linear equation $y = -\left(\frac{26}{35}\right)x + 10$.

(a) What interpretation can be given to the y-intercept of the graph of the equation?

(b) Approximately what percent of college freshmen smoked in 2005?

(c) In what year did approximately 4.8% of college freshmen smoke?

46. Find an equation of the line having x-intercept $(16, 0)$ and y-intercept $(0, 8)$.

47. Find an equation of the line having x-intercept $(.6, 0)$ and y-intercept $(0, .9)$.

48. Find an equation of the line having y-intercept $(0, 5)$ and x-intercept $(4, 0)$.

49. What is the equation of the x-axis?

50. Can a line have more than one x-intercept?

---

[3] *The American Freshman: National Norms*; American Council on Education, University of California-Los Angeles.

51. What is the general form of the equation of a line that is parallel to the x-axis?

52. Give the x- and y-intercepts of the line $\frac{x}{a} + \frac{y}{b} = 1$.

*Every straight line has an equation of the form $cx + dy = e$, where not both c and d are 0. Such an equation is said to be a **general form** of the equation of the line. In Exercises 53–58, find a general form of the given equation.*

53. $y = 2x + 3$ **54.** $x = 5$ **55.** $x = -3$

56. $y = 3x - 4$ **57.** $y = -\frac{2}{3}x - 5$ **58.** $y = 4x - \frac{5}{6}$

59. Show that the straight line with x-intercept $(a, 0)$ and y-intercept $(0, b)$, where a and b are not both zero, has $bx + ay = ab$ as a general form of its equation.

60. Use the result of Exercise 59 to find a general form of the equation of the line having x-intercept $(5, 0)$ and y-intercept $(0, 6)$.

In Exercises 61–68, give the equation of a line having the stated property. Note: There are many answers to each exercise.

61. x-intercept $(9, 0)$ **62.** y-intercept $(0, 10)$

63. passes through the point $(-2, 5)$

64. passes through the point $(3, -3)$

65. crosses the positive part of the y-axis

66. passes through the origin

67. crosses the negative part of the x-axis

68. crosses the positive part of the x-axis

Exercises 69–74 require the use of a graphing calculator.
In Exercises 69–72, (a) graph the line in the standard window $[-10, 10]$ by $[-10, 10]$, (b) use the calculator to find the y-coordinate of the point on the line with x-coordinate 2, (c) use the calculator to determine the two intercepts.

69. $y = -3x + 6$ **70.** $y = .25x - 2$

71. $3y - 2x = 9$ **72.** $2y + 5x = 8$

73. Determine an appropriate window and graph the line $2y + x = 100$.

74. Determine an appropriate window and graph the line $x - 3y = 60$.

Solutions to Practice Problems 1.1

1. Because the numbers are large, make each hatchmark correspond to 100. Then the point $(500, 200)$ is found by starting at the origin, moving 500 units to the right and 200 units up (Fig. 12).

2. Replace x by 4 and y by -7 in the equation $2x - 3y = 1$.
$$2(4) - 3(-7) = 1$$
$$8 + 21 = 1$$
$$29 = 1$$
The equation is not satisfied, so $(4, -7)$ is not on the graph. Similarly, if we substitute $(5, 3)$ into the equation, we find that
$$2 \cdot 5 - 3 \cdot 3 = 1$$
$$10 - 9 = 1$$
$$1 = 1.$$
So the equation is satisfied and $(5, 3)$ is on the graph.

3. The standard form is obtained by solving for y:
$$y = -5x + 10.$$
Thus $m = -5$ and $b = 10$. The y-intercept is $(0, 10)$. To find the x-intercept, set $y = 0$:
$$0 = -5x + 10$$
$$5x = 10$$
$$x = 2.$$
So the x-intercept is $(2, 0)$ (Fig. 13).

4. To find the y-intercept, set $x = 0$; then $y = 3 \cdot 0 = 0$. To find the x-intercept, set $y = 0$; then $3x = 0$ or $x = 0$. The two intercepts are the same point $(0, 0)$. We must therefore plot some other point. Setting $x = 1$, we obtain $y = 3 \cdot 1 = 3$, so another point on the line is $(1, 3)$ (Fig. 14).

Figure 12

Figure 13

Figure 14

1.2 Linear Inequalities

In this section we study the properties of inequalities. Start with a Cartesian coordinate system on the line (Fig. 1). Recall that it is possible to associate with each point of the line a number; and conversely, with each number (positive, negative, or zero) it is possible to associate a point on the line.

Figure 1

Let a and b be any numbers. We say that ***a* is less than *b*** if a lies to the left of b on the line. When a is less than b, we write $a < b$ (read: a is less than b). Thus, for example, $2 < 3$, $-1 < 2$, $-3 < -1$, and $0 < 4$. When a is less than b, we also say that ***b* is greater than *a*** ($b > a$). Thus, for example, $3 > 2$, $2 > -1$, $-1 > -3$, and $4 > 0$. Sometimes it is convenient to have a notation that means that a is no larger than b. The notation used for this is $a \leq b$ (read: a is less than or equal to b). Similarly, the notation $a \geq b$ (read: a is greater than or equal to b) means that a is no smaller than b. The symbols $>$, $<$, $\geq$, and $\leq$ are called **inequality signs**. It is easiest to remember the meaning of these various symbols by noting that the symbols $>$ and $<$ always point toward the smaller of a and b.

An inequality expresses a relationship between the quantities on both of its sides. This relationship is very similar to the relationship expressed by an equation. And just as some problems require solving equations, others require solving inequalities. Our next task will be to state and illustrate the arithmetic operations permissible in dealing with inequalities. These permissible operations form the basis of a technique for solving the inequalities occurring in applications.

> **Inequality Property 1** Suppose that $a < b$ and that c is any number. Then $a + c < b + c$ and $a - c < b - c$. In other words, the same number can be added or subtracted from both sides of the inequality.

For example, start with the inequality $2 < 3$ and add 4 to both sides to get

$$2 + 4 < 3 + 4.$$

That is,

$$6 < 7,$$

a correct inequality.

EXAMPLE 1

Solving a linear inequality Solve the inequality $x + 4 > 3$. That is, determine all values of x for which the inequality holds.

Solution We proceed as we would in dealing with an equation. Isolate x on the left by subtracting 4 from both sides, which is permissible by Inequality Property 1:

$$x + 4 > 3$$
$$(x + 4) - 4 > 3 - 4$$
$$x > -1.$$

That is, the values of x for which the inequality holds are exactly those x greater than -1. ∎

In dealing with an equation, both sides may be multiplied or divided by a number. However, multiplying or dividing an inequality by a number requires some care. The result depends on whether the number is positive or negative. More precisely,

---

Inequality Property 2

2A. If $a < b$ and c is positive, then $ac < bc$.

2B. If $a < b$ and c is negative, then $ac > bc$.

In other words, an inequality may be multiplied by a positive number, just as in the case of equations. But to multiply an inequality by a negative number, it is necessary to reverse the inequality sign. For example, the inequality $-1 < 2$ can be multiplied by 4 to get $-4 < 8$, a correct statement. But if we were to multiply by -4, it would be necessary to reverse the inequality sign, because -4 is negative. In this latter case we would get $4 > -8$, a correct statement.

NOTE ▸ Inequality Properties 1 and 2 are stated using only $<$. However, exactly the same properties hold if $<$ is replaced by $>$, $\leq$, or $\geq$. ■

EXAMPLE 2

Solving a linear inequality Solve the inequality $-3x + 2 \geq -1$.

Solution Treat the inequality as if it were an equation. The goal is to isolate x on one side. To this end, first subtract 2 from both sides (Property 1). This gives

$$(-3x + 2) - 2 \geq -1 - 2$$
$$-3x \geq -3.$$

Next, we multiply by $-\frac{1}{3}$. (This gives x on the left.) But $-\frac{1}{3}$ is negative, so by Property 2B we must reverse the inequality sign. Thus,

$$-\tfrac{1}{3}(-3x) \leq -\tfrac{1}{3}(-3)$$
$$x \leq 1.$$

Therefore, the values of x satisfying the inequality are precisely those values that are ≤ 1. ■

Now Try Exercise 7

The inequalities of greatest interest to us[1] are those in two variables, x and y, and having the form $cx + dy \leq e$ or $cx + dy \geq e$, where c, d, and e are given numbers, with c and d not both 0. We will call such inequalities **linear inequalities**. When $d \neq 0$ (that is, when y actually appears), the inequality can be put into one of the **standard forms** $y \leq mx + b$ or $y \geq mx + b$. When $d = 0$, the inequality can be put into one of the standard forms $x \leq a$ or $x \geq a$. The procedure for putting a linear inequality into standard form is analogous to that for putting a linear equation into standard form.

EXAMPLE 3

Standard form of a linear inequality Put the linear inequality $2x - 3y \geq -9$ into standard form.

Solution Since we want the y-term on the left and all other terms on the right, begin by subtracting $2x$ from both sides:

$$-3y \geq -2x - 9.$$

---

[1]Such inequalities arise in our discussion of linear programming in Chapter 3.

Next, multiply by $-\frac{1}{3}$, remembering to change the inequality sign, since $-\frac{1}{3}$ is negative:

$$y \le -\tfrac{1}{3}(-2x - 9)$$

$$y \le \tfrac{2}{3}x + 3.$$

Now Try Exercise 9   The last inequality is in standard form.   ■

EXAMPLE 4   **Standard form of a linear inequality** Find the standard form of the inequality $\frac{1}{2}x \ge 4$.

Solution   Note that y does not appear in the inequality. Just as was the case in finding the standard form of a linear equation when y does not appear, solve for x. To do this, multiply by 2 to get

$$x \ge 8,$$

Now Try Exercise 13   the standard form.   ■

Graphing Linear Inequalities   Associated with every linear inequality is a set of points in the plane, the set of all those points that satisfy the inequality. This set of points is called the **graph** of the inequality.

EXAMPLE 5   **Solution of a linear inequality** Determine whether or not the given point satisfies the inequality $y \ge -\frac{2}{3}x + 4$.

(a) $(3, 4)$ (b) $(0, 0)$

Solution   Substitute the x-coordinate of the point for x and the y-coordinate for y, and determine if the resulting inequality is correct or not.

(a) $4 \ge -\frac{2}{3}(3) + 4$ (b) $0 \ge -\frac{2}{3}(0) + 4$

  $4 \ge -2 + 4$ $0 \ge 0 + 4$

  $4 \ge 2$ (correct) $0 \ge 4$ (not correct)

Now Try Exercises 15 and 17   Therefore, the point $(3, 4)$ satisfies the inequality and the point $(0, 0)$ does not.   ■

It is easiest to determine the graph of a given inequality after it has been written in standard form. Therefore, let us describe the graphs of each of the standard forms. The easiest to handle are the forms $x \ge a$ and $x \le a$.

A point satisfies the inequality $x \ge a$ if, and only if, its x-coordinate is greater than or equal to a. The y-coordinate can be anything. Therefore, the graph of $x \ge a$ consists of all points to the right of and on the vertical line $x = a$. We will display the graph by crossing out the portion of the plane to the left of the line (see Fig. 2). Similarly, the graph of $x \le a$ consists of the points to the left of and on the line $x = a$. This graph is shown in Fig. 3.

Here is a simple procedure for graphing the other two standard forms.

To graph $y \ge mx + b$ or $y \le mx + b$,

  1. Draw the graph of $y = mx + b$.

  2. Throw away, that is, "cross out," the portion of the plane not satisfying the inequality. The graph of $y \ge mx + b$ consists of all points above or on the line. The graph of $y \le mx + b$ consists of all points below or on the line.

The graphs of the inequalities $y \ge mx + b$ and $y \le mx + b$ are shown in Fig. 4. Some simple reasoning suffices to show why these graphs are correct. Draw the line

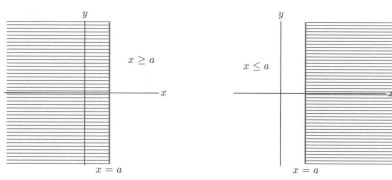

Figure 2   **Figure 3**

$y = mx + b$, as in Fig. 5, and pick any point P above the line. Suppose that P has coordinates (x, y). Let Q be the point on the line that lies directly below P. Then Q has the same first coordinate as P, that is, x. Since Q lies on the line, the second coordinate of Q is $mx + b$. Since the second coordinate of P is clearly larger than the second coordinate of Q, we must have $y \geq mx + b$. Similarly, any point below the line satisfies $y \leq mx + b$. Thus the two graphs are as given in Fig. 4.

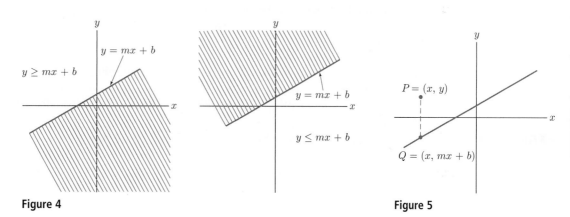

Figure 4   **Figure 5**

EXAMPLE 6

Graphing a linear inequality   Graph the inequality $2x + 3y \geq 15$.

Solution   In order to apply the aforementioned procedure, the inequality must first be put into standard form:

$$2x + 3y \geq 15$$
$$3y \geq -2x + 15 \qquad \text{Subtract } 2x \text{ from both sides.}$$
$$y \geq -\tfrac{2}{3}x + 5 \qquad \text{Divide both sides by 3.}$$

The last inequality is in standard form. Next, we graph the line $y = -\tfrac{2}{3}x + 5$. Its intercepts are $(0, 5)$ and $\left(\tfrac{15}{2}, 0\right)$. Since the inequality is "$y \geq$" we cross out the region below the line and label the region above with the inequality. The graph

Now Try Exercise 31   consists of all points above or on the line (Fig. 6 on the next page).   ∎

EXAMPLE 7

Graphing a linear inequality   Graph the inequality $4x - 2y \geq 12$.

Figure 6

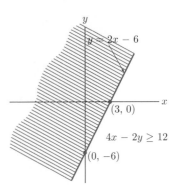

Figure 7

Solution First, put the inequality in standard form:

$$4x - 2y \geq 12$$
$$-2y \geq -4x + 12 \qquad \text{Subtract } 4x \text{ from both sides.}$$
$$y \leq 2x - 6 \qquad \text{Divide both sides by } -2.$$

(Note the change in the inequality sign!). Next, graph $y = 2x - 6$. The intercepts are $(0, -6)$ and $(3, 0)$. Since the inequality is "$y \leq$" the graph consists of all points below or on the line (Fig. 7).   ∎

> Now Try Exercise 27

So far, we have been concerned only with graphing single inequalities. The next example concerns graphing a system of inequalities. That is, it asks us to determine all points of the plane that *simultaneously* satisfy all inequalities of a system.

EXAMPLE 8   **Graphing a system of linear inequalities** Graph the system of inequalities

$$\begin{cases} 2x + 3y \geq 15 \\ 4x - 2y \geq 12 \\ y \geq 0. \end{cases}$$

Solution The first two inequalities have already been graphed in Examples 6 and 7. The graph of $y \geq 0$ consists of all points above or on the x-axis. In Fig. 8, any point that is crossed out is *not* on the graph of at least one inequality. So the points that simultaneously satisfy all three inequalities are those in the remaining clear region and its border.   ∎

> Now Try Exercise 41

> **REMARK** ▶   At first, our convention of crossing out those points *not* on the graph of an inequality (instead of shading the points *on* the graph) may have seemed odd. However, the real advantage of this convention becomes apparent when graphing a system of inequalities. Imagine trying to find the graph of the system of Example 8 if the points *on* the graph of each inequality had been shaded. It would have been necessary to locate the points that had been shaded three times. This is hard to do.   ∎

Figure 8

The graph of a system of inequalities is called a **feasible set**. The feasible set associated to the system of Example 8 is a three-sided, unbounded region.

Given a specific point, we should be able to decide whether or not the point lies in the feasible set. The next example shows how this is done.

EXAMPLE 9

Feasible set of a system of linear inequalities Determine whether the points $(5, 3)$ and $(4, 2)$ are in the feasible set of the system of inequalities of Example 8.

Solution If we had very accurate measuring devices, we could plot the points in the graph of Fig. 8 and determine whether or not they lie in the feasible set. However, there is a simpler and more reliable algebraic method. Just substitute the coordinates of the points into each of the inequalities of the system and see whether or not *all* of the inequalities are satisfied. So doing, we find that $(5, 3)$ is in the feasible set and $(4, 2)$ is not.

$$(5, 3) \quad \begin{cases} 2(5) + 3(3) \geq 15 \\ 4(5) - 2(3) \geq 12 \\ (3) \geq 0 \end{cases} \quad \begin{cases} 19 \geq 15 \\ 14 \geq 12 \\ 3 \geq 0 \end{cases}$$

$$(4, 2) \quad \begin{cases} 2(4) + 3(2) \geq 15 \\ 4(4) - 2(2) \geq 12 \\ (2) \geq 0 \end{cases} \quad \begin{cases} 14 \geq 15 \\ 12 \geq 12 \\ 2 \geq 0 \end{cases}$$

Now Try Exercises 45 and 47   ■

INCORPORATING TECHNOLOGY

GC Graphing calculators use the *style* setting and the **Shade** command to display graphs of linear inequalities. With the TI-83/84 Plus, there is a style icon (initially a line of four dots) to the left of each function in the **Y=** editor. To change the style setting of a function, move the cursor to the style icon and press the ENTER key. Of the seven different icons, the icons ◥ and ◣ specify that the region above and below the line, respectively, be crossed out when the line is graphed. With the TI-89, you specify the style setting of the selected function in the **Y=** editor by pressing 2nd[F6] and selecting **Above** or **Below**. Figure 9 shows the **Y=** editor and the feasible set for Example 9.

(a)   (b) TI-83/84 Plus   (c) TI-89

Figure 9

Regions to the left and right, respectively, of the vertical line $x = k$ can be crossed out with the commands

Shade(c-1,d+1,a,k,2,3)   and   Shade(c-1,d+1,k,b,2,3)   [TI-83/84 Plus]

Shade ymin,ymax,xmin,k   and   Shade ymin,ymax,k,xmax   [TI-89]

where the window setting of the TI-83/84 Plus is $[a, b]$ by $[c, d]$. With the TI-83/84 Plus, the **Shade** command is invoked from the home screen with 2nd[DRAW]. With the TI-89, **Shade** can typed directly into the entry line or selected from the CATALOG menu.   ■

Practice Problems 1.2

1. Graph the inequality $3x - y \geq 3$.

2. Graph the feasible set for the system of inequalities

$$\begin{cases} x \geq 0, \ y \geq 0 \\ x + 2y \leq 4 \\ 4x - 4y \geq -4. \end{cases}$$

EXERCISES 1.2

In Exercises 1–4, state whether the inequality is true or false.

1. $2 \leq -3$ **2.** $-2 \leq 0$ **3.** $7 \leq 7$ **4.** $0 \geq \frac{1}{2}$

In Exercises 5–7, solve for x.

5. $2x - 5 \geq 3$ **6.** $3x - 7 \leq 2$

7. $-5x + 13 \leq -2$

8. Which of the following results from solving $-x + 1 \leq 3$ for x?

   (a) $x \leq 4$ **(b)** $x \leq 2$

   (c) $x \geq -4$ **(d)** $x \geq -2$

In Exercises 9–14, put the linear inequality into standard form.

9. $2x + y \leq 5$ **10.** $-3x + y \geq 1$

11. $5x - \frac{1}{3}y \leq 6$ **12.** $\frac{1}{2}x - y \leq -1$

13. $4x \geq -3$ **14.** $-2x \leq 4$

In Exercises 15–22, determine whether or not the given point satisfies the given inequality.

15. $3x + 5y \leq 12$, $(2,1)$ **16.** $-2x + y \geq 9$, $(3,15)$

17. $y \geq -2x + 7$, $(3,0)$ **18.** $y \leq \frac{1}{2}x + 3$, $(4,6)$

19. $y \leq 3x - 4$, $(3,5)$ **20.** $y \geq x$, $(-3,-2)$

21. $x \geq 5$, $(7,-2)$ **22.** $x \leq 7$, $(0,0)$

In Exercises 23–26, graph the given inequality by crossing out (i.e., discarding) the points not satisfying the inequality.

23. $y \leq \frac{1}{3}x + 1$

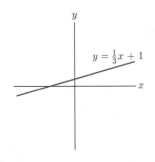

24. $y \geq -x + 1$

25. $x \geq 4$

26. $y \leq 2$

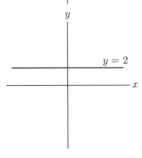

In Exercises 27–38, graph the given inequality.

27. $y \leq 2x + 1$ **28.** $y \geq -3x + 6$

29. $x \geq 2$ **30.** $x \geq 0$

31. $x + 4y \geq 12$ **32.** $4x - 4y \geq 8$

33. $4x - 5y + 25 \geq 0$ **34.** $.1y - x \geq .2$

35. $\frac{1}{2}x - \frac{1}{3}y \leq 1$ **36.** $3y + \frac{1}{2}x \leq 2y + x + 1$

37. $.5x + .4y \leq 2$ **38.** $y - 2x \geq \frac{1}{2}y - 2$

In Exercises 39–44, graph the feasible set for the system of inequalities.

39. $\begin{cases} y \leq 2x - 4 \\ y \geq 0 \end{cases}$ **40.** $\begin{cases} y \geq -\frac{1}{3}x + 1 \\ x \geq 0 \end{cases}$

41. $\begin{cases} x + 2y \geq 2 \\ 3x - y \geq 3 \end{cases}$ **42.** $\begin{cases} 3x + 6y \geq 24 \\ 3x + y \geq 6 \end{cases}$

43. $\begin{cases} x + 5y \leq 10 \\ x + y \leq 3 \\ x \geq 0,\ y \geq 0 \end{cases}$ **44.** $\begin{cases} x + 2y \geq 6 \\ x + y \geq 5 \\ x \geq 1 \end{cases}$

In Exercises 45–48, determine whether the given point is in the feasible set of this system of inequalities:

$$\begin{cases} 6x + 3y \leq 96 \\ x + y \leq 18 \\ 2x + 6y \leq 72 \\ x \geq 0,\ y \geq 0. \end{cases}$$

45. $(8, 7)$ **46.** $(14, 3)$ **47.** $(9, 10)$ **48.** $(16, 0)$

In Exercises 49–52, determine whether the given point is above or below the given line.

49. $y = 2x + 5,\ (3, 9)$ **50.** $3x - y = 4,\ (2, 3)$

51. $7 - 4x + 5y = 0,\ (0, 0)$ **52.** $x = 2y + 5,\ (6, 1)$

53. Give a system of inequalities for which the graph is the region between the pair of lines $8x - 4y - 4 = 0$ and $8x - 4y = 0$.

54. PE The shaded region in Fig. 10 is bounded by four straight lines. Which of the following is NOT an equation of one of the boundary lines?

(a) $y = 0$ (b) $y = 2$ (c) $x = 0$

(d) $2x + 3y = 12$ (e) $3x + 2y = 12$

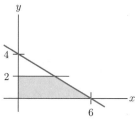

Figure 10

55. PE The shaded region in Fig. 11 is bounded by four straight lines. Which of the following is NOT an equation of one of the boundary lines?

(a) $x = 0$ (b) $y = x$ (c) $y = 5$

(d) $y = 0$ (e) $x + 2y = 6$

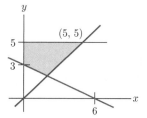

Figure 11

56. PE Which quadrant in Fig. 12 contains no points that satisfy the inequality $x + 2y \geq 6$?

(a) none   (b) I   (c) II   (d) III   (e) IV

Figure 12

57. PE Which quadrant in Fig. 12 contains no points that satisfy the inequality $3y - 2x \geq 6$?

(a) none   (b) I   (c) II   (d) III   (e) IV

Use a graphing calculator to solve Exercises 58–61.

58. Graph the line $4x - 2y = 7$.

(a) Locate the point on the line with x-coordinate 3.6.

(b) Does the point $(3.6, 3.5)$ lie above or below the line? Explain.

59. Graph the line $x + 2y = 11$.

(a) Locate the point on the line with x-coordinate 6.

(b) Does the point $(6, 2.6)$ lie above or below the line? Explain.

60. If your graphing calculator can shade feasible sets of inequalities, display the feasible set in Exercise 39.

61. If your graphing calculator can shade feasible sets of inequalities, display the feasible set in Exercise 42.

Solutions to Practice Problems 1.2

1. Linear inequalities are easiest to graph if they are first put into standard form. Subtract $3x$ from both sides and multiply by -1:

$$3x - y \geq 3$$
$$-y \geq -3x + 3$$
$$y \leq 3x - 3.$$

Now graph the line $y = 3x - 3$ (Fig. 13 on the next page). The graph of the inequality is the portion of the plane below and on the line ("$\leq$" corresponds to below), so throw away (that is, cross out) the portion above the line.

(Continued)

Figure 13

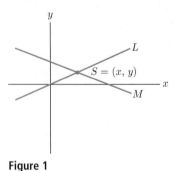

Figure 14

2. Begin by putting the linear inequalities into standard form and then graphing them all on the same coordinate system.

$$\begin{cases} x \geq 0, \ y \geq 0 \\ \quad x + 2y \leq \quad 4 \\ 4x - 4y \geq -4 \end{cases}$$

has standard form

$$\begin{cases} x \geq 0, \ y \geq 0 \\ y \leq -\frac{1}{2}x + 2 \\ y \leq \quad x + 1 \end{cases}$$

A good procedure to follow is to graph all of the linear equations and then cross out the regions to be thrown away one at a time (Fig. 14). The inequalities $x \geq 0$ and $y \geq 0$ arise frequently in applications. The first has the form $x \geq a$, where $a = 0$, and the second has the form $y \geq mx + b$, where $m = 0$ and $b = 0$. To graph them, just cross out all points to the left of the y-axis and all points below the x-axis, respectively.

1.3 The Intersection Point of a Pair of Lines

Figure 1

Suppose that we are given a pair of intersecting straight lines L and M. Let us consider the problem of determining the coordinates of the **point of intersection** $S = (x, y)$ (see Fig. 1). We may as well assume that the equations of L and M are given in standard form. First, let us assume that both lines are in the first standard form — that is, that the equations are

$$L: \ y = mx + b, \qquad M: \ y = nx + c.$$

Since the point S is on both lines, its coordinates satisfy both equations. In particular, we have two expressions for its y-coordinate:

$$y = mx + b = nx + c.$$

The last equality gives an equation from which x can easily be determined. Then the value of y can be determined as $mx + b$ (or $nx + c$). Let us see how this works in a particular example.

EXAMPLE 1

Finding the point of intersection Find the point of intersection of the two lines $y = 2x - 3$ and $y = x + 1$.

Solution To find the x-coordinate of the point of intersection, equate the two expressions for y and solve for x:

$$2x - 3 = x + 1$$

$$x - 3 = 1 \qquad \text{Subtract } x \text{ from both sides.}$$

$$x = 4 \qquad \text{Add 3 to both sides.}$$

To find the value of y, set $x = 4$ in either equation, say the first. Then

$$y = 2 \cdot 4 - 3 = 5.$$

Now Try Exercise 1 | So the point of intersection is $(4, 5)$. ∎

EXAMPLE 2

Finding the point of intersection Find the point of intersection of the two lines $x + 2y = 6$ and $5x + 2y = 18$.

Solution To use the method described, the equations must be in standard form. Solving both equations for y, we get the standard forms

$$y = -\tfrac{1}{2}x + 3$$
$$y = -\tfrac{5}{2}x + 9.$$

Equating the expressions for y gives

$$-\tfrac{1}{2}x + 3 = -\tfrac{5}{2}x + 9$$

$$\tfrac{5}{2}x - \tfrac{1}{2}x + 3 = 9 \qquad \text{Add } \tfrac{5}{2}x \text{ to both sides.}$$

$$2x + 3 = 9 \qquad \text{Combine } x \text{ terms.}$$

$$2x = 6 \qquad \text{Subtract 3 from both sides.}$$

$$x = 3 \qquad \text{Divide both sides by 2.}$$

Setting $x = 3$ in the first equation gives

$$y = -\tfrac{1}{2}(3) + 3 = \tfrac{3}{2}.$$

Now Try Exercise 3 | So the intersection point is $\left(3, \tfrac{3}{2}\right)$. ∎

The preceding method works when both equations have the first standard form $(y = mx + b)$. In case one equation has the standard form $x = a$, things are much simpler. The value of x is then given directly without any work, namely $x = a$. The value of y can be found by substituting a for x in the other equation.

EXAMPLE 3

Finding the point of intersection Find the point of intersection of the lines $y = 2x - 1$ and $x = 2$.

Solution The x-coordinate of the intersection point is 2, and the y-coordinate is $y = 2 \cdot 2 - 1 = 3$. Therefore, the intersection point is $(2, 3)$. ∎

Now Try Exercise 5

The method just introduced may be used to solve systems of two equations in two variables.

EXAMPLE 4

Solving a system of equations Solve the following system of linear equations:

$$\begin{cases} 2x + 3y = 7 \\ 4x - 2y = 9. \end{cases}$$

Solution First convert the equations to standard form:

$$2x + 3y = 7$$
$$3y = -2x + 7 \qquad \text{Subtract } 2x \text{ from both sides.}$$
$$y = -\tfrac{2}{3}x + \tfrac{7}{3} \qquad \text{Divide both sides by 3.}$$

$$4x - 2y = 9$$
$$-2y = -4x + 9 \qquad \text{Subtract } 4x \text{ from both sides.}$$
$$y = 2x - \tfrac{9}{2} \qquad \text{Divide both sides by } -2.$$

Now equate the two expressions for y:

$$2x - \tfrac{9}{2} = -\tfrac{2}{3}x + \tfrac{7}{3}$$
$$\tfrac{8}{3}x - \tfrac{9}{2} = \tfrac{7}{3} \qquad\qquad\quad \text{Add } \tfrac{2}{3}x \text{ to both sides.}$$
$$\tfrac{8}{3}x = \tfrac{7}{3} + \tfrac{9}{2} \qquad\qquad\quad \text{Add } \tfrac{9}{2} \text{ to both sides.}$$
$$\tfrac{8}{3}x = \tfrac{14}{6} + \tfrac{27}{6} = \tfrac{41}{6} \qquad\quad \text{Add fractions on right.}$$
$$x = \tfrac{3}{8} \cdot \tfrac{41}{6} = \tfrac{41}{16} \qquad\qquad \text{Multiply both sides by } \tfrac{3}{8}.$$
$$y = 2x - \tfrac{9}{2} = 2\left(\tfrac{41}{16}\right) - \tfrac{9}{2} \qquad \text{Substitute value for } x \text{ into second equation.}$$
$$y = \tfrac{41}{8} - \tfrac{36}{8} = \tfrac{5}{8} \qquad\qquad \text{Perform arithmetic.}$$

Now Try Exercise 9 So the solution of the given system is $x = \tfrac{41}{16}$, $y = \tfrac{5}{8}$. ∎

Supply and Demand Curves The price p that a commodity sells for is related to the quantity q available. Economists study two kinds of graphs that express relationships between q and p. To describe these graphs, let us plot *quantity* along the horizontal axis and *price* along the vertical axis. The first graph relating q and p is called a **supply curve** (Fig. 2) and expresses the relationship between q and p from a manufacturer's point of view. For every quantity q, the supply curve specifies the price p for which the manufacturer is willing to produce the quantity q. The greater the quantity to be supplied, the higher the price must be. So supply curves rise when viewed from left to right.

Figure 2	Figure 3	Figure 4
Supply curve	Demand curve	

The second curve relating q and p is called a **demand curve** (Fig. 3) and expresses the relationship between q and p from the consumer's viewpoint. For each quantity q, the demand curve gives the price p that must be charged in order for q units of the commodity to be sold. The greater the quantity that must be sold, the lower the price that consumers must be asked to pay. So demand curves fall when viewed from left to right.

Suppose the supply and demand curves for a commodity are drawn on a single coordinate system (Fig. 4). The intersection point (a, b) of the two curves has an economic significance: The quantity produced will stabilize at a units and the price will be b dollars per unit.

EXAMPLE 5

Applying the law of supply and demand Suppose the supply curve for a certain commodity is the straight line whose equation is $p = .0002q + 2$ (p in dollars). Suppose the demand curve for the same commodity is the straight line whose equation is $p = -.0005q + 5.5$. Determine both the quantity of the commodity that will be produced and the price at which it will sell.

Solution We must solve the system of linear equations

$$\begin{cases} p = .0002q + 2 \\ p = -.0005q + 5.5 \end{cases}$$

$.0002q + 2 = -.0005q + 5.5$	
$.0007q + 2 = 5.5$	Add .0005q to both sides.
$.0007q = 3.5$	Subtract 2 from both sides.
$q = \frac{3.5}{.0007} = 5000$	Divide both sides by .0007.
$p = .0002(5000) + 2$	Substitute value for q into first equation.
$p = 1 + 2 = 3$	Perform arithmetic.

Thus 5000 units of the commodity will be produced and it will sell for \$3 per unit.

Now Try Exercise 27   ■

INCORPORATING TECHNOLOGY

GC Graphing utilities have commands that find the intersection point of a pair of lines. Figure 5 shows the result of solving Example 4 on a TI-83/84 Plus with the intersect command of the CALC menu. Since the x-coordinate of the intersection point is assigned to ANS, the x-intercept can be converted to a fraction by pressing MATH 1 ENTER from the home screen. Figure 6 shows the result of solving Example 4 on a TI-89 with the Intersection routine in the menu resulting from pressing F5.   ■

Figure 5. $[-3, 6]$ by $[-3, 3]$

Figure 6. $[-3, 6]$ by $[-3, 3]$

Practice Problems 1.3

Figure 7 shows the feasible set of a system of linear inequalities; its four vertices are labeled A, B, C, and D.

1. Use the method of this section to find the coordinates of the point C.

2. Determine the coordinates of the points A and B by inspection.

3. Find the coordinates of the point D.

Figure 7

EXERCISES 1.3

In Exercises 1–6, find the point of intersection of the given pair of straight lines.

1. $\begin{cases} y = 4x - 5 \\ y = -2x + 7 \end{cases}$ **2.** $\begin{cases} y = 3x - 15 \\ y = -2x + 10 \end{cases}$

3. $\begin{cases} x - 4y = -2 \\ x + 2y = 4 \end{cases}$ **4.** $\begin{cases} 2x - 3y = 3 \\ y = 3 \end{cases}$

5. $\begin{cases} y = \frac{1}{3}x - 1 \\ x = 12 \end{cases}$ **6.** $\begin{cases} 2x - 3y = 3 \\ x = 6 \end{cases}$

7. Does $(6, 4)$ satisfy the following system of linear equations?
$$\begin{cases} x - 3y = -6 \\ 3x - 2y = 10 \end{cases}$$

8. Does $(12, 4)$ satisfy the following system of linear equations?
$$\begin{cases} y = \frac{1}{3}x - 1 \\ x = 12 \end{cases}$$

In Exercises 9–12, solve the systems of linear equations.

9. $\begin{cases} 2x + y = 7 \\ x - y = 3 \end{cases}$ **10.** $\begin{cases} x + 2y = 4 \\ \frac{1}{2}x + \frac{1}{2}y = 3 \end{cases}$

11. $\begin{cases} 5x - 2y = 1 \\ 2x + y = -4 \end{cases}$ **12.** $\begin{cases} x + 2y = 6 \\ x - \frac{1}{3}y = 4 \end{cases}$

In Exercises 13–16, find the coordinates of the vertices of the feasible sets.

13.

14.

15.

16.

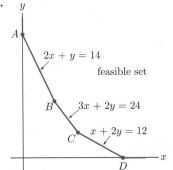

In Exercises 17–22, graph the feasible set for the system of inequalities and find the coordinates of the vertices.

17. $\begin{cases} 2y - x \le 6 \\ x + 2y \ge 10 \\ x \le 6 \end{cases}$ **18.** $\begin{cases} 2x + y \ge 10 \\ x \ge 2 \\ y \ge 2 \end{cases}$

19. $\begin{cases} x + 3y \le 18 \\ 2x + y \le 16 \\ x \ge 0, \ y \ge 0 \end{cases}$ **20.** $\begin{cases} 5x + 2y \ge 14 \\ x + 3y \ge 8 \\ x \ge 0, \ y \ge 0 \end{cases}$

21. $\begin{cases} 4x + y \ge 8 \\ x + y \ge 5 \\ x + 3y \ge 9 \\ x \ge 0, \ y \ge 0 \end{cases}$ **22.** $\begin{cases} x + 4y \le 28 \\ x + y \le 10 \\ 3x + y \le 24 \\ x \ge 0, \ y \ge 0 \end{cases}$

23. Supply Curve The supply curve for a certain commodity is $p = .0001q + .05$.

   (a) What price must be offered in order for 19,500 units of the commodity to be supplied?

   (b) What prices result in no units of the commodity being supplied?

24. Demand Curve The demand curve for a certain commodity is $p = -.001q + 32.5$.

   (a) At what price can 31,500 units of the commodity be sold?

   (b) What quantities are so large that many units of the commodity cannot possibly all be sold no matter how low the price?

25. Supply and Demand Suppose that supply and demand for a certain commodity are described by the supply and demand curves of Exercises 23 and 24. Determine the quantity of the commodity that will be produced and the selling price.

26. Temperature Conversion The precise formula for converting Celsius degrees to Fahrenheit degrees is $F = \frac{9}{5}C + 32$. An easier-to-use formula that approximates the conversion is $F = 2C + 30$.

(a) Compare the values given by the two formulas for a temperature of $5°C$.

(b) Compare the values given by the two formulas for a temperature of $20°C$.

(c) For what Celsius temperature do the two formulas give the same Fahrenheit temperature?

27. Supply and Demand A discount book seller has determined that the supply curve for a certain author's newest paperback book is $p = \frac{1}{300}q + 13$. The demand curve for this book is $p = -.03q + 19$. What quantity of sales would result in supply exactly meeting demand, and for what price should the book be sold?

28. Time Apportionment A plant supervisor must apportion her 40-hour workweek between hours working on the assembly line and hours supervising the work of others. She is paid $12 per hour for working and $15 per hour for supervising. If her earnings for a certain week are $504, how much time does she spend on each task?

29. Calling Card Options A calling card offers two methods of paying for a phone call. Method A charges 1 cent per minute but has a 45-cent connection fee. Method B charges 3.5 cents per minute but has no connection fee. Write the equations that show the total cost, y, of a call of x minutes for methods A and B and determine their intersection point. What does the intersection point represent?

30. Weight Determination PE In a wrestling competition, the total weight of the two contestants is 700 pounds. If twice the weight of the first contestant is 275 pounds more than the weight of the second contestant, what is the weight (in pounds) of the first contestant?

(a) 275 (b) 300 (c) 325 (d) 350 (e) 375

31. Sales Determination PE An appliance store sells a $15''$ TV for $280 and a $19''$ TV of the same brand for $400. During a one-week period the store sold 5 more $19''$ TVs than $15''$ TVs and collected $15,600. What was the total number of TV sets sold?

(a) 42   (b) 43   (c) 44   (d) 45   (e) 46

Exercises 32–37 require the use of a graphing calculator.

In Exercises 32–35, graph the lines and use the Intersect *command to estimate the point of intersection to two decimal places.*

32. $\begin{cases} y = .25x + 1.3 \\ y = -.5x + 4.1 \end{cases}$ **33.** $\begin{cases} y = -\frac{2}{3}x + 4.5 \\ y = \quad 2x \end{cases}$

34. $\begin{cases} x - 4y = -5 \\ 3x - 2y = 4.2 \end{cases}$ **35.** $\begin{cases} 2x + 3y = 5 \\ -4x + 5y = 1 \end{cases}$

In Exercises 36 and 37, (a) graph the feasible set for the system of inequalities (use a window such as ZDecimal *or* ZoomDec *that gives nice values of the coordinates of points); (b) find the coordinates of the vertices of the feasible set; (c) locate the given point with the cursor; (d) determine whether or not the given point lies in the feasible set.*

36. $\begin{cases} -x + 3y \geq 3 \\ .4x + \quad y \geq 3.2 \end{cases}$ $(3.2, 2)$

37. $\begin{cases} 2x + \quad y \geq 5 \\ x - 2y \leq 0 \end{cases}$ $(2.2, 1.4)$

Solutions to Practice Problems 1.3

1. Point C is the point of intersection of the lines with equations $y = -\frac{1}{2}x + 4$ and $3x + y = 9$. To use the method of this section, the second equation must be put into its standard form $y = -3x + 9$. Now equate the two expressions for y and solve.

$$-\tfrac{1}{2}x + 4 = -3x + 9$$
$$\tfrac{5}{2}x = 5$$
$$x = \tfrac{2}{5} \cdot 5 = 2$$
$$y = -\tfrac{1}{2}(2) + 4 = 3$$

Therefore, $C = (2, 3)$.

2. $A = (0, 0)$, because the point A is the origin. $B = (0, 4)$, because it is the y-intercept of the line with equation $y = -\frac{1}{2}x + 4$.

3. D is the x-intercept of the line $3x + y = 9$. Its first coordinate is found by setting $y = 0$ and solving for x.

$$3x + (0) = 9$$
$$x = 3$$

Therefore, $D = (3, 0)$.

1.4 The Slope of a Straight Line

As we have seen, any linear equation can be put into one of the two standard forms, $y = mx + b$ or $x = a$. In this section, let us exclude linear equations whose standard form is of the latter type. *Geometrically, this means that we will consider only nonvertical lines.*

> **DEFINITION** Given a nonvertical line L with equation $y = mx + b$, the number m is called the **slope** of L. That is, the slope is the coefficient of x in the standard form of the equation of the line.

EXAMPLE 1   **Finding the slope of a line from its equation** Find the slopes of the lines having the following equations.

(a) $y = 2x + 1$ (b) $y = -\frac{3}{4}x + 2$ (c) $y = 3$ (d) $-8x + 2y = 4$

Solution (a) $m = 2$.
(b) $m = -\frac{3}{4}$.
(c) When we write the equation in the form $y = 0 \cdot x + 3$, we see that $m = 0$.
(d) First, we put the equation in standard form:

$$-8x + 2y = 4$$
$$2y = 8x + 4 \qquad \text{Add } 8x \text{ to both sides.}$$
$$y = 4x + 2 \qquad \text{Divide both sides by 2.}$$

Now Try Exercise 1   Thus $m = 4$.   ■

The definition of the slope is given in terms of the standard form of the equation of the line. Let us give an alternative definition.

> **DEFINITION Geometric Definition of Slope** Let L be a line passing through the points (x_1, y_1) and (x_2, y_2), where $x_1 \neq x_2$. Then the slope of L is given by the formula
> $$m = \frac{y_2 - y_1}{x_2 - x_1}. \tag{1}$$

That is, the slope is the difference in the y-coordinates divided by the difference in the x-coordinates, with both differences formed in the same order.

Before proving this definition equivalent to the first one given, let us show how it can be used.

EXAMPLE 2   **Finding the slope of a line from two points** Find the slope of the line passing through the points $(1, 3)$ and $(4, 6)$.

Solution We have

$$m = \frac{[\text{difference in } y\text{-coordinates}]}{[\text{difference in } x\text{-coordinates}]} = \frac{6 - 3}{4 - 1} = \frac{3}{3} = 1.$$

Thus $m = 1$. [Note that if we reverse the order of the points and use formula (1) to compute the slope, then we get

$$m = \frac{3 - 6}{1 - 4} = \frac{-3}{-3} = 1,$$

which is the same answer. The order of the points is immaterial. The important concern is to make sure that the differences in the x- and y-coordinates are formed in the same order.

Now Try Exercise 5

The slope of a line does not depend on which pair of points is chosen as (x_1, y_1) and (x_2, y_2). Consider the line $y = 4x - 3$ and two points $(1, 1)$ and $(3, 9)$, which are on the line. Using these two points, we calculate the slope to be

$$m = \frac{9 - 1}{3 - 1} = \frac{8}{2} = 4.$$

Now let's choose two other points on the line, say $(2, 5)$ and $(-1, -7)$, and use these points to determine m. We obtain

$$m = \frac{-7 - 5}{-1 - 2} = \frac{-12}{-3} = 4.$$

The two pairs of points give the same slope.

Justification of Formula (1)   Since (x_1, y_1) and (x_2, y_2) are both on the line, both points satisfy the equation of the line, which has the form $y = mx + b$. Thus

$$y_2 = mx_2 + b$$
$$y_1 = mx_1 + b.$$

Subtracting these two equations gives

$$y_2 - y_1 = mx_2 - mx_1 = m(x_2 - x_1).$$

Dividing by $x_2 - x_1$, we have

$$m = \frac{y_2 - y_1}{x_2 - x_1},$$

which is formula (1). So the two definitions of slope lead to the same number.   ■

Let us now study four of the most important properties of the slope of a straight line. We begin with the **steepness property**, since it provides us with a geometric interpretation for the number m.

m positive

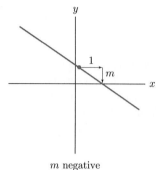

m negative

$m = 0$

Figure 1

Steepness Property   Let the line L have slope m. If we start at any point on the line and move 1 unit to the right, then we must move m units vertically in order to return to the line (Fig. 1). (Of course, if m is positive, then we move up; and if m is negative, we move down.)

EXAMPLE 3

Steepness property of a line   Illustrate the steepness property for each of the lines.
(a) $y = 2x + 1$ **(b)** $y = -\frac{3}{4}x + 2$ **(c)** $y = 3$

Solution   **(a)** Here $m = 2$. So starting from any point on the line, proceeding 1 unit to the right, we must go 2 units up to return to the line (Fig. 2 on the next page).
(b) Here $m = -\frac{3}{4}$. So starting from any point on the line, proceeding 1 unit to the right, we must go $\frac{3}{4}$ unit down to return to the line (Fig. 3).
(c) Here $m = 0$. So going 1 unit to the right requires going 0 units vertically to return to the line (Fig. 4).   ■

Now Try Exercise 51

Figure 2

Figure 3

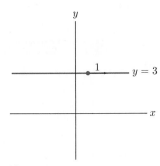

Figure 4

In the next example we introduce a new method for graphing a linear equation. This method relies on the steepness property and is much more efficient than finding two points on the line (e.g., the two intercepts).

EXAMPLE 4

Using the steepness property to graph a line Use the steepness property to draw the graph of $y = \frac{1}{2}x + \frac{3}{2}$.

Solution The y-intercept is $\left(0, \frac{3}{2}\right)$, as we read from the equation. We can find another point on the line using the steepness property. Start at $\left(0, \frac{3}{2}\right)$. Go 1 unit to the right. Since the slope is $\frac{1}{2}$, we must move vertically $\frac{1}{2}$ unit to return to the line. But this locates a second point on the line. So we draw the line through the two points. The

Now Try Exercise 11 entire procedure is illustrated in Fig. 5. ■

Figure 5

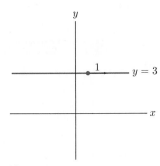

Figure 6

Actually, to use the steepness property to graph an equation, all that is needed is the slope plus *any* point (not necessarily the y-intercept).

EXAMPLE 5

Using the steepness property to graph a line Graph the line of slope -1 which passes through the point $(2, 2)$.

Solution Start at $(2, 2)$, move 1 unit to the right and then -1 unit vertically, that is, 1 unit down. The line through $(2, 2)$ and the resulting point is the desired line (see Fig. 6).

Now Try Exercise 25 ■

Slope measures the steepness of a line. Namely, the slope of a line tells whether it is rising or falling, and how fast. Specifically, lines of positive slope rise as we move from left to right. Lines of negative slope fall, and lines of zero slope stay level. The larger the magnitude of the slope, the steeper the ascent or descent. These facts are directly implied by the steepness property (see Fig. 7).

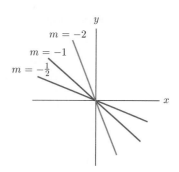

Figure 7

Justification of the Steepness Property   Consider a line with equation $y = mx + b$, and let (x_1, y_1) be any point on the line. If we start from this point and move 1 unit to the right, the first coordinate of the new point is $x_1 + 1$ since the x-coordinate is increased by 1. Now go far enough vertically to return to the line. Denote the y-coordinate of this new point by y_2 (see Fig. 8). We must show that to get y_2, we add m to y_1. That is, $y_2 = y_1 + m$. By equation (1), we can compute m as

Figure 8

$$m = \frac{[\text{difference in } y\text{-coordinates}]}{[\text{difference in } x\text{-coordinates}]} = \frac{y_2 - y_1}{1} = y_2 - y_1.$$

In other words, $y_2 = y_1 + m$, which is what we desired to show.   ■

Often the slopes of the straight lines that occur in applications have interesting and significant interpretations. An application in the field of economics is illustrated in the next example.

EXAMPLE 6

Slope of the cost line   Suppose a manufacturer finds that the cost y of producing x units of a certain commodity is given by the formula $y = 2x + 5000$. What interpretation can be given to the slope of the graph of this equation?

Solution   Suppose that the firm is producing at a certain level and increases production by 1 unit. That is, x is increased by 1 unit. By the steepness property, the value of y then increases by 2, which is the slope of the line whose equation is $y = 2x + 5000$. Thus each additional unit of production costs \$2. (The graph of $y = 2x + 5000$ is called a **cost curve**. It relates the size of production to total cost. The graph is a straight line, and economists call its slope the **marginal cost of production**. The y-coordinate of the y-intercept is called the **fixed cost**. In this case the fixed cost is \$5000, and it includes costs such as rent and insurance which are incurred

Now Try Exercise 27   even if no units are produced.)   ■

In applied problems having time as a variable, the letter t is often used in place of the letter x. If so, straight lines have equations of the form $y = mt + b$ and are graphed on a ty-coordinate system.

EXAMPLE 7

Straight-line depreciation   The federal government allows businesses an income tax deduction for the decrease in value (or **depreciation**) of capital assets (such as buildings and equipment). One method of calculating the depreciation is to take equal amounts over the expected lifetime of the asset. This method is called **straight-line depreciation**. For tax purposes the value V of an asset t years after purchase is figured according to the equation $V = -100{,}000t + 700{,}000$. The expected life of the asset is 5 years.

(a) How much did the asset originally cost?

(b) What is the annual deduction for depreciation?

(c) What is the **salvage value** of the asset? (That is, what is the value of the asset after 5 years?)

Solution (a) The original cost is the value of V at $t = 0$, namely

$$V = -100{,}000(0) + 700{,}000 = 700{,}000.$$

That is, the asset originally cost $700,000.

(b) By the steepness property, each increase of 1 in t causes a decrease in V of 100,000. That is, the value is decreasing by $100,000 per year. So the depreciation deduction is $100,000 each year.

(c) After 5 years, the value of V is given by

$$V = -100{,}000(5) + 700{,}000 = 200{,}000.$$

The salvage value is $200,000. ∎

We have seen in Example 5 how to sketch a straight line when given its slope and one point on it. Let us now see how to find the equation of the line from this data.

> **Point-Slope Formula**   The equation of the straight line passing through (x_1, y_1) and having slope m is given by $y - y_1 = m(x - x_1)$.

EXAMPLE 8   **Finding the equation of a line from its slope and a point on the line**   Find the equation of the line that passes through $(2, 3)$ and has slope $\frac{1}{2}$.

Solution Here $x_1 = 2$, $y_1 = 3$, and $m = \frac{1}{2}$. So the equation is

$$y - 3 = \tfrac{1}{2}(x - 2)$$

$$y - 3 = \tfrac{1}{2}x - 1 \qquad \text{Perform multiplication on right side.}$$

Now Try Exercise 41

$$y = \tfrac{1}{2}x + 2 \qquad \text{Add 3 to both sides.} \qquad ∎$$

EXAMPLE 9   **Finding the equation of a line**   Find the equation of the line through the points $(3, 1)$ and $(6, 0)$.

Solution We can compute the slope from equation (1):

$$[\text{slope}] = \frac{[\text{difference in } y\text{-coordinates}]}{[\text{difference in } x\text{-coordinates}]} = \frac{1 - 0}{3 - 6} = -\frac{1}{3}.$$

Now we can determine the equation from the point-slope formula with $(x_1, y_1) = (3, 1)$ and $m = -\frac{1}{3}$:

$$y - 1 = -\tfrac{1}{3}(x - 3)$$

$$y - 1 = -\tfrac{1}{3}x + 1 \qquad \text{Perform multiplication on right side.}$$

$$y = -\tfrac{1}{3}x + 2 \qquad \text{Add 1 to both sides.}$$

Now Try Exercise 47   [*Question:* What would the equation be if we had chosen $(x_1, y_1) = (6, 0)$?] ∎

EXAMPLE 10

Revenue generated by advertising For each dollar in monthly advertising expenditure, a store experiences a 6-dollar increase in sales revenue. Even without advertising, the store has $30,000 in sales revenue per month. Let x be the number of dollars of advertising expenditures per month and let y be the number of dollars in sales revenue per month.

(a) Find the equation of the line that expresses the relationship between x and y.

(b) If the store spends $10,000 in advertising, what will be the sales revenue for the month?

(c) How much would the store have to spend on advertising to attain $150,000 in sales revenue for the month?

Solution (a) The steepness property tells us that the line has slope $m = 6$. Since $x = 0$ (no advertising expenditures) yields $y = $30,000$, the y-intercept of the line is $(0, 30{,}000)$. Therefore, the standard form of the equation of the line is

$$y = 6x + 30{,}000.$$

(b) If $x = 10{,}000$, then $y = 6(10{,}000) + 30{,}000 = 90{,}000$. Therefore, the sales revenue for the month will be $90,000.

(c) We are given that $y = 150{,}000$, and we must find the value of x for which

$$150{,}000 = 6x + 30{,}000.$$

Solving for x, we obtain $6x = 120{,}000$, and hence $x = $20,000$. To attain $150,000 in sales revenue, the store should invest $20,000 in advertising. ∎

Now Try Exercise 37

Verification of the Point-Slope Formula Let (x, y) be any point on the line passing through the point (x_1, y_1) and having slope m. Then, by equation (1), we have

$$m = \frac{y - y_1}{x - x_1}.$$

Multiplying through by $x - x_1$ gives

$$y - y_1 = m(x - x_1). \tag{2}$$

Thus every point (x, y) on the line satisfies equation (2). So (2) gives the equation of the line through (x_1, y_1) and having slope m. ∎

The next property of slope relates the slopes of two perpendicular lines.

Perpendicular Property When two lines are perpendicular, their slopes are negative reciprocals of one another. That is, if two lines with slopes m and n are perpendicular to one another, then[1]

$$m = -\frac{1}{n}.$$

Conversely, if two lines have slopes that are negative reciprocals of one another, they are perpendicular.

A proof of the perpendicular property is outlined in Exercise 81. Let us show how it can be used to help find equations of lines.

---

[1]If $n = 0$, this formula does not say anything, since $1/0$ is undefined. However, in this case, one line is horizontal and one is vertical, the vertical one having an undefined slope.

EXAMPLE 11   **Perpendicular lines** Find the equation of the line perpendicular to the graph of $y = 2x - 5$ and passing through $(1, 2)$.

Solution   The slope of the graph of $y = 2x - 5$ is 2. By the perpendicular property, the slope of a line perpendicular to it is $-\frac{1}{2}$. If a line has slope $-\frac{1}{2}$ and passes through $(1, 2)$, it has the equation

$$y - 2 = -\tfrac{1}{2}(x - 1) \quad \text{or} \quad y = -\tfrac{1}{2}x + \tfrac{5}{2}$$

▶ Now Try Exercise 19   (by the point-slope formula).   ■

The final property of slopes gives the relationship between slopes of parallel lines. A proof is outlined in Exercise 80.

> **Parallel Property**   Parallel lines have the same slope. Conversely, if two different lines have the same slope, they are parallel.

EXAMPLE 12   **Parallel lines** Find the equation of the line through $(2, 0)$ and parallel to the line whose equation is $y = \frac{1}{3}x - 11$.

Solution   The slope of the line having equation $y = \frac{1}{3}x - 11$ is $\frac{1}{3}$. Therefore, any line parallel to it also has slope $\frac{1}{3}$. Thus the desired line passes through $(2, 0)$ and has slope $\frac{1}{3}$, so its equation is

▶ Now Try Exercise 21 $$y - 0 = \tfrac{1}{3}(x - 2) \quad \text{or} \quad y = \tfrac{1}{3}x - \tfrac{2}{3}.$$ ■

Practice Problems 1.4

*Suppose that the revenue y from selling x units of a certain commodity is given by the formula $y = 4x$. (**Revenue** is the amount of money received from the sale of the commodity.)*

1. What interpretation can be given to the slope of the graph of this equation?

2. (See Example 6.) Find the coordinates of the point of intersection of $y = 4x$ and $y = 2x + 5000$.

3. What interpretation can be given to the value of the x-coordinate of the point found in Problem 2?

EXERCISES 1.4

In Exercises 1–4, find the slope of the line having the given equation.

1. $y = \frac{2}{3}x + 7$

2. $y = -4$

3. $y - 3 = 5(x + 4)$

4. $7x + 5y = 10$

In Exercises 5–8, plot each pair of points, draw the straight line between them, and find the slope.

5. $(3, 4)$, $(7, 9)$

6. $(-2, 1)$, $(3, -3)$

7. $(0, 0)$, $(5, 4)$

8. $(4, 17)$, $(-2, 17)$

9. What is the slope of any line parallel to the y-axis?

10. Why doesn't it make sense to talk about the slope of the line between the two points $(2, 3)$ and $(2, -1)$?

In Exercises 11–14, graph the given linear equation by beginning at the y-intercept, moving 1 unit to the right and m units in the y-direction.

11. $y = -2x + 1$

12. $y = 4x - 2$

13. $y = 3x$

14. $y = -2$

In Exercises 15–22, find the equation of line L.

15.

16.

17.

18.

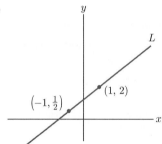

19.

L perpendicular to $y = -4x + 10$

20.

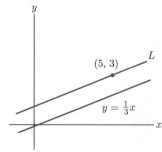

L parallel to $y = \frac{1}{3}x$

21.

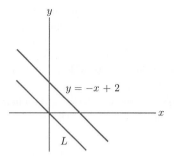

L parallel to $y = -x + 2$

22.

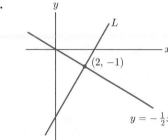

L perpendicular to $y = -\frac{1}{2}x$

23. Find the equation of the line passing through the point $(2, 3)$ and parallel to the x-axis.

24. Find the equation of the line passing through $(0, 0)$ and having slope 1.5.

25. Find the y-intercept of the line passing through the point $(5, 6)$ and having slope $\frac{3}{5}$.

26. Find the slope of the line passing through the point $(1, 4)$ and having y-intercept $(0, 4)$.

27. Weekly Pay A salesperson's weekly pay depends on the volume of sales. If she sells x units of goods, then her pay is $y = 5x + 60$ dollars. Give an interpretation to the slope and the y-intercept of this straight line.

28. Cost Curve A manufacturer has fixed costs (such as rent and insurance) of \$2000 per month. The cost of producing each unit of goods is \$4. Give the linear equation for the cost of producing x units per month.

29. Demand Curve Suppose the price that must be set in order to sell q items is given by the equation $p = -3q + 1200$.

(a) Find and interpret the p-intercept of the graph of the equation.

(b) Find and interpret the q-intercept of the graph of the equation.

(c) Find and interpret the slope of the graph of the equation.

(d) What price must be set in order to sell 350 items?

(e) What quantity will be sold if the price is \$300?

(f) Sketch the graph of the equation.

30. Cricket Chirps Biologists have found that the number of chirps that crickets of a certain species make per minute is related to the temperature. The relationship is very close to linear. At 68°F those crickets chirp about 124 times a minute. At 80°F they chirp about 172 times a minute.

   (a) Find the linear equation relating Fahrenheit temperature F and the number of chirps c.

   (b) If you only count chirps for 15 seconds, how can you quickly estimate the temperature?

31. Cost Equation Suppose that the cost of making 20 radios is $6800 and the cost of making 50 radios is $9500.

   (a) Find the cost equation.

   (b) What is the fixed cost?

   (c) What is the marginal cost of production?

   (d) Sketch the graph of the equation.

Exercises 32–34 are related.

32. Cost Equation Suppose that the total cost y of making x coats is given by the formula $y = 40x + 2400$.

   (a) What is the cost of making 100 coats?

   (b) How many coats can be made for $3600?

   (c) Find and interpret the y-intercept of the graph of the equation.

   (d) Find and interpret the slope of the graph of the equation.

33. Revenue Equation Suppose that the total revenue y from the sale of x coats is given by the formula $y = 100x$.

   (a) What is the revenue if 300 coats are sold?

   (b) How many coats must be sold to have a revenue of $6000?

   (c) Find and interpret the y-intercept of the graph of the equation.

   (d) Find and interpret the slope of the graph of the equation.

34. Profit Equation Consider a coat factory with the cost and revenue equations given in Exercises 32 and 33.

   (a) Find the equation giving the profit y resulting from making and selling x coats.

   (b) Find and interpret the y-intercept of the graph of the equation.

   (c) Find and interpret the x-intercept of the graph of the equation.

   (d) Find and interpret the slope of the graph of the equation.

   (e) How much profit will be made if 80 coats are sold?

   (f) How many coats must be sold to have a profit of $6000?

   (g) Sketch the graph of the equation found in part (a).

35. Heating Oil An apartment complex has a storage tank to hold its heating oil. The tank was filled on January 1, but no more deliveries of oil will be made until sometime in March. Let t denote the number of days after January 1 and let y denote the number of gallons of fuel oil in the tank. Current records show that y and t will be related by the equation $y = 30{,}000 - 400t$.

   (a) Graph the equation $y = 30{,}000 - 400t$.

   (b) How much oil will be in the tank on February 1?

   (c) How much oil will be in the tank on February 15?

   (d) Determine the y-intercept of the graph. Explain its significance.

   (e) Determine the t-intercept of the graph. Explain its significance.

36. Cash Reserves A corporation receives payment for a large contract on July 1, bringing its cash reserves to $2.3 million. Let y denote its cash reserves (in millions) t days after July 1. The corporation's accountants estimate that y and t will be related by the equation $y = 2.3 - .15t$.

   (a) Graph the equation $y = 2.3 - .15t$.

   (b) How much cash does the corporation have on the morning of July 16?

   (c) Determine the y-intercept of the graph. Explain its significance.

   (d) Determine the t-intercept of the graph. Explain its significance.

   (e) Determine the cash reserves on July 4.

   (f) When will the cash reserves be $.8 million?

37. Weekly Pay A furniture salesperson earns $220 a week plus 10% commission on her sales. Let x denote her sales and y her income for a week.

   (a) Express y in terms of x.

   (b) Determine her week's income if she sells $2000 in merchandise that week.

   (c) How much must she sell in a week in order to earn $540?

Find the equations of the following lines.

38. Slope is $-\frac{1}{2}$; y-intercept is $(0, 0)$

39. Slope is 3; y-intercept is $(0, -1)$

40. Slope is $-\frac{1}{3}$; $(6, -2)$ on line

41. Slope is 1; $(1, 2)$ on line

42. Slope is $\frac{1}{2}$; $(2, -3)$ on line

43. Slope is -7; $(5, 0)$ on line

44. Slope is $-\frac{2}{5}$; $(0, 5)$ on line

45. Slope is 0; $(7, 4)$ on line

46. $(5, -3)$ and $(-1, 3)$ on line

47. $(2, 1)$ and $(4, 2)$ on line

48. $(2,-1)$ and $(3,-1)$ on line

49. $(0,0)$ and $(1,-2)$ on line

50. $(3,-1)$ and $(3,1)$ on line

In each of Exercises 51–54 we specify a line by giving the slope and one point on the line. We give the first coordinate of some points on the line. Without deriving the equation of the line, find the second coordinate of each of the points.

51. Slope is 2, $(1,3)$ on line; $(2,\ )$; $(0,\ )$; $(-1,\ )$

52. Slope is -3, $(2,2)$ on line; $(3,\ )$; $(4,\ )$; $(1,\ )$

53. Slope is $-\frac{1}{4}$, $(-1,-1)$ on line; $(0,\ )$; $(1,\ )$; $(-2,\ )$

54. Slope is $\frac{1}{3}$, $(-5,2)$ on line; $(-4,\ )$; $(-3,\ )$; $(-2,\ )$

55. Each of the lines (A), (B), (C), and (D) in Fig. 9 is the graph of one of the linear equations (a), (b), (c), and (d). Match each line with its equation.

(A)

(B)

(C)

(D)

Figure 9

(a) $x+y=1$ **(b)** $x-y=1$

(c) $x+y=-1$ **(d)** $x-y=-1$

56. The following table gives several points on the line $\mathbf{Y_1} = mx + b$. Find m and b.

In Exercises 57–62, give the equation of a line with the stated property. Note: There are many answers to each exercise.

57. rises as you move from left to right

58. falls as you move from left to right

59. has slope 0

60. slope is not defined

61. parallel to the line $2x+3y=4$

62. perpendicular to the line $5x+6y=7$

63. Temperature Conversion Celsius and Fahrenheit temperatures are related by a linear equation. Use the fact that $0°C = 32°F$ and $100°C = 212°F$ to find an equation.

64. Dating of Artifacts An archaeologist dates a bone fragment discovered at a depth of 4 feet as approximately 1500 B.C. and dates a pottery shard at a depth of 8 feet as approximately 2100 B.C. Assuming there is a linear relationship between depths and dates at this archeological site, find the equation that relates depth to date. How deep should the archaeologist dig to look for relics from 3000 B.C.?

65. College Tuition The average college tuition and fees at four-year public colleges increased from $2848 in 1995 to $5685 in 2006. Assuming that average tuition and fees increased linearly with respect to time, find the equation that relates the average tuition and fees, y, to the number of years after 1995, x. What were the average tuition and fees in 2000?

66. College Enrollments Two-year college enrollments increased from 5.2 million in 1990 to 6.5 million in 2005. Assuming that enrollments increased linearly with respect to time, find the equation that relates the enrollment, y, to the number of years after 1990, x. When was the enrollment 6 million?

67. Gas Mileage A certain car gets 25 miles per gallon when the tires are properly inflated. For every pound of pressure that the tires are underinflated, the gas mileage decreases by $\frac{1}{2}$ miles per gallon. Find the equation that relates miles per gallon, y, to the amount the tires are underinflated, x. Use the equation to calculate the gas mileage when the tires are underinflated by 8 pounds of pressure.

68. Home Health Aid Jobs According to the U.S. Department of Labor, home health aid jobs are expected to increase from 787,000 in 2006 to 1,171,000 in 2016. Assuming that the number of home health aid jobs increases linearly during that time, find the equation that relates the number of jobs, y, to the number of years after 2006, x. Use the equation to predict the number of home health aid jobs in 2012.

69. **Bachelor Degrees in Business** According to the U.S. National Center of Educational Statistics, 249,165 bachelor degrees in business were awarded in 1991 and 318,042 were awarded in 2006. If the number of bachelor degrees in business continues to grow linearly, how many bachelor degrees in business will be awarded in 2011?

70. **Pizza Stores** According to the Pizza Marketing Quarterly, the number of U.S. Domino's Pizza stores grew from 4818 in 2001 to 5143 in 2006. If the number of stores continues to grow linearly, when will there be 6000 stores?

71. **Super Bowl Commercials** The average cost of a 30-second advertising slot during the Super Bowl increased linearly from $2.4 million in 2005 to $2.7 million in 2008. Find the equation that relates the cost (in millions of dollars) of a 30-second slot, y, to the number of years after 2000, x. What was the average cost in 2007?

72. Write an inequality whose graph consists of the points on or below the straight line passing through the two points $(2, 5)$ and $(4, 9)$.

73. Write an inequality whose graph consists of the points on or above the line with slope 4 and y-intercept $(0, 3)$.

74. Find a system of inequalities having the feasible set in Fig. 10.

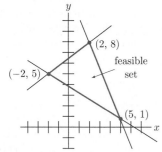

Figure 10

75. Find a system of inequalities having the feasible set in Fig. 11.

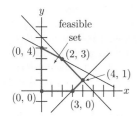

Figure 11

76. Show that the points $(1, 3)$, $(2, 4)$, and $(3, -1)$ are *not* on the same line.

77. For what value of k will the three points $(1, 5)$, $(2, 7)$, and $(3, k)$ be on the same line?

78. Find the value of a for which the line through the points $(a, 1)$ and $(2, -3.1)$ is parallel to the line through the points $(-1, 0)$ and $(3.8, 2.4)$.

79. Rework Exercise 78, where the word "parallel" is replaced by the word "perpendicular."

80. Prove the parallel property. [*Hint*: If $y = mx + b$ and $y = m'x + b'$ are the equations of two lines, then the two lines have a point in common if and only if the equation $mx + b = m'x + b'$ has a solution x.]

81. Prove the perpendicular property. [*Hint*: Without loss of generality, assume that both lines pass through the origin. Use the point-slope formula, the Pythagorean theorem, and Fig. 12.]

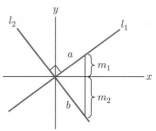

Figure 12

82. **Temperature Conversion** **PE** Figure 13 gives the conversion of temperatures from Centigrade to Fahrenheit. What is the Fahrenheit equivalent of $30°$C?

(a) $85°$F (b) $86°$F (c) $87°$F

(d) $88°$F (e) $89°$F

Figure 13

83. **Shipping Costs** **PE** Figure 14 gives the cost of shipping a package from coast to coast. What is the cost of shipping a 20-pound package?

(a) $15.00 (b) $15.50 (c) $16.00

(d) $16.50 (e) $17.00

Figure 14

84. Costs and Revenue PE A T-shirt company has fixed costs of $25,000 per year. Each T-shirt costs $8.00 to produce and sells for $12.50. How many T-shirts must the company produce and sell each year in order to make a profit of $65,000?

(a) 9200 (b) 11,250 (c) 14,375

(d) 20,000 (e) 25,556

85. Costs and Revenue PE A company produces a single product for which variable costs are $100 per unit and annual fixed costs are $1,000,000. If the product sells for $130 per unit, how many units must the company produce and sell in order to attain an annual profit of $2,000,000?

(a) 10,000 (b) 15,385 (c) 20,000

(d) 66,667 (e) 100,000

86. Demand and Revenue PE Suppose the quantity q of a certain brand of mountain bike sold each week depends on price according to the equation $q = 800 - 4p$. What is the total weekly revenue if a bike sells for $150?

(a) $200 (b) $600 (c) $2000

(d) $30,000 (e) $80,000

87. Demand and Revenue PE Suppose the number n of single-use cameras sold each month varies with the price according to the equation $n = 2200 - 25p$. What is the monthly revenue if the price of each camera is $8?

(a) $200 (b) $2,000 (c) $16,000

(d) $17,600 (e) $18,000

88. Setting a Price PE During 2008 a manufacturer produced 50,000 items that sold for $100 each. The manufacturer had fixed costs of $600,000 and made a profit before income taxes of $400,000. In 2009, rent and insurance combined increased by $200,000. Assuming that the quantity produced and all other costs were unchanged, what should the 2009 price be if the manufacturer is to make the same $400,000 profit before income taxes?

(a) $96 (b) $100 (c) $102 (d) $104 (e) $106

89. Setting a Price PE Rework Exercise 88 with a 2008 fixed cost of $800,000 and a profit before income taxes of $300,000.

(a) $96 (b) $100 (c) $102 (d) $104 (e) $106

Exercises 90–94 require the use of a graphing calculator.

90. Graph the three lines $y = 2x - 3$, $y = 2x$, and $y = 2x + 3$ together and then identify each line without using TRACE.

91. Graph the two lines $y = .5x + 1$ and $y = -2x + 9$ in the standard window $[-10, 10]$ by $[-10, 10]$. Do they appear perpendicular? If not, use **ZSquare** or **ZoomSqr** to obtain true aspect, and look at the graphs.

92. Graph the line $y = -.5x + 2$ with the window **ZDecimal** or **ZoomDec**. Without pressing TRACE, move the cursor to a point on the line. Then move the cursor one unit to the right and down $\frac{1}{2}$ unit to return to the line. If you start at a point on the line and move 2 units to the right, how many units down will you have to move the cursor to return to the line? Test your answer.

93. Graph the three lines $y = 2x + 1$, $y = x + 1$, and $y = .5x + 1$ together and then identify each line without using TRACE.

94. Repeat Exercise 92 for the line $y = .7x - 2$, using "up" instead of "down" and .7 instead of $\frac{1}{2}$.

Solutions to Practice Problems 1.4

1. By the steepness property, whenever x is increased by 1 unit, the value of y is increased by 4 units. Therefore, each additional unit of production brings in $4 of revenue. (The graph of $y = 4x$ is called a **revenue curve** and its slope is called the **marginal revenue of production**.)

2. $\begin{cases} y = 4x \\ y = 2x + 5000 \end{cases}$

Equate expressions for y:

$$4x = 2x + 5000$$
$$2x = 5000$$
$$x = 2500$$
$$y = 4(2500) = 10,000.$$

3. When producing 2500 units, the revenue equals the cost. This value of x is called the **break-even point**. Since profit = (revenue) − (cost), the company will make a profit only if its level of production is greater than the break-even point (Fig. 15).

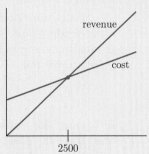

Figure 15

1.5 The Method of Least Squares

Modern people compile graphs of literally thousands of different quantities: the purchasing value of the dollar as a function of time; the pressure of a fixed volume of air as a function of temperature; the average income of people as a function of their years of formal education; or the incidence of strokes as a function of blood pressure. The observed points on such graphs tend to be irregularly distributed due to the complicated nature of the phenomena underlying them as well as to errors made in observation (for example, a given procedure for measuring average income may not count certain groups). In spite of the imperfect nature of the data, we are often faced with the problem of making assessments and predictions based on them. Roughly speaking, this problem amounts to filtering the sources of errors in the data and isolating the basic underlying trend. Frequently, on the basis of a suspicion or a working hypothesis, we may suspect that the underlying trend is linear—that is, the data should lie on a straight line. But which straight line? This is the problem that the **method of least squares** attempts to answer. To be more specific, let us consider the following problem:

> **Problem**   Given observed data points $(x_1, y_1), (x_2, y_2), \ldots, (x_N, y_N)$ in the plane, find the straight line that "best" fits these points.

In order to completely understand the statement of the problem being considered, we must define what it means for a line to "best" fit a set of points. If (x_i, y_i) is one of our observed points, then we will measure how far it is from a given line $y = ax + b$ by the vertical distance, E_i, from the point to the line. (See Fig. 1.)

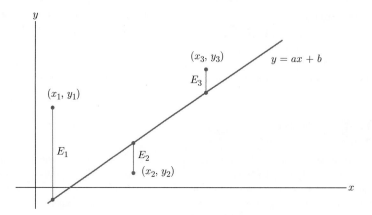

Figure 1. Fitting a line to data points.

Statisticians prefer to work with the square of the vertical distance E_i. The total error in approximating the data points $(x_1, y_1), \ldots, (x_N, y_N)$ by the line $y = ax + b$ is usually measured by the sum E of the squares of the vertical distances from the points to the line,

$$E = E_1^2 + E_2^2 + \cdots + E_N^2.$$

E is called the **least-squares error** of the observed points with respect to the line. If all the observed points lie on the line $y = ax + b$, then all the E_i are zero and the error E is zero. If a given observed point is far away from the line, the corresponding E_i^2 is large and hence makes a large contribution to the error E.

EXAMPLE 1

Finding the least-squares error Determine the least-squares error when the line $y = 1.5x + 3$ is used to approximate the data points $(1, 6)$, $(4, 5)$, and $(6, 14)$.

Solution Figure 2 shows the line, the points, and the vertical distances. The vertical distance of a point from the line is determined by finding the second coordinate of the point on the line having the same x-coordinate as the point. For instance, for the data point $(1, 6)$, the point on the line with x-coordinate 1 has y-coordinate $y = 1.5(1) + 3 = 4.5$ and, therefore, vertical distance $6 - 4.5 = 1.5$. Table 1 summarizes the vertical distances. The table shows that the least-squares error is $1.5^2 + 4^2 + 2^2 = 2.25 + 16 + 4 = 22.25$. ∎

Now Try Exercise 1

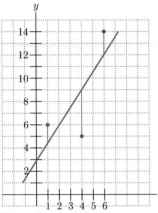

Figure 2

TABLE 1   Vertical distances from the line y =1.5x + 3

Data Point	Point on Line	Vertical Distance
$(1, 6)$	$(1, 4.5)$	1.5
$(4, 5)$	$(4, 9)$	4
$(6, 14)$	$(6, 12)$	2

In general, we cannot expect to find a line $y = mx + b$ that fits the observed points so well that the error E is zero. Actually, this situation will occur only if the observed points lie on a straight line. However, we can rephrase our original problem as follows:

Problem   Given observed data points $(x_1, y_1), (x_2, y_2), \ldots, (x_N, y_N)$ in the plane, find the straight line $y = mx + b$ for which the error E is as small as possible.

This line, called the **least-squares line** or the **regression line**, can be found from the data points with the formulas

$$m = \frac{N \cdot \sum xy - \sum x \cdot \sum y}{N \cdot \sum x^2 - \left(\sum x\right)^2}$$

$$b = \frac{\sum y - m \cdot \sum x}{N},$$

where

$$\sum x = \text{sum of the } x\text{-coordinates of the data points}$$

$$\sum y = \text{sum of the } y\text{-coordinates of the data points}$$

$$\sum xy = \text{sum of the products of the coordinates of the data points}$$

$$\sum x^2 = \text{sum of the squares of the } x\text{-coordinates of the data points}$$

$$N = \text{number of data points.}$$

That is,

$$\sum x = x_1 + x_2 + \cdots + x_N$$

$$\sum y = y_1 + y_2 + \cdots + y_N$$

$$\sum xy = x_1 \cdot y_1 + x_2 \cdot y_2 + \cdots + x_N \cdot y_N$$

$$\sum x^2 = x_1^2 + x_2^2 + \cdots + x_N^2.$$

EXAMPLE 2

Finding the least-squares line   Find the least-squares line for the data points of Example 1.

Solution   The sums are calculated in Table 2 and then used to determine the values of m and b.

TABLE 2			
x	y	xy	x^2
1	6	6	1
4	5	20	16
6	14	84	36
$\sum x = 11$	$\sum y = 25$	$\sum xy = 110$	$\sum x^2 = 53$

$$m = \frac{3 \cdot 110 - 11 \cdot 25}{3 \cdot 53 - 11^2} = \frac{55}{38} \approx 1.45$$

$$b = \frac{25 - \frac{55}{38} \cdot 11}{3} = \frac{38 \cdot 25 - 55 \cdot 11}{38 \cdot 3} = \frac{345}{114} = \frac{115}{38} \approx 3.03$$

Therefore, the equation of the least-squares line is $y = \frac{55}{38}x + \frac{115}{38}$. With this line, the least-squares error can be shown to be about 22.13.

Now Try Exercise 7

INCORPORATING TECHNOLOGY

Obtaining the Least-Squares Line with Technology   Least-squares lines can be obtained with graphing calculators and spreadsheets. For instance, on the TI-83/84 Plus graphing calculator screens in Fig. 3, the data points are entered into lists, the least-squares line is calculated with the item **LinReg(ax + b)** of the STAT/CALC menu, and the data points and line are plotted with [STAT PLOT] and GRAPH. On the TI-89, the least-squares line is calculated with the **LinReg** command found in the MATH/Statistics/Regressions menu. The end of this section and Appendix D contain the details for obtaining least-squares lines with these calculators.

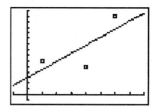

Figure 3.   Obtaining a least-squares line with a TI-83/84 Plus.

Spreadsheet programs, such as Excel, have special functions that calculate the slope and y-intercept of the least-squares line for a collection of data points. In Fig. 4 the least-squares line of Example 2 is calculated and graphed in Excel. The end of this section shows how to obtain the graph in Fig. 4.

The next example obtains a least-squares line and uses the line to make projections.

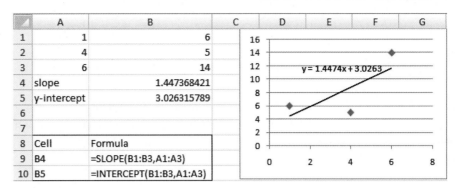

	A	B	C	D	E	F	G
1	1	6					
2	4	5					
3	6	14					
4	slope	1.447368421					
5	y-intercept	3.026315789					
6							
7							
8	Cell	Formula					
9	B4	=SLOPE(B1:B3,A1:A3)					
10	B5	=INTERCEPT(B1:B3,A1:A3)					

Figure 4. Obtaining a least-squares line with Excel.

EXAMPLE 3

Finding and using the least-squares line Table 3 gives the U.S. per capita health care expenditures[1] for several years.

TABLE 3	U.S per capita health care expenditures				
Year	2002	2003	2004	2005	2006
Dollars	5560	5952	6301	6649	7026

(a) Find the least-squares line for this data.

(b) Use the least-squares line to estimate the per capita health care expenditures for the year 2009.

(c) Use the least-squares line to estimate the year in which the per capita health care expenditures will reach \$9000.

Solution (a) The numbers can be made more manageable by counting years beginning with 2002 and measuring dollars in thousands. See Table 4.

TABLE 4	U.S per capita health care expenditures				
Year	0	1	2	3	4
Dollars	5.560	5.952	6.301	6.649	7.026

The slope and y-intercept of the least-squares line can be found with the formulas involving sums or with technology. The sums are calculated in Table 5 and then used to determine the values of m and b. The screens in the margin show the results of solving Example 3 with a graphing calculator.

```
L1      L2      L3      1
0       5.56    ------
1       5.952
2       6.301
3       6.649
4       7.026
        ------
L1(6)=
```

```
LinReg
y=ax+b
a=.3629
b=5.5718
```

TABLE 5			
x	y	xy	x^2
0	5.560	0	0
1	5.952	5.952	1
2	6.301	12.602	4
3	6.649	19.947	9
4	7.026	28.104	16
$\sum x = 10$	$\sum y = 31.488$	$\sum xy = 66.605$	$\sum x^2 = 30$

---

[1]Centers for Medicare and Medicaid Services, NHE Fact Sheet.

$$m = \frac{5 \cdot 66.605 - 10 \cdot 31.488}{5 \cdot 30 - 10^2} = \frac{18.145}{50} = .3629$$

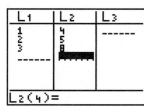

$$b = \frac{31.488 - .3629 \cdot 10}{5} = 5.5718$$

Therefore, the least-squares line is $y = .3629x + 5.5718$.

(b) The year 2009 corresponds to $x = 7$. The value of y is

$$y = .3629(7) + 5.5718 = 8.1121.$$

Therefore, an estimate of per capita health care expenditures in the year 2009 is \$8112.10.

(c) Set the value of y equal to 9 and solve for x.

$$9 = .3629x + 5.5718$$

$$x = \frac{9 - 5.5718}{.3629} \approx 9.45$$

Rounding up, expenditures are projected to reach \$9000 ten years after 2002; that is, in the year 2012. ∎

Now Try Exercise 13

Obtaining the Least-Squares Line with a Graphing Calculator The following steps show how to use a TI-83/84 Plus calculator to find the straight line that minimizes the least-squares error for the points $(1, 4)$, $(2, 5)$, and $(3, 8)$. (See Appendix D for the corresponding steps with the TI-89 calculator.)

1. Press $\boxed{\text{STAT}}$ **1** to obtain a table used for entering the data.
2. If there are no data in columns labeled $\mathbf{L_1}$ and $\mathbf{L_2}$, proceed to step 4.
3. Move the cursor up to $\mathbf{L_1}$ and press $\boxed{\text{CLEAR}}$ $\boxed{\text{ENTER}}$ to delete all data in $\mathbf{L_1}$'s column. Move the cursor right and up to $\mathbf{L_2}$ and press $\boxed{\text{CLEAR}}$ $\boxed{\text{ENTER}}$ to delete all data in $\mathbf{L_2}$'s column.
4. If necessary, move the cursor left to the first blank row of the $\mathbf{L_1}$ column. Press **1** $\boxed{\text{ENTER}}$ **2** $\boxed{\text{ENTER}}$ **3** $\boxed{\text{ENTER}}$ to place the x-coordinates of the three points into the $\mathbf{L_1}$ column.

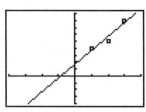

Figure 5

5. Move the cursor right to the $\mathbf{L_2}$ column and press **4** $\boxed{\text{ENTER}}$ **5** $\boxed{\text{ENTER}}$ **8** $\boxed{\text{ENTER}}$ to place the y-coordinates of the three points into the $\mathbf{L_2}$ column. The screen should now appear as in Fig. 5.
6. Press $\boxed{\text{STAT}}$ $\boxed{\blacktriangleright}$ and press the number for **LinReg(ax + b)**.
7. Press $\boxed{\text{ENTER}}$. The screen should now appear as in Fig. 6. The least-squares line is $y = 2x + \frac{5}{3}$. (*Note:* $\frac{5}{3} \approx 1.666666667$.)
8. If desired, the linear function can be assigned to $\mathbf{Y_1}$ with the following steps:

   (a) Press $\boxed{\text{Y=}}$ $\boxed{\text{CLEAR}}$ to erase the current expression in $\mathbf{Y_1}$.

   (b) Press $\boxed{\text{VARS}}$ **5** $\boxed{\blacktriangleright}$ $\boxed{\blacktriangleright}$ and the number for **RegEQ** to assign the linear function to $\mathbf{Y_1}$.

Figure 6

9. The original points can be easily plotted along with the least-squares line. Assume that the linear function has been assigned to $\mathbf{Y_1}$, that all other functions have been cleared or deselected, and that the window has been set to $[-4, 4]$ *by* $[-4, 9]$. Press $\boxed{\text{2nd}}$ $[\text{STAT PLOT}]$ $\boxed{\text{ENTER}}$ $\boxed{\text{ENTER}}$ $\boxed{\text{GRAPH}}$ to see the display in Fig. 7. (*Note 1:* To turn off the point-plotting feature, press $\boxed{\text{2nd}}$ $[\text{STAT PLOT}]$ $\boxed{\text{ENTER}}$ $\boxed{\blacktriangleright}$ $\boxed{\text{ENTER}}$. *Note 2:* The point-plotting feature can be toggled from the $\mathbf{Y=}$ editor by moving the cursor to the word **"Plot1"** on the top line and pressing $\boxed{\text{ENTER}}$.)

Figure 7

Obtaining the Least-Squares Line with an Excel Spreadsheet[2] The following steps obtain the graph in Fig. 4 on page 39.

1. Enter the six numbers in the range A1:B3, and then select the range.
2. (Excel 2007) On the **Insert** tab, in the **Charts** group, click on **Scatter**.
   (Excel 97-2003) Click the **Chart Wizard** button (holds a picture of a histogram) on the toolbar, and click on **XY (Scatter)** in the **Chart type** list box.
3. (Excel 2007) Click on **Scatter with only Markers** in the gallery that opens. *Note*: You can rest the mouse on any chart type to see its name.
   (Excel 97-2003) Click on the **Finish** button in the lower right corner of the window.
4. Right-click on one of the diamond-shaped points in the graph and then click on **Add Trendline**.
5. Click the box in front of **Display equation on chart**.
6. (Excel 2007) Click on the **Close** button.
   (Excel 97-2003) Click on the **OK** button.
7. Click on the legend located to the right of the graph and press the **Del** key.

Practice Problems 1.5

1. Can a vertical distance be negative?

2. Under what condition will a vertical distance be zero?

EXERCISES 1.5

1. Suppose the line $y = 3x + 1$ is used to fit the four data points in Table 6. Complete the table and determine the least-squares error E.

TABLE 6

Data Point	Point on Line	Vertical Distance
$(1, 3)$		
$(2, 6)$		
$(3, 11)$		
$(4, 12)$		

2. Suppose the line $y = -2x + 12$ is used to fit the four data points in Table 7. Complete the table and determine the least-squares error E.

TABLE 7

Data Point	Point on Line	Vertical Distance
$(1, 11)$		
$(2, 7)$		
$(3, 5)$		
$(4, 5)$		

3. Find the least-squares error E for the least-squares line fit to the four points in Fig. 8.

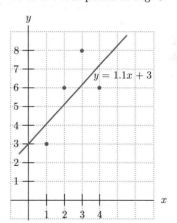

Figure 8

---

[2] "Excel 2007" refers to the latest version of Excel, and "Excel 97-2003" refers to the earlier versions.

4. Find the least-squares error E for the least-squares line fit to the five points in Fig. 9.

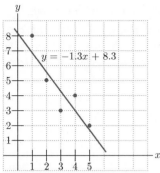

Figure 9

5. Complete Table 8 and find the values of m and b for the straight line that provides the best least-squares fit to the data.

TABLE 8

x	y	xy	x^2
1	7		
2	6		
3	4		
4	3		
$\sum x =$	$\sum y =$	$\sum xy =$	$\sum x^2 =$

6. Complete Table 9 and find the values of m and b for the straight line that provides the best least-squares fit to the data.

TABLE 9

x	y	xy	x^2
1	2		
2	4		
3	7		
4	9		
5	12		
$\sum x =$	$\sum y =$	$\sum xy =$	$\sum x^2 =$

7. Consider the data points $(1,2)$, $(2,5)$, and $(3,11)$. Find the straight line that provides the best least-squares fit to these data.

8. Consider the data points $(1,8)$, $(2,4)$, and $(4,3)$. Find the straight line that provides the best least-squares fit to these data.

9. Consider the data points $(1,9)$, $(2,8)$, $(3,6)$, and $(4,3)$. Find the straight line that provides the best least-squares fit to these data.

10. Consider the data points $(1,5)$, $(2,7)$, $(3,6)$, and $(4,10)$. Find the straight line that provides the best least-squares fit to these data.

Since Exercises 11–16 use real data, they are best answered with a graphing calculator or spreadsheet.

11. Lung Cancer and Smoking The following table[3] gives the crude male death rate for lung cancer in 1950 and the per capita consumption of cigarettes in 1930 in various countries.

Country	Cigarette Consumption (per Capita)	Lung Cancer Deaths (per Million Males)
Norway	250	95
Sweden	300	120
Denmark	350	165
Australia	470	170

(a) Use the method of least-squares to obtain the straight line that best fits these data.

(b) In 1930 the per capita cigarette consumption in Finland was 1100. Use the straight line found in part (a) to estimate the male lung cancer death rate in Finland in 1950.

12. Cost and Usage of Fuel The accompanying table shows the 1999 price of a gallon (in U.S. dollars) of fuel and the average miles driven per automobile for several countries.[4]

Country	Price per Gallon	Average Miles per Automobile
France	$4.01	9090
Germany	$3.78	7752
Japan	$3.65	6009
Sweden	$4.22	9339
United Kingdom	$5.13	10,680

(a) Find the straight line that provides the best least-squares fit to these data.

(b) In 1999, the price of gas in Canada was $2.04 per gallon. Use the straight line of part (a) to estimate the average number of miles automobiles were driven in Canada.

(c) In 1999 the average miles driven in the United States was 11,868. Use the straight line of part (a) to estimate the 1999 price of a gallon of gasoline in the United States.

---

[3]These data were obtained from *Smoking and Health*, Report of the Advisory Committee to the Surgeon General of the Public Health Service, U.S. Department of Health, Education, and Welfare, Washington, D.C., Public Health Service Publication No. 1103, p. 176.
[4]U.S. Department of Transportation, Federal Highway Administration, *Highway Statistics*, 2000.

13. College Graduates The following table gives the percent of persons 25 years and over who have completed four or more years of college.[5]

(a) Use the method of least squares to obtain the straight line that best fits these data.

(b) Estimate the percent for the year 2003.

(c) If the trend determined by the straight line in part (a) continues, when will the percent reach 30?

Year	Percent
1980	17.0
1985	19.4
1990	21.3
1995	23.0
2000	25.6
2005	27.6

14. College Enrollments The following table gives enrollment (in millions) in public colleges in the United States[6] for certain years.

Year	Enrollment
1995	11.1
2000	11.8
2002	12.8
2003	12.9
2004	13.0
2005	13.0
2006	13.3

(a) Use the method of least squares to obtain the straight line that best fits these data.

(b) Estimate the enrollment in 1998.

(c) If the trend determined by the straight line in part (a) continues, when will the enrollment reach 15 million?

15. Life Expectancy The following table is an abbreviated life expectancy table for U.S. males.

Current Age	Life Expectancy
0	75.2
20	76.2
40	77.7
60	80.8
80	88.2

(a) Find the straight line that provides the best least-squares fit to these data.

(b) Use the straight line of part (a) to estimate the life expectancy of a 30-year-old U.S. male. (*Note:* The actual life expectancy is 77.0 years.)

(c) Use the straight line of part (a) to estimate the life expectancy of a 50-year-old U.S. male. (*Note:* The actual life expectancy is 78.9 years.)

(d) Use the straight line of part (a) to estimate the life expectancy of a 90-year-old U.S. male. (*Note:* The actual life expectancy is 94.4 years.)

16. Banking Two Harvard economists studied countries' relationships between the independence of banks and inflation rates from 1955 to 1990.[7] The independence of banks was rated on a scale of -1.5 to 2.5, with -1.5, 0, and 2.5 corresponding to least, average, and most independence, respectively. The following table gives the values for various countries.

Country	Independence Rating	Inflation Rate (%)
New Zealand	-1.4	7.6
Italy	$-.75$	7.2
Belgium	.3	4.0
France	.4	6.0
Canada	.9	4.5
United States	1.6	4.0
Switzerland	2.2	3.1

(a) Use the method of least squares to obtain the straight line that best fits these data.

(b) What relationship between independence of banks and inflation is indicated by the least-squares line?

(c) Japan has a .6 independence rating. Use the least-squares line to estimate Japan's inflation rate.

(d) The inflation rate for Britain is 6.8. Use the least-squares line to estimate Britain's independence rating.

17. Consumer Price Index The following table gives the average price of a pound of potato chips in January of the given years. (*Source:* U.S. Bureau of Labor Statistics, Consumer Price Index.)

Year	Price
1993	$2.83
1996	$3.00
2000	$3.39
2004	$3.43
2008	$3.53

---

[5]U.S. Bureau of the Census.

[6]U.S. Dept. of Education, National Center for Education Statistics, *Digest of Education Statistics, 2007.*

[7]J. Bradford DeLong (Harvard) and L. H. Summers (World Bank).

(a) Use the method of least squares to obtain the straight line that best fits these data.

(b) Estimate the average price of a pound of potato chips in January 1999.

(c) If this trend continues, when will the average price of a pound of potato chips be $3.85?

18. **Greenhouse Gases** Although greenhouse gases are essential to maintaining the temperature of the Earth, an excess of greenhouse gases can raise the temperature to dangerous levels. One of the most threatening greenhouse gases is carbon dioxide (CO_2). The Mauna Loa atmospheric CO_2 measurements constitute the longest continuous record of atmospheric CO_2 concentrations available in the world. The following table shows the concentration of CO_2 (in parts per million) at Mauna Loa, Hawaii for three years.

Year	CO_2 (ppm)
1958	315
1983	342
2008	384

(a) Use the method of least squares to obtain the straight line that best fits these data. (Let $x = 0$ correspond to 1958.)

(b) Estimate the concentration of CO_2 in the year 2000.

(c) If the trend continues, in what year will the concentration of CO_2 reach 398 ppm.

19. Find the best least-squares fit to the points $(5, 4)$ and $(7, 3)$. Show that it is the straight line through the two points.

Solutions to Practice Problems 1.5

1. No. The word "distance" implies a nonnegative number. It is the absolute value of the difference between the y-coordinate of the data point and the y-coordinate of the point on the line.

2. The vertical distance will be zero when the point actually lies on the least-squares line.

CHAPTER SUMMARY

1. Cartesian coordinate systems associate a number with each point of a line and associate a pair of numbers with each point of a plane.

2. The collection of points in the plane that satisfy the linear equation $ax + by = c$ (where a and b are not both zero) lies on a straight line. After this equation is put into one of the standard forms $y = mx + b$ or $x = a$, the graph can be easily drawn.

3. The direction of the inequality sign in an inequality is unchanged when a number is added to or subtracted from both sides of the inequality, or when both sides of the inequality are multiplied by the same positive number. The direction of the inequality sign is reversed when both sides of the inequality are multiplied by the same negative number.

4. The collection of points in the plane that satisfy the linear inequality $ax + by \leq c$ or $ax + by \geq c$ consists of all points on and to one side of the graph of the corresponding linear equation. After this inequality is put into standard form, the graph can be easily pictured by crossing out the half-plane consisting of the points that do not satisfy the inequality.

5. The feasible set of a system of linear inequalities (that

is, the collection of points that satisfy all the inequalities) is best obtained by crossing out the points not satisfied by each inequality.

6. The point of intersection of a pair of lines can be obtained by first converting the equations to standard form and then either equating the two expressions for y or substituting the value of x from the form $x = a$ into the other equation.

7. The slope of the line $y = mx + b$ is the number m. It is also the ratio of the difference between the y-coordinates and the difference between the x-coordinates of any pair of points on the line.

8. The steepness property states that if we start at any point on a line of slope m and move 1 unit to the right, then we must move m units vertically to return to the line.

9. The point-slope formula states that the line of slope m passing through the point (x_1, y_1) has the equation $y - y_1 = m(x - x_1)$.

10. Two nonvertical lines are parallel if, and only if, they have the same slope. Two nonvertical lines are perpendicular if, and only if, the product of their slopes is -1.

11. The method of least squares finds the straight line that gives the best fit to a collection of points in the sense that the sum of the squares of the vertical distances from the points to the line is as small as possible. The slope and y-intercept of the least-squares line are usually found with formulas involving sums of coordinates or by using technology.

REVIEW OF FUNDAMENTAL CONCEPTS

1. How do you determine the coordinates of a point in the plane?

2. What is meant by the graph of an equation in x and y?

3. What is the general form of a linear equation in x and y?

4. What is the standard form of a linear equation in x and y?

5. What is the y-intercept of a line? How do you find the y-intercept from an equation of a line?

6. What is the x-intercept of a line? How do you find the x-intercept from an equation of a line?

7. Give a method for graphing the equation $y = mx + b$.

8. State the inequality properties for addition, subtraction, and multiplication.

9. What are the general and standard forms of a linear inequality in x and y?

10. Explain how to obtain the graph of a linear inequality.

11. What is meant by the feasible set of a system of linear inequalities?

12. Describe how to obtain the point of intersection of two lines.

13. Define the slope of a line, and give a physical description.

14. Suppose you know the slope and the coordinates of a point on a line. How could you draw the line without first finding its equation?

15. What is the point-slope form of the equation of a line?

16. Describe how to find the equation for a line when you know the coordinates of two points on the line.

17. What can you say about the slopes of perpendicular lines?

18. What can you say about the slopes of parallel lines?

19. What is the least-squares line approximation to a set of data points?

KEY FORMULAS

Equation of line with slope m and y-intercept $(0, b)$:

$$y = mx + b$$

Equation of line with slope m and passing through (x_1, y_1):

$$y - y_1 = m(x - x_1)$$

Slope of line passing through (x_1, y_1) and (x_2, y_2):

$$m = \frac{y_2 - y_1}{x_2 - x_1}$$

Let m and n be slopes of parallel lines:

$$m = n$$

Let m and n be slopes of perpendicular lines:

$$m = -\frac{1}{n}$$

Let $y = mx + b$ be the least-squares line for the points $(x_1, y_1), (x_2, y_2), \ldots, (x_N, y_N)$:

$$m = \frac{N \cdot \sum xy - \sum x \cdot \sum y}{N \cdot \sum x^2 - \left(\sum x\right)^2}$$

$$b = \frac{\sum y - m \cdot \sum x}{N},$$

where

$$\sum x = x_1 + x_2 + \ldots + x_N$$

$$\sum y = y_1 + y_2 + \ldots + y_N$$

$$\sum xy = x_1 \cdot y_1 + x_2 \cdot y_2 + \cdots + x_N y_N$$

$$\sum x^2 = x_1^2 + x_2^2 + \cdots + x_N^2.$$

SUPPLEMENTARY EXERCISES

1. What is the equation of the y-axis?

2. Graph the linear equation $y = -\frac{1}{2}x$.

3. Find the point of intersection of the pair of straight lines $x - 5y = 6$ and $3x = 6$.

4. Find the slope of the line having equation $3x - 4y = 8$.

5. Find the equation of the line having y-intercept $(0, 5)$ and x-intercept $(10, 0)$.

6. Graph the linear inequality $x - 3y \geq 12$.

7. Does the point $(1, 2)$ satisfy the linear inequality $3x + 4y \geq 11$?

8. Find the point of intersection of the pair of straight lines $2x - y = 1$ and $x + 2y = 13$.

9. Find the equation of the straight line passing through the point $(15, 16)$ and parallel to the line $2x - 10y = 7$.

10. Find the y-coordinate of the point having x-coordinate 1 and lying on the line $y = 3x + 7$.

11. Find the x-intercept of the straight line with equation $x = 5$.

12. Graph the linear inequality $y \leq 6$.

13. Solve the following system of linear equations:

$$\begin{cases} 3x - 2y = 1 \\ 2x + y = 24. \end{cases}$$

14. Graph the feasible set for the following system of inequalities:

$$\begin{cases} 2y + 7x \geq 28 \\ 2y - x \geq 0 \\ y \leq 8. \end{cases}$$

15. Find the y-intercept of the line passing through the point $(4, 9)$ and having slope $\frac{1}{2}$.

16. **Cost of Moving** The fee charged by a local moving company depends on the amount of time required for the move. If t hours are required, then the fee is $y = 35t + 20$ dollars. Give an interpretation of the slope and y-intercept of this line.

17. Are the points $(1, 2)$, $(2, 0)$, and $(3, 1)$ on the same line?

18. Write an equation of the line with x-intercept $(3, 0)$ and y-intercept $(0, -2)$.

19. **PE** If $x + 7y = 30$ and $x = -2y$, then y equals
   (a) -12 (b) 12 (c) $30/9$ (d) 6 (e) -6

20. Write the inequality whose graph is the half-plane below the line with slope $\frac{2}{3}$ and y-intercept $\left(0, \frac{3}{2}\right)$.

21. Write the inequality whose graph is the half-plane above the line through $(2, -1)$ and $(6, 8.6)$.

22. Solve the system of linear equations

$$\begin{cases} 1.2x + 2.4y = .6 \\ 4.8y - 1.6x = 2.4. \end{cases}$$

23. Find the equation of the line through $(1, 1)$ and the intersection point of the lines $y = -x + 1$ and $y = 2x + 3$.

24. Find all numbers x such that $2x + 3(x - 2) \geq 0$.

25. Graph the equation $x + \frac{1}{2}y = 4$, and give the slope and both intercepts.

26. Do the three graphs of the linear equations $2x - 3y = 1$, $5x + 2y = 0$, and $x + y = 1$ contain a common point?

27. Show that the lines with equations $2x - 3y = 1$ and $3x + 2y = 4$ are perpendicular.

28. Each of the half-planes (A), (B), (C), and (D) is the graph of one of the linear inequalities (a), (b), (c), and (d). Match each half-plane with its inequality.

(A)

(B)

(C)

(D)

(a) $x + y \geq 1$ (b) $x + y \leq 1$

(c) $x - y \leq 1$ (d) $y - x \leq -1$

29. Each of the lines L_1, L_2, and L_3 in Fig. 1 is the graph of one of the equations (a), (b), and (c). Match each of the following equations with its corresponding line.

Figure 1

(a) $4x + y = 17$ (b) $y = x + 2$

(c) $2x + 3y = 11$

30. Find a system of inequalities having the feasible set in Fig. 2 and find the coordinates of the unspecified vertex. [*Hint*: There is a right angle at the vertex $\left(4, \frac{3}{2}\right)$.]

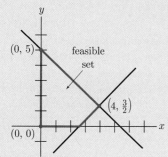

Figure 2

31. Consider the following four equations:

$$p = .01q - 5$$
$$p = .005q + .5$$
$$p = -.01q - 10$$
$$p = -.01q + 5.$$

One is the equation of a supply curve and another is the equation of a demand curve. Identify the two equations and then find the intersection point of those two curves.

32. Find the vertices of the following feasible set.

$$\begin{cases} x \geq 0 \\ y \geq 0 \\ 5x + y \leq 50 \\ 2x + 3y \leq 33 \\ x - 2y \geq -8 \end{cases}$$

33. College Freshmen The percent of college freshmen who enter college intending to eventually obtain a degree in a medical field (M.D., D.O., D.D.S., D.V.M.) has increased steadily in recent years.[1] The percent, y, who entered college x years after 2000 intending to obtain a degree in a medical field is approximated by the linear equation $y = .1x + 8.8$.

(a) What interpretation can be given to the y-intercept of the graph of the equation?

(b) Approximately what percent of college freshmen entering in 2008 intended to eventually obtain a degree in a medical field?

(c) In what year did approximately 9.2% of entering college freshmen intend to eventually obtain a degree in a medical field?

34. Profit Equation For a certain manufacturer, the production and sale of each additional unit yields an additional profit of $10. The sale of 1000 units yields a profit of $4000.

(a) Find the profit equation.

(b) Find the y- and x-intercepts of the graph of the profit equation.

(c) Sketch the graph of the profit equation.

35. Car Rentals One-day car rentals cost $50 plus 10 cents per mile from company A and $40 plus 20 cents per mile from company B.

(a) For each company, give the linear equations for the cost, y, when x miles are driven.

(b) Which company offers the best value when the car is driven for 80 miles?

(c) Which company offers the best value when the car is driven for 160 miles?

(d) For what mileage do the two companies offer the same value?

36. Inflation In 1990, white bread cost an average of $0.69 per pound. In 2007, white bread cost an average of $1.21 per pound. (*Source*: U.S. Bureau of Labor Statistics, Consumer Price Index)

(a) Assuming a linear increase in the price per pound of bread, find the equation that relates the cost, y, to the number of years after 1990, x.

(b) When did white bread cost an average of $1.00 per pound?

37. Graph the linear inequality $x \leq 3y + 2$.

38. Sales Commission A furniture store offers its new employees a weekly salary of $200 plus a 3% commission on sales. After one year, employees receive $100 per week plus a 5% sales commission. For what weekly sales level will the two scales produce the same salary?

[1] *The American Freshman: National Norms*; American Council on Education, University of California-Los Angeles.

39. Find a system of linear inequalities having the feasible set of Fig. 3.

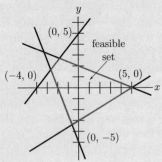

Figure 3

40. Find a system of linear inequalities having the feasible set of Fig. 4.

Figure 4

41. Medical Assistant Jobs According to the U.S. Department of Labor, medical assistant jobs are expected to increase from 417,000 in 2006 to 565,000 in 2016. Assuming that the number of medical assistant jobs increases linearly during that time, find the equation that relates the number of jobs, y, to the number of years after 2006, x. Use the equation to predict the number of medical assistant jobs in 2012.

42. Bachelor Degrees in Education According to the U.S. National Center of Educational Statistics, 110,807 bachelor degrees in education were awarded in 1991 and 107,238 were awarded in 2006. If the number of bachelor degrees in education continues to decline linearly, how many bachelor degrees in education will be awarded in 2010?

43. Soft Drinks According to *Beverage Digest*, Coke Classic's percentage of the soft drink market declined from 20.4 in 2000 to 17.2 in 2007. If the percentage declined linearly during that time, estimate Coke Classic's percentage of the soft drink market in 2005.

44. Life Expectancy The following table gives the 2008 life expectancy at birth for several countries.[2]

	Male	Female
Portugal	74.8	81.5
United States	75.3	81.1
Australia	77.9	83.8
Japan	78.7	85.6

(a) Use the method of least squares to obtain the straight line that best fits these data.

(b) In Norway the life expectancy of men is 77.2 years. Use the least-squares line from (a) to estimate the life expectancy for women.

(c) In France the life expectancy for women is 84.2 years. Use the least-squares line from (a) to estimate the life expectancy for men.

45. Prospective Nurses Students entering college in 2007 expressed the greatest interest in nursing careers in many years. The following table gives the percent of college freshmen in 2003 through 2007 who said that their probable career choice would be in nursing.[3]

(a) Use the method of least squares to obtain the straight line that best fits these data. (Let $x = 0$ represent 2000.)

(b) Estimate the percentage of students who entered college in 2009 whose probable career was in nursing.

(c) If the trend continues, when will 5.4% of freshmen have nursing as their probable career choice?

Year	Percent
2003	3.5
2004	3.9
2005	4.0
2006	4.1
2007	4.3

46. Cancer and Diet The following table[4] gives the (age-adjusted) death rate per 100,000 women from breast cancer and the daily dietary fat intake (in grams per day) for various countries.

Country	Fat Intake	Death Rate
Japan	41	4
Poland	90	10
Finland	118	13
United States	148	21

(a) Use the method of least squares to obtain the straight line that best fits these data.

[2]U.S. Bureau of the Census, International Database.

[3] *The American Freshman*: *National Norms*; American Council on Education, University of California–Los Angeles.

[4]B. S. Reddy et al., "Nutrition and Its Relationship to Cancer," *Advances in Cancer Research* 32:237, 1980.

(b) In Denmark women consume an average of 160 grams of fat per day. Use the least-squares line to estimate the breast cancer death rate.

(c) In New Zealand the breast cancer death rate is 22 women per 100,000. Use the least-squares line to estimate the daily fat intake in New Zealand.

Conceptual Exercises

47. Consider an equation of the form $y = mx + b$. When the value of m remains fixed and the value of b changes, the graph is translated vertically. As the value of b increases, does the graph move up or down?

48. Consider a linear equation of the form $y = mx + b$. When the value of b remains fixed and the value of m changes, the graph rotates about the point $(0, b)$. As the value of m increases, will the graph rotate in a clockwise or counterclockwise direction?

49. When is the x-intercept of a line the same as the y-intercept?

50. What is the difference between a line having undefined slope and zero slope?

51. Does every line have an x-intercept? y-intercept?

52. Suppose you have found the line of best least-squares fit to a collection of points and that you edit the data by adding a point on the line to the data. Will the expanded data have the same least-squares line? Explain the rationale for your conclusion, and then experiment to test whether your conclusion is correct.

CHAPTER TEST

1. Graph the linear equation $y = 3x$.

2. Find the y-coordinate of the point having x-coordinate $\frac{1}{2}$ and lying on the line $y = -2x + 6$.

3. Find the equation of the line through the point $(-1, 3)$ and parallel to the line $y = -2x + 6$.

4. Solve the system of linear equations

$$\begin{cases} 2x - 3y = 9 \\ -3x + 7y = -11. \end{cases}$$

5. Show that the lines $3x - y = 1$ and $-\frac{1}{3}x - 4 = y$ are perpendicular.

6. Graph the inequality $x + y \geq 8$ in the plane.

7. Find the equation of the line of slope 2 that passes through the intersection point of the lines $4x + 5y = 11$ and $2x - 3y = 7$.

8. Find the coordinates of the vertices of the feasible set for the following system of inequalities.

$$\begin{cases} x + y \geq 16 \\ -2x + y \leq 10 \\ 3x + y \leq 75 \\ x \geq 0, \ y \geq 0 \end{cases}$$

9. Sales Commissions Fred sells carpeting. He earns $200 each week plus 5% commission on sales. His sister thinks she has a better job selling carpet because she earns $250 a week plus 3% commission on her sales. For what volume of sales is Fred's sister correct? When is she incorrect?

10. Inflation The following table gives the average price of a pound of Red Delicious apples in January of the given years. (*Source*: U.S. Bureau of Labor Statistics, Consumer Price Index.)

Year	Price
1999	$0.86
2002	$0.88
2005	$0.97
2008	$1.16

(a) Use the method of least squares to obtain the straight line that best fits these data.

(b) Estimate the average price of a pound of Red Delicious apples in January 2004.

(c) If this trend continues, when will the average price of a pound of Red Delicious apples be $1.25?

CHAPTER 1 | PROJECT

Break-Even Analysis

We discussed linear demand curves in Section 1.3. Demand curves normally apply to an entire industry or to a monopolist; that is, a manufacturer that is so large that the quantity it supplies affects the market price of the commodity. We discussed linear cost curves and break-even analysis in Section 1.4. In this chapter project we combine demand curves and cost curves with least-squares lines to extend break-even analysis to a monopolist.

1. Table 1 can be used to obtain the demand curve for a monopolist who manufactures and sells a unique type of camera. The first column gives several production quantities in thousands of cameras and the second column gives the corresponding prices per camera. For instance, in order to sell 200 thousand cameras, the manufacturer must set the price at $316 per camera. Find the least-squares line that best fits these data; that is, find a demand curve for the camera.

TABLE 1

q (thousands)	p (dollars)
100	360
200	316
300	288
400	236
500	200

2. Use the demand curve from part 1 to estimate the price that must be charged in order to sell 350 thousand cameras. Calculate the revenue for this price and quantity. (*Note*: The revenue is the amount of money received from the sale of the cameras.)

3. Use the demand curve to estimate the quantity that can be sold if the price is $300 per camera. Calculate the revenue for this price and quantity.

4. Determine the expression that gives the revenue from producing and selling q thousand cameras. (*Note*: The number of cameras sold will be 1000q.)

5. Assuming that the manufacturer has fixed costs of $8,000,000 and that the variable cost of producing each thousand cameras is $100,000, find the equation of the cost curve.

6. Graph the revenue curve from part 4 and the cost curve from part 5 on a graphing calculator and determine the two points of intersection.

7. What is the break-even point; that is, the lowest value of q for which cost equals revenue?

8. For what values of q will the company make a profit?

MATRICES

We begin this chapter by developing a method for solving systems of linear equations in any number of variables. Our discussion of this method will lead naturally into the study of mathematical objects called *matrices*. The arithmetic and applications of matrices are the main topics of the chapter. We discuss in detail the application of matrix arithmetic to input–output analysis, which can be (and is) used to make production decisions for large businesses and entire economies.

2.1 Solving Systems of Linear Equations, I

In Chapter 1 we presented a method for solving systems of linear equations in two variables. The method of Chapter 1 is very efficient for determining the solutions. Unfortunately, it works only for systems of linear equations having *two* variables. In many applications we meet systems having more than two variables, as the following example illustrates.

EXAMPLE 1

Manufacturing The Upside Down company specializes in making down jackets, ski vests, and comforters. The requirements for down and labor and the profits earned are given in the following chart.

	Down (pounds)	Time (labor-hours)	Profit ($)
Jacket	3	2	6
Vest	2	1	6
Comforter	4	1	2

Each week the company has available 600 pounds of down and 275 labor-hours. It wants to earn a weekly profit of $1150. How many of each item should the company make each week?

Solution The requirements and earnings can be expressed by a system of equations. Let x be the number of jackets, y the number of vests, and z the number of comforters. If 600 pounds of down are used, then

$$[\text{down in jackets}] + [\text{down in vests}] + [\text{down in comforters}] = 600$$
$$3\,[\text{no. jackets}] \ + \ 2\,[\text{no. vests}] \ + \ 4\,[\text{no. comforters}] \ = 600.$$

That is,

$$3x + 2y + 4z = 600.$$

Similarly, the equation for labor is

$$2x + y + z = 275,$$

and the equation for the profit is

$$6x + 6y + 2z = 1150.$$

The numbers x, y, and z must simultaneously satisfy a system of three linear equations in three variables.

$$\begin{cases} 3x + 2y + 4z = \ \ 600 \\ 2x + \ y + \ z = \ \ 275 \\ 6x + 6y + 2z = 1150. \end{cases} \qquad (1)$$

Later we present a method for determining the solution to this system. This method yields the solution $x = 50$, $y = 125$, and $z = 50$. It is easy to confirm that these values of x, y, and z satisfy all three equations:

$$3(50) + 2(125) + 4(50) = \ \ 600$$
$$2(50) + \ (125) + \ (50) = \ \ 275$$
$$6(50) + 6(125) + 2(50) = 1150.$$

Thus, the Upside Down company can make a profit of $1150 by producing 50 jackets, 125 vests, and 50 comforters. ∎

In this section we develop a step-by-step procedure for solving systems of linear equations such as (1). The procedure, called the **Gauss–Jordan elimination method**, consists of repeatedly simplifying the system, using so-called elementary row operations, until the solution stares us in the face!

In the system of linear equations (1) the equations have been written in such a way that the x-terms, the y-terms, and the z-terms lie in different columns. We shall always be careful to display systems of equations with separate columns for each variable. One of the key ideas of the Gauss–Jordan elimination method is to think of the solution as a system of linear equations in its own right. For example, we can write the solution of system (1) as

$$\begin{cases} x & = 50 \\ & y & = 125 \\ & z = 50. \end{cases} \tag{2}$$

This is just a system of linear equations in which the coefficients of most terms are zero! Since the only terms with nonzero coefficients are arranged on a diagonal, such a system is said to be in **diagonal form**.

Our method for solving a system of linear equations consists of repeatedly using three operations that alter the system but do not change the solutions. The operations are used to transform the system into a system in diagonal form. Since the operations involve only elementary arithmetic and are applied to entire equations (i.e., rows of the system), they are called **elementary row operations**. Let us begin our study of the Gauss–Jordan elimination method by introducing these operations.

Elementary Row Operation 1   Interchange any two equations.

This operation is harmless enough. It certainly does not change the solutions of the system.

Elementary Row Operation 2   Multiply an equation by a nonzero number.

For example, if we are given the system of linear equations

$$\begin{cases} 2x - 3y + 4z = 11 \\ 4x - 19y + z = 31 \\ 5x + 7y - z = 12, \end{cases}$$

then we may replace it by a new system obtained by leaving the last two equations unchanged and multiplying the first equation by 3. To accomplish this, multiply each term of the first equation by 3. The transformed system is

$$\begin{cases} 6x - 9y + 12z = 33 \\ 4x - 19y + z = 31 \\ 5x + 7y - z = 12. \end{cases}$$

The operation of multiplying an equation by a nonzero number does not change the solutions of the system. For if a particular set of values of the variables satisfies the original equation, it satisfies the resulting equation, and vice versa.

Elementary row operation 2 may be used to make the coefficient of a particular variable 1.

EXAMPLE 2   **Demonstrating elementary row operation 2**   Replace the system

$$\begin{cases} -5x + 10y + 20z = 4 \\ x \qquad\;\; - 12z = 1 \\ x + y + z = 0 \end{cases}$$

by an equivalent system in which the coefficient of x in the first equation is 1.

Solution   The coefficient of x in the first equation is -5, so we use elementary row operation 2 to multiply the first equation by $-\frac{1}{5}$. Multiplying each term of the first equation by $-\frac{1}{5}$ gives

$$\begin{cases} x - 2y - \ 4z = -\frac{4}{5} \\ x \qquad - 12z = \ \ 1 \\ x + \ y + \ \ z = \ \ 0. \end{cases}$$

Now Try Exercise 1 ■

Another operation that can be performed on a system without changing its solutions is to replace one equation by its sum with some other equation. For example, consider this system of equations:

$$\text{A:} \quad \begin{cases} x + \ y - \ \ 2z = \ \ 3 \\ x + 2y - \ \ 5z = \ \ 4 \\ 5x + 8y - 18z = 14. \end{cases}$$

We can replace the second equation by the sum of the first and the second. Since

$$\begin{array}{r} x + \ y - 2z = 3 \\ + \ \ x + 2y - 5z = 4 \\ \hline 2x + 3y - 7z = 7, \end{array}$$

the resulting system is

$$\text{B:} \quad \begin{cases} x + \ y - \ \ 2z = \ \ 3 \\ 2x + 3y - \ \ 7z = \ \ 7 \\ 5x + 8y - 18z = 14. \end{cases}$$

If a particular choice of x, y, and z satisfies system A, it also satisfies system B. This is because system B results from adding equations. Similarly, system A can be derived from system B by subtracting equations. So any particular solution of system A is a solution of system B, and vice versa.

The operation of adding equations is usually used in conjunction with elementary row operation 2. That is, an equation is changed by adding to it a nonzero multiple of another equation. For example, consider the system

$$\begin{cases} x + \ y - \ \ 2z = \ \ 3 \\ x + 2y - \ \ 5z = \ \ 4 \\ 5x + 8y - 18z = 14. \end{cases}$$

Let us change the second equation by adding to it twice the first. Since

$$\begin{array}{rr} 2(\text{first}) & 2x + 2y - 4z = \ \ 6 \\ + \ (\text{second}) & x + 2y - 5z = \ \ 4 \\ \hline & 3x + 4y - 9z = 10, \end{array}$$

the new second equation is

$$3x + 4y - 9z = 10$$

and the transformed system is

$$\begin{cases} x + \ y - \ \ 2z = \ \ 3 \\ 3x + 4y - \ \ 9z = 10 \\ 5x + 8y - 18z = 14. \end{cases}$$

Since addition of equations and elementary row operation 2 are often used together, let us define a third elementary row operation.

> **Elementary Row Operation 3**   Change an equation by adding to it a multiple of another equation.

For reference, let us summarize the elementary row operations we have just defined.

> **Elementary Row Operations**
>
> **1.** Interchange any two equations.
>
> **2.** Multiply an equation by a nonzero number.
>
> **3.** Change an equation by adding to it a multiple of another equation.

The idea of the Gauss–Jordan elimination method is to transform an arbitrary system of linear equations into diagonal form by repeated applications of the three elementary row operations. To see how the method works, consider the following example.

EXAMPLE 3

Solving a system of equations using Gauss–Jordan elimination   Solve the following system by the Gauss–Jordan elimination method:

$$\begin{cases} x - 3y = 7 \\ -3x + 4y = -1. \end{cases}$$

Solution   Let us transform this system into diagonal form by examining one column at a time, starting from the left. Examine the first column:

$$x$$
$$-3x$$

The coefficient of the top x is 1, which is exactly what it should be for the system to be in diagonal form. So we do nothing to this term. Now examine the next term in the column, $-3x$. In diagonal form this term must be absent. In order to accomplish this, we add a multiple of the first equation to the second. Since the coefficient of x in the second is -3, we add three times the first equation to the second equation in order to cancel the x-term. (Abbreviation: $R_2 + 3R_1$. The R_2 refers to the second equation; that is, the equation in the second row of the system of equations. The expression $R_2 + 3R_1$ means that we are replacing the second equation by the original equation plus 3 times the first equation.)

$$\begin{cases} x - 3y = 7 \\ -3x + 4y = -1 \end{cases} \xrightarrow{\ R_2 + 3R_1\ } \begin{cases} x - 3y = 7 \\ \quad\ - 5y = 20. \end{cases}$$

The first column now has the proper form, so we proceed to the second column. In diagonal form that column will have one nonzero term, namely the second, and the coefficient of y in that term must be 1. To bring this about, multiply the second equation by $-\frac{1}{5}$ (abbreviation: $(-\frac{1}{5})R_2$):

$$\begin{cases} x - 3y = 7 \\ \quad\ - 5y = 20 \end{cases} \xrightarrow{\ (-\frac{1}{5})R_2\ } \begin{cases} x - 3y = 7 \\ \qquad\quad y = -4. \end{cases}$$

The second column still does not have the correct form. We must get rid of the $-3y$-term in the first equation. We do this by adding a multiple of the second equation to the first. Since the coefficient of the term to be canceled is -3, we add three times the second equation to the first:

$$\begin{cases} x - 3y = 7 \\ y = -4 \end{cases} \xrightarrow{R_1 + 3R_2} \begin{cases} x = -5 \\ y = -4. \end{cases}$$

The system is now in diagonal form and the solution can be read off: $x = -5$,

Now Try Exercise 37 $y = -4$. ∎

NOTE The abbreviation for interchanging the first and second equation is $R_1 \leftrightarrow R_2$. ∎

EXAMPLE 4

Solving a system of equations using Gauss–Jordan elimination Use the Gauss–Jordan elimination method to solve the system

$$\begin{cases} 2x - 6y = -8 \\ -5x + 13y = 1. \end{cases}$$

Solution We can perform the calculations in a mechanical way, proceeding column by column from the left:

$$\begin{cases} 2x - 6y = -8 \\ -5x + 13y = 1 \end{cases} \xrightarrow{\frac{1}{2}R_1} \begin{cases} x - 3y = -4 \\ -5x + 13y = 1 \end{cases}$$

$$\xrightarrow{R_2 + 5R_1} \begin{cases} x - 3y = -4 \\ - 2y = -19 \end{cases}$$

$$\xrightarrow{(-\frac{1}{2})R_2} \begin{cases} x - 3y = -4 \\ y = \frac{19}{2} \end{cases}$$

$$\xrightarrow{R_1 + 3R_2} \begin{cases} x = \frac{49}{2} \\ y = \frac{19}{2}. \end{cases}$$

Now Try Exercise 45 So the solution of the system is $x = \frac{49}{2}$, $y = \frac{19}{2}$. ∎

The calculation becomes easier to follow if we omit writing down the variables at each stage and work only with the coefficients. At each stage of the computation, the system is represented by a rectangular array of numbers. For instance, the original system is written[1]

$$\begin{bmatrix} 2 & -6 & | & -8 \\ -5 & 13 & | & 1 \end{bmatrix}.$$

The elementary row operations are performed on the rows of this rectangular array just as if the variables were there. So, for example, the first step in the above solution is to multiply the first equation by $\frac{1}{2}$. This corresponds to multiplying the first row of the array by $\frac{1}{2}$ to get

$$\begin{bmatrix} 1 & -3 & | & -4 \\ -5 & 13 & | & 1 \end{bmatrix}.$$

The diagonal form just corresponds to the array

$$\begin{bmatrix} 1 & 0 & | & \frac{49}{2} \\ 0 & 1 & | & \frac{19}{2} \end{bmatrix}.$$

---

[1] The vertical line between the second and third columns is a placemarker that separates the data obtained from the left- and right-hand sides of the equations. It is inserted for visual convenience.

Note that this array has ones down the diagonal and zeros everywhere else on the left. The solution of the system appears on the right.

A rectangular array of numbers is called a **matrix** (plural: *matrices*). In the next example, we use matrices to carry out the Gauss–Jordan elimination method.

EXAMPLE 5

Solving a system of equations using Gauss–Jordan elimination   Use the Gauss–Jordan elimination method to solve the system

$$\begin{cases} 3x - 6y + 9z = 0 \\ 4x - 6y + 8z = -4 \\ -2x - y + z = 7. \end{cases}$$

Solution   The initial array corresponding to the system is

$$\left[\begin{array}{ccc|c} 3 & -6 & 9 & 0 \\ 4 & -6 & 8 & -4 \\ -2 & -1 & 1 & 7 \end{array}\right].$$

We must use elementary row operations to transform this array into diagonal form—that is, with ones down the diagonal and zeros everywhere else on the left:

$$\left[\begin{array}{ccc|c} 1 & 0 & 0 & * \\ 0 & 1 & 0 & * \\ 0 & 0 & 1 & * \end{array}\right].$$

We proceed one column at a time.

$$\left[\begin{array}{ccc|c} 3 & -6 & 9 & 0 \\ 4 & -6 & 8 & -4 \\ -2 & -1 & 1 & 7 \end{array}\right] \xrightarrow{\frac{1}{3}R_1} \left[\begin{array}{ccc|c} 1 & -2 & 3 & 0 \\ 4 & -6 & 8 & -4 \\ -2 & -1 & 1 & 7 \end{array}\right] \xrightarrow{R_2 + (-4)R_1}$$

$$\left[\begin{array}{ccc|c} 1 & -2 & 3 & 0 \\ 0 & 2 & -4 & -4 \\ -2 & -1 & 1 & 7 \end{array}\right] \xrightarrow{R_3 + 2R_1} \left[\begin{array}{ccc|c} 1 & -2 & 3 & 0 \\ 0 & 2 & -4 & -4 \\ 0 & -5 & 7 & 7 \end{array}\right] \xrightarrow{\frac{1}{2}R_2}$$

$$\left[\begin{array}{ccc|c} 1 & -2 & 3 & 0 \\ 0 & 1 & -2 & -2 \\ 0 & -5 & 7 & 7 \end{array}\right] \xrightarrow{R_1 + 2R_2} \left[\begin{array}{ccc|c} 1 & 0 & -1 & -4 \\ 0 & 1 & -2 & -2 \\ 0 & -5 & 7 & 7 \end{array}\right] \xrightarrow{R_3 + 5R_2}$$

$$\left[\begin{array}{ccc|c} 1 & 0 & -1 & -4 \\ 0 & 1 & -2 & -2 \\ 0 & 0 & -3 & -3 \end{array}\right] \xrightarrow{\left(-\frac{1}{3}\right)R_3} \left[\begin{array}{ccc|c} 1 & 0 & -1 & -4 \\ 0 & 1 & -2 & -2 \\ 0 & 0 & 1 & 1 \end{array}\right] \xrightarrow{R_1 + 1R_3}$$

$$\left[\begin{array}{ccc|c} 1 & 0 & 0 & -3 \\ 0 & 1 & -2 & -2 \\ 0 & 0 & 1 & 1 \end{array}\right] \xrightarrow{R_2 + 2R_3} \left[\begin{array}{ccc|c} 1 & 0 & 0 & -3 \\ 0 & 1 & 0 & 0 \\ 0 & 0 & 1 & 1 \end{array}\right]$$

The last array is in diagonal form, so we just put back the variables and read off the solution:

$$x = -3, \qquad y = 0, \qquad z = 1.$$

Because so much arithmetic has been performed, it is a good idea to check the solution by substituting the values for x, y, and z into each of the equations of the original system. This will uncover any arithmetic errors that may have occurred.

$$\begin{cases} 3x - 6y + 9z = 0 \\ 4x - 6y + 8z = -4 \\ -2x - y + z = 7 \end{cases} \qquad \begin{cases} 3(-3) - 6(0) + 9(1) = 0 \\ 4(-3) - 6(0) + 8(1) = -4 \\ -2(-3) - (0) + (1) = 7 \end{cases}$$

$$\begin{cases} -9 - 0 + 9 = 0 \\ -12 - 0 + 8 = -4 \\ 6 - 0 + 1 = 7 \end{cases}$$

$$\begin{cases} 0 = 0 \\ -4 = -4 \\ 7 = 7 \end{cases}$$

Now Try Exercise 43   So we have indeed found a solution of the system.   ■

REMARK   Note that so far we have not had to use elementary row operation 1, which allows interchange of equations. But in some examples it is definitely needed.

Consider this system:

$$\begin{cases} y + z = 0 \\ 3x - y + z = 6 \\ 6x - z = 3. \end{cases}$$

The first step of the Gauss–Jordan elimination method consists of making the x-coefficient 1 in the first equation. But we cannot do this, since the first equation does not involve x. To remedy this difficulty, just interchange the first two equations to guarantee that the first equation involves x. Now proceed as before. Of course, in terms of the matrix of coefficients, interchanging equations corresponds to interchanging rows of the matrix.   ■

INCORPORATING TECHNOLOGY

GC   Graphing utilities can perform many operations with matrices, including elementary row operations.

TI-83/84 Plus   Pressing 2ND [MATRX] or 2ND [MATRIX] presents the three menus shown in Fig. 1. You define a new matrix or alter an existing matrix with the EDIT menu. You place the name of an existing matrix on the home screen with the NAMES menu. You perform operations on existing matrices with the MATH menu.

With the EDIT menu, you first select one of the names **[A]**, **[B]**, **[C]**, ... for the matrix and then specify the size and fill in the entries as shown in Fig. 2. The three elementary row operations are carried out with commands of the following forms from the MATRX/MATH menu.

Figure 1

rowSwap(*matrix, rowA, rowB*)	Interchange *rowA* and *rowB* of *matrix*
*row(*value, matrix, row*)	Multiply *row* of *matrix* by *value*
*row+(*value, matrix, rowA, rowB*)	Add *value*rowA* to *rowB* of *matrix*

When one of these commands is carried out, the resulting matrix is displayed but the stored matrix is not changed. Therefore, when a sequence of commands is executed to carry out the Gauss–Jordan elimination method, each command should be followed with STO ▶ *matrix* to change the stored matrix. (*Note:* To display the name of a matrix, press 2nd[MATRX], cursor down to the matrix, and press ENTER.)

Figure 2

For instance, if in Example 5 the original matrix is named [A], then the first three row operations are carried out with

$$\texttt{*row(1/3,[A],1)}\boxed{\texttt{STO}}\blacktriangleright\texttt{[A]}$$
$$\texttt{*row+(-4,[A],1,2)}\boxed{\texttt{STO}}\blacktriangleright\texttt{[A]}$$
$$\texttt{*row+(2,[A],1,3)}\boxed{\texttt{STO}}\blacktriangleright\texttt{[A]}.$$

Figure 3

Matrix entries are normally displayed on the calculator as decimals. From the home screen you can display the entries as fractions with a command such as **[A] ▶Frac** or **Ans ▶Frac**. (**▶Frac** is displayed by pressing $\boxed{\texttt{MATH}}$ **1**.) See Fig. 3.

TI-89 Matrices are created and altered with the Data/Matrix editor that is accessed through the $\boxed{\texttt{APPS}}$ key. See Appendix D for details. ∎

ES[2] The systems of linear equations presented in this section can be solved with a device called **Solver**. The steps below use Solver to find the solution to Example 5.

$\boxed{\texttt{NOTE}}$▶ A cell is most easily used in formulas if it has been given a name such as **x**, **y**, or **z**. To name a cell, select it, click on the Name box (located just above the upper-left corner of the spreadsheet), type the name, and press Enter. Single letter names can consist of any letter other than C or R. ∎

1. Give the cells A1, A2, and A3 the names x, y, and z, respectively. (There is no need to place any values into these cells.)

2. In the cells B1, B2, and B3, place the formulas consisting of the left sides of the three equations. For instance, type the formula **=3*x-6*y+9*z** into cell B1.

3. (Excel 2007) On the **Data** tab, in the **Analysis** group, click on **Solver**.
   (Excel 97-2003) Click on Solver in the Tools menu.
   A window titled Solver Parameters will appear. (*Note*: If Solver is not present on your computer, see Appendix C for instructions on installing Solver.)

4. Clear the contents, if any, of the Set Target Cell box. (Ignore any entries appearing in the "Equal To" line.)

5. Type **x**, **y**, **z** into the By Changing Cells box.

6. Click the Add button. An Add Constraint dialog box will appear.
   (a) Enter **$B$1,=,** and **0** into the three boxes and then press the Add button.
   (b) Enter **$B$2,=,** and **–4** into the three boxes and then press the Add button.
   (c) Enter **$B$3,=,** and **7** into the three boxes and then press the OK button. The Solver Parameters window will reappear as shown in Fig. 4 on the next page. *Note*: The entries 0, −4, and 7 are the numbers on the right sides of the equations.

7. Click the Solve button. A window titled Solver Results will appear.

8. Click the OK button. The solution to the system of linear equations will appear in the x, y, and z cells. *Note*: The values may differ slightly from the true values due to rounding errors. For instance, the value for y may appear as something like 2.72E-15 (that is, 2.72×10^{-15}) instead of 0.

---

[2]ES is an abbreviation for "Excel Spreadsheet."

Solver Parameters   ✕

Set Target Cell: [   ] 🔢   [Solve]

Equal To: ⦿ Max   ⦾ Min   ⦾ Value of: [0   ]   [Close]

By Changing Cells:

[x,y,z   ] 🔢   [Guess]

Subject to the Constraints: [Options]

```
$B$1 = 0
$B$2 = -4                               [ Add ]
$B$3 = 7
                                        [ Change ]
                                                    [ Reset All ]
                                        [ Delete ]
                                                    [ Help ]
```

Figure 4

Practice Problems 2.1

1. Determine whether the following systems of linear equations are in diagonal form.

(a) $\begin{cases} x \quad + z = 3 \\ \quad y \quad = 2 \\ \quad\quad z = 7 \end{cases}$ (b) $\begin{cases} x \quad\quad = -1 \\ \quad y \quad = 0 \\ \quad\quad 3z = 4 \end{cases}$

2. Perform the indicated elementary row operation.

(a) $\begin{cases} x - 3y = 2 \\ 2x + 3y = 5 \end{cases} \xrightarrow{R_2 + (-2)R_1}$

(b) $\begin{cases} x + y = 3 \\ -x + 2y = 5 \end{cases} \xrightarrow{R_2 + 1R_1}$

3. State the next elementary row operation that should be performed when applying the Gauss–Jordan elimination method.

(a) $\begin{bmatrix} 0 & 2 & 4 & | & 1 \\ 0 & 3 & -7 & | & 0 \\ 3 & 6 & -3 & | & 3 \end{bmatrix}$

(b) $\begin{bmatrix} 1 & -3 & 4 & | & 5 \\ 0 & 2 & 3 & | & 4 \\ -6 & 5 & -7 & | & 0 \end{bmatrix}$

EXERCISES 2.1

In Exercises 1–8, perform the indicated elementary row operations and give their abbreviations.

1. Operation 2: Multiply the first equation by 2.

$$\begin{cases} \frac{1}{2}x - 3y = 2 \\ 5x + 4y = 1 \end{cases}$$

2. Operation 2: Multiply the second equation by -1.

$$\begin{cases} x + 4y = 6 \\ -y = 2 \end{cases}$$

3. Operation 3: Change the second equation by adding to it 5 times the first equation.

$$\begin{cases} x + 2y = 3 \\ -5x + 4y = 1 \end{cases}$$

4. Operation 3: Change the second equation by adding to it $\left(-\frac{1}{2}\right)$ times the first equation.

$$\begin{cases} x - 6y = 4 \\ \frac{1}{2}x + 2y = 1 \end{cases}$$

5. Operation 3: Change the third equation by adding to it (-4) times the first equation.

$$\begin{cases} x - 2y + z = 0 \\ y - 2z = 4 \\ 4x + y + 3z = 5 \end{cases}$$

6. Operation 3: Change the third equation by adding to it 3 times the second equation.

$$\begin{cases} x + 6y - 4z = 1 \\ y + 3z = 1 \\ -3y + 7z = 2 \end{cases}$$

7. Operation 3: Change the first row by adding to it $\frac{1}{2}$ times the second row.

$$\begin{bmatrix} 1 & -\frac{1}{2} & 3 \\ 0 & 1 & 4 \end{bmatrix}$$

8. Operation 3: Change the third row by adding to it (-4) times the second row.

$$\begin{bmatrix} 1 & 0 & 7 & 9 \\ 0 & 1 & -2 & 3 \\ 0 & 4 & 8 & 5 \end{bmatrix}$$

In Exercises 9–12, write the matrix corresponding to the system of linear equations.

9. $\begin{cases} -3x + 4y = -2 \\ x - 7y = 8 \end{cases}$
10. $\begin{cases} \frac{2}{3}x - 3y = 4 \\ y = -5 \end{cases}$

11. $\begin{cases} x + 13y - 2z = 0 \\ 2x - z = 3 \\ y = 5 \end{cases}$
12. $\begin{cases} y - z = 22 \\ 2x = 17 \\ x - 3y = 12 \end{cases}$

In Exercises 13–16, write the system of linear equations corresponding to the matrix.

13. $\begin{bmatrix} 0 & -2 & 3 \\ 1 & 7 & -4 \end{bmatrix}$
14. $\begin{bmatrix} -5 & \frac{2}{3} & 3 \\ 1 & 7 & -\frac{5}{8} \end{bmatrix}$

15. $\begin{bmatrix} 3 & 2 & 0 & -3 \\ 0 & 1 & -6 & 4 \\ -5 & -1 & 7 & 0 \end{bmatrix}$
16. $\begin{bmatrix} \frac{6}{5} & -1 & 12 & -\frac{2}{3} \\ -1 & 0 & 0 & 5 \\ 0 & 2 & -1 & 6 \end{bmatrix}$

In Exercises 17–22, describe in your own words the meaning of the notation with respect to a matrix.

17. $\frac{1}{3}R_2$
18. $R_2 + (-4)R_1$
19. $R_1 + 3R_2$
20. $(-1)R_1$
21. $R_2 \leftrightarrow R_3$
22. $R_1 \leftrightarrow R_2$

In Exercises 23–28, carry out the indicated elementary row operation.

23. $\begin{bmatrix} 1 & 2 & 0 \\ -3 & 4 & 5 \end{bmatrix} \xrightarrow{R_2 + 3R_1} \begin{bmatrix} & & \\ & & \end{bmatrix}$

24. $\begin{bmatrix} -\frac{1}{2} & 2 & \frac{3}{4} \\ -3 & 4 & 9 \end{bmatrix} \xrightarrow{(-2)R_1} \begin{bmatrix} & & \\ & & \end{bmatrix}$

25. $\begin{bmatrix} \frac{1}{7} & \frac{2}{7} & \frac{3}{7} \\ 3 & -2 & 0 \end{bmatrix} \xrightarrow{7R_1} \begin{bmatrix} & & \\ & & \end{bmatrix}$

26. $\begin{bmatrix} 1 & 3 & -2 \\ 4 & 4 & 5 \end{bmatrix} \xrightarrow{R_2 + (-4)R_1} \begin{bmatrix} & & \\ & & \end{bmatrix}$

27. $\begin{bmatrix} 0 & 1 & 7 \\ 1 & 3 & -5 \end{bmatrix} \xrightarrow{R_1 \leftrightarrow R_2} \begin{bmatrix} & & \\ & & \end{bmatrix}$

28. $\begin{bmatrix} 4 & 5 & 6 \\ -3 & 2 & 0 \end{bmatrix} \xrightarrow{R_1 + 1R_2} \begin{bmatrix} & & \\ & & \end{bmatrix}$

In Exercises 29–36, state the next elementary row operation that should be performed in order to put the matrix into diagonal form. Do not perform the operation.

29. $\begin{bmatrix} 1 & -5 & 1 \\ -2 & 4 & 6 \end{bmatrix}$
30. $\begin{bmatrix} 1 & 3 & 4 \\ 0 & 2 & 6 \end{bmatrix}$

31. $\begin{bmatrix} 1 & 2 & 3 \\ 0 & 1 & 4 \end{bmatrix}$
32. $\begin{bmatrix} 1 & -2 & 5 & 7 \\ 0 & -3 & 6 & 9 \\ 4 & 5 & -6 & 7 \end{bmatrix}$

33. $\begin{bmatrix} 0 & 5 & -3 & 6 \\ 2 & -3 & 4 & 5 \\ 4 & 1 & -7 & 8 \end{bmatrix}$
34. $\begin{bmatrix} 1 & 4 & -2 & 5 \\ 0 & -3 & 6 & 9 \\ 0 & 4 & 3 & 1 \end{bmatrix}$

35. $\begin{bmatrix} 1 & 0 & 3 & 4 \\ 0 & 1 & 2 & 5 \\ 0 & 0 & 1 & 6 \end{bmatrix}$
36. $\begin{bmatrix} 1 & 2 & 4 & 5 \\ 0 & 0 & 3 & 6 \\ 0 & 1 & 1 & 7 \end{bmatrix}$

In Exercises 37–50, solve the linear system by using the Gauss–Jordan elimination method.

37. $\begin{cases} x + 9y = 8 \\ 2x + 8y = 6 \end{cases}$
38. $\begin{cases} \frac{1}{3}x + 2y = 1 \\ -2x - 4y = 6 \end{cases}$

39. $\begin{cases} x - 3y + 4z = 1 \\ 4x - 10y + 10z = 4 \\ -3x + 9y - 5z = -6 \end{cases}$

40. $\begin{cases} \frac{1}{2}x + y = 4 \\ -4x - 7y + 3z = -31 \\ 6x + 14y + 7z = 50 \end{cases}$

41. $\begin{cases} 2x - 2y + 4 = 0 \\ 3x + 4y - 1 = 0 \end{cases}$
42. $\begin{cases} 2x + 3y = 4 \\ -x + 2y = -2 \end{cases}$

43. $\begin{cases} 4x - 4y + 4z = -8 \\ x - 2y - 2z = -1 \\ 2x + y + 3z = 1 \end{cases}$

44. $\begin{cases} x + 2y + 2z - 11 = 0 \\ x - y - z + 4 = 0 \\ 2x + 5y + 9z - 39 = 0 \end{cases}$

45. $\begin{cases} .2x + .3y = 4 \\ .6x + 1.1y = 15 \end{cases}$
46. $\begin{cases} \frac{3}{2}x + 6y = 9 \\ \frac{1}{2}x - \frac{2}{3}y = 11 \end{cases}$

47. $\begin{cases} x + y + 4z = 3 \\ 4x + y - 2z = -6 \\ -3x + 2z = 1 \end{cases}$

48. $\begin{cases} -2x - 3y + 2z = -2 \\ x + y = 3 \\ -x - 3y + 5z = 8 \end{cases}$

49. $\begin{cases} -x + y = -1 \\ x + z = 4 \\ 6x - 3y + 2z = 10 \end{cases}$
50. $\begin{cases} x + 2z = 9 \\ y + z = 1 \\ 3x - 2y = 9 \end{cases}$

51. **PE** A baked potato smothered with cheddar cheese weighs 180 grams and contains 10.5 grams of protein. If cheddar cheese contains 25% protein and a baked potato contains 2% protein, how many grams of cheddar cheese are there?

    (a) 25   (b) 30   (c) 35   (d) 40   (e) 45

52. **PE** A high school math department purchased brand A calculators for $80 each and brand B calculators for $95 each. It purchased a total of 20 calculators at a total cost of $1780. How many brand A calculators did the department purchase?

    (a) 7   (b) 8   (c) 9   (d) 10   (e) 11

Exercises 53 and 54 are multiple choice exercises with five possible choices. Each exercise consists of a question and two statements that may or may not provide sufficient information to answer the question. Select the response below that best describes the situation.

(a) Statement I alone is sufficient to answer the question, but statement II is not sufficient.

(b) Statement II alone is sufficient to answer the question, but statement I is not sufficient.

(c) Both statements together are sufficient to answer the question, but neither alone is sufficient.

(d) Each statement alone is sufficient to answer the question.

(e) Both statements together are not sufficient to answer the question.

53. **PE** A box of golf balls and a golf glove cost a total of $20. How much does the box of balls cost?

    Statement I: The golf glove costs three times as much as the box of golf balls.

    Statement II: The golf glove costs $15.

54. **PE** I have four nickels and three pennies in my pocket. What is the total weight of these coins?

    Statement I: A nickel weighs twice as much as a penny.

    Statement II: The total weight of a nickel and two pennies is 10 grams.

55. **Sales** A street vendor has a total of 350 short and long sleeve T-shirts. If she sells the short sleeve shirts for $10 each and the long sleeve shirts for $14 each, how many of each did she sell if she sold all of her stock for $4300?

56. **Sales** A grocery store carries two brands of bleach. A 96-ounce bottle of the national brand sells for $1.99, while the same size bottle of the store brand sells for $1.79. How many bottles of each brand were sold if a total of 82 bottles were sold for $158.98?

57. **Movie Tickets** A 350-seat movie theater charges $9.25 admission for adults and $6.25 for children. If the theater is full and $2973.50 is collected, how many adults and how many children are in the audience?

58. **Batting Average** A baseball player's batting average is determined by dividing the number of hits by the number of times at bat and multiplying by 1000. (Batting averages are usually, but not necessarily, rounded to the nearest whole number.) For instance, if a player gets 2 hits in 5 times at bat, his batting average is 400: $\left(\frac{2}{5} \times 1000 = 400\right)$. Partway through the season, a player thinks to himself, "If I get a hit in my next time at bat, my average will go up to 250; if I don't get a hit, it will drop to 187.5." How many times has this player batted, how many hits has he had, and what is his current batting average?

59. **Investment Planning** A bank wishes to invest a $100,000 trust fund in three sources: bonds paying 8%; certificates of deposit paying 7%; and first mortgages paying 10%. The bank wishes to realize an $8000 annual income from the investment. A condition of the trust is that the total amount invested in bonds and certificates of deposit must be triple the amount invested in mortgages. How much should the bank invest in each possible category? Let x, y, and z, respectively, be the amounts invested in bonds, certificates of deposit, and first mortgages. Solve the system of equations by the Gauss–Jordan elimination method.

60. **Nutrition Planning** A dietitian wishes to plan a meal around three foods. Each ounce of food I contains 10% of the daily requirements for carbohydrates, 10% for protein, and 15% for vitamin C. Each ounce of food II contains 10% of the daily requirements for carbohydrates, 5% for protein, and 0% for vitamin C. Each ounce of food III contains 10% of the daily requirements for carbohydrates, 25% for protein, and 10% for vitamin C. How many ounces of each food should be served in order to supply exactly the daily requirements for each nutrient? Let x, y, and z, respectively, be the number of ounces of foods I, II, and III.

61. **Candy Assortments** A small candy store makes three types of party mixes. The first type contains 40% nonpareils and 60% peanut clusters, while the second type contains 30% peanut clusters and 70% chocolate covered raisins. The third type consists of 40% nonpareils, 30% peanut clusters, and 30% chocolate covered raisins. If the store has 90 pounds of nonpareils, 100 pounds of peanut clusters, and 120 pounds of chocolate covered raisins available, how many pounds of each type of party mix should be made?

62. **Investment Planning** New parents Jim and Lucy want to start saving for their son's college education. They have $5000 to invest in three different types of plans. A traditional savings account pays 1% annual interest, a certificate of deposit pays 3.6% annual interest, and a prepaid college plan pays 5.5% annual interest. If they want to invest the same amount in the prepaid college fund as in the other two plans together, how much should they invest in each plan to realize an interest income of $195 for the first year?

Exercises 63–68 require the use of a graphing calculator or spreadsheet.

63. Enter the matrix corresponding to the equations in Exercise 3, and change the second row by adding to it 5 times the first row.

64. Enter the matrix from Exercise 5, and change the third row by adding to it (-4) times the first row.

65. Enter the matrix in Exercise 7, and interchange the rows.

66. Enter the matrix corresponding to the linear system in Exercise 45, and multiply the first row by 5.

67. Use technology to solve the system of linear equations in Exercise 47.

68. Use technology to solve the system of linear equations in Exercise 48.

Solutions to Practice Problems 2.1

1. (a) Not in diagonal form, since the first equation contains both x and z.

(b) Not in diagonal form, since the coefficient of z is not 1.

2. (a) Change the system into another system in which the second equation is altered by having (-2)(first equation) added to it. The new system is
$$\begin{cases} x - 3y = 2 \\ 9y = 1. \end{cases}$$
The equation $9y = 1$ was obtained as follows:

$$\begin{array}{ll} (-2)(\text{first equation}) & -2x + 6y = -4 \\ + (\text{second equation}) & \underline{2x + 3y = 5} \\ & 9y = 1. \end{array}$$

(b) Change the second equation by adding to it 1 times the first equation. The result is
$$\begin{cases} x + y = 3 \\ 3y = 8. \end{cases}$$

In general, notation of the form $R_i + kR_j$ specifies that the first row mentioned, R_i, be changed by adding to it a multiple, k, of the second row mentioned, R_j. The row R_j is not changed by the operation.

3. (a) The first row should contain a nonzero number as its first entry. This can be accomplished by interchanging the first and third rows. The notation for this operation is

$$R_1 \leftrightarrow R_3$$

(b) The first column can be put into proper form by eliminating the -6. To accomplish this, multiply the first row by 6 and add this product to the third row. The notation for this operation is

$$R_3 + 6R_1$$

2.2 Solving Systems of Linear Equations, II

In this section we introduce the operation of pivoting and consider systems of linear equations that do not have exactly one solution.

Roughly speaking, the Gauss–Jordan elimination method applied to a matrix proceeds as follows: Consider the columns one at a time, from left to right. For each column use the elementary row operations to transform the appropriate entry to a one and the remaining entries in the column to zeros. (The "appropriate" entry is the first entry in the first column, the second entry in the second column, and so forth.) This sequence of elementary row operations performed for each column is called **pivoting**. More precisely,

Method To pivot a matrix about a given nonzero entry,

1. Transform the given entry into a one.

2. Transform all other entries in the same column into zeros.

Pivoting is used in solving problems other than systems of linear equations. As we shall see in Chapter 4, it is the basis for the simplex method of solving linear programming problems.

EXAMPLE 1   **Pivoting**   Pivot the matrix about the circled element.

$$\left[\begin{array}{cc|c} 18 & \circled{-6} & 15 \\ 5 & -2 & 4 \end{array}\right]$$

Solution   The first step is to transform the -6 to a 1. We do this by multiplying the first row by $-\frac{1}{6}$:

$$\left[\begin{array}{cc|c} 18 & -6 & 15 \\ 5 & -2 & 4 \end{array}\right] \quad \xrightarrow{\left(-\frac{1}{6}\right)R_1} \quad \left[\begin{array}{cc|c} -3 & 1 & -\frac{5}{2} \\ 5 & -2 & 4 \end{array}\right].$$

Next, we transform the -2 (the only remaining entry in column 2) into a 0:

$$\left[\begin{array}{cc|c} -3 & 1 & -\frac{5}{2} \\ 5 & -2 & 4 \end{array}\right] \quad \xrightarrow{R_2 + 2R_1} \quad \left[\begin{array}{cc|c} -3 & 1 & -\frac{5}{2} \\ -1 & 0 & -1 \end{array}\right].$$

The last matrix is the result of pivoting the original matrix about the circled entry.

Now Try Exercise 1   ◼

In terms of pivoting, we can give the following summary of the Gauss–Jordan elimination method.

> **Gauss–Jordan Elimination Method to Transform a System of Linear Equations into Diagonal Form**
>
> **1.** Write down the matrix corresponding to the linear system.
>
> **2.** Make sure that the first entry in the first column is nonzero. Do this by interchanging the first row with one of the rows below it, if necessary.
>
> **3.** Pivot the matrix about the first entry in the first column.
>
> **4.** Make sure that the second entry in the second column is nonzero. Do this by interchanging the second row with one of the rows below it, if necessary.
>
> **5.** Pivot the matrix about the second entry in the second column.
>
> **6.** Continue in this manner.

All the systems considered in the preceding section had only a single solution. In this case we say that the solution is **unique**. Let us now use the Gauss–Jordan elimination method to study the various possibilities other than a unique solution.

EXAMPLE 2   **A system of equations that has no solution**   Find all solutions of the system

$$\begin{cases} x - y + z = 3 \\ x + y - z = 5 \\ -2x + 4y - 4z = 1. \end{cases}$$

Solution We apply the Gauss–Jordan elimination method to the matrix of the system.

$$
\begin{bmatrix}
① & -1 & 1 & \bigm| & 3 \\
1 & 1 & -1 & \bigm| & 5 \\
-2 & 4 & -4 & \bigm| & 1
\end{bmatrix}
\xrightarrow[\;R_3 + 2R_1\;]{\;R_2 + (-1)R_1\;}
\begin{bmatrix}
1 & -1 & 1 & \bigm| & 3 \\
0 & ② & -2 & \bigm| & 2 \\
0 & 2 & -2 & \bigm| & 7
\end{bmatrix}
$$

$$
\xrightarrow[\;R_3 + (-2)R_2\;]{\substack{\frac{1}{2}R_2 \\ R_1 + 1R_2}}
\begin{bmatrix}
1 & 0 & 0 & \bigm| & 4 \\
0 & 1 & -1 & \bigm| & 1 \\
0 & 0 & 0 & \bigm| & 5
\end{bmatrix}
$$

We cannot pivot about the last zero in the third column, so we have carried the method as far as we can. Let us write out the equations corresponding to the last matrix:

$$
\begin{cases}
x & = 4 \\
y - z & = 1 \\
0 & = 5.
\end{cases}
$$

Note that the last equation is a built-in contradiction. The last equation can never be satisfied, no matter what the values of x, y, and z. Thus, the original system has no solution. Systems with no solution can always be detected by the presence of a matrix row of the form $\begin{bmatrix} 0 & 0 & \cdots & 0 & \mid & a \end{bmatrix}$, where a is a nonzero number. ∎

Now Try Exercise 13

EXAMPLE 3   **Solving a system of equations that has infinitely many solutions** Determine all solutions of the system

$$
\begin{cases}
2x + 2y + 4z = 8 \\
x - y + 2z = 2 \\
-x + 5y - 2z = 2.
\end{cases}
$$

Solution We set up the matrix corresponding to the system and perform the appropriate pivoting operations. (The elements pivoted about are circled.)

$$
\begin{bmatrix}
② & 2 & 4 & \bigm| & 8 \\
1 & -1 & 2 & \bigm| & 2 \\
-1 & 5 & -2 & \bigm| & 2
\end{bmatrix}
\xrightarrow[\;R_3 + 1R_1\;]{\substack{\frac{1}{2}R_1 \\ R_2 + (-1)R_1}}
\begin{bmatrix}
1 & 1 & 2 & \bigm| & 4 \\
0 & -2 & 0 & \bigm| & -2 \\
0 & 6 & 0 & \bigm| & 6
\end{bmatrix}
$$

$$
\xrightarrow[\;R_3 + (-6)R_2\;]{\substack{\left(-\frac{1}{2}\right)R_2 \\ R_1 + (-1)R_2}}
\begin{bmatrix}
1 & 0 & 2 & \bigm| & 3 \\
0 & 1 & 0 & \bigm| & 1 \\
0 & 0 & 0 & \bigm| & 0
\end{bmatrix}
$$

Note that our method must terminate here, since there is no way to transform the third entry in the third column into a 1 without disturbing the columns already in appropriate form. The equations corresponding to the last matrix read

$$
\begin{cases}
x & + 2z = 3 \\
y & = 1 \\
0 & = 0.
\end{cases}
$$

The last equation does not involve any of the variables and so may be omitted. This leaves the two equations

$$\begin{cases} x \quad + 2z = 3 \\ \quad y \quad = 1. \end{cases}$$

Now, taking the $2z$-term in the first equation to the right side, we can write the equations

$$\begin{cases} x = 3 - 2z \\ y = 1. \end{cases}$$

The value of y is given: $y = 1$. The value of x is given in terms of z. To find a solution to this system, assign any value to z. Then the first equation gives a value for x and thereby a specific solution to the system. For example, if we take $z = 1$, then the corresponding specific solution is

$$z = 1$$
$$x = 3 - 2(1) = 1$$
$$y = 1.$$

If we take $z = -3$, the corresponding specific solution is

$$z = -3$$
$$x = 3 - 2(-3) = 9$$
$$y = 1.$$

Thus, we see that the original system has infinitely many specific solutions, corresponding to the infinitely many possible different choices for z.

We say that the **general solution** of the system is

$$z = \text{any value}$$
$$x = 3 - 2z$$

Now Try Exercise 15

$$y = 1.$$ ∎

Gauss–Jordan Elimination Method for the Matrix of a Linear System that Cannot be Transformed into Diagonal Form

1. Apply the Gauss–Jordan elimination method to put as many columns as possible into proper form. (A column is in proper form if one entry is 1 and the other entries are 0.) Proceed from left to right, but do not disturb columns that have already been put into proper form. As much as possible, each row should have a 1 in its leftmost nonzero entry. (Such a 1 is called a *leading 1*.) The column for each leading 1 should be to the right of the columns for the leading 1s in the rows above it.

2. If at any time one or more of the rows is of the form $\begin{bmatrix} 0 & 0 & \cdots & 0 \mid a \end{bmatrix}$, where a is a nonzero number, then the linear system has no solution.

3. Otherwise there are infinitely many solutions. Variables corresponding to columns not in proper form can assume any value. The other variables can then be expressed in terms of these variables.

EXAMPLE 4

Solving a system of equations that has infinitely many solutions Find all solutions of the linear system

$$\begin{cases} x + 2y - \ z + 3w = 5 \\ \quad\quad y + 2z + \ w = 7. \end{cases}$$

Solution The Gauss–Jordan elimination method proceeds as follows:

$$\begin{bmatrix} 1 & 2 & -1 & 3 & | & 5 \\ 0 & ① & 2 & 1 & | & 7 \end{bmatrix}$$ (The first column is already in proper form.)

$$\xrightarrow{R_1 + (-2)R_2} \begin{bmatrix} 1 & 0 & -5 & 1 & | & -9 \\ 0 & 1 & 2 & 1 & | & 7 \end{bmatrix}.$$

We cannot do anything further with the third and fourth columns (without disturbing the first two columns), so the corresponding variables, z and w, can assume any values. Writing down the equations corresponding to the last matrix yields

$$\begin{cases} x & - 5z + w = -9 \\ & y + 2z + w = \ \ 7 \end{cases}$$

or

$$z = \text{any value}$$
$$w = \text{any value}$$
$$x = -9 + 5z - w$$
$$y = \ \ 7 - 2z - w$$

To determine a specific solution, let, for example, $z = 1$ and $w = 2$. Then a specific solution of the original system is

$$z = 1$$
$$w = 2$$
$$x = -9 + 5(1) - (2) = -6$$
$$y = \ \ 7 - 2(1) - (2) = \ \ 3$$

Now Try Exercise 19   ■

EXAMPLE 5

Solving a system of equations that has infinitely many solutions Find all solutions of the system of equations

$$\begin{cases} x - \ \ 7y + \ \ z = 3 \\ 2x - 14y + 3z = 4. \end{cases}$$

Solution The first pivot operation is routine:

$$\begin{bmatrix} ① & -7 & 1 & | & 3 \\ 2 & -14 & 3 & | & 4 \end{bmatrix} \xrightarrow{R_2 + (-2)R_1} \begin{bmatrix} 1 & -7 & 1 & | & 3 \\ 0 & 0 & 1 & | & -2 \end{bmatrix}.$$

However, it is impossible to pivot about the zero in the second column. So skip the second column and pivot about the second entry in the third column to get

$$\begin{bmatrix} 1 & -7 & 0 & | & 5 \\ 0 & 0 & 1 & | & -2 \end{bmatrix}.$$

This is as far as we can go. The variable corresponding to the second column, namely y, can assume any value, and the general solution of the system is obtained from the equations

$$\begin{cases} x - 7y & = \ \ 5 \\ z = -2. \end{cases}$$

Therefore, the general solution of the system is

$$y = \text{any value}$$
$$x = 5 + 7y$$
$$z = -2.$$

Now Try Exercise 23

At first it might seem strange that some systems have no solution, some have one, and yet others have infinitely many. The reason for the difference can be explained geometrically. For simplicity, consider the case of systems of two equations in two variables. Each equation in this case has a graph in the xy-plane, and the graph is a straight line. As we have seen, solving the system corresponds to finding the points lying on both lines. There are three possibilities. First, the two lines may intersect. In this case the solution is unique. Second, the two lines may be parallel. Then the two lines do not intersect, and the system has no solution. Finally, the two equations may represent the same line, as, for example, the equations $2x + 3y = 1$ and $4x + 6y = 2$ do. In this case every point on the line is a solution of the system; that is, there are infinitely many solutions (Fig. 1).

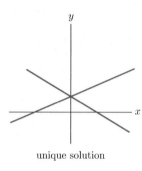

unique solution

no solution

infinitely many solutions

Figure 1

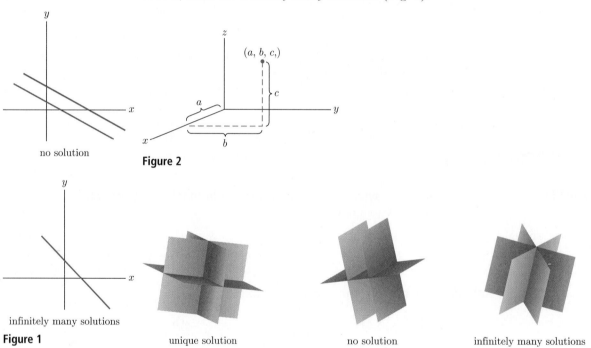

Figure 2

unique solution

no solution

infinitely many solutions

Figure 3

Systems of three equations in three variables can be examined in an analogous way using a 3-dimensional coordinate system. The point having coordinates (a, b, c) is obtained by starting at the origin, moving a units in the x-direction, b units in the y-direction, and then c units in the z-direction (up if c is positive, down if c is negative). See Fig. 2. The collection of points that satisfy a specific linear equation in three variables form a plane. Therefore, the solution of a system of linear equations in three variables consists of all points that are simultaneously on the planes corresponding to each equation. Figure 3 shows some possible configurations for these planes.

INCORPORATING TECHNOLOGY

GC The complete Gauss–Jordan elimination method can be carried out in one step as shown in Figs. 4 and 5 for the matrix of Example 5. The command **rref** is found in the MATRX/MATH menu of the TI-83/84 Plus and in the MATH/Matrix menu of the TI-89. (*Note*: **rref** stands for "reduced row echelon form," the name given to the final form of a matrix that has been completely row reduced.) ∎

Figure 4. TI-83/84 Plus   **Figure 5.** TI-89

ES When Solver is used with a system of linear equations having infinitely many solutions, only one solution is given. When Solver is used with a system of linear equations having no solution, the sentence "Solver could not find a feasible solution." is displayed.

Practice Problems 2.2

1. Find a specific solution to a system of linear equations whose general solution is

$$w = \text{any value}$$
$$y = \text{any value}$$
$$z = 7 + 6w$$
$$x = 26 - 2y + 14w.$$

2. Find all solutions of this system of linear equations.

$$\begin{cases} 2x + 4y - 4z - 4w = 24 \\ -3x - 6y + 10z - 18w = -8 \\ -x - 2y + 4z - 10w = 2 \end{cases}$$

EXERCISES 2.2

In Exercises 1–8, pivot each matrix about the circled element.

1. $\begin{bmatrix} \boxed{2} & -4 & 6 \\ 3 & 7 & 1 \end{bmatrix}$

2. $\begin{bmatrix} 1 & 2 & 3 \\ 4 & \boxed{8} & -12 \end{bmatrix}$

3. $\begin{bmatrix} 7 & 1 & 4 & 5 \\ -1 & 1 & \boxed{2} & 6 \\ 4 & 0 & 2 & 3 \end{bmatrix}$

4. $\begin{bmatrix} 5 & 10 & -10 & 12 \\ 4 & 3 & 6 & 12 \\ 4 & \boxed{-4} & 4 & -16 \end{bmatrix}$

5. $\begin{bmatrix} \boxed{2} & 3 \\ 6 & 0 \\ 1 & 5 \end{bmatrix}$

6. $\begin{bmatrix} 2 & 1 \\ \boxed{-1} & 0 \end{bmatrix}$

7. $\begin{bmatrix} 4 & 3 & 0 \\ \frac{2}{3} & 0 & -2 \\ 1 & 3 & \boxed{6} \end{bmatrix}$

8. $\begin{bmatrix} 1 & 0 & 2 \\ -1 & 1 & \boxed{-2} \\ 1 & 2 & 6 \end{bmatrix}$

In Exercises 9–22, use the Gauss–Jordan elimination method to find all solutions of the systems of linear equations.

9. $\begin{cases} 2x - 4y = 6 \\ -x + 2y = -3 \end{cases}$

10. $\begin{cases} -\frac{1}{2}x + y = \frac{3}{2} \\ -3x + 6y = 10 \end{cases}$

11. $\begin{cases} x + 2y = 5 \\ 3x - y = 1 \\ -x + 3y = 5 \end{cases}$

12. $\begin{cases} x - 6y = 12 \\ -\frac{1}{2}x + 3y = -6 \\ \frac{1}{3}x - 2y = 4 \end{cases}$

13. $\begin{cases} x - y + 3z = 3 \\ -2x + 3y - 11z = -4 \\ x - 2y + 8z = 6 \end{cases}$

14. $\begin{cases} x - 3y + z = 5 \\ -2x + 7y - 6z = -9 \\ x - 2y - 3z = 6 \end{cases}$

15. $\begin{cases} x + y + z = -1 \\ 2x + 3y + 2z = 3 \\ 2x + y + 2z = -7 \end{cases}$ **16.** $\begin{cases} x - 3y + 2z = 10 \\ -x + 3y - z = -6 \\ -x + 3y + 2z = 6 \end{cases}$

17. $\begin{cases} x + 2y + 3z = 4 \\ 5x + 6y + 7z = 8 \\ x + 2y + 3z = 5 \end{cases}$ **18.** $\begin{cases} x + 3y = 7 \\ x + 2y = 5 \\ -x + y = 2 \end{cases}$

19. $\begin{cases} x + y - 2z + 2w = 5 \\ 2x + y - 4z + w = 5 \\ 3x + 4y - 6z + 9w = 20 \\ 4x + 4y - 8z + 8w = 20 \end{cases}$

20. $\begin{cases} 2y + z - w = 1 \\ x - y + z + w = 14 \\ -x - 9y - z + 4w = 11 \\ x + y + z = 9 \end{cases}$

21. $\begin{cases} 6x - 4y = 2 \\ -3x + 3y = 6 \\ 5x + 2y = 39 \end{cases}$ **22.** $\begin{cases} 3x + 2y = 5 \\ -x + 3y = 2 \\ 5x + 2y = 6 \\ 6x + y = 39 \end{cases}$

In Exercises 23–25, find three solutions to the systems of equations.

23. $\begin{cases} x + 2y + z = 5 \\ y + 3z = 9 \end{cases}$ **24.** $\begin{cases} x + 5y + 3z = 9 \\ 2x + 9y + 7z = 5 \end{cases}$

25. $\begin{cases} x + 7y - 3z = 8 \\ z = 5 \end{cases}$

26. Triathlon An out-of-shape athlete runs 6 miles per hour, swims 1 mile per hour, and bikes 10 miles per hour. He entered a triathlon, which requires all three events, and finished 5 hours and 40 minutes later. A friend who runs 8 miles per hour, swims 2 miles per hour, and bikes 15 miles per hour finished the same course in 3 hours and 35 minutes. The total course was 32 miles long. How many miles was each segment (running, swimming, and biking)?

27. Nutrition Planning In a laboratory experiment, a researcher wants to provide a rabbit with exactly 1000 units of vitamin A, exactly 1600 units of vitamin C, and exactly 2400 units of vitamin E. The rabbit is fed a mixture of three foods. Each gram of food 1 contains 2 units of vitamin A, 3 units of vitamin C, and 5 units of vitamin E. Each gram of food 2 contains 4 units of vitamin A, 7 units of vitamin C, and 9 units of vitamin E. Each gram of food 3 contains 6 units of vitamin A, 10 units of vitamin C, and 14 units of vitamin E. How many grams of each food should the rabbit be fed?

28. Nutrition Planning Rework Exercise 27 with the requirement for vitamin E changed to 2000 units.

29. Quilting Granny's Custom Quilts receives an order for a patchwork quilt made from square patches of three types: solid green, solid blue, and floral. The quilt is to be 8 squares by 12 squares, and there must be 15 times as many solid squares as floral squares. If Granny's charges $3 per solid square and $5 per floral square, and if the customer wishes to spend exactly $300, how many of each type of square may be used in the quilt?

30. Purchasing Options Amanda is decorating her new home and wants to buy some house plants. She is interested in three types of plants costing $7, $10, and $13. If she has budgeted exactly $150 for the plants and wants to buy exactly 15 of them, what are her options?

31. Find all solutions to the following system of equations.

$$\begin{cases} x^2 + y^2 + z^2 = 14 \\ x^2 - y^2 + 2z^2 = 15 \\ x^2 + 2y^2 + 3z^2 = 36 \end{cases}$$

32. For what value of k will the following system of linear equations have a solution?

$$\begin{cases} 2x + 6y = 4 \\ x + 7y = 10 \\ kx + 8y = 4 \end{cases}$$

33. For what values(s) of k will the following system of linear equations have no solution? Infinitely many solutions?

$$\begin{cases} 2x - 3y = 4 \\ -6x + 9y = k \end{cases}$$

34. Suppose that after the Gauss–Jordan elimination method has been applied to a matrix corresponding to a system of linear equations, the matrix has a row of all zeros. Must the system have infinitely many solutions?

35. Figure 6 shows the graphs of the equations from a system of three linear equations in two variables. How many solutions does the system have?

(a) three   **(b)** none

(c) infinitely many   **(d)** one

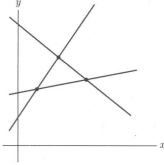

Figure 6

In Exercises 36–40, use a graphing calculator to carry out the tasks.

In Exercises 36–39, graph the three equations together, and determine the number of solutions (exactly one, none, or infinitely many). If there is exactly one solution, estimate the solution.

36. $\begin{cases} 2x + 3y = 5 \\ -3x + 5y = 22 \\ 2x + y = -1 \end{cases}$

37. $\begin{cases} x + y = 10 \\ 2x - 3y = 5 \\ -x + 3y = 2 \end{cases}$

38. $\begin{cases} 3x - 2y = 3 \\ -2x + 4y = 14 \\ x + y = 11 \end{cases}$

39. $\begin{cases} 2x + y = 12 \\ 3x - y = 2 \\ x + 2y = 16 \end{cases}$

40. If your calculator has **rref** or an analogous command, apply the command to the matrix in Example 2. How does the final matrix differ from the one appearing in the text?

Solutions to Practice Problems 2.2

1. Since w and y can each assume any value, select any numbers, say $w = 1$ and $y = 2$. Then $z = 7 + 6(1) = 13$ and $x = 26 - 2(2) + 14(1) = 36$. So $x = 36$, $y = 2$, $z = 13$, $w = 1$ is a specific solution. There are infinitely many different specific solutions since there are infinitely many different choices for w and y.

2. We apply the Gauss–Jordan elimination method to the matrix of the system.

$$\left[\begin{array}{cccc|c} ② & 4 & -4 & -4 & 24 \\ -3 & -6 & 10 & -18 & -8 \\ -1 & -2 & 4 & -10 & 2 \end{array}\right]$$

$$\xrightarrow[\substack{\frac{1}{2}R_1 \\ R_2 + 3R_1 \\ R_3 + 1R_1}]{} \left[\begin{array}{cccc|c} 1 & 2 & -2 & -2 & 12 \\ 0 & 0 & ④ & -24 & 28 \\ 0 & 0 & 2 & -12 & 14 \end{array}\right]$$

$$\xrightarrow[\substack{\frac{1}{4}R_2 \\ R_1 + 2R_2 \\ R_3 + (-2)R_2}]{} \left[\begin{array}{cccc|c} 1 & 2 & 0 & -14 & 26 \\ 0 & 0 & 1 & -6 & 7 \\ 0 & 0 & 0 & 0 & 0 \end{array}\right]$$

The corresponding system of equations is

$$\begin{cases} x + 2y - 14w = 26 \\ z - 6w = 7. \end{cases}$$

The general solution is

$$w = \text{any value}$$
$$y = \text{any value}$$
$$z = 7 + 6w$$
$$x = 26 - 2y + 14w$$

2.3 Arithmetic Operations on Matrices

We introduced matrices in Sections 2.1 and 2.2 to display the coefficients of a system of linear equations. For example, the linear system

$$\begin{cases} 5x - 3y = \frac{1}{2} \\ 4x + 2y = -1 \end{cases}$$

is represented by the matrix

$$\left[\begin{array}{cc|c} 5 & -3 & \frac{1}{2} \\ 4 & 2 & -1 \end{array}\right].$$

After we have become accustomed to using such matrices in solving linear systems, we may omit the vertical line that separates the left and right sides of the equations.

We need only remember that the right side of the equations is recorded in the right column. So, for example, we would write the preceding matrix in the form

$$\begin{bmatrix} 5 & -3 & \frac{1}{2} \\ 4 & 2 & -1 \end{bmatrix}.$$

A matrix is *any* rectangular array of numbers and may be of any size. Here are some examples of matrices of various sizes:

$$\begin{bmatrix} 3 & 7 \\ 0 & -1 \end{bmatrix}, \qquad \begin{bmatrix} 1 \\ 2 \end{bmatrix}, \qquad \begin{bmatrix} 2 & 1 \end{bmatrix}, \qquad \begin{bmatrix} 6 \end{bmatrix}, \qquad \begin{bmatrix} 5 & 7 & -1 \\ 0 & 3 & 5 \\ 6 & 0 & 5 \end{bmatrix}.$$

Examples of matrices abound in everyday life. For example, the newspaper stock market report is a large matrix with several thousand rows, one for each listed stock. The columns of the matrix give the various data about each stock, such as opening and closing price, number of shares traded, and so on. Another example of a matrix is a mileage chart on a road map. The rows and columns are labeled with the names of cities. The number at a given row and column gives the distance between the corresponding cities.

In these everyday examples, matrices are used only to display data. However, the most important applications involve arithmetic operations on matrices—namely, addition, subtraction, and multiplication of matrices. The major goal of this section is to discuss these operations. Before we can do so, however, we need some vocabulary with which to describe matrices.

A matrix is described by its **size**; that is, the number of rows and columns it contains. For example, the matrix

$$\begin{bmatrix} 7 & 5 \\ \frac{1}{2} & -2 \\ 2 & -11 \end{bmatrix}$$

has three rows and two columns and is referred to as a *3 × 2* (read: "three-by-two") *matrix*. The matrix $\begin{bmatrix} 4 & 5 & 0 \end{bmatrix}$ has one row and three columns and is a *1 × 3 matrix*. A matrix with only one row is called a **row matrix**. A matrix, such as

$$\begin{bmatrix} 2 \\ 7 \end{bmatrix},$$

that has only one column is called a **column matrix**. If a matrix has the same number of rows and columns, it is called a **square matrix**. Here are some square matrices of various sizes:

$$\begin{bmatrix} 5 \end{bmatrix}, \qquad \begin{bmatrix} 1 & 2 \\ 3 & 4 \end{bmatrix}, \qquad \begin{bmatrix} 2 & -1 & 0 \\ 3 & 5 & 4 \\ 0 & 3 & -7 \end{bmatrix}.$$

The rows of a matrix are numbered from the top down, and the columns are numbered from left to right. For example, the first row of the matrix

$$A = \begin{bmatrix} 1 & -1 & 0 \\ 2 & 1 & 7 \\ -3 & 2 & 4 \end{bmatrix}$$

is $\begin{bmatrix} 1 & -1 & 0 \end{bmatrix}$, and its third column is

$$\begin{bmatrix} 0 \\ 7 \\ 4 \end{bmatrix}.$$

The numbers in a matrix, called **entries**, may be identified in terms of the row and column containing the entry in question. For example, the entry in the first row, third column of matrix A is 0:

$$\begin{bmatrix} 1 & -1 & 0 \\ 2 & 1 & 7 \\ -3 & 2 & 4 \end{bmatrix};$$

the entry in the second row, first column is 2:

$$\begin{bmatrix} 1 & -1 & 0 \\ 2 & 1 & 7 \\ -3 & 2 & 4 \end{bmatrix};$$

and the entry in the third row, third column is 4:

$$\begin{bmatrix} 1 & -1 & 0 \\ 2 & 1 & 7 \\ -3 & 2 & 4 \end{bmatrix}.$$

We use double-subscripted lowercase letters to indicate the locations of the entries of a matrix. We denote the entry in the ith row, jth column of the matrix A by a_{ij}. For instance, we have $a_{13} = 0$, $a_{21} = 2$, and $a_{33} = 4$.

We say that two matrices A and B are **equal**, denoted $A = B$, provided that they have the same size and that all their corresponding entries are equal.

Addition and Subtraction of Matrices   We define the sum $A + B$ of two matrices A and B only if A and B are two matrices of the same size—that is, if A and B have the same number of rows and the same number of columns. In this case $A + B$ is the matrix formed by adding the corresponding entries of A and B. For example,

$$\begin{bmatrix} 2 & 0 \\ 1 & 1 \\ 5 & 3 \end{bmatrix} + \begin{bmatrix} 5 & 4 \\ 0 & 2 \\ 2 & 6 \end{bmatrix} = \begin{bmatrix} 2+5 & 0+4 \\ 1+0 & 1+2 \\ 5+2 & 3+6 \end{bmatrix} = \begin{bmatrix} 7 & 4 \\ 1 & 3 \\ 7 & 9 \end{bmatrix}.$$

We subtract matrices of the same size by subtracting corresponding entries. Thus, we have

$$\begin{bmatrix} 7 \\ 1 \end{bmatrix} - \begin{bmatrix} 3 \\ 2 \end{bmatrix} = \begin{bmatrix} 7-3 \\ 1-2 \end{bmatrix} = \begin{bmatrix} 4 \\ -1 \end{bmatrix}.$$

Multiplication of Matrices   It might seem that to define the product of two matrices, one would start with two matrices of like size and multiply the corresponding entries. But this definition is not useful, since the calculations that arise in applications require a somewhat more complex multiplication. In the interests of simplicity, we start by defining the product of a row matrix times a column matrix.

If A is a row matrix and B is a column matrix, then we can form the product $A \cdot B$ provided that the two matrices have the same length. The product $A \cdot B$ is the 1×1 matrix obtained by multiplying corresponding entries of A and B and then forming the sum.

We may put this definition into algebraic terms as follows. Suppose that A is the row matrix

$$A = \begin{bmatrix} a_1 & a_2 & \cdots & a_n \end{bmatrix},$$

and B is the column matrix

$$B = \begin{bmatrix} b_1 \\ b_2 \\ \vdots \\ b_n \end{bmatrix}.$$

Note that A and B are both of the same length, namely n. Then

$$A \cdot B = \begin{bmatrix} a_1 & a_2 & \cdots & a_n \end{bmatrix} \cdot \begin{bmatrix} b_1 \\ b_2 \\ \vdots \\ b_n \end{bmatrix}$$

is calculated by multiplying corresponding entries of A and B and forming the sum; that is,

$$A \cdot B = \begin{bmatrix} a_1 b_1 + a_2 b_2 + \cdots + a_n b_n \end{bmatrix}.$$

Notice that the product is a 1×1 matrix, namely a single number in brackets.

Here are some examples of the product of a row matrix times a column matrix:

$$\begin{bmatrix} 3 & \frac{1}{2} \end{bmatrix} \cdot \begin{bmatrix} 1 \\ 4 \end{bmatrix} = \begin{bmatrix} 3 \cdot 1 + \frac{1}{2} \cdot 4 \end{bmatrix} = \begin{bmatrix} 5 \end{bmatrix};$$

$$\begin{bmatrix} 2 & 0 & -1 \end{bmatrix} \cdot \begin{bmatrix} 6 \\ 5 \\ 3 \end{bmatrix} = \begin{bmatrix} 2 \cdot 6 + 0 \cdot 5 + (-1) \cdot 3 \end{bmatrix} = \begin{bmatrix} 9 \end{bmatrix}.$$

In multiplying a row matrix times a column matrix, it helps to use both of your hands. Use your left index finger to point to the first element of the row matrix and your right to point to the first element of the column. Multiply the elements you are pointing to and keep a running total of the products in your head. After each multiplication move your fingers to the next elements of each matrix. With a little practice you should be able to multiply a row times a column quickly and accurately.

The preceding definition of multiplication may seem strange. But products of this sort occur in many down-to-earth problems. Consider, for instance, the next example.

EXAMPLE 1

Total revenue as a matrix product   A dairy farm produces three items—milk, eggs, and cheese. The prices of the three items are $1.50 per gallon, $0.80 per dozen, and $2.00 per pound, respectively. In a certain week the dairy farm sells 30,000 gallons of milk, 2000 dozen eggs, and 5000 pounds of cheese. Represent its total revenue as a matrix product.

Solution   The total revenue equals

$$(1.50)(30,000) + (.80)(2000) + (2)(5000).$$

This suggests that we define two matrices: The first displays the prices of the various items:

$$\begin{bmatrix} 1.50 & .80 & 2 \end{bmatrix}.$$

The second represents the production:

$$\begin{bmatrix} 30,000 \\ 2000 \\ 5000 \end{bmatrix}.$$

Then the revenue for the week, when placed in a 1×1 matrix, equals

$$\begin{bmatrix} 1.50 & .80 & 2 \end{bmatrix} \begin{bmatrix} 30{,}000 \\ 2000 \\ 5000 \end{bmatrix} = \begin{bmatrix} 56{,}600 \end{bmatrix}.$$

Now Try Exercise 71   ■

The principle behind Example 1 is this: Any sum of products of the form $a_1 b_1 + a_2 b_2 + \cdots + a_n b_n$, when placed in a 1×1 matrix, can be written as the matrix product

$$\begin{bmatrix} a_1 b_1 + a_2 b_2 + \cdots + a_n b_n \end{bmatrix} = \begin{bmatrix} a_1 & a_2 & \cdots & a_n \end{bmatrix} \cdot \begin{bmatrix} b_1 \\ b_2 \\ \vdots \\ b_n \end{bmatrix}.$$

Let us illustrate the procedure for multiplying more general matrices by working out a typical product:

$$\begin{bmatrix} 2 & 1 \\ 0 & 1 \\ 1 & 0 \end{bmatrix} \cdot \begin{bmatrix} 1 & 1 \\ 4 & 2 \end{bmatrix}.$$

To obtain the entries of the product, we multiply the rows of the left matrix by the columns of the right matrix, taking care to arrange the products in a specific way to yield a matrix, as follows. Start with the first row on the left, $\begin{bmatrix} 2 & 1 \end{bmatrix}$, and the first column on the right, $\begin{bmatrix} 1 \\ 4 \end{bmatrix}$. Their product is $\begin{bmatrix} 6 \end{bmatrix}$, so we enter 6 as the element in the first row, first column of the product:

$$\begin{bmatrix} 2 & 1 \\ 0 & 1 \\ 1 & 0 \end{bmatrix} \cdot \begin{bmatrix} 1 & 1 \\ 4 & 2 \end{bmatrix} = \begin{bmatrix} 6 & \\ & \end{bmatrix}.$$

The product of the first row of the left matrix and the second column of the right matrix is $\begin{bmatrix} 4 \end{bmatrix}$, so we put a 4 in the first row, second column of the product:

$$\begin{bmatrix} 2 & 1 \\ 0 & 1 \\ 1 & 0 \end{bmatrix} \cdot \begin{bmatrix} 1 & 1 \\ 4 & 2 \end{bmatrix} = \begin{bmatrix} 6 & 4 \\ & \end{bmatrix}.$$

There are no more columns that can be multiplied by the first row, so let us move to the second row and shift back to the first column. Correspondingly, we move down one row in the product:

$$\begin{bmatrix} 2 & 1 \\ 0 & 1 \\ 1 & 0 \end{bmatrix} \cdot \begin{bmatrix} 1 & 1 \\ 4 & 2 \end{bmatrix} = \begin{bmatrix} 6 & 4 \\ 4 & \end{bmatrix};$$

$$\begin{bmatrix} 2 & 1 \\ 0 & 1 \\ 1 & 0 \end{bmatrix} \cdot \begin{bmatrix} 1 & 1 \\ 4 & 2 \end{bmatrix} = \begin{bmatrix} 6 & 4 \\ 4 & 2 \end{bmatrix}.$$

We have now exhausted the second row of the left matrix, so we shift to the third row and correspondingly move down one row in the product:

$$
\begin{bmatrix} 2 & 1 \\ 0 & 1 \\ 1 & 0 \end{bmatrix} \cdot \begin{bmatrix} 1 & 1 \\ 4 & 2 \end{bmatrix} = \begin{bmatrix} 6 & 4 \\ 4 & 2 \\ 1 & \end{bmatrix} ;
$$

$$
\begin{bmatrix} 2 & 1 \\ 0 & 1 \\ 1 & 0 \end{bmatrix} \cdot \begin{bmatrix} 1 & 1 \\ 4 & 2 \end{bmatrix} = \begin{bmatrix} 6 & 4 \\ 4 & 2 \\ 1 & 1 \end{bmatrix} .
$$

Note that we have now multiplied every row of the left matrix by every column of the right matrix. This completes the computation of the product:

$$
\begin{bmatrix} 2 & 1 \\ 0 & 1 \\ 1 & 0 \end{bmatrix} \cdot \begin{bmatrix} 1 & 1 \\ 4 & 2 \end{bmatrix} = \begin{bmatrix} 6 & 4 \\ 4 & 2 \\ 1 & 1 \end{bmatrix} .
$$

EXAMPLE 2

Matrix multiplication Calculate the following product:

$$
\begin{bmatrix} 1 & 5 \\ 3 & 2 \end{bmatrix} \cdot \begin{bmatrix} 1 & 2 \\ 1 & 0 \end{bmatrix} .
$$

Solution

$$
\begin{bmatrix} 1 & 5 \\ 3 & 2 \end{bmatrix} \cdot \begin{bmatrix} 1 & 2 \\ 1 & 0 \end{bmatrix} = \begin{bmatrix} 6 & \\ & \end{bmatrix}
$$

$$
\begin{bmatrix} 1 & 5 \\ 3 & 2 \end{bmatrix} \cdot \begin{bmatrix} 1 & 2 \\ 1 & 0 \end{bmatrix} = \begin{bmatrix} 6 & 2 \\ & \end{bmatrix}
$$

$$
\begin{bmatrix} 1 & 5 \\ 3 & 2 \end{bmatrix} \cdot \begin{bmatrix} 1 & 2 \\ 1 & 0 \end{bmatrix} = \begin{bmatrix} 6 & 2 \\ 5 & \end{bmatrix}
$$

$$
\begin{bmatrix} 1 & 5 \\ 3 & 2 \end{bmatrix} \cdot \begin{bmatrix} 1 & 2 \\ 1 & 0 \end{bmatrix} = \begin{bmatrix} 6 & 2 \\ 5 & 6 \end{bmatrix}
$$

Thus,

$$
\begin{bmatrix} 1 & 5 \\ 3 & 2 \end{bmatrix} \cdot \begin{bmatrix} 1 & 2 \\ 1 & 0 \end{bmatrix} = \begin{bmatrix} 6 & 2 \\ 5 & 6 \end{bmatrix} .
$$

Now Try Exercise 25

Notice that we cannot use the preceding method to compute the product $A \cdot B$ of *any* matrices A and B. For the procedure to work, it is crucial that the number of entries of each row of A be the same as the number of entries of each column of B. (Or, to put it another way, the number of columns of the left matrix must equal the number of rows of the right matrix.) Therefore, in order for us to form the product $A \cdot B$, the sizes of A and B must match up in a special way. If A is $m \times n$ and B is $p \times q$, then the product $A \cdot B$ is defined only in case the "inner" dimensions n and p are equal. In that case, the size of the product is determined by the "outer" dimensions m and q. It is an $m \times q$ matrix:

$$
\underset{m \times n}{A} \quad \cdot \quad \underset{p \times q}{B} \quad = \quad \underset{m \times q}{C}.
$$

equal

So, for example,

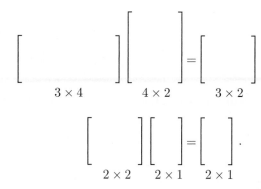

$$
\underset{3 \times 4}{\begin{bmatrix} \end{bmatrix}} \underset{4 \times 2}{\begin{bmatrix} \end{bmatrix}} = \underset{3 \times 2}{\begin{bmatrix} \end{bmatrix}}
$$

$$
\underset{2 \times 2}{\begin{bmatrix} \end{bmatrix}} \underset{2 \times 1}{\begin{bmatrix} \end{bmatrix}} = \underset{2 \times 1}{\begin{bmatrix} \end{bmatrix}}.
$$

If the sizes of A and B do not match up in the way just described, the product $A \cdot B$ is not defined.

EXAMPLE 3

Matrix multiplication Calculate the following products, if defined.

(a) $\begin{bmatrix} 3 & -1 \\ 2 & 0 \\ 1 & 5 \end{bmatrix} \begin{bmatrix} 1 & 0 \\ 5 & -4 \\ 2 & -1 \end{bmatrix}$ (b) $\begin{bmatrix} 3 & -1 \\ 2 & 0 \\ 1 & 5 \end{bmatrix} \begin{bmatrix} 5 & 4 \\ -2 & 3 \end{bmatrix}$

Solution (a) The matrices to be multiplied are 3×2 and 3×2. The inner dimensions do not match, so the product is undefined.

(b) We are asked to multiply a 3×2 matrix times a 2×2 matrix. The inner dimensions match, so the product is defined and has size determined by the outer dimensions, that is, 3×2.

$$
\begin{bmatrix} 3 & -1 \\ 2 & 0 \\ 1 & 5 \end{bmatrix} \begin{bmatrix} 5 & 4 \\ -2 & 3 \end{bmatrix} = \begin{bmatrix} 3 \cdot 5 + (-1) \cdot (-2) & 3 \cdot 4 + (-1) \cdot 3 \\ 2 \cdot 5 + 0 \cdot (-2) & 2 \cdot 4 + 0 \cdot 3 \\ 1 \cdot 5 + 5 \cdot (-2) & 1 \cdot 4 + 5 \cdot 3 \end{bmatrix}
$$

$$
= \begin{bmatrix} 17 & 9 \\ 10 & 8 \\ -5 & 19 \end{bmatrix}
$$

Now Try Exercise 27

Multiplication of matrices has many properties in common with multiplication of ordinary numbers. However, there is at least one important difference. With matrix multiplication, the order of the factors is usually important. For example, the product of a 2×3 matrix times a 3×2 matrix is defined: The product is a 2×2 matrix. If the order is reversed to a 3×2 matrix times a 2×3 matrix, the product is a 3×3 matrix. So reversing the order may change the size of the product. Even when it does not, reversing the order may still change the entries in the product, as the following two products demonstrate:

$$
\begin{bmatrix} 1 & 5 \\ 3 & 2 \end{bmatrix} \begin{bmatrix} 1 & 2 \\ 1 & 0 \end{bmatrix} = \begin{bmatrix} 6 & 2 \\ 5 & 6 \end{bmatrix}; \qquad \begin{bmatrix} 1 & 2 \\ 1 & 0 \end{bmatrix} \begin{bmatrix} 1 & 5 \\ 3 & 2 \end{bmatrix} = \begin{bmatrix} 7 & 9 \\ 1 & 5 \end{bmatrix}.
$$

EXAMPLE 4

Investment earnings An investment trust has investments in three states. Its deposits in each state are divided among bonds, mortgages, and consumer loans. On January 1 the amount (in millions of dollars) of money invested in each category by state is given by the matrix

	Bonds	Mortgages	Consumer loans
State A	10	5	20
State B	30	12	10
State C	15	6	25

The current average yields are 7% for bonds, 9% for mortgages, and 15% for consumer loans. Determine the earnings of the trust from its investments in each state.

Solution Define the matrix of investment yields by

$$\begin{bmatrix} .07 \\ .09 \\ .15 \end{bmatrix} \quad \begin{matrix} \text{Bonds} \\ \text{Mortgages} \\ \text{Consumer loans.} \end{matrix}$$

The amount earned in state A, for instance, is

[amount of bonds][yield of bonds]

+ [amount of mortgages][yield of mortgages]

+ [amount of consumer loans][yield of consumer loans]

$$= (10)(.07) + (5)(.09) + (20)(.15).$$

And this is just the first entry of the product:

$$\begin{bmatrix} 10 & 5 & 20 \\ 30 & 12 & 10 \\ 15 & 6 & 25 \end{bmatrix} \begin{bmatrix} .07 \\ .09 \\ .15 \end{bmatrix} .$$

Similarly, the earnings for the other states are the second and third entries of the product. Carrying out the arithmetic, we find that

$$\begin{bmatrix} 10 & 5 & 20 \\ 30 & 12 & 10 \\ 15 & 6 & 25 \end{bmatrix} \begin{bmatrix} .07 \\ .09 \\ .15 \end{bmatrix} = \begin{bmatrix} 4.15 \\ 4.68 \\ 5.34 \end{bmatrix} .$$

Therefore, the trust earns $4.15 million in state A, $4.68 million in state B, and $5.34 million in state C.   ∎

Now Try Exercise 51(a)

EXAMPLE 5

Manufacturing revenue A clothing manufacturer has factories in Los Angeles, San Antonio, and Newark. Sales (in thousands) during the first quarter of last year are summarized in the production matrix

	Los Angeles	San Antonio	Newark
Coats	12	13	38
Shirts	25	5	26
Sweaters	11	8	8
Ties	5	0	12

During this period the selling price of a coat was $100, of a shirt $10, of a sweater $25, and of a tie $5.

(a) Use a matrix calculation to determine the total revenue produced by each of the factories.

(b) Suppose that the prices had been $110, $8, $20, and $10, respectively. How would this have affected the revenue of each factory?

Solution **(a)** For each factory, we wish to multiply the price of each item by the number produced to arrive at revenue. Since the production figures for the various items of clothing are arranged down the columns, we arrange the prices in a row matrix, ready for multiplication. The price matrix is

$$\begin{bmatrix} 100 & 10 & 25 & 5 \end{bmatrix}.$$

The revenues of the various factories are then the entries of the product

$$\begin{bmatrix} 100 & 10 & 25 & 5 \end{bmatrix} \begin{bmatrix} 12 & 13 & 38 \\ 25 & 5 & 26 \\ 11 & 8 & 8 \\ 5 & 0 & 12 \end{bmatrix} = \begin{matrix} \text{Los Angeles} & \text{San Antonio} & \text{Newark} \\ \begin{bmatrix} 1750 & 1550 & 4320 \end{bmatrix} \end{matrix}.$$

Since the production figures are in thousands, the revenue figures are in thousands of dollars. That is, the Los Angeles factory has revenues of $1,750,000, the San Antonio factory $1,550,000, and the Newark factory $4,320,000.

(b) In a similar way, we determine the revenue of each factory if the price matrix had been $\begin{bmatrix} 110 & 8 & 20 & 10 \end{bmatrix}$.

$$\begin{bmatrix} 110 & 8 & 20 & 10 \end{bmatrix} \begin{bmatrix} 12 & 13 & 38 \\ 25 & 5 & 26 \\ 11 & 8 & 8 \\ 5 & 0 & 12 \end{bmatrix} = \begin{matrix} \text{Los Angeles} & \text{San Antonio} & \text{Newark} \\ \begin{bmatrix} 1790 & 1630 & 4668 \end{bmatrix} \end{matrix}.$$

The change in revenue at each factory can be read from the difference of the revenue matrices:

$$\begin{bmatrix} 1790 & 1630 & 4668 \end{bmatrix} - \begin{bmatrix} 1750 & 1550 & 4320 \end{bmatrix} = \begin{bmatrix} 40 & 80 & 348 \end{bmatrix}.$$

If prices had been as given in (b), revenues of the Los Angeles factory would have increased by $40,000, revenues at San Antonio would have increased by $80,000, and revenues at Newark would have increased by $348,000. ■

Now Try Exercise 55

There are special matrices analogous to the number 1. Such matrices are called *identity matrices*.

> **DEFINITION** The **identity matrix** I_n is the $n \times n$ square matrix with all zeros except for ones down the upper-left-to-lower-right diagonal.

Here are the identity matrices of sizes 2, 3, and 4:

$$I_2 = \begin{bmatrix} 1 & 0 \\ 0 & 1 \end{bmatrix}; \quad I_3 = \begin{bmatrix} 1 & 0 & 0 \\ 0 & 1 & 0 \\ 0 & 0 & 1 \end{bmatrix}; \quad I_4 = \begin{bmatrix} 1 & 0 & 0 & 0 \\ 0 & 1 & 0 & 0 \\ 0 & 0 & 1 & 0 \\ 0 & 0 & 0 & 1 \end{bmatrix}.$$

The characteristic property of an identity matrix is that it plays the role of the number 1; that is,

$$I_n \cdot A = A \cdot I_n = A$$

for all $n \times n$ matrices A.

One of the principal uses of matrices is in dealing with systems of linear equations. Matrices provide a compact way of writing systems, as the next example shows.

EXAMPLE 6

Representing a system of equations as a matrix equation   Write the system of linear equations

$$\begin{cases} -2x + 4y = 2 \\ -3x + 7y = 7 \end{cases}$$

as a matrix equation.

Solution   The system of equations can be written in the form

$$\begin{bmatrix} -2x + 4y \\ -3x + 7y \end{bmatrix} = \begin{bmatrix} 2 \\ 7 \end{bmatrix}.$$

So consider the matrices

$$A = \begin{bmatrix} -2 & 4 \\ -3 & 7 \end{bmatrix}, \qquad X = \begin{bmatrix} x \\ y \end{bmatrix}, \qquad B = \begin{bmatrix} 2 \\ 7 \end{bmatrix}.$$

Notice that

$$AX = \begin{bmatrix} -2 & 4 \\ -3 & 7 \end{bmatrix} \begin{bmatrix} x \\ y \end{bmatrix} = \begin{bmatrix} -2x + 4y \\ -3x + 7y \end{bmatrix}.$$

Thus, AX is a 2×1 column matrix whose entries correspond to the left side of the given system of linear equations. Since the entries of B correspond to the right side of the system of equations, we can rewrite the given system in the form

$$AX = B$$

—that is,

$$\begin{bmatrix} -2 & 4 \\ -3 & 7 \end{bmatrix} \begin{bmatrix} x \\ y \end{bmatrix} = \begin{bmatrix} 2 \\ 7 \end{bmatrix}.$$

Now Try Exercise 39   ■

The matrix A of the preceding example displays the coefficients of the variables x and y, and so it is called the **coefficient matrix** of the system.

INCORPORATING TECHNOLOGY

GC   The arithmetic operations $+$, $-$, and $*$ can be applied to matrices in much the same way as to numbers, as Figs. 1, 2, 4, and 5 show. (*Note:* With the TI-83/84 Plus **[A]*[B]** also can be written as **[A][B]**.) Identity matrices are placed on the home screen with the command **identity** (in the MATRIX/MATH menu of the TI-83/84 Plus and in the MATH/Matrix menu of the TI-89), as shown in Figures 3 and 6. The value in the ith row, jth column of the matrix **[A]** can be displayed with **[A](i,j)** on the TI-83/84 Plus and with **a[i,j]** on the TI-89.   ■

ES   The entries of an $m \times n$ matrix can be typed directly into an m by n range of cells. (In order to insert a fraction, type in a formula such as **=2/3**. A matrix is most easily used in calculations if it has been given a name, such as **A** or **B**. To name a matrix, select it, click on the Name box, type the name, and press Enter. Single-letter names can consist of any letter other than C or R.

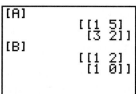

Figure 1

Figure 2

Figure 3

Figure 4

Figure 5

Figure 6

Matrices are added, subtracted, and multiplied with the + operator, the − operator, and the MMULT function, respectively. The following steps carry out these operations on the matrices A and B:

1. Highlight a range of cells having the size of the matrix to be computed.
2. Type **=A+B**, **=A−B**, or **=MMULT(A,B)**.
3. Press Ctrl+Shift+Enter. (*Note*: The plus signs indicate that the three keys should be held down together.) The computed matrix will be displayed in the highlighted block.

Practice Problems 2.3

1. Compute

$$\begin{bmatrix} 3 & 1 & 2 \\ -1 & 0 & \frac{1}{2} \\ 0 & 4 & 1 \end{bmatrix} \begin{bmatrix} 7 & -1 & 0 \\ 5 & 4 & 2 \\ -6 & 0 & 4 \end{bmatrix}.$$

2. Give the system of linear equations that is equivalent to the matrix equation

$$\begin{bmatrix} 3 & -6 \\ 2 & 1 \end{bmatrix} \begin{bmatrix} x \\ y \end{bmatrix} = \begin{bmatrix} 5 \\ 0 \end{bmatrix}.$$

3. Give a matrix equation equivalent to this system of equations:

$$\begin{cases} 8x + 3y = 7 \\ 9x - 2y = -5. \end{cases}$$

EXERCISES 2.3

In Exercises 1–6, give the size and special characteristics of the given matrix (such as square, column, row, identity).

1. $\begin{bmatrix} 3 & 2 & 4 \\ \frac{1}{2} & 0 & 6 \end{bmatrix}$

2. $\begin{bmatrix} 3 \\ -1 \end{bmatrix}$

3. $\begin{bmatrix} 2 & \frac{1}{3} & 0 \end{bmatrix}$

4. $\begin{bmatrix} 1 & 0 \\ 0 & 1 \end{bmatrix}$

5. $\begin{bmatrix} 1 & 0 \\ 0 & 0 \end{bmatrix}$

6. $\begin{bmatrix} 5 \end{bmatrix}$

Exercises 7–10 refer to the 2×3 matrix $A = \begin{bmatrix} 2 & -4 & 6 \\ 0 & 3 & -1 \end{bmatrix}$.

7. Find a_{12} and a_{21}.

8. Find a_{23} and a_{11}.

9. For what values of i and j does $a_{ij} = 6$?

10. For what values of i and j does $a_{ij} = 3$?

In Exercises 11–18, perform the indicated matrix calculations.

11. $\begin{bmatrix} 4 & -2 \\ 3 & 0 \end{bmatrix} + \begin{bmatrix} 5 & 5 \\ 4 & -1 \end{bmatrix}$ **12.** $\begin{bmatrix} 8 \\ -3 \end{bmatrix} + \begin{bmatrix} 5 \\ 6 \end{bmatrix}$

13. $\begin{bmatrix} 2 & 8 \\ \frac{4}{3} & 4 \\ 1 & -2 \end{bmatrix} - \begin{bmatrix} 1 & 5 \\ \frac{1}{3} & 2 \\ -3 & 0 \end{bmatrix}$

14. $\begin{bmatrix} 1 & 0 \\ 0 & 1 \end{bmatrix} - \begin{bmatrix} .8 & .5 \\ .2 & .5 \end{bmatrix}$

15. $\begin{bmatrix} 5 & 3 \end{bmatrix} \begin{bmatrix} 1 \\ 2 \end{bmatrix}$ **16.** $\begin{bmatrix} 1 & 0 & 0 \end{bmatrix} \begin{bmatrix} \frac{1}{2} \\ 6 \\ 2 \end{bmatrix}$

17. $\begin{bmatrix} 6 & 1 & 5 \end{bmatrix} \begin{bmatrix} \frac{1}{2} \\ -3 \\ 2 \end{bmatrix}$ **18.** $\begin{bmatrix} 0 & 0 \end{bmatrix} \begin{bmatrix} 5 \\ -3 \end{bmatrix}$

In Exercises 19–24, the sizes of two matrices are given. Tell whether or not the product AB is defined. If so, give its size.

19. A, 3×4; B, 4×5 **20.** A, 3×3; B, 3×4

21. A, 3×2; B, 3×2 **22.** A, 1×1; B, 1×1

23. A, 3×3; B, 3×1 **24.** A, 4×2; B, 3×4

In Exercises 25–34, perform the multiplication.

25. $\begin{bmatrix} 3 & 1 \\ 0 & 2 \end{bmatrix} \begin{bmatrix} 1 & 4 \\ 3 & 5 \end{bmatrix}$ **26.** $\begin{bmatrix} 4 & -1 \\ 2 & \frac{1}{2} \end{bmatrix} \begin{bmatrix} 3 \\ 2 \end{bmatrix}$

27. $\begin{bmatrix} 4 & 1 & 0 \\ -2 & 0 & 3 \\ 1 & 5 & -1 \end{bmatrix} \begin{bmatrix} 5 \\ 1 \\ 2 \end{bmatrix}$ **28.** $\begin{bmatrix} 0 & 0 \\ 0 & 0 \\ 0 & 0 \end{bmatrix} \begin{bmatrix} 1 & 2 \\ 3 & 4 \end{bmatrix}$

29. $\begin{bmatrix} 1 & 0 \\ 0 & 1 \end{bmatrix} \begin{bmatrix} 5 & 6 \\ 7 & 8 \end{bmatrix}$ **30.** $\begin{bmatrix} 1 & 2 \\ 1 & 3 \end{bmatrix} \begin{bmatrix} 3 & -2 \\ -1 & 1 \end{bmatrix}$

31. $\begin{bmatrix} .6 & .3 \\ .4 & .7 \end{bmatrix} \begin{bmatrix} .6 & .3 \\ .4 & .7 \end{bmatrix}$

32. $\begin{bmatrix} 0 & 1 & 2 \\ -1 & 4 & \frac{1}{2} \\ 1 & 3 & 0 \end{bmatrix} \begin{bmatrix} 3 & -1 & 5 \\ 0 & 2 & 2 \\ 4 & -6 & 0 \end{bmatrix}$

33. $\begin{bmatrix} 2 & -1 & 4 \\ 0 & 1 & 0 \\ \frac{1}{2} & 3 & -2 \end{bmatrix} \begin{bmatrix} 4 & 8 & 0 \\ 3 & -1 & 2 \\ 5 & 0 & 1 \end{bmatrix}$

34. $\begin{bmatrix} 1 & 0 & 0 \\ 0 & 1 & 0 \\ 0 & 0 & 1 \end{bmatrix} \begin{bmatrix} 1 \\ 2 \\ 3 \end{bmatrix}$

In Exercises 35–38, give the system of linear equations that is equivalent to the matrix equation. Do not solve.

35. $\begin{bmatrix} 2 & 3 \\ 4 & 5 \end{bmatrix} \begin{bmatrix} x \\ y \end{bmatrix} = \begin{bmatrix} 6 \\ 7 \end{bmatrix}$ **36.** $\begin{bmatrix} -3 & 4 \\ 0 & 1 \end{bmatrix} \begin{bmatrix} x \\ y \end{bmatrix} = \begin{bmatrix} 1 \\ 1 \end{bmatrix}$

37. $\begin{bmatrix} 1 & 2 & 3 \\ 4 & 5 & 6 \\ 7 & 8 & 9 \end{bmatrix} \begin{bmatrix} x \\ y \\ z \end{bmatrix} = \begin{bmatrix} 10 \\ 11 \\ 12 \end{bmatrix}$

38. $\begin{bmatrix} 1 & 0 & 0 \\ 0 & 1 & 0 \\ 0 & 0 & 1 \end{bmatrix} \begin{bmatrix} x \\ y \\ z \end{bmatrix} = \begin{bmatrix} 1 \\ 2 \\ 3 \end{bmatrix}$

In Exercises 39–42, write the given system of linear equations in matrix form.

39. $\begin{cases} 3x + 2y = -1 \\ 7x - y = 2 \end{cases}$ **40.** $\begin{cases} 5x - 2y = 6 \\ -2x + 4y = 0 \end{cases}$

41. $\begin{cases} x - 2y + 3z = 5 \\ y + z = 6 \\ z = 2 \end{cases}$ **42.** $\begin{cases} -2x + 4y - z = 5 \\ x + 6y + 3z = -1 \\ 7x + 4z = 8 \end{cases}$

The distributive law *says that* $(A+B)C = AC+BC$. *That is, adding A and B and then multiplying on the right by C gives the same result as first multiplying each of A and B on the right by C and then adding. In Exercises 43 and 44, verify the distributive law for the given matrices.*

43. $A = \begin{bmatrix} 1 & 2 \\ 0 & 3 \end{bmatrix}$, $B = \begin{bmatrix} 3 & -2 \\ 4 & 5 \end{bmatrix}$, $C = \begin{bmatrix} 1 & 6 \\ 2 & 0 \end{bmatrix}$

44. $A = \begin{bmatrix} 1 & 0 & 0 \\ 0 & 1 & 0 \\ 0 & 0 & 1 \end{bmatrix}$, $B = \begin{bmatrix} 2 & 1 & 3 \\ 0 & 5 & -1 \\ 3 & 6 & 0 \end{bmatrix}$, $C = \begin{bmatrix} 0 \\ 3 \\ -4 \end{bmatrix}$

Two $n \times n$ matrices A and B *are called* inverses *(of one another) if both products AB and BA equal* I_n. *Check that the pairs of matrices in Exercises 45 and 46 are inverses.*

45. $\begin{bmatrix} 3 & -1 \\ -1 & \frac{1}{2} \end{bmatrix}$, $\begin{bmatrix} 1 & 2 \\ 2 & 6 \end{bmatrix}$

46. $\begin{bmatrix} 2 & 8 & -11 \\ -1 & -5 & 7 \\ 1 & 2 & -3 \end{bmatrix}$, $\begin{bmatrix} 1 & 2 & 1 \\ 4 & 5 & -3 \\ 3 & 4 & -2 \end{bmatrix}$

47. Wardrobe Costs The quantities of pants, shirts, and jackets owned by Mike and Don are given by the matrix A, and the costs of these items are given by matrix B.

	Pants	Shirts	Jackets	
Mike	6	8	2	$= A$
Don	2	5	3	

Pants	20	
Shirts	15	$= B$
Jackets	50	

(a) Calculate the matrix AB.

(b) Interpret the entries of the matrix AB.

48. Retail Sales Two stores sell the exact same brand and style of a dresser, a nightstand, and a bookcase. Matrix A gives the retail prices (in dollars) for the items. Matrix B gives the number of each item sold at each store in one month.

$$A = \begin{matrix} \text{Dresser} & \text{Nightstand} & \text{Bookcase} \\ [\quad 250 & 80 & 60 \quad] \end{matrix}$$

$$B = \begin{matrix} & \text{Store 1} & \text{Store 2} & \\ & 40 & 35 & \text{Dresser} \\ & 30 & 35 & \text{Nightstand} \\ & 50 & 75 & \text{Bookcase} \end{matrix}$$

(a) Calculate AB.

(b) Interpret the entries of AB.

49. Retail Sales A candy shop sells various items for the price per pound (in dollars) indicated in matrix A. Matrix B gives the number of pounds of peanuts, raisins, and espresso beans used in a week. Matrix C gives the total number of pounds of plain, milk chocolate-covered, and dark chocolate-covered items sold each week.

$$A = \begin{matrix} \text{Plain} & \text{Milk} & \text{Dark} & \\ 3 & 3 & 5.8 & \text{Peanuts} \\ 2.5 & 3.5 & 6 & \text{Raisins} \\ 9 & 8 & 9.5 & \text{Espresso beans} \end{matrix}$$

$$B = \begin{matrix} \text{Peanuts} & \text{Raisins} & \text{Espresso beans} \\ [\quad 210 & 175 & 135 \quad] \end{matrix}$$

$$C = \begin{matrix} 105 & \text{Plain} \\ 390 & \text{Milk} \\ 285 & \text{Dark} \end{matrix}$$

Determine and interpret the following matrices.

(a) BA **(b)** AC

50. Wholesale and Retail Sales A company has three appliance stores that sell washers, dryers, and stoves. Matrices A and B give the wholesale and retail prices of these items, respectively. Matrices C and D give the quantities of these items sold by the three stores in September and October, respectively.

$$A = \begin{matrix} \text{Washers} & \text{Dryers} & \text{Stoves} \\ [\quad 300 & 250 & 450 \quad] \end{matrix}$$

$$B = \begin{matrix} \text{Washers} & \text{Dryers} & \text{Stoves} \\ [\quad 500 & 450 & 750 \quad] \end{matrix}$$

$$C = \begin{matrix} & \text{Store 1} & \text{Store 2} & \text{Store 3} & \\ & 30 & 40 & 20 & \text{Washers} \\ & 20 & 30 & 10 & \text{Dryers} \\ & 10 & 5 & 35 & \text{Stoves} \end{matrix}$$

$$D = \begin{matrix} & \text{Store 1} & \text{Store 2} & \text{Store 3} & \\ & 20 & 50 & 30 & \text{Washers} \\ & 30 & 10 & 20 & \text{Dryers} \\ & 10 & 20 & 30 & \text{Stoves} \end{matrix}$$

Determine and interpret the following matrices.

(a) AC	**(b)** AD
(c) BC	**(d)** BD
(e) $B - A$	**(f)** $(B-A)C$
(g) $(B-A)D$	**(h)** $C + D$
(i) $(B-A)(C+D)$	

51. Course Grades Three professors teaching the same course have entirely different grading policies. The percentage of students given each grade by the professors is summarized in the following matrix:

	Grade				
	A	B	C	D	F
Prof. I	25	35	30	10	0
Prof. II	10	20	40	20	10
Prof. III	5	10	20	40	25

(a) The point values of the grades are A = 4, B = 3, C = 2, D = 1, and F = 0. Use matrix multiplication to determine the average grade given by each professor.

(b) Professor I has 240 students, professor II has 120 students, and professor III has 40 students. Use matrix multiplication to determine the numbers of A's, B's, C's, D's, and F's given.

52. Semester Grades A professor bases semester grades on four 100-point items: homework, quizzes, a midterm exam, and a final exam. Students may choose one of three schemes summarized in the following matrix for weighting the points from the four items. Use matrix multiplication to determine the most advantageous weighting scheme for a student who earned 97 points on homework, 72 points on the quizzes, 83 points on the midterm exam, and 75 points on the final exam.

	Items			
	Hw	Qu	ME	FE
Scheme I	.10	.10	.30	.50
Scheme II	.10	.20	.30	.40
Scheme III	.15	.15	.35	.35

53. Voter Analysis In a certain town the proportions of voters voting Democratic and Republican by various age groups is summarized by this matrix:

$$
A = \begin{array}{c} \text{Under 30} \\ \text{30–50} \\ \text{Over 50} \end{array}
\begin{array}{cc} \text{Dem.} & \text{Rep.} \\ \left[\begin{array}{cc} .65 & .35 \\ .55 & .45 \\ .45 & .55 \end{array} \right] \end{array}
$$

The population of voters in the town by age group is given by the matrix

$$
B = \left[\begin{array}{ccc} \underbrace{6000}_{\substack{\text{Under} \\ 30}} & \underbrace{8000}_{\substack{\text{30–50}}} & \underbrace{4000}_{\substack{\text{Over} \\ 50}} \end{array} \right].
$$

Interpret the entries of the matrix product BA.

54. Voter Analysis Refer to Exercise 53.

   (a) Using the given data, which party would win and what would be the percentage of the winning vote?

   (b) Suppose that the population of the town shifted toward older residents as reflected in the population matrix $B = \begin{bmatrix} 2000 & 4000 & 12{,}000 \end{bmatrix}$. What would be the result of the election now?

55. Labor Costs Suppose that a contractor employs carpenters, bricklayers, and plumbers, working three shifts per day. The number of labor-hours employed in each of the shifts is summarized in the following matrix:

	\multicolumn{3}{c}{Shift}		
	1	2	3
Carpenters	50	20	10
Bricklayers	30	30	15
Plumbers	20	20	5

Labor in shift 1 costs $10 per hour, in shift 2 $15 per hour, and in shift 3 $20 per hour. Use matrix multiplication to compute the amount spent on each type of labor.

56. Epidemiology A flu epidemic hits a large city. Each resident of the city is either sick, well, or a carrier. The proportion of people in each of the categories is expressed by the following matrix:

	\multicolumn{3}{c}{Age}
	0–10	10–30	Over 30
Well	.70	.70	.60
Sick	.10	.20	.30
Carrier	.20	.10	.10

= A.

The population of the city is distributed by age and sex as follows:

		Male	Female
	0–10	60,000	65,000
Age	10–30	100,000	110,000
	Over 30	200,000	230,000

= B.

   (a) Compute AB.

   (b) How many sick males are there?

   (c) How many female carriers are there?

57. Nutrition Analysis Mikey's diet consists of food X and food Y. The matrix N represents the number of units of nutrients 1, 2, and 3 per ounce for each of the foods.

$$
N = \begin{array}{cc} & \begin{array}{ccc} 1 & 2 & 3 \end{array} \\ \begin{bmatrix} 60 & 50 & 38 \\ 42 & 50 & 67 \end{bmatrix} & \begin{array}{c} X \\ Y \end{array} \end{array}
$$

The matrices B, L, and D represent the number of ounces of each food that Mikey eats each day for breakfast, lunch, and dinner, respectively.

$$
B = \begin{array}{cc} X & Y \\ \begin{bmatrix} 2 & 1 \end{bmatrix} \end{array} \quad
L = \begin{array}{cc} X & Y \\ \begin{bmatrix} 1 & 3 \end{bmatrix} \end{array} \quad
D = \begin{array}{cc} X & Y \\ \begin{bmatrix} 2 & 4 \end{bmatrix} \end{array}
$$

Calculate and interpret the following.

   (a) BN (b) LN (c) DN

   (d) $B+L+D$ (e) $(B+L+D)N$

58. Bakery Sales A bakery makes three types of cookies, I, II, and III. Each type of cookie is made from the four ingredients A, B, C, and D. The number of units of each ingredient used in each type of cookie is given by the matrix M. The cost per unit of each of the four ingredients (in cents) is given by the matrix N. The selling price for each of the cookies (in cents) is given by the matrix S. The baker receives an order for 10 type I cookies, 20 type II cookies, and 15 type III cookies, as represented by the matrix R.

$$
M = \begin{array}{c} \\ \text{I} \\ \text{II} \\ \text{III} \end{array}
\begin{array}{cccc} A & B & C & D \\ \begin{bmatrix} 1 & 0 & 2 & 4 \\ 3 & 2 & 1 & 1 \\ 2 & 5 & 3 & 1 \end{bmatrix} \end{array}
\quad
N = \begin{bmatrix} 10 \\ 20 \\ 15 \\ 17 \end{bmatrix} \begin{array}{c} A \\ B \\ C \\ D \end{array}
$$

$$
S = \begin{bmatrix} 175 \\ 150 \\ 225 \end{bmatrix} \begin{array}{c} \text{I} \\ \text{II} \\ \text{III} \end{array}
\quad
R = \begin{array}{c} \\ \end{array} \begin{array}{ccc} \text{I} & \text{II} & \text{III} \\ \begin{bmatrix} 10 & 20 & 15 \end{bmatrix} \end{array}
$$

Calculate and interpret the following.

   (a) RM (b) MN (c) RMN

   (d) $S - MN$ (e) $R(S - MN)$ (f) RS

59. Revenue A community fitness center has a pool and a weight room. The admission prices (in dollars) for residents and nonresidents are given by the matrix

$$
P = \begin{bmatrix} 4.50 \\ 5.00 \end{bmatrix} \begin{array}{c} \text{Residents} \\ \text{Nonresidents} \end{array}.
$$

The average daily numbers of customers for the fitness center are given by the matrix

$$
A = \begin{array}{cc} & \begin{array}{cc} \text{Residents} & \text{Nonresidents} \end{array} \\ \begin{bmatrix} 90 & 63 \\ 78 & 59 \end{bmatrix} & \begin{array}{c} \text{Pool} \\ \text{Weight room} \end{array} \end{array}
$$

   (a) Compute AP.

(b) What is the average amount of money taken in by the pool each day?

60. **Production Planning** A company makes radios and TV sets. Each radio requires 3 hours of assembly and $\frac{1}{2}$ hour of packaging, while each TV set requires 5 hours of assembly and 1 hour of packaging.

   (a) Write a matrix T representing the required time for assembly and packaging of radios and TV sets.

   (b) The company receives an order from a retail outlet for 30 radios and 20 TV sets. Find a matrix S so that either ST or TS gives the total assembly time and the total packaging time required to fill the order. What is the total assembly time? What is the total packaging time?

61. **Production Planning** A bakery sells Boston cream pies and carrot cakes. Each Boston cream pie requires 30 minutes preparation time, 30 minutes baking time, and 15 minutes for finishing. Each carrot cake requires 45 minutes preparation time, 50 minutes baking time, and 10 minutes for finishing.

   (a) Write a matrix T representing the required time for preparation, baking, and finishing for the Boston cream pies and the carrot cakes.

   (b) The bakery receives an order for 20 Boston cream pies and 8 carrot cakes for a large party. Find a matrix S so that either ST or TS gives the total preparation, baking, and finishing times required to fill this order.

   (c) What is the total baking time? What is the total finishing time?

62. **Time Requirements** A beauty salon offers manicures and pedicures. A manicure requires 20 minutes for preparation, 5 minutes for lacquering, and 15 minutes for drying. A pedicure requires 30 minutes for preparation, 5 minutes for lacquering, and 20 minutes for drying.

   (a) Construct a matrix T representing the time required for preparation, lacquering, and drying for manicures and pedicures.

   (b) Suppose the salon will be giving manicures and pedicures to a large wedding party. If 15 members of the wedding party want manicures and 9 want pedicures, find a matrix S so that either ST or TS gives the total amount of time required for each of the three steps.

   (c) What is the total time required for drying?

63. **Production and Revenue** The J.E. Carrying Company makes two types of backpacks. The larger Huge One backpack requires 2 hours for cutting, 3 hours for sewing, and 2 hours for finishing, and sells for $32. The smaller Regular Joe backpack requires 1.5 hours for cutting, 2 hours for sewing, and 1 hour for finishing, and sells for $24.

(a) Construct a matrix T representing the time required for each of the three steps in making the backpacks.

(b) Construct a matrix S representing the sales prices for the two types of backpacks.

(c) Suppose the J.E. Carrying Company receives an order for 27 Huge One backpacks and 56 Regular Joe backpacks. Construct a matrix A so that either AT or TA gives the total time required to construct the backpacks in this order, and either AS or SA gives the total revenue generated by this order.

(d) How much total time is needed for sewing to fill this order?

(e) What is the total revenue for this order?

64. **MP3 Sales** A store sells three types of MP3 players. Matrix A contains information about size (in gigabytes), battery life (in hours), and weight (in ounces) of the three MP3 players. Matrix B contains the sales prices (in dollars) of the MP3 players, while matrix C contains the number of each type of player sold in one week.

$$
A = \begin{matrix}
& \text{Type I} & \text{Type II} & \text{Type III} & \\
& \begin{bmatrix} 4 & 8 & 2 \\ 33 & 20 & 15 \\ 2 & 1.7 & .9 \end{bmatrix} & & & \begin{matrix} \text{Size} \\ \text{Battery Life} \\ \text{Weight} \end{matrix}
\end{matrix}
$$

$$
B = \begin{matrix}
\text{Type I} & \text{Type II} & \text{Type III} \\
\begin{bmatrix} 100 & 180 & 60 \end{bmatrix}
\end{matrix}
$$

$$
C = \begin{bmatrix} 25 \\ 16 \\ 32 \end{bmatrix} \begin{matrix} \text{Type I} \\ \text{Type II} \\ \text{Type III} \end{matrix}
$$

Calculate and interpret the following

(a) BC (b) AC

(c) the row 2, column 1 entry of AC

65. Make up an application whose answer is that the total cost is given by

$$
\begin{bmatrix} 20 & 30 \end{bmatrix} \begin{bmatrix} 600 \\ 700 \end{bmatrix}.
$$

66. Find the values of a and b for which $A \cdot B = I_3$, where

$$
A = \begin{bmatrix} 3 & 2 & 0 \\ 1 & 1 & 0 \\ 0 & 0 & 1 \end{bmatrix} \quad \text{and} \quad B = \begin{bmatrix} a & b & 0 \\ -1 & 3 & 0 \\ 0 & 0 & 1 \end{bmatrix}.
$$

In Exercises 67 and 68, determine the matrix B based on the screen shown.

67.

```
[A]
      [[1  5  -4]
       [3  2  25]]
[A]+[B]
      [[4   3  -3]
       [-2  8  32]]
```

68.

```
[A]
      [[1  5  -4]
       [3  2  25]]
[A]-[B]
      [[-4  1  -1]
       [3   3  23]]
```

69. If A is a 3×4 matrix and $A(BB)$ is defined, what is the size of matrix B?

70. If B is a 3×5 matrix and $(AA)B$ is defined, what is the size of matrix A?

71. **School Enrollments** Table 1 gives the number of public school teachers (elementary and secondary) and the average number of pupils per teacher for three mid-Atlantic states in 2006. Set up a product of two matrices that gives the total number of pupils in the three states.

TABLE 1   Teachers and Pupils

	Delaware	Maryland	Virginia
Teachers	7998	56,685	96,158
Pupils per teacher	15.1	15.2	12.6

72. **Population** Table 2 gives the area and 2008 population density for three West-Coast states. Set up a product of two matrices that gives total population of the three states.

TABLE 2   State Areas and Densities

	California	Oregon	Washington
Land Area (sq. mi.)	155,959	95,997	66,544
Pop. Density (per sq. mile)	234.4	39.0	97.2

In Exercises 73–80, use a graphing calculator or spreadsheet to carry out the matrix operations.

In Exercises 73–80, calculate the given expression, where

$$A = \begin{bmatrix} .4 & 7 & -3 \\ 19 & .5 & 1.6 \\ -9 & 11 & 2 \end{bmatrix}, \qquad B = \begin{bmatrix} 6 & -9 & .3 \\ 1.5 & 22 & -4 \\ -5 & 6.6 & 14 \end{bmatrix},$$

and

$$C = \begin{bmatrix} 2.4 & 8 & -.2 \\ -11 & .3 & 6 \\ 7 & -4 & 5.1 \end{bmatrix}.$$

73. AB 74. BA

75. $A(B + C)$ 76. $AB + AC$

77. A^2 (that is, AA)   78. A^3 (that is, AAA)

79. Calculate $[A]^{\wedge}2$ and $[A]^{\wedge}3$. Compare your results with your answers in Exercises 77 and 78.

80. Try multiplying matrices A and B, where the number of columns of A differs from the number of rows of B. How does your calculator or spreadsheet respond?

Solutions to Practice Problems 2.3

1. Answer:

$$\begin{bmatrix} 3 & 1 & 2 \\ -1 & 0 & \frac{1}{2} \\ 0 & 4 & 1 \end{bmatrix} \begin{bmatrix} 7 & -1 & 0 \\ 5 & 4 & 2 \\ -6 & 0 & 4 \end{bmatrix}$$

$$= \begin{bmatrix} 14 & 1 & 10 \\ -10 & 1 & 2 \\ 14 & 16 & 12 \end{bmatrix}.$$

The systematic steps to be taken are as follows:

(a) Determine the size of the product matrix. Since we have a

$$\text{(3)} \times 3 \quad \text{times a} \quad 3 \times \text{(3)},$$
$$\llcorner\text{ outer dimensions }\lrcorner$$

the size of the product is given by the outer dimensions or 3×3. Begin by drawing a 3×3 rectangular array.

(Continued)

(b) Find the entries one at a time. To find the entry in the first row, first column of the product, look at the first row of the left matrix and the first column of the right matrix and form their product.

$$\begin{bmatrix} 3 & 1 & 2 \\ -1 & 0 & \frac{1}{2} \\ 0 & 4 & 1 \end{bmatrix} \begin{bmatrix} 7 & -1 & 0 \\ 5 & 4 & 2 \\ -6 & 0 & 4 \end{bmatrix}$$

$$= \begin{bmatrix} 14 & & \\ & & \\ & & \end{bmatrix}$$

since $3 \cdot 7 + 1 \cdot 5 + 2(-6) = 14$. In general, to find the entry in the ith row, jth column of the product, put one finger on the ith row of the left matrix and another finger on the jth column of the right matrix. Then multiply the row matrix times the column matrix to get the desired entry.

2. Denote the three matrices by A, X, and B, respectively. Since b_{11} (the entry of the first row, first column of B) is 5, this means that

$$\begin{bmatrix} \text{first row of } A \end{bmatrix} \begin{bmatrix} \text{first} \\ \text{column} \\ \text{of } X \end{bmatrix} = \begin{bmatrix} b_{11} \end{bmatrix}.$$

That is,

$$\begin{bmatrix} 3 & -6 \end{bmatrix} \begin{bmatrix} x \\ y \end{bmatrix} = \begin{bmatrix} 5 \end{bmatrix} \quad \text{or} \quad 3x - 6y = 5.$$

Similarly, $b_{21} = 0$ says that $2x + y = 0$. Therefore, the corresponding system of linear equations is

$$\begin{cases} 3x - 6y = 5 \\ 2x + \ y = 0. \end{cases}$$

3. The coefficient matrix is

$$\begin{bmatrix} 8 & 3 \\ 9 & -2 \end{bmatrix}.$$

So the system is equivalent to the matrix equation

$$\begin{bmatrix} 8 & 3 \\ 9 & -2 \end{bmatrix} \begin{bmatrix} x \\ y \end{bmatrix} = \begin{bmatrix} 7 \\ -5 \end{bmatrix}.$$

2.4 The Inverse of a Matrix

In Section 2.3 we introduced the operations of addition, subtraction, and multiplication of matrices. In this section let us pursue the algebra of matrices a bit further and consider equations involving matrices. Specifically, we consider equations of the form

$$AX = B, \tag{1}$$

where A and B are given matrices and X is an unknown matrix whose entries are to be determined. Such equations among matrices are intimately bound up with the theory of systems of linear equations. Indeed, we described the connection in a special case in Example 6 of Section 2.3. In that example we wrote the system of linear equations

$$\begin{cases} -2x + 4y = 2 \\ -3x + 7y = 7 \end{cases}$$

as a matrix equation of the form (1), where

$$A = \begin{bmatrix} -2 & 4 \\ -3 & 7 \end{bmatrix}, \qquad B = \begin{bmatrix} 2 \\ 7 \end{bmatrix}, \qquad X = \begin{bmatrix} x \\ y \end{bmatrix}.$$

Note that by determining the entries (x and y) of the unknown matrix X, we solve the system of linear equations. We will return to this example after we have made a complete study of the matrix equation (1).

As motivation for our solution of equation (1), let us consider the analogous equation among numbers:

$$ax = b,$$

where a and b are given numbers[1] and x is to be determined. Let us examine its solution in great detail. Multiply both sides by $1/a$. (Note that $1/a$ makes sense, since $a \neq 0$.)

$$\left(\frac{1}{a}\right) \cdot (ax) = \frac{1}{a} \cdot b$$

$$\left(\frac{1}{a} \cdot a\right) \cdot x = \frac{1}{a} \cdot b$$

$$1 \cdot x = \frac{1}{a} \cdot b$$

$$x = \frac{1}{a} \cdot b$$

Let us model our solution of equation (1) on the preceding calculation. To do so, we need to multiply both sides of the equation by a matrix that plays the same role in matrix arithmetic as $1/a$ plays in ordinary arithmetic. Our first task then will be to introduce this matrix and study its properties.

The number $1/a$ has the following relationship to the number a:

$$\frac{1}{a} \cdot a = a \cdot \frac{1}{a} = 1. \tag{2}$$

The matrix analog of the number 1 is an identity matrix I. This prompts us to generalize equation (2) to matrices as follows. Suppose that we are given a square matrix A. Then the **inverse** of A, denoted A^{-1}, is a square matrix with the property

$$A^{-1}A = I \quad \text{and} \quad AA^{-1} = I, \tag{3}$$

where I is an identity matrix of the same size as A. The matrix A^{-1} is the matrix analog of the number $1/a$. It can be shown that a matrix A has at most one inverse. (However, A may not have an inverse at all; see Example 3.)

If we are given a matrix A, then it is easy to determine whether or not a given matrix is its inverse. Merely check equation (3) with the given matrix substituted for A^{-1}. For example, if

$$A = \begin{bmatrix} -2 & 4 \\ -3 & 7 \end{bmatrix}, \quad \text{then} \quad A^{-1} = \begin{bmatrix} -\frac{7}{2} & 2 \\ -\frac{3}{2} & 1 \end{bmatrix}.$$

Indeed, we have

$$\underbrace{\begin{bmatrix} -\frac{7}{2} & 2 \\ -\frac{3}{2} & 1 \end{bmatrix}}_{A^{-1}} \underbrace{\begin{bmatrix} -2 & 4 \\ -3 & 7 \end{bmatrix}}_{A} = \begin{bmatrix} 7-6 & -14+14 \\ 3-3 & -6+7 \end{bmatrix} = \underbrace{\begin{bmatrix} 1 & 0 \\ 0 & 1 \end{bmatrix}}_{I_2}$$

and

$$\underbrace{\begin{bmatrix} -2 & 4 \\ -3 & 7 \end{bmatrix}}_{A} \underbrace{\begin{bmatrix} -\frac{7}{2} & 2 \\ -\frac{3}{2} & 1 \end{bmatrix}}_{A^{-1}} = \begin{bmatrix} 7-6 & -4+4 \\ \frac{21}{2}-\frac{21}{2} & -6+7 \end{bmatrix} = \underbrace{\begin{bmatrix} 1 & 0 \\ 0 & 1 \end{bmatrix}}_{I_2}.$$

The inverse of a matrix can be calculated using Gauss–Jordan elimination, as the next example illustrates.

---

[1] We may as well assume that $a \neq 0$. Otherwise, x does not occur.

EXAMPLE 1

Finding the inverse of a matrix Let

$$A = \begin{bmatrix} 3 & 1 \\ 5 & 2 \end{bmatrix}.$$

Determine A^{-1}.

Solution Since A is a 2×2 matrix, A^{-1} is also a 2×2 matrix and satisfies

$$AA^{-1} = I_2 \quad \text{and} \quad A^{-1}A = I_2, \tag{4}$$

where $I_2 = \begin{bmatrix} 1 & 0 \\ 0 & 1 \end{bmatrix}$ is the 2×2 identity matrix. Suppose that

$$A^{-1} = \begin{bmatrix} x & y \\ z & w \end{bmatrix}.$$

Then the first equation of (4) reads

$$\begin{bmatrix} 3 & 1 \\ 5 & 2 \end{bmatrix} \begin{bmatrix} x & y \\ z & w \end{bmatrix} = \begin{bmatrix} 1 & 0 \\ 0 & 1 \end{bmatrix}.$$

Multiplying out the matrices on the left gives

$$\begin{bmatrix} 3x + z & 3y + w \\ 5x + 2z & 5y + 2w \end{bmatrix} = \begin{bmatrix} 1 & 0 \\ 0 & 1 \end{bmatrix}.$$

Now equate corresponding elements in the two matrices to obtain the equations

$$\begin{cases} 3x + z = 1 \\ 5x + 2z = 0, \end{cases} \qquad \begin{cases} 3y + w = 0 \\ 5y + 2w = 1. \end{cases}$$

Notice that the equations break up into two pairs of linear equations, each pair involving only two variables. Solving these two systems of linear equations yields $x = 2$, $z = -5$, $y = -1$, and $w = 3$. Therefore,

$$A^{-1} = \begin{bmatrix} 2 & -1 \\ -5 & 3 \end{bmatrix}.$$

Indeed, we may readily verify that

$$\begin{bmatrix} 3 & 1 \\ 5 & 2 \end{bmatrix} \begin{bmatrix} 2 & -1 \\ -5 & 3 \end{bmatrix} = \begin{bmatrix} 1 & 0 \\ 0 & 1 \end{bmatrix}$$

$$\begin{bmatrix} 2 & -1 \\ -5 & 3 \end{bmatrix} \begin{bmatrix} 3 & 1 \\ 5 & 2 \end{bmatrix} = \begin{bmatrix} 1 & 0 \\ 0 & 1 \end{bmatrix}.$$

Now Try Exercise 3

The preceding method can be used to calculate the inverse of matrices of any size, although it involves considerable calculation. We provide a rather efficient computational method for calculating A^{-1} in the next section. For now, however, let us be content with the above method. Using it, we can derive a general formula for A^{-1} in the case where A is a 2×2 matrix.

To determine the inverse of a 2×2 matrix, let

$$A = \begin{bmatrix} a & b \\ c & d \end{bmatrix}.$$

Let $D = ad - bc$, and assume that $D \neq 0$. Then A^{-1} is given by the formula

$$A^{-1} = \begin{bmatrix} \dfrac{d}{D} & -\dfrac{b}{D} \\ -\dfrac{c}{D} & \dfrac{a}{D} \end{bmatrix}. \tag{5}$$

We will omit the derivation of this formula. It proceeds along lines similar to those of Example 1. Notice that formula (5) involves division by D. Since division by 0 is not permissible, it is necessary that $D \neq 0$ for formula (5) to be applied. We discuss the case $D = 0$ in Example 3.

Obtaining equation (5) can be reduced to a simple step-by-step procedure.

To determine the inverse of $\begin{bmatrix} a & b \\ c & d \end{bmatrix}$ if $D = ad - bc \neq 0$,

1. Interchange a and d to get $\begin{bmatrix} d & b \\ c & a \end{bmatrix}.$

2. Change the signs of b and c to get $\begin{bmatrix} d & -b \\ -c & a \end{bmatrix}.$

3. Divide all entries by D to get $\begin{bmatrix} \dfrac{d}{D} & -\dfrac{b}{D} \\ -\dfrac{c}{D} & \dfrac{a}{D} \end{bmatrix}.$

EXAMPLE 2   **Using the formula for the inverse of a 2 x 2 matrix**   Calculate the inverse of

$$\begin{bmatrix} -2 & 4 \\ -3 & 7 \end{bmatrix}.$$

Solution $D = (-2) \cdot 7 - 4 \cdot (-3) = -2$, so $D \neq 0$, and we may use the preceding computation.

1. Interchange a and d:

$$\begin{bmatrix} 7 & 4 \\ -3 & -2 \end{bmatrix}.$$

2. Change the signs of b and c:

$$\begin{bmatrix} 7 & -4 \\ 3 & -2 \end{bmatrix}.$$

3. Divide all entries by $D = -2$:

$$\begin{bmatrix} -\frac{7}{2} & 2 \\ -\frac{3}{2} & 1 \end{bmatrix}.$$

Thus

$$\begin{bmatrix} -2 & 4 \\ -3 & 7 \end{bmatrix}^{-1} = \begin{bmatrix} -\frac{7}{2} & 2 \\ -\frac{3}{2} & 1 \end{bmatrix}.$$

Now Try Exercise 5 ∎

Not every square matrix has an inverse. Indeed, it may be impossible to satisfy equation (3) for any choice of A^{-1}. This phenomenon can even occur in the case of 2×2 matrices. Here one can show that *if $D = 0$, then the matrix does not have an inverse.* The next example illustrates this phenomenon in a special case.

EXAMPLE 3

Showing that a 2 x 2 matrix does not have an inverse   Show that

$$\begin{bmatrix} 1 & 1 \\ 1 & 1 \end{bmatrix}$$

does not have an inverse.

Solution Note first that $D = 1 \cdot 1 - 1 \cdot 1 = 0$, so the inverse cannot be computed via equation (5). Suppose that the given matrix did have an inverse, say

$$\begin{bmatrix} s & t \\ u & v \end{bmatrix}.$$

Then the following equation would hold:

$$\begin{bmatrix} s & t \\ u & v \end{bmatrix} \begin{bmatrix} 1 & 1 \\ 1 & 1 \end{bmatrix} = \begin{bmatrix} 1 & 0 \\ 0 & 1 \end{bmatrix}.$$

On multiplying out the two matrices on the left, we get the equation

$$\begin{bmatrix} s+t & s+t \\ u+v & u+v \end{bmatrix} = \begin{bmatrix} 1 & 0 \\ 0 & 1 \end{bmatrix},$$

so that, on equating entries in the first row:

$$s + t = 1, \qquad s + t = 0.$$

But $s + t$ cannot equal both 1 and 0. So we reach a contradiction, and therefore
Now Try Exercise 23   the original matrix cannot have an inverse. ∎

We were led to introduce the inverse of a matrix from a discussion of the matrix equation $AX = B$. Let us now return to that discussion. Suppose that A and B are given matrices and that we wish to solve the matrix equation

$$AX = B$$

for the unknown matrix X. Suppose further that A has an inverse A^{-1}. Multiply both sides of the equation on the left by A^{-1} to obtain

$$A^{-1} \cdot AX = A^{-1}B.$$

Because $A^{-1} \cdot A = I$, we have

$$IX = A^{-1}B$$
$$X = A^{-1}B.$$

Thus the matrix X is found by simply multiplying B on the left by A^{-1}, and we can summarize our findings as follows:

> **Solving a Matrix Equation**   If the matrix A has an inverse, then the solution of the matrix equation
>
> $$AX = B \quad \text{is given by} \quad X = A^{-1}B.$$

Matrix equations can be used to solve systems of linear equations, as illustrated in the next example.

EXAMPLE 4

Using a matrix inverse to solve a system of equations   Use a matrix equation to solve the system of linear equations

$$\begin{cases} -2x + 4y = 2 \\ -3x + 7y = 7. \end{cases}$$

Solution   In Example 6 of Section 2.3 we saw that the system could be written as a matrix equation:

$$\underset{A}{\begin{bmatrix} -2 & 4 \\ -3 & 7 \end{bmatrix}} \underset{X}{\begin{bmatrix} x \\ y \end{bmatrix}} = \underset{B}{\begin{bmatrix} 2 \\ 7 \end{bmatrix}}.$$

We happen to know A^{-1} from Example 2, namely

$$A^{-1} = \begin{bmatrix} -\frac{7}{2} & 2 \\ -\frac{3}{2} & 1 \end{bmatrix}.$$

So we may compute the matrix $X = A^{-1}B$:

$$X = \begin{bmatrix} x \\ y \end{bmatrix} = \begin{bmatrix} -\frac{7}{2} & 2 \\ -\frac{3}{2} & 1 \end{bmatrix} \begin{bmatrix} 2 \\ 7 \end{bmatrix} = \begin{bmatrix} 7 \\ 4 \end{bmatrix}.$$

Now Try Exercise 11   Thus, the solution of the system is $x = 7$, $y = 4$.   ∎

EXAMPLE 5

Analyzing marriage trends   Let x and y denote the number of married and single adults in a certain town as of January 1. Let m and s denote the corresponding numbers for the following year. A statistical survey shows that x, y, m, and s are related by the equations

$$.9x + .2y = m$$
$$.1x + .8y = \ s.$$

In a given year there were found to be 490,000 married adults and 147,000 single adults.

(a) How many married adults were there in the preceding year?

(b) How many married adults were there two years ago?

Solution   (a) The given equations can be written in the matrix form

$$AX = B,$$

where

$$A = \begin{bmatrix} .9 & .2 \\ .1 & .8 \end{bmatrix}, \qquad X = \begin{bmatrix} x \\ y \end{bmatrix}, \qquad B = \begin{bmatrix} m \\ s \end{bmatrix}.$$

We are given that $B = \begin{bmatrix} 490{,}000 \\ 147{,}000 \end{bmatrix}$. So, since

$$X = A^{-1}B \quad \text{and} \quad A^{-1} = \begin{bmatrix} \frac{8}{7} & -\frac{2}{7} \\ -\frac{1}{7} & \frac{9}{7} \end{bmatrix},$$

we have

$$X = \begin{bmatrix} \frac{8}{7} & -\frac{2}{7} \\ -\frac{1}{7} & \frac{9}{7} \end{bmatrix} \begin{bmatrix} 490{,}000 \\ 147{,}000 \end{bmatrix} = \begin{bmatrix} 518{,}000 \\ 119{,}000 \end{bmatrix}.$$

Thus last year there were 518,000 married adults and 119,000 single adults.

(b) We deduce x and y for two years ago from the values of m and s for last year, namely $m = 518{,}000$, $s = 119{,}000$.

$$X = A^{-1}B = \begin{bmatrix} \frac{8}{7} & -\frac{2}{7} \\ -\frac{1}{7} & \frac{9}{7} \end{bmatrix} \begin{bmatrix} 518{,}000 \\ 119{,}000 \end{bmatrix} = \begin{bmatrix} 558{,}000 \\ 79{,}000 \end{bmatrix}.$$

That is, two years ago there were 558,000 married adults and 79,000 single adults.

Now Try Exercise 17

EXAMPLE 6

Using a matrix inverse to solve systems of equations In Section 2.5 we will show that if

$$A = \begin{bmatrix} 4 & -2 & 3 \\ 8 & -3 & 5 \\ 7 & -2 & 4 \end{bmatrix}, \quad \text{then} \quad A^{-1} = \begin{bmatrix} -2 & 2 & -1 \\ 3 & -5 & 4 \\ 5 & -6 & 4 \end{bmatrix}.$$

(a) Use this fact to solve the system of linear equations

$$\begin{cases} 4x - 2y + 3z = 1 \\ 8x - 3y + 5z = 4 \\ 7x - 2y + 4z = 5. \end{cases}$$

(b) Solve the system of equations

$$\begin{cases} 4x - 2y + 3z = 4 \\ 8x - 3y + 5z = 7 \\ 7x - 2y + 4z = 6. \end{cases}$$

Solution (a) The system can be written in the matrix form

$$\underset{A}{\begin{bmatrix} 4 & -2 & 3 \\ 8 & -3 & 5 \\ 7 & -2 & 4 \end{bmatrix}} \underset{X}{\begin{bmatrix} x \\ y \\ z \end{bmatrix}} = \underset{B}{\begin{bmatrix} 1 \\ 4 \\ 5 \end{bmatrix}}.$$

The solution of this matrix equation is $X = A^{-1}B$, or

$$\begin{bmatrix} x \\ y \\ z \end{bmatrix} = \begin{bmatrix} -2 & 2 & -1 \\ 3 & -5 & 4 \\ 5 & -6 & 4 \end{bmatrix} \begin{bmatrix} 1 \\ 4 \\ 5 \end{bmatrix} = \begin{bmatrix} 1 \\ 3 \\ 1 \end{bmatrix}.$$

Thus the solution of the system is $x = 1$, $y = 3$, $z = 1$.

(b) This system has the same left-hand side as the preceding system, so its solution is

$$\begin{bmatrix} x \\ y \\ z \end{bmatrix} = \begin{bmatrix} -2 & 2 & -1 \\ 3 & -5 & 4 \\ 5 & -6 & 4 \end{bmatrix} \begin{bmatrix} 4 \\ 7 \\ 6 \end{bmatrix} = \begin{bmatrix} 0 \\ 1 \\ 2 \end{bmatrix}.$$

 Now Try Exercise 19   That is, the solution of the system is $x = 0$, $y = 1$, $z = 2$.   ■

Using the method of matrix equations to solve a system of linear equations is especially efficient if one wishes to solve a number of systems all having the same left-hand sides but different right-hand sides. For then A^{-1} must be computed only once for all the systems under consideration. (This point is useful in Exercises 19–22.)

 INCORPORATING TECHNOLOGY

GC (TI-83/84 Plus)   The inverse of a square matrix can be obtained directly with the inverse key $\boxed{x^{-1}}$. See Fig. 1. (*Note*: Do not use **[A]**$^{\wedge}$**-1**.)

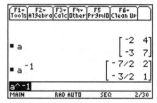

Figure 1   **Figure 2**

(TI-89)   The inverse of a square matrix can be obtained directly by raising the matrix to the -1 power. See Fig. 2.   ■

ES   To obtain the inverse of the $n \times n$ matrix named A, select an n by n square of cells where you would like the inverse matrix to be displayed, type **=MINVERSE(A)**, and press Crtl+Shift+Enter.

Practice Problems 2.4

1. Show that the inverse of

$$\begin{bmatrix} -4 & 1 & 2 \\ 7 & -1 & -4 \\ -\frac{1}{2} & 0 & \frac{1}{2} \end{bmatrix} \text{ is } \begin{bmatrix} 1 & 1 & 4 \\ 3 & 2 & 4 \\ 1 & 1 & 6 \end{bmatrix}.$$

2. Use the method of this section to solve the system of linear equations

$$\begin{cases} .8x + .6y = 5 \\ .2x + .4y = 2. \end{cases}$$

EXERCISES 2.4

In Exercises 1 and 2, use the fact that

$$\begin{bmatrix} 2 & 2 \\ \frac{1}{2} & 1 \end{bmatrix}^{-1} = \begin{bmatrix} 1 & -2 \\ -\frac{1}{2} & 2 \end{bmatrix}.$$

1. Solve $\begin{cases} 2x + 2y = 4 \\ \frac{1}{2}x + y = 1. \end{cases}$

2. Solve $\begin{cases} 2x + 2y = 14 \\ \frac{1}{2}x + y = 4. \end{cases}$

In Exercises 3–10, find the inverse of the given matrix.

3. $\begin{bmatrix} 7 & 2 \\ 3 & 1 \end{bmatrix}$ **4.** $\begin{bmatrix} 2 & 3 \\ 5 & 7 \end{bmatrix}$

5. $\begin{bmatrix} 6 & 2 \\ 5 & 2 \end{bmatrix}$ **6.** $\begin{bmatrix} 1 & .5 \\ 0 & .5 \end{bmatrix}$

7. $\begin{bmatrix} .7 & .2 \\ .3 & .8 \end{bmatrix}$ **8.** $\begin{bmatrix} 0 & 1 \\ 1 & 0 \end{bmatrix}$

9. $\begin{bmatrix} 3 \end{bmatrix}$ **10.** $\begin{bmatrix} .2 \end{bmatrix}$

In Exercises 11–14, use the method of this section to solve the system of linear equations.

11. $\begin{cases} x + 2y = 3 \\ 2x + 6y = 5 \end{cases}$ **12.** $\begin{cases} 5x + 3y = 1 \\ 7x + 4y = 2 \end{cases}$

13. $\begin{cases} \frac{1}{2}x + 2y = 4 \\ 3x + 16y = 0 \end{cases}$ **14.** $\begin{cases} .8x + .6y = 2 \\ .2x + .4y = 1 \end{cases}$

15. Marriage Trends It is found that the number of married and single adults in a certain town are subject to the following statistics. Suppose that x and y denote the number of married and single adults, respectively, in a given year (say as of January 1) and let m, s denote the corresponding numbers for the following year. Then

$$.8x + .3y = m$$
$$.2x + .7y = s.$$

(a) Write this system of equations in matrix form.

(b) Solve the resulting matrix equation for $X = \begin{bmatrix} x \\ y \end{bmatrix}$.

(c) Suppose that in a given year there were found to be 100,000 married adults and 50,000 single adults. How many married (respectively, single) adults were there the preceding year?

(d) How many married (respectively, single) adults were there two years ago?

16. Epidemiology A flu epidemic is spreading through a town of 48,000 people. It is found that if x and y denote the numbers of people sick and well in a given week, respectively, and if s and w denote the corresponding numbers for the following week, then

$$\tfrac{1}{3}x + \tfrac{1}{4}y = s$$
$$\tfrac{2}{3}x + \tfrac{3}{4}y = w.$$

(a) Write this system of equations in matrix form.

(b) Solve the resulting matrix equation for $X = \begin{bmatrix} x \\ y \end{bmatrix}$.

(c) Suppose that 13,000 people are sick in a given week. How many were sick the preceding week?

(d) Same question as part (c), except assume that 14,000 are sick.

17. Housing Trends Statistics show that at a certain university, 70% of the students who live on campus during a given semester will remain on campus the following semester, and 90% of students living off campus during a given semester will remain off campus the following semester. Let x and y denote the number of students who live on and off campus this semester, and let u and v be the corresponding numbers for the next semester. Then

$$.7x + .1y = u$$
$$.3x + .9y = v.$$

(a) Write this system of equations in matrix form.

(b) Solve the resulting matrix equation for $\begin{bmatrix} x \\ y \end{bmatrix}$.

(c) Suppose that out of a group of 9000 students, 6000 currently live on campus and 3000 live off campus. How many lived on campus last semester? How many will live off campus next semester?

18. Performance on Tests A teacher estimates that of the students who pass a test, 80% will pass the next test, while of the students who fail a test, 50% will pass the next test. Let x and y denote the number of students who pass and fail a given test, and let u and v be the corresponding numbers for the following test.

(a) Write a matrix equation relating $\begin{bmatrix} x \\ y \end{bmatrix}$ to $\begin{bmatrix} u \\ v \end{bmatrix}$.

(b) Suppose that 25 of the teacher's students pass the third test and 8 fail the third test. How many students will pass the fourth test? Approximately how many passed the second test?

In Exercises 19 and 20, use the fact that

$$\begin{bmatrix} 1 & 2 & 2 \\ 1 & 3 & 2 \\ 1 & 2 & 3 \end{bmatrix}^{-1} = \begin{bmatrix} 5 & -2 & -2 \\ -1 & 1 & 0 \\ -1 & 0 & 1 \end{bmatrix}.$$

19. Solve $\begin{cases} x + 2y + 2z = 1 \\ x + 3y + 2z = -1 \\ x + 2y + 3z = -1. \end{cases}$

20. Solve $\begin{cases} x + 2y + 2z = 1 \\ x + 3y + 2z = 0 \\ x + 2y + 3z = 0. \end{cases}$

In Exercises 21 and 22, use the fact that

$$\begin{bmatrix} 9 & 0 & 2 & 0 \\ -20 & -9 & -5 & 5 \\ 4 & 0 & 1 & 0 \\ -4 & -2 & -1 & 1 \end{bmatrix}^{-1} = \begin{bmatrix} 1 & 0 & -2 & 0 \\ 0 & 1 & 0 & -5 \\ -4 & 0 & 9 & 0 \\ 0 & 2 & 1 & -9 \end{bmatrix}.$$

21. Solve $\begin{cases} 9x + 2z = 1 \\ -20x - 9y - 5z + 5w = 0 \\ 4x + z = 0 \\ -4x - 2y - z + w = -1. \end{cases}$

22. Solve $\begin{cases} 9x + 2z = 2 \\ -20x - 9y - 5z + 5w = 1 \\ 4x + z = 3 \\ -4x - 2y - z + w = 0. \end{cases}$

23. Without computing D, show that the matrix $\begin{bmatrix} 6 & 3 \\ 2 & 1 \end{bmatrix}$ does not have an inverse.

24. If $A^{-1} = \begin{bmatrix} 2 & 7 \\ 1 & -3 \end{bmatrix}$, what is the matrix A?

25. Age Distribution There are two age groups for a particular species of organism. Group I consists of all organisms aged under 1 year, while group II consists of all organisms aged from 1 to 2 years. No organism survives more than 2 years. The average number of offspring per year born to each member of group I is 1, while the average number of organisms per year born to each member of group II is 2. Nine-tenths of group I survive to enter group II each year.

   (a) Let x and y represent the initial number of organisms in groups I and II, respectively. Let a and b represent the number of organisms in groups I and II, respectively, after one year. Write a matrix equation relating $\begin{bmatrix} x \\ y \end{bmatrix}$ to $\begin{bmatrix} a \\ b \end{bmatrix}$.

   (b) If there are initially 450,000 organisms in group I and 360,000 organisms in group II, calculate the number of organisms in each of the groups after 1 year and after 2 years.

   (c) Suppose that at a certain time there were 810,000 organisms in group I and 630,000 organisms in group II. Determine the population of each group 1 year earlier.

26. If $A^2 = \begin{bmatrix} -2 & -1 \\ 2 & -1 \end{bmatrix}$ and $A^3 = \begin{bmatrix} -2 & 1 \\ -2 & -3 \end{bmatrix}$, what is A?

27. Show that if AB is a matrix of all zeros and A has an inverse, then B is a matrix of all zeros.

28. Consider the matrices $A = \begin{bmatrix} 3 & 1 \\ 5 & 2 \end{bmatrix}$ and $B = \begin{bmatrix} 6 & 2 \\ 5 & 2 \end{bmatrix}$. Show that $(AB)^{-1} = B^{-1}A^{-1}$.

29. Find a 2×2 matrix A and a 2×1 column matrix B for which $AX = B$ has no solution.

30. Find a 2×2 matrix A and a 2×1 column matrix B for which $AX = B$ has infinitely many solutions.

In Exercises 31–39 use a graphing calculator or spreadsheet.

In Exercises 31–34, use the inverse operation to find the inverse of the given matrix. Display the entries as fractions.

31. $\begin{bmatrix} .2 & 3 \\ 4 & 1.6 \end{bmatrix}$ **32.** $\begin{bmatrix} -12 & 3.3 \\ 6 & .4 \end{bmatrix}$

33. $\begin{bmatrix} .6 & 3 & -7 \\ 2.5 & -1 & 4 \\ -2 & .3 & 9 \end{bmatrix}$ **34.** $\begin{bmatrix} 5 & 2.3 & 6 \\ 1.2 & 5 & -7 \\ -3 & -4 & 6.5 \end{bmatrix}$

In Exercises 35–38, calculate the answer using $[A]^{-1} * [B]$ and give the answer using fractions.

35. $\begin{cases} 2x - 4y + 7z = 11 \\ x + 3y - 5z = -9 \\ 3x - y + 3z = 7 \end{cases}$

36. $\begin{cases} 5x + 2y - 3z = 1 \\ 4x - y + z = 22 \\ -x + 5y - 6z = 4 \end{cases}$

37. $\begin{cases} 2x + 7z + 5w = 10 \\ 5x - y + 3z = -2 \\ x + 2y - 2w = 0 \\ 3x - 4y + 2z - 5w = -18 \end{cases}$

38. $\begin{cases} x + 4y - z + 2w = 9 \\ 3x - 8y + 2z + 4w = -2 \\ -x - 3y + 7z - 6w = 10 \\ 4x + 2y - 3z + w = -6 \end{cases}$

39. Try finding the inverse of a matrix that does not have an inverse. How does your calculator or spreadsheet respond?

Solutions to Practice Problems 2.4

1. To see if this matrix is indeed the inverse, multiply it by the original matrix and find out if the products are identity matrices.

$$\begin{bmatrix} 1 & 1 & 4 \\ 3 & 2 & 4 \\ 1 & 1 & 6 \end{bmatrix} \begin{bmatrix} -4 & 1 & 2 \\ 7 & -1 & -4 \\ -\frac{1}{2} & 0 & \frac{1}{2} \end{bmatrix} = \begin{bmatrix} 1 & 0 & 0 \\ 0 & 1 & 0 \\ 0 & 0 & 1 \end{bmatrix},$$

(an identity matrix)

$$\begin{bmatrix} -4 & 1 & 2 \\ 7 & -1 & -4 \\ -\frac{1}{2} & 0 & \frac{1}{2} \end{bmatrix} \begin{bmatrix} 1 & 1 & 4 \\ 3 & 2 & 4 \\ 1 & 1 & 6 \end{bmatrix} = \begin{bmatrix} 1 & 0 & 0 \\ 0 & 1 & 0 \\ 0 & 0 & 1 \end{bmatrix}.$$

(Continued)

2. The matrix form of this system is

$$\begin{bmatrix} .8 & .6 \\ .2 & .4 \end{bmatrix} \begin{bmatrix} x \\ y \end{bmatrix} = \begin{bmatrix} 5 \\ 2 \end{bmatrix}.$$

Therefore, the solution is

$$\begin{bmatrix} x \\ y \end{bmatrix} = \begin{bmatrix} .8 & .6 \\ .2 & .4 \end{bmatrix}^{-1} \begin{bmatrix} 5 \\ 2 \end{bmatrix}.$$

To compute the inverse of the 2×2 matrix, first compute D.

$$D = ad - bc = (.8)(.4) - (.6)(.2) = .32 - .12 = .2$$

Thus,

$$\begin{bmatrix} .8 & .6 \\ .2 & .4 \end{bmatrix}^{-1} = \begin{bmatrix} .4/.2 & -.6/.2 \\ -.2/.2 & .8/.2 \end{bmatrix} = \begin{bmatrix} 2 & -3 \\ -1 & 4 \end{bmatrix}.$$

Therefore,

$$\begin{bmatrix} x \\ y \end{bmatrix} = \begin{bmatrix} 2 & -3 \\ -1 & 4 \end{bmatrix} \begin{bmatrix} 5 \\ 2 \end{bmatrix} = \begin{bmatrix} 4 \\ 3 \end{bmatrix},$$

so the solution is $x = 4$, $y = 3$.

2.5 The Gauss–Jordan Method for Calculating Inverses

Of the several popular methods for finding the inverse of a matrix, the **Gauss–Jordan method** is probably the easiest to describe. It can be used on square matrices of any size. Also, the mechanical nature of the computations allows this method to be programmed for a computer with relative ease. We shall illustrate the procedure with a 2×2 matrix, whose inverse can also be calculated using the method of the previous section. Let

$$A = \begin{bmatrix} \frac{1}{2} & 1 \\ 1 & 3 \end{bmatrix}.$$

It is simple to check that

$$A^{-1} = \begin{bmatrix} 6 & -2 \\ -2 & 1 \end{bmatrix}.$$

Let us now derive this result using the Gauss–Jordan method.

Step 1 Write down the matrix A, and on its right append an identity matrix of the same size.

This is most conveniently done by placing I_2 beside A in a single matrix.

$$\begin{bmatrix} \underbrace{\begin{matrix} \frac{1}{2} & 1 \\ 1 & 3 \end{matrix}}_{A} & \bigg| & \underbrace{\begin{matrix} 1 & 0 \\ 0 & 1 \end{matrix}}_{I_2} \end{bmatrix}$$

Step 2 Perform elementary row operations on the left-hand matrix so as to transform it into an identity matrix. Each operation performed on the left-hand matrix is also performed on the right-hand matrix.

This step proceeds exactly like the Gauss–Jordan elimination method and may be most conveniently expressed in terms of pivoting.

$$\left[\begin{array}{cc|cc} \tfrac{1}{2} & 1 & 1 & 0 \\ 1 & 3 & 0 & 1 \end{array}\right], \quad \left[\begin{array}{cc|cc} 1 & 2 & 2 & 0 \\ 0 & 1 & -2 & 1 \end{array}\right], \quad \left[\begin{array}{cc|cc} 1 & 0 & 6 & -2 \\ 0 & 1 & -2 & 1 \end{array}\right]$$

Step 3   When the matrix on the left becomes an identity matrix, the matrix on the right is the desired inverse.

So, from the last matrix of our calculation above, we have

$$A^{-1} = \begin{bmatrix} 6 & -2 \\ -2 & 1 \end{bmatrix}.$$

This is the same result obtained earlier.
    We will demonstrate why the preceding method works after some further examples.

EXAMPLE 1

Finding the inverse of a matrix using the Gauss–Jordan method   Find the inverse of the matrix

$$A = \begin{bmatrix} 4 & -2 & 3 \\ 8 & -3 & 5 \\ 7 & -2 & 4 \end{bmatrix}.$$

Solution

$$\left[\begin{array}{ccc|ccc} 4 & -2 & 3 & 1 & 0 & 0 \\ 8 & -3 & 5 & 0 & 1 & 0 \\ 7 & -2 & 4 & 0 & 0 & 1 \end{array}\right]$$

$$\left[\begin{array}{ccc|ccc} 1 & -\tfrac{1}{2} & \tfrac{3}{4} & \tfrac{1}{4} & 0 & 0 \\ 0 & 1 & -1 & -2 & 1 & 0 \\ 0 & \tfrac{3}{2} & -\tfrac{5}{4} & -\tfrac{7}{4} & 0 & 1 \end{array}\right]$$

$$\left[\begin{array}{ccc|ccc} 1 & 0 & \tfrac{1}{4} & -\tfrac{3}{4} & \tfrac{1}{2} & 0 \\ 0 & 1 & -1 & -2 & 1 & 0 \\ 0 & 0 & \tfrac{1}{4} & \tfrac{5}{4} & -\tfrac{3}{2} & 1 \end{array}\right]$$

$$\left[\begin{array}{ccc|ccc} 1 & 0 & 0 & -2 & 2 & -1 \\ 0 & 1 & 0 & 3 & -5 & 4 \\ 0 & 0 & 1 & 5 & -6 & 4 \end{array}\right]$$

Therefore,

$$A^{-1} = \begin{bmatrix} -2 & 2 & -1 \\ 3 & -5 & 4 \\ 5 & -6 & 4 \end{bmatrix}.$$

Now Try Exercise 7

Not all square matrices have inverses. If a matrix does not have an inverse, this will become apparent when applying the Gauss–Jordan method. At some point there will be no way to continue transforming the left-hand matrix into an identity matrix. This is illustrated in the next example.

EXAMPLE 2   **Demonstrating that a matrix does not have an inverse**   Find the inverse of the matrix

$$A = \begin{bmatrix} 1 & 3 & 2 \\ 0 & 1 & 4 \\ 1 & 5 & 10 \end{bmatrix}.$$

Solution

$$\left[\begin{array}{ccc|ccc} \boxed{1} & 3 & 2 & 1 & 0 & 0 \\ 0 & 1 & 4 & 0 & 1 & 0 \\ 1 & 5 & 10 & 0 & 0 & 1 \end{array}\right]$$

$$\left[\begin{array}{ccc|ccc} 1 & 3 & 2 & 1 & 0 & 0 \\ 0 & \boxed{1} & 4 & 0 & 1 & 0 \\ 0 & 2 & 8 & -1 & 0 & 1 \end{array}\right]$$

$$\left[\begin{array}{ccc|ccc} 1 & 0 & -10 & 1 & -3 & 0 \\ 0 & 1 & 4 & 0 & 1 & 0 \\ 0 & 0 & 0 & -1 & -2 & 1 \end{array}\right]$$

Since the third row of the left-hand matrix has only zero entries, it is impossible to complete the Gauss–Jordan method. Therefore, the matrix A has no inverse matrix.   ∎

Now Try Exercise 9

Verification of the Gauss–Jordan Method for Calculating Inverses   In Section 2.4 we showed how to calculate the inverse by solving several systems of linear equations. Actually, the Gauss–Jordan method is just an organized way of going about the calculation. To see why, let us consider a concrete example:

$$A = \begin{bmatrix} 4 & -2 & 3 \\ 8 & -3 & 5 \\ 7 & -2 & 4 \end{bmatrix}.$$

We wish to determine A^{-1}, so regard it as a matrix of unknowns:

$$A^{-1} = \begin{bmatrix} x_1 & x_2 & x_3 \\ y_1 & y_2 & y_3 \\ z_1 & z_2 & z_3 \end{bmatrix}.$$

The statement $AA^{-1} = I_3$ is

$$\begin{bmatrix} 4 & -2 & 3 \\ 8 & -3 & 5 \\ 7 & -2 & 4 \end{bmatrix} \begin{bmatrix} x_1 & x_2 & x_3 \\ y_1 & y_2 & y_3 \\ z_1 & z_2 & z_3 \end{bmatrix} = \begin{bmatrix} 1 & 0 & 0 \\ 0 & 1 & 0 \\ 0 & 0 & 1 \end{bmatrix}.$$

Multiplying out the matrices on the left and comparing the result with the matrix on the right give us nine equations, namely

$$\begin{cases} 4x_1 - 2y_1 + 3z_1 = 1 \\ 8x_1 - 3y_1 + 5z_1 = 0 \\ 7x_1 - 2y_1 + 4z_1 = 0 \end{cases}$$

$$\begin{cases} 4x_2 - 2y_2 + 3z_2 = 0 \\ 8x_2 - 3y_2 + 5z_2 = 1 \\ 7x_2 - 2y_2 + 4z_2 = 0 \end{cases}$$

$$\begin{cases} 4x_3 - 2y_3 + 3z_3 = 0 \\ 8x_3 - 3y_3 + 5z_3 = 0 \\ 7x_3 - 2y_3 + 4z_3 = 1. \end{cases}$$

Notice that each system of equations corresponds to one column of unknowns in A^{-1}. More precisely, if we set

$$X_1 = \begin{bmatrix} x_1 \\ y_1 \\ z_1 \end{bmatrix}, \qquad X_2 = \begin{bmatrix} x_2 \\ y_2 \\ z_2 \end{bmatrix}, \qquad X_3 = \begin{bmatrix} x_3 \\ y_3 \\ z_3 \end{bmatrix},$$

then the preceding three systems have the respective matrix forms

$$AX_1 = \begin{bmatrix} 1 \\ 0 \\ 0 \end{bmatrix}, \qquad AX_2 = \begin{bmatrix} 0 \\ 1 \\ 0 \end{bmatrix}, \qquad AX_3 = \begin{bmatrix} 0 \\ 0 \\ 1 \end{bmatrix}.$$

Now imagine the process of applying Gauss–Jordan elimination to solve these three systems. We apply elementary row operations to the matrices

$$\left[A \;\middle|\; \begin{matrix} 1 \\ 0 \\ 0 \end{matrix} \right], \qquad \left[A \;\middle|\; \begin{matrix} 0 \\ 1 \\ 0 \end{matrix} \right], \qquad \left[A \;\middle|\; \begin{matrix} 0 \\ 0 \\ 1 \end{matrix} \right].$$

The process ends when we convert A into the identity matrix, at which point the solutions may be read off the right column. So the procedure ends with the matrices

$$\begin{bmatrix} I_3 & | & X_1 \end{bmatrix}, \qquad \begin{bmatrix} I_3 & | & X_2 \end{bmatrix}, \qquad \begin{bmatrix} I_3 & | & X_3 \end{bmatrix}.$$

Realize, however, that at each step of the three Gauss–Jordan eliminations we are performing the same operations, since all three start with the matrix A on the left. So, in order to save calculations, perform the three Gauss–Jordan eliminations simultaneously by performing the row operations on the composite matrix

$$\left[A \;\middle|\; \begin{matrix} 1 & 0 & 0 \\ 0 & 1 & 0 \\ 0 & 0 & 1 \end{matrix} \right] = \begin{bmatrix} A & | & I_3 \end{bmatrix}.$$

The procedure ends when this matrix is converted into

$$\begin{bmatrix} I_3 & | & X_1 & X_2 & X_3 \end{bmatrix}.$$

That is, since $A^{-1} = \begin{bmatrix} X_1 & X_2 & X_3 \end{bmatrix}$, the procedure ends with A^{-1} on the right. This is the reasoning behind the Gauss–Jordan method of calculating inverses. ∎

Practice Problems 2.5

1. Use the Gauss–Jordan method to calculate the inverse of the matrix

$$\begin{bmatrix} 1 & 0 & 2 \\ 0 & 1 & -4 \\ 0 & 0 & 2 \end{bmatrix}.$$

2. Solve the system of linear equations

$$\begin{cases} x & + 2z = 4 \\ & y - 4z = 6 \\ & 2z = 9. \end{cases}$$

EXERCISES 2.5

In Exercises 1–12, use the Gauss–Jordan method to compute the inverse of the matrix.

1. $\begin{bmatrix} 7 & 3 \\ 5 & 2 \end{bmatrix}$ **2.** $\begin{bmatrix} 5 & -2 \\ 6 & 2 \end{bmatrix}$

3. $\begin{bmatrix} 2 & 3 \\ -4 & -7 \end{bmatrix}$ **4.** $\begin{bmatrix} 1 & -3 \\ 0 & 1 \end{bmatrix}$

5. $\begin{bmatrix} 2 & -4 \\ -1 & 2 \end{bmatrix}$ **6.** $\begin{bmatrix} 1 & 3 & 1 \\ -1 & 2 & 0 \\ 2 & 11 & 3 \end{bmatrix}$

7. $\begin{bmatrix} 1 & 2 & -2 \\ 1 & 1 & 1 \\ 0 & 0 & 1 \end{bmatrix}$ **8.** $\begin{bmatrix} 2 & 2 & 0 \\ 0 & -2 & 0 \\ 3 & 0 & 1 \end{bmatrix}$

9. $\begin{bmatrix} -2 & 5 & 2 \\ 1 & -3 & -1 \\ -1 & 2 & 1 \end{bmatrix}$ **10.** $\begin{bmatrix} 1 & 0 & 0 \\ 2 & 1 & -2 \\ -1 & 2 & 1 \end{bmatrix}$

11. $\begin{bmatrix} 1 & 6 & 0 & 0 \\ 1 & 5 & 0 & 0 \\ 0 & 0 & 4 & 2 \\ 0 & 0 & 50 & 2 \end{bmatrix}$ **12.** $\begin{bmatrix} 6 & 0 & 2 & 0 \\ -6 & 1 & 0 & 1 \\ 1 & 0 & 1 & 0 \\ -9 & 0 & -1 & 1 \end{bmatrix}$

In Exercises 13–16, use matrix inversion to solve the systems of linear equations.

13. $\begin{cases} x + y + 2z = 3 \\ 3x + 2y + 2z = 4 \\ x + y + 3z = 5 \end{cases}$ **14.** $\begin{cases} x + 2y + 3z = 4 \\ 3x + 5y + 5z = 3 \\ 2x + 4y + 2z = 4 \end{cases}$

15. $\begin{cases} x & - 2z - 2w = 0 \\ y & - 5w = 1 \\ -4x & + 9z + 9w = 2 \\ 2y + z - 8w = 3 \end{cases}$

16. $\begin{cases} y + 2z = 1 \\ 2x + y + 3z = 2 \\ x + y + 2z = 3 \end{cases}$

17. If $A^{-1} = \begin{bmatrix} 2 & 7 \\ 1 & 3 \end{bmatrix}$, what is the matrix A?

18. Find the 2×2 matrix C for which $AC = B$, where

$$A = \begin{bmatrix} 3 & 2 \\ 4 & 3 \end{bmatrix} \quad \text{and} \quad B = \begin{bmatrix} 5 & 6 \\ 1 & 7 \end{bmatrix}.$$

19. Find a 2×2 matrix A for which

$$A \begin{bmatrix} 2 \\ 1 \end{bmatrix} = \begin{bmatrix} -1 \\ 4 \end{bmatrix} \quad \text{and} \quad A \begin{bmatrix} 5 \\ 3 \end{bmatrix} = \begin{bmatrix} 0 \\ 2 \end{bmatrix}.$$

20. Let

$$A = \begin{bmatrix} 7 & 4 \\ 3 & 2 \end{bmatrix} \quad \text{and} \quad B = \begin{bmatrix} 1 & 5 \\ -3 & 4 \end{bmatrix}.$$

Each of the equations $AX = B$ and $XA = B$ has a 2×2 matrix X as a solution. Find X in each case and explain why the two answers are different.

Solutions to Practice Problems 2.5

1. First write the given matrix beside an identity matrix of the same size

$$\left[\begin{array}{ccc|ccc} 1 & 0 & 2 & 1 & 0 & 0 \\ 0 & 1 & -4 & 0 & 1 & 0 \\ 0 & 0 & 2 & 0 & 0 & 1 \end{array}\right].$$

The object is to use elementary row operations to transform the 3×3 matrix on the left into the identity matrix. The first two columns are already in the correct form.

(Continued)

$$\begin{bmatrix} 1 & 0 & 2 & | & 1 & 0 & 0 \\ 0 & 1 & -4 & | & 0 & 1 & 0 \\ 0 & 0 & 2 & | & 0 & 0 & 1 \end{bmatrix}$$

$$\xrightarrow{\frac{1}{2}R_3} \begin{bmatrix} 1 & 0 & 2 & | & 1 & 0 & 0 \\ 0 & 1 & -4 & | & 0 & 1 & 0 \\ 0 & 0 & 1 & | & 0 & 0 & \frac{1}{2} \end{bmatrix}$$

$$\xrightarrow{R_1 + (-2)R_3} \begin{bmatrix} 1 & 0 & 0 & | & 1 & 0 & -1 \\ 0 & 1 & -4 & | & 0 & 1 & 0 \\ 0 & 0 & 1 & | & 0 & 0 & \frac{1}{2} \end{bmatrix}$$

$$\xrightarrow{R_2 + (4)R_3} \begin{bmatrix} 1 & 0 & 0 & | & 1 & 0 & -1 \\ 0 & 1 & 0 & | & 0 & 1 & 2 \\ 0 & 0 & 1 & | & 0 & 0 & \frac{1}{2} \end{bmatrix}$$

Thus the inverse of the given matrix is

$$\begin{bmatrix} 1 & 0 & -1 \\ 0 & 1 & 2 \\ 0 & 0 & \frac{1}{2} \end{bmatrix}.$$

2. The matrix form of this system of equations is $AX = B$, where A is the matrix whose inverse was found in Problem 1, and

$$B = \begin{bmatrix} 4 \\ 6 \\ 9 \end{bmatrix}.$$

Therefore, $X = A^{-1}B$, so that

$$\begin{bmatrix} x \\ y \\ z \end{bmatrix} = \begin{bmatrix} 1 & 0 & -1 \\ 0 & 1 & 2 \\ 0 & 0 & \frac{1}{2} \end{bmatrix} \begin{bmatrix} 4 \\ 6 \\ 9 \end{bmatrix} = \begin{bmatrix} -5 \\ 24 \\ \frac{9}{2} \end{bmatrix}.$$

So the solution of the system is $x = -5$, $y = 24$, $z = \frac{9}{2}$.

2.6 Input–Output Analysis

In recent years matrix arithmetic has played an ever-increasing role in economics, especially in that branch of economics called **input–output analysis**. Pioneered by the Harvard economist Vassily Leontieff, input–output analysis is used to analyze an economy in order to meet given consumption and export demands. As we shall see, such analysis leads to matrix calculations and in particular to inverses. Input–output analysis has been of such great significance that Leontieff was awarded the 1973 Nobel Prize in economics for his fundamental work in the subject.

Suppose that we divide an economy into a number of industries—transportation, agriculture, steel, and so on. Each industry produces a certain output using certain raw materials (or input). The input of each industry is made up in part by the outputs of other industries. For example, in order to produce food, agriculture uses as input the output of many industries, such as transportation (tractors and trucks) and oil (gasoline and fertilizers). This interdependence among the industries of the economy is summarized in a matrix—an **input–output matrix**. There is one column for each industry's input requirements. The entries in the column reflect the amount of input required from each of the industries. A typical input–output matrix looks like this:

Input requirements of:

Industry 1 Industry 2 Industry 3 ...

$$\text{From} \quad \begin{matrix} \text{Industry 1} \\ \text{Industry 2} \\ \text{Industry 3} \\ \vdots \end{matrix} \begin{bmatrix} \quad & \quad & \quad \\ \quad & \quad & \quad \\ \quad & \quad & \quad \end{bmatrix}.$$

It is most convenient to express the entries of this matrix in monetary terms. That is, each column gives the dollar values of the various inputs needed by an industry in order to produce $1 worth of output.

There are consumers (other than the industries themselves) who want to purchase some of the output of these industries. The quantity of goods that these consumers want (or demand) is called the **final demand** on the economy. The final demand can be represented by a column matrix, with one entry for each industry, indicating the amount of consumable output demanded from the industry:

$$\left[\text{final demand}\right] = \begin{bmatrix} \text{amount from industry 1} \\ \text{amount from industry 2} \\ \vdots \end{bmatrix}.$$

We shall consider the situation in which the final-demand matrix is given and it is necessary to determine how much output should be produced by each industry in order to provide the needed inputs of the various industries and also to satisfy the final demand. The proper level of output can be computed using matrix calculations, as illustrated in the next example.

EXAMPLE 1

Determining industrial production Suppose that an economy is composed of only three industries—coal, steel, and electricity. Each of these industries depends on the others for some of its raw materials. Suppose that to make $1 of coal, it takes no coal, but $.02 of steel and $.01 of electricity; to make $1 of steel, it takes $.15 of coal, $.03 of steel, and $.08 of electricity; and to make $1 of electricity, it takes $.43 of coal, $.20 of steel, and $.05 of electricity. How much should each industry produce to allow for consumption (not used for production) at these levels: $2 billion coal, $1 billion steel, $3 billion electricity?

Solution Put all the data indicating the interdependence of the industries in a matrix. In each industry's column, put the amount of input from each of the industries needed to produce $1 of output in that particular industry:

$$\begin{array}{cccc} & \text{Coal} & \text{Steel} & \text{Electricity} \\ \begin{matrix} \text{Coal} \\ \text{Steel} \\ \text{Electricity} \end{matrix} & \begin{bmatrix} 0 & .15 & .43 \\ .02 & .03 & .20 \\ .01 & .08 & .05 \end{bmatrix} & = A. \end{array}$$

This matrix is the input–output matrix corresponding to the economy. Let D denote the final-demand matrix. Then, letting the numbers in D stand for billions of dollars, we have

$$D = \begin{bmatrix} 2 \\ 1 \\ 3 \end{bmatrix}.$$

Suppose that the coal industry produces x billion dollars of output, the steel industry y billion dollars, and the electrical industry z billion dollars. Our problem is to determine the x, y, and z that yield the desired amounts left over from the production process. As an example, consider coal. The amount of coal that can be consumed or exported is just

$$x - \left[\text{amount of coal used in production}\right].$$

To determine the amount of coal used in production, refer to the input–output matrix. Production of x billion dollars of coal takes $0 \cdot x$ billion dollars of coal; production of y billion dollars of steel takes $.15y$ billion dollars of coal; and production of z billion dollars of electricity takes $.43z$ billion dollars of coal. Thus,

$$[\text{amount of coal used in production}] = 0 \cdot x + .15y + .43z.$$

This quantity should be recognized as the first entry of a matrix product. Namely, if we let

$$X = \begin{bmatrix} x \\ y \\ z \end{bmatrix},$$

then

$$\begin{bmatrix} \text{coal} \\ \text{steel} \\ \text{electricity} \end{bmatrix}_{\text{used in production}} = \begin{bmatrix} 0 & .15 & .43 \\ .02 & .03 & .20 \\ .01 & .08 & .05 \end{bmatrix} \begin{bmatrix} x \\ y \\ z \end{bmatrix} = AX.$$

The equations for the amounts of steel and electricity used in production are obtained in a manner similar to the equation for coal. But then the amount of each output available for purposes other than production is $X - AX$. That is, we have the matrix equation

$$X - AX = D.$$

To solve this equation for X, proceed as follows. Since $IX = X$, write the equation in the form

$$IX - AX = D$$

$$(I - A)X = D$$

$$X = (I - A)^{-1}D. \tag{1}$$

So, in other words, X may be found by multiplying D on the left by $(I - A)^{-1}$. Let us now do the arithmetic.

$$I - A = \begin{bmatrix} 1 & 0 & 0 \\ 0 & 1 & 0 \\ 0 & 0 & 1 \end{bmatrix} - \begin{bmatrix} 0 & .15 & .43 \\ .02 & .03 & .20 \\ .01 & .08 & .05 \end{bmatrix} = \begin{bmatrix} 1 & -.15 & -.43 \\ -.02 & .97 & -.20 \\ -.01 & -.08 & .95 \end{bmatrix}$$

Applying the Gauss–Jordan method, we find that

$$(I - A)^{-1} = \begin{bmatrix} 1.01 & .20 & .50 \\ .02 & 1.05 & .23 \\ .01 & .09 & 1.08 \end{bmatrix},$$

where all figures are carried to two decimal places (Exercise 9). Therefore,

$$X = (I - A)^{-1}D = \begin{bmatrix} 1.01 & .20 & .50 \\ .02 & 1.05 & .23 \\ .01 & .09 & 1.08 \end{bmatrix} \begin{bmatrix} 2 \\ 1 \\ 3 \end{bmatrix} = \begin{bmatrix} 3.72 \\ 1.78 \\ 3.35 \end{bmatrix}.$$

In other words, coal should produce $3.72 billion worth of output, steel $1.78 billion, and electricity $3.35 billion. This output will meet the required final demands from each industry.

Now Try Exercise 5

The preceding analysis is useful in studying not only entire economies but also segments of economies and even individual companies.

EXAMPLE 2

Determining production for a conglomerate A conglomerate has three divisions, which produce computers, semiconductors, and business forms. For each $1 of output, the computer division needs $.02 worth of computers, $.20 worth of semiconductors, and $.10 worth of business forms. For each $1 of output, the semiconductor division needs $.02 worth of computers, $.01 worth of semiconductors, and $.02 worth of business forms. For each $1 of output, the business forms division requires $.10 worth of computers and $.01 worth of business forms. The conglomerate estimates the sales demand to be $300,000,000 for the computer division, $100,000,000 for the semiconductor division, and $200,000,000 for the business forms division. At what level should each division produce in order to satisfy this demand?

Solution The conglomerate can be viewed as a miniature economy and its sales as the final demand. The input–output matrix for this "economy" is

$$
\begin{array}{c}
\\
\\
\text{Computers} \\
\text{Semiconductors} \\
\text{Business forms}
\end{array}
\begin{array}{ccc}
\text{Computers} & \text{Semiconductors} & \begin{array}{c}\text{Business} \\ \text{forms}\end{array} \\
\left[\begin{array}{ccc}
.02 & .02 & .10 \\
.20 & .01 & 0 \\
.10 & .02 & .01
\end{array}\right] = A.
\end{array}
$$

The final-demand matrix is

$$
D = \begin{bmatrix} 3 \\ 1 \\ 2 \end{bmatrix},
$$

where the demand is expressed in hundreds of millions of dollars. By equation (1) the matrix X, giving the desired levels of production for the various divisions, is given by

$$
X = (I - A)^{-1}D.
$$

But

$$
I - A = \begin{bmatrix}
.98 & -.02 & -.10 \\
-.20 & .99 & 0 \\
-.10 & -.02 & .99
\end{bmatrix},
$$

so that (Exercise 10)

$$
(I - A)^{-1} = \begin{bmatrix}
1.04 & .02 & .10 \\
.21 & 1.01 & .02 \\
.11 & .02 & 1.02
\end{bmatrix}
\quad \text{and} \quad
(I - A)^{-1}D = \begin{bmatrix} 3.34 \\ 1.68 \\ 2.39 \end{bmatrix}.
$$

Therefore,

$$
X = \begin{bmatrix} 3.34 \\ 1.68 \\ 2.39 \end{bmatrix}.
$$

That is, the computer division should produce $334,000,000, the semiconductor division $168,000,000, and the business forms division $239,000,000. ∎

Now Try Exercise 7

Input–output analysis is usually applied to the entire economy of a country having hundreds of industries. The resulting matrix equation $(I - A)X = D$ could be solved by the Gauss–Jordan elimination method. However, it is best to find the inverse of $I - A$ and solve for X as we have done in the examples of this section. Over a short period, D might change but A is unlikely to change. Therefore, the proper outputs to satisfy the new demand can easily be determined by using the already computed inverse of $I - A$.

The Closed Leontieff Model   The foregoing description of an economy is usually called the **open Leontieff model** since it views exports as an activity that takes place external to the economy. However, it is possible to consider exports as yet another industry in the economy. Instead of describing exports by a demand column D, we describe it by a column in the input–output matrix. That is, the export column describes how each dollar of exports is divided among the various industries. Since exports are now regarded as another industry, each of the original columns has an additional entry, namely the amount of output from the export industry (that is, imports) used to produce \$1 of goods (of the industry corresponding to the column). If A denotes the expanded input–output matrix and X the production matrix (as before), then AX is the matrix describing the total demand experienced by each of the industries. In order for the economy to function efficiently, the total amount demanded by the various industries should equal the amount produced. That is, the production matrix must satisfy the equation

$$AX = X.$$

By studying the solutions to this equation, it is possible to determine the equilibrium states of the economy—that is, the production matrices X for which the amounts produced exactly equal the amounts needed by the various industries. The model just described is called the **closed Leontieff model**.

We may expand the closed Leontieff model to include the effects of labor and monetary phenomena by considering labor and banking as yet further industries to be incorporated in the input–output matrix.

INCORPORATING TECHNOLOGY

GC   With a graphing calculator, the matrix $(I - A)^{-1}D$ can be calculated with a single press of the ENTER key. Figures 1 and 2 show the calculation for the matrices of Example 2.   ■

Figure 1

Figure 2

ES   To display the matrix $(I - A)^{-1}D$ on an Excel spreadsheet, select a column of n cells, type the formula **=MMULT(MINVERSE(I-A),D)** and press Ctrl+Shift+Enter. (Here D is an $n \times 1$ matrix, I is the $n \times n$ identity matrix, and A is an $n \times n$ square matrix.)

Practice Problems 2.6

1. Let

$$I = \begin{bmatrix} 1 & 0 & 0 \\ 0 & 1 & 0 \\ 0 & 0 & 1 \end{bmatrix}, \quad A = \begin{bmatrix} .1 & 0 & .1 \\ .2 & .1 & .1 \\ .1 & .2 & 0 \end{bmatrix},$$

$$X = \begin{bmatrix} x \\ y \\ z \end{bmatrix}, \quad D = \begin{bmatrix} 100 \\ 200 \\ 50 \end{bmatrix}.$$

Solve the matrix equation

$$(I - A)X = D.$$

2. Let I, A, and X be as in Problem 1, but let

$$D = \begin{bmatrix} 300 \\ 100 \\ 100 \end{bmatrix}.$$

Solve the matrix equation $(I - A)X = D$.

EXERCISES 2.6

Three-Sector Economy *In Exercises 1–4, suppose a simplified economy consisting of the three sectors Manufacturing, Energy, and Services has the input-output matrix*

$$\begin{array}{c} M \\ E \\ S \end{array} \begin{bmatrix} .3 & .1 & .2 \\ .2 & .25 & .15 \\ .1 & .2 & .15 \end{bmatrix}.$$

$$\begin{array}{ccc} M & E & S \end{array}$$

1. How many cents of energy are required to produce $1 worth of manufactured goods?

2. How many cents of energy are required to produce $1 worth of services?

3. Which sector of the economy requires the greatest amount of services in order to produce $1 worth of output?

4. What is the dollar amount of the energy costs needed to produce 10 million dollars worth of goods from each sector?

5. **Industrial Production** Suppose that in the economy of Example 1 the demand for electricity triples and the demand for coal doubles, whereas the demand for steel increases only by 50%. At what levels should the various industries produce in order to satisfy the new demand?

6. **Conglomerate** Suppose that the conglomerate of Example 2 is faced with an increase of 50% in demand for computers, a doubling in demand for semiconductors, and a decrease of 50% in demand for business forms. At what levels should the various divisions produce in order to satisfy the new demand?

7. **Conglomerate** Suppose that the conglomerate of Example 2 experiences a doubling in the demand for business forms. At what levels should the computer and semiconductor divisions produce?

8. **Multinational Corporation** A multinational corporation does business in the United States, Canada, and England. Its branches in one country purchase goods from the branches in other countries according to the matrix

		Branch in:	
	United States	Canada	England
Purchase from: United States	.02	0	.02
Canada	.01	.03	.01
England	.03	0	.01

where the entries in the matrix represent proportions of total sales by the respective branch. The external sales by each of the offices are $800,000,000 for the U.S. branch, $300,000,000 for the Canadian branch, and $1,400,000,000 for the English branch. At what level should each of the branches produce in order to satisfy the total demand?

9. Show that to two decimal places

$$\begin{bmatrix} 1 & -.15 & -.43 \\ -.02 & .97 & -.20 \\ -.01 & -.08 & .95 \end{bmatrix}^{-1} = \begin{bmatrix} 1.01 & .20 & .50 \\ .02 & 1.05 & .23 \\ .01 & .09 & 1.08 \end{bmatrix}.$$

10. Show that to two decimal places

$$\begin{bmatrix} .98 & -.02 & -.10 \\ -.20 & .99 & 0 \\ -.10 & -.02 & .99 \end{bmatrix}^{-1} = \begin{bmatrix} 1.04 & .02 & .10 \\ .21 & 1.01 & .02 \\ .11 & .02 & 1.02 \end{bmatrix}.$$

11. **Two-Sector Economy** A simplified economy consists of the two sectors Transportation and Energy. For each $1 worth of output, the transportation sector requires $.25 worth of input from the transportation sector and $.20 of input from the energy sector. For each $1 worth of output, the energy sector requires $.30 from the transportation sector and $.15 from the energy sector.

    (a) Give the input-output matrix A for this economy.

    (b) Determine the matrix $(I - A)^{-1}$. (Round entries to two decimal places.)

    (c) At what level of output should each sector produce to meet a demand for $5 billion worth of transportation and $3 billion worth of energy?

12. **Three-Sector Economy** An economy consists of the three sectors agriculture, energy, and manufacturing. For each $1 worth of output, the agriculture sector requires $.08 worth of input from the agriculture sector, $.10 worth of input from the energy sector, and $.20 worth of input from the manufacturing sector. For each $1 worth of output, the energy sector requires $.15 worth of input from the agriculture sector, $.14 worth of input from the energy sector, and $.10 worth of input from the manufacturing sector. For each $1 worth of output, the manufacturing sector requires $.25 worth of input from the agriculture sector, $.12 worth of input from the energy sector, and $.05 worth of input from the manufacturing sector.

(a) Give the input-output matrix A for this economy.

(b) Determine the matrix $(I - A)^{-1}$. (Round entries to two decimal places.)

(c) At what level of output should each sector produce to meet a demand for $4 billion worth of agriculture, $3 billion worth of energy, and $2 billion worth of manufacturing?

13. **Two-Product Corporation** A corporation has a plastics division and an industrial equipment division. For each $1 worth of output, the plastics division needs $.02 worth of plastics and $.10 worth of equipment. For each $1 worth of output, the industrial equipment division needs $.01 worth of plastics and $.05 worth of equipment. At what level should the divisions produce to meet a demand for $930,000 worth of plastics and $465,000 worth of industrial equipment?

14. **Two-Product Corporation** Rework Exercise 13 under the condition that the demand for plastics is $1,860,000 and the demand for industrial equipment is $2,790,000.

15. **Three-Sector Industry** An industrial system involves manufacturing, transportation, and agriculture. The interdependence of the three industries is given by the input-output matrix

$$
\begin{array}{ccc}
M & T & A \\
\end{array}
$$
$$
\begin{bmatrix}
.4 & .3 & .1 \\
.2 & .2 & .2 \\
.1 & .1 & .4
\end{bmatrix}
\begin{array}{c}
M \\
T \\
A
\end{array}
$$

At what levels must the industries produce to satisfy a demand for $100 million worth of manufactured goods,

$80 million of transportation, and $200 million worth of agricultural products?

16. **Localized Economy** A town has a merchant, a baker, and a farmer. To produce $1 worth of output, the merchant requires $.30 worth of baked goods and $.40 worth of the farmer's products. To produce $1 worth of output, the baker requires $.50 worth of the merchant's goods, $.10 worth of his own goods, and $.30 worth of the farmer's goods. To produce $1 worth of output, the farmer requires $.30 worth of the merchant's goods, $.20 worth of baked goods, and $.30 worth of his own products. How much should the merchant, baker, and farmer produce to meet a demand for $20,000 worth of output from the merchant, $15,000 worth of output from the baker, and $18,000 worth of output from the farmer?

17. The matrix $(I - A)^{-1}$ from Example 1 is given in Exercise 9. Show that if the final demand for coal is increased by one billion dollars, then the additional amounts (in billions of dollars) that must be produced by each of the three industries is given by the first column of $(I - A)^{-1}$.

$$
\text{Hint: } (I - A)^{-1} \begin{bmatrix} 3 \\ 1 \\ 3 \end{bmatrix} = (I - A)^{-1} \left(\begin{bmatrix} 2 \\ 1 \\ 3 \end{bmatrix} + \begin{bmatrix} 1 \\ 0 \\ 0 \end{bmatrix} \right).
$$

18. Refer to Exercise 17. Interpret the significance of the second and third columns of $(I - A)^{-1}$.

In the following exercises, use a graphing calculator or a spreadsheet to carry out the matrix operations.

In Exercises 19 and 20, use the input–output matrix A and the final-demand matrix D to find the production matrix X for the open Leontieff model. Round your answers to two decimal places.

19. $A = \begin{bmatrix} .1 & .2 & .4 \\ .05 & .3 & .25 \\ .15 & .1 & .2 \end{bmatrix}, D = \begin{bmatrix} 3 \\ 7 \\ 4 \end{bmatrix}.$

20. $A = \begin{bmatrix} .2 & .35 & .15 & .05 \\ .1 & .1 & .3 & .2 \\ .075 & .2 & .05 & .1 \\ .3 & .04 & .1 & .15 \end{bmatrix}, D = \begin{bmatrix} 5 \\ 2 \\ 1 \\ 7 \end{bmatrix}$

Solutions to Practice Problems 2.6

1. The equation $(I - A)X = D$ has the form $CX = D$, where C is the matrix $I - A$. From Section 2.4 we know that $X = C^{-1}D$. That is, $X = (I - A)^{-1}D$. Now

$$I - A = \begin{bmatrix} 1 & 0 & 0 \\ 0 & 1 & 0 \\ 0 & 0 & 1 \end{bmatrix} - \begin{bmatrix} .1 & 0 & .1 \\ .2 & .1 & .1 \\ .1 & .2 & 0 \end{bmatrix}$$

$$= \begin{bmatrix} .9 & 0 & -.1 \\ -.2 & .9 & -.1 \\ -.1 & -.2 & 1 \end{bmatrix}.$$

Using the Gauss–Jordan method to find the inverse of this matrix, we have (to two decimal places)

$$(I - A)^{-1} = \begin{bmatrix} 1.13 & .03 & .12 \\ .27 & 1.14 & .14 \\ .17 & .23 & 1.04 \end{bmatrix}.$$

Therefore, rounding to the nearest integer, we have

$$X = (I - A)^{-1}D = \begin{bmatrix} 1.13 & .03 & .12 \\ .27 & 1.14 & .14 \\ .17 & .23 & 1.04 \end{bmatrix} \begin{bmatrix} 100 \\ 200 \\ 50 \end{bmatrix}$$

$$= \begin{bmatrix} 125 \\ 262 \\ 115 \end{bmatrix}.$$

2. We have $X = (I - A)^{-1}D$, where $(I - A)^{-1}$ is as computed in Problem 1. So

$$X = (I - A)^{-1}D = \begin{bmatrix} 1.13 & .03 & .12 \\ .27 & 1.14 & .14 \\ .17 & .23 & 1.04 \end{bmatrix} \begin{bmatrix} 300 \\ 100 \\ 100 \end{bmatrix}$$

$$= \begin{bmatrix} 354 \\ 209 \\ 178 \end{bmatrix}.$$

CHAPTER SUMMARY

1. The three elementary row operations for a system of linear equations (or a matrix) are as follows:

   (a) Interchange any two equations (rows).

   (b) Multiply an equation (row) by a nonzero number.

   (c) Change an equation (row) by adding to it a multiple of another equation (row).

2. When an elementary row operation is applied to a system of linear equations the solutions remain the same. The Gauss–Jordan elimination method is a systematic process that applies a sequence of elementary row operations until the solutions can be easily obtained.

3. The process of pivoting on a specific element of a matrix is to apply a sequence of elementary row operations so that the specific element becomes 1 and the other elements in its column become 0. To apply the Gauss–Jordan elimination method, proceed from left to right and perform pivots on as many columns to the left of the vertical line as possible, with the specific elements for the pivots coming from different rows.

4. After a matrix corresponding to a system of linear equations has been completely reduced with the Gauss–Jordan elimination method, all the solutions to the system of linear equations can be obtained. If the matrix on the left of the vertical line is an identity matrix, then there is a unique solution. If one row of the matrix is of the form $0 \ \ 0 \ \ 0 \ \cdots \ 0 \mid a$, where a is a nonzero number, then there is no solution. Otherwise, there are infinitely many solutions. In this case, variables corresponding to columns that have not been pivoted can assume any values, and the values of the other variables can be expressed in terms of those variables.

5. A matrix of size $m \times n$ has m rows and n columns.

6. Matrices of the same size can be added (or subtracted) by adding (or subtracting) corresponding elements.

7. The product of an $m \times n$ matrix and an $n \times r$ matrix is the $m \times r$ matrix whose ijth element is obtained by multiplying the ith row of the first matrix by the jth column of the second matrix. (The product of each row and column is calculated as the sum of the products of successive entries.)

8. The inverse of a square matrix A is a square matrix A^{-1} with the property that $A^{-1}A = I$ and $AA^{-1} = I$, where I is an identity matrix.

9. A 2×2 matrix $\begin{bmatrix} a & b \\ c & d \end{bmatrix}$ has an inverse if $D = ad - bc \neq 0$. If so, the inverse matrix is

$$\begin{bmatrix} \dfrac{d}{D} & -\dfrac{b}{D} \\[2ex] -\dfrac{c}{D} & \dfrac{a}{D} \end{bmatrix}.$$

10. A system of linear equations can be written in the form $AX = B$, where A is a rectangular matrix of coefficients of the variables, X is a column of variables, and

B is a column matrix of the constants from the right side of the system. If the matrix A has an inverse, then the solution of the equation is given by $X = A^{-1}B$.

11. To calculate the inverse of a matrix by the Gauss–Jordan method, append an identity matrix to the right of the original matrix and perform pivots to reduce the original matrix to an identity matrix. The matrix on the right will then be the inverse of the original matrix. (If the original matrix cannot be reduced to an identity matrix, then the original matrix does not have an inverse.)

12. An input–output matrix has rows and columns labeled with the different industries in an economy. The ijth entry of the matrix gives the cost of the input from the industry in row i used in the production of $1 worth of the output of industry in column j.

13. If A is an input–output matrix and D is a demand matrix giving the dollar values of the outputs from the various industries to be supplied to outside customers, then the matrix $X = (I - A)^{-1}D$ gives the amounts that must be produced by the various industries in order to meet the demand.

REVIEW OF FUNDAMENTAL CONCEPTS

1. What is meant by a solution to a system of linear equations?

2. What is a matrix?

3. State the three elementary row operations on equations or matrices.

4. What does it mean for a system of equations or a matrix to be in diagonal form?

5. What is meant by pivoting a matrix about a nonzero entry?

6. State the Gauss–Jordan elimination method for transforming a system of linear equations into diagonal form.

7. What is a row matrix? Column matrix? Square matrix? Identity matrix, I_n?

8. What is meant by a_{ij}, the ijth entry of a matrix?

9. Define the sum and difference of two matrices.

10. Define the product of two matrices.

11. Define the inverse of a matrix, A^{-1}.

12. Give the formula for the inverse of a 2×2 matrix.

13. Explain how to use the inverse of a matrix to solve a system of linear equations.

14. Describe the steps of the Gauss–Jordan method for calculating the inverse of a matrix.

15. What is an input–output matrix and a final-demand matrix?

16. Explain how to solve an input–output analysis problem.

KEY FORMULAS

Inverse of $\begin{bmatrix} a & b \\ c & d \end{bmatrix}$ is $\begin{bmatrix} \dfrac{d}{D} & -\dfrac{b}{D} \\ -\dfrac{c}{D} & \dfrac{a}{D} \end{bmatrix}$, where $D = ad - bc \neq 0$.

Solution of $AX = B$, where A has an inverse is $X = A^{-1}B$.
If A is the input–output matrix for an economy and D is the demand matrix, then the proper production amounts for each sector are given by $X = (I - A)^{-1}D$.

SUPPLEMENTARY EXERCISES

In Exercises 1 and 2, pivot each matrix around the circled element.

1. $\begin{bmatrix} ③ & -6 & 1 \\ 2 & 4 & 6 \end{bmatrix}$

2. $\begin{bmatrix} -5 & -3 & 1 \\ 4 & ② & 0 \\ 0 & 6 & 7 \end{bmatrix}$

In Exercises 3–8, use the Gauss–Jordan elimination method to find all solutions of the systems of linear equations.

3. $\begin{cases} \frac{1}{2}x - y = -3 \\ 4x - 5y = -9 \end{cases}$

4. $\begin{cases} 3x + 9z = 42 \\ 2x + y + 6z = 30 \\ -x + 3y - 2z = -20 \end{cases}$

5. $\begin{cases} 3x - 6y + 6z = -5 \\ -2x + 3y - 5z = \frac{7}{3} \\ x + y + 10z = 3 \end{cases}$

6. $\begin{cases} 3x + 6y - 9z = 1 \\ 2x + 4y - 6z = 1 \\ 3x + 4y + 5z = 0 \end{cases}$

7. $\begin{cases} x + 2y - 5z + 3w = 16 \\ -5x - 7y + 13z - 9w = -50 \\ -x + y - 7z + 2w = 9 \\ 3x + 4y - 7z + 6w = 33 \end{cases}$

8. $\begin{cases} 5x - 10y = 5 \\ 3x - 8y = -3 \\ -3x + 7y = 0 \end{cases}$

In Exercises 9 and 10, perform the indicated matrix operations.

9. $\begin{bmatrix} 2 \\ -1 \\ 0 \end{bmatrix} + \begin{bmatrix} 3 \\ 4 \\ 7 \end{bmatrix}$ **10.** $\begin{bmatrix} 1 & 3 & -2 \\ 4 & 0 & -1 \end{bmatrix} \begin{bmatrix} 3 & 5 \\ 1 & 0 \\ 0 & -6 \end{bmatrix}$

11. Find the inverse of the appropriate matrix, and use it to solve the system of equations

$$\begin{cases} 3x + 2y = 0 \\ 5x + 4y = 2. \end{cases}$$

12. The matrices

$$\begin{bmatrix} 4 & -2 & 3 \\ 8 & -3 & 5 \\ 7 & -2 & 4 \end{bmatrix} \text{ and } \begin{bmatrix} -2 & 2 & -1 \\ 3 & -5 & 4 \\ 5 & -6 & 4 \end{bmatrix}$$

are inverses of each other. Use these matrices to solve the following systems of linear equations.

(a) $\begin{cases} -2x + 2y - z = 1 \\ 3x - 5y + 4z = 0 \\ 5x - 6y + 4z = 3 \end{cases}$

(b) $\begin{cases} 4x - 2y + 3z = 0 \\ 8x - 3y + 5z = -1 \\ 7x - 2y + 4z = 2 \end{cases}$

In Exercises 13 and 14, use the Gauss–Jordan method to calculate the inverses of the following matrices.

13. $\begin{bmatrix} 2 & 6 \\ 1 & 2 \end{bmatrix}$ **14.** $\begin{bmatrix} 1 & 1 & 1 \\ 3 & 4 & 3 \\ 1 & 1 & 2 \end{bmatrix}$

15. Crop Allocation Farmer Brown has 1000 acres of land on which he plans to grow corn, wheat, and soybeans. The cost of cultivating these crops is $206 per acre for corn, $85 per acre for wheat, and $97 per acre for soybeans. If Farmer Brown wishes to use all his available land and his entire budget of $151,500, and if he wishes to plant the same number of acres of corn as wheat and soybeans combined, how many acres of each crop can he grow?

16. Equipment Sales A company makes backyard playground equipment like swing sets, slides, and play sets. The cost (in dollars) to make a specific style of each piece is given in matrix C. The sales price (in dollars) for each piece is given in matrix S. Two stores sell these specific pieces and matrix A gives the quantities sold during one month.

$$C = \begin{bmatrix} 165 \\ 65 \\ 210 \end{bmatrix} \begin{matrix} \text{Swing set} \\ \text{Slide} \\ \text{Play set} \end{matrix}$$

$$S = \begin{bmatrix} 200 \\ 80 \\ 250 \end{bmatrix} \begin{matrix} \text{Swing set} \\ \text{Slide} \\ \text{Play set} \end{matrix}$$

	Swing set	Slide	Play set
$A = $	15	20	8
	10	17	12

Determine and interpret the following matrices.

(a) AC **(b)** AS **(c)** $S - C$ **(d)** $A(S - C)$

17. Investment Earnings Teresa and Patrick want to invest money in three different college savings plans. Matrix A contains the percentages (in decimal form) invested in bonds, stocks, and a conservative fixed income fund for each of the three different plans. Matrix B gives the total amount invested in each of the three savings plans and matrix C gives the rates of return (in decimal form) for one year and for five years.

	Bonds	Stocks	Fixed Income	
$A = $	.50	.43	.07	Plan 1
	.45	.26	.29	Plan 2
	.40	.40	.20	Plan 3

	Plan 1	Plan 2	Plan 3
$B = [$	5000	8000	10,000 $]$

	One Year	Five Year	
$C = $	.0032	.1119	Plan 1
	.0233	.0976	Plan 2
	.0320	.0467	Plan 3

Calculate and interpret the following

(a) BA **(b)** BC

(c) the row 1, column 2 entry of BA

(d) the row 1, column 1 entry of BC

18. Job Earnings Sara, Quinn, Tamia, and Zack are working at the pool this summer. One week they spend the following amounts of time at three different tasks.

	Concessions	Front Desk	Cleaning	
$A = $	11	7	12	Sara
	9	5	16	Quinn
	13	8	9	Tamia
	13	7	10	Zack

The hourly pay (in dollars) for the three different tasks is given by

$$B = \begin{bmatrix} 8 \\ 6 \\ 9 \end{bmatrix} \begin{matrix} \text{Concessions} \\ \text{Front Desk} \\ \text{Cleaning} \end{matrix}$$

(a) Calculate and interpret the matrix AB.

(b) Who earned the most that week? Who earned the least?

(c) If the hourly pay for concessions is changed to $9 and the hourly pay for cleaning is changed to $8, who earns the most that week?

(d) How many hours did Sara work that week?

19. **Fruit Baskets** The produce department at a grocery store makes fruit baskets of apples, bananas, and oranges. The cost for each apple is $.85, for each banana is $.20, and for each orange is $.76. Suppose each basket needs to have 18 pieces of fruit and costs $9 to make. How many apples, bananas, and oranges are in each basket if the number of bananas in each basket is the same as the number of apples and oranges together?

20. **Nuclear Disarmament** In an arms race between two superpowers, each nation takes stock of its own and its enemy's nuclear arsenal each year. Each nation has the policy of dismantling a certain percentage of its stockpile each year and adding that same percentage of its competitor's stockpile. Nation A dismantles 20% and nation B dismantles 10%. Suppose that the current stockpiles of nations A and B are 10,000 and 7000 weapons, respectively.

(a) What will the stockpiles be in each of the next two years?

(b) What were the stockpiles in each of the preceding two years?

(c) Show that the "missile gap" between the superpowers decreases by 30% each year under these policies. Show that the total number of weapons decreases each year if nation A begins with the most weapons, and the total number of weapons increases if nation B begins with the most weapons.

21. **Two-Sector Economy** The economy of a small country can be regarded as consisting of two industries, I and

II, whose input–output matrix is

$$A = \begin{bmatrix} .4 & .2 \\ .1 & .3 \end{bmatrix}.$$

How many units should be produced by each industry in order to meet a demand for 8 units from industry I and 12 units from industry II?

22. **Coins PE** Joe has $3.30 in his pocket made up of nickels, dimes, and quarters. There are 30 coins and there are five times as many dimes as quarters. How many quarters does Joe have?

(a) 4   (b) 5   (c) 6   (d) 7   (e) 8

Conceptual Exercises

23. Identify each statement as true or false.

(a) If a system of linear equations has two different solutions, it must have infinitely many solutions.

(b) If a system of linear equations has more equations than variables, it cannot have a unique solution.

(c) If a system of linear equations has more variables than equations, then it must have infinitely many solutions.

24. Make up a system of two linear equations that has infinitely many solutions. No solution.

25. If the product of two numbers is zero, then one of the numbers must be zero. If the two matrices A and B are such that AB is a matrix of all zeros, must A or B be a matrix of all zeros?

26. Suppose that we try to solve the matrix equation $AX = B$ by using matrix inversion but find that even though the matrix A is a square matrix, it has no inverse. What can be said about the outcome from solving the associated system of linear equations by the Gauss–Jordan elimination method?

27. Why should the numbers in a single column of an input–output matrix have a sum that is less than 1?

CHAPTER TEST

1. Solve the following system of linear equations by using the Gauss–Jordan elimination method.

$$\begin{cases} x + 2y + z = 5 \\ 2x - y + z = -5 \\ -3x + y - 2z = 8 \end{cases}$$

2. Each of the following is the final matrix of a Gauss–Jordan elimination process. Give the solutions to the corresponding systems of linear equations.

(a) $\begin{bmatrix} 1 & 0 & 0 & | & 4 \\ 0 & 1 & 0 & | & -3 \\ 0 & 0 & 1 & | & 6 \end{bmatrix}$ (b) $\begin{bmatrix} 1 & 0 & 0 & | & 2 \\ 0 & 1 & 0 & | & 3 \\ 0 & 0 & 1 & | & 5 \end{bmatrix}$

(c) $\begin{bmatrix} 1 & 0 & 0 & | & 1 \\ 0 & 1 & 0 & | & -3 \\ 0 & 0 & 1 & | & 4 \\ 0 & 0 & 0 & | & 2 \end{bmatrix}$ (d) $\begin{bmatrix} 1 & 0 & -1 & | & 2 \\ 0 & 1 & 2 & | & 2 \end{bmatrix}$

(e) $\begin{bmatrix} 1 & 2 & 0 & | & 0 \\ 0 & 0 & 1 & | & 0 \\ 0 & 0 & 0 & | & 0 \end{bmatrix}$

3. The following is the general solution to a system of linear equations. Find a *specific* solution.

$$\begin{cases} w = \text{any value} \\ z = \text{any value} \\ y = 2x + w - z \\ x = w + z \end{cases}$$

4. Find three solutions to the system

$$\begin{cases} x + y - 2z = 15 \\ \phantom{x + {}} y + 4z = 6. \end{cases}$$

5. Let matrices A, B, and C be defined as shown. Calculate the following matrices whenever they are defined: $A + B$, $A + C$, AB, AC, BC.

$$A = \begin{bmatrix} 2 & 1 & 0 \\ 3 & 2 & 1 \end{bmatrix} \quad B = \begin{bmatrix} -1 & 1 \\ 0 & 1 \\ 1 & -1 \end{bmatrix} \quad C = \begin{bmatrix} 0 & 1 & 2 \\ -1 & 1 & 1 \end{bmatrix}$$

6. **Resource Allocation** Making a large decorative plate for retail sale takes $\frac{1}{2}$ hour molding time, 3 hours oven time, and 4 hours painting time. Vases require 1 hour molding time, 2.5 hours oven time, and 3 hours painting time. Bowls require 1 hour molding time, 2 hours oven time, and 2 hours painting time. We intend to produce x plates, y vases, and z bowls.

(a) Write three equations expressing molding time (m), oven time (v), and painting time (p) needed in terms of x, y, and z.

(b) Write the system as a matrix equation.

(c) Determine the number of hours each of molding time, oven time, and painting time to produce 100 plates, 300 vases, and 200 bowls.

7. Find A^{-1} if it exists, where

$$A = \begin{bmatrix} 1 & 2 & 1 \\ 0 & 1 & 1 \\ 1 & -1 & 0 \end{bmatrix}.$$

8. **College Tuition** The freshman class at State University has 1500 students. Out-of-state students pay $10,000 tuition, while in-state students are charged $4500 for tuition. The school collected $12,800,000 in tuition. How many students are in-state?

9. **Three-Sector Economy** In an economic system, each of three industries depends on the others for raw materials. To make $1 of processed wood requires 30¢ wood, 20¢ steel, and 10¢ coal. To make $1 of steel requires no wood, 30¢ steel, and 20¢ coal. To make $1 of coal requires 10¢ wood, 20¢ steel, and 5¢ coal. To allow for $1 consumption in wood, $4 consumption in steel, and $2 consumption in coal, what levels of production for wood, steel, and coal are required?

CHAPTER 2 | PROJECT

Population Dynamics

In 1991 the U.S. Fish and Wildlife Service proposed logging restrictions on nearly 12 million acres of Pacific Northwest forest to help save the endangered northern spotted owl. This decision caused considerable controversy between the logging industry and environmentalists.

Mathematical ecologists created a mathematical model to analyze the population dynamics of the spotted owl.[1] They divided the female owl population into three categories— juvenile (up to one year old), subadult (1 to 2 years old), and adult (over 2 years old). Suppose that in a certain region there are currently 2950 female spotted owls made up of 650 juveniles, 200 subadults, and 2100 adults. The ecologists used matrices to project the changes in the population from year to year. The original numbers can be displayed in the column matrix

$$X_0 = \begin{bmatrix} 650 \\ 200 \\ 2100 \end{bmatrix}_0 .$$

The populations after one year are given by the column matrix

$$X_1 = \begin{bmatrix} 693 \\ 117 \\ 2116 \end{bmatrix}_1 .$$

The subscript 1 tells us that the matrix gives the population after one year. The column matrices for subsequent years will have subscripts 2, 3, 4, etc.

1. How many subadult females are there after one year?

2. Did the total population of females increase or decrease during the year?

Let A denote the matrix

$$\begin{bmatrix} 0 & 0 & .33 \\ .18 & 0 & 0 \\ 0 & .71 & .94 \end{bmatrix} .$$

According to the mathematical model, subsequent population distributions are generated by multiplication on the left by A. That is,

$$A \cdot X_0 = X_1, \quad A \cdot X_1 = X_2, \quad A \cdot X_2 = X_3, \ldots .$$

If the population distribution at any time is given by $\begin{bmatrix} j \\ s \\ a \end{bmatrix}$, then the distribution one year later is $A \cdot \begin{bmatrix} j \\ s \\ a \end{bmatrix}$.

3. Fill in the blanks in the following statements.
   (a) Each year _____ juvenile females are born for each 100 adult females.
   (b) Each year _____% of the juvenile females survive to become subadults.
   (c) Each year _____% of the subadults survive to become adults and _____% of the adults survive.

---

[1]Lamberson, R. H., R. McKelvey, B. R. Noon, and C. Voss, "A Dynamic Analysis of Northern Spotted Owl Viability in a Fragmented Forest Landscape," *Conservation Biology*, Vol. 6, No. 4, December 1992; 505–512.

4. Calculate the column matrices X_2, X_3, X_4, and X_5. (*Note*: With a graphing calculator you can specify matrix **[A]** to be the 3×3 matrix A and specify **[B]** to be the initial 3×1 population matrix X_0. Display **[B]** in the home screen and then enter the command **[A]*Ans**. Each press of the ENTER key will generate the next population distribution matrix. *Tip*: Prior to generating the matrices invoke the MODE list and set Float to 0 so that all numbers in the population matrices will be rounded to whole numbers.)

5. Refer to item 4. Is the total female population increasing, decreasing, or neither during the first five years?

6. Explain why calculating **[A]$^\wedge$50*[B]** gives the column matrix for the population distribution after 50 years.

7. Find the projected population matrix after 50 years; after 100 years; after 150 years. Based on this mathematical model, what do you conclude about the prospects for the northern spotted owl?

In this model, the main impediment to the survival of the owl is the number .18 in the second row of matrix A. This number is low for two reasons. The first year of life is precarious for most animals living in the wild. In addition, juvenile owls must eventually leave the nest and establish their own territory. If much of the forest near their original home has been cleared, then they are vulnerable to predators while searching for a new home.

8. Suppose that due to better forest management, the number .18 can be increased to .26. Find the total female population for the first five years under this new assumption. Repeat item 7 and determine if extinction will be avoided under the new assumption.

LINEAR PROGRAMMING, A GEOMETRIC APPROACH

Linear programming is a method for solving problems in which a linear function (representing cost, profit, distance, weight, or the like) is to be maximized or minimized. Such problems are called **optimization problems**. As we shall see, these problems, when translated into mathematical language, involve systems of linear inequalities, systems of linear equations, and eventually (in Chapter 4) matrices.

3.1 A Linear Programming Problem

Let us begin with a detailed discussion of a typical problem that can be solved by linear programming.

Furniture Manufacturing Problem   A furniture manufacturer makes two types of furniture—chairs and sofas. For simplicity, divide the production process into three distinct operations—carpentry, finishing, and upholstery. The amount of labor required for each operation varies. Manufacture of a chair requires 6 hours of carpentry, 1 hour of finishing, and 2 hours of upholstery. Manufacture of a sofa requires 3 hours of carpentry, 1 hour of finishing, and 6 hours of upholstery. Due to limited availability of skilled labor as well as of tools and equipment, the factory has available each day 96 labor-hours for carpentry, 18 labor-hours for finishing,

117

and 72 labor-hours for upholstery. The profit per chair is $80 and the profit per sofa $70. How many chairs and how many sofas should be produced each day to maximize the profit?

It is often helpful to tabulate data given in verbal problems. Our first step, then, is to construct a chart.

	Chair	Sofa	Available time
Carpentry	6 hours	3 hours	96 labor-hours
Finishing	1 hour	1 hour	18 labor-hours
Upholstery	2 hours	6 hours	72 labor-hours
Profit	$80	$70	

The next step is to translate the problem into mathematical language. As you know, this is done by identifying what is unknown and denoting the unknown quantities by letters. Since the problem asks for the optimal number of chairs and sofas to be produced each day, there are two unknowns—the number of chairs produced each day and the number of sofas produced each day. Let x denote the number of chairs and y the number of sofas.

To achieve a large profit, one need only manufacture a large number of chairs and sofas. But due to restricted availability of tools and labor, the factory cannot manufacture an unlimited quantity of furniture. Let us translate the restrictions into mathematical language. Each of the first three rows of the chart gives one restriction. The first row says that the amount of carpentry required is 6 hours for each chair and 3 hours for each sofa. Also, there are available only 96 labor-hours of carpentry per day. We can compute the total number of labor-hours of carpentry required per day to produce x chairs and y sofas as follows:

$[\text{number of labor-hours per day of carpentry}]$

$$= (\text{number of hours carpentry per chair}) \cdot (\text{number of chairs per day})$$

$$+ (\text{number of hours carpentry per sofa}) \cdot (\text{number of sofas per day})$$

$$= 6 \cdot x + 3 \cdot y.$$

The requirement that at most 96 labor-hours of carpentry be used per day means that x and y must satisfy the inequality

$$6x + 3y \leq 96. \tag{1}$$

The second row of the chart gives a restriction imposed by finishing. Since 1 hour of finishing is required for each chair and sofa, and since at most 18 labor-hours of finishing are available per day, the same reasoning as used to derive inequality (1) yields

$$x + y \leq 18. \tag{2}$$

Similarly, the third row of the chart gives the restriction due to upholstery:

$$2x + 6y \leq 72. \tag{3}$$

Further restrictions are given by the fact that the numbers of chairs and sofas must be nonnegative:

$$x \geq 0, \qquad y \geq 0. \tag{4}$$

Now that we have written down the restrictions constraining x and y, let us express the profit (which is to be maximized) in terms of x and y. The profit comes from two sources—chairs and sofas. Therefore,

$$\begin{aligned}
[\text{profit}] &= [\text{profit from chairs}] + [\text{profit from sofas}] \\
&= [\text{profit per chair}] \cdot [\text{number of chairs}] \\
&\quad + [\text{profit per sofa}] \cdot [\text{number of sofas}] \\
&= 80x + 70y.
\end{aligned} \tag{5}$$

Since the objective of the problem is to optimize profit, the expression $80x + 70y$ is called the **objective function**. Combining (1) to (5), we arrive at the following:

Furniture Manufacturing Problem—Mathematical Formulation Find numbers x and y for which the objective function $80x + 70y$ is as large as possible, and for which all the following inequalities hold simultaneously:

$$\begin{cases}
6x + 3y \le 96 \\
x + y \le 18 \\
2x + 6y \le 72 \\
x \ge 0, \quad y \ge 0
\end{cases} \tag{6}$$

We may describe this mathematical problem in the following general way. We are required to maximize an expression in a certain number of variables, where the variables are subject to restrictions in the form of one or more inequalities. Problems of this sort are called *mathematical programming problems*. Actually, general mathematical programming problems can be quite involved, and their solutions may require very sophisticated mathematical ideas. However, this is not the case with the furniture manufacturing problem. What makes it a rather simple mathematical programming problem is that both the expression to be maximized and the inequalities are linear. For this reason the furniture manufacturing problem is called a **linear programming problem**. The theory of linear programming is a fairly recent advance in mathematics. It was developed over the last 70 years to deal with the increasingly more complicated problems of our technological society. The 1975 Nobel Prize in economics was awarded to Kantorovich and Koopmans for their pioneering work in the field of linear programming.

We will solve the furniture manufacturing problem in Section 3.2, where we develop a general technique for handling similar linear programming problems. At this point it is worthwhile to attempt to gain some insights into the problem and possible methods for attacking it.

It seems clear that a factory will operate most efficiently when its labor is fully utilized. Let us therefore take the operations one at a time and determine the conditions on x and y that fully utilize the three kinds of labor. The restriction on carpentry asserts that

$$6x + 3y \le 96.$$

If x and y were chosen so that $6x + 3y$ is actually *less* than 96, we would leave the carpenters idle some of the time, a waste of labor. Thus it would seem reasonable to choose x and y to satisfy

$$6x + 3y = 96.$$

Similarly, to utilize all the finishers' time, x and y must satisfy

$$x + y = 18,$$

and to utilize all the upholsterers' time, we must have

$$2x + 6y = 72.$$

Thus, if no labor is to be wasted, then x and y must satisfy the system of equations

$$\begin{cases} 6x + 3y = 96 \\ x + y = 18 \\ 2x + 6y = 72 \end{cases} \tag{7}$$

Let us now graph the three equations of (7), which represent the conditions for full utilization of all forms of labor. (See the following chart and Fig. 1.)

Equation	Standard form	x-Intercept	y-Intercept
$6x + 3y = 96$	$y = -2x + 32$	$(16, 0)$	$(0, 32)$
$x + y = 18$	$y = -x + 18$	$(18, 0)$	$(0, 18)$
$2x + 6y = 72$	$y = -\frac{1}{3}x + 12$	$(36, 0)$	$(0, 12)$

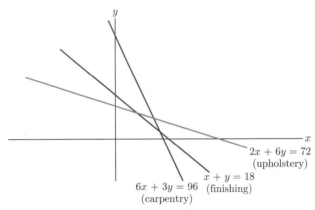

$2x + 6y = 72$
(upholstery)

$x + y = 18$

$6x + 3y = 96$ (finishing)
(carpentry)

Figure 1

What does Fig. 1 say about the furniture manufacturing problem? Each particular pair of numbers (x, y) is called a **production schedule**. Each of the lines in Fig. 1 gives the production schedules that fully utilize one of the types of labor. Notice that the three lines do not have a common intersection point. This means that there is *no* production schedule that *simultaneously* makes full use of all three types of labor. In any production schedule at least some of the labor-hours must be wasted. This is not a solution to the furniture manufacturing problem, but it is a valuable insight. It says that in the inequalities of (6) not all of the corresponding equations can hold. This suggests that we take a closer look at the system of inequalities.

The standard forms of the inequalities (6) are

$$\begin{cases} y \leq -2x + 32 \\ y \leq -x + 18 \\ y \leq -\frac{1}{3}x + 12 \\ x \geq 0, \quad y \geq 0 \end{cases}$$

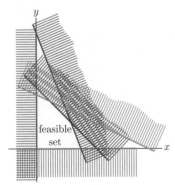

feasible set

Figure 2

By using the techniques of Section 1.2, we arrive at a feasible set for the preceding system of inequalities, as shown in Fig. 2.

The feasible set for the furniture manufacturing problem is a bounded, five-sided region. The points on and inside the boundary of this feasible set give the production schedules that satisfy all the restrictions. In Section 3.2 we show how to pick out a particular point of the feasible set that corresponds to a maximum profit.

Practice Problems 3.1

1. Determine whether the following points are in the feasible set of the furniture manufacturing problem:
   (a) $(10, 9)$;   **(b)** $(14, 4)$.

2. A physical fitness enthusiast decides to devote her exercise time to a combination of jogging and cycling. She wants to earn aerobic points (a measure of the benefit of the exercise to strengthening the heart and lungs) and also to achieve relaxation and enjoyment. She jogs at 6 miles per hour and cycles at 18 miles per hour. An hour of jogging earns 12 aerobic points, and an hour of cycling earns 9 aerobic points. Each week she would like to earn at least 36 aerobic points, cover at least 54 miles, and cycle at least as much as she jogs.

(a) Fill in the following chart.

(b) Let x be the number of hours of jogging and y the number of hours of cycling each week. Referring to the chart, give the inequalities that x and y must satisfy due to miles covered and aerobic points.

(c) Give the inequalities that x and y must satisfy due to her preference for cycling and also due to the fact that x and y cannot be negative.

(d) Express the time required as a linear function of x and y.

(e) Graph the feasible set for the system of linear inequalities.

	One hour of jogging	One hour of cycling	Requirement
Miles covered			
Aerobic points			
Time required			

EXERCISES 3.1

In Exercises 1–4, determine whether the given point is in the feasible set of the furniture manufacturing problem. (The inequalities are as follows.)

$$\begin{cases} 6x + 3y \le 96; & 2x + 6y \le 72 \\ x + y \le 18; & x \ge 0, \ y \ge 0 \end{cases}$$

1. $(8, 7)$ 2. $(14, 3)$ 3. $(9, 10)$ 4. $(16, 0)$

5. **Shipping** A truck traveling from New York to Baltimore is to be loaded with two types of cargo. Each crate of cargo A is 4 cubic feet in volume, weighs 100 pounds, and earns $13 for the driver. Each crate of cargo B is 3 cubic feet in volume, weighs 200 pounds, and earns $9 for the driver. The truck can carry no more than 300 cubic feet of crates and no more than 10,000 pounds. Also, the number of crates of cargo B must be less than or equal to twice the number of crates of cargo A.

   (a) Fill in the following chart.

	A	B	Truck capacity
Volume			
Weight			
Earnings			

   (b) Let x be the number of crates of cargo A and y the number of crates of cargo B. Referring to the chart, give the two inequalities that x and y must satisfy because of the truck's capacity for volume and weight.

   (c) Give the inequalities that x and y must satisfy because of the last sentence of the problem and also because x and y cannot be negative.

   (d) Express the earnings from carrying x crates of cargo A and y crates of cargo B.

   (e) Graph the feasible set for the shipping problem.

6. **Mining** A coal company owns mines in two different locations. Each day mine 1 produces 4 tons of anthracite (hard coal), 4 tons of ordinary coal, and 7 tons of bituminous (soft) coal. Each day mine 2 produces 10 tons of anthracite, 5 tons of ordinary coal, and 5 tons of bituminous coal. It costs the company $150 per day to operate mine 1 and $200 per day to operate mine 2. An order is received for 80 tons of anthracite, 60 tons of ordinary coal, and 75 tons of bituminous coal.

   (a) Fill in the following chart.

	Mine 1	Mine 2	Ordered
Anthracite			
Ordinary			
Bituminous			
Daily cost			

(b) Let x be the number of days mine 1 should be operated and y the number of days mine 2 should be operated. Refer to the chart and give three inequalities that x and y must satisfy to fill the order.

(c) Give other requirements that x and y must satisfy.

(d) Find the cost of operating mine 1 for x days and mine 2 for y days.

(e) Graph the feasible set for the mining problem.

7. Exam Strategy A student is taking an exam consisting of 10 essay questions and 50 short-answer questions. He has 90 minutes to take the exam and knows he cannot possibly answer every question. The essay questions are worth 20 points each and the short-answer questions are worth 5 points each. An essay question takes 10 minutes to answer and a short-answer question takes 2 minutes. The student must do at least 3 essay questions and at least 10 short-answer questions.

(a) Fill in the following chart.

	Essay questions	Short-answer questions	Available
Time to answer			
Quantity Required			
Worth			

(b) Let x be the number of essay questions to be answered and y the number of short-answer questions to be answered. Refer to the chart and give the inequality that x and y must satisfy due to the amount of time available.

(c) Give the inequalities that x and y must satisfy because of the numbers of each type of question and also because of the minimum number of each type of question that must be answered.

(d) Give an expression for the score obtained from answering x essay questions and y short-answer questions.

(e) Graph the feasible set for the exam strategy problem.

8. Political Campaign—Resource Allocation A local politician has budgeted at most $80,000 for her media campaign. She plans to distribute these funds between TV ads and radio ads. Each 1-minute TV ad is expected to be seen by 20,000 viewers, and each 1-minute radio ad is expected to be heard by 4000 listeners. Each minute of TV time costs $8000 and each minute of radio time costs $2000. She has been advised to use at most 90% of her media campaign budget on television ads.

(a) Fill in the following chart. (*Note:* Fill in only the first entry of the last column.)

	One-minute TV ads	One-minute radio ads	Money available
Cost			
Audience reached			

(b) Let x be the number of minutes of TV ads and let y be the number of minutes of radio ads. Refer to the chart and give an inequality that x and y must satisfy due to the amount of money available.

(c) Give the inequality that x must satisfy due to the limitation on the amount of money to be spent on TV ads. Also, give the inequalities that x and y must satisfy because x and y cannot be negative.

(d) Give an expression for the audience reached by x minutes of TV ads and y minutes of radio ads.

(e) Graph the feasible set for the political campaign problem.

9. Nutrition—Dairy Cows A dairy farmer concludes that his small herd of cows will need at least 4550 pounds of protein in their winter feed, at least 26,880 pounds of total digestible nutrients (TDN), and at least 43,200 international units (IUs) of vitamin A. Each pound of alfalfa hay provides .13 pound of protein, .48 pound of TDN, and 2.16 IUs of vitamin A. Each pound of ground ears of corn supplies .065 pound of protein, .96 pound of TDN, and no vitamin A. Alfalfa hay costs $1 per 100-pound sack. Ground ears of corn costs $1.60 per 100-pound sack.

(a) Fill in the following chart.

	Alfalfa	Corn	Requirements
Protein			
TDN			
Vitamin A			
Cost/lb			

(b) Let x be the number of pounds of alfalfa hay and y be the number of pounds of ground ears of corn to be bought. Give the inequalities that x and y must satisfy.

(c) Graph the feasible set for the system of linear inequalities.

(d) Express the cost of buying x pounds of alfalfa hay and y pounds of ground ears of corn.

10. Manufacturing—Resource Allocation A clothing manufacturer makes denim and hooded fleece jackets. Each denim jacket requires 2 labor-hours for cutting the pieces, 2 labor-hours for sewing, and 1 labor-hour for finishing. Each hooded fleece jacket requires 1 labor-hour for cutting, 4 labor-hours for sewing, and 1 labor-hour for finishing. There are 42 labor-hours for cutting,

90 labor-hours for sewing, and 27 labor-hours for finishing available each day. The profit is $9 per denim jacket and $5 per hooded fleece jacket.

(a) Fill in the following chart.

	Denim	Hooded fleece	Available hours
Cutting			
Sewing			
Finishing			
Profit			

(b) Let x be the number of denim jackets made each day. Let y be the number of hooded fleece jackets made each day. Refer to the chart and give three inequalities that x and y must satisfy due to the available labor-hours.

(c) Give other requirements that x and y must satisfy.

(d) Find the profit in making x denim jackets and y hooded fleece jackets.

(e) Graph the feasible set for the clothing problem.

Solutions to Practice Problems 3.1

1. A point is in the feasible set of a system of inequalities if it satisfies every inequality. Either the original form or the standard form of the inequalities may be used. The original forms of the inequalities of the furniture manufacturing problem are

$$\begin{cases} 6x + 3y \le 96 \\ x + y \le 18 \\ 2x + 6y \le 72 \\ x \ge 0, \quad y \ge 0 \end{cases}$$

(a) $(10, 9)$
$$\begin{cases} 6(10) + 3(9) \le 96 \\ 10 + 9 \le 18 \\ 2(10) + 6(9) \le 72 \\ 10 \ge 0, \quad 9 \ge 0; \end{cases} \quad \begin{cases} 87 \le 96 \\ 19 \le 18 \\ 74 \le 72 \\ 10 \ge 0, \quad 9 \ge 0 \end{cases} \quad \begin{array}{l} \text{true} \\ \text{false} \\ \text{false} \\ \text{true} \end{array}$$

(b) $(14, 4)$
$$\begin{cases} 6(14) + 3(4) \le 96 \\ 14 + 4 \le 18 \\ 2(14) + 6(4) \le 72 \\ 14 \ge 0, \quad 4 \ge 0; \end{cases} \quad \begin{cases} 96 \le 96 \\ 18 \le 18 \\ 52 \le 72 \\ 14 \ge 0, \quad 4 \ge 0 \end{cases} \quad \begin{array}{l} \text{true} \\ \text{true} \\ \text{true} \\ \text{true} \end{array}$$

Therefore, $(14, 4)$ is in the feasible set and $(10, 9)$ is not.

2. (a)

	One hour of jogging	One hour of cycling	Requirement
Miles covered	6	18	54
Aerobic points	12	9	36
Time required	1	1	

(b) Miles covered: $6x + 18y \ge 54$
Aerobic points: $12x + 9y \ge 36$

(c) $y \ge x, x \ge 0$. It is not necessary to list $y \ge 0$ since this is automatically assured if the other two inequalities hold.

(d) $x + y$. (An objective of the exercise program might be to minimize $x + y$.)

(e)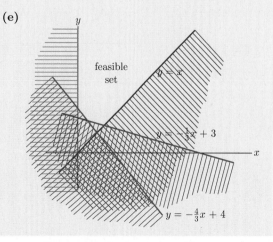

3.2 Linear Programming I

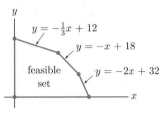

Figure 1

We have shown that the feasible set for the furniture manufacturing problem—that is, the set of points corresponding to production schedules satisfying all five restriction inequalities—consists of the points in the interior and on the boundary of the five-sided region drawn in Fig. 1. For reference, we have labeled each line segment with the equation of the line to which it belongs. The line segments intersect in five points, each of which is a corner of the feasible set. Such a corner is called a **vertex**. Somehow, we must pick out of the feasible set an **optimal point**—that is, a point corresponding to a production schedule that yields a maximum profit. To assist us in this task, we have the following result[1]:

Fundamental Theorem of Linear Programming   The maximum (or minimum) value of the objective function is achieved at one of the vertices of the feasible set.

This result does not completely solve the furniture manufacturing problem for us, but it comes close. It tells us that an optimal production schedule (a, b) corresponds to one of the five points labeled A–E in Fig. 2. So to complete the solution of the furniture manufacturing problem, it suffices to find the coordinates of the five points, evaluate the profit at each, and then choose the point corresponding to the maximum profit.

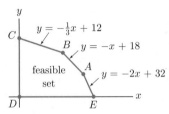

Figure 2

Solution of the Furniture Manufacturing Problem   Let us begin by determining the coordinates of the points A–E in Fig. 2. Remembering that the x-axis has the equation $y = 0$ and the y-axis the equation $x = 0$, we see from Fig. 2 that the coordinates of A–E can be found as intersections of the following lines:

$$A : \begin{cases} y = -x + 18 \\ y = -2x + 32 \end{cases}$$

$$B : \begin{cases} y = -x + 18 \\ y = -\frac{1}{3}x + 12 \end{cases}$$

$$C : \begin{cases} y = -\frac{1}{3}x + 12 \\ x = 0 \end{cases}$$

$$D : \begin{cases} y = 0 \\ x = 0 \end{cases}$$

$$E : \begin{cases} y = 0 \\ y = -2x + 32 \end{cases}$$

The point D is clearly $(0, 0)$, and C is clearly the point $(0, 12)$. We obtain A from

$-x + 18 = -2x + 32$	Equate two equations of lines through A.
$x + 18 = 32$	Add $2x$ to both sides.
$x = 14$	Subtract 18 from both sides.
$y = -x + 18 = -(14) + 18 = 4$	Substitute 14 for x in first equation.

---

[1]For a verification, see Section 3.3.

Hence $A = (14, 4)$. Similarly, we obtain B from

$$-x + 18 = -\tfrac{1}{3}x + 12 \qquad \text{Equate two equations of lines through } B.$$
$$-\tfrac{2}{3}x + 18 = 12 \qquad \text{Add } \tfrac{1}{3}x \text{ to both sides.}$$
$$-\tfrac{2}{3}x = -6 \qquad \text{Subtract 18 from both sides.}$$
$$x = (-\tfrac{3}{2})(-6) = 9 \qquad \text{Multiply both sides by } -\tfrac{3}{2}.$$
$$y = -x + 18 = -(9) + 18 = 9 \qquad \text{Substitute 9 for } x \text{ in first equation.}$$

so $B = (9, 9)$. Finally, E is obtained from

$$0 = -2x + 32 \quad \text{Equate two equations of lines through } E.$$
$$2x = 32 \quad \text{Add } 2x \text{ to both sides.}$$
$$x = 16 \quad \text{Divide both sides by 2.}$$
$$y = 0 \quad y = 0 \text{ is a given equation.}$$

and thus $E = (16, 0)$. We have displayed the vertices in Fig. 3 and listed them in Table 1. In the second column we have evaluated the profit, which is given by $80x + 70y$, at each of the vertices. Note that the largest profit occurs at the vertex $(14, 4)$, so the solution of the linear programming problem is $x = 14$, $y = 4$. In other words, the factory should produce 14 chairs and 4 sofas each day in order to achieve maximum profit, and the maximum profit is \$1400 per day.

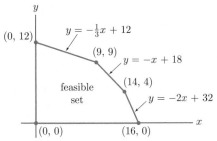

TABLE 1	
Vertex	**Profit $= 80x + 70y$**
$(14, 4)$	$80(14) + 70(4) = 1400$
$(9, 9)$	$80(9) + 70(9) = 1350$
$(0, 12)$	$80(0) + 70(12) = 840$
$(0, 0)$	$80(0) + 70(0) = 0$
$(16, 0)$	$80(16) + 70(0) = 1280$

Figure 3

The furniture manufacturing problem is one particular example of a linear programming problem. Generally, such problems involve finding the values of x and y that maximize (or minimize) a particular linear expression in x and y (the objective function) and where x and y are chosen so as to satisfy one or more restrictions in the form of linear inequalities. On the basis of our experience with the furniture manufacturing problem, we can summarize the steps to be followed in approaching *any* linear programming problem.

Step 1 Translate the problem into mathematical language.

    A. Organize the data.

    B. Identify the unknown quantities and define corresponding variables.

    C. Translate the restrictions into linear inequalities.

    D. Form the objective function.

Step 2   Graph the feasible set.

   A. Put the inequalities in standard form.

   B. Graph the straight line corresponding to each inequality.

   C. Determine the side of the line belonging to the graph of each inequality. Cross out the other side. The remaining region is the feasible set.

Step 3   Determine the vertices of the feasible set.

Step 4   Evaluate the objective function at each vertex. Determine the optimal point.

Linear programming can be applied to many problems. The Army Corps of Engineers has used linear programming to plan the location of a series of dams so as to maximize the resulting hydroelectric power production. The restrictions were to provide adequate flood control and irrigation. Public transit companies have used linear programming to plan routes and schedule buses in order to maximize services. The restrictions in this case arose from the limitations on labor, equipment, and funding. The petroleum industry uses linear programming in the refining and blending of gasoline. Profit is maximized subject to restrictions on availability of raw materials, refining capacity, and product specifications. Some large advertising firms have used linear programming in media selection. The problem consists of determining how much to spend in each medium in order to maximize the number of consumers reached. The restrictions come from limitations on the budget and the relative costs of different media. Linear programming has also been used by psychologists to design an optimal battery of tests. The problem is to maximize the correlation between test scores and the characteristic that is to be predicted. The restrictions are imposed by the length and cost of the testing.

Linear programming is also used by dietitians in planning meals for large numbers of people. The object is to minimize the cost of the diet, and the restrictions reflect the minimum daily requirements of the various nutrients considered in the diet. The next example is representative of this type of problem. Whereas in actual practice many nutritional factors are considered, we shall simplify the problem by considering only three: protein, calories, and riboflavin.

EXAMPLE 1

Nutrition—People   Suppose a person decides to make rice and soybeans part of his staple diet. The object is to design a lowest-cost diet that provides certain minimum levels of protein, calories, and vitamin B_2 (riboflavin). Suppose that one cup of uncooked rice costs 21 cents and contains 15 grams of protein, 810 calories, and $\frac{1}{9}$ milligram of riboflavin. On the other hand, one cup of uncooked soybeans costs 14 cents and contains 22.5 grams of protein, 270 calories, and $\frac{1}{3}$ milligram of riboflavin. Suppose that the minimum daily requirements are 90 grams of protein, 1620 calories, and 1 milligram of riboflavin. Design the lowest-cost diet meeting these specifications.

Solution   We solve the problem by following steps 1–4. The first step is to translate the problem into mathematical language, and the first part of this step is to organize the data, preferably into a chart (Table 2).

Now that we have organized the data, we ask for the unknowns. We wish to know how many cups each of rice and soybeans should comprise the diet, so we

TABLE 2

	Rice	Soybeans	Required level per day
Protein (grams/cup)	15	22.5	90
Calories (per cup)	810	270	1620
Riboflavin (milligrams/cup)	$\frac{1}{9}$	$\frac{1}{3}$	1
Cost (cents/cup)	21	14	

identify appropriate variables:

$$x = \text{number of cups of rice per day}$$

$$y = \text{number of cups of soybeans per day.}$$

Next, we obtain the restrictions on the variables. There is one restriction corresponding to each nutrient. That is, there is one restriction for each of the first three rows of the chart. If x cups of rice and y cups of soybeans are consumed, the amount of protein is $15x + 22.5y$ grams. Thus, from the first row of the chart, $15x + 22.5y \geq 90$, a restriction expressing the fact that there must be at least 90 grams of protein per day. Similarly, the restrictions for calories and riboflavin lead to the inequalities $810x + 270y \geq 1620$ and $\frac{1}{9}x + \frac{1}{3}y \geq 1$, respectively. As in the furniture manufacturing problem, x and y cannot be negative, so there are two further restrictions: $x \geq 0$, $y \geq 0$. In all, there are five restrictions:

$$\begin{cases} 15x + 22.5y \geq 90 \\ 810x + 270y \geq 1620 \\ \frac{1}{9}x + \frac{1}{3}y \geq 1 \\ x \geq 0, \quad y \geq 0 \end{cases} \qquad (1)$$

Now that we have the restrictions, we form the objective function, which tells us what we want to maximize or minimize. Since we wish to minimize cost, we express cost in terms of x and y. Now x cups of rice cost $21x$ cents and y cups of soybeans cost $14y$ cents, so the objective function is given by

$$[\text{cost}] = 21x + 14y. \qquad (2)$$

The problem can finally be stated in mathematical form: Minimize the objective function (2) subject to the restrictions (1). This completes the first step of the solution process.

The second step requires that we graph each of the inequalities (1). In Table 3 on the next page we have summarized all the steps necessary to obtain the information from which to draw the graphs. We have sketched the graphs in Fig. 4. From Fig. 4(b) we see that the feasible set is an unbounded, five-sided region. There are four vertices, two of which are known from Table 3, since they are intercepts of boundary lines. Label the remaining two vertices A and B (Fig. 5).

The third step of the solution process consists of determining the coordinates of A and B. From Fig. 5, these coordinates can be found by solving the following systems of equations:

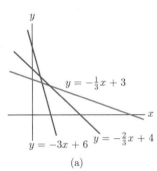

$y = -\frac{1}{3}x + 3$

$y = -3x + 6$ $\qquad$ $y = -\frac{2}{3}x + 4$

(a)

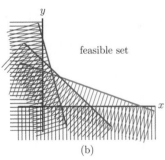

feasible set

(b)

Figure 4

$(0, 6)$

$y = -3x + 6$

A

$y = -\frac{2}{3}x + 4$

B

$y = -\frac{1}{3}x + 3$

$(9, 0)$

Figure 5

To find A solve: $\begin{cases} y = -3x + 6 \\ y = -\frac{2}{3}x + 4 \end{cases}$ $\qquad$ To find B solve: $\begin{cases} y = -\frac{2}{3}x + 4 \\ y = -\frac{1}{3}x + 3 \end{cases}$

TABLE 3

Inequality	Standard form	Line	Intercepts x	y	Graph
$15x + 22.5y \geq 90$	$y \geq -\frac{2}{3}x + 4$	$y = -\frac{2}{3}x + 4$	$(6,0)$	$(0,4)$	above
$810x + 270y \geq 1620$	$y \geq -3x + 6$	$y = -3x + 6$	$(2,0)$	$(0,6)$	above
$\frac{1}{9}x + \frac{1}{3}y \geq 1$	$y \geq -\frac{1}{3}x + 3$	$y = -\frac{1}{3}x + 3$	$(9,0)$	$(0,3)$	above
$x \geq 0$	$x \geq 0$	$x = 0$	$(0,0)$	—	right
$y \geq 0$	$y \geq 0$	$y = 0$	—	$(0,0)$	above

To solve the first system, equate the two expressions for y:

$$-\tfrac{2}{3}x + 4 = -3x + 6$$

$$3x - \tfrac{2}{3}x = 6 - 4 \qquad \text{Add } 3x \text{ and subtract 4 from both sides.}$$

$$\tfrac{7}{3}x = 2 \qquad \text{Combine terms.}$$

$$x = \tfrac{3}{7} \cdot 2 = \tfrac{6}{7} \qquad \text{Multiply both sides by } \tfrac{3}{7}.$$

$$y = -3x + 6 = -3\left(\tfrac{6}{7}\right) + 6 = \tfrac{24}{7} \qquad \text{Substitute } \tfrac{6}{7} \text{ for } x \text{ in first equation.}$$

Therefore, $A = \left(\tfrac{6}{7}, \tfrac{24}{7}\right)$.

Similarly, we find B:

$$-\tfrac{2}{3}x + 4 = -\tfrac{1}{3}x + 3 \qquad \text{Equate the two expressions for } y.$$

$$\tfrac{1}{3}x - \tfrac{2}{3}x = 3 - 4 \qquad \text{Add } \tfrac{1}{3}x \text{ and subtract 4 from both sides.}$$

$$-\tfrac{1}{3}x = -1 \qquad \text{Combine terms.}$$

$$x = (-3) \cdot (-1) = 3 \qquad \text{Multiply both sides by } -3.$$

$$y = -\tfrac{2}{3}x + 4 = -\tfrac{2}{3}(3) + 4 = 2 \qquad \text{Substitute 3 for } x \text{ in first equation.}$$

Therefore, $B = (3,2)$.

TABLE 4

Vertex	Cost $= 21x + 14y$
$(0,6)$	$21 \cdot 0 + 14 \cdot 6 = 84$
$\left(\tfrac{6}{7}, \tfrac{24}{7}\right)$	$21 \cdot \tfrac{6}{7} + 14 \cdot \tfrac{24}{7} = 66$
$(3,2)$	$21 \cdot 3 + 14 \cdot 2 = 91$
$(9,0)$	$21 \cdot 9 + 14 \cdot 0 = 189$

The fourth step consists of evaluating the objective function, in this case $21x + 14y$, at each vertex. From Table 4 we see that the minimum cost is achieved at the vertex $\left(\tfrac{6}{7}, \tfrac{24}{7}\right)$. So the optimal diet—that is, the one that gives nutrients at the desired levels but at minimum cost—is the one that has $\tfrac{6}{7}$ cup of rice per day and $\tfrac{24}{7}$ cups of soybeans per day.

Now Try Exercise 31   ■

NOTE ▶ We have assumed that all linear programming problems have solutions. Although every linear programming problem presented in this text has a solution, there are problems that have no optimal feasible solution. This can happen in two ways. First, there might be no points in the feasible set. Second, feasible solutions to the system of inequalities might exist, but the objective function might not have a maximum (or minimum) value within the feasible set. See Exercises 40 and 41. ■

INCORPORATING TECHNOLOGY

GC   Graphing calculators can draw a feasible set, determine the vertices of the feasible set, and evaluate the objective function at the vertices. Figures 6 to 8 show how some of these tasks can be carried out on a TI-83/84 Plus for the furniture manufacturing problem. ■

Figure 6. $[0, 18]$ *by* $[0, 14]$

Figure 7

L1	L2	**L3**	◆ 3
14	4	1400	
9	9	1350	
0	12	840	
0	0	0	
16	0	1280	
------	------	------	
L3 ="80L1+70L2"			

Figure 8

	A	B
1		=6*x+3*y
2		=x+y
3		=2*x+6*y
4		=x
5		=y
6		=80*x+70*y

Figure 9

ES   Solver can be used to solve linear programming problems. Each linear inequality should be written with the variables on the left and a constant on the right. For instance, the linear inequalitites for the furniture manufacturing problem should be written as near the top of page 119. In Fig. 9, the cells A1 and A2 have been named x and y, respectively. The figure shows the formulas that are typed into column B. The formulas entered into the first five cells of column B are the left sides of the inequalities and the formula entered into cell B6 is the objective function.

To obtain the solution of the linear programming problem, invoke Solver and fill in the Solver Parameters window as shown in Fig. 10. The cell containing the objective function is the target cell, and the Max button is selected since the objective function is to be maximized. The rest of the window is completed in much the same way as when solving a system of linear equations. (For instance, to enter a constraint, click the Add button and fill in the Add Constraint dialog box that appears.) Fig. 11 shows the answer generated after the Solve and then the OK buttons have been clicked.

Solver Parameters

Set Target Cell: $B$6

Equal To: ● Max   ○ Min   ○ Value of: [   ]

By Changing Cells:

x,y

Subject to the Constraints:

$B$1 <= 96
$B$2 <= 18
$B$3 <= 72
x >= 0
y >= 0

[Solve] [Close] [Guess] [Options] [Add] [Change] [Reset All] [Delete] [Help]

Figure 10

	A	B
1	14	96
2	4	18
3		52
4		14
5		4
6		1400

Figure 11

Practice Problems 3.2

1. The feasible set for the nutrition problem is shown in Fig. 12. The cost is $21x + 14y$. *Without* using the fundamental theorem of linear programming, explain why the cost could not possibly be minimized at the point $(4, 4)$.

2. Rework the nutrition problem assuming that the cost of rice is changed to 7 cents per cup.

feasible set

• $(4, 4)$

Figure 12

EXERCISES 3.2

For each of the feasible sets in Exercises 1–4, determine x and y so that the objective function $4x + 3y$ is maximized.

1.

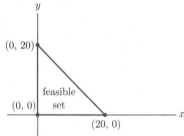

$(0, 20)$

feasible set

$(0, 0)$

$(20, 0)$

2.

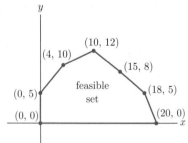

$(10, 12)$

$(4, 10)$

$(15, 8)$

$(0, 5)$

feasible set

$(18, 5)$

$(0, 0)$

$(20, 0)$

3.

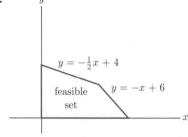

$y = -\frac{1}{2}x + 4$

feasible set

$y = -x + 6$

4.

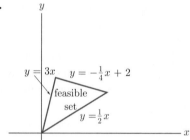

$y = 3x$ $y = -\frac{1}{4}x + 2$

feasible set

$y = \frac{1}{2}x$

In Exercises 5–8, find the values of x and y that maximize the given objective function for the feasible set in Fig. 13.

5. $x + 2y$ **6.** $x + y$

7. $2x + y$ **8.** $3 - x - y$

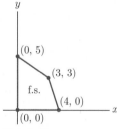

$(0, 5)$

$(3, 3)$

f.s.

$(4, 0)$

$(0, 0)$

Figure 13

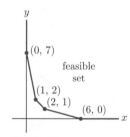

$(0, 7)$

feasible set

$(1, 2)$

$(2, 1)$

$(6, 0)$

Figure 14

In Exercises 9–12, find the values of x and y that minimize the given objective function for the feasible set in Fig. 14.

9. $8x + y$ **10.** $3x + 2y$

11. $2x + 3y$ **12.** $x + 8y$

13. Shipping Refer to Exercises 3.1, Problem 5. How many crates of each cargo should be shipped in order to satisfy the shipping requirements and yield the greatest earnings? (See the graph of the feasible set in Fig. 15.)

Shipping problem

Figure 15

14. Mining Refer to Exercises 3.1, Problem 6. Find the number of days that each mine should be operated in order to fill the order at the least cost. (See the graph of the feasible set in Fig. 16.)

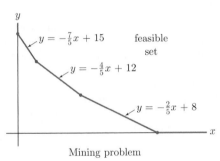

Mining problem

Figure 16

15. Exam Strategy Refer to Exercises 3.1, Problem 7. How many of each type of question should the student do to maximize the total score? (See the graph of the feasible set in Fig. 17.)

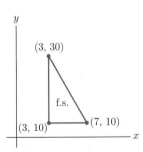

Exam strategy problem

Figure 17

16. Political Campaign—Resource Allocation Refer to Exercises 3.1, Problem 8. How should the media funds be allocated so as to maximize the total audience? (See the graph of the feasible set in Fig. 18.)

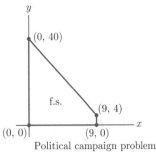

Political campaign problem

Figure 18

17. Nutrition—Dairy Cows Refer to Exercises 3.1, Problem 9. How many pounds of each food should be purchased in order to meet the nutritional requirements at the least cost? (See the graph of the feasible set in Fig. 19.)

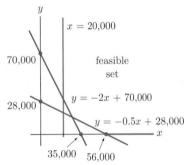

Figure 19

18. Manufacturing-Resource Allocation Refer to Exercises 3.1, Problem 10. How many of each type of jacket should be made to maximize the profit? (See the graph of the feasible set in Fig. 20.)

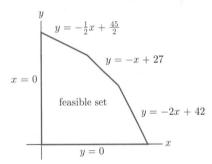

Figure 20

(Furniture Manufacturing) In Exercises 19 and 20, rework the furniture manufacturing problem, where everything is the same except that the profit per chair is changed to the given value. (See Table 1 for vertices.)

19. $150 **20.** $60

21. Minimize the objective function $3x + 4y$ subject to the constraints

$$\begin{cases} 2x + y \geq 10 \\ x + 2y \geq 14 \\ x \geq 0, \quad y \geq 0 \end{cases}$$

22. Maximize the objective function $7x + 4y$ subject to the constraints

$$\begin{cases} 3x + 2y \leq 36 \\ x + 4y \leq 32 \\ x \geq 0, \quad y \geq 0 \end{cases}$$

23. Maximize the objective function $2x + 5y$ subject to the constraints

$$\begin{cases} x + 2y \leq 20 \\ 3x + 2y \geq 24 \\ x \leq 6 \\ x \geq 0, \quad y \geq 0 \end{cases}$$

24. Minimize the objective function $2x + 3y$ subject to the constraints

$$\begin{cases} x + y \geq 10 \\ y \leq x \\ x \leq 8 \end{cases}$$

25. Maximize the objective function $100x + 150y$ subject to the constraints

$$\begin{cases} x + 3y \leq 120 \\ 35x + 10y \leq 780 \\ x \leq 20 \\ x \geq 0, \quad y \geq 0 \end{cases}$$

26. Minimize the objective function $\frac{1}{2}x + \frac{3}{4}y$ subject to the constraints

$$\begin{cases} 2x + 2y \geq 8 \\ 3x + 5y \geq 16 \\ x \geq 0, \quad y \geq 0 \end{cases}$$

27. Minimize the objective function $7x + 4y$ subject to the constraints

$$\begin{cases} y \geq -2x + 11 \\ y \leq -x + 10 \\ y \leq -\frac{1}{3}x + 6 \\ y \geq -\frac{1}{4}x + 4 \end{cases}$$

28. Maximize the objective function $x + 2y$ subject to the constraints

$$\begin{cases} y \leq -x + 100 \\ y \geq \frac{1}{3}x + 20 \\ y \leq x \end{cases}$$

29. Manufacturing—Resource Allocation Infotron Inc. makes electronic hockey and soccer games. Each hockey game requires 2 labor-hours of assembly and 2 labor-hours of testing. Each soccer game requires 3 labor-hours of assembly and 1 labor-hour of testing. Each day there are 42 labor-hours available for assembly and 26 labor-hours available for testing. How many of each game should Infotron produce each day to maximize its total daily output?

30. Manufacturing—Production Planning An electronics company has factories in Cleveland and Toledo that manufacture three-head and four-head VCRs. Each day the Cleveland factory produces 500 three-head VCRs and 300 four-head VCRs at a cost of $18,000. Each day the Toledo factory produces 300 of each type of VCR at a cost of $15,000. An order is received for 25,000 three-head VCRs and 21,000 four-head VCRs. For how many days should each factory operate to fill the order at the least cost?

31. Nutrition—People A nutritionist, working for NASA, must meet certain nutritional requirements and yet keep the weight of the food at a minimum. He is considering a combination of two foods, which are packaged in tubes. Each tube of food A contains 4 units of protein, 2 units of carbohydrates, and 2 units of fat and weighs 3 pounds. Each tube of food B contains 3 units of protein, 6 units of carbohydrates, and 1 unit of fat and weighs 2 pounds. The requirement calls for 42 units of protein, 30 units of carbohydrates, and 18 units of fat. How many tubes of each food should be supplied to the astronauts?

32. Construction—Resource Allocation A contractor builds two types of homes. The first type requires one lot, $12,000 capital, and 150 labor-days to build and is sold for a profit of $2400. The second type of home requires one lot, $32,000 capital, and 200 labor-days to build and is sold for a profit of $3400. The contractor owns 150 lots and has available for the job $2,880,000 capital and 24,000 labor-days. How many homes of each type should she build to realize the greatest profit?

33. Packaging—Product Mix The Beautiful Day Fruit Juice Company makes two varieties of fruit drink. The table below shows the composition and profit per can for each variety. Each week the company has available 9000 ounces of pineapple juice, 2400 ounces of orange juice, and 1400 ounces of apricot juice. How many cans of Fruit Delight and of Heavenly Punch should be produced each week to maximize the total profit?

	Fruit Delight	Heavenly Punch
Pineapple juice	10 ounces	10 ounces
Orange juice	3 ounces	2 ounces
Apricot juice	1 ounce	2 ounces
Profit	$.40	$.60

34. Manufacturing—Resource Allocation The Bluejay Lacrosse Stick Company makes two kinds of lacrosse sticks. The table below shows the labor requirements and profits for each type of lacrosse stick. Each day the company has available 120 labor-hours for cutting, 150 labor-hours for stringing, and 140 labor-hours for finishing. How many lacrosse sticks of each type should be manufactured each day to maximize the total profit?

	Attack	Defense
Cutting	2 labor-hours	1 labor-hour
Stringing	1 labor-hour	3 labor-hours
Finishing	2 labor-hours	2 labor-hours
Profit	$16	$20

35. Agriculture—Crop Planning A farmer has 100 acres on which to plant oats or corn. Each acre of oats requires $18 capital and 2 hours of labor. Each acre of corn requires $36 capital and 6 hours of labor. Labor costs are $8 per hour. The farmer has $2100 available for capital and $2400 available for labor. If the revenue is $55 from each acre of oats and $125 from each acre of corn, what planting combination will produce the greatest total profit? (Profit here is revenue plus leftover capital and labor cash reserve.) What is the maximum profit?

36. Manufacturing—Resource Allocation A company makes two items, I_1 and I_2, from three raw materials, M_1, M_2, and M_3. Item I_1 uses 3 ounces of M_1, 2 ounces of M_2, and 2 ounces of M_3. Item I_2 uses 4 ounces of M_1, 1 ounce of M_2, and 3 ounces of M_3. The profit on item I_1 is $8 and on item I_2 is $6. The company has a daily supply of 40 ounces of M_1, 20 ounces of M_2, and 60 ounces of M_3.

(a) How many of items I_1 and I_2 should be made each day to maximize profit?

(b) What is the maximum profit?

(c) How many ounces of each raw material are used?

(d) If the profit on item I_1 increases to $13, how many of items I_1 and I_2 should be made each day to maximize profit?

37. Agriculture—Crop Planning Suppose that the farmer of Exercise 35 can allocate the $4500 available for capital and labor however he or she wants.

(a) Without solving the linear programming problem, explain why the optimal profit cannot be less than what was found in Exercise 35.

(b) Find the optimal solution in the new situation. Does it provide more profit than in Exercise 35?

38. Nutrition Pavan wants to add a sliced carrot and sliced green pepper salad to his dinner each day that will help him meet some of his nutritional needs. The nutritional

information and costs per cup are contained in the table below. He would like his salad to contain at least 15 g of fiber, 100 mg of calcium, and 100 mg of Vitamin C. How many cups of sliced carrots and peppers should he use to make his salad for the least cost?

	Fiber	Calcium	Vitamin C	Cost
Carrots	3.4 g	40 mg	7.2 mg	$.21
Green peppers	1.6 g	9 mg	74.0 mg	$.42

39. Manufacturing The E-JEM Company produces two types of laptop computer bags. The regular version requires $32 in capital, 4 hours of labor, and sells for $46. The deluxe version requires $38 in capital, 6 hours of labor, and sells for $55. How many of each type of bag should the company produce in order to maximize their revenue if they have $2100 in capital and 280 labor hours available?

40. Consider the following linear programming problem: Maximize $M = 10x + 6y$ subject to the constraints

$$\begin{cases} x + y \geq 6 \\ x \geq 0, \quad y \geq 0 \end{cases}$$

(a) Sketch the feasible set.

(b) Determine three points in the feasible set and calculate M at each of them.

(c) Show that the objective function attains no maximum value for points in the feasible set.

41. Consider the following linear programming problem: Minimize $M = 10x + 6y$ subject to the constraints

$$\begin{cases} x + y \geq 6 \\ 4x + 3y \leq 4 \\ x \geq 0, \quad y \geq 0 \end{cases}$$

(a) Sketch the feasible set for the linear programming problem.

(b) Determine a point of the feasible set.

Exercises 42 and 43 require a spreadsheet.

42. Use an electronic spreadsheet such as Excel to solve Exercise 21.

43. Use an electronic spreadsheet such as Excel to solve Exercise 22.

Solutions to Practice Problems 3.2

1. The point P in Fig. 21 has a smaller value of x and a smaller value of y than $(4,4)$ and is still in the feasible set. It therefore corresponds to a lower cost than $(4,4)$ and still meets the requirements. We conclude that no interior point of the feasible set could possibly be an optimal point. This geometric argument indicates that an optimal point might be one that juts out far—that is, a vertex.

Figure 21

2. The system of linear inequalities, feasible set, and vertices will all be the same as before. Only the objective function changes. The new objective function is $7x + 14y$. The minimum cost occurs when using 3 cups of rice and 2 cups of soybeans.

Vertex	Cost $= 7x + 14y$
$(0,6)$	84
$\left(\frac{6}{7}, \frac{24}{7}\right)$	54
$(3,2)$	49
$(9,0)$	63

3.3 Linear Programming II

In this section we apply the technique of linear programming to the design of a portfolio for a retirement fund and to the transportation of goods from warehouses to retail outlets. The significant new feature of each of these problems is that, on the surface, they appear to involve more than two variables. However, they can be translated into mathematical language so that only two variables are required.

EXAMPLE 1   **Investment planning**   A pension fund has $30 million to invest. The money is to be divided among Treasury notes, bonds, and stocks. The rules for administration of the fund require that at least $3 million be invested in each type of investment, that at least half the money be invested in Treasury notes and bonds, and that the amount invested in bonds not exceed twice the amount invested in Treasury notes. The annual yields for the various investments are 7% for Treasury notes, 8% for bonds, and 9% for stocks. How should the money be allocated among the various investments to produce the largest return?

Solution   First, let us agree that all numbers stand for millions. That is, we write 30 to stand for 30 million dollars. This will save us from writing many zeros. In examining the problem, we find that very little organization needs to be done. The rules for administration of the fund are written in a form from which inequalities can be read right off. Let us just summarize the remaining data in the first row of a chart (Table 1).

TABLE 1			
	Treasury notes	**Bonds**	**Stocks**
Yield	.07	.08	.09
Variables	x	y	$30 - (x + y)$

There appear to be three variables—the amounts to be invested in each of the three categories. However, since the three investments must total 30, we need only two variables. Let $x =$ the amount to be invested in Treasury notes and $y =$ the amount to be invested in bonds. Then the amount to be invested in stocks is $30 - (x + y)$. We have displayed the variables in Table 1.

Now for the restrictions. Since at least 3 (million dollars) must be invested in each category, we have the three inequalities

$$x \geq 3$$
$$y \geq 3$$
$$30 - (x + y) \geq 3.$$

Moreover, since at least half the money, or 15, must be invested in Treasury notes and bonds, we must have

$$x + y \geq 15.$$

Finally, since the amount invested in bonds must not exceed twice the amount invested in Treasury notes, we must have

$$y \leq 2x.$$

(In this example we do not need to state that $x \geq 0$, $y \geq 0$, since we have already required that they be greater than or equal to 3.) Thus there are five restriction inequalities:

$$\begin{cases} x \geq 3, \quad y \geq 3 \\ 30 - (x + y) \geq \quad 3 \\ \qquad x + y \geq 15 \\ \qquad\qquad y \leq 2x \end{cases} \tag{1}$$

Next, we form the objective function, which in this case equals the total return on the investment. Since x dollars is invested at 7%, y dollars at 8%, and $30 - (x + y)$ dollars at 9%, the total return is

$$\begin{aligned} [\text{return}] &= .07x + .08y + .09[30 - (x + y)] \\ &= .07x + .08y + 2.7 - .09x - .09y \\ &= 2.7 - .02x - .01y. \end{aligned} \tag{2}$$

So the mathematical statement of the problem is: Maximize the objective function (2) subject to the restrictions (1).

The next step of the solution is to graph the inequalities (1). The necessary information is tabulated in Table 2.

One point about the chart is worth noting: It contains enough data to graph each of the lines, with the exception of $y = 2x$. The reason is that the x- and

TABLE 2

Inequality	Standard form	Line	Intercepts x	y	Graph
$x \geq 3$	$x \geq 3$	$x = 3$	$(3, 0)$	—	Right of line
$y \geq 3$	$y \geq 3$	$y = 3$	—	$(0, 3)$	Above line
$30 - (x + y) \geq 3$	$y \leq -x + 27$	$y = -x + 27$	$(27, 0)$	$(0, 27)$	Below line
$x + y \geq 15$	$y \geq -x + 15$	$y = -x + 15$	$(15, 0)$	$(0, 15)$	Above line
$y \leq 2x$	$y \leq 2x$	$y = 2x$	$(0, 0)$	$(0, 0)$	Below line

(a)

Figure 1

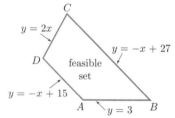

Figure 2

y-intercepts of this line are the same, $(0,0)$. So to graph $y = 2x$, we must find an additional point on the line. For example, if we set $x = 2$, then $y = 4$, so $(2,4)$ is on the line. In Fig. 1(a) we have drawn the various lines, and in Fig. 1(b) we have crossed out the appropriate regions to produce the graph of the system. The feasible set, as well as the equations of the various lines that make up its boundary, are shown in Fig. 2. From Fig. 2 we find the pairs of equations that determine each of the vertices A–D. This is the third step of the solution procedure.

$$A: \begin{cases} y = 3 \\ y = -x + 15 \end{cases} \qquad B: \begin{cases} y = 3 \\ y = -x + 27 \end{cases}$$

$$C: \begin{cases} y = -x + 27 \\ y = 2x \end{cases} \qquad D: \begin{cases} y = 2x \\ y = -x + 15 \end{cases}$$

A and B are the easiest to determine. To find A, we must solve

$$3 = -x + 15$$
$$x = 12 \qquad \text{Add } x \text{ and subtract 3 from both sides.}$$
$$y = 3 \qquad \text{Given by first equation.}$$

Therefore, $A = (12,3)$. Similarly, $B = (24,3)$. To find C, we must solve

$$2x = -x + 27$$
$$3x = 27 \qquad \text{Add } x \text{ to both sides.}$$
$$x = 9 \qquad \text{Divide both sides by 3.}$$
$$y = 2x = 2(9) = 18 \quad \text{Substitute 9 for } x \text{ in second equation.}$$

Therefore, $C = (9,18)$. Similarly, $D = (5,10)$.

Finally, we list the four vertices and evaluate the objective function (2) at each one. The results are summarized in Table 3.

TABLE 3	
Vertex	**Return $= 2.7 - .02x - .01y$**
$(5,10)$	$2.7 - .02(5) - .01(10) = \$2.5$ million
$(9,18)$	$2.7 - .02(9) - .01(18) = \$2.34$ million
$(24,3)$	$2.7 - .02(24) - .01(3) = \$2.19$ million
$(12,3)$	$2.7 - .02(12) - .01(3) = \$2.43$ million

It is clear that the largest return occurs when $x = 5$, $y = 10$. In other words, $5 million should be invested in Treasury notes, $10 million in bonds, and $30 - (x+y) = 30 - (5 + 10) = \$15$ million in stocks.

Now Try Exercise 23

Linear programming is of use not only in analyzing investments but in the fields of transportation and shipping. It is often used to plan routes, determine locations of warehouses, and develop efficient procedures for getting goods to people. Many linear programming problems of this variety can be formulated as *transportation problems*. A typical transportation problem involves determining the least-cost scheme for delivering a commodity stocked in a number of different warehouses to a number of different locations, say retail stores. Of course, in practical applications, it is necessary to consider problems involving perhaps dozens or even hundreds of warehouses, and possibly just as many delivery locations. For problems on such a grand scale, the methods developed so far are inadequate. For one thing, the number of variables required is usually more than two. We must wait until Chapter 4 for methods that apply to such problems. However, the next example gives an instance of a transportation problem that does not involve too many warehouses or too many delivery points. It gives the flavor of general transportation problems.

EXAMPLE 2   **Transportation—Shipping** Suppose that a Maryland TV dealer has stores in Annapolis and Rockville and warehouses in College Park and Baltimore. The cost of shipping a TV set from College Park to Annapolis is $6; from College Park to Rockville, $3; from Baltimore to Annapolis, $9; and from Baltimore to Rockville, $5. Suppose that the Annapolis store orders 25 TV sets and the Rockville store 30. Suppose further that the College Park warehouse has a stock of 45 sets and the Baltimore warehouse 40. What is the most economical way to supply the requested TV sets to the two stores?

Solution The first step in solving a linear programming problem is to translate it into mathematical language. And the first part of this step is to organize the information given, preferably in the form of a chart. In this case, since the problem is geographic, we draw a schematic diagram, as in Fig. 3, which shows the flow of goods between warehouses and retail stores. By each route, we have written the cost. Below each warehouse we have written down its stock and below each retail store the number of TV sets it ordered.

Figure 3

Next, let us determine the variables. It appears initially that four variables are required, namely the number of TV sets to be shipped over each route. However, a closer look shows that only two variables are required. For if x denotes the number of TV sets to be shipped from College Park to Rockville, then since Rockville ordered 30 sets, the number shipped from Baltimore to Rockville is $30 - x$. Similarly, if y denotes the number of sets shipped from College Park to Annapolis, then the number shipped from Baltimore to Annapolis is $25 - y$. We have written the appropriate shipment sizes beside the various routes in Fig. 3.

As the third part of the translation process, let us write down the restrictions on the variables. Basically, there are two kinds of restrictions: None of x, y, $30 - x$,

$25 - y$ can be negative, and a warehouse cannot ship more TV sets than it has in stock. Referring to Fig. 3, we see that College Park ships $x + y$ sets, so that $x + y \leq 45$. Similarly, Baltimore ships $(30 - x) + (25 - y)$ sets, so that $(30 - x) + (25 - y) \leq 40$. Simplifying this inequality, we get

$$
\begin{aligned}
55 - x - y &\leq 40 \\
-x - y &\leq -15 \\
x + y &\geq 15
\end{aligned}
$$

The inequality $30 - x \geq 0$ can be simplified to $x \leq 30$, and the inequality $25 - y \geq 0$ can be written $y \leq 25$. So our restriction inequalities are these:

$$
\begin{cases}
x \geq 0, \quad y \geq 0 \\
x \leq 30, \quad y \leq 25 \\
x + y \leq 45 \\
x + y \geq 15
\end{cases}
\tag{3}
$$

The final step in the translation process is to form the objective function. In this problem we are attempting to minimize cost, so the objective function must express the cost in terms of x and y. Refer again to Fig. 3. There are x sets going from College Park to Rockville, and each costs \$3 to transport, so the cost of delivering these x sets is $3x$. Similarly, the costs of making the other deliveries are $6y$, $5(30 - x)$, and $9(25 - y)$. Thus the objective function is

$$
\begin{aligned}
[\text{cost}] &= 3x + 6y + 5(30 - x) + 9(25 - y) \\
&= 3x + 6y + 150 - 5x + 225 - 9y \\
&= 375 - 2x - 3y.
\end{aligned}
\tag{4}
$$

So the mathematical problem we must solve is as follows: Find x and y that minimize the objective function (4) and satisfy the restrictions (3).

To solve the mathematical problem, we must graph the system of inequalities in (3). Four of the inequalities have graphs determined by horizontal or vertical lines. The only inequalities involving any work are $x + y \geq 15$ and $x + y \leq 45$. And even these are very easy to graph. The result is the graph in Fig. 4.

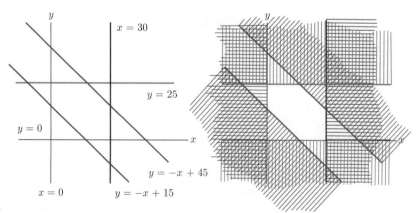

Figure 4

In Fig. 5 we have drawn the feasible set and have labeled each boundary line with its equation. The vertices A–F are now simple to determine. First, A and F are the intercepts of the line $y = -x + 15$. Therefore, $A = (15, 0)$ and $F = (0, 15)$. Since B is the x-intercept of the line $x = 30$, we have $B = (30, 0)$. Similarly, $E = (0, 25)$. Since C is on the line $x = 30$, its x-coordinate is 30. Its y-coordinate is $y = -30 + 45 = 15$, so $C = (30, 15)$. Similarly, since D has y-coordinate 25, its x-coordinate is given by $25 = -x + 45$ or $x = 20$. Thus $D = (20, 25)$.

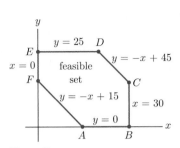

TABLE 4	
Vertex	**Cost $= 375 - 2x - 3y$**
$(0, 25)$	300
$(0, 15)$	330
$(15, 0)$	345
$(30, 0)$	315
$(30, 15)$	270
$(20, 25)$	260

Figure 5

We have listed in Table 4 the vertices A–F as well as the cost corresponding to each one. The minimum cost of $260 occurs at the vertex $(20, 25)$. So $x = 20$, $y = 25$ yields the minimum of the objective function. In other words, 20 TV sets should be shipped from College Park to Rockville and 25 from College Park to Annapolis, $30 - x = 10$ from Baltimore to Rockville, and $25 - y = 0$ from Baltimore to Annapolis. This solves our problem. ∎

Now Try Exercise 25

Remarks Concerning the Transportation Problem Note that the highest-cost route is the one from Baltimore to Annapolis. The solution we have obtained eliminates any shipments over this route. One might infer from this that one should always avoid the most expensive route. But this is not correct reasoning. To see why, reconsider Example 2, except change the cost of transporting a TV set from Baltimore to Annapolis from $9 to $7. The Baltimore–Annapolis route is still the most expensive. However, in this case the minimum cost is not obtained by eliminating the Baltimore–Annapolis route. For the revised problem, the linear inequalities stay the same. So the feasible set and the vertices remain the same. The only change is in the objective function, which now is given by

$$\left[\text{cost}\right] = 3x + 6y + 5(30 - x) + 7(25 - y) = 325 - 2x - y.$$

The costs at the various vertices are given in Table 5. So the minimum cost of $250 is achieved when $x = 30$, $y = 15$, $30 - x = 0$, and $25 - y = 10$. Note that 10 sets are being shipped from Baltimore to Annapolis, even though this is the most expensive route.

TABLE 5	
Vertex	**Cost $= 325 - 2x - y$**
$(0, 25)$	300
$(0, 15)$	310
$(15, 0)$	295
$(30, 0)$	265
$(30, 15)$	250
$(20, 25)$	260

It is even possible for the cost function to be optimized simultaneously at two different vertices. For example, if the cost from Baltimore to Annapolis is $8 and all other data are the same as in Example 2, then the optimal cost is $260 and is achieved at both vertices $(30, 15)$ and $(20, 25)$. ∎

Verification of the Fundamental Theorem The fundamental theorem of linear programming asserts that the objective function assumes its optimal value at a vertex of the feasible set. Let us verify this fact. For simplicity, we give the argument only in a special case, namely for the furniture manufacturing problem. However, this is for convenience of exposition only. The same argument given in the following example may be used to prove the fundamental theorem in general. Our argument relies on the parallel property for straight lines, which asserts that parallel lines have the same slope.

EXAMPLE 3

Proof of the Fundamental Theorem of Linear Programming Prove the fundamental theorem of linear programming in the special case of the furniture manufacturing problem.

Solution The profit derived from producing x chairs and y sofas is $80x + 70y$ dollars. Let us examine all those production schedules having a given profit. As an example, consider a profit of \$2800. Then x and y must satisfy $80x + 70y = 2800$. That is, (x, y) must lie on the line whose equation is $80x + 70y = 2800$, or in standard form, $y = -\frac{8}{7}x + 40$. The slope of this line is $-\frac{8}{7}$ and its y-intercept is $(0, 40)$. We have drawn this line in Fig. 6(a), in which we have also drawn the feasible set for the furniture manufacturing problem. Note two fundamental facts: (1) Every production schedule on the line corresponds to a profit of \$2800. (2) The line lies above the feasible set. In particular, no production schedule on the line satisfies all the restrictions of the problem. The difficulty is that \$2800 is too high a profit for which to ask.

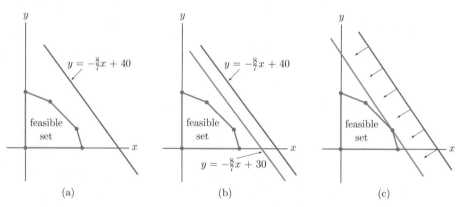

Figure 6   (a)   (b)   (c)

So now lower the profit, say, to \$2100. In this case the production schedule (x, y) lies on the line $80x + 70y = 2100$, or in standard form, $y = -\frac{8}{7}x + 30$. This line is drawn in Fig. 6(b). Note that since both lines have slope $-\frac{8}{7}$, they are parallel by the parallel property. Actually, if we look at the production schedules yielding any fixed profit p, then they will lie along a line of slope $-\frac{8}{7}$, which is parallel to the two lines already drawn. For if the production schedule (x, y) yields a profit p, then

$$80x + 70y = p \quad \text{or} \quad y = -\frac{8}{7}x + \frac{p}{70}.$$

In other words, (x, y) lies on a line of slope $-\frac{8}{7}$ and y-intercept $(0, p/70)$. In particular, all the "lines of constant profit" are parallel to one another. So let us go back to the line of \$2800 profit. It does not touch the feasible set. So now lower the profit and therefore translate the line downward parallel to itself. Next lower the profit until we first touch the feasible set. This line now touches the feasible set at a vertex [Fig. 6(c)]. And this vertex corresponds to the optimal production schedule, since any other point of the feasible set lies on a "line of constant profit" corresponding to an even-lower profit. This shows why the fundamental theorem of linear programming is true.

Now Try Exercise 1

Range of Optimality   The objective function for the furniture manufacturing problem is $80x + 70y$, and the optimal production schedule is $(14, 4)$. The numbers 80 and 70 in the objective function were the profits per chair and sofa, respectively. If the profit per chair is increased to \$90 and all other numbers in the problem remain the same, then the optimal production schedule will still be $(14, 4)$. Actually, if

$$70 \leq [\text{profit per chair}] \leq 140,$$

then the production schedule $(14, 4)$ will still provide an optimal solution. The interval $[70, 140]$ is called the **range of optimality** for the profit per chair. (Exercise 34 shows how to use the concept developed in Example 3 to calculate ranges of optimality.) Since $80 - 70 = 10$ and $140 - 80 = 60$, the profit per chair can be decreased by as much as \$10 or increased by as much as \$60 while still keeping $(14, 4)$ as an optimal production schedule. We say that the **allowable decrease** for the profit per chair is 10 and the **allowable increase** is 60. The range of optimality for the profit per sofa is $[40, 80]$. Therefore, the profit per sofa has an allowable decrease of 30 and an allowable increase of 10.

If the objective function is parallel to one of the boundary lines of the feasible set, there will be infinitely many solutions—all points on that boundary line segment provide optimal values for the objective function. At least one such point is a vertex of the feasible set.

EXAMPLE 4   **Transportation—Shipping**   Reconsider the TV shipping problem discussed in Example 2 with the cost of shipping from Baltimore to Annapolis now \$8 and all other data the same as in Example 2. Minimize the shipping costs.

Solution   The cost function to be minimized is now

$$[\text{cost}] = 350 - 2x - 2y.$$

Note that for any fixed value of the cost, the slope of the objective function is -1. The feasible set is identical to that of Example 2 (Fig. 5). The slope of the boundary line $y = -x + 45$ is also -1. A check of the vertices of the feasible set (Table 6) shows that the minimal cost of \$260 is achieved at the two vertices $C = (30, 15)$ and $D = (20, 25)$. In fact, the cost of \$260 is achieved at every point on the boundary line joining these two vertices. Let's verify this in two cases. The points $(25, 20)$ and $(28, 17)$ both lie on the line $y = -x + 45$ and produce a cost of \$260. Figure 7 illustrates the result.

TABLE 6	
Vertex	Cost $= 350 - 2x - 2y$
$(0, 25)$	300
$(0, 15)$	320
$(15, 0)$	320
$(30, 0)$	290
$(30, 15)$	260
$(20, 25)$	260

Figure 7

INCORPORATING TECHNOLOGY

Figure 8

GC Graphing calculators can draw accurate feasible sets and accurate lines of constant profit (or cost). These precise drawings often permit us to select the optimal vertex by inspection. Figure 8 shows a TI-83/84 Plus screen for the shipping problem of Example 2. The thick line is the line of constant cost, $253. As the thick line is lowered, the point $(20, 25)$ is selected. A similar screen can be produced with the TI-89. ∎

ES Solver can be asked to provide allowable increases and decreases for the coefficients of the objective function along with the solution. After the Solver Parameters window has been filled in, click the Options button to invoke the Solver Options window. In the Solver Options window, click on the box labeled "Assume Linear Model" and then click the OK button to return to the Solver Parameters window. As before, click on the Solve button to invoke the Solver Results window. In this window, click on Sensitivity in the Reports list, and then click on the OK button. The requested information will be contained in a table in a sheet named "Sensitivity Report 1." See Table 7. The sheet contains a second table that is discussed at the end of Section 4.4.

TABLE 7 The first table of the sensitivity sheet

Adjustable Cells

Cell	Name	Final Value	Reduced Cost	Objective Coefficient	Allowable Increase	Allowable Decrease
$A$1	x	14	0	80	60	10
$A$2	y	4	0	70	10	30

Practice Problems 3.3

Problems 1–3 refer to Example 1. Translate the statement into an inequality.

1. The amount to be invested in bonds is at most $5 million more than the amount to be invested in Treasury notes.

2. No more than $25 million should be invested in stocks and bonds.

3. Rework Example 1, assuming that the yield for Treasury notes goes up to 8%.

4. A linear programming problem has objective function $\left[\text{cost}\right] = 5x + 10y$, which is to be minimized. Figure 9 shows the feasible set and the straight line of all combinations of x and y for which $\left[\text{cost}\right] = \$20$.

    (a) Give the linear equation (in standard form) of the line of constant cost c.

(b) As c increases, does the line of constant cost c move up or down?

(c) By inspection, find the vertex of the feasible set that gives the optimal solution.

Figure 9

EXERCISES 3.3

1. Figure 10(a) shows the feasible set of the nutrition problem of Section 3.2 and the straight line of all combinations of rice and soybeans for which the cost is 42 cents.

   (a) The objective function is $21x + 14y$. Give the linear equation (in standard form) of the line of constant cost c.

   (b) As c increases, does the line of constant cost move up or down?

   (c) By inspection, find the vertex of the feasible set that gives the optimal solution.

2. Figure 10(b) shows the feasible set of the transportation problem of Example 2 and the straight line of all combinations of shipments for which the transportation cost is $240.

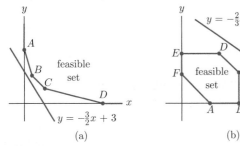

(a)   (b)

Figure 10

(a) The objective function is $\left[\text{cost}\right] = 375 - 2x - 3y$. Give the linear equation (in standard form) of the line of constant cost c.

(b) As c increases, does the line of constant cost move up or down?

(c) By inspection, find the vertex of the feasible set that gives the optimal solution.

Consider the feasible set in Fig. 11(a). In Exercises 3–6, find an objective function of the form $ax + by$ that has its greatest value at the given point.

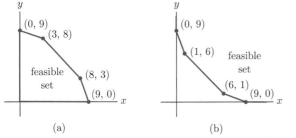

(a)   (b)

Figure 11

3. $(9, 0)$ 4. $(3, 8)$ 5. $(8, 3)$ 6. $(0, 9)$

Consider the feasible set in Fig. 11(b). In Exercises 7–10, find an objective function of the form $ax + by$ that has its least value at the given point.

7. $(9, 0)$ 8. $(1, 6)$ 9. $(6, 1)$ 10. $(0, 9)$

Consider the feasible set in Fig. 12(a), where three of the boundary lines are labeled with their slopes. In Exercises 11–14, find the point at which the given objective function has its greatest value.

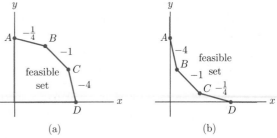

(a)   (b)

Figure 12

11. $3x + 2y$ 12. $2x + 10y$

13. $10x + 2y$ 14. $2x + 3y$

Consider the feasible set in Fig. 12(b), where three of the boundary lines are labeled with their slopes. In Exercises 15–18, find the point at which the given objective function has its least value.

15. $2x + 10y$ 16. $10x + 2y$

17. $2x + 3y$ 18. $3x + 2y$

19. Consider the feasible set in Fig. 13. For what values of k will the objective function $x + ky$ be maximized at the vertex $(3, 4)$?

Figure 13   **Figure 14**

20. Consider the feasible set in Fig. 14. Explain why the objective function $ax + by$, with a and b positive, must have its maximum value at point E.

21. **Nutrition—Animal** Mr. Smith decides to feed his pet Doberman pinscher a combination of two dog foods. Each can of brand A contains 3 units of protein, 1 unit of carbohydrates, and 2 units of fat and costs 80 cents. Each can of brand B contains 1 unit of protein, 1 unit of carbohydrates, and 6 units of fat and costs 50 cents. Mr. Smith feels that each day his dog should have at least 6 units of protein, 4 units of carbohydrates, and 12 units of fat. How many cans of each dog food should he give to his dog each day to provide the minimum requirements at the least cost?

22. Oil Production An oil company owns two refineries. Refinery I produces each day 100 barrels of high-grade oil, 200 barrels of medium-grade oil, and 300 barrels of low-grade oil and costs $10,000 to operate. Refinery II produces each day 200 barrels of high-grade, 100 barrels of medium-grade, and 200 barrels of low-grade oil and costs $9000 to operate. An order is received for 1000 barrels of high-grade oil, 1000 barrels of medium-grade oil, and 1800 barrels of low-grade oil. How many days should each refinery be operated to fill the order at the least cost?

23. Investment Planning Mr. Jones has $9000 to invest in three types of stocks: low-risk, medium-risk, and high-risk. He invests according to three principles. The amount invested in low-risk stocks will be at most $1000 more than the amount invested in medium-risk stocks. At least $5000 will be invested in low- and medium-risk stocks. No more than $7000 will be invested in medium- and high-risk stocks. The expected yields are 6% for low-risk stocks, 7% for medium-risk stocks, and 8% for high-risk stocks. How much money should Mr. Jones invest in each type of stock to maximize his total expected yield?

24. Shipping—Product Mix A produce dealer in Florida ships oranges, grapefruits, and avocados to New York by truck. Each truckload consists of 100 crates, of which at least 20 crates must be oranges, at least 10 crates must be grapefruits, at least 30 crates must be avocados, and there must be at least as many crates of oranges as grapefruits. The profit per crate is $5 for oranges, $6 for grapefruits, and $4 for avocados. How many crates of each type should be shipped to maximize the profit? [*Hint*: Let x = number of crates of oranges, y = number of crates of grapefruit. Then $100 - x - y$ = number of crates of avocados.]

25. Transportation—Shipping A foreign-car dealer with warehouses in New York and Baltimore receives orders from dealers in Philadelphia and Trenton. The dealer in Philadelphia needs 4 cars and the dealer in Trenton needs 7. The New York warehouse has 6 cars and the Baltimore warehouse has 8. The cost of shipping cars from Baltimore to Philadelphia is $120 per car, from Baltimore to Trenton $90 per car, from New York to Philadelphia $100 per car, and from New York to Trenton $70 per car. Find the number of cars to be shipped from each warehouse to each dealer to minimize the shipping cost. (*Hint*: Let x = number of cars to be shipped from Baltimore to Philadelphia, y = number of cars to be shipped from Baltimore to Trenton, $4 - x$ = number of cars to be shipped from New York to Philadelphia, and $7 - y$ = number of cars to be shipped from New York to Trenton.)

26. Manufacturing—Production Planning An automobile manufacturer has assembly plants in Detroit and Cleveland, each of which can assemble cars and trucks. The Detroit plant can assemble at most 800 vehicles in one day at a cost of $1200 per car and $2100 per truck. The Cleveland plant can assemble at most 500 vehicles in one day at a cost of $1000 per car and $2000 per truck. A rush order is received for 600 cars and 300 trucks. How many vehicles of each type should each plant produce to fill the order at the least cost? (*Hint*: Let x = number of cars to be produced in Detroit, y = number of trucks to be produced in Detroit, $600 - x$ = number of cars to be produced in Cleveland, and $300 - y$ = number of trucks to be produced in Cleveland.)

27. Manufacturing—Production Planning An oil refinery produces gasoline, jet fuel, and diesel fuel. The profits per gallon from the sale of these fuels are $.15, $.12, and $.10, respectively. The refinery has a contract with an airline to deliver a minimum of 20,000 gallons per day of jet fuel and/or gasoline (or some of each). It has a contract with a trucking firm to deliver a minimum of 50,000 gallons per day of diesel fuel and/or gasoline (or some of each). The refinery can produce 100,000 gallons of fuel per day, distributed among the fuels in any fashion. It wishes to produce at least 5000 gallons per day of each fuel. How many gallons of each should be produced to maximize the daily profit?

28. Manufacturing—Production Planning Suppose that a price war reduces the profits of gasoline in Exercise 27 to $.05 per gallon and that the profits on jet fuel and diesel fuel are unchanged. How many gallons of each fuel should now be produced to maximize the profit?

29. Shipping—Resource Allocation A shipping company is buying new trucks. The high-capacity trucks cost $50,000 and hold 320 cases of merchandise. The low-capacity trucks cost $30,000 and hold 200 cases of merchandise. The company has budgeted $1,080,000 for the new trucks and has a maximum of 30 people qualified to drive the trucks. Due to availability limitations, the company can purchase at most 15 high-capacity trucks. How many of each type of truck should the company purchase to maximize the number of cases of merchandise that can be shipped simultaneously?

30. Shipping—Resource Allocation Suppose that the shipping company of Exercise 29 needs to buy enough new trucks to be able to ship 11,200 cases of merchandise. Of course, the company is willing to increase its budget.

(a) How many of each type of truck should the company purchase to minimize cost?

(b) What if the company hires 23 additional qualified drivers?

31. Transportation—Shipping A major coffee supplier has warehouses in Seattle and San José. The coffee supplier receives orders from coffee retailers in Salt Lake City and Reno. The retailer in Salt Lake City needs 400 pounds of coffee, and the retailer in Reno needs 350 pounds of coffee. The Seattle warehouse has 700 pounds available, and the warehouse in San José has 500 pounds available. The cost of shipping from Seattle to Salt Lake City is $2.50 per pound, from Seattle to Reno $3 per pound, from San José to Salt Lake City $4 per pound, and from San José to Reno $2 per pound. Find the number of pounds to be shipped from each warehouse to each retailer to minimize the cost.

32. **Transportation—Shipping** Suppose that the coffee supplier's costs in Exercise 31 change so that the cost of shipping from Seattle to Salt Lake City is $3 per pound, from Seattle to Reno $3 per pound, from San José to Salt Lake City $3.50 per pound, and from San José to Reno $2.50 per pound. How many pounds should be shipped from each warehouse to each retailer to minimize the cost?

33. **Packaging—Product Mix** A pet store sells three different starter kits for 10-gallon aquariums. The following table shows the contents of each kit. The store has 54 filters, 100 pounds of gravel, and 53 packages of fish food available. If the store makes as many of kit I as kits II and III together, how many of each kit should be created to maximize profit?

	Kit I	Kit II	Kit III
Filters	1	2	1
Gravel (pounds)	2	2	3
Fish food (packages)	1	0	2
Profit	$7	$10	$13

34. Refer to Fig. 6 in Example 3. As the lines of constant profit were lowered, the final line had slope $-\frac{8}{7}$ and passed through the optimal vertex of the feasible set. Figure 15 shows that as long as the slope of the final line is between -2 and -1, the optimal solution would still be $(14, 4)$.

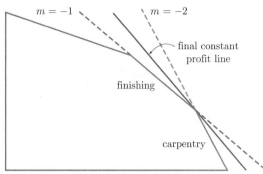

Figure 15

(a) Suppose that the profit per chair is changed from $80 to $$A$, but that the profit per sofa remains at $70. Show that the lines of constant profit will each have slope $-\frac{A}{70}$.

(b) Show that when

$$-2 \le -\frac{A}{70} \le -1,$$

then $70 \le A \le 140$. Conclude that the interval $[70, 140]$ is the range of optimality for the profit per chair.

(c) Use similar reasoning to show that the range of optimality for the profit per sofa is $[40, 80]$.

Exercise 35 requires a spreadsheet.

35. Use an electronic spreadsheet such as Excel to create a sensitivity report for the nutrition problem of Example 1 of Section 3.2. Use the report to determine the range of optimality for the cost of rice and for the cost of soybeans.

Solutions to Practice Problems 3.3

1. Amount invested in bonds $= y$. Five million dollars more than the amount invested in Treasury notes is $x + 5$. Therefore, $y \le x + 5$.

2. Amount invested in stocks $= 30 - (x + y)$.
   Amount invested in bonds $= y$.
   Therefore,
   $$30 - (x + y) + y \le 25$$
   $$30 - x \le 25$$
   $$x \ge 5.$$

3. The feasible set stays the same but the return becomes
   $$[\text{return}] = .08x + .08y + .09[30 - (x + y)]$$
   $$= .08x + .08y + 2.7 - .09x - .09y$$
   $$= 2.7 - .01x - .01y.$$

When the return is evaluated at each of the vertices of the feasible set, the greatest return is achieved at two vertices. Either of these vertices yields an optimal solution.

(x, y)	$2.7 - .01x - .01y$
$(5, 10)$	2.55
$(12, 3)$	2.55
$(24, 3)$	2.43
$(9, 18)$	2.43

(Continued)

4. (a) The values of x and y for which the cost is c dollars satisfy $5x + 10y = c$. The standard form of this linear equation is $y = -\frac{1}{2}x + \frac{c}{10}$.

(b) The line $y = -\frac{1}{2}x + \frac{c}{10}$ has slope $-\frac{1}{2}$ and y-intercept $(0, c/10)$. As c increases, the slope stays the same, but the y-intercept moves up. Therefore, the line moves up.

(c) The line of constant cost \$20 does not contain any points of the feasible set, so such a low cost cannot be achieved. Increase the cost until the line of constant cost just touches the feasible set. As c increases, the line moves up (keeping the same slope) and first touches the feasible set at vertex C. Therefore, taking x and y to be the coordinates of C yields the minimum cost.

CHAPTER SUMMARY

1. A linear programming problem asks us to find the point (or points) in the feasible set of a system of linear inequalities at which the value of a linear expression involving the variables, called the objective function, is either maximized or minimized.

2. The fundamental theorem of linear programming states that the optimal value of the objective function for a linear programming problem occurs at a vertex of the feasible set.

3. To solve a linear programming word problem, assign variables to the unknown quantities, translate the restrictions into a system of linear inequalities involving no more than two variables, form an objective function for the quantity to be optimized, graph the feasible set, determine the vertices of the feasible set, evaluate the objective function at each vertex, and identify the vertex that gives the optimal value.

REVIEW OF FUNDAMENTAL CONCEPTS

1. What is the nature of a linear programming problem?

2. What is the role of the objective function in a linear programming problem?

3. State the fundamental theorem of linear programming.

4. Give the four-step procedure for solving a linear programming problem.

SUPPLEMENTARY EXERCISES

1. **Travel—Resource Allocation** Terrapin Airlines wants to fly 1400 members of a ski club to Colorado. The airline owns two types of planes. Type A can carry 50 passengers, requires 3 flight attendants, and costs \$14,000 for the trip. Type B can carry 300 passengers, requires 4 flight attendants, and costs \$90,000 for the trip. If the airline must use at least as many type A planes as type B and has available only 42 flight attendants, how many planes of each type should be used to minimize the cost for the trip?

2. **Nutrition—People** A nutritionist is designing a new breakfast cereal using wheat germ and enriched oat flour as the basic ingredients. The table below shows the nutritional information and costs per ounce. The nutritionist wants each serving of the cereal to have at least 7 milligrams of niacin, 9 milligrams of iron, and 1 milligram of thiamin. How many ounces of wheat germ and how many ounces of enriched oat flour should be used in each serving to meet the nutritional requirements at the least cost?

	Wheat germ	Oat flour
Niacin	2 mg	3 mg
Iron	3 mg	3 mg
Thiamin	.5 mg	.25 mg
Cost	\$.06	\$.08

3. **Manufacturing—Resource Allocation** An automobile manufacturer makes hardtops and sports cars. The table below shows the labor requirements and profits per automobile. During each day 360 labor-hours are available to assemble, 50 labor-hours to paint, and 40 labor-hours to upholster automobiles. How many hardtops and sports cars should be produced each day to

maximize the total profit?

	Hardtops	Sports cars
Assemble	8 labor-hours	18 labor-hours
Paint	2 labor-hours	2 labor-hours
Upholster	2 labor-hours	1 labor-hours
Profit	$90	$100

4. **Packaging—Product Mix** A confectioner makes two raisin–nut mixtures. A box of mixture A contains 6 ounces of peanuts, 1 ounce of raisins, and 4 ounces of cashews and sells for $4.25. A box of mixture B contains 12 ounces of peanuts, 3 ounces of raisins, and 2 ounces of cashews and sells for $6.55. He has available 5400 ounces of peanuts, 1200 ounces of raisins, and 2400 ounces of cashews. How many boxes of each mixture should he make to maximize revenue?

5. **Publishing—Product Mix** A textbook publisher puts out 72 new books each year, which are classified as elementary, intermediate, and advanced. The company's policy for new books is to publish at least four advanced books, at least three times as many elementary books as intermediate books, and at least twice as many intermediate books as advanced books. On the average, the annual profits are $8000 for each elementary book, $7000 for each intermediate book, and $1000 for each advanced book. How many new books of each type should be published to maximize the annual profit while conforming to company policy?

6. **Shipping—Resource Allocation** A computer company has two manufacturing plants, one in Rochester and one in Queens. Transporting a computer from Rochester to the retail outlet takes 15 hours and costs $15, while transporting a computer from Queens to the retail outlet takes 20 hours and costs $30. The profit on each computer manufactured in Rochester is $40, and the profit on each computer manufactured in Queens is $30. The Rochester plant has 80 computers available, and the Queens plant has 120 computers available. If there are 2100 hours and $3000 allotted for transporting the computers, how many computers should be sent to the retail outlet from each of the two plants to maximize the company's profits?

7. **Transportation—Shipping** An appliance company has two warehouses and two retail outlets. Warehouse A has 400 refrigerators, and warehouse B has 300 refrigerators. Outlet I needs 200 refrigerators, and outlet II needs 300 refrigerators. It costs $36 to ship a refrigerator from warehouse A to outlet I and $30 to ship a refrigerator from warehouse A to outlet II. It costs $30 to ship a refrigerator from warehouse B to outlet I and $25 to ship a refrigerator from warehouse B to outlet II. How should the company ship the refrigerators to minimize the cost?

8. **Investment Planning** Portia has $10,000 to invest. She is considering a certificate of deposit (CD) that is expected to yield 5%, a mutual fund expected to yield 7%, and stocks expected to yield 9%. The amount invested in the mutual fund can be no more than the amount invested in the CD and stocks together. The amount in the mutual fund and stocks must be no more than $8000. How much should Portia invest in each investment vehicle to maximize her total expected yield?

Conceptual Exercises

9. Suppose a constraint is added to a cost minimization problem. Is it possible for the new optimal cost to be greater than the original optimal cost? Is it possible for the new optimal cost to be less than the original optimal cost?

10. Suppose a constraint is removed from a profit maximization problem. Is it possible for the new optimal profit to be greater than the original optimal profit? Is it possible for the new optimal profit to be less than the original optimal profit?

11. Make up a linear programming problem for which the objective function assumes neither a minimum nor a maximum value.

12. Explain why a linear programming problem will always have a solution if the feasible set is bounded.

13. Suppose the maximum value of an objective function occurs at two vertices. Explain why every point on the line segment between the two vertices yields a maximum value of the objective function.

CHAPTER TEST

1. Describe the four main steps for solving a linear programming problem graphically.

2. Determine the objective function and the constraints for the following linear programming problems. *Do not solve the problems.*

   (a) **Manufacturing—Resource Allocation** A video game company makes two types of hockey games at two different manufacturing plants. Plant A can produce 20 type I games and 10 type II games per hour. Plant B can produce 30 type I games and 20 type II games per hour. It costs $70 per hour to operate plant A and $90 per hour to operate Plant B. The company needs 300 type I hockey games and 200 type II hockey games per day. How many hours per day should each plant spend on producing these games in order to meet the company's need and minimize production costs?

(b) **Investment Planning** Mabel plans to invest a total of $500,000 in mutual funds, bonds, and certificates of deposit (CDs). The annual yields for mutual funds, bonds, and CDs are 7%, 6%, and 4.5%, respectively. She wishes to invest at least $150,000 in bonds and no more than $200,000 in CDs. She will invest at least half as much money in mutual funds as she does in bonds. How should she allocate the $500,000 so as to maximize her total annual yield?

3. (a) Graph the feasible set for the following linear programming problem. Maximize $3x + 2y$ subject to the constraints

$$\begin{cases} x + 2y \geq 10 \\ 2x + y \geq 8 \\ x \geq 0, \quad y \geq 0 \end{cases}$$

(b) Does the linear programming problem in part (a) have a solution? Explain.

4. Find the coordinates of the vertices of the following feasible set.

$$\begin{cases} x + y \leq 12 \\ 5x + 7y \leq 70 \\ x \leq 9 \\ x \geq 0, \quad y \geq 0 \end{cases}$$

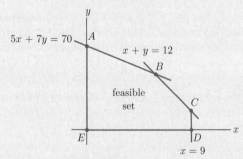

5. For the following feasible set, determine x and y so that the objective function $20x - 10y$ is

(a) maximized

(b) minimized.

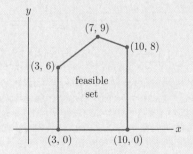

6. Suppose the objective function for a linear programming problem is $[\text{cost}] = 8x + 5y$. The feasible set for the linear programming problem is shown, along with the straight line of all combinations of x and y for which the cost is $3200.

(a) Give the linear equation (in standard form) of the line of constant cost shown in the figure.

(b) Give the linear equation (in standard form) of the line of constant cost c.

(c) As c decreases, does the line of constant cost move up or down?

(d) By inspection, determine the vertex of the feasible set that results in the minimum cost.

7. Consider the feasible set shown, where three of the boundary lines are labeled with their slopes. Find the point at which the objective function $5x + 8y$ has its least value.

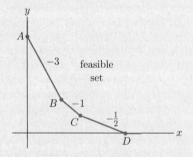

8. **Resource Allocation** A small craft shop makes toy stuffed bears and silk flower wreaths. Each bear requires 3 hours of preparation time, 6 hours of assembly time, and 2 hours of finishing time. Each wreath requires 2 hours of preparation time, 5 hours of assembly time, and 3 hours of finishing time. There are 36 hours of preparation time, 78 hours of assembly time, and 42 hours of finishing time available each week. If each bear earns a profit of $10 and each wreath earns a profit of $8, how many of each should be crafted to maximize the profit?

CHAPTER 3 | PROJECT

Shadow Prices

When a mathematician is presented with a linear programming problem, he or she will not only determine the optimal solution but will also supply what are called **shadow prices** for each constraint. This chapter project develops the concept of a shadow price.

Consider the furniture manufacturing problem. The constraint for finishing is $x + y \leq 18$. The number 18 came from the fact that 18 hours are available for finishing each day. Suppose you could increase the number of hours available for finishing by one hour. The shadow price for the finishing constraint is the maximum price you would be willing to pay for that additional hour.

1. What is the new inequality for the finishing constraint? What is its corresponding linear equation?

2. The figure shows the graph of the original feasible set for the furniture manufacturing problem drawn with a red boundary. The blue line segments show the change in the feasible set when the new finishing constraint is used. Find the coordinates of the points A and B.

3. Determine the optimal solution for the revised linear programming problem. What is the new maximum profit? By how much was the profit increased due to the additional hour for finishing?

4. What is the shadow price for the finishing constraint?

5. Return to the original furniture manufacturing problem and assume that one additional hour is available for carpentry. Solve the altered problem and determine the shadow price for the carpentry constraint.

6. Use your knowledge of the solution of the original furniture manufacturing problem and the definition of shadow price to explain why the shadow price for the upholstery constraint is 0. (*Hint*: No computation is necessary.)

7. Fill in the blanks in the following sentence. The shadow price associated with a constraint can be interpreted as the change in value of the _____ _____ per unit change of the constraint's right-hand-side resource.

SETS AND COUNTING

In this chapter we introduce some ideas useful in the study of probability (Chapter 6). Our first topic, the theory of sets, will provide a convenient language and notation in which to discuss probability. Using set theory, we develop a number of counting principles that can also be applied to computing probabilities.

5.1 Sets

In many applied problems one must consider collections of various sorts of objects. For example, a survey of unemployment might consider the collection of all U.S. cities with current unemployment greater than 7%. A study of birthrates might consider the collection of countries with a current birthrate less than 20 per 1000 population. Such collections are examples of sets. A **set** is any collection of objects. The objects, which may be countries, cities, years, numbers, letters, or anything else, are called the **elements** of the set. A set is often specified by a listing of its elements inside a pair of braces. For example, the set whose elements are the first six letters of the alphabet is written

$$\{a, b, c, d, e, f\}.$$

Similarly, the set whose elements are the even numbers between 1 and 11 is written

$$\{2, 4, 6, 8, 10\}.$$

We can also specify a set by giving a description of its elements (without actually listing the elements). For example, the set $\{a, b, c, d, e, f\}$ can also be written

{the first six letters of the alphabet},

and the set $\{2, 4, 6, 8, 10\}$ can be written

{all even numbers between 1 and 11}.

For convenience, we usually denote sets by capital letters, A, B, C, and so on. The great diversity of sets is illustrated by the following examples.

1. Let $C = \{$possible sequences of outcomes of tossing a coin three times$\}$. If we let H denote "heads" and T denote "tails," the various sequences can be easily described:

$$C = \{\text{HHH}, \text{THH}, \text{HTH}, \text{HHT}, \text{TTH}, \text{THT}, \text{HTT}, \text{TTT}\},$$

where, for instance, THH means "first toss tails, second toss heads, third toss heads."

2. Let $B = \{$license plate numbers consisting of three letters followed by three digits$\}$. Some typical elements of B are

SBG 602, GXZ 179, YHJ 006.

The number of elements in B is sufficiently large so that listing all of them is impractical. However, in this chapter we develop a technique that allows us to calculate the number of elements of B.

3. The graph of the equation $y = x^2$ is the set of all points (a, b) in the plane for which $b = a^2$. This set has infinitely many elements.

Sets arise in many practical contexts, as the next example shows.

EXAMPLE 1

Listing the elements of a set Table 1 gives the rate of inflation, as measured by the percentage change in the consumer price index, for the years from 1988 to 2007. Let

$A = \{$years from 1988 to 2007 in which inflation was above 4%$\}$

$B = \{$years from 1988 to 2007 in which inflation was below 3%$\}$.

Determine the elements of A and B.

Solution By reading Table 1, we see that

$$A = \{1988, 1989, 1990, 1991\}$$

Now Try Exercises 9(a) and (b)

$$B = \{1994, 1995, 1997, 1998, 1999, 2001, 2002, 2003, 2004, 2007\}. \quad \blacksquare$$

Suppose that we are given two sets, A and B. Then it is possible to form new sets from A and B.

DEFINITION **Union and Intersection of Two Sets** The **union** of A and B, written $A \cup B$ and pronounced "A union B," is defined as follows:

$A \cup B$ is the set of all elements that belong to either A or B (or both).

The **intersection** of A and B, written $A \cap B$ and pronounced "A intersection B," is defined as follows:

$A \cap B$ is the set of all elements that belong to both A and B.

TABLE 1

Year	Inflation (%)	Year	Inflation (%)
1988	4.1	1998	1.6
1989	4.8	1999	2.2
1990	5.4	2000	3.4
1991	4.2	2001	2.8
1992	3.0	2002	1.6
1993	3.0	2003	2.3
1994	2.6	2004	2.7
1995	2.8	2005	3.4
1996	3.0	2006	3.2
1997	2.3	2007	2.8

For example, let $A = \{1,2,3,4\}$ and $B = \{1,3,5,7,11\}$. Then

$$A \cup B = \{1,2,3,4,5,7,11\}$$
$$A \cap B = \{1,3\}.$$

EXAMPLE 2

The intersection and union of sets Table 2 on the next page gives the rates of unemployment and inflation for the years from 1994 to 2007. Let

$A = \{$years from 1994 to 2007 in which unemployment is at least 5%$\}$

$B = \{$years from 1994 to 2007 in which the inflation rate is at least 3%$\}$.

(a) Describe the sets $A \cap B$ and $A \cup B$.

(b) Determine the elements of A, B, $A \cap B$, and $A \cup B$.

Solution (a) From the descriptions of A and B, we have

$A \cap B = \{$years from 1994 to 2007 in which unemployment is at least 5% and inflation is at least 3%$\}$

$A \cup B = \{$years from 1994 to 2007 in which either unemployment is at least 5% or inflation is at least 3% (or both)$\}$.

(b) From the table we see that

$$A = \{1994, 1995, 1996, 2002, 2003, 2004, 2005\}$$
$$B = \{1996, 2000, 2005, 2006\}$$
$$A \cap B = \{1996, 2005\}$$

Now Try Exercises 9(c) and (d)

$$A \cup B = \{1994, 1995, 1996, 2000, 2002, 2003, 2004, 2005, 2006\}. \quad\blacksquare$$

We have defined the union and the intersection of two sets. In a similar manner, we can define the union and intersection of any number of sets. For example, if A, B, and C are three sets, then their union, denoted $A \cup B \cup C$, is the set whose elements are precisely those that belong to at least one of the sets A, B, and C. Similarly, the intersection of A, B, and C, denoted $A \cap B \cap C$, is the set consisting of those elements that belong to all the sets A, B, and C. In a similar way, we may define the union and intersection of more than three sets.

Suppose we are given a set A. We may form new sets by selecting elements from A. Sets formed in this way are called *subsets* of A.

TABLE 2		
Year	Unemployment (%)	Inflation (%)
1994	6.1	2.6
1995	5.6	2.8
1996	5.4	3.0
1997	4.9	2.3
1998	4.5	1.6
1999	4.2	2.2
2000	4.0	3.4
2001	4.7	2.8
2002	5.8	1.6
2003	6.0	2.3
2004	5.5	2.7
2005	5.1	3.4
2006	4.6	3.2
2007	4.6	2.8

DEFINITION Subset of a Set The set B is a **subset** of the set A, written $B \subseteq A$ and pronounced "B is a subset of A," provided every element of B is an element of A.

For example, $\{1, 3\} \subseteq \{1, 2, 3\}$.

One set that is considered very often is the set that contains no elements at all. This set is called the **empty set** (or *null set*) and is written $\emptyset$. The empty set is a subset of every set.[1]

EXAMPLE 3

Listing the subsets of a set Let $A = \{a, b, c\}$. Find all subsets of A.

Solution Since A contains three elements, every subset of A has at most three elements. We look for subsets according to the number of elements:

Number of elements in subset	Possible subsets
0	$\emptyset$
1	$\{a\}, \{b\}, \{c\}$
2	$\{a, b\}, \{a, c\}, \{b, c\}$
3	$\{a, b, c\}$

Thus we see that A has eight subsets, namely those listed on the right. (Note that we count A as a subset of itself.)

Now Try Exercise 5

It is usually convenient to regard all sets involved in a particular discussion as subsets of a single larger set. Thus, for example, if a problem involves the sets $\{a, b, c\}, \{e, f\}, \{g\}, \{b, x, y\}$, then we can regard all of these as subsets of the set

$$U = \{\text{all letters of the alphabet}\}.$$

---

[1]Here is why: Let A be any set. Every element of $\emptyset$ also belongs to A. If you do not agree, then you must produce an element of $\emptyset$ that does not belong to A. But you cannot, since $\emptyset$ has no elements. So $\emptyset \subseteq A$.

Since U contains all elements being discussed, it is called a **universal set** (for the particular problem). In this book we shall specify the particular universal set we have in mind or it will be clearly defined by the context.

The set A contained in the universal set U has a counterpart, called its complement.

DEFINITION Complement of a Set The **complement** of A, written A' and pronounced "A complement," is defined as follows:

A' is the set of all elements in the universal set U that do not belong to A.

For example, let $U = \{1, 2, 3, 4, 5, 6, 7, 8, 9\}$ and $A = \{2, 4, 6, 8\}$. Then

$$A' = \{1, 3, 5, 7, 9\}.$$

EXAMPLE 4

Finding the complement of a set Let $U = \{a, b, c, d, e, f, g\}$, $S = \{a, b, c\}$, and $T = \{a, c, d\}$. List the elements of the following sets.

(a) S' (b) T' (c) $(S \cap T)'$ (d) $S' \cap T'$ (e) $S' \cup T'$

Solution (a) S' consists of those elements of U that are not in S, so $S' = \{d, e, f, g\}$.

(b) Similarly, $T' = \{b, e, f, g\}$.

(c) To determine $(S \cap T)'$, we must first determine $S \cap T$:

$$S \cap T = \{a, c\}.$$

Then we determine the complement of this set:

$$(S \cap T)' = \{b, d, e, f, g\}.$$

(d) We determined S' and T' in parts (a) and (b). The set $S' \cap T'$ consists of the elements that belong to both S' and T'. Therefore, referring to parts (a) and (b), we have

$$S' \cap T' = \{e, f, g\}.$$

(e) Since $S' \cup T'$ consists of the elements that belong to S' or T' (or both),

Now Try Exercises 9(e) and (f)

$$S' \cup T' = \{b, d, e, f, g\}. \qquad \blacksquare$$

NOTE ▶ The results of parts (c) and (d) show that in general $(S \cap T)'$ *is not* the same as $S' \cap T'$. In the next section, we show that $(S \cap T)'$ *is* the same as $S' \cup T'$. ∎

The Greek letter $\in$ (epsilon) is commonly used with sets as a shorthand for "is an element of." For instance, if $S = \{\text{H}, \text{T}\}$, then $\text{H} \in S$. The letter $\in$ should not be confused with the symbol $\subseteq$. For instance, $\text{H} \in S$, but $\{\text{H}\} \subseteq S$. The symbol $\notin$ is shorthand for "is not an element of." The letter $\in$ can be used to define union, intersection, complement, and subset.

DEFINITION

$A \cup B$ is the set of all x such that $x \in A$ or $x \in B$.

$A \cap B$ is the set of all x such that $x \in A$ and $x \in B$.

A' is the set of all $x \in U$ such that $x \notin A$.

$B \subseteq A$ if $x \in A$ whenever $x \in B$.

Practice Problems 5.1

1. Let $U = \{a, b, c, d, e, f, g\}$, $R = \{a, b, c, d\}$, $S = \{c, d, e\}$, and $T = \{c, e, g\}$. List the elements of the following sets.

   (a) R' (b) $R \cap S$

   (c) $(R \cap S) \cap T$ (d) $R \cap (S \cap T)$

2. Let $U = \{$all Nobel Prize winners$\}$, $W = \{$women

   who have won Nobel Prizes$\}$, $A = \{$Americans who have won Nobel Prizes$\}$, $L = \{$winners of the Nobel Prize in literature$\}$. Describe the following sets.

   (a) W' (b) $A \cap L'$ (c) $W \cap A \cap L'$

3. Refer to Problem 2. Use set-theoretic notation to describe $\{$Nobel Prize winners who are American men or recipients of the Nobel Prize in literature$\}$.

EXERCISES 5.1

1. Let $U = \{1, 2, 3, 4, 5, 6, 7\}$, $S = \{1, 2, 3, 4\}$, and $T = \{1, 3, 5, 7\}$. List the elements of the following sets.
   (a) S' (b) $S \cup T$ (c) $S \cap T$ (d) $S' \cap T$

2. Let $U = \{1, 2, 3, 4, 5\}$, $S = \{1, 2, 3\}$, and $T = \{5\}$. List the elements of the following sets.
   (a) S' (b) $S \cup T$ (c) $S \cap T$ (d) $S' \cap T$

3. Let $U = \{$all letters of the alphabet$\}$, $R = \{a, b, c\}$, $S = \{c, d, e, f\}$, and $T = \{x, y, z\}$. List the elements of the following sets.
   (a) $R \cup S$ (b) $R \cap S$ (c) $S \cap T$

4. Let $U = \{a, b, c, d, e, f, g\}$, $R = \{a\}$, $S = \{a, b\}$, and $T = \{b, d, e, f, g\}$. List the elements of the following sets.
   (a) $R \cup S$ (b) $R \cap S$ (c) T' (d) $T' \cup S$

5. List all subsets of the set $\{1, 2\}$.

6. List all subsets of the set $\{1\}$.

7. **College Students** Let $U = \{$all college students$\}$, $M = \{$all male college students$\}$, and $F = \{$all college students who like football$\}$. Describe the elements of the following sets.
   (a) $M \cap F$ (b) M' (c) $M' \cap F'$ (d) $M \cup F$

8. **Corporations** Let $U = \{$all corporations$\}$, $S = \{$all corporations with headquarters in New York City$\}$, and $T = \{$all privately owned corporations$\}$. Describe the elements of the following sets.
   (a) S' (b) T' (c) $S \cap T$ (d) $S \cap T'$

9. **S&P Index** The Standard and Poor's Index measures the price of a certain collection of 500 stocks. Table 3 compares the percentage change in the index during the first 5 business days of certain years with the percentage change for the entire year. Let $U = \{$all years from 1980 to 2007$\}$, $S = \{$all years during which the index increased by 2% or more during the first 5 days$\}$, and $T = \{$all years for which the index increased by 16% or more during the entire year$\}$. List the elements of the following sets.
   (a) S (b) T (c) $S \cap T$
   (d) $S \cup T$ (e) $S' \cap T$ (f) $S \cap T'$

10. **S&P Index** Refer to Table 3. Let $U = \{$all years from 1980 to 2007$\}$, $A = \{$all years during which the index declined during the first 5 days$\}$, and $B = \{$all years during which the index declined for the entire year$\}$. List the elements of the following sets.
    (a) A (b) B (c) $A \cap B$
    (d) $A' \cap B$ (e) $A \cap B'$

11. **S&P Index** Refer to Exercise 9. Describe verbally the fact that $S \cap T'$ has three elements.

12. **S&P Index** Refer to Exercise 10. Describe verbally the fact that $A \cap B'$ has nine elements.

13. Let $U = \{a, b, c, d, e, f\}$, $R = \{a, b, c\}$, $S = \{a, c, e\}$, and $T = \{e, f\}$. List the elements of the following sets.
    (a) $(R \cup S)'$ (b) $R \cup S \cup T$
    (c) $R \cap S \cap T$ (d) $R \cap S \cap T'$
    (e) $R' \cap S \cap T$ (f) $S \cup T$
    (g) $(R \cup S) \cap (R \cup T)$
    (h) $(R \cap S) \cup (R \cap T)$
    (i) $R' \cap T'$

14. Let $U = \{1, 2, 3, 4, 5\}$, $R = \{1, 3, 5\}$, $S = \{3, 4, 5\}$, and $T = \{2, 4\}$. List the elements of the following sets.
    (a) $R \cap S \cap T$ (b) $R \cap S \cap T'$ (c) $R \cap S' \cap T$
    (d) $R' \cap T$ (e) $R \cup S$ (f) $R' \cup R$
    (g) $(S \cap T)'$ (h) $S' \cup T'$

In Exercises 15–20, simplify the given expression.

15. $(S')'$ 16. $S \cap S'$ 17. $S \cup S'$
18. $S \cap \varnothing$ 19. $T \cap S \cap T'$ 20. $S \cup \varnothing$

Corporation *A large corporation classifies its many divisions by their performance in the preceding year. Let $P = \{$divisions that made a profit$\}$, $L = \{$divisions that had an increase in labor costs$\}$, and $T = \{$divisions whose total revenue increased$\}$. Describe the sets in Exercises 21–26 using set-theoretic notation.*

21. $\{$divisions that had increases in labor costs or total revenue$\}$

22. $\{$divisions that did not make a profit$\}$

TABLE 3 Percentage change in the Standard and Poor's index

Year	Percent change for first 5 days	Percent change for year	Year	Percent change for first 5 days	Percent change for year
2007	-0.4	3.5	1993	-1.5	7.1
2006	3.0	13.6	1992	0.2	4.5
2005	-2.1	3.0	1991	-4.6	26.3
2004	1.8	9.0	1990	0.1	-6.6
2003	3.4	26.4	1989	1.2	27.3
2002	1.1	-23.4	1988	-1.5	12.4
2001	-1.9	-13.0	1987	6.2	2.0
2000	-1.9	-10.1	1986	-1.6	14.6
1999	3.7	19.5	1985	-1.9	26.3
1998	-1.5	26.7	1984	2.4	1.4
1997	1.0	31.0	1983	3.3	17.3
1996	0.4	20.3	1982	-2.4	14.8
1995	0.3	34.1	1981	-2.0	-9.7
1994	0.7	-1.5	1980	0.9	25.8

23. {divisions that made a profit despite an increase in labor costs}

24. {divisions that had an increase in labor costs and either were unprofitable or did not increase their total revenue}

25. {profitable divisions with increases in labor costs and total revenue}

26. {divisions that were unprofitable or did not have increases in either labor costs or total revenue}

Automobile Insurance *An automobile insurance company classifies applicants by their driving records for the previous three years. Let $S = \{$applicants who have received speeding tickets$\}$, $A = \{$applicants who have caused accidents$\}$, and $D = \{$applicants who have been arrested for driving while intoxicated$\}$. Describe the sets in Exercises 27–32 using set-theoretic notation.*

27. {applicants who have not received speeding tickets}

28. {applicants who have caused accidents and been arrested for drunk driving}

29. {applicants who have received speeding tickets, caused accidents, or been arrested for drunk driving}

30. {applicants who have not been arrested for drunk driving but have received speeding tickets or have caused accidents}

31. {applicants who have not both caused accidents and received speeding tickets but who have been arrested for drunk driving}

32. {applicants who have not caused accidents or have not been arrested for drunk driving}

College Teachers and Students *Let $U = \{$people at Mount College$\}$, $A = \{$students at Mount College$\}$, $B = \{$teachers*
at Mount College$\}$, $C = \{$females at Mount College$\}$, and $D = \{$males at Mount College$\}$. Describe verbally the sets in Exercises 33–40.*

33. $A \cap D$ **34.** $B \cap C$ **35.** $A \cap B$ **36.** $B \cup C$

37. $A \cup C'$ **38.** $(A \cap D)'$ **39.** D' **40.** $D \cap U$

Ice Cream Preferences *Let $U = \{$all people$\}$, $S = \{$people who like strawberry ice cream$\}$, $V = \{$people who like vanilla ice cream$\}$, and $C = \{$people who like chocolate ice cream$\}$. Describe the sets in Exercises 41–46 using set-theoretic notation.*

41. {people who don't like strawberry ice cream}

42. {people who like vanilla but not chocolate ice cream}

43. {people who like vanilla or chocolate but not strawberry ice cream}

44. {people who don't like any of the three flavors of ice cream}

45. {people who like neither chocolate nor vanilla ice cream}

46. {people who like only strawberry ice cream}

47. Let U be the set of vertices in Fig. 1 on the next page. Let $R = \{$vertices (x, y) with $x > 0\}$, $S = \{$vertices (x, y) with $y > 0\}$, and $T = \{$vertices (x, y) with $x \leq y\}$. List the elements of the following sets.

  (a) R **(b)** S **(c)** T

  (d) $R' \cup S$ **(e)** $R' \cap T$ **(f)** $R \cap S \cap T$

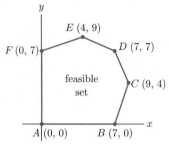

Figure 1

48. **Topping Choices** Sam ordered a baked potato at a restaurant. The waitress offered him butter, cheese, and chives as toppings. How many different ways could he have his potato? List them.

49. Let $S = \{1, 3, 5, 7\}$ and $T = \{2, 5, 7\}$. Give an example of a subset of T that is not a subset of S.

50. Suppose that S and T are subsets of the set U. Under what circumstance will $S \cap T = T$?

51. Suppose that S and T are subsets of the set U. Under what circumstance will $S \cup T = T$?

52. Find three subsets of the set of integers from 1 through 10, R, S, and T, such that $R \cup (S \cap T)$ is different from $(R \cup S) \cap T$.

In Exercises 53–60, determine if the statement is true or false.

53. $5 \in \{3, 5, 7\}$ 54. $\{1, 3\} \subseteq \{1, 2, 3\}$
55. $\{b\} \subseteq \{b, c\}$ 56. $0 \in \{1, 2, 3\}$
57. $0 \in \emptyset$ 58. $\emptyset \subseteq \{a, b, c\}$
59. $\{b, c\} \subseteq \{b, c\}$ 60. $1 \notin \{1\}$

Solutions to Practice Problems 5.1

1. (a) $\{e, f, g\}$ (b) $\{c, d\}$

   (c) $\{c\}$. This problem asks for the intersection of two sets. The first set is $R \cap S = \{c, d\}$ and the second set is $T = \{c, e, g\}$. The intersection of these sets is $\{c\}$.

   (d) $\{c\}$. Here again the problem asks for the intersection of two sets. However, now the first set is $R = \{a, b, c, d\}$ and the second set is $S \cap T = \{c, e\}$. The intersection of these sets is $\{c\}$.

   [*Note:* It should be expected that the set $(R \cap S) \cap T$ is the same as the set $R \cap (S \cap T)$, for each set consists of those elements that are in all three sets. Therefore, each of these sets equals the set $R \cap S \cap T$.]

2. (a) $W' = \{$men who have won Nobel Prizes$\}$. This is so since W' consists of those elements of U that are not in W—that is, those Nobel Prize winners who are not women.

   (b) $A \cap L' = \{$Americans who have received Nobel Prizes in fields other than literature$\}$.

   (c) $W \cap A \cap L' = \{$American women who have received Nobel Prizes in fields other than literature$\}$. This is so since to qualify for $W \cap A \cap L'$, a Nobel Prize winner must simultaneously be in W, in A, and in L'—that is, a woman, an American, and not a winner of the Nobel Prize in literature.

3. $(A \cap W') \cup L$

5.2 A Fundamental Principle of Counting

A counting problem is one that requires us to determine the number of elements in a set S. Counting problems arise in many applications of mathematics and comprise the mathematical field of **combinatorics**. We shall study a number of different sorts of counting problems in the remainder of this chapter.

If S is any set, we will denote the number of elements in S by $n(S)$. For example, if $S = \{1, 7, 11\}$, then $n(S) = 3$, and if $S = \{a, b, c, d, e, f, g, h, i\}$, then $n(S) = 9$. Of course, if $S = \emptyset$, the empty set, then $n(S) = 0$. (The empty set contains no elements.)

Let us begin by stating one of the fundamental principles of counting, the *inclusion–exclusion principle*.

Inclusion–Exclusion Principle   Let S and T be sets. Then
$$n(S \cup T) = n(S) + n(T) - n(S \cap T). \qquad (1)$$

Notice that formula (1) connects the four quantities $n(S \cup T)$, $n(S)$, $n(T)$, and $n(S \cap T)$. Given any three, the remaining quantity can be determined by using this formula.

To test the plausibility of the inclusion–exclusion principle, consider this example. Let $S = \{a, b, c, d, e\}$ and $T = \{a, c, g, h\}$. Then

$$S \cup T = \{a, b, c, d, e, g, h\} \qquad n(S \cup T) = 7$$
$$S \cap T = \{a, c\} \qquad n(S \cap T) = 2.$$

In this case the inclusion–exclusion principle reads

$$n(S \cup T) = n(S) + n(T) - n(S \cap T)$$
$$7 \quad = \quad 5 \quad + \quad 4 \quad - \quad 2,$$

which is correct.

Here is the reason for the validity of the inclusion–exclusion principle: The left side of formula (1) is $n(S \cup T)$, the number of elements in either S or T (or both). As a first approximation to this number, add the number of elements in S to the number of elements in T, obtaining $n(S) + n(T)$. However, if an element lies in both S and T, it is counted twice—once in $n(S)$ and again in $n(T)$. To make up for this double counting we must subtract the number of elements counted twice, namely $n(S \cap T)$. So doing gives us $n(S) + n(T) - n(S \cap T)$ as the number of elements in $S \cup T$.

When S and T have no elements in common, the inclusion–exclusion principle reduces to a simple sum.

Special Case of the Inclusion–Exclusion Principle   If $S \cap T = \emptyset$, then
$$n(S \cup T) = n(S) + n(T).$$

The next example illustrates a typical use of the inclusion–exclusion principle in an applied problem.

EXAMPLE 1

Using the inclusion–exclusion principle   In the year 2007, *Executive* magazine surveyed the presidents of the 500 largest corporations in the United States. Of these 500 people, 310 had degrees (of any sort) in business, 238 had undergraduate degrees in business, and 184 had graduate degrees in business. How many presidents had both undergraduate and graduate degrees in business?

Solution Let

$$S = \{\text{presidents with an undergraduate degree in business}\}$$
$$T = \{\text{presidents with a graduate degree in business}\}.$$

Then

$$S \cup T = \{\text{presidents with at least one degree in business}\}$$
$$S \cap T = \{\text{presidents with both undergraduate and graduate degrees in business}\}.$$

From the data given we have

$$n(S) = 238 \qquad n(T) = 184 \qquad n(S \cup T) = 310.$$

The problem asks for $n(S \cap T)$. By the inclusion–exclusion principle we have

$$n(S \cup T) = n(S) + n(T) - n(S \cap T)$$

$$310 = 238 + 184 - n(S \cap T)$$

$$n(S \cap T) = 112.$$

That is, exactly 112 of the presidents had both undergraduate and graduate degrees
in business.

Now Try Exercise 9

It is possible to visualize sets geometrically by means of drawings known as
Venn diagrams. Such graphical representations of sets are very useful tools in
solving counting problems. In order to describe Venn diagrams, let us begin with a
single set S contained in a universal set U. Draw a rectangle and view its points as
the elements of U [Fig. 1(a)]. To show that S is a subset of U, we draw a circle inside
the rectangle and view S as the set of points in the circle [Fig. 1(b)]. The resulting
diagram is called a Venn diagram of S. It illustrates the proper relationship between
S and U. Since S' consists of those elements of U that are not in S, we may view
the portion of the rectangle that is outside of the circle as representing S' [Fig. 1(c)].

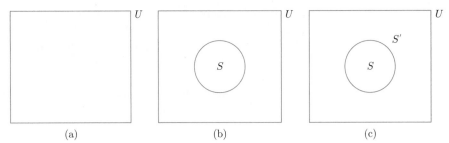

(a)   (b)   (c)

Figure 1

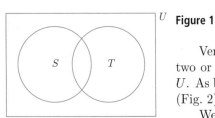

Figure 2

Venn diagrams are particularly useful for visualizing the relationship between
two or three sets. Suppose that we are given two sets S and T in a universal set
U. As before, we represent each of the sets by means of a circle inside the rectangle
(Fig. 2).

We can now illustrate a number of sets by shading in appropriate regions of the
rectangle. For instance, in Fig. 3 we have shaded the regions corresponding to T,
$S \cup T$, and $S \cap T$, respectively.

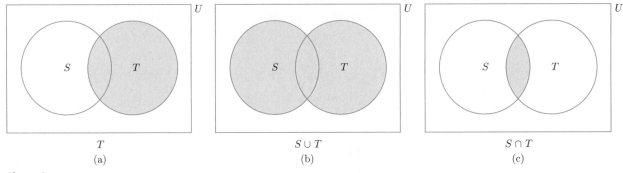

T $S \cup T$ $S \cap T$

(a)   (b)   (c)

Figure 3

EXAMPLE 2

Shading portions of a Venn diagram Shade the portions of the rectangle corresponding to the sets

(a) $S \cap T'$ **(b)** $(S \cap T')'$

Solution **(a)** $S \cap T'$ consists of the points in S and in T', that is, the points in S and not in T. So we shade the points that are in the circle S but are not in the circle T [Fig. 4(a)].

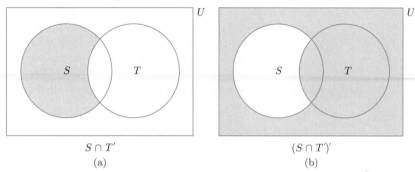

Figure 4

$S \cap T'$
(a)

$(S \cap T')'$
(b)

(b) $(S \cap T')'$ is the complement of the set $S \cap T'$. Therefore, it consists of exactly those points not shaded in Fig. 4(a). [See Fig. 4(b).]

Now Try Exercises 15 and 19

In a similar manner, Venn diagrams can illustrate intersections and unions of three sets. Some representative regions are shaded in Fig. 5.

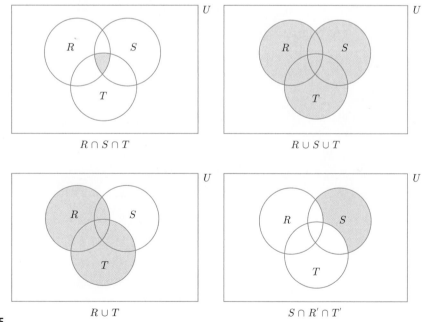

$R \cap S \cap T$

$R \cup S \cup T$

$R \cup T$

$S \cap R' \cap T'$

Figure 5

There are many formulas expressing relationships between intersections and unions of sets. Possibly the most fundamental are the two formulas known as *De Morgan's laws*.

De Morgan's Laws   Let S and T be sets. Then

$$(S \cup T)' = S' \cap T' \quad \text{and} \quad (S \cap T)' = S' \cup T'. \tag{2}$$

In other words, De Morgan's laws state that to form the complement of a union (or intersection), form the complements of the individual sets and change unions to intersections (or intersections to unions).

Verification of De Morgan's Laws   Let us use Venn diagrams to describe $(S \cup T)'$. In Fig. 6(a) we have shaded the region corresponding to $S \cup T$. In Fig. 6(b) we have shaded the region corresponding to $(S \cup T)'$. On the other hand, in Fig. 6(c) we have shaded the region corresponding to S' and in Fig. 6(d) the region corresponding to T'. By considering the common shaded regions of Fig. 6(c) and (d), we arrive at the shaded region corresponding to $S' \cap T'$ [Fig. 6(e)]. Note that this is the same region as shaded in Fig. 6(b). Therefore,

$$(S \cup T)' = S' \cap T'.$$

This verifies the first of De Morgan's laws. The proof of the second law is similar.   ■

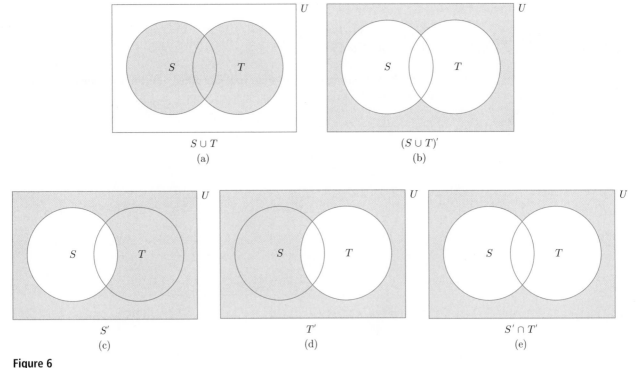

Figure 6

Practice Problems 5.2

1. Draw a two-circle Venn diagram and shade the portion corresponding to the set $(S \cap T') \cup (S \cap T)$.

2. What does the inclusion–exclusion principle conclude when T is a subset of S?

EXERCISES 5.2

1. Find $n(S \cup T)$, given that $n(S) = 5$, $n(T) = 4$, and $n(S \cap T) = 2$.

2. Find $n(S \cup T)$, given that $n(S) = 17$, $n(T) = 13$, and $n(S \cap T) = 9$.

3. Find $n(S \cap T)$, given that $n(S) = 7$, $n(T) = 8$, and $n(S \cup T) = 15$.

4. Find $n(S \cap T)$, given that $n(S) = 4$, $n(T) = 12$, and $n(S \cup T) = 15$.

5. Find $n(S)$, given that $n(T) = 7$, $n(S \cap T) = 5$, and $n(S \cup T) = 13$.

6. Find $n(T)$, given that $n(S) = 14$, $n(S \cap T) = 6$, and $n(S \cup T) = 14$.

7. If $n(S) = n(S \cap T)$, what can you conclude about S and T?

8. If $n(S) = n(S \cup T)$, what can you conclude about S and T?

9. **Languages** Suppose that each of the 245 million adults in South America is fluent in Portuguese or Spanish. If 134 million are fluent in Portuguese and 130 million are fluent in Spanish, how many are fluent in both languages?

10. **Course Enrollments** Suppose that all of the 1000 first-year students at a certain college are enrolled in a math or an English course. Suppose that 400 are taking both math and English and 600 are taking English. How many are taking a math course?

11. **Symmetry of Letters** Of the 26 capital letters of the alphabet, 11 have vertical symmetry (for instance, A, M, and T), 9 have horizontal symmetry (such as B, C, and D), and 4 have both (H, I, O, X). How many letters have no symmetry?

12. **Magazine Subscriptions** A survey of employees in a certain company revealed that 300 people subscribe to *Newsweek*, 200 subscribe to *Time*, and 50 subscribe to both. How many people subscribe to at least one of these magazines?

13. **Automobile Options** Motors Inc. manufactured 325 cars with automatic transmissions, 216 with power steering, and 89 with both of these options. How many cars were manufactured with at least one of the two options?

14. **Investments** A survey of 100 investors in stocks and bonds revealed that 80 investors owned stocks and 70 owned bonds. How many investors owned both stocks and bonds?

In Exercises 15–26, draw a two-circle Venn diagram and shade the portion corresponding to the set.

15. $S' \cap T$

16. $S' \cap T'$

17. $S \cup T'$

18. $S' \cup T'$

19. $(S' \cap T)'$

20. $(S \cap T)'$

21. $(S \cap T') \cup (S' \cap T)$

22. $(S \cap T) \cup (S' \cap T')$

23. $S \cup (S \cap T)$

24. $S \cup (T' \cup S)$

25. $S \cup S'$

26. $S \cap S'$

In Exercises 27–38, draw a three-circle Venn diagram and shade the portion corresponding to the set.

27. $R \cap S \cap T'$

28. $R' \cap S' \cap T$

29. $R \cup (S \cap T)$

30. $R \cap (S \cup T)$

31. $R \cap (S' \cup T)$

32. $R' \cup (S \cap T')$

33. $R \cap T$

34. $S \cap T'$

35. $R' \cap S' \cap T'$

36. $(R \cup S \cup T)'$

37. $(R \cap T) \cup (S \cap T')$

38. $(R \cup S') \cap (R \cup T')$

In Exercises 39–44, use De Morgan's laws to simplify the given expression.

39. $S' \cup (S \cap T)'$

40. $T \cap (S \cup T)'$

41. $(S' \cup T)'$

42. $(S' \cap T')'$

43. $T \cup (S \cap T)'$

44. $(S' \cap T)' \cup S$

In Exercises 45–50, give a set-theoretic expression that describes the shaded portion of the Venn diagram.

45.

46.

47.

48.

49.

50.
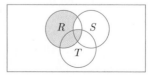

By drawing a Venn diagram, replace each of the expressions in Exercises 51–53 with one involving at most one union and the complement symbol applied only to R, S, and T.

51. $(T \cap S) \cup (T \cap R) \cup (R \cap S') \cup (T \cap R' \cap S')$
52. $(R \cap S) \cup (S \cap T) \cup (R \cap S' \cap T')$
53. $((R \cap S') \cup (S \cap T') \cup (T \cap R'))'$

Citizenship *Assume the universal set U is the set of all people living in the United States. Let A be the set of all citizens, B be the set of all legal aliens, and C be the set of all illegal aliens. Let D be the set of all children under 5 years of age, E be the set of children from 5 to 18 years old, and F be the set of everyone over the age of 18. Let G be the set of all people who are employed. Describe in words the sets in Exercises 54–59.*

54. $E \cap G \cap B$ **55.** $C' \cup (G \cap F)$ **56.** $A \cap (F \cup G)$

57. $F \cap G'$ **58.** $A \cap B$ **59.** $(A' \cup B) \cap G'$

Solutions to Practice Problems 5.2

1. $(S \cap T') \cup (S \cap T)$ is given as a union of two sets, $S \cap T'$ and $S \cap T$. The Venn diagrams for these two sets are given in Fig. 7(a) and (b). The desired set consists of the elements that are in one or the other (or both) of the two sets. Therefore, its Venn diagram is obtained by shading everything that is shaded in either Fig. 7(a) or (b) [see Fig. 7(c)]. [*Note:* Looking at Fig. 7(c) reveals that $(S \cap T') \cup (S \cap T)$ and S are the same set. Often Venn diagrams can be used to simplify complicated set-theoretic expressions.]

2. Not much. When $T \subseteq S$, $S \cup T = S$ and $S \cap T = T$. The inclusion–exclusion principle becomes

$$n(S \cup T) = n(S) + n(T) - n(S \cap T)$$
$$n(S) = n(S) + n(T) - n(T)$$
$$n(S) = n(S)$$

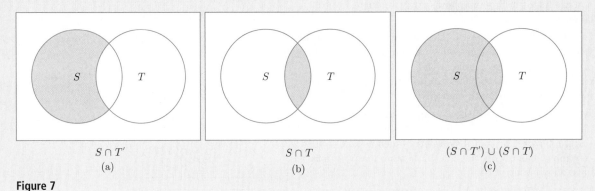

$$S \cap T'$$
(a)

$$S \cap T$$
(b)

$$(S \cap T') \cup (S \cap T)$$
(c)

Figure 7

5.3 Venn Diagrams and Counting

In this section we discuss the use of Venn diagrams in solving counting problems. The techniques developed are especially useful in analyzing survey data.

Each Venn diagram divides the universal set U into a certain number of regions. For example, the Venn diagram for a single set divides U into two regions—the inside and outside of the circle [Fig. 1(a)]. The Venn diagram for two sets divides U into four regions [Fig. 1(b)]. And the Venn diagram for three sets divides U into eight regions [Fig. 1(c)]. Each of the regions is called a **basic region** for the Venn diagram. Knowing the number of elements in each basic region is of great use in many applied problems. As an illustration consider the following example.

(a)

(b)

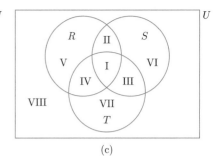
(c)

Figure 1

EXAMPLE 1   **Nobel prize laureates** Let

$$U = \{\text{Nobel Prize laureates during the period 1901–2007}\}$$
$$A = \{\text{American Nobel Prize laureates during the period 1901–2007}\}$$
$$C = \{\text{Chemistry Nobel Prize laureates during the period 1901–2007}\}$$
$$P = \{\text{Nobel Peace Prize laureates during the period 1901–2007}\}.$$

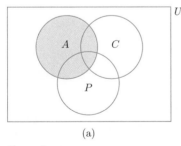

Figure 2

These sets are illustrated in the Venn diagram of Fig. 2 in which each basic region has been labeled with the number of elements in it.

(a) How many Americans received a Nobel Prize during the period 1901–2007?

(b) How many Americans received Nobel Prizes in fields other than chemistry and peace during this period?

(c) How many Americans received the Nobel Peace Prize during this period?

(d) How many people received Nobel Prizes during this period?

Solution (a) The number of Americans who received a Nobel Prize is the total contained in the circle A, which is

$$223 + 25 + 1 + 56 = 305 \quad [\text{Fig. 3(a)}].$$

(a)

(b)

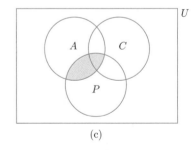
(c)

Figure 3

(b) The question asks for the number of Nobel laureates in A but not in C and not in P. So start with the A circle and eliminate those basic regions belonging to C or P [Fig. 3(b)]. There remains a single basic region with 223 Nobel laureates. Note that this region corresponds to $A \cap C' \cap P'$.

(c) The question asks for the number of elements in both A and P—that is, $n(A \cap P)$. But $A \cap P$ comprises two basic regions [Fig. 3(c)]. Thus, to compute $n(A \cap P)$ we add the numbers in these basic regions to obtain $25 + 1 = 26$ Americans who have received the Nobel Peace Prize.

(d) The number of recipients is just $n(U)$, and we obtain it by adding together the numbers corresponding to the basic regions. We obtain

$$310 + 223 + 56 + 1 + 25 + 93 + 0 + 89 = 797.$$

One need not always be given the number of elements in each of the basic regions of a Venn diagram. Very often these data can be deduced from given information.

EXAMPLE 2

Corporate presidents Consider the set of 500 corporate presidents of Example 1, Section 5.2.

(a) Draw a Venn diagram displaying the given data, and determine the number of elements in each basic region.

(b) Determine the number of presidents having exactly one degree (graduate or undergraduate) in business.

Solution **(a)** Recall that we defined the following sets:

$$S = \{\text{presidents with an undergraduate degree in business}\}$$
$$T = \{\text{presidents with a graduate degree in business}\}.$$

We were given the following data:

$$n(S) = 238 \qquad n(T) = 184 \qquad n(S \cup T) = 310.$$

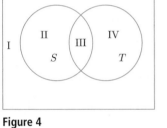

Figure 4

We draw a Venn diagram corresponding to S and T (Fig. 4). Notice that none of the given information corresponds to a basic region of the Venn diagram. So we must use our wits to determine the number of presidents in each of the regions I–IV. Region I is the complement of $S \cup T$, so it contains

$$n(U) - n(S \cup T) = 500 - 310 = 190$$

presidents. Region III is just $S \cap T$. By using the inclusion–exclusion principle, in Example 1, Section 5.2, we determined that $n(S \cap T) = 112$. Now the total number of presidents in II and III combined equals $n(S)$, or 238. Therefore, the number of presidents in II is

$$238 - 112 = 126.$$

Similarly, the number of presidents in IV is

$$184 - 112 = 72.$$

Thus we may fill in the data to obtain a completed Venn diagram (Fig. 5).

Figure 5

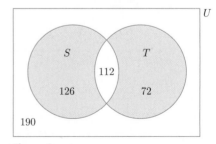

Figure 6

(b) The number of people with exactly one business degree corresponds to the shaded region in Fig. 6. Adding together the number of presidents in each of these regions gives $126 + 72 = 198$ presidents with exactly one business degree.

Now Try Exercise 23

Here is another example illustrating the procedure for determining the number of elements in each of the basic regions of a Venn diagram.

EXAMPLE 3

Advertising media   An advertising agency finds that the media use of its 170 clients is as follows:

115 use television (T) 95 use radio and magazines
100 use radio (R) 85 use television and magazines
130 use magazines (M) 70 use all three.
75 use television and radio

Use these data to complete the Venn diagram in Fig. 7 to display the clients' use of mass media.

Solution   Of the various data given, only the last item corresponds to one of the eight basic regions of the Venn diagram, namely the "70" corresponding to the use of all three media. So we begin by entering this number in the diagram [Fig. 8(a)]. We can fill in the rest of the Venn diagram by working with the remaining information one piece at a time in the reverse order that it is given. Since 85 clients advertise in television and magazines, $85 - 70 = 15$ advertise in television and magazines but not on radio. The appropriate region is labeled in Fig. 8(b). In Fig. 8(c) the next two pieces of information have been used in the same way to fill in two more basic regions. In Fig. 8(c) we observe that three of the four basic regions comprising M have been filled in. Since $n(M) = 130$, we deduce that the number of clients advertising only in magazines is $130 - (15 + 70 + 25) = 130 - 110 = 20$ [Fig. 9(a)]. By similar reasoning the number of clients using only radio advertising and the number using only television advertising can be determined [Fig. 9(b)]. Adding together the numbers in the three circles gives the number of clients utilizing television, radio, or magazines as $25 + 5 + 0 + 15 + 70 + 25 + 20 = 160$. Since there were 170 clients in total, the remainder—or $170 - 160 = 10$ clients—use none of these media. Figure 9(c) gives a complete display of the data. ∎

$n(U) = 170$

Figure 7

Now Try Exercise 31(a)

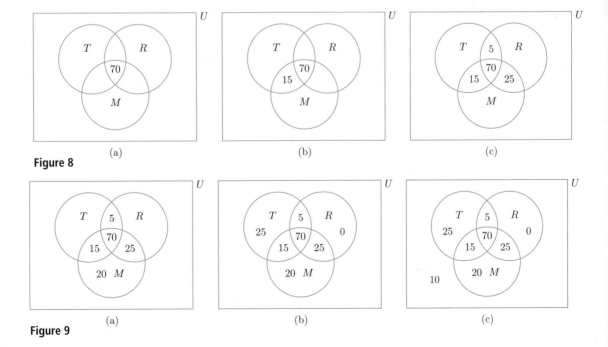

(a)   (b)   (c)

Figure 8

(a)   (b)   (c)

Figure 9

Practice Problems 5.3

1. Of the 1000 first-year students at a certain college, 700 take mathematics courses, 300 take mathematics and economics courses, and 200 do not take any mathematics or economics courses. Represent these data in a Venn diagram.

2. Refer to the Venn diagram from Problem 1.
   (a) How many of the first-year students take an economics course?
   (b) How many take an economics course but not a mathematics course?

EXERCISES 5.3

Family Library *The Venn diagram in Fig. 10 classifies the 100 books in a family's library as Hardback, Fiction, and Children's. Exercises 1–10 refer to this Venn diagram.*

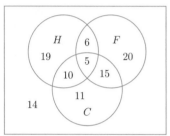

Figure 10

1. How many books are hardback fiction?
2. How many books are paperback fiction?
3. How many books are fiction?
4. How many books are nonfiction?
5. How many books are paperback nonfiction children's books?
6. How many books are adult hardback nonfiction?
7. How many books are either hardback or fiction?
8. How many hardback books are either fiction or children's books?
9. How many children's books are either hardback or fiction?
10. How many books are either hardback, fiction, or children's books?

In Exercises 11–22, let R, S, and T be subsets of the universal set U. Draw an appropriate Venn diagram and use the given data to determine the number of elements in each basic region.

11. $n(U) = 14$, $n(S) = 5$, $n(T) = 6$, $n(S \cap T) = 2$.
12. $n(U) = 20$, $n(S) = 11$, $n(T) = 7$, $n(S \cap T) = 7$.
13. $n(U) = 20$, $n(S) = 12$, $n(T) = 14$, $n(S \cup T) = 18$.
14. $n(S') = 6$, $n(S \cup T) = 10$, $n(S \cap T) = 5$, $n(T) = 7$.
15. $n(U) = 75$, $n(S) = 15$, $n(T) = 25$, $n(S' \cap T') = 40$.
16. $n(S) = 9$, $n(T) = 11$, $n(S \cap T) = 5$, $n(S') = 13$.
17. $n(S) = 3$, $n(S \cup T) = 6$, $n(T) = 4$, $n(S' \cup T') = 9$.

18. $n(U) = 15$, $n(S) = 8$, $n(T) = 9$, $n(S \cup T) = 14$.
19. $n(U) = 44$, $n(R) = 17$, $n(S) = 17$, $n(T) = 17$, $n(R \cap S) = 7$, $n(R \cap T) = 6$, $n(S \cap T) = 5$, $n(R \cap S \cap T) = 2$.
20. $n(U) = 29$, $n(R) = 10$, $n(S) = 12$, $n(T) = 10$, $n(R \cap S) = 1$, $n(R \cap T) = 5$, $n(S \cap T) = 4$, $n(R \cap S \cap T) = 1$.
21. $n(R') = 22$, $n(R \cup S) = 21$, $n(S) = 14$, $n(T) = 22$, $n(R \cap S) = 7$, $n(S \cap T) = 9$, $n(R \cap T) = 11$, $n(R \cap S \cap T) = 5$.
22. $n(U) = 64$, $n(R \cup S \cup T) = 45$, $n(R) = 22$, $n(T) = 26$, $n(R \cap S) = 4$, $n(S \cap T) = 6$, $n(R \cap T) = 8$, $n(R \cap S \cap T) = 1$.

23. **Music Preferences** A survey of 70 high school students revealed that 35 like rock music, 15 like hip-hop music, and 5 like both. How many of the students surveyed do not like either rock or hip-hop music?

24. **Nobel Prize Laureates** A total of 797 Nobel Prizes had been awarded by 2007. Fifteen of the 101 prizes in literature were awarded to Scandinavians. Scandinavians received a total of 55 awards. How many Nobel Prizes outside of literature have been awarded to non-Scandinavians?

25. **Analysis of Sonnet** One of Shakespeare's sonnets has a verb in 11 of its 14 lines, an adjective in 9 lines, and both in 7 lines. How many lines have a verb but no adjective? An adjective but no verb? Neither an adjective nor a verb?

Exam Performance *The results from an exam taken by 130 students were as follows:*

90 students correctly answered the first question
62 students correctly answered the second question
50 students correctly answered both questions.

Exercises 26–30 refer to these students.

26. How many students correctly answered either the first or second question?

27. How many students did not answer either of the two questions correctly?

28. How many students answered either the first or the second question correctly, but not both?

29. How many students answered the second question correctly, but not the first?

30. How many students missed the second question?

31. Class Enrollment Out of 35 students in a finite math class, 22 are male, 19 are business majors, 27 are first-year students, 14 are male business majors, 17 are male first-year students, 15 are first-year students who are business majors, and 11 are male first-year business majors.

    (a) Use these data to complete a Venn diagram displaying the characteristics of the students.

    (b) How many upper class female non-business majors are in the class?

    (c) How many female business majors are in the class?

32. Exercise Preferences A survey of 100 college faculty who exercise regularly found that 45 jog, 30 swim, 20 cycle, 6 jog and swim, 1 jogs and cycles, 5 swim and cycle, and 1 does all three. How many of the faculty members do not do any of these activities? How many just jog?

News Dissemination *A merchant surveyed 400 people to determine from where they found out about an upcoming sale. The results of the survey follow:*

> *180 from the Internet*
> *190 from television*
> *190 from newspapers*
> *80 from Internet and television*
> *90 from Internet and newspapers*
> *50 from television and newspapers*
> *30 from all three sources.*

Exercises 33–38 refer to the people in this survey.

33. How many people learned of the sale from newspapers or the Internet, but not both?

34. How many people learned of the sale only from newspapers?

35. How many people learned of the sale from the Internet or television but not newspapers?

36. How many people learned of the sale from at least two of the three media?

37. How many people learned of the sale from exactly one of the three media?

38. How many people learned of the sale from the Internet and television but not newspapers?

39. Course Enrollments PE Table 1 shows the number of students enrolled in each of three science courses at Gotham College. Although no students are enrolled in all three courses, 15 are enrolled in both Chemistry and Physics, 10 are enrolled in both Physics and Biology, and 5 are enrolled in both Biology and Chemistry. How many students are enrolled in at least one of these science courses?

    (a) 75   **(b)** 80   **(c)** 90   **(d)** 100   **(e)** 130

TABLE 1	
Course	**Enrollment**
Chemistry	60
Physics	40
Biology	30

Foreign Language Courses *A survey in a local high school shows that of the 4000 students in the school,*

> *2000 take French (F)*
> *3000 take Spanish (S)*
> *500 take Latin (L)*
> *1500 take both French and Spanish*
> *300 take both French and Latin*
> *200 take Spanish and Latin*
> *50 take all three languages.*

Use a Venn diagram to find the number of people in the sets given in Exercises 40–44.

40. $L \cap (F \cup S)$ **41.** $(L \cup F \cup S)'$ **42.** L'

43. $L \cup S \cup F'$ **44.** $F \cap S' \cap L'$

45. Voting Preferences One hundred college students were surveyed after voting in an election involving a Democrat and a Republican. Fifty were first-year students, 55 voted Democratic, and 25 were non-first-year students who voted Republican. How many first-year students voted Democratic?

46. Union Membership and Education Status A group of 100 workers were asked if they were college graduates and if they belonged to a union. Sixty were not college graduates, 20 were nonunion college graduates, and 30 were union members. How many of the workers were neither college graduates nor union members?

47. Diagnostic Test Results A class of 30 students was given a diagnostic test on the first day of a mathematics course. At the end of the semester, only 2 of the 21 students who had passed the diagnostic test failed the course. A total of 23 students passed the course. How many students managed to pass the course even though they failed the diagnostic test?

48. Air-Traffic Controllers A group of applicants for training as air-traffic controllers consists of 35 pilots, 20 veterans, 30 pilots who were not veterans, and 50 people who were neither veterans nor pilots. How large was the group?

College Majors *A group of 52 students has the following characteristics:*

> *5 are male biology majors*
> *15 are female biology majors*
> *12 are females majoring in a field other than biology.*

Exercises 49–54 refer to these students. (Hint: The creation of the Venn diagram requires the inclusion–exclusion principle.)

49. How many of the students are either male or are biology majors?

50. How many of the students are male?

51. How many of the students are female?

52. How many of the students are biology majors?

53. How many of the male students are not biology majors?

54. How many of the students are not biology majors?

Music Preferences *A campus radio station surveyed 190 students to determine the genres of music they liked. The survey results follow:*

> *114 like rock*
> *50 like country*
> *15 like rock and jazz*
> *11 like jazz and country*
> *20 like jazz only*
> *10 like rock and jazz, but not country*
> *9 like rock and country, but not jazz*
> *20 don't like any of the three types of music*

Exercises 55–62 refer to the students in this survey. (Note: The creation of the Venn diagram requires the inclusion–exclusion principle.)

55. How many students like rock only?

56. How many students like country but not rock?

57. How many students like jazz and country but not rock?

58. How many students like jazz or country but not rock?

59. How many students like exactly one of the genres?

60. How many students like all three genres?

61. How many students like at least two of the three genres?

62. How many students do not like either rock or country?

63. Magazine Preferences One hundred and eighty business executives were surveyed to determine if they regularly read *Fortune*, *Time*, or *Money* magazines. Seventy-five read *Fortune*, 70 read *Time*, 55 read *Money*, 45 read exactly two of the three magazines, 25 read *Fortune* and *Time*, 25 read *Time* and *Money*, and 5 read all three magazines. How many read none of the three magazines?

64. Small Businesses A survey of the characteristics of 100 small businesses that had failed revealed that 95 of them either were undercapitalized, had inexperienced management, or had a poor location. Four of the businesses had all three of these characteristics. Forty businesses were undercapitalized but had experienced management and good location. Fifteen businesses had inexperienced management but sufficient capitalization and good location. Seven were undercapitalized and had inexperienced management. Nine were undercapitalized and had poor location. Ten had inexperienced management and poor location. How many of the businesses had poor location? Which of the three characteristics was most prevalent in the failed businesses?

65. Music Each of the 100 students attending a conservatory of music plays at least one of three instruments: piano, violin, and clarinet. 65 play the piano, 42 play the violin, 28 play the clarinet, 20 play the piano and the violin, 10 play the violin and the clarinet, and 8 play the piano and the clarinet. How many play all three instruments? *Hint*: Let x represent the number of students who play all three instruments.

Solutions to Practice Problems 5.3

1. Draw a Venn diagram with two circles, one for mathematics (M) and one for economics (E) [Fig. 11(a)]. This Venn diagram has four basic regions, and our goal is to label each basic region with the proper number of students. The numbers for two of the basic regions are given directly. Since "300 take mathematics and economics," $n(M \cap E) = 300$. Since "200 do not take any mathematics or economics courses," $n((M \cup E)') = 200$ [Fig. 11(b)]. Now "700 take mathematics courses." Since M is made up of two basic regions and one region has 300 elements, the other basic region of M must contain 400 elements [Fig. 11(c)]. At this point all but one of the basic regions have been labeled and $400 + 300 + 200 = 900$ students have been accounted for. Since there is a total of 1000 students, the remaining basic region has 100 students [Fig. 11(d)].

2. (a) 400. "Economics" refers to the entire circle E, which is made up of two basic regions, one having 300 elements and the other 100. (A common error is to interpret the question as asking for the number of first-year students who take economics exclusively and therefore give the answer 100. To say that a person takes an economics course does not imply anything about the person's enrollment in mathematics courses.)

(b) 100

(Continued)

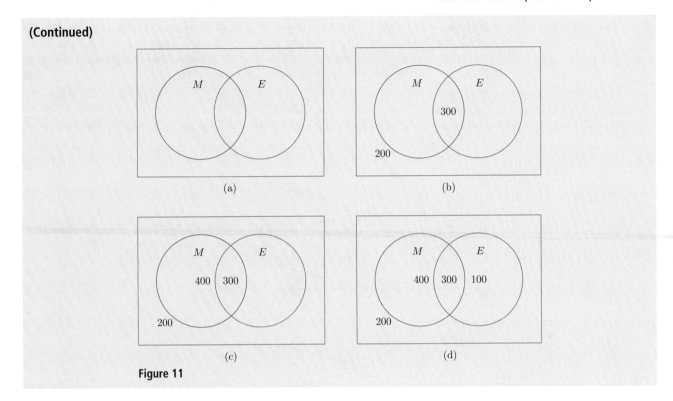

Figure 11

5.4 The Multiplication Principle

In this section we introduce a second fundamental principle of counting, the *multiplication principle*. By way of motivation, consider the following example.

EXAMPLE 1

Counting paths through a maze A medical researcher wishes to test the effect of a drug on a rat's perception by studying the rat's ability to run a maze while under the influence of the drug. The maze is constructed so that to arrive at the exit point C, the rat must pass through a central point B. There are five paths from the entry point A to B, and three paths from B to C. In how many different ways can the rat run the maze from A to C? (See Fig. 1.)

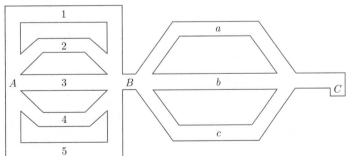

Figure 1

Solution The paths from A to B have been labeled 1 through 5, and the paths from B to C have been labeled a through c. The various paths through the maze can be schematically represented as in Fig. 2. The diagram shows that there are five ways to go from A to B. For each of these five ways, there are three ways to go from B to C. So there are five groups of three paths each, and therefore $5 \cdot 3 = 15$ possible paths from A to C. (A diagram such as Fig. 2, called a **tree diagram**, is useful in enumerating the various possibilities in counting problems.) ∎

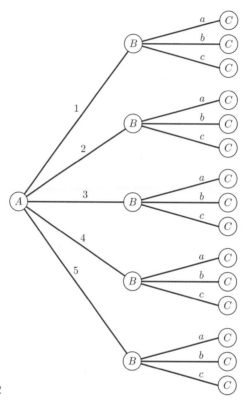

Figure 2

In the preceding problem, selecting a path is a task that can be broken up into two consecutive choices.

Choose path from A to B	Choose path from B to C
Choice 1	Choice 2

The first choice can be performed in five ways and, after the first choice has been carried out, the second can be performed in three ways. And we determined that the entire task can be performed in $5 \cdot 3 = 15$ ways. The same reasoning as just used yields the following useful counting principle:

Multiplication Principle   Suppose that a task is composed of two consecutive choices. If choice 1 can be performed in m ways and, for each of these, choice 2 can be performed in n ways, then the complete task can be performed in $m \cdot n$ ways.

EXAMPLE 2

Counting routes for a trip   An airline passenger must fly from New York to Frankfurt via London. There are 8 flights leaving New York for London. All of these provide connections on any one of 19 flights from London to Frankfurt. In how many different ways can the passenger book reservations?

Solution The task "fly from New York to Frankfurt" is composed of two consecutive choices:

Select a flight from New York to London	Select a flight from London to Frankfurt
Choice 1	Choice 2

From the data given, the multiplication principle implies that the task can be accomplished in $8 \cdot 19 = 152$ ways.

Now Try Exercise 1

It is possible to generalize the multiplication principle to tasks consisting of more than two choices.

> **Generalized Multiplication Principle** Suppose that a task consists of t choices performed consecutively. Suppose that choice 1 can be performed in m_1 ways; for each of these, choice 2 in m_2 ways; for each of these, choice 3 in m_3 ways; and so forth. Then the task can be performed in
>
> $$m_1 \cdot m_2 \cdot m_3 \cdot \cdots \cdot m_t \quad \text{ways.}$$

EXAMPLE 3

Officers for a board of directors A corporation has a board of directors consisting of 10 members. The board must select from among its members a chairperson, vice chairperson, and secretary. In how many ways can this be done?

Solution The task "select the three officers" can be divided into three consecutive choices:

Select chairperson	Select vice chairperson	Select secretary

Since there are 10 directors, choice 1 can be performed in 10 ways. After the chairperson has been selected, there are 9 directors left as possible candidates for vice chairperson, so that for each way of performing choice 1, choice 2 can be performed in 9 ways. After this has been done, there are 8 directors who are possible candidates for secretary, so choice 3 can be performed in 8 ways. By the generalized multiplication principle, the number of possible ways to perform the sequence of three choices equals $10 \cdot 9 \cdot 8$, or 720. So the officers of the board can be selected in 720 ways.

Now Try Exercise 13

In Example 3 we made important use of the phrase "for each of these" in the generalized multiplication principle. The choice "select a vice chairperson" can be performed in 10 ways, since any member of the board is eligible. However, when we view the selection process as a sequence of choices of which "select a vice chairperson" is the second choice, the situation has changed. *For each way that the first choice is performed, one person will have been used up; hence there will be only 9 possibilities for choosing the vice chairperson.*

EXAMPLE 4

Posing for a group picture In how many ways can a baseball team of nine players arrange themselves in a line for a group picture?

Solution Choose the players by their place in the picture, say from left to right. The first can be chosen in nine ways; for each of these outcomes the second can be chosen in eight ways; for each of these outcomes the third can be chosen in seven ways; and so forth. So the number of possible arrangements is

Now Try Exercise 24

$$9 \cdot 8 \cdot 7 \cdot 6 \cdot 5 \cdot 4 \cdot 3 \cdot 2 \cdot 1 = 362,880.$$

EXAMPLE 5   **License plates** A certain state uses automobile license plates that consist of three letters followed by three digits. How many such license plates are there?

Solution The task in this case, "form a license plate," consists of a sequence of six choices: three for choosing letters and three for choosing digits. Each letter can be chosen in 26 ways and each digit in 10 ways. So the number of license plates is

Now Try Exercise 33

$$26 \cdot 26 \cdot 26 \cdot 10 \cdot 10 \cdot 10 = 17,576,000.$$

■

Practice Problems 5.4

1. There are six seats available in a sedan. In how many ways can six people be seated if only three can drive?

2. A multiple-choice exam contains 10 questions, each having 3 possible answers. How many different ways are there of completing the exam?

EXERCISES 5.4

1. **Routes** If there are three routes from College Park to Baltimore and five routes from Baltimore to New York, how many routes are there from College Park to New York via Baltimore?

2. **Choosing an Outfit** How many different outfits consisting of a coat and a hat can be chosen from two coats and three hats?

3. **Two-Letter Words** How many different two-letter words (including nonsense words) can be formed when repetition of letters is allowed?

4. **Two-Letter Words** How many different two-letter words (including nonsense words) can be formed such that the two letters are distinct?

5. **Railroad Tickets** A railway has 20 stations. If the names of the point of departure and the destination are printed on each ticket, how many different kinds of single tickets must be printed?

6. **Railroad Tickets** Refer to Exercise 5. How many different kinds of tickets are needed if each ticket may be used in either direction between two stations?

7. **Gloves** A man has five different pairs of gloves. In how many ways can he select a right-hand glove and a left-hand glove that do not match?

8. **License Plates** How many license plates consisting of two letters followed by four digits are possible?

9. **Group Picture** How many ways can five people be arranged in a line for a group picture?

10. **Arranging Books** In how many different ways can four books be arranged on a bookshelf?

11. **Coin Tosses** Toss a coin six times and observe the sequence of heads or tails that results. How many different sequences are possible?

12. **Coin Tosses** Refer to Exercise 11. In how many of the sequences are the first and last tosses identical?

13. **Winners** Twenty athletes enter an Olympic event. How many different possibilities are there for winning the Gold Medal, Silver Medal, and Bronze Medal?

14. **Ranking Teams** A sportswriter is asked to rank eight teams. How many different orderings are possible?

15. **Electing Captains** In how many different ways can a 30-member football team select a captain and an assistant captain?

16. **Selecting an Outfit** How many different outfits can be selected from two coats, three hats, and two scarves?

17. **Rearranging Letters** How many different words (including nonsense words) can be formed using the four letters of the word "MATH"?

18. **Travel Options** If you can travel from Frederick, Maryland, to Baltimore, Maryland, by car, bus, or train and from Baltimore to London by airplane or ship, how many different ways are there to go from Frederick to London?

19. **Exam Questions** An exam contains five "true or false" questions. In how many different ways can the exam be completed?

20. **Pairs of Initials** A company has 700 employees. Explain why there must be two people with the same pair of initials.

21. **Serial Numbers** A computer manufacturer assigns serial numbers to its computers. The first symbol of a serial number is either A, B, or C, indicating the manufacturing plant. The second and third symbols taken together are one of the numbers $01, 02, \ldots, 12$, indicating the month of manufacture. The final four symbols are digits. How many possible serial numbers are there?

22. **Forming Words** How many four-letter words (including nonsense words) can be made from the letters of "statistics," assuming that each word may not have repeated letters?

23. **Forming Words** How many four-letter words (including nonsense words) can be made from the letters h, o, t, s, m, x, and e for each of the following conditions?

    (a) Letters can be repeated.

    (b) Letters cannot be repeated.

    (c) Words must begin with an h, and repetitions are allowed.

    (d) Words must end with a vowel, and repetitions are not allowed.

24. **Group Picture** A group of five boys and three girls is to be photographed.

    (a) How many ways can they be arranged in one row?

    (b) How many ways can they be arranged with the girls in the front row and the boys in the back row?

25. **Batting Orders** The manager of a Little League baseball team has picked the nine starting players for a game. How many different batting orders are possible under each of the following conditions?

    (a) There are no restrictions.

    (b) The pitcher must bat last.

    (c) The pitcher must bat last, the catcher eighth, and the shortstop first.

26. **Shading of Venn Diagrams** How many different ways can a Venn diagram with two circles be shaded?

27. **Shading of Venn Diagrams** How many different ways can a Venn diagram with three circles be shaded?

28. **Club Officers** A club can elect a member as president and a different member as treasurer in 506 different ways. How many members does the club have?

29. **Exam Questions** An exam contains six true or false statements. In how many ways can the exam be completed if leaving the answer blank is also an option?

30. **Test Volunteers** A physiologist wants to test the effects of exercise and meditation on blood pressure. She devises four different exercise programs and three different meditation programs. If she wants 10 subjects for each combination of exercise and meditation program, how many volunteers must she recruit?

31. **Menu Selections** A college student eats all his meals at a restaurant offering six breakfast specials, seven lunch specials, and four dinner specials. How many days can he go without repeating an entire day's menu selection?

32. **Entrances** A classroom building has 7 different doors. In how many ways can a student enter by one door and exit by a different door?

33. **License Plates** A California license plate consists of a digit followed by three letters, and then three digits. How many such license plates are there?

34. **Sweaters** A clothing store offers three styles of sweaters with each sweater available in six colors. How many different sweaters are there?

35. **Area Codes** Before 1995, three-digit area codes for the United States had the following restrictions:

    (a) Neither 0 nor 1 could be used as the first digit.

    (b) 0 or 1 had to be used for the second digit.

    (c) There were no restrictions on the third digit.
    How many different area codes were possible?

36. **Area Codes** Refer to Exercise 35. Beginning in 1995, restriction (b) was lifted and any digit could be used in the second position. How many different area codes are possible?

37. **Handshakes** Two ten-member basketball teams play a game. After the game, each of the members of the winning team shakes hands once with each member of both teams. How many handshakes take place?

38. **Chair Varieties** A furniture manufacturer makes three types of upholstered chairs and offers 20 fabrics. How many different chairs are available?

39. **Colored Houses** Six houses in a row are each to be painted with one of the colors red, blue, green, and yellow. In how many different ways can the houses be painted so that no two adjacent houses are of the same color?

40. **Numbers** How many three-digit odd numbers can be formed using the digits 1, 2, 3, 4, 5, 6, and 7?

41. **Exam Questions** Each of the 10 questions on a multiple-choice exam has four possible answers. How many different ways are there for a student to answer the questions? Assume that every question must be answered.

42. **Mismatched Shoes** Fred has 10 different pairs of shoes. In how many ways can he put on a pair of shoes that do not match?

43. **Transportation Options** Suppose that Jack wants to go from Florida to Maine via New York and can travel each leg of the journey by bus, car, train, or airplane. How many different ways can Jack make the trip?

44. **Menu Selections** A restaurant menu lists 6 appetizers, 10 entrées, and 5 desserts. How many ways can a diner select a three-course meal?

45. **Band Selections PE** In how many arrangements can a band play three waltzes and three tangos in a row without repeating any song, such that the first, third, and fifth songs are waltzes?

    (a) 6   (b) 12   (c) 16   (d) 36   (e) 720

46. **Milk Delivery** How many ways can a milkman deliver 10 distinguishable bottles of milk on a street containing five houses?

47. **Computer Options** A computer manufacturer offers a computer with a choice of four types of monitors, two types of keyboards, and three types of hard drives. How many different computers are offered?

48. **Ballots** Seven candidates for mayor, 4 candidates for city council president, and 12 propositions are being put before the electorate. How many different ballots could be cast, assuming that every voter votes on each of the items? If voters can choose to leave any item blank, how many different ballots are possible?

49. **Gift Wrapping** The gift-wrap desk at a large department store offers 5 box sizes, 10 wrapping papers, 7 colors of ribbon in two widths, and 9 special items to be added on the bow. How many different ways are there to gift-wrap a package assuming that the customer must choose at least a box but need not choose any of the other offerings?

50. **Selecting Fruit** José was told to get a dozen oranges, eight apples, and a half-pound of grapes. When he gets to the store he finds five varieties of oranges, five varieties of apples, and two varieties of grapes. Assuming that he buys only one variety of each type of fruit, how many different bags of fruit could he bring home?

51. **College Applications** Allison is preparing her applications for college. She will apply to three community colleges and has to fill out five parts to each of those applications. She will apply to three four-year schools, each of which has a six-part application. How many application segments must she complete?

52. **Car Options** An automobile dealer is offering five models of a particular car. On each model the customer may choose cloth or leather seats, each available in three colors, automatic or manual transmission, and a regular or a satellite radio. The car can be ordered in any one of eight exterior colors. How many different cars can be ordered?

53. **Game of Clue** In the game of *Clue*, there are six suspects in a murder that was committed in any one of nine rooms, using any one of six weapons. How many scenarios are possible?

54. **Numbers** James chooses a number from 1 to 100 (inclusive), Janet chooses a number between 1 and 100 that is divisible by 7, and Sandy chooses a number between 1 and 100 that is divisible by 21. How many triples of numbers are possible?

55. **Numbers** How many four-digit numbers can be formed using the digits $\{1, 2, 3, 4, 5, 6, 7\}$ if adjacent digits must be different?

56. **Fruit Baskets** A grocery store makes up fruit baskets using as many as four apples, three pears, and four oranges. A basket must contain at least one piece of fruit. How many different fruit selections are possible?

57. **Social Security Numbers** How many Social Security numbers are available if the only restriction is that the number 000-00-0000 cannot be assigned?

58. **Displaying Paintings** An art gallery has two paintings by each of four artists. In how many ways can the eight paintings be displayed in a row if paintings by the same artist must be adjacent to each other?

59. **Paths to Texas** Consider the following triangular display of letters. Start with the letter T at the top and move down the triangle to a letter S at the bottom. From any given letter move only to one of the letters directly below it on the left or right. How many different paths spell *TEXAS*?

$$
\begin{array}{ccccccccc}
 & & & & T & & & & \\
 & & & E & & E & & & \\
 & & X & & X & & X & & \\
 & A & & A & & A & & A & \\
S & & S & & S & & S & & S
\end{array}
$$

60. **Choosing an Outfit** A girl dresses in the morning in a blouse, a skirt, and shoes. She always wears standard white socks. She wants to wear a different combination on every day of the year. If she has the same number of blouses, skirts, and pairs of shoes, how many of each article would she need to have a different combination every day? (From *The Mathematics Teacher*, February 1996)

61. **Seating Arrangements** Three couples go on a movie date. In how many ways can they be seated in a row of six seats so that each couple is seated together?

62. **Three-Letter Words** How many different three-letter words (including nonsense words) are there in which successive letters are different?

63. **Seating Arrangements** A panel of eight experts is to present opposing arguments in a discussion of legalizing marijuana for medical purposes. The four proponents arrive first and sit in such a way that the panelists will alternate pro and con. In how many ways can the four proponents be seated? In how many ways can all eight panelists be seated?

64. **Call Letters** TV and radio stations east of the Mississippi River have call letters beginning with the letter W. How many different three- or four-letter call letters are possible?

A number is said to be a palindrome *if it reads the same backwards as forwards (e.g., 58485).*

65. **Palindromes** How many 5-digit numbers are palindromes?

66. **Palindromes** How many 6-digit numbers are palindromes?

67. Give an example of a counting problem whose solution is obtained by multiplying 5 by 6.

Solutions to Practice Problems 5.4

1. 360. Pretend that you are given the task of seating the six people. This task consists of six choices performed consecutively, as shown in Table 1. After you have performed choice 1, five people will remain, and any one of these five can be seated in the middle front seat. After choice 2, four people remain, and so on. By the generalized multiplication principle, the task can be performed in $3 \cdot 5 \cdot 4 \cdot 3 \cdot 2 \cdot 1 = 360$ ways.

2. 3^{10}. The task of answering the questions consists of 10 consecutive choices, each of which can be performed in three ways. Therefore, by the generalized multiplication principle, the task can be performed in

$$\underbrace{3 \cdot 3 \cdot 3 \cdot \ \cdots \ \cdot 3}_{10 \text{ terms}} \quad \text{ways.}$$

(*Note:* The answer can be left as 3^{10} or can be multiplied out to 59,049.)

TABLE 1

Choice	Number of ways choice can be performed
1: Select person to drive	3
2: Select person for middle front seat	5
3: Select person for right front seat	4
4: Select person for left rear seat	3
5: Select person for middle rear seat	2
6: Select person for right rear seat	1

5.5 Permutations and Combinations

In preceding sections we have solved a variety of counting problems using Venn diagrams and the generalized multiplication principle. Let us now turn our attention to two types of counting problems that occur very frequently and that can be solved using formulas derived from the generalized multiplication principle. These problems involve what are called permutations and combinations, which are particular types of arrangements of elements of a set. The sorts of arrangements we have in mind are illustrated in two problems:

Problem A   How many words (by which we mean strings of letters) of two distinct letters can be formed from the letters $\{a, b, c\}$?

Problem B   A construction crew has three members. A team of two must be chosen for a particular job. In how many ways can the team be chosen?

Each of the two problems can be solved by enumerating all possibilities.

Solution of Problem A   There are six possible words, namely

$$ab \quad ac \quad ba \quad bc \quad ca \quad cb.$$

Solution of Problem B   Designate the three crew members by a, b, and c. Then there are three possible two-person teams, namely

$$\{a, b\} \quad \{a, c\} \quad \{b, c\}.$$

(Note that $\{b, a\}$, the team consisting of b and a, is the same as the team $\{a, b\}$.)

   We deliberately set up both problems using the same letters in order to facilitate comparison. Both problems are concerned with counting the numbers of arrangements of the elements of the set $\{a, b, c\}$, taken two at a time, without allowing repetition (for example, *aa* was not allowed). However, in Problem A the order of the arrangement mattered, whereas in Problem B it did not. Arrangements of the sort considered in Problem A are called *permutations*, whereas those in Problem B are called *combinations*.

More precisely, suppose that we are given a set of n objects.[1] Then a **permutation of n objects taken r at a time** is an arrangement of r of the n objects in a specific order. So, for example, Problem A was concerned with permutations of the three objects, a, b, c ($n = 3$), taken two at a time ($r = 2$). A **combination of n objects taken r at a time** is a selection of r objects from among the n, with order disregarded. Thus, for example, in Problem B we considered combinations of the three objects a, b, c ($n = 3$), taken two at a time ($r = 2$).

It is convenient to introduce the following notation for counting permutations and combinations. Let

$P(n, r) =$ the number of permutations of n objects taken r at a time

$C(n, r) =$ the number of combinations of n objects taken r at a time.

Thus, for example, from our solutions to Problems A and B, we have

$$P(3, 2) = 6 \qquad C(3, 2) = 3.$$

Very simple formulas for $P(n, r)$ and $C(n, r)$ allow us to calculate these quantities for any n and r. Let us begin by stating the formula for $P(n, r)$. For $r = 1, 2, 3$, respectively,

$$P(n, 1) = n$$
$$P(n, 2) = n(n - 1) \qquad \text{(two factors)},$$
$$P(n, 3) = n(n - 1)(n - 2) \qquad \text{(three factors)}.$$

Continuing, we obtain the following formula:

Permutation Formula   The number of permutations of n objects taken r at a time is

$$P(n, r) = n(n - 1)(n - 2) \cdot \cdots \cdot (n - r + 1) \qquad (r \text{ factors}). \qquad (1)$$

This formula is verified at the end of this section.

EXAMPLE 1   **Applying the permutation formula**   Compute the following numbers.
(a) $P(100, 2)$ (b) $P(6, 4)$ (c) $P(5, 5)$

Solution (a) Here $n = 100$, $r = 2$. So we take the product of two factors, beginning with 100:
$$P(100, 2) = 100 \cdot 99 = 9900.$$

(b) $P(6, 4) = 6 \cdot 5 \cdot 4 \cdot 3 = 360$

▶ Now Try Exercise 1   (c) $P(5, 5) = 5 \cdot 4 \cdot 3 \cdot 2 \cdot 1 = 120$ ■

In order to state the formula for $C(n, r)$, we must introduce some further notation. Suppose that r is any positive integer. We denote by $r!$ (read "r factorial") the product of all positive integers from r down to 1:

$$r! = r \cdot (r - 1) \cdot \cdots \cdot 2 \cdot 1.$$

---
[1] All are assumed to be different.

For instance,

$$1! = 1$$

$$2! = 2 \cdot 1 = 2$$

$$3! = 3 \cdot 2 \cdot 1 = 6$$

$$4! = 4 \cdot 3 \cdot 2 \cdot 1 = 24$$

$$5! = 5 \cdot 4 \cdot 3 \cdot 2 \cdot 1 = 120.$$

In terms of this notation we can state a very simple formula for $C(n, r)$, the number of combinations of n things taken r at a time.

> **Combination Formula**   The number of combinations of n objects taken r at a time is
> $$C(n, r) = \frac{P(n, r)}{r!} = \frac{n(n-1) \cdot \cdots \cdot (n-r+1)}{r(r-1) \cdot \cdots \cdot 1} \tag{2}$$

This formula is verified at the end of this section.

EXAMPLE 2   **Applying the combination formula**   Compute the following numbers.

(a) $C(100, 2)$ (b) $C(6, 4)$ (c) $C(5, 5)$

Solution   (a) $C(100, 2) = \dfrac{P(100, 2)}{2!} = \dfrac{100 \cdot 99}{2 \cdot 1} = 4950$

(b) $C(6, 4) = \dfrac{P(6, 4)}{4!} = \dfrac{6 \cdot 5 \cdot 4 \cdot 3}{4 \cdot 3 \cdot 2 \cdot 1} = 15$

Now Try Exercise 5   (c) $C(5, 5) = \dfrac{P(5, 5)}{5!} = \dfrac{5 \cdot 4 \cdot 3 \cdot 2 \cdot 1}{5 \cdot 4 \cdot 3 \cdot 2 \cdot 1} = 1$ ■

EXAMPLE 3   **Applying the permutation and combination formulas**   Solve Problems A and B using formulas (1) and (2).

Solution   The number of two-letter words that can be formed from the three letters a, b, and c is equal to $P(3, 2) = 3 \cdot 2 = 6$, in agreement with our previous solution.

The number of two-worker teams that can be formed from three individuals is equal to $C(3, 2)$, and

$$C(3, 2) = \frac{P(3, 2)}{2!} = \frac{3 \cdot 2}{2 \cdot 1} = 3,$$

in agreement with our previous result.   ■

EXAMPLE 4   **Selecting a committee**   The board of directors of a corporation has 10 members. In how many ways can they choose a committee of 3 board members to negotiate a merger?

Solution   Since the committee of three involves no ordering of its members, we are concerned here with combinations. The number of combinations of 10 people taken 3 at a time is $C(10, 3)$, which is

$$C(10, 3) = \frac{10 \cdot 9 \cdot 8}{3 \cdot 2 \cdot 1} = 120.$$

Now Try Exercise 51   Thus there are 120 possibilities for the committee.   ■

EXAMPLE 5   **Outcomes of a horse race**   Eight horses are entered in a race in which a first, second, and third prize will be awarded. Assuming no ties, how many different outcomes are possible?

Solution   In this example we are considering ordered arrangements of three horses, so we are dealing with permutations. The number of permutations of eight horses taken three at a time is

$$P(8,3) = 8 \cdot 7 \cdot 6 = 336,$$

Now Try Exercise 44   so the number of possible outcomes of the race is 336.   ∎

EXAMPLE 6   **Polling sample**   A political pollster wishes to survey 1500 individuals chosen from a sample of 5,000,000 adults. In how many ways can the 1500 individuals be chosen?

Solution   No ordering of the 1500 individuals is involved, so we are dealing with combinations. So the number in question is $C(5{,}000{,}000, 1500)$, a number too large to be written down in digit form. (It has several thousand digits!) But it could be calculated

Now Try Exercise 45   with the aid of a computer.   ∎

EXAMPLE 7   **Selecting club officers**   A club has 10 members. In how many ways can they choose a slate of four officers, consisting of a president, vice president, secretary, and treasurer?

Solution   In this problem we are dealing with an ordering of four members. (The first is the president, the second the vice president, and so on.) So we are dealing with permutations, and the number of ways of choosing the officers is

Now Try Exercise 25 $$P(10,4) = 10 \cdot 9 \cdot 8 \cdot 7 = 5040.$$ ∎

Verification of the Formulas for $P(n,r)$ and $C(n,r)$ Let us first derive the formula for $P(n,r)$, the number of permutations of n objects taken r at a time. The task of choosing r objects (in a given order) consists of r consecutive choices (Fig. 1). The first choice can be performed in n ways. For each way that the first choice is performed, one object will have been used up and so we can perform the second choice in $n-1$ ways, and so on. For each way of performing the sequence of choices $1, 2, 3, \ldots, r-1$, the rth choice can be performed in $n - (r-1) = n - r + 1$ ways. By the generalized multiplication principle, the task of choosing the r objects from among the n can be performed in

$$n(n-1) \cdot \cdots \cdot (n-r+1) \quad \text{ways.}$$

That is,

$$P(n,r) = n(n-1) \cdot \cdots \cdot (n-r+1),$$

which is formula (1).

Let us now verify the formula for $C(n,r)$, the number of combinations of n objects taken r at a time. Each such combination is a set of r objects and therefore can be ordered in

$$P(r,r) = r(r-1) \cdot \cdots \cdot 2 \cdot 1 = r!$$

Choose 1st object		Choose 2nd object	...	Choose rth object

Figure 1   Choice 1   Choice 2   Choice r

ways by formula (1). In other words, each different combination of r objects gives rise to $r!$ permutations of the same r objects. On the other hand, each permutation of n objects taken r at a time gives rise to a combination of n objects taken r at a time, by simply ignoring the order of the permutation. Thus, if we start with the $P(n, r)$ permutations, we will have all the combinations of n objects taken r at a time, with each combination repeated $r!$ times. Thus

$$P(n, r) = r! \, C(n, r).$$

On dividing both sides of the equation by $r!$, we obtain formula (2).

INCORPORATING TECHNOLOGY

GC   Most graphing calculators have commands to compute $P(n, r)$, $C(n, r)$, and $n!$. For instance, the MATH key on the TI-83/84 Plus leads to the PRB menu of Fig. 2, which contains the commands **nPr**, **nCr**, and **!**. Figure 3 shows how these commands are used. *Note:* The number **8.799226775E15** represents $8.799226775 \times 10^{15}$. On the TI-89, the first three items on the MATH/Probability menu are **!**, **nPr**, and **nCr**. Figure 4 shows how these commands are used.   ■

Figure 2

Figure 3

Figure 4

ES   The values of $n!$, $P(n, r)$, and $C(n, r)$ are calculated in an Excel spreadsheet with the functions $\text{FACT}(n)$, $\text{PERMUT}(n, r)$, and $\text{COMBIN}(n, r)$.

Practice Problems 5.5

1. Calculate the following values.

   (a) $5!$ **(b)** $P(5, 5)$ **(c)** $P(7, 3)$ **(d)** $C(7, 3)$

2. A newborn child is to be given a first name and a middle name from a selection of 10 names. How many different possibilities are there?

EXERCISES 5.5

For Exercises 1–20, calculate the values.

1. $P(4, 2)$
2. $P(5, 1)$
3. $P(6, 3)$
4. $P(5, 4)$
5. $C(10, 3)$
6. $C(12, 2)$
7. $C(5, 4)$
8. $C(6, 3)$
9. $P(7, 1)$
10. $P(5, 5)$
11. $P(n, 1)$
12. $P(n, 2)$
13. $C(4, 4)$
14. $C(n, 2)$
15. $C(n, n - 2)$
16. $C(n, 1)$
17. $6!$
18. $\dfrac{10!}{4!}$
19. $\dfrac{9!}{7!}$
20. $7!$

21. **Group Picture** In how many ways can four people line up in a row for a group picture?

22. **Contest Winners** How many different outcomes of "winner" and "runner-up" are possible if there are six contestants in a pie-eating contest?

23. **Book Selection** How many different selections of two books can be made from a set of nine books?

24. **Pizza Varieties** A pizza parlor offers five toppings for the plain cheese base of the pizzas. How many different pizzas are possible that use three of the toppings?

25. **Contest Winners** How many ways are there to choose first, second, and third prizes in an art contest with 15 entrants?

26. **Waiting in Line** In how many ways can six people line up at a single counter to order food at McDonald's?

27. **Banana Split Options** A deluxe chocolate banana split is made with three scoops of chocolate ice cream, one banana, and a choice of 4 out of 10 possible toppings. How many different deluxe chocolate banana splits can be ordered?

28. **Selecting Sweaters** Suppose that you own 10 sweaters. How many ways can you select four of them to take on a trip?

29. **Selecting Sweaters** Suppose that you own 10 sweaters and are going on a trip. How many ways can you select six of them to leave at home?

30. **Selecting Sweaters** Why do Exercises 28 and 29 have the same answer?

31. **Player Introductions** The five starting players of a basketball team are introduced one at a time. In how many different ways can they be introduced?

32. **Supreme Court Decisions** In how many different ways can the nine members of the Supreme Court reach a six-to-three decision?

33. **Conference Games** In an eight-team football conference, each team plays every other team exactly once. How many games must be played?

34. **Choosing Exam Questions** A student is required to work exactly five problems from an eight-problem exam. In how many ways can the problems be chosen?

35. **Arranging Books** How many ways can you arrange 5 of 10 books on a shelf?

36. **Selecting Books** How many ways can you choose 5 of your 10 books to put in your backpack?

37. **Guest Lists** How many ways can you choose 5 out of 10 friends to invite to a dinner party?

38. **Giving Gifts** How many ways can you distribute $1, $2, $5, $10, $20 to 5 of your 10 friends? Assume that no one gets more than one bill.

39. **CD Changer** Suppose that you have 35 CDs and your CD player has five slots numbered 1 through 5. How many ways can you fill your CD player?

40. **Job Interviews** Of the 20 applicants for a job, 4 will be selected for intensive interviews. In how many ways can the selection be made?

41. **Diskettes** In a batch of 100 computer diskettes, 7 are defective. A sample of three diskettes is to be selected from the batch. How many samples are possible? How many of the samples consist of all defective diskettes?

42. **Course Selection** A student must choose five courses out of seven that he would like to take. How many possibilities are there?

43. **Three-Letter Words** How many different three-letter words are there having no repetition of letters?

44. **Ranking Teams** A sportswriter makes a preseason guess of the top 5 football teams (in order) from among 40 major teams. How many different possibilities are there?

45. **Senate Committees** In how many different ways can a committee of 5 senators be selected from the 100 members of the U.S. Senate?

46. **Race Winners** Theoretically, how many possibilities are there for first, second, and third places in a marathon race with 1000 entries?

Poker Hands *Exercises 47–50 refer to poker hands. A poker hand consists of 5 cards selected from a deck of 52 cards.*

47. How many different poker hands are there?

48. How many different poker hands consist entirely of aces and kings?

49. How many different poker hands consist entirely of clubs?

50. How many different poker hands consist entirely of red cards?

51. **Choosing a Board of Directors** A fraternity has 20 members. In how many ways can it choose a three-person board of directors?

52. **Choosing Appetizers** A restaurant offers an "appetizer-plate special" consisting of five selections from its list of appetizers. If there are more than 700 different possible appetizer-plate specials, what is the least possible number of appetizers?

53. **Distributing Sandwiches** Five students order different sandwiches at a campus eatery. The waiter forgets who ordered what and gives out the sandwiches at random. In how many different ways can the sandwiches be distributed?

54. **Nautical Signals** A nautical signal consists of three flags arranged vertically on a flagpole. If a sailor has flags of six different colors, how many different signals are possible?

55. **Selecting Colleges** A high school student decides to apply to four of the eight Ivy League colleges. In how many possible ways can the four colleges be selected?

56. **Numbers** In how many six digit numbers are the digits strictly decreasing when read from left to right? *Hint*: Start with the number 9876543210 and remove four digits.

57. **Choosing Candy** Two children, Moe and Joe, are allowed to select candy from a plate of nine pieces of candy. Moe, being younger, is allowed to choose first but can only take two candies. Joe is then allowed to take three of the remaining candies. Joe complains that he has fewer options than Moe. Is Joe correct? How many options will each child have?

58. Franchises In how many ways can three new basketball franchises be distributed to the five cities that have applied for them?

59. Picture Arrangements A nursery school teacher has collected a picture from each of the 12 children in the class. She wants to hang the pictures in four rows of three. How many different arrangements are possible?

60. Racetrack Betting Most racetracks have "compound" bets on two or more horses. An *exacta* is a bet in which the first and second finishers in a race are specified in order. A *quinella* is a bet on the first two finishers in a race, with order not specified. With a field of nine horses, how many different exacta bets can be placed? Quinella bets?

61. Arranging Books In how many ways can five mathematics books and four novels be placed on a bookshelf if the mathematics books must be together?

62. Arranging Books George has three books by each of his four favorite authors. In how many ways can the books be placed on a shelf if books by the same author must be together?

63. Arranging Paintings An art gallery has seven paintings by a new artist. The director wants to place four of them in a row on one wall of the gallery. How many different arrangements are possible?

64. Baseball Lineup On a children's baseball team, there are four players who can play at any of the following infield positions: catcher, first base, third base, and shortstop. There are five possible pitchers, none of whom plays any other position. And there are four players that can play any of the three outfield positions (right, left, center) or second base. In how many ways can the coach assign players to positions?

65. Batting Orders How many batting orders are possible for a team of nine baseball players in which the pitcher always bats last and the first baseman bats in either the third or fourth spot?

66. Selecting Performers A cabaret show is put together by a manager who wishes to present two comedians and three singers. He can choose from 14 comedians and 20 singers. In how many ways can he select the acts for the show?

67. Performance Order The cabaret show manager of Exercise 66 also controls the order of the five acts he selects. In how many ways can he organize the program once he has decided on which acts to present?

68. MRI Processing Seven patients are waiting to have an MRI scan, but there is time to process only three of them before the office closes for the day. In how many ways can the three patients be chosen?

69. Poker Hands How many five-card combinations from a standard playing-card deck have cards from exactly two suits?

70. Ten-Letter Words A 10-letter word consists of 4 A's and 6 B's. How many different words are possible if no two A's can be next to each other? *Hint*: Start with $BBBBBB$ and decide where to insert the A's.

71. ZIP Codes How many five-digit ZIP codes are possible in which the product of the digits is even? (From *The Mathematics Teacher*, February 1997)

72. League Games In a six-team softball league, each team plays every other team three times during the season. How many games must be scheduled?

73. Handshakes At a party, everyone shakes hands with everyone else. If 45 handshakes take place, how many people are at the party?

74. Distributing Jerseys PE Each of the 25 contestants in a race wears a jersey in either a single color or a pair of colors. What is the minimum number of colors so that no two contestants have the same color jersey?
(a) 5 **(b)** 6 **(c)** 7 **(d)** 25 **(e)** 50

75. Side Dishes A restaurant offers its customers a choice of 3 side dishes with each meal. The side dishes can be chosen from a list of fifteen possibilities with duplications allowed. For instance, a customer can order two sides of mashed potatoes and one side of string beans. Show that there are 680 possible options for the three side dishes.

76. Ice Cream Specials An ice cream parlor offers a special consisting of three scoops of ice cream chosen from 16 different flavors. Duplication of flavors is allowed. For instance, one possibility is two scoops of chocolate and one scoop of vanilla. Show that there are 816 different possible options for the special.

When the New York State lottery (Lotto) was first established, a contestant had to select six numbers from 1 to 49. A few years later the numbers 50 through 54 were added. In March 2007, the numbers 55 through 59 were added.

77. Lotto The number of possible combinations of six numbers selected from 1 to 59 is approximately _____ times the number of combinations selected from 1 through 49.
(a) 2 **(b)** 3 **(c)** 10 **(d)** 100

78. Lotto Drawings for Lotto are held twice per week. Suppose you decide to purchase 110 tickets for each drawing and never use the same combination twice. Approximately how many years would be required before you would have bet on every possible combination?
(a) 100 **(b)** 1000 **(c)** 2000 **(d)** 4000

79. Triangles How many distinct triangles can be constructed by connecting three different vertices of a cube?

80. Explain why $P(n, r)$ also can be calculated as $\frac{n!}{(n-r)!}$.

In Exercises 81–83, use a graphing calculator or spreadsheet to calculate the answers.

81. **Course Options** Students attending a college that operates on the semester system choose five courses each semester from a catalog containing 752 courses. The students who attend a college on the trimester system choose three courses each term from 937 courses in the catalog. Assume all courses are taught every term. In the standard four-year undergraduate program, which students have a greater number of different programs?

82. **Arranging Microchips** A computer manufacturer has 50 distinct microchips to place into a rectangular array that is 5 units wide by 10 units long.

  (a) In how many ways can the chips be arranged?

  (b) Ten of the chips control special functions. How many arrangements are possible if these must occupy the first column?

  (c) Find the number of arrangements having no special-function chips in the first column.

83. **Lottery**

  (a) Calculate the number of possible lottery tickets if the player must choose five distinct numbers from 0 to 44, inclusive, where the order does not matter. The winner must match all five.

  (b) Calculate the number of lottery tickets if the player must choose four distinct numbers from 0 to 99, inclusive, where the order does not matter. The winner must match all four.

  (c) In which lottery does the player have a better chance of choosing the randomly selected winning numbers?

  (d) Find the answer to (c) if the order in which the numbers appear on the ticket must match the order on the winning ticket.

Solutions to Practice Problems 5.5

1. (a) $5! = 5 \cdot 4 \cdot 3 \cdot 2 \cdot 1 = 120$

  (b) $P(5,5) = 5 \cdot 4 \cdot 3 \cdot 2 \cdot 1 = 120$
     [$P(n,n)$ is the same as $n!$]

  (c) $P(7,3) = \underbrace{7 \cdot 6 \cdot 5}_{3 \text{ factors}} = 210$

     [$P(n,r)$ is the product of the first r factors in the descending expansion of $n!$.]

  (d) $C(7,3) = \dfrac{7 \cdot 6 \cdot 5}{3 \cdot 2 \cdot 1} = \dfrac{7 \cdot \cancel{6} \cdot 5}{\cancel{3} \cdot \cancel{2} \cdot 1} = 35$

     [A convenient procedure to follow when calculating $C(n,r)$ is first to write the product expansion of $r!$ in the denominator and then to write in the numerator an integer from the descending expansion of $n!$ above each integer in the denominator.]

2. 90. The first question to be asked here is whether permutations or combinations are involved. Two names are to be selected, and the order of the names is important. (The name Amanda Beth is different from the name Beth Amanda.) Since the problem asks for arrangements of 10 names taken 2 at a time in a *specific order*, the number of arrangements is $P(10,2) = 10 \cdot 9 = 90$. In general, order is important if a different outcome results when two items in the selection are interchanged.

5.6 Further Counting Problems

In Section 5.5 we introduced permutations and combinations and developed formulas for counting all permutations (or combinations) of a given type. Many counting problems can be formulated in terms of permutations or combinations. But to use the formulas of Section 5.5 successfully, we must be able to recognize these problems when they occur and to translate them into a form in which the formulas may be applied. In this section we practice doing that. We consider five typical applications giving rise to permutations or combinations. At first glance, the first two applications may seem to have little practical significance. However, they suggest a common way to "model" outcomes of real-life situations having two equally likely results.

As our first application, consider a coin-tossing experiment in which we toss a coin a fixed number of times. We can describe the outcome of the experiment as a sequence of "heads" and "tails." For instance, if a coin is tossed three times, then one possible outcome is "heads on the first toss, tails on the second toss, and tails on third toss." This outcome can be abbreviated as HTT. We can use the methods of the preceding section to count the number of possible outcomes having various prescribed properties.

EXAMPLE 1

Tossing a coin ten times Suppose that an experiment consists of tossing a coin 10 times and observing the sequence of heads and tails.

(a) How many different outcomes are possible?

(b) How many different outcomes have exactly four heads?

Solution (a) Visualize each outcome of the experiment as a sequence of 10 boxes, where each box contains one letter, H or T, with the first box recording the result of the first toss, the second box recording the result of the second toss, and so forth.

$$\boxed{H}\boxed{T}\boxed{H}\boxed{T}\boxed{T}\boxed{T}\boxed{H}\boxed{T}\boxed{H}\boxed{T}$$
$$1 \quad 2 \quad 3 \quad 4 \quad 5 \quad 6 \quad 7 \quad 8 \quad 9 \quad 10$$

Each box can be filled in two ways. So by the generalized multiplication principle, the sequence of 10 boxes can be filled in

$$\underbrace{2 \cdot 2 \cdot \,\cdots\, \cdot 2}_{\text{10 factors}} = 2^{10}$$

ways. So there are $2^{10} = 1024$ different possible outcomes.

(b) An outcome with 4 heads corresponds to filling the boxes with 4 H's and 6 T's. A particular outcome is determined as soon as we decide where to place the H's. The 4 boxes to receive H's can be selected from the 10 boxes in $C(10, 4)$ ways. So the number of outcomes with 4 heads is

Now Try Exercises 1(a) and (b)

$$C(10, 4) = \frac{10 \cdot 9 \cdot 8 \cdot 7}{4 \cdot 3 \cdot 2 \cdot 1} = 210. \qquad \blacksquare$$

Ideas similar to those applied in Example 1 are useful in counting even more complicated sets of outcomes of coin-tossing experiments. The second part of our next example highlights a trick that can often save time and effort.

EXAMPLE 2

Tossing a coin ten times Consider the coin-tossing experiment of Example 1.

(a) How many different outcomes have at most two heads?

(b) How many different outcomes have at least three heads?

Solution (a) The outcomes with at most two heads are those having 0, 1, or 2 heads. Let us count the number of these outcomes separately:

0 heads: There is 1 outcome, namely T T T T T T T T T T.

1 head: To determine such an outcome, we just select the box in which to put the single H. And this can be done in $C(10, 1) = 10$ ways.

2 heads: To determine such an outcome, we just select the boxes in which to put the two H's. And this can be done in $C(10, 2) = (10 \cdot 9)/(2 \cdot 1) = 45$ ways.

Adding up all the possible outcomes, we see that the number of outcomes with at most two heads is equal to $1 + 10 + 45 = 56$.

(b) "At least three heads" refers to an outcome with either 3, 4, 5, 6, 7, 8, 9, or 10 heads. The total number of such outcomes is

$$C(10, 3) + C(10, 4) + \cdots + C(10, 10).$$

This sum can, of course, be calculated, but there is a less tedious way to solve the problem. Just start with all outcomes [1024 of them by Example 1(a)] and subtract those with at most two heads [56 of them by part (a)]. So the number of outcomes with at least three heads is $1024 - 56 = 968$. ∎

Now Try Exercises 1(c) and (d)

NOTE ▶ The solution to part (b) of Example 2 employs a useful counting technique. Sometimes it is easier to count the number of elements in the complement of a set and then subtract it from the total number of possibilities. ∎

Let us now turn to a different sort of counting problem, namely one that involves counting the number of paths between two points.

EXAMPLE 3   **Routes through a city** In Fig. 1 we have drawn a partial map of the streets in a certain city. A tourist wishes to walk from point A to point B. We have drawn two possible routes from A to B. What is the total number of routes (with no backtracking) from A to B?

Figure 1

Solution Any particular route can be described by giving the directions of each block walked in the appropriate order. For instance, the route on the left of Fig. 1 is described as "a block south, a block south, a block east, a block east, a block east, a block south, a block east." Using S for south and E for east, this route can be designated by the string of letters SSEEESE. Similarly, the route on the right is ESESEES. Note that each route is then described by a string of seven letters, of which three are S's (we must go three blocks south) and four are E's (we must go four blocks east). Selecting a route is thus the same as placing three S's in a string of seven boxes:

$$\boxed{}\,\boxed{S}\,\boxed{}\,\boxed{S}\,\boxed{}\,\boxed{}\,\boxed{S}$$

The three boxes to receive S's can be selected in $C(7,3) = 35$ ways. So the number of paths from A to B is 35. ∎

Now Try Exercise 3

Let us now move on to a third type of counting problem. Suppose that we have an urn in which there are a certain number of red balls and a certain number of white balls. We perform an experiment that consists of selecting a number of balls from the urn and observing the color distribution of the sample selected. (This model may be used, for example, to describe the process of selecting people to be polled in a survey. The different colors correspond to different opinions.) By using familiar counting techniques we can calculate the number of possible samples having a given color distribution. The next example illustrates a typical computation.

EXAMPLE 4   **Selecting balls from an urn** An urn contains 25 numbered balls, of which 15 are red and 10 are white. A sample of 5 balls is to be selected.

(a) How many different samples are possible?

(b) How many samples contain all red balls?

(c) How many samples contain 3 red balls and 2 white balls?

(d) How many samples contain at least 4 red balls?

Solution (a) A sample is just an unordered selection of 5 balls out of 25. There are $C(25,5)$ such samples. Numerically, we have

$$C(25,5) = \frac{25 \cdot 24 \cdot 23 \cdot 22 \cdot 21}{5 \cdot 4 \cdot 3 \cdot 2 \cdot 1} = 53{,}130$$

samples.

(b) To form a sample of all red balls we must select 5 balls from the 15 red ones. This can be done in $C(15,5)$ ways—that is, in

$$C(15,5) = \frac{15 \cdot 14 \cdot 13 \cdot 12 \cdot 11}{5 \cdot 4 \cdot 3 \cdot 2 \cdot 1} = 3003$$

ways.

(c) To answer this question we use both the multiplication principle and the formula for $C(n,r)$. We form a sample of 3 red balls and 2 white balls using a sequence of two choices:

Select 3 red balls	Select 2 white balls
Choice 1	Choice 2

The first choice can be performed in $C(15,3)$ ways and the second in $C(10,2)$ ways. Thus the total number of samples having 3 red and 2 white balls is $C(15,3) \cdot C(10,2)$. That is,

$$C(15,3) = \frac{15 \cdot 14 \cdot 13}{3 \cdot 2 \cdot 1} = 455$$

$$C(10,2) = \frac{10 \cdot 9}{2 \cdot 1} = 45$$

$$C(15,3) \cdot C(10,2) = 455 \cdot 45 = 20{,}475.$$

So the number of possible samples is 20,475.

(d) A sample with at least 4 red balls has either 4 or 5 red balls. By part (b) the number of samples with 5 red balls is 3003. Using the same reasoning as in part (c), the number of samples with 4 red balls is $C(15,4) \cdot C(10,1) = 1365 \cdot 10 = 13{,}650$. Thus the total number of samples having at least 4 red balls is $13{,}650 + 3003 = 16{,}653$.   ∎

Now Try Exercise 5

Practice Problems 5.6

1. **School Board** A newspaper reporter wants an indication of how the 15 members of the school board feel about a certain proposal. She decides to question a sample of 6 of the board members.

    (a) How many different samples are possible?

    (b) Suppose that 10 of the board members support the proposal and 5 oppose it. How many of the samples reflect the distribution of the board? That is, in how many of the samples do 4 people support the proposal and 2 oppose it?

2. **Free Throws** A basketball player shoots eight free throws and lists the sequence of results of each trial in order. Let S represent "success" and F represent "failure." Then, for instance, FFSSSSSS represents the outcome of missing the first two shots and hitting the rest.

    (a) How many different outcomes are possible?

    (b) How many of the outcomes have six successes?

EXERCISES 5.6

1. **Heads and Tails** An experiment consists of tossing a coin six times and observing the sequence of heads and tails.

   (a) How many different outcomes are possible?

   (b) How many different outcomes have exactly three heads?

   (c) How many different outcomes have more heads than tails?

   (d) How many different outcomes have at least two heads?

2. **Routes through City Streets** Refer to the map in Fig. 2. How many routes are there from A to B?

Figure 2   **Figure 3**

3. **Routes through City Streets** Refer to the map in Fig. 3. How many routes are there from A to B?

4. **Selecting Balls from an Urn** An urn contains 12 numbered balls, of which 8 are red and 4 are white. A sample of 4 balls is to be selected.

   (a) How many different samples are possible?

   (b) How many samples contain all red balls?

   (c) How many samples contain 2 red balls and 2 white balls?

   (d) How many samples contain at least 3 red balls?

   (e) How many samples contain a different number of red balls than white balls?

5. **Selecting Apples** A bag of 10 apples contains 2 rotten apples and 8 good apples. A shopper selects a sample of 3 apples from the bag.

   (a) How many different samples are possible?

   (b) How many samples contain all good apples?

   (c) How many samples contain at least 1 rotten apple?

6. **Heads and Tails** An experiment consists of tossing a coin 8 times and observing the sequence of heads and tails.

   (a) How many different outcomes are possible?

   (b) How many different outcomes have exactly 3 heads?

   (c) How many different outcomes have at least 2 heads?

   (d) How many different outcomes have 4 heads or 5 heads?

7. **Dorm Assignments** How many ways can a group of 100 students be assigned to dorms A, B, and C, with 25 assigned to dorm A, 40 to dorm B, and 35 to dorm C?

8. **World Series** In the World Series the American League team ("A") and the National League team ("N") play until one team wins four games. If the sequence of winners is designated by letters (NAAAA means the National League won the first game and lost the next four), how many different sequences are possible?

9. **Routes through City Streets** Refer to the map in Fig. 3. How many of the routes from A to B pass through the point C?

10. **Selecting Fuses** A package contains 100 fuses, of which 10 are defective. A sample of 5 fuses is selected at random.

    (a) How many different samples are there?

    (b) How many of the samples contain 2 defective fuses?

    (c) How many of the samples contain at least 1 defective fuse?

11. **Senate Committees** In how many ways can a committee of 5 senators be selected from the 100 members of the U.S. Senate so that no two committee members are from the same state?

12. **Exam Questions** An exam contains five "true or false" questions. How many of the 32 different ways of answering these questions contain 3 or more correct answers?

13. **Exam Questions** A student is required to work exactly 6 problems from a 10-problem exam and must work exactly 3 of the first 4 problems. In how many ways can the six problems be chosen?

14. **Arranging Books** The new book shelf at a library contains two novels, six biographies, and four how-to books. In how many ways can the books be arranged on the shelf if the books for each category are placed together?

15. **Jury Selection** In how many ways can 12 jurors and 2 alternates be chosen from a group of 20 prospective jurors?

16. **Subcommittee Selection** A committee has four male and five female members. In how many ways can a subcommittee consisting of two males and two females be selected?

17. **Investment Portfolio** In how many ways can an investor put together a portfolio of five stocks and six bonds selected from her favorite nine stocks and eight bonds?

18. **Game Outcomes** A football team plays 10 games. In how many ways can these games result in five wins, four losses, and one tie?

19. **Marketing Calls** A telemarketer makes 15 phone calls in 1 hour. In how many ways can the outcomes of the calls be three sales, eight no-sales, and four no-answers?

20. **Free-Throws** During practice, a basketball player shoots 10 free-throws. In how many ways can the outcomes result in seven hits and three misses?

21. **License Plates** A license plate contains six letters with no repetitions allowed. How many different license plates are possible?

22. **Technology Options** A college mathematics department has 15 calculus classes. Five classes will use graphing calculators and four classes will use computer software. In how many different ways can the classes be selected?

23. **Three-Letter Words** How many different three-letter words (i.e., sequences of letters) can be formed from the letters of the word JUPITER?

24. **Seven-Letter Words** The shortest word containing all five vowels is SEQUOIA. How many seven-letter sequences of letters, with no repeated letters, contain all five vowels?

25. **Arranging Letters** In how many arrangements of the letters in the word ABSTEMIOUS are the vowels in alphabetical order?

26. **Teaching Assignments** Out of a group of 20 senior education majors at the University of Maryland, five will be selected to student-teach in Montgomery County, four will be selected to student-teach in Prince Georges County, and three will be selected to student-teach in Howard County. In how many ways can this be done?

27. **Group Picture** The student council at Gotham College is made up of four freshmen, five sophomores, six juniors, and seven seniors. A yearbook photographer would like to line up three council members from each class for a picture. How many different pictures are possible if each group of classmates stands together?

28. **Delivery Schedule** A truck driver has to deliver bread to five grocery stores. In how many different ways can he schedule the order of his stops?

29. **Delivery Schedule** Suppose that the stores in Exercise 28 are located in two towns far enough apart that the driver wants to make all stops in one town before going on to the next. In how many different ways can he schedule the order of his stops if the larger town has three stores?

30. **Job Allocation** Of the 14 new programmers hired by a major software company, 3 will be selected to work on programming languages, 4 will be selected to work on word processing software, and 5 will be selected to work on spreadsheet software. In how many ways can this be done?

31. **Poker** How many poker hands consist of 3 aces and 2 kings?

32. **Poker** How many poker hands consist of 2 aces, 2 cards of another denomination, and 1 card of a third denomination?

33. **Poker** How many poker hands consist of 3 cards of one denomination and 2 cards of another denomination? (Such a poker hand is called a "full house.")

34. **Poker** How many poker hands consist of 2 cards of one denomination, 2 cards of another (different) denomination, and 1 card of a third denomination? (Such a poker hand is called "two pairs.")

35. **Detour-Prone ZIP Codes** A five-digit ZIP code is said to be detour-prone if it looks like a valid and different ZIP code when read upside down (Fig. 4). For instance, 68901 and 88111 are detour-prone, whereas 32145 and 10801 are not. How many of the 10^5 possible ZIP code numbers are detour-prone?

Figure 4

36. **Dorm Assignments** In how many ways can a residence director assign six students to four dormitory rooms if two rooms are doubles, two rooms are singles, and two of the students cannot be placed together?

37. **Committee Selection** A class has 12 students, of which 3 are seniors. How many committees of size 4 can be selected if at least one member of each committee must be a senior?

38. **Dance Routines** A dance team knows 15 routines of which 8 are tap, 5 are ballet, and 2 are modern. The program can consist of any five routines. In how many ways can the manager choose which routines to present if there are no restrictions?

39. **Dance Routines** Refer to Exercise 38. In how many ways can the manager choose the routines if at least one routine of each type must be included?

40. **Seating Arrangements** In how many ways can 6 married couples sit in a row if men and women alternate?

41. **Seating Arrangements** In how many ways can 6 married couples sit in a row if no 2 women sit next to each other?

42. **Family Dinner** A family has 6 members. In how many different ways can exactly three of them come to dinner? In how many different ways can three or more of them come to dinner?

43. **Family Dinner** A family has 6 members. How many different family groups can come to dinner?

44. **Placemat Arrangement** A family has 6 members. Each member has a placemat with his or her name on it. In how many ways can the placemats be placed around a round table?

45. Selecting Marbles There are 8 marbles in a bag, numbered 1 through 8. Three (1, 2, 3) are blue and five (4, 5, 6, 7, 8) are white. Choose three marbles from the bag. In how many samples will the number of blue marbles chosen exceed the number of white marbles chosen?

46. Handshakes In a room of 10 people, each person shakes hands with 5 people. How many handshakes take place?

47. English Words How many four-digit sequences of letters could possibly be an English word? *Note*: A word in the English language must contain at least one of the five vowels.

In Exercises 48–51, use a graphing calculator or spreadsheet to calculate the answers.

48. Class Formation The dean at a small college wishes to form an experimental section of General Psychology with 22 students chosen from 20 women and 18 men interested in social science.

(a) How many different such classes are possible?

(b) The dean decides the class should have 12 women and 10 men. Compare the number of possible classes to the solution to (a).

49. Bridge A bridge hand contains 13 cards. What percentage of bridge hands contains all four aces?

50. Bridge Which is more likely—a bridge hand with four aces or one with exactly two kings and two queens?

51. Bridge Which is more likely—a bridge hand with four aces or one with the two red kings, the two red queens, and no other kings or queens?

Solutions to Practice Problems 5.6

1. (a) $C(15,6)$. Each sample is an unordered selection of 15 objects taken 6 at a time.

(b) $C(10,4) \cdot C(5,2)$. Asking for the number of samples of a certain type is the same as asking for the number of ways that the task of forming such a sample can be performed. This task is composed of two consecutive choices. Choice 1, selecting 4 people from among the 10 that support the proposal, can be performed in $C(10,4)$ ways. Choice 2, selecting 2 people from among the 5 people that oppose the proposal, can be performed in $C(5,2)$ ways. Therefore, by the multiplication principle, the complete task can be performed in $C(10,4) \cdot C(5,2)$ ways. [*Note*: $C(15,6) = 5005$ and $C(10,4) \cdot C(5,2) = 2100$. Therefore, less than half of the possible samples reflect the true distribution of the school board.]

2. (a) 2^8 or 256. Apply the generalized multiplication principle.

(b) $C(8,6)$ or 28. Each outcome having 6 successes corresponds to a sequence of 8 letters of which 6 are S's and 2 are F's. Such an outcome is specified by selecting the 6 locations for the S's from among the 8 locations, and this has $C(8,6)$ possibilities.

5.7 The Binomial Theorem

In Sections 5.5 and 5.6 we dealt with permutations and combinations and, in particular, derived a formula for $C(n, r)$, the number of combinations of n objects taken r at a time. Namely, we have

$$C(n, r) = \frac{P(n, r)}{r!} = \frac{n(n - 1) \cdot \cdots \cdot (n - r + 1)}{r!}. \tag{1}$$

Actually, formula (1) was verified in case both n and r are positive integers. But it is useful to consider $C(n, r)$ also in case $r = 0$. In this case we are considering the number of combinations of n things taken 0 at a time. There is clearly only one such combination: the one containing no elements. Therefore,

$$C(n, 0) = 1. \tag{2}$$

Here is another convenient formula for $C(n, r)$:

$$C(n, r) = \frac{n!}{r! \, (n - r)!}. \tag{3}$$

For instance, according to formula (3),

$$C(8,3) = \frac{8!}{3!\,(8-3)!} = \frac{8!}{3!\,5!} = \frac{8\cdot7\cdot6\cdot\cancel{5}\cdot\cancel{4}\cdot\cancel{3}\cdot\cancel{2}\cdot\cancel{1}}{3\cdot2\cdot1\cdot\cancel{5}\cdot\cancel{4}\cdot\cancel{3}\cdot\cancel{2}\cdot\cancel{1}} = \frac{8\cdot7\cdot6}{3\cdot2\cdot1},$$

which agrees with the result given by formula (1).

Verification of Formula (3)   Note that

$$n(n-1)\cdot\cdots\cdot(n-r+1) =$$

$$\frac{n(n-1)\cdot\cdots\cdot(n-r+1)\cancel{(n-r)}\cancel{(n-r-1)}\cdot\cdots\cdot\cancel{2}\cdot\cancel{1}}{\cancel{(n-r)}\cancel{(n-r-1)}\cdot\cdots\cdot\cancel{2}\cdot\cancel{1}} = \frac{n!}{(n-r)!}.$$

Then, by formula (1), we have

$$C(n,r) = \frac{n(n-1)\cdot\cdots\cdot(n-r+1)}{r!} = \frac{\frac{n!}{(n-r)!}}{r!} = \frac{n!}{r!\,(n-r)!},$$

which is formula (3).   ∎

Note that for $r = 0$, formula (3) reads

$$C(n,0) = \frac{n!}{0!\,(n-0)!} = \frac{n!}{0!\,n!} = \frac{1}{0!}.$$

Let us agree that the value of $0!$ is 1. Then the right-hand side of the equation above is 1, so that formula (3) also holds for $r = 0$.

Formula (3) can be used to prove many facts about $C(n,r)$. For example, the following formula is useful in calculating $C(n,r)$ for large values of r:

$$C(n,r) = C(n,n-r). \tag{4}$$

Suppose that we wish to calculate $C(100,98)$. If we apply formula (4), we have

$$C(100,98) = C(100,100-98) = C(100,2) = \frac{100\cdot99}{2\cdot1} = 4950.$$

Verification of Formula (4)   Apply formula (3) to evaluate $C(n,n-r)$:

$$C(n,n-r) = \frac{n!}{(n-r)!\,(n-(n-r))!} = \frac{n!}{(n-r)!\,r!}$$

$$= C(n,r) \quad \text{[by formula (3) again]}.$$

The formula is intuitively reasonable since each time we select a subset of r elements we are selecting a subset of $n-r$ elements to be excluded. Thus there are as many subsets of $n-r$ elements as there are subsets of r elements.   ∎

An alternative notation for $C(n,r)$ is $\binom{n}{r}$. Thus, for example,

$$\binom{5}{2} = C(5,2) = \frac{5\cdot4}{2\cdot1} = 10.$$

The symbol $\binom{n}{r}$ is called a **binomial coefficient**. To discover why, let us tabulate the values of $\binom{n}{r}$ for some small values of n and r.

$$n = 2: \quad \binom{2}{0} = 1 \quad \binom{2}{1} = 2 \quad \binom{2}{2} = 1$$

$$n = 3: \quad \binom{3}{0} = 1 \quad \binom{3}{1} = 3 \quad \binom{3}{2} = 3 \quad \binom{3}{3} = 1$$

$$n = 4: \quad \binom{4}{0} = 1 \quad \binom{4}{1} = 4 \quad \binom{4}{2} = 6 \quad \binom{4}{3} = 4 \quad \binom{4}{4} = 1$$

$$n = 5: \quad \binom{5}{0} = 1 \quad \binom{5}{1} = 5 \quad \binom{5}{2} = 10 \quad \binom{5}{3} = 10 \quad \binom{5}{4} = 5 \quad \binom{5}{5} = 1$$

Each row consists of the coefficients that arise in expanding $(x + y)^n$. To see this, inspect the results of expanding $(x + y)^n$ for $n = 2, 3, 4$, and 5:

$$(x + y)^2 = x^2 + 2xy + y^2$$
$$(x + y)^3 = x^3 + 3x^2y + 3xy^2 + y^3$$
$$(x + y)^4 = x^4 + 4x^3y + 6x^2y^2 + 4xy^3 + y^4$$
$$(x + y)^5 = x^5 + 5x^4y + 10x^3y^2 + 10x^2y^3 + 5xy^4 + y^5.$$

Compare the coefficients in any row with the values in the corresponding row of binomial coefficients. Note that they are the same. Thus we see that the binomial coefficients arise as coefficients in multiplying out powers of the binomial $x + y$; hence the name *binomial coefficient*.

What we observed for the exponents $n = 2, 3, 4$, and 5 holds true for any positive integer n. We have the following result, a proof of which is given at the end of this section.

Binomial Theorem

$$(x + y)^n = \binom{n}{0}x^n + \binom{n}{1}x^{n-1}y + \binom{n}{2}x^{n-2}y^2 + \cdots + \binom{n}{n-1}xy^{n-1} + \binom{n}{n}y^n$$

EXAMPLE 1

Applying the binomial theorem Expand $(x + y)^6$.

Solution By the binomial theorem,

$$(x + y)^6 = \binom{6}{0}x^6 + \binom{6}{1}x^5y + \binom{6}{2}x^4y^2 + \binom{6}{3}x^3y^3$$

$$+ \binom{6}{4}x^2y^4 + \binom{6}{5}xy^5 + \binom{6}{6}y^6.$$

Furthermore,

$$\binom{6}{0} = 1 \qquad \binom{6}{1} = \frac{6}{1} = 6 \qquad \binom{6}{2} = \frac{6 \cdot 5}{2 \cdot 1} = 15$$

$$\binom{6}{3} = \frac{6 \cdot 5 \cdot 4}{3 \cdot 2 \cdot 1} = 20 \qquad \binom{6}{4} = \frac{6 \cdot 5 \cdot 4 \cdot 3}{4 \cdot 3 \cdot 2 \cdot 1} = 15$$

$$\binom{6}{5} = \frac{6 \cdot 5 \cdot 4 \cdot 3 \cdot 2}{5 \cdot 4 \cdot 3 \cdot 2 \cdot 1} = 6 \qquad \binom{6}{6} = \frac{6 \cdot 5 \cdot 4 \cdot 3 \cdot 2 \cdot 1}{6 \cdot 5 \cdot 4 \cdot 3 \cdot 2 \cdot 1} = 1.$$

Thus

Now Try Exercise 19

$$(x+y)^6 = x^6 + 6x^5y + 15x^4y^2 + 20x^3y^3 + 15x^2y^4 + 6xy^5 + y^6.$$ ■

The binomial theorem can be used to count the number of subsets of a set, as shown in the next example.

EXAMPLE 2   **Counting the number of subsets of a set**   Determine the number of subsets of a set with five elements.

Solution   Let us count the number of subsets of each possible size. A subset of r elements can be chosen in $\binom{5}{r}$ ways, since $C(5,r) = \binom{5}{r}$. So the set has $\binom{5}{0}$ subsets with 0 elements, $\binom{5}{1}$ subsets with 1 element, $\binom{5}{2}$ subsets with 2 elements, and so on. Therefore, the total number of subsets is

$$\binom{5}{0} + \binom{5}{1} + \binom{5}{2} + \binom{5}{3} + \binom{5}{4} + \binom{5}{5}.$$

On the other hand, the binomial theorem for $n = 5$ gives

$$(x+y)^5 = \binom{5}{0}x^5 + \binom{5}{1}x^4y + \binom{5}{2}x^3y^2 + \binom{5}{3}x^2y^3 + \binom{5}{4}xy^4 + \binom{5}{5}y^5.$$

Set $x = 1$ and $y = 1$ in this formula.

$$(1+1)^5 = \binom{5}{0}1^5 + \binom{5}{1}1^4 \cdot 1 + \binom{5}{2}1^3 \cdot 1^2 + \binom{5}{3}1^2 \cdot 1^3 + \binom{5}{4}1 \cdot 1^4 + \binom{5}{5}1^5$$

$$2^5 = \binom{5}{0} + \binom{5}{1} + \binom{5}{2} + \binom{5}{3} + \binom{5}{4} + \binom{5}{5}$$

Now Try Exercise 27

Thus the total number of subsets of a set with five elements (the right side) equals $2^5 = 32$. ■

There is nothing special about the number 5 in the preceding example. An analogous argument gives the following result:

A set of n elements has 2^n subsets.

EXAMPLE 3   **Counting pizza options**   A pizza parlor offers a plain cheese pizza to which any number of six possible toppings can be added. How many different pizzas can be ordered?

Solution   Ordering a pizza requires selecting a subset of the six possible toppings. Since the set of six toppings has 2^6 different subsets, there are 2^6 or 64 different pizzas. (Note that the plain cheese pizza corresponds to selecting the empty subset of toppings.)

Now Try Exercise 31 ■

Proof of the Binomial Theorem   Note that

$$(x+y)^n = \underbrace{(x+y)(x+y) \cdot \cdots \cdot (x+y)}_{n \text{ factors}}.$$

Multiplying out these factors involves forming all products, where one term is selected from each factor, and then combining like products. For instance,

$$(x+y)(x+y)(x+y) = x \cdot x \cdot x + x \cdot x \cdot y + x \cdot y \cdot x + y \cdot x \cdot x$$
$$+ x \cdot y \cdot y + y \cdot x \cdot y + y \cdot y \cdot x + y \cdot y \cdot y.$$

The first product on the right, $x \cdot x \cdot x$, is obtained by selecting the x-term from each of the three factors. The next term, $x \cdot x \cdot y$, is obtained by selecting the x-terms from the first two factors and the y-term from the third. The next product, $x \cdot y \cdot x$, is obtained by selecting the x-terms from the first and third factors and the y-term from the second. And so on. There are as many products containing two x's and one y as there are ways of selecting the factor from which to pick the y-term—namely $\binom{3}{1}$.

In general, when multiplying the n factors $(x+y)(x+y)\cdots(x+y)$, the number of products having k y's (and therefore $(n-k)$ x's) is equal to the number of different ways of selecting the k factors from which to take the y-term—that is, $\binom{n}{k}$. Therefore, the coefficient of $x^{n-k}y^k$ is $\binom{n}{k}$. This proves the binomial theorem. ∎

Practice Problems 5.7

1. Calculate $\binom{12}{8}$.

2. An ice cream parlor offers 10 flavors of ice cream and 5 toppings. How many different servings are possible

if each serving consists of one flavor of ice cream and as many toppings as desired?

EXERCISES 5.7

Calculate the value for each of Exercises 1–18.

1. $\binom{6}{2}$ **2.** $\binom{7}{3}$ **3.** $\binom{8}{1}$ **4.** $\binom{9}{9}$

5. $\binom{18}{16}$ **6.** $\binom{25}{24}$ **7.** $\binom{7}{0}$ **8.** $\binom{6}{1}$

9. $\binom{8}{8}$ **10.** $\binom{9}{0}$ **11.** $\binom{n}{n-1}$

12. $\binom{n}{n}$ **13.** $0!$ **14.** $1!$

15. $n \cdot (n-1)!$ **16.** $\dfrac{n!}{n}$

17. $\binom{6}{0} + \binom{6}{1} + \binom{6}{2} + \binom{6}{3} + \binom{6}{4} + \binom{6}{5} + \binom{6}{6}$

18. $\binom{7}{0} + \binom{7}{1} + \binom{7}{2} + \binom{7}{3} + \binom{7}{4} + \binom{7}{5} + \binom{7}{6} + \binom{7}{7}$

19. Determine the first three terms in the binomial expansion of $(x+y)^{10}$.

20. Determine the first three terms in the binomial expansion of $(x+y)^{20}$.

21. Determine the last three terms in the binomial expansion of $(x+y)^{15}$.

22. Determine the last three terms in the binomial expansion of $(x+y)^{12}$.

23. Determine the middle term in the binomial expansion of $(x+y)^{20}$.

24. Determine the middle term in the binomial expansion of $(x+y)^{10}$.

25. Determine the coefficient of x^4y^7 in the binomial expansion of $(x+y)^{11}$.

26. Determine the coefficient of x^8y^5 in the binomial expansion of $(x+y)^{13}$.

27. How many different subsets can be chosen from a set of six elements?

28. How many different subsets can be chosen from a set of 100 elements?

29. Restaurant Tip How many different tips could you leave in a restaurant if you had a nickel, a dime, a quarter, and a half-dollar?

30. Pizza Options A pizza parlor offers mushrooms, green peppers, onions, and sausage as toppings for the plain cheese base. How many different types of pizzas can be made?

31. Cable TV Options A cable TV franchise offers 20 basic channels plus a selection (at an extra cost per channel) from a collection of 5 premium channels. How many different options are available to the subscriber?

32. Salad Options A salad bar offers a base of lettuce to which tomatoes, chickpeas, beets, pinto beans, olives, and green peppers can be added. Five salad dressings are available. How many different salads are possible? (Assume that each salad contains at least lettuce and at most one salad dressing.)

33. Book Selection In how many ways can a selection of at least one book be made from a set of eight books?

34. Dessert Choices In how many ways can a selection of at most five desserts be made from a dessert trolley containing six desserts?

35. **Pizza Options** Armand's Chicago Pizzeria offers thin-crust and deep-dish pizzas in 9-, 12-, and 14-inch sizes, with 15 possible toppings. How many different types of pizzas can be ordered?

36. **CD Selection** In how many ways can a selection of at least two CDs be made from a set of seven CDs?

37. **Appetizers Selection** In how many ways can a selection of at most five appetizers be made from a menu containing seven appetizers?

38. **Ice Cream Sundaes** An ice cream parlor offers four flavors of ice cream, three sauces, and two types of nuts. How many different sundaes consisting of a single flavor of ice cream plus one or more toppings are possible?

39. How many subsets of the set $\{a, b, c, d, e\}$ do not contain the letter c?

40. How many subsets of the set $\{1, 2, 3, 4, 5\}$ do not contain an even digit?

41. **Lab Projects** Students in a physics class are required to complete at least two out of a collection of eight lab projects. In how many ways can a student satisfy the requirement?

42. Suppose that a set has an odd number of elements. Explain why half of the subsets will have an odd number of elements.

43. **Seminar Attendance** How many different groups of students can show up for a seminar with an enrollment of 12?

44. **Menu Planning** In planning a menu, a dietitian must choose 2 carbohydrates from the 7 available ones, 3 vegetables from the 10 available ones, and 1 protein from the 5 available ones. How many menus are possible?

45. Show that in a Venn diagram containing three sets, there are eight basic regions. Use binomial coefficients to explain why.

46. **Car Showroom** A car dealership has 20 different models that could be placed on display in the showroom, but it has room for at most 5 of these. In how many ways can the manager choose the "show cars"? (Assume that at least 1 car will be shown.)

47. **Car Showroom** A car dealership has 20 different models, of which 8 are two-door and 12 are four-door vehicles. In how many ways can the manager choose three of the two-door and two of the four-door models for a showroom display?

48. **Car Sales** In how many ways can a car dealership with 20 cars available on a particular day make at least one sale?

49. What is the coefficient of y^4 in the expansion of $(x - 3y)^7$?

50. **(a)** Use equation (4) to show that

$$\binom{5}{0} - \binom{5}{1} + \binom{5}{2} - \binom{5}{3} + \binom{5}{4} - \binom{5}{5} = 0.$$

(b) For what values of n can equation (4) be used to show that

$$\binom{n}{0} - \binom{n}{1} + \binom{n}{2} - \binom{n}{3} + \cdots \pm \binom{n}{n} = 0?$$

(c) Use the binomial theorem to prove the result in part (a). *Hint*: Apply the binomial theorem to $(x + y)^5$ with $x = 1$ and $y = -1$.

(d) For what values of n can the binomial theorem be used to prove the result in part (b)?

51. **Club Contingent** The Scrabble club at Gotham College agrees to be represented at a national intercollegiate Scrabble tournament. The contingent can consist of as many members of the club as desired, but must consist of at least one person. If the club has 15 members, how many different contingents are possible?

Solutions to Practice Problems 5.7

1. 495. $\binom{12}{8}$ is the same as $C(12, 8)$, which equals $C(12, 12 - 8)$ or $C(12, 4)$.

$$C(12, 4) = \frac{12 \cdot 11 \cdot 10 \cdot 9}{4 \cdot 3 \cdot 2 \cdot 1} = \frac{\cancel{12} \cdot 11 \cdot \overset{5}{\cancel{10}} \cdot 9}{\cancel{4} \cdot \cancel{3} \cdot \cancel{2} \cdot 1} = 495$$

2. 320. The task of deciding what sort of serving to have consists of two choices. The first choice, selecting the flavor of ice cream, can be performed in 10 ways. The second choice, selecting the toppings, can be performed in 2^5 or 32 ways, since selecting the toppings amounts to selecting a subset from the set of 5 toppings, and a set of 5 elements has 2^5 subsets. (Notice that selecting the empty subset corresponds to ordering a plain dish of ice cream.) By the multiplication principle, the task can be performed in $10 \cdot 32 = 320$ ways.

5.8 Multinomial Coefficients and Partitions

Permutation and combination problems are only two of the many types of counting problems. By appropriately generalizing the binomial coefficients to the *multinomial coefficients*, we can consider certain generalizations of combinations, namely *partitions*. To introduce the notion of a partition, let us return to combinations and look at them from another viewpoint. Suppose that we consider combinations of n objects taken r at a time. View the n objects as the elements of a set S. Then each combination determines an ordered division of S into two subsets, S_1 and S_2, the first containing the r elements selected and the second containing the $n-r$ elements remaining (Fig. 1). We see that

$$S = S_1 \cup S_2 \quad \text{and} \quad n(S_1) + n(S_2) = n.$$

Figure 1

This ordered division is called an **ordered partition of type $(r, n-r)$**. We know that the number of such partitions is just the number of ways of selecting the first subset, that is, $n!/[r!(n-r)!]$. If we let $n_1 = n(S_1) = r$ and $n_2 = n(S_2) = n - r$, then we find that the number of ordered partitions of type (n_1, n_2) is $n!/n_1! n_2!$.

We may generalize the aforementioned situation as follows: Let S be a set of n elements. An **ordered partition of S of type $(n_1, n_2, \ldots, n_m)$** is a decomposition of S into m subsets (given in a specific order) $S_1, S_2, \ldots, S_m$, where no two of these intersect and where

$$n(S_1) = n_1, \qquad n(S_2) = n_2, \qquad \ldots \quad , n(S_m) = n_m$$

(Fig. 2). Since S has n elements, we clearly must have $n = n_1 + n_2 + \cdots + n_m$.

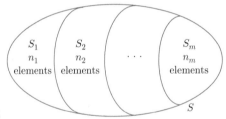

Figure 2

EXAMPLE 1

Ordered partitions of a set List all ordered partitions of $S = \{a, b, c, d\}$ of type $(1, 1, 2)$.

Solution

$$(\{a\}, \{b\}, \{c, d\}) \qquad (\{c\}, \{a\}, \{b, d\})$$
$$(\{a\}, \{c\}, \{b, d\}) \qquad (\{c\}, \{b\}, \{a, d\})$$
$$(\{a\}, \{d\}, \{b, c\}) \qquad (\{c\}, \{d\}, \{a, b\})$$
$$(\{b\}, \{a\}, \{c, d\}) \qquad (\{d\}, \{a\}, \{b, c\})$$
$$(\{b\}, \{c\}, \{a, d\}) \qquad (\{d\}, \{b\}, \{a, c\})$$
$$(\{b\}, \{d\}, \{a, c\}) \qquad (\{d\}, \{c\}, \{a, b\})$$

Note that the ordered partition $(\{a\}, \{b\}, \{c, d\})$ is different from the ordered partition $(\{b\}, \{a\}, \{c, d\})$, since in the first S_1 is $\{a\}$, whereas in the second S_1 is $\{b\}$. The order in which the subsets are given is significant. ∎

We saw earlier that the number of ordered partitions of type (n_1, n_2) for a set of n elements is $n!/n_1! n_2!$. This result generalizes.

Number of Ordered Partitions of Type ($n_1, n_2, \ldots, n_m$)   Let S be a set of n elements. Then the number of ordered partitions of S of type $(n_1, n_2, \ldots, n_m)$ where $n_1 + n_2 + \cdots + n_m = n$ is

$$\frac{n!}{n_1! \, n_2! \cdots n_m!}. \tag{1}$$

The number of ordered partitions of type $(n_1, n_2, \ldots, n_m)$ for a set of n elements is often denoted

$$\binom{n}{n_1, n_2, \ldots, n_m}.$$

Using the preceding notation, result (1) says that

$$\binom{n}{n_1, n_2, \ldots, n_m} = \frac{n!}{n_1! \, n_2! \cdots n_m!}.$$

The binomial coefficient $\binom{n}{n_1}$ can also be written $\binom{n}{n_1, n_2}$. The number

$$\binom{n}{n_1, n_2, \ldots, n_m}$$

is known as a **multinomial coefficient** since it appears as the coefficient of $x_1^{n_1} x_2^{n_2} \cdots x_m^{n_m}$ in the expansion of $(x_1 + x_2 + \cdots + x_m)^n$.

EXAMPLE 2   **Ordered partitions of a set**   Let S be a set of four elements. Use the formula in (1) to determine the number of ordered partitions of S of type $(1, 1, 2)$.

Solution   Here $n = 4$, $n_1 = 1$, $n_2 = 1$, and $n_3 = 2$. Therefore, the number of ordered partitions of type $(1, 1, 2)$ is

$$\binom{4}{1, 1, 2} = \frac{4!}{1! \, 1! \, 2!} = \frac{4 \cdot 3 \cdot 2 \cdot 1}{1 \cdot 1 \cdot 2 \cdot 1} = 12.$$

Now Try Exercise 1   This result is the same as obtained in Example 1 by enumeration.   ■

EXAMPLE 3   **Assigning tasks to construction workers**   A work crew consists of 12 construction workers, all having the same skills. A construction job requires four welders, three concrete workers, three heavy equipment operators, and two bricklayers. In how many ways can the 12 workers be assigned to the required tasks?

Solution   Each assignment of jobs corresponds to an ordered partition of the type $(4, 3, 3, 2)$. The number of such ordered partitions is

Now Try Exercise 15

$$\binom{12}{4, 3, 3, 2} = \frac{12!}{4! \, 3! \, 3! \, 2!} = 277,200.$$ ■

Sometimes all of the m subsets of an ordered partition are required to have the same number of elements. If the set has n elements and each of the m subsets has r elements, then the number of ordered partitions of type

$$(\underbrace{r, r, \ldots, r}_{m})$$

is

$$\binom{n}{r, r, \ldots, r} = \frac{n!}{r! \, r! \cdots r!} = \frac{n!}{(r!)^m}. \tag{2}$$

EXAMPLE 4   **Counting the number of bridge hands**   In the game of bridge, four players seated in a specific order are each dealt 13 cards. How many different possibilities are there for the hands dealt to the players?

Solution   Each deal results in an ordered partition of the 52 cards of type $(13, 13, 13, 13)$. The number of such partitions is

$$\binom{52}{13, 13, 13, 13} = \frac{52!}{(13!)^4}.$$

This number is approximately 5.36×10^{28}.   ∎

Unordered Partitions   Determining the number of unordered partitions of a certain type is a complex matter. We will restrict our attention to the special case in which each subset is of the same size.

EXAMPLE 5   **Unordered partitions of a set**   List all unordered partitions of $S = \{a, b, c, d\}$ of type $(2, 2)$.

Solution

$$(\{a, b\}, \{c, d\})$$
$$(\{a, c\}, \{b, d\})$$
$$(\{a, d\}, \{b, c\})$$ ∎

Note that the partition $(\{c, d\}, \{a, b\})$ is the same as the partition $(\{a, b\}, \{c, d\})$ when order is not taken into account.

Number of Unordered Partitions of Type ($r, r, \ldots, r$)   Let S be a set of n elements where $n = m \cdot r$. Then the number of unordered partitions of S of type $(r, r, \ldots, r)$ is

$$\frac{1}{m!} \cdot \frac{n!}{(r!)^m}. \tag{3}$$

Formula (3) follows from the fact that each unordered partition of the m subsets gives rise to $m!$ ordered partitions. Therefore,

$(m!)$ [number of unordered partitions] $=$ [number of ordered partitions]

or

$$[\text{number of unordered partitions}] = \frac{1}{m!} \cdot [\text{number of ordered partitions}]$$

$$= \frac{1}{m!} \cdot \frac{n!}{(r!)^m} \quad [\text{by formula (2)}].$$

EXAMPLE 6   **Unordered partitions of a set**   Let S be a set of four elements. Use formula (3) to determine the number of unordered partitions of S of type $(2, 2)$.

Solution   Here $n = 4$, $r = 2$, and $m = 2$. Therefore, the number of unordered partitions of type $(2, 2)$ is

$$\frac{1}{2!} \cdot \frac{4!}{(2!)^2} = \frac{1}{2} \cdot \frac{4 \cdot 3 \cdot 2 \cdot 1}{(2 \cdot 1)^2} = 3.$$

Now Try Exercise 11   This result is the same as that obtained in Example 5 by enumeration.   ∎

EXAMPLE 7

Grouping construction workers A construction crew contains 12 workers, all having similar skills. In how many ways can the workers be divided into four groups of three?

Solution The order of the four groups is not relevant. (It does not matter which is labeled S_1 and which S_2, and so on. Only the composition of the groups is important.) Applying formula (3) with $n = 12$, $r = 3$, and $m = 4$, we see that the number of ways is

$$\frac{1}{m!} \cdot \frac{n!}{(r!)^m} = \frac{1}{4!} \cdot \frac{12!}{(3!)^4}$$

$$= \frac{1}{\cancel{4} \cdot \cancel{3} \cdot \cancel{2} \cdot \cancel{1}} \cdot \frac{12 \cdot 11 \cdot 10 \cdot 9 \cdot 8 \cdot 7 \cdot 6 \cdot 5 \cdot \cancel{4} \cdot \cancel{3} \cdot \cancel{2} \cdot \cancel{1}}{6^4}$$

$$= \frac{\overset{2}{\cancel{12}} \cdot 11 \cdot 10 \cdot \overset{}{\cancel{9}} \cdot \overset{2}{\cancel{8}} \cdot 7 \cdot \cancel{6} \cdot 5}{\cancel{6} \cdot \cancel{6} \cdot \cancel{6} \cdot \cancel{6}} = 15,400.$$

Now Try Exercise 19

Practice Problems 5.8

1. A foundation wishes to award one grant of $100,000, two grants of $10,000, five grants of $5000, and five grants of $2000. Its list of potential grant recipients has been narrowed to 13 possibilities. In how many ways can the awards be made?

2. In how many different ways can six medical interns be put into three groups of two and assigned to

   (a) The radiology, neurology, and surgery departments?

   (b) Share living quarters?

EXERCISES 5.8

Let S be a set of n elements. Determine the number of ordered partitions of the types in Exercises 1–10.

1. $n = 5$; $(3, 1, 1)$

2. $n = 5$; $(2, 1, 2)$

3. $n = 6$; $(2, 1, 2, 1)$

4. $n = 6$; $(3, 3)$

5. $n = 7$; $(3, 2, 2)$

6. $n = 7$; $(4, 1, 2)$

7. $n = 12$; $(4, 4, 4)$

8. $n = 8$; $(3, 3, 2)$

9. $n = 12$; $(5, 3, 2, 2)$

10. $n = 8$; $(2, 2, 2, 2)$

Let S be a set of n elements. Determine the number of unordered partitions of the types in Exercises 11–14.

11. $n = 15$; $(3, 3, 3, 3, 3)$

12. $n = 10$; $(5, 5)$

13. $n = 18$; $(6, 6, 6)$

14. $n = 12$; $(4, 4, 4)$

15. **Stock Reports** A brokerage house regularly reports the behavior of a group of 20 stocks, each stock being reported as "up," "down," or "unchanged." How many different reports can show seven stocks up, five stocks down, and eight stocks unchanged?

16. **Investment Ratings** An investment advisory service rates investments as A, AA, and AAA. On a certain week, it rates 15 investments. In how many ways can it rate five investments in each of the categories?

17. **Observation Groups** A psychology experiment observes groups of four individuals. In how many ways can an experimenter choose 5 groups of 4 from among 20 subjects?

18. **Weather** In a certain month (of 30 days) it rains 10 days, snows 2 days, and is clear 18 days. In how many ways can such weather be distributed over the month?

19. **Orientation Groups** During orientation, new students are divided into groups of five people. In how many ways can 4 groups be chosen from among 20 people?

20. **Awarding Prizes** Of the nine contestants in a contest, three will receive cars, three will receive TV sets, and three will receive radios. In how many different ways can the prizes be awarded?

21. **Job Promotions** A corporation has four employees that it wants to place in high executive positions. One will become president, one will become vice president, and two will be appointed to the board of directors. In how many different ways can this be accomplished?

22. **Forming Committees** The 10 members of a city council decide to form two committees of six to study zoning ordinances and street-repair schedules, with an overlap of two committee members. In how many ways can the committees be formed? (*Hint*: Specify three groups, not two.)

23. **Field Trip** In how many ways can the 14 children in a third-grade class be paired up for a trip to a museum?

24. **Work Schedule** A sales representative must travel to three cities twice each in the next 10 days. Her non-travel days are spent in the office. In how many different ways can she schedule her travel, assuming that she does not want to spend four consecutive days in the office?

25. **Basketball Teams** Ten students in a physical education class are to be divided into five-member teams for a

basketball game. In how many ways can the two teams be selected?

26. Derive formula (1) using the generalized multiplication principle and the formula for $\binom{n}{r}$. (*Hint*: First select the elements of S_1, then the elements of S_2, and so on.)

In Exercises 27 and 28, use a graphing calculator or spreadsheet to calculate the answers.

27. **Assignments to Seminars** Calculate the number of ways that 38 students can be assigned to four seminars of size 10, 12, 10, and 6, respectively.

28. **Campaign Tasks** Calculate the number of ways that 65 phone numbers can be distributed to 5 campaign workers if each worker gets the same number of names.

Solutions to Practice Problems 5.8

1. Each choice of recipients is an ordered partition of the 13 finalists into a first subset of one ($100,000 award), a second subset of two ($10,000 award), a third subset of five ($5000 award), and a fourth subset of five ($2000 award). The number of ways to choose the recipients is thus

$$\binom{13}{1,2,5,5} = \frac{13!}{1!\,2!\,5!\,5!}$$

$$= \frac{13 \cdot 12 \cdot 11 \cdot \cancel{10}^{3} \cdot \cancel{9} \cdot \cancel{8} \cdot 7 \cdot 6 \cdot \cancel{5 \cdot 4 \cdot 3 \cdot 2 \cdot 1}}{1 \cdot \cancel{2} \cdot 1 \cdot \cancel{5} \cdot \cancel{4} \cdot \cancel{3} \cdot \cancel{2} \cdot 1 \cdot \cancel{5 \cdot 4 \cdot 3 \cdot 2 \cdot 1}}$$

$$= 13 \cdot 12 \cdot 11 \cdot 3 \cdot 7 \cdot 6 = 216{,}216.$$

2. Each partition is of the type $(2,2,2)$. In part (a) the order of the subsets is important, whereas in part (b) the order is irrelevant. Consider the partitions

$$(\{\text{Dr. A, Dr. B}\}\,,\ \{\text{Dr. C, Dr. D}\},\ \{\text{Dr. E, Dr. F}\})$$

and

$$(\{\text{Dr. C, Dr. D}\}\,,\ \{\text{Dr. A, Dr. B}\},\ \{\text{Dr. E, Dr. F}\}).$$

With respect to part (a) these two partitions are different since in one Drs. A and B are assigned to the radiology department and in the other they are assigned to the neurology department. With respect to part (b), these two partitions are the same since, for instance, Drs. A and B are roommates in both partitions. Therefore, the answers are

(a) $\binom{6}{2,2,2} = \frac{6!}{(2!)^3} = \frac{6 \cdot 5 \cdot \cancel{4} \cdot 3 \cdot \cancel{2} \cdot 1}{\cancel{2} \cdot \cancel{2} \cdot \cancel{2}} = 90.$

(b) $\frac{1}{3!} \cdot \frac{6!}{(2!)^3} = \frac{1}{\cancel{6}} \cdot \frac{\cancel{6} \cdot 5 \cdot \cancel{4} \cdot 3 \cdot \cancel{2} \cdot 1}{\cancel{2} \cdot \cancel{2} \cdot \cancel{2}} = 15.$

CHAPTER SUMMARY

1. A *set* is a collection of objects. Each object is called an *element* of the set. The *empty set* is the set containing no objects.

2. The *union* of two sets is the set consisting of all elements that belong to **at least one** of the sets. The *intersection* of two sets is the set consisting of all elements that belong to **both** of the sets.

3. Set A is a *subset* of set B (written $A \subseteq B$) if every element of set A is also an element of set B. In each situation or problem, all sets are considered to be subsets of a *universal set*. The set of all elements in the

universal set that do not belong to the set A is called the *complement of* A, denoted A'.

4. The inclusion-exclusion principle says that the number of elements in the union of two sets is the sum of the number of elements in each set minus the number of elements in their intersection.

5. A Venn diagram consists of a rectangle containing overlapping circles and is used to illustrate set operations. The rectangle represents the universal set and the circles represent subsets of the universal set.

6. De Morgan's laws state that the complement of the union (intersection) of two sets is the intersection (union) of their complements.

7. The multiplication principle states that the number of ways a sequence of several choices can be performed is the product of the number of ways each individual choice can be performed.

8. The number of ordered arrangements, each called a *permutation*, of n objects taken r at a time is

$$P(n,r) = n(n-1)(n-2)\cdots(n-r+1).$$

9. The number of unordered arrangements, each called a *combination*, of n objects taken r at a time is

$$C(n,r) = \frac{P(n,r)}{r!} = \frac{n(n-1)(n-2)\cdots(n-r+1)}{r(r-1)\cdots 1}.$$

$C(n,r)$ is also denoted $\binom{n}{r}$.

10. The formula $C(n,r) = C(n,n-r)$ simplifies the computation of $C(n,r)$ when r is greater than $\frac{n}{2}$.

11. The binomial theorem states that

$$(x+y)^n = \binom{n}{0}x^n + \binom{n}{1}x^{n-1}y + \binom{n}{2}x^{n-2}y^2$$
$$+ \cdots + \binom{n}{n-1}xy^{n-1} + \binom{n}{n}y^n.$$

12. A set of n elements has 2^n subsets.

13. Let S be a set of n elements, and suppose that $n = n_1 + n_2 + \cdots + n_m$ where each number in the sum is a positive integer. Then the number of ordered partitions of S into subsets of sizes $n_1, n_2, \ldots, n_m$ is

$$\frac{n!}{n_1! \, n_2! \cdots n_m!}.$$

This number is also denoted

$$\binom{n}{n_1, n_2, \ldots, n_m}.$$

14. Let S be a set of n elements, where $n = m \cdot r$. Then the number of unordered partitions of S into m subsets of size r is $\dfrac{1}{m!} \cdot \dfrac{n!}{(r!)^m}$.

REVIEW OF FUNDAMENTAL CONCEPTS

1. What is a set?

2. What is a subset of a set?

3. What is an element of a set?

4. Define a universal set.

5. Define the empty set.

6. Use a Venn diagram to draw the complement of a set A.

7. Use a Venn diagram to draw the sets $A \cap B$ and $A \cup B$.

8. Use a Venn diagram to draw the sets $A \cap (B \cup C)$ and $A \cup (B \cap C)$.

9. State the generalized multiplication principle for counting.

10. What is meant by a permutation of n items taken r at a time?

11. How would you calculate the number of permutations of n items taken r at a time?

12. What is the difference between a permutation and a combination?

13. How would you calculate the number of combinations of n items taken r at a time?

14. Give a formula that can be used to calculate each of the following:

$$n! \qquad \binom{n}{r} \qquad C(n,r) \qquad P(n,r).$$

15. State the binomial theorem.

16. If a set contains n elements, how many subsets does it have?

17. Explain what is meant by an ordered partition of a set.

18. Explain how to calculate the number of ordered partitions of a set.

19. Give a formula that can be used to calculate

$$\binom{n}{n_1, n_2, \ldots, n_m}.$$

KEY FORMULAS

Inclusion–Exclusion Principle:

$$n(S \cup T) = n(S) + n(T) - n(S \cap T)$$

De Morgan's Law:

$$(S \cup T)' = S' \cap T' \quad \text{and} \quad (S \cap T)' = S' \cup T'$$

Permutations:

$$P(n, r) = n(n - 1)(n - 2) \cdots \cdot (n - r + 1) \quad (r \text{ factors})$$

Combinations:

$$C(n, r) = \frac{P(n, r)}{r!} = \frac{n(n-1) \cdots \cdot (n - r + 1)}{r(r - 1) \cdots \cdot 1}$$

$$= \frac{n!}{r!(n - r)!}$$

A Property of Binomial Coefficients: $C(n, r) = C(n, n - r)$

Binomial Theorem:

$$(x + y)^n = \binom{n}{0}x^n + \binom{n}{1}x^{n-1}y + \binom{n}{2}x^{n-2}y^2$$

$$+ \cdots + \binom{n}{n-1}xy^{n-1} + \binom{n}{n}y^n$$

Number of subsets in a set of n elements: 2^n

Number of Ordered Partitions of Type $(n_1, n_2, \ldots, n_m)$, where $n = n_1 + \cdots + n_m$:

$$\frac{n!}{n_1!\, n_2! \cdots n_m!}$$

Number of Unordered Partitions of Type $(r, r, \ldots, r)$, where there are m r's and $n = m \cdot r$:

$$\frac{1}{m!} \cdot \frac{n!}{(r!)^m}$$

SUPPLEMENTARY EXERCISES

1. List all subsets of the set $\{a, b\}$.

2. Draw a two-circle Venn diagram and shade the portion corresponding to the set $(S \cup T')'$.

3. **Tennis Finalists** There are 16 contestants in a tennis tournament. How many different possibilities are there for the two people who will play in the final round?

4. **Team Picture** In how many ways can a coach and five basketball players line up in a row for a picture if the coach insists on standing at one of the ends of the row?

5. Draw a three-circle Venn diagram and shade the portion corresponding to the set $R' \cap (S \cup T)$.

6. Calculate the first three terms in the binomial expansion of $(x + y)^{12}$.

7. **Balls in an Urn** An urn contains 14 numbered balls, of which 8 are red and 6 are green. How many different possibilities are there for selecting a sample of 5 balls in which 3 are red and 2 are green?

8. **Testing a Drug** Sixty people with a certain medical condition were given pills. Fifteen of these people received placebos. Forty people showed improvement, and 30 of these people received an actual drug. How many of the people who received the drug showed no improvement?

9. **Appliance Purchase** An appliance store carries seven different types of washing machines and five different types of dryers. How many different combinations are possible for a customer who wants to purchase a washing machine and a dryer?

10. **Contest Prizes** There are 12 contestants in a contest. Two will receive trips around the world, four will receive cars, and six will receive TV sets. In how many different ways can the prizes be awarded?

11. **Languages** Out of a group of 115 applicants for jobs at the World Bank, 70 speak French, 65 speak Spanish, 65 speak German, 45 speak French and Spanish, 35 speak Spanish and German, 40 speak French and German, and 35 speak all three languages. How many of the people speak none of the three languages?

12. Calculate $\binom{17}{15}$.

Environmental Poll *The 100 members of the Earth Club were asked what they felt the club's priorities should be in the coming year: clean water, clean air, or recycling. The responses were 45 for clean water, 30 for clean air, 42 for recycling, 13 for both clean air and clean water, 20 for clean air and recycling, 16 for clean water and recycling, and 9 for all three. Exercises 13–20 refer to this poll.*

13. How many members thought the priority should be clean air only?

14. How many members thought the priority should be clean water or clean air, but not both?

15. How many members thought the priority should be clean water or recycling but not clean air?

16. How many members thought the priority should be clean air and recycling but not clean water?

17. How many members thought the priority should be exactly one of the three issues?

18. How many members thought recycling should not be a priority?

19. How many members thought the priority should be recycling but not clean air?

20. How many members thought the priority should be something other than one of these three issues?

21. **Nine-Letter Words** How many different nine-letter words (i.e., sequences of letters) can be made using four S's and five T's?

22. **Passing an Exam** Forty people take an exam. How many different possibilities are there for the set of people who pass the exam?

23. **Winter Sports** A survey at a small New England college showed that 400 students skied, 300 played ice hockey, and 150 did both. How many students participated in at least one of these sports?

24. **Meal Choices** How many different meals can be chosen if there are 6 appetizers, 10 main dishes, and 8 desserts, assuming a meal consists of one item from each category?

25. **Test Scoring** On an essay test there are 5 questions worth 20 points each. In how many ways can a student get 10 points on one question, 15 points on each of three questions, and 20 points on another question?

26. **Seven-Digit Numbers** How many seven-digit numbers are even and have a 3 in the hundreds place?

27. **Telephone Numbers** How many telephone numbers are theoretically possible if all numbers are of the form *abc-def-ghij* and neither of the first two leading digits (*a* and *d*) is zero?

28. Calculate the number of different strings of letters of length at least 1 but less than 11.

29. How many strings of length 8 can be formed from the symbols *a*, *b*, *c*, *d*, and *e*? How many of the strings have at least one *e*?

30. **Basketball Teams** How many different 5-person basketball teams can be formed from a pool of 12 players?

31. **Selecting Students** Fourteen students in the 100-student eighth grade are to be chosen to tour the United Nations. How many different groups of 14 are possible?

32. **Journal Subscriptions** In one ZIP code, there are 40,000 households. Of them, 4000 households get *Fancy Diet Magazine*, 10,000 households get *Clean Living Journal*, and 1500 households get both publications. How many households get neither?

33. **Computer Program** At each stage in a decision process, a computer program has three branches. There are 10 stages at which these branches appear. How many different paths could the process follow?

34. **Filling Jobs** Sixty people apply for 10 job openings. In how many ways can all the jobs be filled?

35. **Generating Tests** A computerized test generator can generate any one of 5 problems for each of the 10 areas being tested. How many different tests can be generated?

36. If a string of six letters cannot contain any vowels (a, e, i, o, u), how many strings are possible?

37. **Choosing Delegations** How many different 4-person delegations can be chosen from 10 ambassadors?

38. **Subdividing a Class** In how many ways can a teacher divide a class of 21 students into groups of 7 students each?

39. **Distributing Candy** In how many ways can 14 different candies be distributed to 14 scouts?

40. **Senate Subdivision** In how many ways can 100 senators be divided into groups of 20 each?

41. **Senate Subdivision** In how many ways can 100 senators be assigned to groups of 20 each if the 2 senators from the state of New York cannot be in the same group?

42. If every team in a ten-team softball league plays every other team three times, how many games are played?

43. How many diagonals does an *n*-sided polygon have?

44. **Racetrack Betting** Racetracks have a compound bet called the *daily double*, in which the bettor tries to select the winners of the first two races. If 8 horses compete in the first race and 6 horses compete in the second race, determine the possible number of daily double bets.

45. **Hat Displays** A designer of a window display wants to form a pyramid with 15 hats. She wants to place the five men's hats in the bottom row, the four women's hats in the next row, next the three baseball caps, then the two berets, and a clown's hat at the top. All the hats are different. How many displays are possible?

46. **Seat Assignments** In how many ways can 5 people be assigned to seats in a 12-seat room?

47. **Poker** A poker hand consists of five cards. How many different poker hands contain all cards of the same suit? (Such a hand is called a "flush.")

48. How many three-digit numbers are there in which no two digits are alike?

49. How many three-digit numbers are there in which exactly two digits are alike?

50. **Poker** How many hands of five cards contain exactly three aces?

51. **Greek-Letter Societies** Fraternity and sorority names consist of two or three letters from the Greek alphabet. How many different names are there in which no letter appears more than once? (The Greek alphabet contains 24 letters.)

Party Guests *In Exercises 52–54 suppose there are three boys and three girls at a party.*

52. How many different pairings of the six into three boy-girl pairs can be formed?

53. In how many ways can they be seated in a row such that no person is seated next to someone of the same sex?

54. In how many ways can they be seated at a round table such that no person is seated next to someone of the same sex?

55. **Feasible Set** If 10 lines are drawn in the plane so that none of them are parallel and no three lines intersect at the same point, how many points of intersection are there? If each of these 10 lines forms the boundary of the bounded feasible set of a system of linear inequalities, how many of the intersections occur outside the feasible set?

56. **Splitting Classes** Two elementary school teachers have 24 students each. The first teacher splits his students into four groups of six. The second teacher splits her students into six groups of four. Which teacher has more options?

57. **Consultation Schedule** A consulting engineer agrees to spend three days at Widgets International, four days at Gadgets Unlimited, and three days at Doodads Incorporated in the next two workweeks. In how many different ways can she schedule her consultations?

58. **Arranging Books** A set of books can be arranged on a bookshelf in 120 different ways. How many books are in the set?

59. **Batting Order** How many batting orders are possible in a nine-member baseball team if the catcher must bat fourth and the pitcher last?

60. **Choosing Committees** In how many ways can a committee of 5 people be chosen from 12 married couples if

    (a) The committee must consist of two men and three women?

    (b) A husband and wife cannot both serve on the committee?

61. **Voting** Suppose that you are voting in an election for state delegate. Two state delegates are to be elected from among seven candidates. In how many different ways can you cast your ballot? (*Note*: You may vote for two candidates. However, some people "single-shoot," and others don't pull any levers.)

62. **Spelling Algebraic** The object is to start with the letter A on top and to move down the diagram to the C at the bottom. From any given letter, move only to one of the letters directly below it on the left or right. If these rules are followed, how many different paths spell *ALGEBRAIC*?

$$A$$
$$L \quad L$$
$$G \quad G \quad G$$
$$E \quad E \quad E \quad E$$
$$B \quad B \quad B \quad B \quad B$$
$$R \quad R \quad R \quad R$$
$$A \quad A \quad A$$
$$I \quad I$$
$$C$$

63. **Call Letters** The call letters of radio stations in the U.S. consist of either three or four letters, where the first letter is K or W. How many different call letters are possible?

In Exercises 64–66, use a graphing calculator or spreadsheet to calculate the answer.

64. **Arranging Students** A group of students can be arranged in a row of seats in 479,001,600 ways. How many students are there?

65. **Assigning Jobs** There are 25 people in a department who must be deployed to work on three projects requiring 10, 9, and 6 people. All the people are eligible for all jobs. Calculate the number of ways this can be done.

66. **License Plates**

    (a) Calculate the number of license plates that can be formed using three distinct letters and three distinct numbers in any order.

    (b) Compare the solution to (a) with the number of license plates consisting of three distinct letters followed by three distinct numbers. (See Section 4, Example 5.)

Conceptual Exercises

67. What is the relationship between the two sets A and B if $A \cap B = \varnothing$?

68. What is the relationship between the two sets A and B if $n(A \cup B) = n(A) + n(B)$?

69. Explain why $n \cdot (n-1)! = n!$.

70. Use the result in Exercise 69 to explain why 0! is defined to be 1.

71. Express in your own words the difference between a permutation and a combination.

72. Consider a group of 10 people. Without doing any computation, explain why the number of committees of size 6 is equal to the number of committees of 4 people.

73. Without doing any computation, explain why $C(10, 3) = C(10, 7)$.

74. Without doing any computation, explain why $C(10, 4) + C(10, 5) = C(11, 5)$. *Hint*: Suppose a committee of size 5 is to be chosen from a pool of 11 people, and John Doe is one of the people. How many committees are there which include John? How many committees are there that don't include John?

CHAPTER TEST

1. Calculate each of the following:

    (a) $4!$ (b) $P(7,3)$ (c) $C(18,16)$

    (d) $\binom{6}{0}$ (e) $\binom{5}{2,1,2}$

2. True or false?

    (a) $\{a,b\} = \{b,a,b\}$.

    (b) If $A \cup B = A$, then $A \cap B = B$.

    (c) $(A \cap B)' = A' \cap B'$.

3. Let $U = \{a,b,c,d,e\}$, $S = \{b,c,d\}$, and $T = \{a,c,e\}$. List the elements of the following sets.

    (a) $S' \cap T$ (b) $(S \cup T)'$

4. Let

$$U = \{\text{all people}\}$$
$$C = \{\text{certified public accountants}\}$$
$$E = \{\text{self-employed people}\}.$$

    Describe verbally the sets $C \cap E$ and $C \cup E'$.

5. Draw a three-circle Venn diagram and shade the portion corresponding to the set $A \cap (B' \cup C)$.

6. **Group Membership** The Choral Society and the Drama Club at State University hold a joint party. Of the 60 people attending, 40 are members of the Choral Society and 30 are members of the Drama Club. How many are members of both groups?

7. **Freshmen Survey** Out of a group of 100 college freshmen, 9 are education majors, 43 describe themselves as middle-of-the-road politically, and 82 did volunteer work during the past year. Of the education majors, 4 describe themselves as middle-of-the-road politically and 6 did volunteer work during the past year. Thirty-two students did volunteer work during the past year and describe themselves as middle-of-the-road politically. Three freshmen are education majors who describe themselves as middle-of-the-road politically and who did volunteer work during the past year. How many of the freshmen did not meet any of the three

criteria? (*Note*: The data for this problem are based on a survey conducted in the fall semester of 2007 by the American Council of Education.)

8. **Executive Positions** An Internet company is considering three candidates for CEO, five candidates for CFO, and four candidates for marketing director. In how many different ways can these positions be filled?

9. **Exam Questions**

    (a) In choosing problems for an exam consisting of 10 true/false questions, a teacher uses a data bank of 20 easy and 30 hard questions. How many ways can he select the questions for an exam consisting of 5 questions of each type?

    (b) A student who is totally unprepared for the exam decides to answer six of the questions true and the remainder false without even reading the questions. How many different ways can he answer the questions?

10. How many three-digit numbers can be formed from the numbers $\{1,2,3,4,5,6,7\}$ if no digit is repeated?

11. **Family Picture** A family consisting of two parents and four children is to be seated in a row for a picture. How many different arrangements are possible in which the children are seated together?

12. **Selecting Students** The 30 students in a math class consist of 10 science majors and 20 humanities majors. In how many ways can a group of 6 students be selected so that 3 students from each type of major are in the group?

13. Determine the coefficient of $x^7 y^5$ in the binomial expansion of $(x+y)^{12}$.

14. **Hot Dogs** The most popular condiments for hot dogs are mustard, ketchup, onions, relish, chili, sauerkraut, and mayonnaise. How many types of hot dogs can be ordered?

15. **Assigning Volunteers** In how many ways can eight volunteers be assigned to four pairs for visiting the sick?

CHAPTER 5 | PROJECT

Pascal's Triangle

In the following triangular table, known as **Pascal's triangle**, the entries in the nth row are the binomial coefficients $\binom{n}{0}, \binom{n}{1}, \binom{n}{2}, \ldots, \binom{n}{n}$.

							1							0th row
						1		1						1st row
					1		2		1					2nd row
				1		3		3		1				3rd row
			1		4		6		4		1			4th row
		1		5		10		10		5		1		5th row
	1		6		15		20		15		6		1	6th row
1		7		21		35		35		21		7		1

7th row for the last row.

Observe that each number (other than the ones) is the sum of the two numbers directly above it. For example, in the 5th row the number 5 is the sum of the numbers 1 and 4 from the 4th row, and the number 10 is the sum of the numbers 4 and 6 from the 4th row. This fact is known as **Pascal's formula**. Namely, the formula says that

$$\binom{n}{r} = \binom{n-1}{r-1} + \binom{n-1}{r}.$$

1. For what values of n and r does Pascal's formula say that the number 10 in the triangle above is the sum of the numbers 4 and 6?

2. Derive Pascal's formula from the fact that $C(n,r) = \dfrac{n!}{r!\,(n-r)!}$.

3. Derive Pascal's formula from the fact that $C(n,r)$ is the number of ways of selecting r objects from a set of n objects. (*Hint:* Let x denote the nth object of the set. Count the number of ways a subset of r objects containing x can be selected and then count the number of ways a subset of r objects not containing x can be selected.)

4. Use Pascal's formula to extend Pascal's triangle to the 12th row. Determine the values of $\binom{12}{5}$ and $\binom{12}{6}$ from the extended triangle.

5. (a) Show that for any positive integer n,

$$\binom{n}{0} + \binom{n}{1} + \binom{n}{2} + \binom{n}{3} + \cdots + \binom{n}{n} = 2^n.$$

Hint: Apply the binomial theorem to $(x+y)^n$ with $x = 1$, $y = 1$.

(b) Show that for any positive integer n,

$$\binom{n}{0} - \binom{n}{1} + \binom{n}{2} - \binom{n}{3} + \cdots \pm \binom{n}{n} = 0.$$

Hint: Apply the binomial theorem to $(x+y)^n$ with $x = 1$, $y = -1$.

(c) Show that for the 7th row of Pascal's triangle, the sum of the even-numbered elements equals the sum of the odd-numbered elements; that is,

$$\binom{7}{0} + \binom{7}{2} + \binom{7}{4} + \binom{7}{6} = \binom{7}{1} + \binom{7}{3} + \binom{7}{5} + \binom{7}{7}.$$

(d) Use the result of parts (a) and (b) to show that for any row of Pascal's triangle, the sum of the even-numbered elements equals the sum of the odd-numbered elements, and give that common sum for the nth row in terms of n. [*Hint*: Add the two equations in parts (a) and (b).]

(e) Suppose S is a set of n elements. Use the result of part (d) to determine the number of subsets of S that have an even number of elements.

6. (a) Show that for any positive integer n,

$$1 + 2 + 4 + 8 + \cdots + 2^n = 2^{n+1} - 1.$$

(*Hint*: Let $S = 1 + 2 + 4 + 8 + \cdots + 2^n$, multiply both sides of the equation by 2, and subtract the first equation from the second.)

(b) Show that the sum of the elements of any row of Pascal's triangle equals one more than the sum of the elements of all previous rows.

7. (a) Consider the 7th row of Pascal's triangle. Observe that each interior number (that is, a number other than 1) is divisible by 7. For what values of n, for $1 \le n \le 12$, are the interior numbers of the nth row divisible by n?

(b) Confirm that each of the values of n from part (a) is a prime number. (*Note*: A number p is a *prime* number if the only positive integers that divide it are p and 1.) Prove that if p is a prime number, then each interior number of the pth row of Pascal's triangle is divisible by p. [*Hint*: Use the fact that $\binom{p}{r} = \frac{p(p-1)(p-2)\cdots(p-r+1)}{1\cdot2\cdot3\cdots\cdot r}$.]

(c) Show that for any prime number p, the sum of the interior numbers of the pth row is $2^p - 2$.

(d) Calculate $2^p - 2$ for $p = 7$ and show that it is a multiple of 7.

(e) Use the results of parts (b) and (c) to show that for any prime number p, $2^p - 2$ is a multiple of p. (*Note*: This is a special case of Fermat's theorem, which states that for any prime number p and any integer a, $a^p - a$ is a multiple of p.)

8. There are 4 odd numbers in the 6th row of Pascal's triangle $(1, 15, 15, 1)$ and $4 = 2^2$ is a power of 2. For the 0th through 12th rows of Pascal's triangle, show that the number of odd numbers in each row is a power of 2.

In Fig. 1(a) each odd number in the first eight rows of Pascal's triangle has been replaced by a dot and each even number has been replaced by a space. In Fig. 1(b) the pattern for the first four rows is shown in blue. Notice that this pattern appears twice in the next four rows, with the two appearances separated by an inverted triangle. Figure 1(c) shows the locations of the odd numbers in the first 16 rows of Pascal's triangle, and Fig. 1(d) shows that the pattern for the first eight rows appears twice in the next eight rows separated by an inverted triangle. Figure 2 on the next page demonstrates that the first 32 rows of Pascal's triangle have the same property.

(a)   (b)   (c)   (d)

Figure 1

9. Assume that the property shown in Figs. 1 and 2 continues to hold for subsequent rows of Pascal's triangle. Use this result to explain why the number of odd numbers in each row of Pascal's triangle is a power of 2.

(a)   (b)

Figure 2

PROBABILITY

In this chapter we discuss probability, the mathematics of chance. We consider the basic concepts that allow us to associate realistic probabilities to random events that we see in both our personal and professional lives.

6.1 Introduction

Uncertainty faces us every day. We wake up in the morning and check the weather report (60% chance of rain). We decide on our breakfast cereal (oatmeal might reduce cholesterol). We choose the route to school or work (average delay on Route 450 is 20 minutes, average delay on the alternate is 15 minutes). We call our stockbroker and check the bank rates to decide how to handle our paycheck. We get a flat tire on the way to an important date (what's the chance of that?). And so on.

Many events in the world around us exhibit a random character. Yet, by repeated observations of such events we can often discern long-term patterns that persist despite random, short-term fluctuations. Probability is the branch of mathematics devoted to the study of such events.

Human beings have always been interested in games of chance and gambling. We have evidence that games such as dice have been in existence since 3000 B.C. But the mathematical treatment of such games did not begin until the fifteenth century in Italy. The French contributed to the literature in the seventeenth century in an attempt to calculate probabilities and develop the theory. The foundations of modern probability theory are generally credited to Kolmogorov, the Russian mathematician, who in 1933 proposed the axioms on which the present subject of probability rests. Even now in the twenty-first century, contemporary mathematicians continue to develop new ideas that are applied to such varied areas as investment and risk analysis, card shuffling, diagnostic medical procedures, cryptography, and the efficacy of treatment modalities in medical and social programs. To obtain an idea of the sorts of events that are considered, let us consider a concrete example from the field of medicine.

Suppose that we wish to analyze the reliability of a skin test for active pulmonary tuberculosis. Unfortunately, such a test is not completely reliable. On one hand, the test may be negative even for a person with tuberculosis. On the other hand, the test may be positive for a person who does not have tuberculosis. For the moment, let us concentrate on errors of the first sort and consider only individuals actually having tuberculosis. Suppose that by observing the results of the test on increasingly large populations of tuberculosis patients we accumulate the data shown in Table 1. Note that out of each group of tuberculosis patients the test fails to identify a certain number. However, the data do exhibit a pattern. It appears that out of a very large population of tuberculosis patients the skin test will successfully identify about 98% of them. In fact, it appears that as the size of the population is increased, the relative frequency m/N more and more closely approximates the number .98. In a situation like this, we say that the skin test detects tuberculosis with a 98% likelihood or that the *probability* that the test detects tuberculosis (when present) is .98.

TABLE 1

Number of tuberculosis patients N	Number of positive test results m	Relative frequency of positive test results m/N
100	97	.97
500	494	.988
1000	981	.981
10,000	9806	.9806
50,000	49,008	.98016
100,000	98,005	.98005

More generally, the **probability of an event** is a number that expresses the long-run likelihood that the event will occur. Such numbers are always chosen to lie between 0 and 1. The smaller the probability, the less likely the event is to occur. So, for example, an event having probability .1 is rather unlikely to occur; an event with probability .9 is very likely to occur; and an event with probability .5 is just as likely to occur as not.

We assign probabilities to events on the following intuitive basis: The probability of an event should represent the long-run proportion of the time that the event can be expected to occur. For example, an event with probability .9 can be expected to occur 90% of the time, and an event with probability .1 can be expected to occur 10% of the time.

As we shall see, many real-life problems require us to calculate probabilities from known data. Here is one example that arises in connection with the skin test for tuberculosis.

> **Medical Diagnosis** A clinic tests for active pulmonary tuberculosis. If a person has tuberculosis, the probability of a positive test result is .98. If a person does not have tuberculosis, the probability of a negative test result is .99. The incidence of tuberculosis in a certain city is 2 cases per 10,000 population. Suppose that an individual is tested and a positive result is noted. What is the probability that the individual actually has active pulmonary tuberculosis?

Before we can solve this problem, it will be necessary to do considerable preliminary work. We begin this work in Section 6.2, where we introduce a convenient language for discussing events and the process of observing them. In Section 6.3 we introduce probabilities of events, and in Sections 6.4, 6.5, 6.6, and 6.7 we develop methods for calculating probabilities of various sorts of events. The solution of the medical diagnosis problem is presented in Section 6.6. Section 6.8 is devoted to the simulation of simple experiments.

6.2 Experiments, Outcomes, Sample Spaces, and Events

The events whose probabilities we wish to compute all arise as outcomes of various experiments. So as our first step in developing probability theory, let us define *experiments*, *outcomes*, *events*, and the associated concept *sample spaces*.

> **DEFINITIONS** An **experiment** is an activity with an observable result.
> Each possible result is called an **outcome** of the experiment.
> The set of all possible outcomes is called the **sample space** of the experiment.
> An **event** is a subset of the sample space. (We say that the event E has occurred when the outcome of the experiment is an element of E.)

EXAMPLE 1   **Rolling a die** Illustrate the definitions above for the experiment of rolling a die and observing the number on the uppermost face.

Solution   (a) The possible outcomes are the numbers 1, 2, 3, 4, 5, and 6.

(b) The sample space is $\{1, 2, 3, 4, 5, 6\}$

(c) One possible event is $\{2, 4, 6\}$. This event also can be described as "the event that the outcome is an even number." ∎

EXAMPLE 2   **Rolling a pair of dice** Illustrate the definitions above for the experiment of rolling two dice, one red and one green, and observing the number on the uppermost face of each.

Solution   (a) Each outcome of the experiment can be regarded as an ordered pair of numbers, the first representing the number on the red die and the second the number on the green die. Thus, for example, the pair of numbers $(3, 5)$ represents the outcome "3 on the red die, 5 on the green die." That is, each outcome is an ordered pair of numbers (r, g), where r and g are each one of the numbers 1, 2, 3, 4, 5, 6.

(b) The sample space, which has 36 elements, is as follows:

$$\{(1,1), (1,2), (1,3), (1,4), (1,5), (1,6),$$
$$(2,1), (2,2), (2,3), (2,4), (2,5), (2,6),$$
$$(3,1), (3,2), (3,3), (3,4), (3,5), (3,6),$$
$$(4,1), (4,2), (4,3), (4,4), (4,5), (4,6),$$
$$(5,1), (5,2), (5,3), (5,4), (5,5), (5,6),$$
$$(6,1), (6,2), (6,3), (6,4), (6,5), (6,6)\}.$$

(c) One possible event is $\{(1,4), (2,3), (3,2), (4,1)\}$. This event also can be described as "the event that the sum of the two numbers is 5." ■

Now Try Exercise 3(a)

EXAMPLE 3   **Number of people in a queue**   Once an hour a supermarket manager observes the number of people standing in checkout lines. The store has space for at most 30 customers to wait in line. Illustrate the above definitions for this situation.

Solution   (a) The possible outcomes are the numbers 0, 1, 2, 3, ..., 30.

(b) The sample space is $\{0, 1, 2, 3, \ldots, 30\}$.

(c) One possible event is $\{0, 1, 2, 3, 4, 5\}$. This event also can be described as "the event that there are at most five people standing in the line." ■

EXAMPLE 4   **Sample space for pollutant levels**   The Environmental Protection Agency orders Middle States Edison Corporation to install "scrubbers" to remove the pollutants from its smokestacks. To monitor the effectiveness of the scrubbers, the corporation installs monitoring devices to record the levels of sulfur dioxide, particulate matter, and oxides of nitrogen in the smokestack emissions. Consider the monitoring operation as an experiment. Describe the associated sample space.

Solution   Each reading of the instruments consists of an ordered triple of numbers (x, y, z), where x = level of sulfur dioxide, y = level of particulate matter, and z = level of oxides of nitrogen. The sample space thus consists of all possible triples (x, y, z), where $x \geq 0$, $y \geq 0$, and $z \geq 0$. ■

Now Try Exercise 7(a)

The sample spaces in Examples 1, 2, and 3 are *finite*. That is, the associated experiments have only a finite number of possible outcomes. However, the sample space of Example 4 is *infinite*, since there are infinitely many triples (x, y, z), where $x \geq 0$, $y \geq 0$, and $z \geq 0$.

EXAMPLE 5   **Tossing a coin three times**   Suppose that an experiment consists of tossing a coin three times and observing the sequence of heads and tails. (Order counts.)

(a) Determine the sample space S.

(b) Determine the event E = "exactly two heads."

Solution   (a) Denote "heads" by H and "tails" by T. Then a typical outcome of the experiment is a sequence of H's and T's. So, for instance, the sequence HTT would stand for a head followed by two tails. We exhibit all such sequences and arrive at the sample space S:

$$S = \{\text{HHH, HHT, HTH, THH, HTT, THT, TTH, TTT}\}.$$

Now Try Exercise 3(b)

(b) Here are the outcomes in which exactly two heads occur: HHT, HTH, THH. Therefore, event E is

$$E = \{\text{HHT, HTH, THH}\}.$$ ∎

EXAMPLE 6

Political poll A political poll surveys a group of people to determine their income levels and political affiliations. People are classified as either low-, middle-, or upper-level income and as either Democrat, Republican, or Independent.

(a) Find the sample space corresponding to the poll.

(b) Determine the event $E_1 =$ "Independent."

(c) Determine the event $E_2 =$ "low income and not Independent."

(d) Determine the event $E_3 =$ "neither upper income nor Independent."

Solution **(a)** Let us abbreviate low, middle, and upper income, respectively, by the letters L, M, and U, respectively. And let us abbreviate Democrat, Republican, and Independent by the letters D, R, and I, respectively. Then a response to the poll can be represented as a pair of letters. For example, the pair (L, D) refers to a low-income-level Democrat. The sample space S is then given by

$$S = \{\text{(L, D), (L, R), (L, I), (M, D), (M, R), (M, I), (U, D), (U, R), (U, I)}\}.$$

(b) For event E_1 the income level may be anything, but the political affiliation is Independent. Thus

$$E_1 = \{\text{(L, I), (M, I), (U, I)}\}.$$

(c) For event E_2 the income level is low and the political affiliation may be either Democrat or Republican, so that

$$E_2 = \{\text{(L, D), (L, R)}\}.$$

(d) For event E_3 the income level may be either low or middle and the political affiliation may be Democrat or Republican. Thus

Now Try Exercise 9

$$E_3 = \{\text{(L, D), (L, R), (M, D), (M, R)}\}.$$ ∎

The *New York Times* of November 21, 1996 reported that in the New York City public schools with total enrollment of 1.06 million students, 88.1% of the students are in regular classrooms, 4.5% get part-time special education, and 7.4% get full-time special education. Students in New York City attend schools in one of the five boroughs (Manhattan, Bronx, Brooklyn, Queens, Staten Island). If we choose a student at random, we can determine whether the student is in a regular classroom (C), gets part-time special education (P), or gets full-time special education (F). Likewise, for each student we can determine in what borough (M, Bx, Bk, Q, SI) the student goes to school. The sample space is

$$S = \{\text{(C, M), (C, Bx), (C, Bk), (C, Q), (C, SI),}$$
$$\text{(P, M), (P, Bx), (P, Bk), (P, Q), (P, SI),}$$
$$\text{(F, M), (F, Bx), (F, Bk), (F, Q), (F, SI)}\}.$$

A student corresponding to the sample point (F, Bk) is getting full-time special education in Brooklyn.

As we have seen, an event is a subset of the sample space. Two events are worthy of special mention. The first is the event corresponding to the empty set, Ø. This is called the **impossible event**, since it can never occur. The second special event is the set S, the sample space itself. Every outcome is an element of S, so S always occurs. For this reason S is called the **certain event**.

One particular advantage of defining experiments and events in terms of sets is that it allows us to define new events from given ones by applying the operations of set theory. When so doing we always let the sample space S play the role of universal set. (All outcomes belong to the universal set.)

If E and F are events, then so are $E \cup F$, $E \cap F$, and E'. For example, consider the die-rolling experiment of Example 1. Then

$$S = \{1, 2, 3, 4, 5, 6\}.$$

Let E and F be the events given by

$$E = \{3, 4, 5, 6\} \qquad F = \{1, 4, 6\}.$$

Then we have

$$E \cup F = \{1, 3, 4, 5, 6\}$$
$$E \cap F = \{4, 6\}$$
$$E' = \{1, 2\}.$$

Let us interpret the events $E \cup F$, $E \cap F$, and E' using Venn diagrams. In Fig. 1 we have drawn a Venn diagram for $E \cup F$. Note that $E \cup F$ occurs precisely when the experimental outcome belongs to the shaded region—that is, to either E or F. Thus we have the following result.

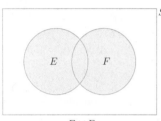

$E \cup F$

Figure 1

DEFINITION Union of Two Events The event $E \cup F$ occurs precisely when either E or F (or both) occurs.

Similarly, we can interpret the event $E \cap F$. This event occurs when the experimental outcome belongs to the shaded region of Fig. 2—that is, to both E and F. Thus we have an interpretation for $E \cap F$:

DEFINITION Intersection of Two Events The event $E \cap F$ occurs precisely when both E and F occur.

Finally, the event E' consists of all those outcomes not in E (Fig. 3). Therefore, we have

DEFINITION Complement of an Event The event E' occurs precisely when E does not occur.

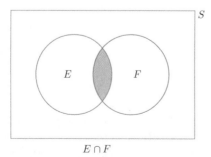

$E \cap F$

Figure 2

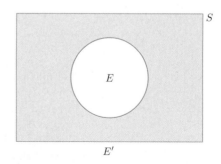

E'

Figure 3

EXAMPLE 7   **Events related to pollution control**   Consider the pollution monitoring described in Example 4. Let E, F, and G be the events

$$E = \text{“level of sulfur dioxide} \geq 100\text{”}$$

$$F = \text{“level of particulate matter} \leq 50\text{”}$$

$$G = \text{“level of oxides of nitrogen} \leq 30.\text{”}$$

Describe the following events.

(a) $E \cap F$ **(b)** E' **(c)** $E \cup G$ **(d)** $E' \cap F \cap G$

Solution   **(a)** $E \cap F = $ “level of sulfur dioxide ≥ 100 *and* level of particulate matter ≤ 50.”
(b) $E' = $ “level of sulfur dioxide < 100.”
(c) $E \cup G = $ “level of sulfur dioxide ≥ 100 *or* level of oxides of nitrogen ≤ 30.”
(d) $E' \cap F \cap G = $ “level of sulfur dioxide < 100 *and* level of particulate matter ≤ 50 *and* level of oxides of nitrogen ≤ 30.”

Now Try Exercise 7(b)

Suppose that E and F are events in a sample space S. We say that E and F are **mutually exclusive** (or *disjoint*) provided that $E \cap F = \emptyset$. In terms of Venn diagrams, we may represent a pair of mutually exclusive events as a pair of circles with no points in common (Fig. 4). If the events E and F are mutually exclusive, then E and F cannot simultaneously occur; if E occurs, then F does not; and if F occurs, then E does not.

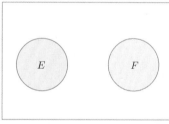

Figure 4 E and F are mutually exclusive.

EXAMPLE 8   **Determining whether events are mutually exclusive**   Let $S = \{a, b, c, d, e, f, g\}$ be a sample space, and let $E = \{a, b, c\}$, $F = \{e, f, g\}$, and $G = \{c, d, f\}$.
(a) Are E and F mutually exclusive?
(b) Are F and G mutually exclusive?

Solution   **(a)** $E \cap F = \emptyset$, and so E and F are mutually exclusive.
Now Try Exercise 11   **(b)** $F \cap G = \{f\}$, and so F and G are *not* mutually exclusive.

Practice Problems 6.2

1. Light Bulbs A machine produces light bulbs. As part of a quality control procedure, a sample of five light bulbs is collected each hour and the number of defective light bulbs among these is observed.

(a) What is the sample space for this experiment?

(b) Describe the event “there are at most two defective light bulbs” as a subset of the sample space.

(Continued)

2. **Citrus Fruit** Suppose that there are two crates of citrus fruit and each crate contains oranges, grapefruit, and tangelos. An experiment consists of selecting a crate and then selecting a piece of fruit from that crate. Both the crate and the type of fruit are noted.

Refer to the crates as crate I and crate II.

(a) What is the sample space for this experiment?

(b) Describe the event "a tangelo is selected" as a subset of the sample space.

EXERCISES 6.2

1. **Committee Selection** A committee of two people is to be selected from five people, R, S, T, U, and V.

   (a) What is the sample space for this experiment?

   (b) Describe the event "R is on the committee" as a subset of the sample space.

   (c) Describe the event "neither R nor S is on the committee" as a subset of the sample space.

2. A letter is selected at random from the word "MISSISSIPPI."

   (a) What is the sample space for this experiment?

   (b) Describe the event "the letter chosen is a vowel" as a subset of the sample space.

3. **Heads and Tails** An experiment consists of tossing a coin two times and observing the sequence of heads and tails.

   (a) What is the sample space of this experiment?

   (b) Describe the event "the first toss is a head" as a subset of the sample space.

4. **Four-Sided Dice** A pair of four-sided dice, each with the numbers from 1 to 4 on their sides, are rolled and the numbers facing down are observed.

   (a) List the sample space.

   (b) Describe each of the following events as a subset of the sample space.
   - (i) Both numbers are even.
   - (ii) At least one number is even.
   - (iii) Neither number is less than or equal to 2.
   - (iv) The sum of the numbers is 6.
   - (v) The sum of the numbers is greater than or equal to 5.
   - (vi) The numbers are the same.
   - (vii) A 2 or 3 occurs, but not both 2 and 3.
   - (viii) No 4 appears.

5. **Selecting from Urns** Suppose that we have two urns—call them urn I and urn II—each containing red balls and white balls. An experiment consists of selecting an urn and then selecting a ball from that urn and noting its color.

   (a) What is a suitable sample space for this experiment?

   (b) Describe the event "urn I is selected" as a subset of the sample space.

6. **Coin Tosses** An experiment consists of tossing a coin four times and observing the sequence of heads and tails.

   (a) What is the sample space of this experiment?

   (b) Determine the event $E_1 =$ "more heads than tails occur."

   (c) Determine the event $E_2 =$ "the first toss is a head."

   (d) Determine the event $E_1 \cap E_2$.

7. **Efficiency Studies** A corporation efficiency expert records the time it takes an assembly line worker to perform a particular task. Let E be the event "more than 5 minutes," F the event "less than 8 minutes," and G the event "less than 4 minutes."

   (a) Describe the sample space for this experiment.

   (b) Describe the events $E \cap F$, $E \cap G$, E', F', $E' \cap F$, $E' \cap F \cap G$, and $E \cup F$.

8. **Product Reliability** A manufacturer of kitchen appliances tests the reliability of its refrigerators by recording in a laboratory test the elapsed time between consecutive failures. Let E be the event "more than nine months" and F the event "less than two years." Describe the events $E \cap F$, E', and F'.

9. **Student Poll** A campus survey is taken to correlate the number of years that students have been on campus with their political leanings. Students are classified as first-year, sophomore, junior, or senior and as conservative or liberal.

   (a) Find the sample space corresponding to the poll.

   (b) Determine the event $E_1 =$ "conservative."

   (c) Determine the event $E_2 =$ "junior and liberal."

   (d) Determine the event $E_3 =$ "neither first-year nor conservative."

10. **Automobiles** An experiment consists of selecting a car at random from a college parking lot and observing the color and make. Let E be the event "the car is red," F be the event "the car is a Chevrolet," G be the event "the car is a green Ford," and H be the event "the car is black or a Chrysler."

(a) Which of the following pairs of events are mutually exclusive?

    (i) E and F (ii) E and G
   (iii) F and G (iv) E and H
    (v) F and H (vi) G and H
  (vii) E' and G (viii) F' and H'

(b) Describe each of the following events:

    (i) $E \cap F$ (ii) $E \cup F$
   (iii) E' (iv) F'
    (v) G' (vi) H'
   (vii) $E \cup G$ (viii) $E \cap G$
    (ix) $E \cap H$ (x) $E \cup H$
    (xi) $G \cap H$ (xii) $E' \cap F'$
  (xiii) $E' \cup G'$

11. Let $S = \{1, 2, 3, 4, 5, 6\}$ be a sample space,

$$E = \{1, 2\} \qquad F = \{2, 3\} \qquad G = \{1, 5, 6\}.$$

  (a) Are E and F mutually exclusive?

  (b) Are F and G mutually exclusive?

12. Show that if E is any event, and E' its complement, then E and E' are mutually exclusive.

13. Let $S = \{a, b, c\}$ be a sample space. Determine all possible events associated with S.

14. Let S be a sample space with n outcomes. How many events are associated with S?

15. Let $S = \{1, 2, 3, 4\}$ be a sample space, $E = \{1\}$, and $F = \{2, 3\}$. Are the events $E \cup F$ and $E' \cap F'$ mutually exclusive?

16. Let S be any sample space, and E, F any events associated with S. Are the events $E \cup F$ and $E' \cap F'$ mutually exclusive? (*Hint*: Apply De Morgan's laws.)

17. **Coin Tosses** Suppose that 10 coins are tossed and the number of heads observed.

  (a) Describe the sample space for this experiment.

  (b) Describe the event "more heads than tails" in terms of the sample space.

18. **Coin Tosses** Suppose that three nickels and three dimes are tossed and the numbers of heads from each group recorded.

  (a) Describe the sample space for this experiment.

  (b) Describe the event "more heads on the nickels than on the dimes" in terms of the sample space.

19. **Genetic Traits** An experiment consists of observing the eye color and gender of the students at a certain school. Let E be the event "blue eyes," F the event "male," and G the event "brown eyes and female."

  (a) Are E and F mutually exclusive?

  (b) Are E and G mutually exclusive?

  (c) Are F and G mutually exclusive?

20. **Genetic Traits** Consider the experiment and events of Exercise 19. Describe the following events.

  (a) $E \cup F$ (b) $E \cap G$ (c) E'

  (d) F' (e) $(G \cup F) \cap E$ (f) $G' \cap E$

21. **Shuttle Bus** Suppose you observe the number of passengers arriving at a Metro station on a shuttle bus that holds up to 8 passengers. Describe the sample space.

22. **Dice** A pair of dice is rolled and the sum of the numbers on the two uppermost faces is observed. What is the sample space of this experiment?

23. **Selecting Balls from an Urn** An urn contains balls numbered 1 through 9. Suppose you draw a ball from the urn, observe its number, replace the ball, draw a ball again, and observe its number. Give an example of an output of the experiment. How large is the sample space?

24. **Selecting Balls from an Urn** Repeat Exercise 23 in the case that the first ball is not replaced.

25. **NBA Draft Lottery** In the NBA, the fourteen basketball teams that did not make the playoffs participate in the draft lottery. Ping pong balls numbered 1 through 14 are placed in a lottery machine and a sample of four balls is drawn randomly to determine which team will have the first overall draft pick. The combination $\{11, 12, 13, 14\}$ is ignored if it is drawn. (*Note*: Each team is assigned between 5 and 250 combinations prior to the drawing in order of their regular season record.) Give an example of an outcome of the draw. In 2008, the Chicago Bulls, who had the ninth worst record in the NBA and were assigned 17 combinations, won the first overall pick. What percentage of the combinations was assigned to the Chicago Bulls?

26. Suppose a coin is tossed and a die is rolled and the face and number appearing are observed. How many outcomes are in the sample space?

27. **The Game of Clue** *Clue* is a board game in which players are given the opportunity to solve a murder that has six suspects, six possible weapons, and nine possible rooms where the murder may have occurred. The six suspects are Colonel Mustard, Miss Scarlet, Professor Plum, Mrs. White, Mr. Green, and Mrs. Peacock. Determine a sample space for the choice of murderer. Discuss how to form a sample space with the entire solution to the murder, giving murderer, weapon, and site.

  (a) How many outcomes would the sample space for the entire solution have?

Let E be the event that the murder occurred in the library. Let F be the event that the weapon was a gun.

  (b) Describe $E \cap F$.   (c) Describe $E \cup F$.

1. (a) $\{0, 1, 2, 3, 4, 5\}$. The sample space is the set of all outcomes of the experiment. At first glance it might seem that each outcome is a set of five light bulbs. What is observed, however, is not the specific sample but rather the number of defective bulbs in the sample. Therefore, the outcome must be a number.

(b) $\{0, 1, 2\}$. "At most 2" means "2 or less."

2. (a) {(crate I, orange), (crate I, grapefruit), (crate I, tangelo), (crate II, orange), (crate II, grapefruit), (crate II, tangelo)}. Two selections are being made and both should be recorded.

(b) {(crate I, tangelo), (crate II, tangelo)}. This set consists of those outcomes in which a tangelo is selected.

6.3 Assignment of Probabilities

In Section 6.2 we introduced the sample space of an experiment and used it to describe events. We complete our description of experiments by introducing probabilities associated to events. For the remainder of this chapter, let us limit our discussion to experiments with only a finite number of outcomes.[1]

What do we mean when we say that the probability of getting a "head" on a toss of a fair coin is 50%? What is meant by the statement that the chance was 1 in 100 of choosing a particular number from the numbers $0, 1, 2, 3, \ldots, 97, 98, 99$? Similar notions are used every day. Probability occurs in the news, in strategies used in games and in war, and in decisions that involve medical treatments, insurance policies, and all kinds of risk.

Suppose that you took a coin and tossed it 152 times and kept track of the results on a chart recording the number of heads and tails as you tossed. You might try this with a real coin, or as we will see later, with a simulation device of some kind. Assume that the tally looked like this:

	Number	Relative frequency
Heads	67	$67/152 = 44\%$
Tails	85	$85/152 = 56\%$
Total	152	1 or 100%

How "fair" does the coin seem to be? We have computed the actual relative frequency of the two outcomes and noted that heads occurs on about 44% of the tosses, and tails on about 56% of the tosses. For this experiment, the **experimental probability**, or **relative frequency**, of heads is 44%.

This experiment is just that—an experiment—and repeating it would generally yield different tallies and different experimental probabilities. But if the coin is fair, the probability assigned to these two outcomes is the fixed theoretical value of 50% for heads and 50% for tails. What this tells us is that in theory, if a fair coin is tossed many, many times, heads will occur about 50% of the time. The experimental probability (relative frequency) of an event may be quite different from the probability.

Suppose that an experiment has a sample space S consisting of a finite number of outcomes $s_1, s_2, \ldots, s_N$. To each outcome we associate a number, called the *probability* of the outcome, which represents the likelihood that the outcome will occur. Suppose that to the outcome s_1 we associate the probability p_1, to the outcome s_2 the probability p_2, and so forth. We can summarize these data in a

---

[1] This restriction will remain in effect until our discussion of the normal distribution in Section 7.6.

chart of the following sort:

Outcome	Probability
s_1	p_1
s_2	p_2
$\vdots$	$\vdots$
s_N	p_N

Such a chart is called the **probability distribution** for the experiment. The numbers $p_1, p_2, \ldots, p_N$ are chosen so that each probability represents the long-run proportion of trials in which the associated outcome can be expected to occur. Central to our assignment of probabilities is the requirement that the total probability is 1. That is,

$$p_1 + p_2 + \cdots + p_N = 1.$$

The next three examples illustrate some methods for determining probability distributions.

EXAMPLE 1   **Probability distribution for coin toss**   Toss an unbiased coin and observe the side that faces upward. Determine the probability distribution for this experiment.

Solution   Since the coin is unbiased, we expect each of the outcomes "heads" and "tails" to be equally likely. We assign the two outcomes equal probabilities, namely $\frac{1}{2}$. The probability distribution is

Outcome	Probability
Heads	$\frac{1}{2}$
Tails	$\frac{1}{2}$

EXAMPLE 2   **Probability distribution for roll of a die**   Roll a die and observe the side that faces upward. Determine the probability distribution for this experiment.

Solution   There are six possible outcomes, namely 1, 2, 3, 4, 5, 6. Assuming that the die is unbiased, these outcomes are equally likely. So we assign to each outcome the probability $\frac{1}{6}$. Here is the probability distribution for the experiment:

Outcome	Probability	Outcome	Probability
1	$\frac{1}{6}$	4	$\frac{1}{6}$
2	$\frac{1}{6}$	5	$\frac{1}{6}$
3	$\frac{1}{6}$	6	$\frac{1}{6}$

Probabilities may be assigned to the elements of a sample space using common sense about the physical nature of the experiment. The fair coin has two sides, both equally likely to be face up. The balanced die has six equally probable faces. However, it may not be possible to use intuition alone to decide on a realistic probability to assign to individual sample elements. Sometimes it is necessary to conduct an experiment and use the data to shed light on the long-run relative frequency with which events occur. The following example demonstrates this technique.

EXAMPLE 3   **Probability distribution for traffic volume**   Traffic engineers measure the volume of traffic on a major highway during the rush hour from 5 to 6 P.M. By observing the number of cars that pass a fixed point for 300 consecutive weekdays, they collect the following data:

Number of cars observed	Frequency observed
at most 1000	30
1001–3000	45
3001–5000	135
5001–7000	75
more than 7000	15

(a) Describe the sample space associated to this experiment.

(b) Assign a probability distribution to this experiment.

Solution (a) The experiment consists of counting the number of cars during rush hour on 300 weekdays and assigning each day to a category depending on the number of cars observed on that day. So, for instance, if we observe 6241 cars on a particular day, we add one to the tally for the category 5001–7000. We let

$$s_1 = \text{"at most 1000 cars"}$$

$$s_2 = \text{"1001–3000 cars"}$$

$$s_3 = \text{"3001–5000 cars"}$$

$$s_4 = \text{"5001–7000 cars"}$$

$$s_5 = \text{"more than 7000 cars."}$$

The sample space is

$$S = \{s_1, s_2, s_3, s_4, s_5\}.$$

(b) For each outcome we use the available data to compute its relative frequency. For example, on 30 days of the 300 observed, the number of cars passing the fixed point is at most 1000. So the outcome s_1 occurred in $30/300 = 10\%$ of the observations. If we assume that the 300 consecutive observations are representative of rush hours in general, it seems reasonable to assign to the outcome s_1 the probability .10. Similarly, we can assign probabilities to the other outcomes based on the percentages of observations in which they occur.

Outcome	Probability
s_1	$\frac{30}{300} = .10$
s_2	$\frac{45}{300} = .15$
s_3	$\frac{135}{300} = .45$
s_4	$\frac{75}{300} = .25$
s_5	$\frac{15}{300} = .05$

■

This method of assigning probabilities to outcomes is valid only insofar as the observed trials are "representative." If such probability models are to be used for planning roadways or traffic patterns, they would have to be tested extensively to be sure that the probabilities are realistic representations of the long-run frequency of events.

In fact, in many instances we cannot rely on intuition or perform such experiments to help us in assigning probabilities; instead, we must use our knowledge of sets and counting to construct a theoretical model of the experiment along with associated probabilities. We need to keep in mind that certain fundamental properties must hold when the set of outcomes (the sample space) is a finite set. These can be observed in the following probability distribution for the number of heads in four tosses of a fair coin:

Events	Probability
0 heads	$\frac{1}{16}$
1 head	$\frac{4}{16} = \frac{1}{4}$
2 heads	$\frac{6}{16} = \frac{3}{8}$
3 heads	$\frac{4}{16} = \frac{1}{4}$
4 heads	$\frac{1}{16}$
Total	1

Note that the column labeled "Events" contains all possible outcomes in the sample space. Also, all of the entries in the probability column are nonnegative numbers between 0 and 1. Furthermore, the sum of the probabilities is 1. These properties hold for every probability distribution.

Let an experiment have outcomes $s_1, s_2, \ldots, s_N$ with respective probabilities $p_1, p_2, p_3, \ldots, p_N$. Then the numbers $p_1, p_2, p_3, \ldots, p_N$ must satisfy two basic properties

Fundamental Property 1   Each of the numbers $p_1, p_2, \ldots, p_N$ is between 0 and 1.

Fundamental Property 2 $p_1 + p_2 + \cdots + p_N = 1$.

Roughly speaking, Fundamental Property 1 says that the likelihood of each outcome lies between 0% and 100%, whereas Fundamental Property 2 says that there is a 100% likelihood that one of the outcomes $s_1, s_2, \ldots, s_N$ will occur. The two fundamental properties may be easily verified for the probability distributions of Examples 1, 2, and 3.

EXAMPLE 3 (Continued)

Verify that the probabilities assigned to the outcomes of Example 3 satisfy Fundamental Properties 1 and 2.

Solution   The probabilities are .10, .15, .45, .25, and .05. Clearly, each is between 0 and 1, so Property 1 is satisfied. Adding the probabilities shows that their sum is 1, satisfying Property 2. ∎

Suppose that we are given an experiment with a finite number of outcomes. Let us now assign to each event E a probability, which we denote by $\Pr(E)$. If E consists of a single outcome, say $E = \{s\}$, then E is called an **elementary event**. In this case we associate to E the probability of the outcome s. If E consists of more than one outcome, we may compute $\Pr(E)$ via the **addition principle**.

> **Addition Principle**   Suppose that an event E consists of the finite number of outcomes $s, t, u, \ldots, z$. That is,
>
> $$E = \{s, t, u, \ldots, z\}.$$
>
> Then
>
> $$\Pr(E) = \Pr(s) + \Pr(t) + \Pr(u) + \cdots + \Pr(z).$$

We supplement the addition principle with the convention that the probability of the impossible event $\emptyset$ is 0. This is certainly reasonable, since the impossible event never occurs.

EXAMPLE 4   **Probability distribution for the number of boys in two-child families**   Observe two-child families. Describe the sample space for counting the number of boys, and assign probabilities to each outcome.

Solution   The sample space $S = \{\text{GG, GB, BG, BB}\}$ describes the sex and birth order in two-child families. (Here, for instance, GB denotes the birth sequence "first child is a girl, second child is a boy.") If we assume that each of the four outcomes in S is equally likely to occur, we should assign probability $\frac{1}{4}$ to each outcome. Then

$$\Pr(\text{no boys}) = \Pr(\text{GG}) = \tfrac{1}{4}$$

$$\Pr(\text{one boy}) = \Pr(\text{GB}) + \Pr(\text{BG}) = \tfrac{1}{4} + \tfrac{1}{4} = \tfrac{1}{2}$$

$$\Pr(\text{two boys}) = \Pr(\text{BB}) = \tfrac{1}{4}.$$

We are making a reasonable assignment of probabilities here, although U.S. statistics show that 51% of all live births are boys and 49% are girls. If we wish to take many years of census data into account for a more accurate model, we would not assign equal probabilities to each outcome in S.   ■

EXAMPLE 5   **Probability associated with a die**   Suppose that we roll a die and observe the side that faces upward. What is the probability that an odd number will occur?

Solution   The event "odd number occurs" corresponds to the subset of the sample space given by

$$E = \{1, 3, 5\}.$$

That is, the event occurs if a 1, 3, or 5 appears on the side that faces upward. By the addition principle,

$$\Pr(E) = \Pr(1) + \Pr(3) + \Pr(5).$$

As we observed in Example 2, each of the outcomes in the die-rolling experiment has probability $\frac{1}{6}$. Therefore,

$$\Pr(E) = \tfrac{1}{6} + \tfrac{1}{6} + \tfrac{1}{6} = \tfrac{1}{2}.$$

Now Try Exercise 5   So we expect an odd number to occur approximately half of the time.   ■

EXAMPLE 6   **A paradox**   In the December 1, 1996 issue of *Parade* magazine, Marilyn vos Savant presented the following question in her column *Ask Marilyn*. "A woman and a man (who are unrelated) each has two children. At least one of the woman's children is a boy, and the man's older child is a boy. Does the chance that the woman has two boys equal the chance that the man has two boys?"

Solution   The answer is NO. The sample space for the man is $\{BB, GB\}$ and each outcome has the same probability, $\frac{1}{2}$. Therefore, his likelihood of having two boys is $\Pr(BB) = \frac{1}{2}$. The sample space for the woman is $\{BB, GB, BG\}$ and each outcome has the same probability, $\frac{1}{3}$. Therefore, her likelihood of having two boys is $\Pr(BB) = \frac{1}{3}$.

A *paradox* is a statement that is counter to many people's intuition and yet is actually true. After the column was published, Marilyn vos Savant received many letters from irate readers criticizing her answer. They reasoned that among families with at least one boy, the other child is just as likely to be a boy as a girl. Therefore, they concluded incorrectly that the probability is $\frac{1}{2}$ in each case.   ■

Now Try Exercise 33

EXAMPLE 7

Probability associated with traffic volume   Consider the traffic study of Example 3. What is the probability that at most 5000 cars will use the highway during rush hour?

Solution   The event

"at most 5000 cars"

is the same as

$$\{s_1, s_2, s_3\},$$

where we use the same notation for the outcomes as we used in Example 3. Thus the probability of the event is

$$\Pr(s_1) + \Pr(s_2) + \Pr(s_3) = .10 + .15 + .45 = .70.$$

Therefore, we expect that traffic will involve at most 5000 cars in approximately 70% of the rush hours.   ■

Now Try Exercise 23(a)

EXAMPLE 8

Probability associated with the roll of a pair of dice   Suppose that we roll a red die and a green die and observe the numbers on the sides that face upward.

(a) Calculate the probabilities of the elementary events.

(b) Calculate the probability that the two dice show the same number.

Solution   (a)   As shown in Example 2 of Section 6.2, the sample space consists of 36 pairs of numbers:

$$S = \{(1,1), (1,2), \ldots, (6,5), (6,6)\}.$$

Each of these pairs is equally likely to occur. (How could the dice show favoritism to a particular pair?) Therefore, each outcome is expected to occur about $\frac{1}{36}$ of the time, and the probability of each elementary event is $\frac{1}{36}$.

(b)   The event

$$E = \text{"both dice show the same number"}$$

consists of six outcomes:

$$E = \{(1,1), (2,2), (3,3), (4,4), (5,5), (6,6)\}.$$

Thus, by the addition principle,

Now Try Exercise 3

$$\Pr(E) = \frac{1}{36} + \frac{1}{36} + \frac{1}{36} + \frac{1}{36} + \frac{1}{36} + \frac{1}{36} = \frac{6}{36} = \frac{1}{6}.$$ ■

EXAMPLE 9

Probability associated with a small lottery   A person playing a certain lottery can win $100, $10, or $1, can break even, or can lose $10. These five outcomes with their corresponding probabilities are given by the probability distribution in Table 1 on the next page.

(a) Which outcome has the greatest probability?

(b) Which outcome has the least probability?

(c) What is the probability that the person will win some money?

Solution (a) Table 1 reveals that the outcome −10 has the greatest probability, .50. (A person playing the lottery repeatedly can expect to lose $10 about 50% of the time.) This outcome is just as likely to occur as not.

TABLE 1

Winnings	Probability
100	.02
10	.05
1	.40
0	.03
−10	.50

(b) The outcome 100 has the least probability, .02. A person playing the lottery can expect to win $100 about 2% of the time. (This outcome is quite unlikely to occur.)

(c) We are asked to determine the probability that the event E occurs, where $E = \{100, 10, 1\}$. By the addition principle,

$$\begin{aligned} \Pr(E) &= \Pr(100) + \Pr(10) + \Pr(1) \\ &= \quad .02 \quad + \quad .05 \quad + \quad .40 \\ &= \quad .47. \end{aligned}$$

Here is a useful formula that relates $\Pr(E \cup F)$ to $\Pr(E \cap F)$:

Inclusion–Exclusion Principle   Let E and F be any events. Then

$$\Pr(E \cup F) = \Pr(E) + \Pr(F) - \Pr(E \cap F).$$

In particular, if E and F are mutually exclusive, then

$$\Pr(E \cup F) = \Pr(E) + \Pr(F).$$

Note the similarity of this principle to the principle of the same name that was used in Section 5.2 to count the elements in a set.

EXAMPLE 10   **Resource availability**   A factory needs two raw materials. The probability of not having an adequate supply of material A is .05, whereas the probability of not having an adequate supply of material B is .03. A study determines that the probability of a shortage of both A and B is .01. What proportion of the time can the factory operate?

Solution Let E be the event "shortage of A" and F the event "shortage of B." We are given that

$$\Pr(E) = .05 \qquad \Pr(F) = .03 \qquad \Pr(E \cap F) = .01.$$

The factory can operate only if it has both raw materials. Therefore, we must calculate the proportion of the time in which there is no shortage of material A or material B. A shortage of A or B is the event $E \cup F$. By the inclusion–exclusion principle,

$$\begin{aligned} \Pr(E \cup F) &= \Pr(E) + \Pr(F) - \Pr(E \cap F) \\ &= \quad .05 \quad + \quad .03 \quad - \quad .01 \\ &= \quad .07. \end{aligned}$$

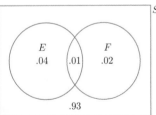

Figure 1

Now Try Exercise 21

Thus the factory is likely to be short of one raw material or the other 7% of the time. Therefore, the factory can expect to operate 93% of the time.

Probabilities involving unions and intersections of events are often conveniently displayed in a Venn diagram. Figure 1 displays the probabilities from Example 10.

Odds   Probability expresses the likelihood of an event occurring as a number from 0 to 1. Odds provide another way to express the likelihood. Odds gives the likelihood as a pair of integers contrasting the chances in favor of the event to the chances against the event. As an example, we say that the odds in favor of obtaining a *three* when rolling a die are 1 to 5. (There is 1 way for the event to be achieved and 5 ways for the event to fail.)

As another example, if a meteorologist says that the odds for rain tomorrow are 3 to 4, he means that on days when weather conditions are similar to today's, we can expect 3 tomorrows with rain for every 4 without rain. In general, when we say that the odds in favor of event E occurring are a to b, we expect that in $a + b$ trials the event would occur a times and fail to occur b times.

> **Converting between Odds and Probabilities**   If the odds in favor of the event E occurring are a to b, then
> $$\Pr(E) = \frac{a}{a+b}.$$
> If $\Pr(E) = p$, then the odds in favor of E are found by reducing the fraction $\frac{p}{1-p}$ to the form $\frac{a}{b}$, where a and b are integers having no common divisor. Then the odds in favor of E are
> $$a \text{ to } b.$$

EXAMPLE 11   **Chance of rain**   Suppose that the odds of rain tomorrow are 5 to 3. What is the probability that rain will occur?

Solution   The probability that rain will occur is

> Now Try Exercise 11

$$\frac{5}{5+3} = \frac{5}{8}.$$
∎

EXAMPLE 12   **Rolling a pair of dice**   The probability of obtaining a sum of eight or more when rolling a pair of dice is $\frac{15}{36}$. What are the odds of obtaining a sum of eight or more?

Solution   With $p = \frac{15}{36}$,

$$\frac{p}{1-p} = \frac{\dfrac{15}{36}}{1 - \dfrac{15}{36}} = \frac{\dfrac{15}{36}}{\dfrac{21}{36}} = \frac{15}{21} = \frac{5}{7}.$$

> Now Try Exercise 13

Therefore, the odds in favor of obtaining a sum of eight or more are 5 to 7. ∎

Odds are often stated as *odds against*. This is always the case with gambling odds. If the odds in favor of an event are a to b, then the odds against the event are b to a. For instance, in Las Vegas roulette, the odds against winning when *red* is bet are 10 to 9. Casinos also have the concept of *house odds*, that are different from true odds. House odds are always in the form m to 1 where m is the amount of money a player wins on a one dollar bet. For instance, the house odds on a *red* bet are 1 to 1. If the ball lands on red, the player wins $1 (in addition to getting his $1 bet back).

Big numbers are easier to get a handle on than small numbers. For instance, the odds of winning the Powerball Lottery with a single ticket are 1 to 146,107,961 and the probability of winning the lottery is .000000006844254. We can easily pronounce the large number in the odds, and we have a reasonable idea of how large 146 million dollars is. But, how does one even pronounce the small probability? One way to pronounce it is 6,844,254 quadrillionths. But very few people have a good feel for how small that number is. Therefore, odds are usually preferable to probabilities in the discussion of highly unlikely events.

Paradoxes   Counterintuitive results abound in probability. Example 6 (two-boy families) provides one illustration. Some other examples of counterintuitive results discussed in this book are as follows.

- *The Famous Birthday Problem*   In a group as small as 23 people, the probability that at least two people have the same birthday is greater that $\frac{1}{2}$. See Example 6, Exercise 61, and Exercise 62 of Section 6.4.
- *Suit Distribution in Bridge*   The most likely distribution of suits in a bridge hand is not 4-3-3-3; that is, four cards of one suit and three cards of each of the other suits. See Exercise 55 in Section 6.4.
- *Medical Diagnosis*   Even with highly reliable tests, a person who tests positive for a certain disease might have a very low probability of actually having the disease. See Example 2 of Section 6.6.
- *Matches Consisting of Multiple Games*   You can have a higher probability than your opponent of winning each game, yet your opponent can have a higher probability of winning the match. See Exercises 38 and 39 of Section 6.6.
- *Tennis Tournament*   Under certain circumstances you have your best chance of winning a tennis tournament if you play most of your games against the best possible opponent. See the first project at the end of Chapter 6.
- *Gender Bias in College Admissions*   In 1973, the University of California at Berkeley was sued for discrimination against women in graduate school admissions. That year 44% of male applicants were admitted and only 30% of female applicants. However, admission is decided by departments and nearly every department favored the female applicants. The second project at the end of Chapter 6 shows how the probability of admission for women can be higher than for men in *every* department and yet the probability of admission for men will be higher in the university as a whole.
- *Family Composition*   A family of four children is more likely to consist of three children of one sex and one of the other, than to consist of two boys and two girls. See Exercise 29 in Section 7.3.

Practice Problems 6.3

1. **T-Maze** A mouse is put into a T-maze (a maze shaped like a "T") (Fig. 2). If he turns to the left he receives cheese, and if he turns to the right he receives a mild shock. This trial is done twice with the same mouse and the directions of the turns recorded.

   (a) What is the sample space for this experiment?

   (b) Why would it not be reasonable to assign each outcome the same probability?

2. What are the odds in favor of an event that is just as likely to occur as not?

3. Suppose that E and F are any events. Show that
$$\Pr(E) = \Pr(E \cap F) + \Pr(E \cap F').$$

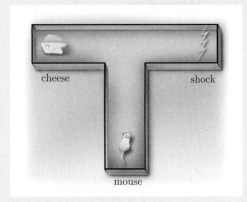

Figure 2

(Continued)

4. The New York State lottery (Lotto) requires a contestant to select six numbers from 1 to 59. The probability of the same combination of six numbers occurring twice in one year is exceptionally low. Lotto system books advise people to avoid number combinations that have been drawn before. What is your assessment of this advice?

EXERCISES 6.3

1. **Word Frequencies** There are 774,746 words in the Bible. The word "and" occurs 46,277 times and the word "Lord" occurs 1855 times.[2] Suppose that a word is selected at random from the Bible.

   (a) What is the probability that the word is "and"?

   (b) What is the probability that the word is "and" or "Lord"?

   (c) What is the probability that the word is neither "and" nor "Lord"?

2. **Heads and Tails** An experiment consists of tossing a coin two times and observing the sequence of heads and tails. Each of the four outcomes has the same probability of occurring.

   (a) What is the probability that "HH" is the outcome?

   (b) What is the probability of the event "at least one head"?

3. **Dice** Suppose that a red die and a green die are rolled and the numbers on the sides that face upward are observed. (See Example 8.)

   (a) What is the probability that the numbers add up to 8?

   (b) What is the probability that the sum of the numbers is less than 5?

4. **U.S. States** A state is selected at random from the 50 states of the United States. What is the probability that it is one of the six New England states?

5. **Roulette** The modern American roulette wheel has 38 slots, which are labeled with 36 numbers evenly divided between red and black, plus two green numbers 0 and 00. What is the probability that the ball lands on a green number?

6. **Selecting a Number** An experiment consists of selecting a number at random from the set of numbers $\{1, 2, 3, 4, 5, 6, 7, 8, 9\}$. Find the probability that the number selected is

   (a) Less than 4.　　(b) Odd.

   (c) Less than 4 or odd.

7. **Horse Race** Three horses, call them A, B, and C, are going to race against each other. The probability that A will win is $\frac{1}{3}$ and the probability that B will win is $\frac{1}{2}$.

   (a) What is the probability that C will win? (Assume that there are no ties.)

   (b) What are the odds that C will win?

8. Which of the following probabilities are feasible for an experiment having sample space $\{s_1, s_2, s_3\}$?

   (a) $\Pr(s_1) = .4$, $\Pr(s_2) = .4$, $\Pr(s_3) = .4$

   (b) $\Pr(s_1) = .5$, $\Pr(s_2) = .7$, $\Pr(s_3) = -.2$

   (c) $\Pr(s_1) = 2$, $\Pr(s_2) = 1$, $\Pr(s_3) = \frac{1}{2}$

   (d) $\Pr(s_1) = \frac{1}{4}$, $\Pr(s_2) = \frac{1}{2}$, $\Pr(s_3) = \frac{1}{4}$

9. An experiment with outcomes s_1, s_2, s_3, s_4 is described by the following probability table:

Outcome	Probability
s_1	.1
s_2	.6
s_3	.2
s_4	.1

   (a) What is $\Pr(\{s_1, s_2\})$?

   (b) What is $\Pr(\{s_2, s_4\})$?

10. An experiment with outcomes $s_1, s_2, s_3, s_4, s_5, s_6$ is described by the following probability table:

Outcome	Probability
s_1	.05
s_2	.25
s_3	.05
s_4	.01
s_5	.63
s_6	.01

    Let $E = \{s_1, s_2\}$ and $F = \{s_3, s_5, s_6\}$.

    (a) Determine $\Pr(E)$ and $\Pr(F)$.

    (b) Determine $\Pr(E')$.

    (c) Determine $\Pr(E \cap F)$.

    (d) Determine $\Pr(E \cup F)$.

11. Convert the following odds to probabilities.

    (a) 10 to 1　　(b) 1 to 2　　(c) 4 to 5

---

[2] According to *The People's Almanac* by Wallechinsky and Wallace (New York: Doubleday, 1975).

12. Poker In poker, the probability of being dealt a hand containing a pair of jacks or better is about $\frac{1}{6}$. What are the corresponding odds?

13. Candy Bars Nine percent of all candy bars sold in the United States are Snickers™ bars. What are the odds that a randomly selected candy bar purchased is a Snickers™ bar?

14. Birth States The odds of Americans living in the state where they were born is 17 to 8. What is the probability that an American selected at random lives in his or her birth state?

15. Horse Race If the odds for Secretariat to win a horse race are 11 to 7, what is the probability that Secretariat wins? Loses?

16. Class Election Four people are running for class president: Liz, Sam, Sue, and Tom. The probabilities of Sam, Sue, and Tom winning are .18, .23, and .31, respectively.

    (a) What is the probability of Liz winning?

    (b) What is the probability that a boy wins?

    (c) What is the probability that Tom loses?

    (d) What are the odds that Sue loses?

    (e) What are the odds that a girl wins?

    (f) What are the odds that Sam wins?

17. Let E and F be events for which $\Pr(E) = .6$, $\Pr(F) = .5$, and $\Pr(E \cap F) = .4$. Find

    (a) $\Pr(E \cup F)$

    (b) $\Pr(E \cap F')$ (*Hint*: Make a Venn diagram similar to Fig. 1.)

18. Let E and F be events for which $\Pr(E) = .4$, $\Pr(F) = .5$, and $\Pr(E \cap F') = .3$. Find

    (a) $\Pr(E \cap F)$ **(b)** $\Pr(E \cup F)$

19. Suppose $\Pr(E) = .4$ and $\Pr(F) = .5$, where E and F are mutually exclusive. Find $\Pr(E \cup F)$.

20. Pair of Dice Suppose a pair of dice is rolled. The probability is $\frac{1}{6}$ that the sum of the numbers on the uppermost faces is 7, and the probability is $\frac{1}{18}$ that the sum is 11. Find the probability that the sum is 7 or 11.

21. Grades Joe feels that the probability of getting an A in history is .7, the probability of getting an A in psychology is .8, and the probability of getting an A in history or psychology is .9. What is the probability that he will get an A in both subjects?

22. Suppose $\Pr(E) = .5$, $\Pr(F) = .6$, and $\Pr(E \cup F) = .9$. Find $\Pr(E \cap F)$.

23. Supermarket Queue A statistical analysis of the wait (in minutes) at the checkout line of a certain supermarket yields the following probability distribution:

Wait (in minutes)	Probability
At most 3	.10
More than 3 and at most 5	.20
More than 5 and at most 10	.25
More than 10 and at most 15	.25
More than 15	.20

    (a) What is the probability of waiting more than 3 minutes but at most 15?

    (b) If you observed the waiting times of a representative sample of 10,000 supermarket customers, approximately how many would you expect to wait for more than 3 minutes but at most 15?

24. What is the probability of the certain event?

25. College Applications The following table was derived from a survey of college freshmen attending baccalaureate colleges and universities. Each probability is the likelihood that a randomly selected freshman applied to the specified number of colleges. For instance, 17% of the freshmen applied to just one college and therefore the probability that a student selected at random applied to just one college is .17. Convert these data into a probability distribution.

Number of Colleges Applied to	Probability
1	.17
2 or less	.29
3 or less	.43
4 or less	.59
20 or less	1

Source: The American Freshman: National Norms for Fall 2007, Los Angeles, Calif.: American Council on Education, 2008.

26. College Applications Refer to the data of Exercise 25. What is the probability that a student applied to three or more colleges?

27. Employees' Ages In a study of the ages of its employees, over a period of several years a university finds the following:

Age (years)	Probability
20–34	.15
20–49	.70
20–64	.90
20–79	1.00

    (a) Find the probability associated with each of the events: 20–34 years, 35–49 years, 50–64 years, and 65–79 years.

    (b) Find the probability that an employee selected at random is at least 50 years old.

28. House Sales A realtor analyzes the office's sales over the past two years. She sorts the sales by the age of the house at the time of sale.

Age	Number of Houses Sold
1–2	1200
3–4	1570
5–6	1600
7–8	1520
9–10	1480

(a) Determine the probability that a sale chosen at random is a house between five and six years old.

(b) What are the odds that the house is less than seven years old?

29. Computer Usage Computer usage in a community is segmented by the kind of use:

Kind of use	Frequency
School only	20%
Work only	22%
Home computer only	20%
No computer anywhere	17%

(a) Explain why the percentages listed above do not add up to 100%.

(b) What is the probability that someone in the community uses a computer?

30. According to Food Processing Magazine (December 2007), the colors in a bag of milk chocolate M&M's have the following distribution:

Color	Probability
Brown	.3
Yellow	.2
Red	.2
Orange	.1
Blue	.1
Green	.1

(a) What is the probability of randomly selecting a blue or yellow M&M?

(b) What is the probability of randomly selecting a brown, orange, or red M&M?

31. College Freshmen Eighty-two percent of the students who entered college in the fall of 2007 had attended public schools. What are the odds that a randomly selected college freshman in the fall of 2007 attended a public school?

32. Odds of an Earthquake The probability that there will be a major earthquake in the San Francisco area during the next 30 years is .7. What are the corresponding odds?

33. Bookies Gamblers usually give odds *against* an event happening. For instance, if a bookie gives the odds 4 to 1 that the Yankees win the next World Series, he is stating that the probability that the Yankees will win are $\frac{1}{5}$ or .2. Also, if a bettor bets $1 that the Yankees will win and the Yankees do win, then the bettor will receive $5 (his original bet + a profit of $4). The following are typical odds set by a bookie for the eventual winner in a fictitious four-team league: Sparks (5 to 3), Meteors (3 to 1), Asteroids (3 to 2), Suns (4 to 1).

(a) Convert the odds to probabilities of winning for each team.

(b) Add the four probabilities.

(c) Explain why the answer to (b) makes sense.

34. Coin Toss A fair coin is tossed twice and we are told that at least one of the tosses is a head. What is the probability that both tosses are heads?

35. Zodiac Signs A high school astrology club has 13 members. What is the probability that two or more members have the same zodiac sign? *Note*: There are twelve zodiac signs.

36. Birth Day A basketball team has eight players. What is the probability that at least two of them were born on the same day of the week?

37. Absent-Minded Attendant Twenty people check their coats at a restaurant's coat-check counter. If the attendant returns the coats to the people at random, what is the probability that exactly 19 of the people receive the correct coat?

38. Tennis The probability that Alice beats Ben in a game of tennis is twice the probability that Ben beats Alice. Determine the two probabilities.

Solutions to Practice Problems 6.3

1. (a) {LL, LR, RR, RL}. Here LL means that the mouse turned left both times, LR means that the mouse turned left the first time and right the second, and so on.

(b) The mouse will learn something from the first trial. If he turned left the first time and got rewarded, then he is more likely to turn left again on the second trial. Hence LL should have a greater probability than LR. Similarly, RL should be more likely than RR.

(Continued)

2. 1 to 1. An event that is just as likely to occur as not has probability $\frac{1}{2}$ and $\frac{.5}{1-.5} = \frac{.5}{.5} = \frac{1}{1}$.

3. The sets $(E \cap F)$ and $(E \cap F')$ have no elements in common and so are mutually exclusive. Since $E = (E \cap F) \cup (E \cap F')$, the result follows from the inclusion–exclusion principle.

4. The ping pong balls don't remember what combinations they produced in the past. Any combination of six numbers is just as likely to occur as any other combination.

6.4 Calculating Probabilities of Events

As mentioned in Section 6.3, there are several ways to assign probabilities to the events of a sample space. One way is to perform the experiment many times and assign probabilities based on empirical data. Sometimes our intuition about situations suffices, as in simple coin-tossing experiments. But we frequently are faced with forming a model of an experiment to assign probabilities consistent with Fundamental Properties 1 and 2. This section shows how the counting techniques of Chapter 5 may be used to extend these ideas to more complex situations. In addition, the exceptionally wide range of applications that make use of probability theory is illustrated.

Experiments with Equally Likely Outcomes   In the experiments associated to many common applications, all outcomes are **equally likely**—that is, they all have the same probability. This is the case, for example, if we toss an unbiased coin or select a person at random from a population. If a sample space has N equally likely outcomes, then the probability of each outcome is $1/N$ (since the probabilities must add up to 1). If we use this fact, the probability of any event is easy to compute. Namely, suppose that E is an event consisting of M outcomes. Then, by the addition principle,

$$\Pr(E) = \underbrace{\frac{1}{N} + \frac{1}{N} + \cdots + \frac{1}{N}}_{M \text{ times}} = \frac{M}{N}.$$

We can restate this fundamental result as follows:

Let S be a sample space consisting of N equally likely outcomes. Let E be any event. Then

$$\Pr(E) = \frac{[\text{number of outcomes in } E]}{N}. \tag{1}$$

In order to apply formula (1) in particular examples, it is necessary to compute N, the number of equally likely outcomes in the sample space, and [number of outcomes in E]. Often these quantities can be determined using the counting techniques of Chapter 5. Some illustrative computations are provided in Examples 1 through 7 here.

We should mention that, although the urn and dice problems considered in this section and the next might seem artificial and removed from applications, many applied problems can be described in mathematical terms as urn or dice experiments. We begin our discussion with two examples involving abstract urn problems. Then in two more examples we show the utility of urn models by applying them to quality control and medical screening problems (Examples 3 and 5, respectively).

EXAMPLE 1

Selecting balls from an urn An urn contains eight white balls and two green balls. A sample of three balls is selected at random. What is the probability of selecting only white balls?

Solution The experiment consists of selecting 3 balls from the 10. Since the order in which the 3 balls are selected is immaterial, the samples are combinations of 10 balls taken 3 at a time. The total number of samples is therefore $C(10,3)$, and this is N, the number of elements in the sample space. Since the selection of the sample is random, all samples are equally likely, and thus we can use formula (1) to compute the probability of any event. The problem asks us to compute the probability of the event $E =$ "all three balls selected are white." Since there are 8 white balls, the number of different samples in which all are white is $C(8,3)$. Thus

$$\Pr(E) = \frac{[\text{number of outcomes in } E]}{N} = \frac{C(8,3)}{C(10,3)} = \frac{56}{120} = \frac{7}{15}. \qquad \blacksquare$$

EXAMPLE 2

Selecting balls from an urn An urn contains eight white balls and two green balls. A sample of three balls is selected at random. What is the probability that the sample contains at least one green ball?

Solution As in Example 1, there are $N = C(10,3)$ equally likely outcomes. Let F be the event "at least one green ball is selected." Let us determine the number of different outcomes in F. These outcomes contain either one or two green balls. There are $C(2,1)$ ways to select one green ball from two; and for each of these, there are $C(8,2)$ ways to select two white balls from eight. By the multiplication principle, the number of samples containing one green ball equals $C(2,1) \cdot C(8,2)$. Similarly, the number of samples containing two green balls equals $C(2,2) \cdot C(8,1)$. Note that although the sample size is 3, there are only two green balls in the urn. Since the sampling is done without replacement, no sample can have more than two greens. Therefore, the number of outcomes in F—namely the number of samples having at least one green ball—equals

$$C(2,1) \cdot C(8,2) + C(2,2) \cdot C(8,1) = 2 \cdot 28 + 1 \cdot 8 = 64,$$

so

Now Try Exercise 9

$$\Pr(F) = \frac{[\text{number of outcomes in } F]}{N} = \frac{64}{C(10,3)} = \frac{64}{120} = \frac{8}{15}. \qquad \blacksquare$$

EXAMPLE 3

Quality control A toy manufacturer inspects boxes of toys before shipment. Each box contains 10 toys. The inspection procedure consists of randomly selecting three toys from the box. If any are defective, the box is not shipped. Suppose that a given box has two defective toys. What is the probability that it will be shipped?

Solution This problem is not really new! We solved it in disguise as Example 1. The urn can be regarded as a box of toys, and the balls as individual toys. The white balls are nondefective toys and the green balls defective toys. The random selection of three balls from the urn is just the inspection procedure. And the event "all three balls selected are white" corresponds to the box being shipped. As we calculated previously, the probability of this event is $\frac{7}{15}$. (Since $\frac{7}{15} \approx .47$, there is approximately a 47% chance of shipping a box with two defective toys. This inspection procedure is not particularly effective!) $\blacksquare$

Now Try Exercise 7

EXAMPLE 4   **Selecting students**   A professor is randomly choosing a group of three students to do an oral presentation. In her class of 10 students, 2 are on the debate team. What is the chance that the professor chooses at least one of the debaters for the group?

Solution   This is the same as Example 2. Just think of the debate team members as the green balls and the others in the class as white balls. The chance of getting at least one debate team member in the group is $\frac{8}{15} \approx .53$.   ■

Now Try Exercise 29

EXAMPLE 5   **Medical screening**   Suppose that a cruise ship returns to the United States from the Far East. Unknown to anyone, 4 of its 600 passengers have contracted a rare disease. Suppose that the Public Health Service screens 20 passengers, selected at random, to see whether the disease is present aboard ship. What is the probability that the presence of the disease will escape detection?

Solution   The sample space consists of samples of 20 drawn from among the 600 passengers. There are $C(600, 20)$ such samples. The number of samples containing none of the sick passengers is $C(596, 20)$. Therefore, the probability of not detecting the disease is

$$\frac{C(596, 20)}{C(600, 20)} = \frac{\dfrac{596!}{20! \, 576!}}{\dfrac{600!}{20! \, 580!}} = \frac{596!}{600!} \cdot \frac{580!}{576!}$$

$$= \frac{596!}{600 \cdot 599 \cdot 598 \cdot 597 \cdot 596!} \cdot \frac{580 \cdot 579 \cdot 578 \cdot 577 \cdot 576!}{576!}$$

$$= \frac{580 \cdot 579 \cdot 578 \cdot 577}{600 \cdot 599 \cdot 598 \cdot 597} \approx .87.$$

Now Try Exercise 13

So there is approximately an 87% chance that the disease will escape detection.   ■

The Complement Rule   The **complement rule** relates the probability of an event E to the probability of its complement E'. When applied together with counting techniques, it often simplifies computation of probabilities.

> **Complement Rule**   Let E be any event, E' its complement. Then
> $$\Pr(E) = 1 - \Pr(E').$$

For example, recall Example 1. We determined the probability of the event

$$E = \text{"all three balls selected are white"}$$

associated to the experiment of selecting three balls from an urn containing eight white balls and two green balls. We found that $\Pr(E) = \frac{7}{15}$. On the other hand, in Example 2 we determined the probability of the event

$$F = \text{"at least one green ball is selected."}$$

The event E is the complement of F:

$$E = F'.$$

So, by the complement rule,

$$\Pr(F) = 1 - \Pr(F') = 1 - \Pr(E) = 1 - \tfrac{7}{15} = \tfrac{8}{15},$$

in agreement with the calculations of Example 2.

The complement rule is especially useful in situations where $\Pr(E')$ is easier to compute than $\Pr(E)$. One of these situations arises in the celebrated *birthday problem*.

EXAMPLE 6

The famous "birthday problem" A group of five people is to be selected at random. What is the probability that two or more of them have the same birthday?

Solution For simplicity we ignore February 29. Furthermore, we assume that each of the 365 days in a year is an equally likely birthday (not an unreasonable assumption). The experiment we have in mind is this. Pick out five people and observe their birthdays. The outcomes of this experiment are strings of five dates, corresponding to the birthdays. For example, one outcome of the experiment is

(June 2, April 6, Dec. 20, Feb. 12, Aug. 5).

Each birth date has 365 different possibilities. So, by the generalized multiplication principle, the total number N of possible outcomes of the experiment is

$$N = 365 \cdot 365 \cdot 365 \cdot 365 \cdot 365 = 365^5.$$

Let E be the event "at least two people have the same birthday." It is very difficult to calculate directly the number of outcomes in E. However, it is comparatively simple to compute the number of outcomes in E' and hence to compute $\Pr(E')$. This is because E' is the event "all five birthdays are different." An outcome in E' can be selected in a sequence of five steps:

Select a day	Select a different day	Select yet a different day	Select yet a different day	Select yet a different day

These five steps will result in a sequence of five different birthdays. The first step can be performed in 365 ways; for each of these, the next step in 364; for each of these, the next step in 363; for each of these, the next step in 362; and for each of these, the last step in 361 ways. Therefore, E' contains $365 \cdot 364 \cdot 363 \cdot 362 \cdot 361$ [or $P(365, 5)$] outcomes, and

$$\Pr(E') = \frac{365 \cdot 364 \cdot 363 \cdot 362 \cdot 361}{365^5} \approx .973.$$

By the complement rule,

$$\Pr(E) = 1 - \Pr(E') \approx 1 - .973 = .027.$$

So the likelihood is about 2.7% that two or more of the five people will have the same birthday. ■

Now Try Exercise 15

The experiment of Example 6 can be repeated using samples of 8, 10, 20, or any number of people. As before, let E be the event "at least two people have the same birthday," so that $E' = $ "all the birthdays are different." If a sample of r people is used, then the same reasoning as used previously yields

$$\Pr(E') = \frac{365 \cdot 364 \cdot \,\cdots\, \cdot (365 - r + 1)}{365^r}.$$

Table 1 on the next page gives the values of $\Pr(E) = 1 - \Pr(E')$ for various values of r. You may be surprised by the numbers in the table. Even with as few as 23 people

TABLE 1   Probability that, in a randomly selected group of r people, at least two will have the same birthday

r	5	10	15	20	22	23	25	30	40	50
$\Pr(E)$	.027	.117	.253	.411	.476	.507	.569	.706	.891	.970

it is more likely than not that at least two people have the same birthday. With a sample of 50 people we are almost certain to have two with the same birthday. (Try this experiment in your dormitory or class.)

EXAMPLE 7   **Rolling a die five times**   A die is rolled five times. What is the probability of obtaining exactly three 4's?

Solution   There are $6^5 = 7776$ possible outcomes when a die is rolled five times. These are equally likely to occur. The event we seek is $E =$ "three 4's." How many outcomes are in E? There are $1 \cdot 1 \cdot 1 \cdot 5 \cdot 5 = 25$ ways to get three 4's followed by two rolls yielding anything except 4. But the three 4's need not appear in the first three rolls. What if the 4's appear as 4xx44? The number of possibilities is $1 \cdot 5 \cdot 5 \cdot 1 \cdot 1 = 25$. Thus we need to determine in how many positions these three 4's can appear in the sequence of five rolls. That is just $C(5, 3) = 10$. Therefore, E contains $(10)(25)$ elements, and

$$\Pr(\text{exactly three 4's in five rolls of a die}) = \frac{(10)(25)}{7776} \approx .03.$$

Thus there is about a 3% chance that in five rolls of a fair die we obtain three 4's.

Now Try Exercise 31

Verification of the Complement Rule   If S is the sample space, then $\Pr(S) = 1$, $E \cup E' = S$, and $E \cap E' = \emptyset$. Therefore, by the inclusion–exclusion principle,

$$\Pr(S) = \Pr(E \cup E') = \Pr(E) + \Pr(E').$$

So we have

$$1 = \Pr(E) + \Pr(E') \quad \text{and} \quad \Pr(E) = 1 - \Pr(E').$$

Practice Problems 6.4

1. **Children** A couple decides to have four children. What is the probability that among the children there will be at least one boy and at least one girl?

2. **(a)** Find the probability that all the numbers are different in three spins of a roulette wheel. [*Note:* A roulette wheel has 38 numbers.]

(b) Guess how many spins are required in order that the probability that all the numbers are different will be less than .5.

EXERCISES 6.4

1. **Course Selection** Each of three people randomly chooses one of three calculus sections to take (A, B, or C).

   (a) What is the probability that they all choose the same one?

   (b) What is the probability that they each choose a different section?

2. **Track Positions** Michael and Christopher are among seven contestants in a race to be run on a seven-lane track. If the runners are assigned to the lanes at random, what is the probability that Michael will be assigned to the inside lane and Christopher will be assigned to the outside lane?

3. Suppose you are asked to choose a whole number between 1 and 13, inclusive.

   (a) What is the probability that it is odd?

   (b) What is the probability that it is even?

   (c) What is the probability that it is a multiple of 3?

   (d) What is the probability that it is odd or a multiple of 3?

4. Five numbers are chosen at random from the whole numbers between 1 and 13, inclusive, with replacement.

   (a) What is the probability that all the numbers are even?

   (b) What is the probability that all the numbers are odd?

   (c) What is the probability that at least one of the numbers is odd?

5. Five numbers are chosen at random from the whole numbers between 1 and 13, inclusive, without replacement.

   (a) What is the probability that all the numbers are even?

   (b) What is the probability that all the numbers are odd?

   (c) What is the probability that at least one of the numbers is odd?

6. **Balls in an Urn** An urn contains 40 balls, some red and some white. If the probability of selecting a red ball is .45, how many red balls are in the urn?

7. **Quality Control** A factory produces fuses, which are packaged in boxes of 10. Three fuses are selected at random from each box for inspection. The box is rejected if at least one of these three fuses is defective. What is the probability that a box containing five defective fuses will be rejected?

8. **Balls in an Urn** An urn contains six white balls and five red balls. A sample of four balls is selected at random from the urn. What is the probability that the sample contains two white balls and two red balls?

9. **Balls in an Urn** An urn contains five red balls and four white balls. A sample of two balls is selected at random from the urn. What is the probability that at least one of the balls is red?

10. **Opinion Polling** Of the nine members of the board of trustees of a college, five agree with the president on a certain issue. The president selects three trustees at random and asks for their opinions. What is the probability that at least two of them will agree with him?

Selecting Students *Exercises 11–14 refer to a classroom of children (12 boys and 10 girls) in which seven students are chosen to go to the blackboard.*

11. What is the probability that at least two girls are chosen?

12. What is the probability that more boys than girls are chosen?

13. What is the probability that no boys are chosen?

14. What is the probability that the first three children chosen are boys?

15. **Date Conflict** Without consultation, each of four organizations announces a one-day convention to be held during June. Find the probability that at least two organizations specify the same day for their convention.

16. Five letters are selected from the alphabet, one at a time with replacement, to form a five-letter "word." What is the probability that the "word" has five different letters?

17. **Track Position** Michael is one of seven contestants entered in two races to be run on a seven-lane track. If in each race the runners are assigned to the lanes at random, what is the probability that Michael will be assigned to the inside lane at least once?

18. **Hotel Choices** An airport limousine has four passengers and stops at six different hotels. What is the probability that two or more people will be staying at the same hotel? (Assume that each person is just as likely to stay in one hotel as another.)

19. **Weather Conditions** In a certain agricultural region the probability of a drought during the growing season is .2, the probability of a severe cold spell is .15, and the probability of both is .1. Find the probability of

   (a) either a drought or a severe cold spell.

   (b) neither a drought nor a severe cold spell.

   (c) not having a drought.

20. **Coin Tosses** A coin is to be tossed seven times. What is the probability of obtaining four heads and three tails?

21. Let E and F be events such that

$$\Pr(E) = .3 \quad \Pr(F') = .6 \quad \text{and} \quad \Pr(E \cup F) = .7.$$

   What is $\Pr(E \cap F)$?

22. **Manufacturing Defects** In a certain manufacturing process the probability of a type I defect is .12, the probability of a type II defect is .22, and the probability of having both types of defects is .02. Find the probability of having neither type of defect.

23. **Socks** A man has six different pairs of socks, from which he selects two socks at random. What is the probability that the selected socks will match?

24. **Opinion Polling** Of the 15 members on a Senate committee, 10 plan to vote "yes" and 5 plan to vote "no" on an important issue. A reporter attempts to predict the outcome of the vote by questioning six of the senators. Find the probability that this sample is precisely representative of the final vote. That is, find the probability that four of the six senators questioned plan to vote "yes."

25. Group Picture A man, a woman, and their three children randomly stand in a row for a family picture. What is the probability that the parents will be standing next to each other?

26. Poker Hands In poker the probabilities of being dealt a flush, a straight, and a straight flush are .0019654, .0039246, and .0000154, respectively. What is the probability of being dealt a straight or a flush?

27. Street Routes Figure 1 shows a partial map of the streets in a certain city. A tourist starts at point A and selects at random a path to point B. (We shall assume that he walks only south and east.) Find the probability that

(a) he passes through point C.

(b) he passes through point D.

(c) he passes through point C and point D.

(d) he passes through point C or point D.

Figure 1

28. Boys and Girls A couple decides to have four children. What is the probability that they will have more girls than boys?

29. Committee Selection A law firm has six senior and four junior partners. A committee of three partners is selected at random to represent the firm at a conference. What is the probability that at least one of the junior partners is on the committee?

30. Rotten Tomato A bag contains nine tomatoes, of which one is rotten. A sample of three tomatoes is selected at random. What is the probability that the sample contains the rotten tomato?

31. Coin Tosses A coin is to be tossed six times. What is the probability of obtaining exactly three heads?

32. Book Selection A vacationer has brought along four novels and four nonfiction books. One day the person selects two at random to take to the beach. What is the probability that both are novels?

Illinois Lotto *Exercises 33 and 34*[1] *refer to the Illinois Lottery Lotto game. In this game, the player chooses six different integers from 1 to 40. If the six match (in any order) the six different integers drawn by the lottery, the player wins the grand prize jackpot, which starts at $1 million and grows weekly until won. Multiple winners split the pot equally. For each $1 bet, the player must pick two (presumably different) sets of six integers.*

33. What is the probability of winning the Illinois Lottery Lotto with a $1 bet?

34. In the game week ending June 18, 1983, 2 million people bought $1 tickets and 78 people matched all six winning integers and split the jackpot. If all numbers were selected randomly, the likelihood of having so many joint winners would be about 10^{-115}. Can you think of any reason that such an unlikely event occurred? (*Note*: The winning numbers were 7, 13, 14, 21, 28, and 35.) What would be the best strategy in selecting the numbers to ensure that in the event you won, you would probably not have to share the jackpot with too many people?

35. Senate Committee The U.S. Senate consists of two senators from each of the 50 states. Five senators are to be selected at random to form a committee. What is the probability that no two members of the committee are from the same state?

36. Subcommittees A politician knows that a committee vote is stacked against her, 6 to 3. However, she has the option of letting a randomly selected subcommittee decide the issue. Show that the smaller the subcommittee is, the better her chances of winning the vote. (Consider only subcommittees with an odd number of members, so that tie votes are precluded.)

37. Birthdays What is the probability that in a group of 25 people at least one person has a birthday on June 13? Why is your answer different from the probability displayed in Table 1 for $r = 25$?

38. Letter Positions What is the probability that a random arrangement of the letters in the word GEESE has all the E's adjacent to one another?

39. Guest List Fred is having a dinner party and is limited to 10 guests. He has 16 men friends and 12 women friends, including Laura and Mary.

(a) If Fred chooses his guests at random, what is the probability that Mary and Laura are invited?

(b) If Fred decides to invite 5 men and 5 women, what is the probability that Mary and Laura are invited?

40. Baseball Predictions In the American League, the East, Central, and West divisions consist of 5, 5, and 4 baseball teams, respectively. A sportswriter predicts the winner of each of the three divisions by choosing a team completely at random in each division. What is the probability that the sportswriter will predict at least one winner correctly?

41. Baseball Predictions Suppose that the sportswriter in Exercise 40 eliminates from each division one team that clearly has no chance of winning and predicts a winner at random from the remaining teams. Assuming

---

the eliminated teams don't end up surprising anyone, what is the writer's chance of predicting at least one winner?

42. **Baseball Predictions** Suppose that the sportswriter in Exercise 40 simply puts the 14 team names in a hat and draws 3 completely at random. Does this increase or decrease the writer's chance of picking at least one winner?

43. **Powerball Lottery** The winner of the Powerball[2] lottery must correctly pick a set of 5 numbers from 1 through 55 and then correctly pick one number (called the Powerball) from 1 through 42.

    (a) What are the odds of winning the Powerball lottery?

    (b) What is the probability of winning the Powerball lottery?

44. **License Plate Game** Johnny and Doyle are driving along on a lightly traveled road. Johnny proposes the following game. They will look at the license plates of oncoming cars and focus on the last two digits. For instance, the license plates ABC512 or 7412BG would yield 12, and the license plate XY406T would yield the number 6. Johnny bets Doyle that at least two of the next fifteen cars will yield the same number. What is the probability that Johnny wins? Assume that each of the 100 possible numbers is equally likely to occur.

45. **Numbers** Two distinct numbers are selected at random from the set $\{1, 2, 3, 4, 5, 6, 7\}$. What is the probability that their product is an even number? *Hint*: First find the probability that the product is odd.

46. **Matching Socks** Ten white socks and six red socks are in a drawer. If two socks are selected at random, what is the probability that both socks are the same color?

47. **British Lottery** In the British lottery, a player pays 1 euro for a ticket and selects 6 numbers from the numbers 1 through 49. If he matches exactly three of the six numbers drawn, he receives 10 euros. What is the probability of selecting exactly three of the six numbers drawn?

48. **Swiss Lottery** The winning combination in the Swiss lottery consists of six numbers drawn from the numbers 1 through 45. What is the probability that a single ticket has no matches?

49. **Place Settings** Fred has five place settings consisting of a dinner plate, a salad plate, and a bowl. Each setting is a different color. If Fred randomly selects a dinner plate, a salad plate, and a bowl, what is the probability that they all have different colors?

50. **Balls in an Urn** An urn contains red balls and white balls. The probability of removing two red balls, without replacement, from the urn is $\frac{2}{5}$. The probability of removing three red balls, without replacement, from

the urn is $\frac{1}{5}$. Explain why there must be two more red balls than white balls. How many red balls were in the urn? *Hint*: Let r be the number of red balls in the urn, and let w be the number of white balls in the urn. Show that $r = w + 2$.

51. **Blink of an Eye** Suppose that blinking causes a person's eyes to be closed 10% of the time. If a photographer takes a picture of three people, what is the probability that all three people will have their eyes open?

52. **Blink of an Eye** Refer to Exercise 51. If the photographer takes two pictures of the three people, what is the probability that at least one of the pictures will be good?

A poker hand consists of five cards drawn from a deck of 52 cards. Each card has one of 13 denominations (2, 3, 4, ..., 10, Jack, Queen, King, Ace) and one of four suits (Spades, Hearts, Diamonds, Clubs).

53. **Poker** Determine the probability of each of the following types of poker hands.

    (a) Full house (three cards of one denomination and two cards of another denomination)

    (b) Three of a kind (three cards of one denomination and two cards of distinct denominations, both different than the denomination of the triple)

54. **Poker** Determine the probability of each of the following types of poker hands.

    (a) Two pairs (two cards of one denomination, two cards of a different denomination, and one card of a denomination other than those two denominations)

    (b) One pair (two cards of one denomination and three cards of distinct denominations, where each of the three cards has a different denomination than the denomination of the pair)

55. **Bridge** In a bridge hand, what is the probability of each of the following suit distributions?

    (a) 4-3-3-3. That is, four cards of one suit and three cards of each of the other three suits. *Hint*: The number of hands having this distribution is $4 \cdot C(13, 4) \cdot C(13, 3) \cdot C(13, 3) \cdot C(13, 3)$.

    (b) 4-4-3-2. That is, four cards of each of two suits, three cards of another suit, and two cards of the remaining suit.

In Exercises 56–63, use a graphing calculator or spreadsheet to calculate the probabilities.

56. **Pick a Card** Find the probability that at least two people in a group of size $n = 5$ select the same card when drawing from a 52-card deck with replacement. Determine for what size group the probability of such a match first exceeds .5.

---

[2]Powerball drawings are held twice a week. If you buy 50 tickets for each drawing, you can expect to win once every 5000 years.

57. Balls in an Urn Two balls are to be selected at random without replacement from an urn that contains 40 balls, some red and some white. If the probability of selecting two red balls is .1, how many red balls are in the urn?

58. Presidential Choices There were 16 presidents of the Continental Congresses from 1774 to 1788. Each of the five students in a seminar in American history chooses one of these on which to do a report. If all presidents are equally likely to be chosen, calculate the probability that at least two students choose the same president.

59. Rolling a Die A die is rolled 24 times.

   (a) How many 3's would you expect?

   (b) Calculate the probability of getting exactly four 3's.

60. Term Papers A political science class has 20 students, each of whom chooses a topic from a list for a term paper. How big a pool of topics is necessary for the probability of at least one duplicate to drop below 50%?

61. Birthday Problem Consider the discussion of the general birthday problem following Example 6.

   (a) Verify that 23 is the smallest value of r for which the probability that at least two people have the same birthday in a group of r randomly selected people is $\geq .5$.

   (b) Find the smallest value of r for which the probability that at least two people have the same birthday in a group of r randomly selected people is $\geq .6$.

62. Birthday Problem Johnny Carson, host of The Tonight Show from 1962–1992, discussed the birthday problem during one of his monologues. To test the hypothesis, he asked the audience if any of them were born on his birthday, October 23. Carson was surprised that no one in the audience of 100 people shared his birthday. What was wrong with Carson's reasoning? What is the probability that one or more people in the audience were born on October 23? How large would the audience have to have been so that the probability that someone in the audience had the same birthday as Carson was at least 50 percent?

63. Blink of an Eye Refer to Exercise 51. How many pictures must the photographer take so that the probability of obtaining at least one good picture is at least 99.9 percent?

Solutions to Practice Problems 6.4

1. Each possible outcome is a string of four letters composed of B's and G's. By the generalized multiplication principle, there are 2^4 or 16 possible outcomes. Let E be the event "children of both sexes." Then $E' = \{BBBB, GGGG\}$, and

$$\Pr(E') = \frac{[\text{number of outcomes in } E']}{[\text{total number of outcomes}]} = \frac{2}{16} = \frac{1}{8}.$$

Therefore,

$$\Pr(E) = 1 - \Pr(E') = 1 - \frac{1}{8} = \frac{7}{8}.$$

So the probability is 87.5% that they will have children of both sexes.

2. (a) Each sequence of three numbers is just as likely to occur as any other. Therefore,

$$\Pr(\text{numbers different})$$
$$= \frac{[\text{number of outcomes with numbers different}]}{[\text{number of possible outcomes}]}$$
$$= \frac{38 \cdot 37 \cdot 36}{38^3} \approx .92.$$

(b) 8

6.5 Conditional Probability and Independence

The probability of an event depends, often in a critical way, on the sample space in question. In this section we explore this dependence in some detail by introducing what are called *conditional probabilities*.

To illustrate the dependence of probabilities on the sample space, consider the following example.

EXAMPLE 1   **College students** Suppose that a certain mathematics class contains 26 students. Of these, 14 are economics majors, 15 are first-year students, and 7 are neither. Suppose that a person is selected at random from the class.

(a) What is the probability that the person is both an economics major and a first-year student?

(b) Suppose we are given the additional information that the person selected is a first-year student. What is the probability that he or she is also an economics major?

Solution Let E denote the set of economics majors and F the set of first-year students. A complete Venn diagram of the class can be obtained with the techniques of Section 5.3. See Fig. 1.

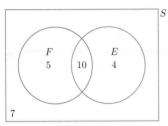

(a) In selecting a student from the class, the sample space consists of all 26 students. Since the choice is random, all students are equally likely to be selected. The event "economics major and first-year student" corresponds to the set $E \cap F$ of the Venn diagram. Therefore,

$$\Pr(E \cap F) = \frac{[\text{number of outcomes in } E \cap F]}{[\text{number of possible outcomes}]} = \frac{10}{26} = \frac{5}{13}.$$

Figure 1

So the probability of selecting a first-year economics major is $\frac{5}{13}$.

(b) If we know that the student selected is a first-year student, then the possible outcomes of the experiment are restricted. They must belong to F. In other words, given the additional information, we must alter the sample space from "all students" to "first-year students." Since each of the 15 first-year students is equally likely to be selected, and since 10 of the 15 first-year students are economics majors, the probability of choosing an economics major under these circumstances is equal to $\frac{10}{15} = \frac{2}{3}$. ∎

Let us consider Example 1 more carefully. In part (a) the sample space is the set of all students in the mathematics class, E is the event "student is an economics major" and F is the event "student is a first-year student." On the other hand, part (b) poses a condition, "student is a first-year student." The condition is satisfied by every element of F. We are being asked to find the **conditional probability** of E given F, written $\Pr(E|F)$. To do this we shall restrict our attention to the new (restricted) sample space, now just the elements of F. Thus, we consider only first-year students and ask, of these, what is the probability of choosing an economics major? We assign a value to $\Pr(E|F)$ via the following formula:

DEFINITION Conditional Probability

$$\Pr(E|F) = \frac{\Pr(E \cap F)}{\Pr(F)}, \qquad (1)$$

provided that $\Pr(F) \neq 0$.

We will provide an intuitive justification of this formula shortly. However, we first give an application.

EXAMPLE 2

Earnings and education Twenty percent of the employees of Acme Steel Company are college graduates. Of all its employees, 25% earn more than $50,000 per year, and 15% are college graduates earning more than $50,000. What is the probability that an employee selected at random earns more than $50,000 per year, given that he or she is a college graduate?

Solution Let H and C be the events

$$H = \text{"earns more than \$50,000 per year"}$$
$$C = \text{"college graduate."}$$

We are asked to calculate $\Pr(H|C)$. The given data are

$$\Pr(H) = .25 \qquad \Pr(C) = .20 \qquad \Pr(H \cap C) = .15.$$

By formula (1), we have

$$\Pr(H|C) = \frac{\Pr(H \cap C)}{\Pr(C)} = \frac{.15}{.20} = \frac{3}{4}.$$

Now Try Exercise 13(b) — Thus $\frac{3}{4}$ of all college graduates at Acme Steel earn more than \$50,000 per year. ∎

Suppose that an experiment has N equally likely outcomes. Then we may apply the following formula to calculate $\Pr(E|F)$.

Conditional Probability in Case of Equally Likely Outcomes

$$\Pr(E|F) = \frac{[\text{number of outcomes in } E \cap F]}{[\text{number of outcomes in } F]}, \qquad (2)$$

provided that $[\text{number of outcomes in } F] \neq 0$.

This formula was actually used in Example 1(b) to compute $\Pr(E|F)$. In that example each student had the same likelihood of being selected.

Let us now justify formulas (1) and (2).

Justification of Formula (1) Formula (1) is a definition of conditional probability and as such does not really need any justification. (We can make whatever definitions we choose!) However, let us proceed intuitively and show that the definition is reasonable, in the sense that formula (1) gives the expected long-run proportion of occurrences of E given that F occurs. Assume that our experiment is performed repeatedly, say for 10,000 trials. We would expect F to occur in approximately $10,000 \Pr(F)$ trials. Among these, the trials for which E also occurs are exactly those for which both E and F occur. In other words, the trials for which E also occurs are exactly those for which the event $E \cap F$ occurs; and this event has probability $\Pr(E \cap F)$. Therefore, out of the original 10,000 trials, there should be approximately $10,000 \Pr(E \cap F)$ in which E and F both occur. Thus, considering only those trials in which F occurs, the proportion in which E also occurs is

$$\frac{10,000 \Pr(E \cap F)}{10,000 \Pr(F)} = \frac{\Pr(E \cap F)}{\Pr(F)}.$$

Thus, at least intuitively, it seems reasonable to define $\Pr(E|F)$ by formula (1). ∎

Justification of Formula (2) Suppose that the number of outcomes of the experiment is N. Then

$$\Pr(F) = \frac{[\text{number of outcomes in } F]}{N}$$

$$\Pr(E \cap F) = \frac{[\text{number of outcomes in } E \cap F]}{N}.$$

Therefore, using formula (1), we have

$$\Pr(E|F) = \frac{\Pr(E \cap F)}{\Pr(F)}$$

$$= \frac{\dfrac{[\text{number of outcomes in } E \cap F]}{N}}{\dfrac{[\text{number of outcomes in } F]}{N}}$$

$$= \frac{[\text{number of outcomes in } E \cap F]}{[\text{number of outcomes in } F]}. \qquad \blacksquare$$

From formula (1), multiplying both sides of the equation by $\Pr(F)$, we can deduce the following useful fact.

> **Product Rule**   If $\Pr(F) \neq 0$,
> $$\Pr(E \cap F) = \Pr(F) \cdot \Pr(E|F). \qquad (3)$$

The next example illustrates the use of this rule.

EXAMPLE 3   **Color-blind males**   Assume that a certain school contains an equal number of female and male students and that 5% of the male population is color-blind. Find the probability that a randomly selected student is a color-blind male.

Solution   Let $M =$ "male" and $B =$ "color-blind." We wish to calculate $\Pr(B \cap M)$. From the given data,
$$\Pr(M) = .5 \quad \text{and} \quad \Pr(B|M) = .05.$$

Therefore, by the product rule,
$$\Pr(B \cap M) = \Pr(M) \cdot \Pr(B|M) = (.5)(.05) = .025. \qquad \blacksquare$$

Often an event G can be described as a sequence of two other events E and F. That is, G occurs if F occurs and then E occurs. The product rule allows us to compute the probability of G as the probability of F times the conditional probability $\Pr(E|F)$. The next example illustrates this point.

EXAMPLE 4   **Cards**   A sequence of two playing cards is drawn at random (without replacement) from a standard deck of 52 cards. What is the probability that the first card is red and the second is black?

Solution   The event in question is a sequence of two events, namely,
$$F = \text{"the first card is red"}$$
$$E = \text{"the second card is black."}$$

Since half the deck consists of red cards, $\Pr(F) = \frac{1}{2}$. If we are given that F occurs, then there are only 51 cards left in the deck, of which 26 are black, so
$$\Pr(E|F) = \tfrac{26}{51}.$$

By the product rule
$$\Pr(E \cap F) = \Pr(F) \cdot \Pr(E|F) = \tfrac{1}{2} \cdot \tfrac{26}{51} = \tfrac{13}{51}. \qquad \blacksquare$$

The product rule may be generalized to sequences of three events E_1, E_2, and E_3:

$$\Pr(E_1 \cap E_2 \cap E_3) = \Pr(E_1) \cdot \Pr(E_2|E_1) \cdot \Pr(E_3|E_1 \cap E_2).$$

Similar formulas hold for sequences of four or more events.

One of the most important applications of conditional probability is in the discussion of independent events. Intuitively, two events are **independent** of each other if the occurrence of one has no effect on the likelihood that the other will occur. For example, suppose that we roll a die twice. Let the events E and F be

$$F = \text{"first roll is a 6"}$$
$$E = \text{"second roll is a 3."}$$

Then intuitively these events are independent of one another. Rolling a 6 on the first roll has no effect whatsoever on the outcome of the second roll. On the other hand, suppose that we draw a sequence of two cards at random (without replacement) from a deck. Then the events

$$F = \text{"first card is red"}$$
$$E = \text{"second card is black"}$$

are not independent of one another, at least intuitively. Indeed, whether or not we draw a red on the first card affects the likelihood of drawing a black on the second.

The notion of independence of events is easily formulated. If E and F are events in a sample space and $\Pr(F) \neq 0$, then the product rule states that $\Pr(E \cap F) = \Pr(E|F) \cdot \Pr(F)$. However, if the occurrence of event F does not affect the likelihood of the occurrence of event E, we would expect that $\Pr(E|F) = \Pr(E)$. Substitution then shows that $\Pr(E \cap F) = \Pr(E) \cdot \Pr(F)$.

DEFINITION Let E and F be events. We say that E and F are **independent** provided that
$$\Pr(E \cap F) = \Pr(E) \cdot \Pr(F).$$

If $\Pr(E) \neq 0$ and $\Pr(F) \neq 0$, then our definition is equivalent to the intuitive statement of independence stated in terms of conditional probability. The two may be used interchangeably.

Let E and F be events with nonzero probability. E and F are *independent* provided that
$$\Pr(E|F) = \Pr(E) \quad \text{and} \quad \Pr(F|E) = \Pr(F).$$

EXAMPLE 5

Two rolls of a die An experiment consists of observing the outcome of two consecutive rolls of a die. Let E and F be the events

$$E = \text{"the first roll is a 3"}$$
$$F = \text{"the second roll is a 6."}$$

Show that these events are independent.

Solution Clearly, $\Pr(E) = \Pr(F) = \frac{1}{6}$. To compute $\Pr(E|F)$, assume that F occurs. Then there are six possible outcomes:

$$F = \{(1,6), (2,6), (3,6), (4,6), (5,6), (6,6)\},$$

and all outcomes are equally likely. Moreover,

$$E \cap F = \{(3,6)\},$$

so that

$$\Pr(E|F) = \frac{[\text{number of outcomes in } E \cap F]}{[\text{number of outcomes in } F]} = \frac{1}{6} = \Pr(E).$$

Similarly, $\Pr(F|E) = \Pr(F)$. So E and F are independent events, in agreement with our intuition. ■

EXAMPLE 6   **Cards** Suppose that an experiment consists of observing the results of drawing two consecutive cards from a 52-card deck. Let E and F be the events

$$E = \text{"second card is black"}$$
$$F = \text{"first card is red."}$$

Are these events independent?

Solution There are the same number of outcomes with the second card red as with the second card black, so $\Pr(E) = \frac{1}{2}$. To compute $\Pr(E|F)$, note that if F occurs, then there are 51 equally likely choices for the second card, of which 26 are black, so that $\Pr(E|F) = \frac{26}{51}$. Note that $\Pr(E|F) \neq \Pr(E)$, so E and F are not independent, in agreement with our intuition. ■

Now Try Exercise 5

EXAMPLE 7   **Heads and tails** Suppose that we toss a coin three times and record the sequence of heads and tails. Let E be the event "at most one head occurs" and F the event "both heads and tails occur." Are E and F independent?

Solution Using the abbreviations H for "heads" and T for "tails," we have

$$E = \{\text{TTT, HTT, THT, TTH}\}$$
$$F = \{\text{HTT, HTH, HHT, THH, THT, TTH}\}$$
$$E \cap F = \{\text{HTT, THT, TTH}\}.$$

The sample space contains eight equally likely outcomes, so that

$$\Pr(E) = \frac{1}{2} \qquad \Pr(F) = \frac{3}{4} \qquad \Pr(E \cap F) = \frac{3}{8}.$$

Moreover,

$$\Pr(E) \cdot \Pr(F) = \frac{1}{2} \cdot \frac{3}{4} = \frac{3}{8},$$

Now Try Exercise 19   which equals $\Pr(E \cap F)$. So E and F are independent. ■

EXAMPLE 8   **Probabilities associated with four-children families** Suppose that a family has four children. Let E be the event "at most one boy" and F the event "at least one child of each sex." Are E and F independent?

Solution Let B stand for "boy" and G for "girl." Then

$$E = \{\text{GGGG, GGGB, GGBG, GBGG, BGGG}\}$$
$$F = \{\text{GGGB, GGBG, GBGG, BGGG, BBBG, BBGB, BGBB,}$$
$$\text{GBBB, BBGG, BGBG, BGGB, GBBG, GBGB, GGBB}\},$$

and the sample space consists of 16 equally likely outcomes. Furthermore,

$$E \cap F = \{\text{GGGB, GGBG, GBGG, BGGG}\}.$$

Therefore,

$$\Pr(E) = \tfrac{5}{16} \qquad \Pr(F) = \tfrac{7}{8} \qquad \Pr(E \cap F) = \tfrac{1}{4}.$$

In this example

$$\Pr(E) \cdot \Pr(F) = \tfrac{5}{16} \cdot \tfrac{7}{8} \neq \Pr(E \cap F).$$

Now Try Exercise 53   So E and F are *not* independent events.

Examples 7 and 8 are similar, yet the events they describe are independent in one case and not the other. Although intuition is frequently a big help, in complex problems we shall need to use the definition of independence to verify that our intuition is correct.

EXAMPLE 9   **Reliability of a calculator**   A new calculator is designed to be extra reliable by having two independent calculating units. The probability that a given calculating unit fails within the first 1000 hours of operation is .001. What is the probability that at least one calculating unit will operate without failure for the first 1000 hours of operation?

Solution   Let

$$E = \text{``calculating unit 1 fails in first 1000 hours''}$$
$$F = \text{``calculating unit 2 fails in first 1000 hours.''}$$

Then E and F are independent events, since the calculating units are independent of one another. Therefore,

$$\Pr(E \cap F) = \Pr(E) \cdot \Pr(F) = (.001)^2 = .000001$$
$$\Pr((E \cap F)') = 1 - .000001 = .999999.$$

Since $(E \cap F)' = $ "not both calculating units fail in first 1000 hours," the desired
Now Try Exercise 17   probability is .999999.

The concept of independent events can be extended to more than two events:

DEFINITION   A set of events is said to be **independent** if, for each collection of events chosen from them, say $E_1, E_2, \ldots, E_n$, we have
$$\Pr(E_1 \cap E_2 \cap \cdots \cap E_n) = \Pr(E_1) \cdot \Pr(E_2) \cdot \cdots \cdot \Pr(E_n).$$

EXAMPLE 10   **Probabilities associated with independent events**   Three events A, B, and C are independent; $\Pr(A) = .5$, $\Pr(B) = .3$, and $\Pr(C) = .2$.
(a) Calculate $\Pr(A \cap B \cap C)$.   **(b)** Calculate $\Pr(A \cap C)$.

Solution   **(a)** $\Pr(A \cap B \cap C) = \Pr(A) \cdot \Pr(B) \cdot \Pr(C) = (.5)(.3)(.2) = .03.$
(b) $\Pr(A \cap C) = \Pr(A) \cdot \Pr(C) = (.5)(.2) = .1.$

We shall leave as an exercise the intuitively reasonable result that if E and F are independent events, so are E and F', E' and F, and E' and F'. This result also generalizes to any collection of independent events.

EXAMPLE 11   **Quality control** A company manufactures stereo components. Experience shows that defects in manufacture are independent of one another. Quality control studies reveal that

2% of CD players are defective,

3% of amplifiers are defective,

7% of speakers are defective.

A system consists of a CD player, an amplifier, and two speakers. What is the probability that the system is not defective?

Solution Let C, A, S_1, and S_2 be events corresponding to defective CD player, amplifier, speaker 1, and speaker 2, respectively. Then

$$\Pr(C) = .02 \qquad \Pr(A) = .03 \qquad \Pr(S_1) = \Pr(S_2) = .07.$$

We wish to calculate $\Pr(C' \cap A' \cap S_1' \cap S_2')$. By the complement rule we have

$$\Pr(C') = .98 \qquad \Pr(A') = .97 \qquad \Pr(S_1') = \Pr(S_2') = .93.$$

Since we have assumed that C, A, S_1, and S_2 are independent, so are C', A', S_1', and S_2'. Therefore,

$$\Pr(C' \cap A' \cap S_1' \cap S_2') = \Pr(C') \cdot \Pr(A') \cdot \Pr(S_1') \cdot \Pr(S_2')$$
$$= (.98)(.97)(.93)^2 \approx .822.$$

Now Try Exercise 9   Thus there is an 82.2% chance that the system is not defective. ∎

Practice Problems 6.5

1. **Cards** Suppose there are three cards: one red on both sides; one white on both sides; and one having a side of each color. A card is selected at random and placed on a table. If the up side is red, what is the probability that the down side is red? (Try guessing at the answer before working it using the formula for conditional probability.)

2. Show that if events E and F are independent of each other, then so are E and F'. [*Hint:* Since $E \cap F$ and $E \cap F'$ are mutually exclusive, we have

$$\Pr(E) = \Pr(E \cap F) + \Pr(E \cap F').]$$

EXERCISES 6.5

In Exercises 1–4, let S be a sample space and E and F events associated with S. Suppose that $\Pr(E) = .5$, $\Pr(F) = .3$, *and* $\Pr(E \cap F) = .1$.

1. Calculate $\Pr(E|F)$ and $\Pr(F|E)$.

2. Are E and F independent events? Explain.

3. Calculate $\Pr(E|F')$.

4. Calculate $\Pr(E'|F')$.

5. **Epidemiology** A doctor studies the known cancer patients in a certain town. The probability that a randomly chosen resident has cancer is found to be .001. It is found that 30% of the town works for Ajax Chemical Company. The probability that an employee of Ajax has cancer is equal to .003. Are the events "has cancer" and "works for Ajax" independent of one another?

6. **Value of College** The proportion of individuals in a certain city earning more than $35,000 per year is .25. The proportion of individuals earning more than $35,000 and having a college degree is .10. Suppose that a person is randomly chosen and he turns out to be earning more than $35,000. What is the probability that he is a college graduate?

7. **Medical Tests** A medical screening program administers three independent medical tests. Of the persons taking the tests, 80% pass test I, 75% pass test II, and 60% pass test III. A participant is chosen at random.

(a) What is the probability that she will pass all three tests?

(b) What is the probability that she will pass at least two of the three tests?

8. **System Reliability** A stereo system contains 50 transistors. The probability that a given transistor will fail in 100,000 hours of use is .0005. Assume that the failures of the various transistors are independent of one another. What is the probability that no transistor will fail during the first 100,000 hours of use?

9. **System Reliability** A TV set contains five circuit boards of type A, five of type B, and three of type C. The probability of failing in its first 5000 hours of use is .01 for a type A circuit board, .02 for a type B circuit board, and .025 for a type C circuit board. Assuming that the failures of the various circuit boards are independent of one another, compute the probability that no circuit board fails in the first 5000 hours of use.

10. **Light Bulbs** A certain brand of a long-life bulb has probability .01 of burning out in less than 1000 hours. Suppose that we wish to light a corridor with a number of independent bulbs in such a way that at least one of the bulbs remains lit for 1000 consecutive hours. What is the minimum number of bulbs needed to ensure that the probability of success is at least .99999?

11. Let E and F be events with $\Pr(E) = \frac{1}{2}$, $\Pr(F) = \frac{1}{3}$, and $\Pr(E \cap F) = \frac{1}{4}$. Compute $\Pr(E|F)$ and $\Pr(F|E)$.

12. Let E and F be events with $\Pr(E) = .3$, $\Pr(F) = .6$, and $\Pr(E \cup F) = .7$. Find
   (a) $\Pr(E \cap F)$ (b) $\Pr(E|F)$ (c) $\Pr(F|E)$
   (d) $\Pr(E' \cap F)$ (e) $\Pr(E'|F)$

13. **Opinion Polling** Of the registered voters in a certain town, 50% are Democrats, 40% favor a school loan, and 30% are Democrats who favor a school loan. Suppose that a registered voter is selected at random from the town.
   (a) What is the probability that the person is not a Democrat and opposes the school loan?
   (b) What is the conditional probability that the person favors the school loan given that he or she is a Democrat?
   (c) What is the conditional probability that the person is a Democrat given that he or she favors the school loan?

14. **Game Attendance** Of the students at a certain college, 50% regularly attend the football games, 30% are first-year students, and 40% are upper-class students who do not regularly attend football games. Suppose that a student is selected at random.
   (a) What is the probability that the person both is a first-year student and regularly attends football games?

(b) What is the conditional probability that the person regularly attends football games given that he is a first-year student?

(c) What is the conditional probability that the person is a first-year student given that he regularly attends football games?

15. **Coin Tosses** A coin is tossed three times. What is the conditional probability that the outcome is HHH given that at least two heads occur?

16. **Balls in an Urn** Two balls are selected at random from an urn containing two white balls and three red balls. What is the conditional probability that both balls are white given that at least one of them is white?

17. **Life Expectancies** The probabilities that a person A and a person B will live an additional 15 years are .8 and .7, respectively. Assuming that their lifespans are independent, what is the probability that A or B will live an additional 15 years?

18. **Spread of a Rumor** Jane has two friends who do not know each other. Each of them has heard the same rumor. The probability that each will tell Jane is 60%. What is the probability that Jane does not hear the rumor from either of these friends?

19. **Balls in an Urn** A sample of two balls is drawn from an urn containing two white balls and three red balls. Are the events "the sample contains at least one white ball" and "the sample contains balls of both colors" independent?

20. **Fishing** The probability that a fisherman catches a tuna in any one excursion is .15. What is the probability that he catches a tuna on each of three excursions? on at least one of three excursions?

21. **Prizes** The probability that a prize appears in a box of breakfast cereal is .005. What is the probability that two boxes of cereal contain at least one prize?

22. **Guessing on an Exam** A "true–false" exam has 10 questions. Assuming that the questions are independent and that a student is guessing, find the probability that she gets 100%.

23. **CD Players** Suppose that in Sleepy Valley only 30% of those over 50 years old own CD players. Find the probability that among four randomly chosen people in that age group none owns a CD player.

24. Assume that A and B are events in a sample space and that $\Pr(A) = .40$ and $\Pr(B|A) = .25$. Find $\Pr(A \cap B)$. With the further assumption that $\Pr(B) = .30$, find $\Pr(A \cup B)$, $\Pr(A' \cap B)$, and $\Pr(A|B)$.

25. Show that if events E and F are independent of each other, then so are E' and F'.

26. Show that if E and F are independent events, then

$$\Pr(E \cup F) = 1 - \Pr(E') \cdot \Pr(F').$$

27. Free-Throws A basketball player makes each free-throw with a probability of .6 and is on the line for a one-and-one free throw. (That is, a second throw is allowed only if the first is successful.) What is the probability that the player will score 0 points? 1 point? 2 points? Assume that the two throws are independent.

28. Let $\Pr(F) > 0$.

   (a) Show that $\Pr(E'|F) = 1 - \Pr(E|F)$.

   (b) Find an example for which

   $$\Pr(E|F') \neq 1 - \Pr(E|F).$$

29. Use the inclusion–exclusion principle for (nonconditional) probabilities to show that if E, F, and G are events in S, then

$$\Pr(E \cup F|G) = \Pr(E|G) + \Pr(F|G) - \Pr(E \cap F|G).$$

30. Marriage Statistics The percentage of the U.S. male population that has ever been married is given in Table 1. Explain how the table relates to the idea of conditional probability by giving a precise definition of "% ever married among 25- to 29-year-olds."

TABLE 1

Ages	Percent ever married
18–19	2.3
20–24	13.3
25–29	42.6
30–34	66.6
35–44	79.2
45–54	87.6

Source: U.S. Census Bureau, *America's Families and Living Arrangements: 2006.*

31. Mortality Rates Two communities are being compared as to their annual death rates. Community A is in the Sunbelt and community B is in Alaska.

Community A: Population: 120,000
   Number of deaths: 12,000
Community B: Population: 90,000
   Number of deaths: 4500

   (a) Find the death rate in community A. Note that this is a conditional probability, namely

   $$\Pr(\text{death}|A).$$

   (b) Express the probability you found in part (a) as a death rate per 1000 in the population of community A.

   (c) Find $\Pr(\text{death}|B)$ and compare to part (b).

32. Blood Tests A hospital uses two tests to classify blood. Every blood sample is subjected to both tests. The first test correctly identifies blood type with probability .7, and the second test correctly identifies blood type with probability .8. The probability that at least one of the tests correctly identifies the blood type is .9.

   (a) Find the probability that both tests correctly identify the blood type.

   (b) Determine the probability that the second test is correct given that the first test is correct.

   (c) Determine the probability that the first test is correct given that the second test is correct.

   (d) Are the events "test I correctly identifies the blood type" and "test II correctly identifies the blood type" independent?

33. E.R. Waits Sixty-five percent of the patients in the emergency room of a hospital are seen by a physician immediately. The remainder are kept waiting in the waiting room. Eighty percent of those kept waiting are seen within 2 hours. Seventy-five percent of those seen immediately are admitted to the hospital. Forty percent of those seen within 2 hours (but not immediately) are admitted to the hospital, and 10% of those who wait more than 2 hours are admitted to the hospital. Let A be the event "the patient is seen immediately." Let B be the event "the patient is not seen immediately but is seen within 2 hours." Let C be the event "the patient waits more than 2 hours." Let H be the event "the patient is admitted to the hospital."

   (a) Find $\Pr(B)$. **(b)** Find $\Pr(C)$. **(c)** Find $\Pr(H)$.

34. Course Choices Out of 250 students interviewed at a community college, 90 were taking mathematics but not computer science, 160 were taking mathematics, and 50 were taking neither mathematics nor computer science. Find the probability that a student chosen at random was

   (a) taking just computer science.

   (b) taking mathematics or computer science, but not both.

   (c) taking computer science.

   (d) not taking mathematics.

   (e) taking mathematics, given that the student was taking computer science.

   (f) taking computer science, given that the student was taking mathematics.

   (g) taking mathematics, given that the student was taking computer science or mathematics.

   (h) taking computer science, given that the student was not taking mathematics.

   (i) not taking mathematics, given that the student was not taking computer science.

35. Sports Choices Out of 250 third-grade boys, 120 played baseball, 140 played soccer, and 50 played both. Find the probability that a boy chosen at random

   (a) did not play either sport.

(b) played exactly one sport.

(c) played soccer but not baseball.

(d) played soccer, given that he played baseball.

(e) played baseball, given that he did not play soccer.

(f) did not play soccer, given that he did not play baseball.

36. **Voting** Table 2 shows the number of voting-age U.S. citizens (in millions) by gender and their participation in the 2006 congressional election. Find the probability that a voting-age citizen selected at random

(a) voted.   (b) is male.

(c) is female, given that they voted.

(d) voted, given that they are male.

TABLE 2

	Voted	Did not vote	Totals
Male	45.2	61.3	106.5
Female	51.0	63.1	114.1
Totals	96.2	124.4	220.6

Source: U.S. Census Bureau.

37. **Advanced Degrees** Table 3 shows the number of advanced degrees (in thousands) earned in the U.S. during a recent year by gender and type of degree. Find the probability that a person selected at random who received an advanced degree

(a) received a master's degree.

(b) is male.

(c) is female, given that they received a bachelor's degree.

(d) received a doctor's degree, given that they are male.

TABLE 3

	Bachelor's	Master's	Doctor's
Male	573	211	24
Female	775	301	22

Source: National Center for Education Statistics.

38. **Student Employment** Table 4 provides some information about students at a certain college. Find the probability that a student selected at random is

(a) a senior.

(b) working full time.

(c) working part time, given that the student is a first-year student.

(d) a first-year student, given that the student does not work.

(e) a junior or senior, given that the student does not work.

(f) working part time or full time, given that the student is a sophomore or a junior.

TABLE 4

	Works full time	Works part time	Not working
First-year	130	460	210
Sophomore	100	500	150
Junior	80	420	100
Senior	200	300	50

39. **Party Affiliation** Table 5 describes the voters in a certain district. Find the probability that a voter chosen at random is a

(a) Democrat.

(b) male.

(c) Independent, given that the voter is female.

(d) male, given that the voter is a Republican.

(e) female, given that the voter is not an Independent.

(f) Democrat, given that the voter is not a Republican.

TABLE 5

	Democrat	Republican	Independent
Male	400	700	300
Female	600	300	200

40. **Opinion Poll** Table 6 shows the responses when 300 people were asked if they thought executives were paid too much. Find the probability that a person selected at random from those surveyed

(a) answered yes.

(b) is male.

(c) is female, given that they answered yes.

(d) answered no, given that he is male.

TABLE 6

	Yes	No	Neutral
Male	75	39	36
Female	91	16	43

41. **Baseball** A baseball player's batting average changes every time he goes to bat, and therefore should not be used as the probability of him getting a hit. However, we can still make a subjective assessment of his ability.

(a) If a player with .3 probability of getting a hit bats four times in a game and each at-bat is an independent event, what is the probability of the player getting at least one hit in the game?

(b) What is the probability of the player in part (a) starting off the season with at least one hit in each of the first 10 games?

(c) If there are 20 players with .3 probability of getting a hit, what is the probability that at least one of them will start the season with a 10-game hitting streak?

42. Military Personnel Table 7 shows the numbers of officers and enlisted persons on active military duty on May 31, 2008. Let E be the event that a person selected at random from the active-duty military personnel is enlisted, and let N be the event that a person selected at random from the active-duty military personnel is in the Navy.

TABLE 7

	Army	Navy	Marine Corps	Air Force
Officer	86,028	52,153	20,048	65,276
Enlisted	436,145	275,960	170,603	259,021

(a) Find each of the following probabilities: $\Pr(E)$, $\Pr(N)$, $\Pr(E \cap N)$, $\Pr(E|N)$, $\Pr(N|E)$.

(b) Are the events E and N independent?

43. Balls in an Urn An urn contains 10 red balls and 15 white balls. A ball is selected at random from the urn and not replaced. Then, a second ball is selected. Show that the probability that the second ball is red is the same as the probability that the first ball is red.

44. Choosing Numbers Juan randomly chooses a positive integer that is divisible by 7 and is less than 70. Chita randomly selects a positive integer less than 70 that is divisible by 11. What is the probability that they choose the same number?

45. Bag of Marbles A bag contains four blue marbles, three white marbles, and six red marbles. Three marbles are selected from the bag. What is the probability they are all red? What is the probability that they are all the same color?

46. Spinners A spinner on a wheel with the numbers 2, 5, 6, and 9 in segments of equal area is spun at random. Another spinner on a wheel with equal segments marked with numbers 3, 7, and 8 is also spun. What is the probability that the sum of the two numbers chosen by the spinners is odd?

47. Sandwiches Horatio goes to the deli for sandwiches and orders two roast beef sandwiches and two ham sandwiches. They are wrapped and put into a paper bag. What is the probability that two sandwiches chosen at random will both be roast beef? What is the probability that the two sandwiches chosen at random will be alike?

48. Numbers Ten slips of paper have numbers 1 through 10. Sue chooses two slips at random. What is the probability that the sum of the numbers chosen is even?

49. Bag of Marbles A bag contains five red marbles and eight white marbles. If a sample of four marbles contains at least one white marble, what is the probability that all the marbles in the sample are white?

50. Cards Eight people each have a deck of well-shuffled cards. Each chooses a card at random from his or her own deck. What is the probability that there is at least one match?

51. Prize Drawing One hundred attendees at a conference put their calling cards into a glass bowl for a drawing. Fred cheats and puts in three of his cards to increase his chance of winning. Just before the drawing, it is announced that a second card will be drawn for a second prize after the first card is drawn. What is the probability that Fred will win both prizes and therefore be revealed to have cheated?

52. Conditional Probabilities Suppose a male is selected at random from the adult male population. Let F be the event "he played varsity sports in college." Which of the following two probabilities is greater?

(a) $\Pr(\text{"he works in a bank and is an avid sports fan"}|F)$

(b) $\Pr(\text{"he works in a bank"}|F)$

53. Roll a Die Roll a die and consider the following two events: $E = \{2, 4, 6\}$, $F = \{3, 6\}$. Are the events E and F independent?

54. Balls in an Urn An urn contains both red and white balls. A ball is selected at random from the urn and not replaced. Then, a second ball is selected. Show that the sequence of colors "red, white" has the same probability of occurring as the sequence "white, red."

55. Children A newly married couple decides to keep having children until they have a girl. What is the probability that the couple will have at least five children? *Note*: Assume no multiple births.

56. Rolling Dice What is the probability that at least one of the dice shows a 1 or a 2 when four dice are rolled?

57. Lottery Suppose you decide to bet $1000 in a weekly lottery for which the probability of winning the jackpot is p, where p is very small. Are your chances of winning the jackpot better if you bet 1000 different combinations in a single lottery or bet a single combination in 1000 successive weekly lotteries? To answer this question, determine the following:

(a) the probability of winning the jackpot when you bet 1000 different combinations in a single lottery.

(b) the probability of winning the jackpot at least once when you bet a single combination in 1000 successive weekly lotteries.

Note: $(1-p)^{1000} \approx 1 - 1000p + 499{,}500p^2$.

58. Roulette If you bet on the number 7 in roulette, the probability of winning on a single spin of the wheel is $\frac{1}{38}$. Suppose you bet on "7" for 38 consecutive spins.

(a) Which of the following numbers do you think is closest to the probability of winning at least once: 1, .64, or .5?

(b) Calculate the probability of winning at least once.

59. **Coin Toss** A biased coin shows heads with probability .6. What is the probability of obtaining the sequence HT in two tosses of the coin? TH? Could this coin be used at the start of a football game to fairly determine which team is to kick off?

60. **Gold and Silver Coins** Consider three boxes where one box contains two gold coins, one box contains two silver coins, and one box contains a gold coin and a silver coin. Suppose you select a box at random and then select a coin at random from that box. If the coin is gold, what is the probability that the other coin in the box is gold?

61. **Coin Toss** A coin is tossed five times. Is the outcome HTHHT more likely to occur than the outcome HHHHH?

62. **Rolling a Die** Suppose you roll a die six times and obtain a 1 each time. What is the probability that the next roll will produce a 1?

In Exercises 63–66, use a graphing calculator or spreadsheet to calculate the probabilities.

63. **Gender and Unemployment** Consider Table 8, with figures in thousands, pertaining to the 2008 American civilian labor force (age 20^+). Determine if gender and unemployment status are independent by finding the probabilities $\Pr(W)$, $\Pr(U)$, and $\Pr(W \cap U)$.

64. **Bridge** A bridge hand consists of 13 cards selected from a deck of 52 cards.

    (a) How many possible bridge hands contain at least one ace?

(b) How many possible bridge hands contain the ace of spades?

(c) Let E = "the hand contains at least two aces." Let F = "the hand contains at least one ace." Let G = "the hand contains the ace of spades." Which is the greater probability: $\Pr(E|F)$ or $\Pr(E|G)$?

65. **Cards**

    (a) Find the probability of drawing four aces from a deck of 52 cards in four repeated draws without replacement.

    (b) Calculate the probability of drawing two red queens followed by two red kings in four draws from the deck without replacement.

    (c) Which of the two events in (a) or (b) is more likely?

66. **Roulette** Find that value of N for which the probability of winning in Exercise 58 at least once in N trials is about .5.

TABLE 8			
	Employed (E)	Unemployed (U)	Totals
Men (M)	74,998	4038	79,036
Women (W)	65,238	3208	68,446
Totals	140,236	7246	147,482

Source: U.S. Bureau of Labor Statistics.

Solutions to Practice Problems 6.5

1. $\frac{2}{3}$. Let F be the event that the up side is red and E the event that the down side is red. $\Pr(F) = \frac{1}{2}$ since half the faces are red. $F \cap E$ is the event that both sides of the card are red—that is, that the card that is red on both sides was selected, an event with probability $\frac{1}{3}$. By (2),

$$\Pr(E|F) = \frac{\Pr(E \cap F)}{\Pr(F)} = \frac{\frac{1}{3}}{\frac{1}{2}} = \frac{2}{3}.$$

(A common error is to conclude that the answer is $\frac{1}{2}$ since the card must be either the red/red card or the red/white card, and each of them is equally likely to have been selected. The correct probability is intuitively evident when you realize that two-thirds of the

time the card will have the same color on the bottom as on the top.)

2. By the hint,

$$\Pr(E \cap F') = \Pr(E) - \Pr(E \cap F)$$
$$= \Pr(E) - \Pr(E) \cdot \Pr(F)$$
$$\text{(since } E \text{ and } F \text{ are independent)}$$
$$= \Pr(E)[1 - \Pr(F)]$$
$$= \Pr(E) \cdot \Pr(F')$$
$$\text{(by the complement rule).}$$

Therefore, E and F' are independent events.

6.6 Tree Diagrams

In solving many probability problems, it is helpful to represent the various events and their associated probabilities by a **tree diagram**. To explain this useful notion, suppose that we wish to compute the probability of an event that results from performing a sequence of experiments. The various outcomes of each experiment are represented as branches emanating from a point. For example, Fig. 1 represents an experiment with three outcomes. Notice that each branch has been labeled with the probability of the associated outcome. For example, the probability of outcome 1 is .5.

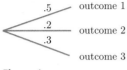

Figure 1

We represent experiments performed one after another by stringing together diagrams of the sort shown in Fig. 1, proceeding from left to right. For example, the diagram in Fig. 2 indicates that first we perform experiment A, having three outcomes, labeled 1–3. If the outcome is 1 or 2, we perform experiment B. If the outcome is 3, we perform experiment C. The probabilities on the right are conditional probabilities. For example, the top probability is the probability of outcome a (of B) given outcome 1 (of A). The probability of a sequence of outcomes may then be computed by multiplying the probabilities along a path. For example, to calculate the probability of outcome 2 followed by outcome b, we must calculate $\Pr(2 \text{ and } b) = \Pr(2) \cdot \Pr(b|2)$. To carry out this calculation, trace out the sequence of outcomes. Multiplying the probabilities along the path gives $(.2)(.6) = .12$—the probability of outcome 2 followed by outcome b.

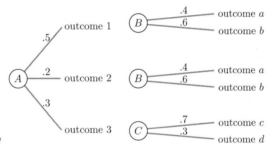

Figure 2

The next example illustrates the use of tree diagrams in calculating probabilities.

EXAMPLE 1

Political polling A pollster is hired by a presidential candidate to determine his support among the voters of Pennsylvania's two big cities: Philadelphia and Pittsburgh. The pollster designs the following sampling technique: Select one of the cities at random and then poll a voter selected at random from that city. Suppose that in Philadelphia two-fifths of the voters favor the Republican candidate and three-fifths favor the Democratic candidate. Suppose that in Pittsburgh two-thirds of the voters favor the Republican candidate and one-third favor the Democratic candidate.

(a) Draw a tree diagram describing the survey.

(b) Find the probability that the voter polled is from Philadelphia and favors the Republican candidate.

(c) Find the probability that the voter favors the Republican candidate.

(d) Find the probability that the voter is from Philadelphia, given that he or she favors the Republican candidate.

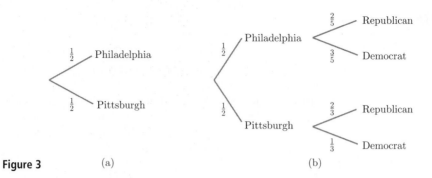

Figure 3   (a)   (b)

Solution **(a)** The survey proceeds in two steps: First, select a city, and second, select and poll a voter. Figure 3(a) shows the possible outcomes of the first step and the associated probabilities. For each outcome of the first step there are two possibilities for the second step: The person selected could favor the Republican or the Democrat. In Fig. 3(b) we have represented these possibilities by drawing branches emanating from each of the outcomes of the first step. The probabilities on the new branches are actually conditional probabilities. For instance,

$$\tfrac{2}{5} = \text{Pr}(\text{Rep}|\text{Phila}),$$

the probability that the voter favors the Republican candidate, given that the voter is from Philadelphia.

(b) $\text{Pr}(\text{Phila} \cap \text{Rep}) = \text{Pr}(\text{Phila}) \cdot \text{Pr}(\text{Rep}|\text{Phila}) = \tfrac{1}{2} \cdot \tfrac{2}{5} = \tfrac{1}{5}.$

That is, the probability is $\tfrac{1}{5}$ that the combined outcome corresponds to the blue path in Fig. 4(a). We have written the probability $\tfrac{1}{5}$ at the end of the path to which it corresponds.

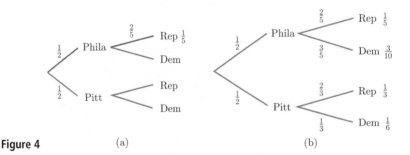

Figure 4   (a)   (b)

(c) In Fig. 4(b) we have computed the probabilities for each path of the tree as in part (b). Namely, the probability for a given path is the product of the probabilities for each of its segments. We are asked for Pr(Rep). There are two paths through the tree leading to Republican, namely

Philadelphia ∩ Republican   or   Pittsburgh ∩ Republican.

The probabilities of these two paths are $\tfrac{1}{5}$ and $\tfrac{1}{3}$, respectively. So the probability that the Republican is favored equals $\tfrac{1}{5} + \tfrac{1}{3} = \tfrac{8}{15}.$

(d) Here we are asked for Pr(Phila|Rep). By the definition of conditional probability,

Now Try Exercise 13

$$\text{Pr}(\text{Phila}|\text{Rep}) = \frac{\text{Pr}(\text{Phila} \cap \text{Rep})}{\text{Pr}(\text{Rep})} = \frac{\tfrac{1}{5}}{\tfrac{8}{15}} = \frac{3}{8}.$$ ∎

Note that from part (c) we might be led to conclude that the Republican candidate is leading, with $\frac{8}{15}$ of the vote. However, we must always be careful when interpreting surveys. The results depend heavily on the survey design. For example, the survey drew half of its sample from each of the cities. However, Philadelphia is a much larger city and is leaning toward the Democratic candidate—so much so, in fact, that in terms of popular vote the Democratic candidate would win, contrary to our expectations drawn from (c). A pollster must be very careful in designing the procedure for selecting people.

We now finally solve the medical diagnosis problem introduced in Section 6.1.

EXAMPLE 2

Medical screening Suppose that the reliability of a skin test for active pulmonary tuberculosis (TB) is specified as follows: Of people with TB, 98% have a positive reaction and 2% have a negative reaction; of people free of TB, 99% have a negative reaction and 1% have a positive reaction.[1] From a large population of which 2 per 10,000 persons have TB, a person is selected at random and given a skin test, which turns out to be positive. What is the probability that the person has active pulmonary tuberculosis?

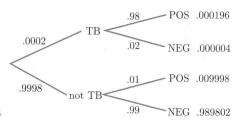

Figure 5

Solution The given data are organized in Fig. 5. The procedure called for is as follows: First select a person at random from the population. There are two possible outcomes: The person has TB,

$$\Pr(\text{TB}) = \frac{2}{10,000} = .0002,$$

or the person does not have TB,

$$\Pr(\text{not TB}) = 1 - .0002 = .9998.$$

For each of these two possibilities, the possible test results and conditional probabilities are given. Multiplying the probabilities along each of the paths through the tree gives the probabilities of the different outcomes. The resulting probabilities are written on the right in Fig. 5. The problem asks for the conditional probability that a person has TB, given that the test is positive. By definition,

$$\Pr(\text{TB}|\text{POS}) = \frac{\Pr(\text{TB} \cap \text{POS})}{\Pr(\text{POS})} = \frac{.000196}{.000196 + .009998} = \frac{.000196}{.010194} \approx .02.$$

Therefore, the probability is .02 that a person with a positive skin test has TB.[2] In other words, although the skin test is quite reliable, only about 2% of those with a positive test turn out to have active TB. This result must be taken into account

---

[1]The probability that a person with the disease has a positive test is called the *sensitivity* of the test. The probability that a disease-free person has a negative test is called the *specificity* of the test. In this case the sensitivity and specificity of the skin test are .98 and .99, respectively.

[2]The probability that a person who tests positive actually has the disease is called the *predictive value of the positive test*.

when large-scale medical diagnostic tests are planned. Because the group of people without TB is so much larger than the group with TB, the small error in the former group is magnified to the point where it dominates the calculation. ∎

Now Try Exercise 31

NOTE▶ The numerical data presented in Example 2 are only approximate. Variations in air quality for different localities within the United States cause variations in the incidence of TB and the reliability of skin tests. ∎

Tree diagrams come in all shapes and sizes. Three or more branches might emanate from a single point, for example, and some trees may not have the symmetry of those in Examples 1 and 2. Tree diagrams arise whenever an activity can be thought of as a sequence of simpler activities.

EXAMPLE 3

Quality control A box contains five good light bulbs and two defective ones. Bulbs are selected one at a time (without replacement) until a good bulb is found. Find the probability that the number of bulbs selected is (i) one, (ii) two, (iii) three.

Figure 6   (a)   (b)   (c)

Solution The initial situation in the box is shown in Fig. 6(a). A bulb selected at random will be good (G) with probability $\frac{5}{7}$ and defective (D) with probability $\frac{2}{7}$. If a good bulb is selected, the activity stops. Otherwise, the situation is as shown in Fig. 6(b), and a bulb selected at random has probability $\frac{5}{6}$ of being good and probability $\frac{1}{6}$ of being defective. If the second bulb is good, the activity stops. If the second bulb is defective, then the situation is as shown in Fig. 6(c). At this point a bulb has probability 1 of being good.

The tree diagram corresponding to the sequence of activities is given in Fig. 7. Each of the three paths has a different length. The probability associated with the length of each path has been computed by multiplying the probabilities for its branches. The first path corresponds to the situation where only one bulb is selected, the second path corresponds to two bulbs, and the third path to three bulbs. Therefore,

Figure 7

Now Try Exercise 11

(i) $\Pr(1) = \frac{5}{7}$ (ii) $\Pr(2) = \frac{5}{21}$ (iii) $\Pr(3) = \frac{1}{21}$.   ∎

Practice Problems 6.6

Fifty percent of the students enrolled in a business statistics course had previously taken a finite mathematics course. Thirty percent of these students received an A for the statistics course, whereas 20% of the other students received an A for the statistics course.

1. Draw a tree diagram and label it with the appropriate probabilities.

2. What is the probability that a student selected at

random previously took a finite mathematics course and did not receive an A in the statistics course?

3. What is the probability that a student selected at random received an A in the statistics course?

4. What is the conditional probability that a student previously took a finite mathematics course, given that he or she received an A in the statistics course?

EXERCISES 6.6

In Exercises 1–4, draw trees representing the sequence of experiments.

1. Experiment I is performed. Outcome *a* occurs with probability .3, and outcome *b* occurs with probability .7. Then experiment II is performed. Its outcome *c* occurs with probability .6, and its outcome *d* occurs with probability .4.

2. Experiment I is performed twice. The three outcomes of experiment I are equally likely.

3. **Quality Control** A stereo repair shop uses a two-step diagnostic procedure to repair amplifiers. Step I locates the problem in an amplifier with probability .8. Step II (which is executed only if step I fails to locate the problem) locates the problem with probability .6.

4. **Personnel Categories** A training program is used by a corporation to direct hirees to appropriate jobs. The program consists of two steps. Step I identifies 30% as management trainees, 60% as nonmanagerial workers, and 10% to be fired. In step II, 75% of the management trainees are assigned to managerial positions, 20% are assigned to nonmanagerial positions, and 5% are fired. In step II, 60% of the nonmanagerial workers are kept in the same category, 10% are assigned to management positions, and 30% are fired.

5. **Quality Control** Refer to Exercise 3. What is the probability that the procedure will fail to locate the problem?

6. **Personnel Categories** Refer to Exercise 4. What is the probability that a randomly chosen hiree will be assigned to a management position at the end of the training period?

7. **Personnel Categories** Refer to Exercise 4. What is the probability that a randomly chosen hiree will be fired by the end of the training period?

8. **Personnel Categories** Refer to Exercise 4. What is the probability that a randomly chosen hiree will be designated a management trainee but *not* be appointed to a management position?

9. **Selecting from Urns** Suppose that we have a white urn containing two white balls and one red ball and we

have a red urn containing one white ball and three red balls. An experiment consists of selecting at random a ball from the white urn and then (without replacing the first ball) selecting at random a ball from the urn having the color of the first ball. Find the probability that the second ball is red.

10. **Cards, Coins, Dice** A card is drawn from a 52-card deck. If the card is a picture card, we toss a coin. If the card is not a picture card, we roll a die. Find the probability that we end the sequence with a "6" on the die. Find the probability that we end the sequence with a "head" on the coin.

11. **Cards** A card is drawn from a 52-card deck. We continue to draw until we have drawn a king or until we have drawn five cards, whichever comes first. Draw a tree diagram that illustrates the experiment. Put the appropriate probabilities on the tree. Find the probability that the drawing ends before the fourth draw.

12. **Final Exams** There are three sections of a mathematics course available at convenient times for a student. There is a 20% chance that Professor Jones gives a final exam, a 10% chance that Professor Cates gives a final exam, and a 5% chance that Professor Smithson gives a final. At other times there are two biology sections, and in those the probabilities of a final are 20% and 13%. Find the probability that a student who randomly chooses one mathematics course and one biology course has to take at least one final examination.

13. **Quality Control** Twenty percent of the library books in the fiction section are worn and need replacement. Ten percent of the nonfiction holdings are worn and need replacement. The library's holdings are 40% fiction and 60% nonfiction. Use a tree diagram to find the probability that a book chosen at random from this library is worn and needs replacement.

14. **School Bussing** Draw a tree diagram that illustrates the following. Three-fifths of kindergarten children are bussed to school, while two-fifths of the first to fifth graders are bussed. The school has grades K through 5, and 17.5% of the students are in kindergarten. De-

termine the probability that a child chosen at random from the school is bussed to school.

15. **Color Blindness** Color blindness is a sex-linked, inherited condition that is much more common among men than women. Suppose that 5% of all men and .4% of all women are color-blind. A person is chosen at random and found to be color-blind. What is the probability that the person is male? (You may assume that 50% of the population are men and 50% are women.)

16. **T-maze** A mouse is put into a T-maze (a maze shaped like a "T"). In this maze he has the choice of turning to the left and being rewarded with cheese or going to the right and receiving a mild shock. Before any conditioning takes place (i.e., on trial 1), the mouse is equally likely to go to the left or to the right. After the first trial his decision is influenced by what happened on the previous trial. If he receives cheese on any trial, the probabilities of his going to the left or right become .9 and .1, respectively, on the following trial. If he receives the electric shock on any trial, the probabilities of his going to the left or right on the next trial become .7 and .3, respectively. What is the probability that the mouse will turn left on the second trial?

17. **T-maze** Refer to Exercise 16. What is the probability that the mouse will turn left on the third trial?

18. **Manufacturing** A factory has two machines that produce bolts. Machine I produces 60% of the daily output of bolts, and 3% of its bolts are defective. Machine II produces 40% of the daily output, and 2% of its bolts are defective.

   (a) What is the probability that a bolt selected at random will be defective?

   (b) If a bolt is selected at random and found to be defective, what is the probability that it was produced by machine I?

19. **Heads or Tails** Three ordinary quarters and a fake quarter with two heads are placed in a hat. One quarter is selected at random and tossed twice. If the outcome is "HH," what is the probability that the fake quarter was selected?

20. **Medical Diagnosis** Suppose that the reliability of a test for hepatitis is specified as follows: Of people with hepatitis, 95% have a positive reaction and 5% have a negative reaction; of people free of hepatitis, 90% have a negative reaction and 10% have a positive reaction. From a large population of which .05% of the people have hepatitis, a person is selected at random and given the test. If the test is positive, what is the probability that the person actually has hepatitis?

21. **Tennis** Kim has a strong first serve; whenever it is good (that is, in) she wins the point 75% of the time. Whenever her second serve is good, she wins the point 50% of the time. Sixty percent of her first serves and 75% of her second serves are good.

   (a) What is the probability that Kim wins the point when she serves?

   (b) If Kim wins a service point, what is the probability that her first serve was good?

22. **Accidental Nuclear War** Suppose that during any year the probability of an accidental nuclear war is .0001 (provided, of course, that there hasn't been one in a previous year). Draw a tree diagram representing the possibilities for the next three years. What is the probability that there will be an accidental nuclear war during the next three years?

23. **Accidental Nuclear War** Refer to Exercise 22. What is the probability that there will be an accidental nuclear war during the next n years?

24. **Coin Tosses** A coin is to be tossed at most five times. The tosser wins as soon as the number of heads exceeds the number of tails and loses as soon as three tails have been tossed. Use a tree diagram for this game to calculate the probability of winning.

25. **Cards** Suppose that instead of tossing a coin, the player in Exercise 24 draws up to five cards from a deck consisting only of three red and three black cards. The player wins as soon as the number of red cards exceeds the number of black cards and loses as soon as three black cards have been drawn. Does the tree diagram for the card game have the same shape as the tree diagram for the coin game? Is there any difference in the probability of winning? If so, which game has the greater probability of winning?

26. **Cards** A man has been guessing the colors of cards drawn from a standard deck. During the first 50 draws he kept track of the number of cards of each color. What is the probability of guessing the color of the fifty-first card?

27. **Genetics** Traits passed from generation to generation are carried by genes. For a certain type of pea plant, the color of the flower produced by the plant (either red or white) is determined by a pair of genes. Each gene is of one of the types C (dominant gene) or c (recessive gene). Plants for which both genes are of type c (said to have genotype cc) produce white flowers. All other plants—that is, plants of genotypes CC and Cc—produce red flowers. When two plants are crossed, the offspring receives one gene from each parent.

   (a) Suppose you cross two pea plants of genotype Cc. What is the probability that the offspring produces white flowers? red flowers?

   (b) Suppose you have a batch of red-flowering pea plants, of which 60% have genotype Cc and 40% have genotype CC. If you select one of these plants at random and cross it with a white-flowering pea plant, what is the probability that the offspring will produce red flowers?

28. Genetics Refer to Exercise 27. Suppose a batch of 99 pea plants contains 33 plants of each of the three genotypes.

(a) If you select one of these plants at random and cross it with a white-flowering pea plant, what is the probability that the offspring will produce white flowers?

(b) If you select one of the 99 pea plants at random, cross it with a white-flowering pea plant, and the offspring produces red flowers, what is the probability that the selected plant had genotype Cc?

29. College Faculty At a local college, four sections of economics are taught during the day and two sections are taught at night. Seventy-five percent of the day sections are taught by full-time faculty. Forty percent of the evening sections are taught by full-time faculty. If Jane has a part-time teacher for her economics course, what is the probability that she is taking a night class?

30. U.S. Car Production Car production in the United States in 2005 was distributed among car manufacturers as follows.

U.S. car production	Type		Percentage of type by brand
60%	Domestic	Chrysler	23%
		Ford	31%
		General Motors	46%
40%	Foreign	Honda	20%
		Toyota	32%
		Other	48%

Source: U.S. Light Vehicle Production by Manufacturer (*Ward's AutoInfo Bank*).

This means that 60% of the cars produced in the United States were manufactured by domestic companies; of them, 23% were Chryslers, 31% were Fords, and 46% were General Motors products.

(a) A 2005 automobile is chosen at random. What is the probability that it is a General Motors car?

(b) What is the probability that a randomly selected 2005 automobile is a Ford or a Toyota?

Exercises 31 and 32 refer to Example 2.

31. Medical Screening Find the predictive value of the negative skin test; that is, the probability of a true negative.

32. Medical Screening The predictive values of a diagnostic test do not depend entirely on the sensitivity and specificity of the test. They also depend on the prevalence of the disease being tested for. Find the predictive values of the positive and negative skin tests if 2 out of 100 people in the population have tuberculosis.

33. Balls in an Urn Urn I contains 5 red balls and 5 white balls. Urn II contains 12 white balls. A ball is selected at random from urn I and placed in urn II. Then a ball is selected at random from urn II. What is the probability that the second ball is white?

34. Balls in an Urn An urn contains five red balls and three green balls. One ball is selected at random and then replaced by a ball of the other color. Then a second ball is selected at random. What is the probability that the second ball is green?

35. Coin Tosses Two people toss two coins each. What is the probability that they get the same number of heads?

36. Quality Control A light bulb manufacturer knows that .05% of all bulbs manufactured are defective. A testing machine is 99% effective; that is, 99% of good bulbs will be declared fine and 99% of flawed bulbs will be declared defective. If a randomly selected light bulb is tested and found to be defective, what is the probability that it actually is defective?

37. Tennis When a tennis player hits his first serve as hard as possible (called a *blast*), he gets the ball in (that is; within bounds) 60% of the time. When the blast first serve is in, he wins the point 80% of the time. When the first serve is out, his gentler second serve wins the point 45% of the time. Draw a tree diagram representing the probabilities of winning the point for the first two serves. Use the tree diagram to determine the probability that the server eventually wins the point when his first serve is a blast.

38. Golf Bud is a very consistent golfer. On par three holes, he always scores a 4. Lou, on the other hand, is quite erratic. On par three holes, Lou scores a 3 seventy percent of the time and scores a 6 thirty percent of the time.

(a) If Bud and Lou play a single par three hole together, who is more likely to win; that is, to have the lowest score?

(b) If Bud and Lou play two consecutive par three holes, who is more likely to have the lowest total score?

39. Pinball Stan and Oliver are playing adjacent pinball machines. Stan is very consistent and scores 400 points each game. Oliver is a bit more aggressive and scores 401 points 99% of the time and 0 points (tilt) the rest of the time.

(a) If they each play one game, what is the probability that Oliver wins; that is, scores the most points?

(b) What is the probability that Oliver has scored the most total points after each person has played 400 games? *Hint*: Stan will have scored 160,000 points. If Oliver loses one or more games, he will have fewer total points than Stan.

40. Selecting from Urns An urn contains 4 red marbles and 3 green marbles. One marble is removed, its color noted, and the marble is not replaced. A second marble is removed and its color noted.

  (a) What is the probability that both marbles are red? green?

  (b) What is the probability that exactly one marble is red?

41. Drug Testing Suppose 500 athletes are tested for a drug, one in ten has used the drug, the test has a 99% specificity, and the test has a 100% sensitivity. That is,

the probability of a false positive is 1% and there is no chance that a user of the drug will go undetected. If an athlete in the group tests positive, what is the probability that he or she has used the drug?

42. Selecting from a Bag A bag is equally likely to contain either one white ball or one red ball. A white ball is added to the bag and then a ball is selected at random from the bag. If the selected ball is white, what is the probability that the bag originally contained a white ball? (*Note*: This problem has been attributed to Lewis Carroll.)

Solutions to Practice Problems 6.6

1.

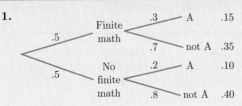

2. The event "finite math and not A" corresponds to

the second path of the tree diagram, which has probability .35.

3. This event is satisfied by the first or third paths and therefore has probability $.15 + .10 = .25$.

4. $\Pr(\text{finite math}|A) = \dfrac{\Pr(\text{finite math and A})}{\Pr(A)} = \dfrac{.15}{.25} = .6$.

6.7 Bayes' Theorem

Let us reconsider the polling survey in Example 1(d) of Section 6.6 (see Fig. 1). Given that the person chosen at random favors the Republican candidate, what is the probability that the respondent is from Philadelphia? We found this probability, $\Pr(\text{Phila}|\text{Rep})$, by finding

$$\frac{\Pr(\text{Phila} \cap \text{Rep})}{\Pr(\text{Rep})}.$$

Let us analyze the components of this calculation. First, recall that

$$\Pr(\text{Phila} \cap \text{Rep}) = \Pr(\text{Phila}) \cdot \Pr(\text{Rep}|\text{Phila}).$$

Second,

$$\Pr(\text{Rep}) = \Pr(\text{Phila} \cap \text{Rep}) + \Pr(\text{Pitt} \cap \text{Rep})$$

$$= \Pr(\text{Phila}) \cdot \Pr(\text{Rep}|\text{Phila}) + \Pr(\text{Pitt}) \cdot \Pr(\text{Rep}|\text{Pitt}),$$

by using the tree diagram. Denote the events "Phila," "Pitt," "Rep," and "Dem" by the letters A, B, R, and D, respectively. Then

$$\Pr(\text{Phila}|\text{Rep}) = \Pr(A|R)$$

$$= \frac{\Pr(A \cap R)}{\Pr(R)}$$

$$= \frac{\Pr(A) \cdot \Pr(R|A)}{\Pr(A) \cdot \Pr(R|A) + \Pr(B) \cdot \Pr(R|B)}.$$

This is a special case of Bayes' theorem.

Figure 1

We summarize a simple form of Bayes' theorem. Suppose that A is an event in S, and B_1 and B_2 are mutually exclusive events such that $B_1 \cup B_2 = S$. Then

$$\Pr(B_1|A) = \frac{\Pr(B_1) \cdot \Pr(A|B_1)}{\Pr(B_1) \cdot \Pr(A|B_1) + \Pr(B_2) \cdot \Pr(A|B_2)}.$$

We have the same type of result for the situation in which we have three mutually exclusive sets B_1, B_2, and B_3 whose union is all of S. We state Bayes' theorem for that case and leave the general case for n mutually exclusive sets for the end of the section.

Figure 2

Bayes' Theorem ($n = 3$)   If B_1, B_2, and B_3 are mutually exclusive events, and $B_1 \cup B_2 \cup B_3 = S$, then for any event A in S,

$$\Pr(B_1|A) = \frac{\Pr(B_1) \cdot \Pr(A|B_1)}{\Pr(B_1) \cdot \Pr(A|B_1) + \Pr(B_2) \cdot \Pr(A|B_2) + \Pr(B_3) \cdot \Pr(A|B_3)}.$$

See Fig. 2.

EXAMPLE 1

Medical screening   Solve the tuberculosis skin test problem of Example 2 of Section 6.6 by using Bayes' theorem.

Solution   The observed event A is "positive skin test result." There are two possible events leading to A—namely,

$$B_1 = \text{"person has tuberculosis"}$$

$$B_2 = \text{"person does not have tuberculosis."}$$

We wish to calculate $\Pr(B_1|A)$. From the data given we have

$$\Pr(B_1) = \frac{2}{10,000} = .0002$$

$$\Pr(B_2) = .9998$$

$$\Pr(A|B_1) = \Pr(\text{POS}|\text{TB}) = .98$$

$$\Pr(A|B_2) = \Pr(\text{POS}|\text{not TB}) = .01.$$

Therefore, by Bayes' theorem,

$$\Pr(B_1|A) = \frac{\Pr(B_1)\Pr(A|B_1)}{\Pr(B_1)\Pr(A|B_1) + \Pr(B_2)\Pr(A|B_2)}$$

$$= \frac{(.0002)(.98)}{(.0002)(.98) + (.9998)(.01)} \approx .02,$$

Now Try Exercise 11   in agreement with our calculation of Example 2 of Section 6.6.   ■

The advantages of Bayes' theorem over the use of tree diagrams are that (1) we do not need to draw the tree diagram to calculate the desired probability, and (2) we need not compute extraneous probabilities. These advantages become significant in dealing with experiments having many outcomes.

EXAMPLE 2

Quality control   A printer has seven book-binding machines. For each machine, Table 1 on the next page gives the proportion of the total book production that it binds and the probability that the machine produces a defective binding. For instance, machine 1 binds 10% of the books and produces a defective binding with

TABLE 1

Machine	Proportion of books bound	Probability of defective binding
1	.10	.03
2	.05	.03
3	.20	.02
4	.15	.02
5	.25	.01
6	.15	.02
7	.10	.03

probability .03. Suppose that a book is selected at random and found to have a defective binding. What is the probability that it was bound by machine 1?

Solution In this example we have seven mutually exclusive events whose union is the entire sample space (the book was bound by one, and only one, of the seven machines). Bayes' theorem can be extended to any finite number of B_i's.

Let B_i $(i = 1, 2, \ldots, 7)$ be the event that the book was bound by machine i, and let A be the event that the book has a defective binding. Then, for example,

$$\Pr(B_1) = .10 \quad \text{and} \quad \Pr(A|B_1) = .03.$$

The problem asks for the reversed conditional probability, $\Pr(B_1|A)$. By Bayes' theorem,

$$\Pr(B_1|A) = \frac{\Pr(B_1)\Pr(A|B_1)}{\Pr(B_1)\Pr(A|B_1) + \Pr(B_2)\Pr(A|B_2) + \cdots + \Pr(B_7)\Pr(A|B_7)}$$

$$= \frac{(.10)(.03)}{(.10)(.03) + (.05)(.03) + (.20)(.02) + (.15)(.02) + (.25)(.01) + (.15)(.02) + (.10)(.03)}$$

$$= \frac{.003}{.02} = .15.$$

Now Try Exercise 1

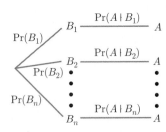

Figure 3

Derivation of Bayes' Theorem   To derive Bayes' theorem in general, we consider a two-stage tree. Suppose that at the first stage there are the events $B_1, B_2, \ldots, B_n$, which are mutually exclusive and exhaust all possibilities. Let us examine only the paths of the tree leading to event A at the second stage of the experiment (see Fig. 3). Suppose we are given that the event A occurs. What is $\Pr(B_1|A)$? First, consider $\Pr(B_1 \cap A)$. This can be seen from Fig. 3 to be $\Pr(B_1) \cdot \Pr(A|B_1)$. Next we calculate $\Pr(A)$. Recall that A occurs at stage 2, preceded at stage 1 by either event $B_1, B_2, \ldots$, or B_n. Since $B_1, B_2, \ldots, B_n$ are mutually exclusive,

$$\Pr(A) = \Pr(B_1 \cap A) + \Pr(B_2 \cap A) + \cdots + \Pr(B_n \cap A).$$

Each of the elements in the sum can be calculated by the product rule, or directly from Fig. 3:

$$\Pr(B_1 \cap A) = \Pr(B_1) \cdot \Pr(A|B_1)$$
$$\Pr(B_2 \cap A) = \Pr(B_2) \cdot \Pr(A|B_2)$$
$$\vdots$$
$$\Pr(B_n \cap A) = \Pr(B_n) \cdot \Pr(A|B_n).$$

The result is the following:

> **Bayes' Theorem**   If $B_1, B_2, \ldots, B_n$ are mutually exclusive events, and if $B_1 \cup B_2 \cup \cdots \cup B_n = S$, then for any event A in S,
>
> $$\Pr(B_1|A) = \frac{\Pr(B_1) \cdot \Pr(A|B_1)}{\Pr(B_1) \cdot \Pr(A|B_1) + \Pr(B_2) \cdot \Pr(A|B_2) + \cdots + \Pr(B_n) \cdot \Pr(A|B_n)}$$
>
> $$\Pr(B_2|A) = \frac{\Pr(B_2) \cdot \Pr(A|B_2)}{\Pr(B_1) \cdot \Pr(A|B_1) + \Pr(B_2) \cdot \Pr(A|B_2) + \cdots + \Pr(B_n) \cdot \Pr(A|B_n)},$$
>
> and so forth.

Practice Problems 6.7

Quality Control *Refer to Example 2. Suppose that a book is selected at random and found to have a defective binding.*

1. What is the probability that the book was bound by machine 2?

2. By what machine is the book most likely to have been bound?

EXERCISES 6.7

1. **Accident Rates** An automobile insurance company has determined the accident rate (probability of having at least one accident during a year) for various age groups (see Table 2). Suppose that a policyholder calls in to report an accident. What is the probability that he or she is over 60?

TABLE 2

Age group	Proportion of total insured	Accident rate
Under 21	.05	.06
21–30	.10	.04
31–40	.25	.02
41–50	.20	.015
51–60	.30	.025
Over 60	.10	.04

2. **Quality Control** An electronic device has six different types of transistors. For each type of transistor, Table 3 gives the proportion of the total number of transistors of that type and the failure rate (probability of failing within one year). If a transistor fails, what is the probability that it is type 1?

TABLE 3

Type	Proportion of total	Failure rate
1	.30	.0002
2	.25	.0004
3	.20	.0005
4	.10	.001
5	.05	.002
6	.10	.004

3. **Student Performance** The enrollment in a certain course is 10% first-year students, 30% sophomores, 40% juniors, and 20% seniors. Past experience has shown that the likelihood of receiving an A in the course is .2 for first-year students, .4 for sophomores, .3 for juniors, and .1 for seniors. Find the probability that a student who receives an A is a sophomore.

4. **Larceny Rates** A metropolitan police department maintains statistics of larcenies reported in the various precincts of the city. It records the proportion of the city population in each precinct and the precinct larceny rate (= the proportion of the precinct population reporting a larceny within the past year). These statistics are summarized in Table 4. A larceny victim is randomly chosen from the city population. What is

the probability he or she comes from Precinct 3?

TABLE 4

Precinct	Proportion of population	Larceny rate
1	.20	.01
2	.10	.02
3	.40	.05
4	.30	.04

5. **Cars and Income** Table 5 gives the distribution of incomes and shows the proportion of two-car families by income level for a certain suburban county. Suppose that a randomly chosen family has two or more cars. What is the probability that its income is at least $75,000 per year?

TABLE 5

Annual family income	Proportion of people	Proportion having two or more cars
< $30,000	.10	.2
$30,000–$44,999	.20	.5
$45,000–$59,999	.35	.6
$60,000–$74,999	.30	.75
≥ $75,000	.05	.9

6. **Voter Turnout** Table 6 gives the distribution of voter registration and voter turnouts for a certain city. A randomly chosen person is questioned at the polls. What is the probability that the person is an Independent?

TABLE 6

	Proportion registered	Proportion turnout
Democrat	.50	.4
Republican	.20	.5
Independent	.30	.7

7. **Mathematics Exam** In a calculus course, the instructor gave an algebra exam on the first day of class to help students determine whether or not they had enrolled in the appropriate course. Eighty percent of the students in the class passed the exam. Forty percent of those who passed the exam on the first day of class earned an *A* in the course, whereas only twenty percent of those who failed the exam earned an *A* in the course. What is the probability that a student selected at random passed the exam on the first day of class, given that he or she earned an *A* in the course?

8. **Demographics** Table 7 shows the percentages of various portions of the U.S. population in 2008 based on age and gender. Suppose that a person is chosen at random from the entire population.

TABLE 7

Age Group	U.S. Population % of population	% male
Under 5 yrs	7	51
5–19 yrs	21	51
20–44 yrs	35	51
45–64 yrs	25	49
Over 64 yrs	12	42

(a) What is the probability that the person chosen is male?

(b) Given that the person chosen is male, find the probability that he is between 5 and 19 years old.

9. **Bilingual Employees** A multinational company has five divisions: A, B, C, D, and E. The percentage of employees from each division who speak at least two languages fluently is shown in Table 8.

TABLE 8

Division	Number of employees	Percentage of employees who are bilingual
A	20,000	20
B	15,000	15
C	25,000	12
D	30,000	10
E	10,000	10
Total	100,000	

(a) Find the probability that an employee selected at random is bilingual.

(b) Find the probability that a bilingual employee selected at random works for division C.

10. **Customized Dice** A specially made pair of dice has only one- and two-spots on the faces. One of the dice has three faces with a one-spot and three faces with a two-spot. The other die has two faces with a one-spot and four faces with a two-spot. One of the dice is selected at random and then rolled six times. If a two-spot shows up only once, what is the probability that it is the die with four two-spots?

Exercises 11–15 refer to diagnostic tests. A false negative in a diagnostic test is a test result that is negative even though the patient has the condition. A false positive, on the other hand, is a test result that is positive although the patient does not have the condition.

11. **Mammogram Accuracy** The *New York Times* of January 24, 1997, discusses the recommendation of a special panel concerning mammograms for women in their 40s. About 2% of women aged 40 to 49 years old develop

breast cancer in their 40s. But the mammogram used for women in that age group has a high rate of false positives and false negatives; the false positive rate is .30, and the false negative rate is .25. If a woman in her 40s has a positive mammogram, what is the probability that she actually has breast cancer?

12. **Drug Testing** A drug-testing laboratory produces false negative results 2% of the time and false positive results 5% of the time. Suppose that the laboratory has been hired by a company in which 10% of the employees use drugs.

   (a) If an employee tests positive for drug use, what is the probability that he or she actually uses drugs?

   (b) What is the probability that a nondrug user will test positive for drug use twice in a row?

   (c) What is the probability that someone who tests positive twice in a row is not a drug user?

13. **Pregnancy Test** An over-the-counter pregnancy test claims to be 99% accurate. Actually, what the insert says is that if the test is performed properly, it is 99% sure to detect a pregnancy.

   (a) What is the probability of a false negative?

   (b) Let us assume that the probability is 98% that the test result is negative for a woman who is not pregnant. If the woman estimates that her chances of being pregnant are about 40% and the test result is positive, what is the probability that she is actually pregnant?

14. **Medical Testing** A test for a condition has a high probability of false positives, 20%. Its rate of false negatives is 10%. The condition is estimated to exist in 65% of all patients sent for screening. If the test is positive, what is the chance the patient has the condition? Suppose that the condition is much more rare in the population—say Pr(condition) = .30. Given the same testing situation, what is Pr(condition|pos)?

15. **Steroid Testing** It is estimated that 10% of Olympic athletes use steroids. The test currently being used to detect steroids is said to be 93% effective in correctly detecting steroids in users. It yields false positives in only 2% of the tests. A country's best weightlifter tests positive. What is the probability that he actually takes steroids?

16. **Cookie Jars** There are two cookie jars on the shelf in the kitchen. The red one has 10 chocolate-chip cookies

and 15 gingersnaps. The blue jar has 20 chocolate-chip cookies and 10 gingersnaps. James goes down in the middle of the night and without turning on the light chooses a jar at random and then chooses a cookie at random. If the cookie is chocolate chip, what is the probability that he got the cookie from the blue jar?

17. **Cards** Thirteen cards are dealt from a deck of 52 cards.

   (a) What is the probability that the ace of spades is one of the 13 cards?

   (b) Suppose one of the 13 cards is chosen at random and found *not* to be the ace of spades. What is the probability that *none* of the 13 cards is the ace of spades?

   (c) Suppose the experiment in part (b) is repeated a total of 10 times (replacing the card looked at each time), and the ace of spades is not seen. What is the probability that the ace of spades actually *is* one of the 13 cards?

18. **College Majors** There are three sections of English 101. In Section I there are 25 students, of whom 5 are mathematics majors. In Section II there are 20 students, of whom 6 are mathematics majors. In Section III there are 35 students, of whom 5 are mathematics majors. A student in English 101 is chosen at random. Find the probability that the student is from Section I, given that he or she is a mathematics major.

19. **Scholarship Winners** Twenty percent of the contestants in a scholarship competition come from Pylesville High School, 40% come from Millerville High School, and the remainder come from Lakeside High School. Two percent of the Pylesville students are among the scholarship winners; 3% of the Millerville contestants and 5% of the Lakeside contestants win.

   (a) If a winner is chosen at random, what is the probability that he or she is from Lakeside?

   (b) What percentage of the winners are from Pylesville?

20. **Manufacturing Reliability** Ten percent of the pens made by Apex are defective. Only 5% of the pens made by its competitor, B-ink, are defective. Since Apex pens are cheaper than B-ink pens, an office orders 70% of its stock from Apex and 30% from B-ink. A pen is chosen at random and found to be defective. What is the probability that it was produced by Apex?

Solutions to Practice Problems 6.7

1. The problem asks for $\Pr(B_2|A)$. Bayes' theorem gives this probability as a quotient with numerator $\Pr(B_2)\Pr(A|B_2)$ and the same denominator as in the solution to Example 2. Therefore,

$$\Pr(B_2|A) = \frac{\Pr(B_2)\Pr(A|B_2)}{.02} = \frac{(.05)(.03)}{.02} = .075.$$

2. To solve this problem we must compute the seven conditional probabilities

$$\Pr(B_1|A), \ \Pr(B_2|A), \ \ldots, \ \Pr(B_7|A)$$

and see which one is the largest. The first two have already been computed. Using the method of the preceding problem we find that

$$\Pr(B_3|A) = .20, \ \Pr(B_4|A) = .15, \ \Pr(B_5|A) = .125,$$
$$\Pr(B_6|A) = .15, \ \text{and} \ \Pr(B_7|A) = .15.$$

Therefore, the book was most likely bound by machine 3.

6.8 Simulation

Simulation is a method of imitating an experiment by using an artificial device to substitute for the real thing. The technique is used often in industrial and scientific applications. For example, in the 1970s Deaconess Hospital in St. Louis was planning to add an extension to the hospital with 144 medical-surgical beds. The planners knew that an increase in the number of beds would require additional operating rooms and recovery room beds. By studying the pattern of patients already being treated in the existing hospital, Homer H. Schmitz and N. K. Kwak[1] constructed a mathematical model to imitate the rate of flow of patients through the planned hospital (with the additional beds) to see what the typical operating suite schedule would look like. But they did not use patients! They used random numbers and a computer in their simulation model. They built a model in which they could vary the number of operating rooms and adjust the schedule. By repeating the experiment many times, they found the optimal number of new operating rooms and recovery room beds to complement the added beds.

Calculators have a command, usually called **rand** or **randInt**, that can be used to select a number at random from a specified set of numbers. Each number in the set is just as likely to be selected as any other. Although random number tables are generally available and many of the techniques discussed here can be used with such tables, we recommend using a graphing calculator or a computer if at all possible when doing simulations. On the TI-83/84 Plus, the command **randInt(1,n)** generates a random integer from 1 through n, and **randInt(1,n,r)** generates a list of r random numbers. (The command **randInt** is the fifth item on the MATH/PRB menu.) On the TI-89, the command **rand(n)** generates a random integer from 1 through n, and **seq(rand(n),x,1,r)** generates a list of r random numbers. (The command **rand** is the fourth item on the MATH/Probability menu and the command **seq** is the first element on the MATH/List menu.) On either calculator, after the list of random numbers has been assigned to a list variable, the command **SortA(*list*)** on the TI-83/84 Plus or **SortA *list*** on the TI-89 sorts the list in ascending order. (**SortA** is found on the LIST/OPS menu of the TI-83/84 Plus, and on the MATH/List menu of the TI-89.) Some examples of the use of these commands follows:

---

[1]Homer H. Schmitz and N. K. Kwak, "Monte Carlo simulation of operating-room and recovery-room usage," *Operations Research* **20**, 1972, pp. 1171–1180.

1. *Simulate the roll of a single die*:

   `randInt(1,6)`   TI-83/84 Plus
   `rand(6)`   TI-89

2. *Simulate the sum for a roll of a pair of dice*:

   `randInt(1,6) + randInt(1,6)`   TI-83/84 Plus
   `rand(6) + rand(6)`   TI-89

3. *Simulate ten rolls of a pair of dice*:

   `randInt(1,6,10) + randInt(1,6,10)`   TI-83/84 Plus
   `seq(rand(6) + rand(6),x,1,10)`   TI-89

4. *Simulate the selection of a ball from an urn containing 7 white balls and 3 red balls*: Think of the white balls as numbered from 1 to 7 and the red balls as numbered from 8 to 10.

   `randInt(1,10)`   TI-83/84 Plus
   `rand(10)`   TI-89

5. *Simulate the outcome of a free throw by Michael Jordan, who had an 83% free-throw average*: Consider each shot as a random whole number from 1 to 100, where a number from 1 to 83 represents a successful free throw and a number from 84 to 100 represents a miss.

   `randInt(1,100)`   TI-83/84 Plus
   `rand(100)`   TI-89

On an Excel spreadsheet, the formula =**RAND**() produces a randomly selected number from 0 to 1, excluding 1. The formula =**RANDBETWEEN**(m,n) produces a randomly selected whole number from m to n. The Random Number Generation routine that is part of the Data Analysis tool generates a random sample from a probability distribution. (See Appendix C for details.) *Note*: The RAND-BETWEEN function is only available if the Analysis ToolPak has been installed.

EXAMPLE 1

Heads and tails Simulate 7 tosses of a fair coin. Then count the number of heads and tails.

Solution (*Graphing Calculator*) We will generate and sort seven numbers that are each either 1 or 2. The number 1 will be interpreted as a Heads and the number 2 will be interpreted as a Tails. See Figures 1 and 2. This simulation of 7 coins tosses yields 4 Heads and 3 Tails on the TI-83/84 Plus, and 5 Heads and 2 Tails on the TI-89.

**INCORPORATING
TECHNOLOGY**

Figure 1

Figure 2

(*Electronic Spreadsheet*) In Fig. 3 on the next page, each cell in the range A1:G1 was generated with the equation =**RANDBETWEEN**(1,2). If we interpret **1** as a Heads and **2** as a Tails, then 3 Heads (and therefore 4 Tails) were produced. The COUNTIF function counts the number of ones appearing in the range of cells. ∎

	A	B	C	D	E	F	G
1	2	1	1	2	1	2	2
2	3						

A2 f_x =COUNTIF(A1:G1,"=1")

Figure 3. Example 1 solved with a spreadsheet.

EXAMPLE 2

Seventy-two rolls of a die Simulate 72 rolls of a fair die, and tabulate the results. Compare your results with the theoretical probabilities.

Solution (*Graphing Calculator*) Generate the 72 random whole numbers from 1 to 6 and store them in L_1. On the TI-83/84 Plus, you may tally the results by setting the STATPLOT as shown in Fig. 4 and setting the WINDOW to $[0,8]$ *by* $[-10,30]$ to allow the maximum frequency to show in the bar graph. Such a result is shown in Fig. 5. The GRAPH key will sketch a special type of bar graph indicating the number of tosses resulting in each of the possible outcomes, 1, 2, 3, 4, 5, and 6. Use the TRACE command and the cursor to determine the number of items in each of the bars. In Fig. 5, for example, we can read from the graph that there are $n = 9$ rolls that are greater than or equal to 2 and less than 3 (for a die, this means exactly 2). Figure 6 shows a similar simulation on a TI-89.

Figure 4

Figure 5

Figure 6

Since the probability of each outcome is $\frac{1}{6}$ and the number of tosses is 72, we would expect that each of the outcomes would occur $(\frac{1}{6})(72) = 12$ times. Observations of the graph or a survey of the generated list will give us the actual number of occurrences in each simulation of 72 tosses.

(*Electronic Spreadsheet*) In Fig. 7, each cell in column B has the content $=1/6$. The Random Number Generation routine from the Data Analysis tool used the probability distribution in A1:B6 to generate the random sample in D1:L8. Then the Histogram routine from the Analysis ToolPak used the random sample and the numbers in column A to create the frequency distribution table in N1:O7. (See Appendix C for details.)

Now Try Exercise 1

EXAMPLE 3

Simulation of recovery room Patients having surgery fall into three categories. Sixty percent of them require two hours in the recovery room, 30% require one hour in the recovery room, and the remainder require a half-hour. Simulate the number of hours of recovery room time required by 25 patients.

Solution (*Graphing Calculator*) One technique is to generate 25 random whole numbers from 1 to 10. Numbers 1 to 6 represent a patient who requires two hours in the recovery room, numbers 7 to 9 represent a patient who requires one hour in the recovery room, and the number 10 represents a patient needing a half-hour in the recovery room. After the 25 random numbers are generated, they can be sorted

	A	B	C	D	E	F	G	H	I	J	K	L	M	N	O
1	1	0.166667		5	5	6	4	3	1	3	3	4		Bin	Frequency
2	2	0.166667		3	2	3	1	1	3	5	1	5		1	13
3	3	0.166667		1	4	4	6	3	4	5	4	4		2	9
4	4	0.166667		3	6	6	3	3	6	1	3	4		3	21
5	5	0.166667		3	4	2	2	2	3	5	3	2		4	13
6	6	0.166667		3	5	4	5	3	3	1	3	3		5	9
7	Prob. Dist.			6	4	2	2	5	4	3	4	1		6	7
8				1	1	1	6	3	1	2	1	2			

Figure 7. Example 2 solved with a spreadsheet.

and then displayed. The right-arrow key can be used to scroll along the list so that we can count all those random entries from 1 to 6, those from 7 to 9, and the 10s. Here is one possible outcome:

$$1, 1, 2, 2, 2, 4, 4, 4, 4, 5, 5, 5, 5, 5, 6, \quad 7, 7, 8, 8, 8, 9, \quad 10, 10, 10, 10,$$

giving 15 patients who require two hours, 6 patients who require one hour, and 4 patients who require a half-hour of recovery time. The total amount of time in the recovery room needed by these patients is $15(2) + 6(1) + 4(\frac{1}{2}) = 38$ hours.

(*Electronic Spreadsheet*) In Fig. 8, the Random Number Generation routine from the Data Analysis tool used the probability distribution in A1:B3 to generate the random sample in D1:H5. Then, the Histogram routine from the Analysis ToolPak used the random sample and the numbers in column A to create the frequency distribution table in J1:K4. The total amount of time in the recovery room needed by these patients is $3(\frac{1}{2}) + 4(1) + 18(2) = 41.5$ hours. ∎

Now Try Exercise 5

	A	B	C	D	E	F	G	H	I	J	K
1	1/2	0.1		1	2	2	2	2		Bin	Frequency
2	1	0.3		2	0.5	2	1	2		1/2	3
3	2	0.6		2	2	2	2	1		1	4
4	Prob. Dist.			2	2	1	0.5	2		2	18
5				2	0.5	2	2	2			

Figure 8. Example 3 solved with a spreadsheet.

EXAMPLE 4

Simulation of a queue Customers steadily arrive at a bank during the hour from 9 A.M. to 10 A.M. so that the line of customers is never empty. There are three tellers, and each customer requires a varying amount of time with a teller. For simplicity, we assume that 40% of the customers need 3 minutes, 50% need 5 minutes, and 10% need 8 minutes. Each customer enters the queue at the end and goes to the first available teller when reaching the front of the queue. Simulate the service process.

(a) Show how many of the first 20 customers each of the tellers is able to service on a random day and in that hour.

(b) If all 20 customers were at the bank when it opened at 9 A.M., what was the average time spent at the bank once it opened?

**INCORPORATING
TECHNOLOGY**

Solution **(a)** (*Graphing Calculator*) We generate 20 random whole numbers from 1 to 10. We consider numbers 1 to 4 as representing customers requiring 3 minutes, numbers 5 to 9 as customers requiring 5 minutes, and 10 as customers needing 8 minutes. We do not sort them, because we want to preserve the randomness of their arrival. Here is a typical list:

Cust. #: $1, 2, 3, 4, 5, 6, 7, 8, 9, 10, 11, 12, 13, 14, 15, 16, 17, 18, 19, 20$
Random #: $10, 7, 2, 3, 1, 6, 4, 3, 1, 10, \ 6, \ 5, \ 2, \ 3, \ 7, \ 7, 10, 10, \ 5, \ 5.$

To determine the schedule, let the tellers be A, B, and C. Then the first customer goes to teller A. Since her random number is 10, she requires 8 minutes, occupying teller A until 9:08. Meanwhile, the second customer, with random number 7, goes to teller B, where he needs 5 minutes. He occupies teller B until 9:05. Then customer #3, with random number 2, goes to teller C until 9:03. Since teller C finishes first, customer #4 steps up to C at 9:03. That customer (with random number 3) requires 3 minutes and leaves teller C at 9:06. In case two tellers are free at the same moment, let us use the convention that the tellers are chosen in alphabetical order, with A first. From Table 1, we see that teller A served 6 of the first 20 customers, teller B served 6, and C served 8 customers. They completed the first 20 transactions at 9:34 A.M.

(*Electronic Spreadsheet*) In Fig. 9, the Random Number Generation routine from the Data Analysis tool could have used the probability distribution in A1:B3 to generate the random sample in E1:X2, the same sequence of random numbers presented in the third column of Table 1. Table 1 can be used as before (with the second column removed) to obtain the same answer.

	A	B	C	D	E	F	G	H	I	J	K	L	M	N	O	P	Q	R	S	T	U	V	W	X
1	3	0.4		Cust. #:	1	2	3	4	5	6	7	8	9	10	11	12	13	14	15	16	17	18	19	20
2	5	0.5		Random #:	8	5	3	3	3	5	3	3	3	8	5	5	3	3	5	5	8	8	5	5
3	8	0.1																						
4	Prob. Dist.																								

Figure 9. The random sample in Example 4(a) generated with a spreadsheet.

(b) We can find the average amount of time spent after the bank opened by totaling the time spent by all customers (use the number of minutes after 9 A.M. in the "End time" column) and dividing by 20, the number of customers. This gives $(8 + 5 + 3 + 6 + 8 + 11 + 11 + 11 + 14 + 19 + 16 + 19 + 19 + 22 + 24 + 24 + 30 + 32 + 29 + 34)/20 = 17.25$ minutes. Thus, on the average, a person who was at the bank at 9 A.M. required 17.25 minutes after the bank opened to be served and to complete his transaction.   ∎

Now Try Exercise 7

The simulation should be repeated many times to determine the typical outcome. So you might simulate 50 days from 9 A.M. to 10 A.M. to see how long it takes to service the first 20 customers and, on the average, how long a customer spends in the bank if he or she is one of the first 20 people there when the bank opens. It might be useful to see the effect of using four tellers or see what happens when the probabilities of the service times are defined differently.

In practice, the arrival times of the customers are also random and can be built into the simulation. A time-and-motion study would be used to determine the appropriate probabilistic model of the arrival process.

TABLE 1

Customer #	Random #	Time req.	Teller	Start time	End time
1	10	8	A	9:00	9:08
2	7	5	B	9:00	9:05
3	2	3	C	9:00	9:03
4	3	3	C	9:03	9:06
5	1	3	B	9:05	9:08
6	6	5	C	9:06	9:11
7	4	3	A	9:08	9:11
8	3	3	B	9:08	9:11
9	1	3	A	9:11	9:14
10	10	8	B	9:11	9:19
11	6	5	C	9:11	9:16
12	5	5	A	9:14	9:19
13	2	3	C	9:16	9:19
14	3	3	A	9:19	9:22
15	7	5	B	9:19	9:24
16	7	5	C	9:19	9:24
17	10	8	A	9:22	9:30
18	10	8	B	9:24	9:32
19	5	5	C	9:24	9:29
20	5	5	C	9:29	9:34

EXERCISES 6.8

1. **Rolling a Die** Simulate 36 rolls of a fair die. Give the relative frequency and the corresponding theoretical probability of each of the outcomes and compare them.

2. **Rolling Dice** Simulate 96 rolls of a pair of dice where the sum is observed. Give the relative frequency and the corresponding theoretical probability of each of the outcomes. Make a table showing your results. Repeat the experiment 6 times and consider the total as if 576 rolls were simulated. [*Note*: $(6)(96) = 576$.]

3. **Free-Throws** Simulate 10 free-throws for Kobe Bryant, whose free throw average in 2008 was 81%. How many of the shots were successful?

4. **Baseball** A baseball player is a .331 hitter. Simulate 10 at-bats for this player and tell how many hits he gets. (Being a .331 hitter means that 33.1% of his at-bats result in a hit.)

5. **Test Taking** A student who has not studied for a 10-question multiple-choice test, with 4 choices among the answers (a, b, c, d) for each question, decides to simulate such a test and answer the questions according to a simulation in which each choice of answer has the same probability. Use a calculator to generate a simulated answer sheet. Assume the correct answers are a, b, b, c, d, d, a, c, b, a. What is the student's score?

6. **Balls in an Urn** In sampling 4 balls at random from an urn containing 30 balls, *without replacement* after each draw, we consider the balls as numbered 1 to 30. In selecting random whole numbers from 1 to 30, we ignore any number that has already been selected and continue the selection until we obtain a sample of size 4. Assume there are 20 red balls and 10 green balls in the urn. Draw 10 samples of size 4 and tabulate the number of red balls in each sample. Compare your results with the theoretical probability.

7. **Registration Queue** Students are queued up at the registrar's office when the registration windows open at 8 A.M. There are four open windows; students approach the first open window as they advance to the front of the queue. Assume that 10% of the students require 5 minutes of service time, 30% of the students require 7 minutes of service time, 40% require 10 minutes, and 20% require 15 minutes. Simulate the service of the first 20 students in a random queue. Show the schedule of service at the four windows (A, B, C, D), determine how long it takes to process these students, and give the average time from 8 A.M. to leaving the service window.

8. **Bank Queue** Simulate the bank queue of Example 4 using four tellers. Give the time needed to process the

first 20 customers and the average time spent by each customer in the bank after 9 A.M.

9. **Gas Queue** A gas station with four self-serve pumps has determined that 80% of all customers completely fill their gas tanks and the remaining 20% fill their tank with a fixed dollar amount's worth of fuel. Suppose that it takes an average of 5 minutes for a complete fill-up and 3 minutes for a partial fill-up. Suppose also

that from 5 PM until 6 PM customers arrive steadily so that there is always a line and that the next customer in line proceeds to the next available pump. Simulate this process for 30 customers.

10. **Rolling Three Dice** Simulate 108 rolls of three dice, and show the frequency of each possible sum of the faces: $3, 4, \ldots, 18$.

CHAPTER SUMMARY

1. The *sample space* of an experiment is the set of all possible outcomes of the experiment. Each subset of the sample space is called an *event*. We say that an event *occurs* when the outcome is an element of the event.

2. The event $E \cup F$ occurs when either E or F (or both) occurs. The event $E \cap F$ occurs when both E and F occur. The event E' occurs when E does not occur.

3. Two events are *mutually exclusive* if they cannot both occur at the same time.

4. A *probability distribution* for a finite sample space associates a probability with each outcome of the sample space. Each probability is a number between 0 and 1, and the sum of the probabilities is 1. The probability of an event is the sum of the probabilities of the outcomes in the event.

5. The inclusion-exclusion principle states that the probability of the union of two events is the sum of the probabilities of the events minus the probability of their intersection. If the two events are mutually exclusive, the probability of the union is just the sum of the probabilities of the events.

6. We say that the *odds* in favor of an event are a to b if the probability of the event is $a/(a + b)$. Intuitively, the event is expected to occur a times for every b times it does not occur.

7. For a sample space with a finite number of equally likely outcomes, the probability of an event is the number of elements in the event divided by the number of elements in the sample space.

8. The probability of the complement of an event is 1 minus the probability of the event.

9. $\Pr(E|F)$, the conditional probability that E occurs given that F occurs, is computed as $\Pr(E \cap F)/\Pr(F)$. For a sample space with a finite number of equally likely outcomes, it can be computed as $n(E \cap F)/n(F)$.

10. The product rule states that if $\Pr(F) \neq 0$, then $\Pr(E \cap F) = \Pr(F) \cdot \Pr(E|F)$.

11. E and F are *independent* events if $\Pr(E \cap F) = \Pr(E) \cdot \Pr(F)$. Equivalently, E and F [with $\Pr(F) \neq 0$] are independent events if $\Pr(E|F) = \Pr(E)$.

12. A collection of events is said to be *independent* if for each collection of events chosen from them, the probability that all the events occur equals the product of the probabilities that each occurs.

13. Tree diagrams provide a useful device for determining probabilities of combined outcomes in a sequence of experiments.

14. Bayes' theorem states that if $B_1, B_2, \ldots, B_n$ are mutually exclusive events whose union is the entire sample space and A is an event, then for each event B_i,

$$\Pr(B_i|A) = \frac{\Pr(B_i)\Pr(A|B_i)}{\Pr(B_1)\Pr(A|B_1) + \cdots + \Pr(B_n)\Pr(A|B_n)}.$$

15. The ability to generate random numbers allows us to simulate the outcomes of experiments.

REVIEW OF FUNDAMENTAL CONCEPTS

1. Describe how to form a sample space for an experiment.

2. Using the language of sets and assuming that A and B are events in a sample space S, write the following events in set notation: $(A$ or $B)$; $(A$ and $B)$; not A.

3. In a sample space, what is the probability of the empty set?

4. What subset in a sample space corresponds to the certain event?

5. Draw Venn diagrams for the events $(A$ or $B)$, $(A$ and $B)$, (not A).

6. Write a formula for the probability of the event $A \cup B$ assuming that you know $\Pr(A)$, $\Pr(B)$, and $\Pr(A \cap B)$.

7. Explain the difference between mutually exclusive events and independent events.

8. State the addition principle.

9. Suppose the probability of an event is k/n. What are

the odds that the event will occur?

10. Suppose the odds that an event occurs are a to b. What is the probability that the event will occur?

11. State the inclusion–exclusion principle for two events.

12. What is the definition of $\Pr(E|F)$?

13. What is Bayes' Theorem?

14. What is a tree diagram?

KEY FORMULAS

Addition Principle:

$$\Pr(E) = \Pr(s) + \Pr(t) + \Pr(u) + \cdots + \Pr(z),$$

where the event E consists of the finite number of outcomes $s, t, u, \ldots, z$

Inclusion–Exclusion Principle:

$$\Pr(E \cup F) = \Pr(E) + \Pr(F) - \Pr(E \cap F)$$

Mutually Exclusive Events: $\Pr(E \cup F) = \Pr(E) + \Pr(F)$, when E and F are mutually exclusive.

Converting Odds to a Probability: If the odds in favor of an event E are a to b, then $\Pr(E) = \dfrac{a}{a+b}$.

Conditional Probability for Equally Likely Outcomes:

$$\Pr(E|F) = \frac{n(E \cap F)}{n(F)}$$

Product Rule: If $\Pr(F) \neq 0$, then $\Pr(E \cap F) = \Pr(F) \cdot \Pr(E|F)$.

Independent Events: If E and F are independent events with nonzero probabilities, then $\Pr(E|F) = \Pr(E)$ and $\Pr(F|E) = \Pr(F)$.

Bayes' Theorem: If $B_1, B_2, \ldots, B_n$ are mutually exclusive events, and if $B_1 \cup B_2 \cup \cdots \cup B_n = S$, then for any event A in S,

$$\Pr(B_k|A) = \frac{\Pr(B_k) \cdot \Pr(A|B_k)}{\Pr(B_1) \cdot \Pr(A|B_1) + \cdots + \Pr(B_n) \cdot \Pr(A|B_n)}$$

for $k = 1, 2, \ldots, n$.

SUPPLEMENTARY EXERCISES

1. Coin Tosses A coin is to be tossed five times. What is the probability of obtaining at least one head?

2. Coin Tosses Suppose that we toss a coin three times and observe the sequence of heads and tails. Let E be the event that "the first toss lands heads" and F the event that "there are more heads than tails." Are E and F independent?

3. Prizes Each box of a certain brand of candy contains either a toy airplane or a toy gun. If one-third of the boxes contain an airplane and two-thirds contain a gun, what is the probability that a person who buys two boxes of candy will receive both an airplane and a gun?

4. Committee Selection A committee consists of five men and five women. If three people are selected at random from the committee, what is the probability that they all will be men?

5. Public and Private Colleges Out of the 50 colleges in a certain state, 25 are private, 15 offer engineering majors, and 5 are private colleges offering engineering majors. If a college is selected at random, what is the conditional probability that it offers an engineering major given that it is a public college?

6. Tax Audits An auditing procedure for income tax returns has the following characteristics: If the return is incorrect, the probability is 90% that it will be rejected; if the return is correct, the probability is 95% that it

will be accepted. Suppose that 80% of all income tax returns are correct. If a return is audited and rejected, what is the probability that the return was actually correct?

7. Numbers A number is chosen at random from the numbers 1 to 100. What is the probability that the number is divisible by 5?

8. Numbers A number is chosen at random from the numbers 1 to 10,000. What is the probability that the number is divisible by 5?

9. Numbers A number is chosen at random from the numbers 1 to 10,000. What is the probability that the number is divisible by 3 or 5?

10. Numbers A number is chosen at random from the numbers 1 to 10,000. What is the probability that the number is divisible by 3 or 12?

11. Seating Arrangements Jack and Hugo attend a party at which there are two tables of 8 for dinner. If guests are assigned to seats at random, what is the probability that Jack and Hugo will be seated at the same table?

12. Student Honors Five students are to receive special honors at commencement. Of the five, two are engineering majors.

   (a) What is the probability that the two engineering majors will be called up as the first two students to receive their awards?

(b) What is the probability that the two engineering majors will be called up consecutively to receive their awards?

13. **Exam Questions** Prior to taking an essay examination, students are given 10 questions to prepare. Six of the 10 will appear on the exam. One student decides to prepare only eight of the questions. Assume that the questions are equally likely to be chosen by the professor.

   (a) What is the probability that she has prepared every question appearing on the test?

   (b) What is the probability that both questions she did not prepare appear on the test?

14. **Code Words** A collection of code words consists of all strings of seven characters, where each of the first three characters can be any letter or digit and each of the last four characters must be a digit. For example, 7A32765 is allowed but 7A3B765 is not.

   (a) What is the probability that a code word chosen at random begins with ABC?

   (b) What is the probability that a code word chosen at random ends with 6578?

   (c) What is the probability that a code word chosen at random ends with a four-digit number divisible by 3?

   (d) What is the probability that a code word chosen at random consists of three letters followed by four even digits?

15. **Archery** Two archers shoot at a moving target. One can hit the target with probability $\frac{1}{4}$ and the other with probability $\frac{1}{3}$. Assuming that their efforts are independent events, what is the probability that

   (a) Both will hit the target?

   (b) At least one will hit the target?

16. If the odds in favor of an event are 7 to 5, what is the probability that the event will occur?

17. **Olympic Swimmers** In an Olympic swimming event, two of the seven contestants are American. The contestants are randomly assigned to lanes 1 through 7. What is the probability that the Americans are assigned to the first two lanes?

18. **Balls in an Urn** An urn contains three balls numbered 1, 2, and 3. Balls are drawn one at a time without replacement until the sum of the numbers drawn is four or more. Find the probability of stopping after exactly two balls are drawn.

19. **Dice** A red die and a green die are rolled as a pair. Let E be the event that "the red die shows a 2" and let F be the event that "the sum of the numbers is 8." Are the events E and F independent?

20. Let E and F be events with $\Pr(E) = .4$, $\Pr(F) = .3$, and $\Pr(E \cup F) = .5$. Find $\Pr(E|F)$.

21. **Weighing Produce** A supermarket has three employees who package and weigh produce. Employee A records the correct weight 98% of the time. Employees B and C record the correct weight 97% and 95% of the time, respectively. Employees A, B, and C handle 40%, 40%, and 20% of the packaging, respectively. A customer complains about the incorrect weight recorded on a package he has purchased. What is the probability that the package was weighed by employee C?

22. **Days of Week** Three people are chosen at random. What is the probability that at least two of them were born on the same day of the week?

23. Let B and A be independent events for which the probability that at least one of them occurs is $\frac{1}{2}$ and the probability that B occurs but A does not occur is $\frac{1}{3}$. Find $\Pr(A)$.

24. **Balls in an Urn** An urn contains 10 balls numbered 1 through 10. Seven balls are drawn one at a time at random without replacement. Find the probability that exactly three odd-numbered balls are drawn and they occur on odd-numbered draws from the urn.

25. **Bills in Envelopes** Each of three sealed opaque envelopes contains two bills. One envelope contains two $1 bills, another contains two $5 bills, and the third contains a $1 bill and a $5 bill. An envelope is selected at random and a bill is taken from the envelope at random. If it is a $5 bill, what is the probability that the other bill in the envelope is also a $5 bill?

26. **Carnival Game** A carnival huckster has placed a coin under one of three cups and asks you to guess which cup contains the coin. After you select a cup, he removes one of the unselected cups, which he guarantees does not contain the coin. You may now either stay with your original choice or switch to the other remaining cup. What decision will give you the greater probability of winning?

27. **Commuting Time** The odds of an American worker living within 20 minutes of work are 13 to 12. What is the probability that a worker selected at random lives within 20 minutes of work?

28. **Demographics** Twenty-six percent of all Americans are under 18 years old. What are the odds that a person selected at random is under 18?

29. **Letters** If the nine letters A, C, D, E, I, N, O, T, and U are arranged to form a word, what is the probability that it will be one of the meaningful words EDUCATION, AUCTIONED, or CAUTIONED?

30. **Dragons** An island contains an equal number of one-headed, two-headed, and three-headed dragons. If a dragon head is picked at random, what is the likelihood of its belonging to a one-headed dragon?

31. **Coin Tosses** Two players each toss a coin three times. What is the probability that they get the same number of tails?

32. Dice Suppose that a pair of dice is rolled. Given that a double does not occur, what is the probability that one die shows a three?

33. Left-Handedness According to *Bottom Line Personal* of March 30, 1991, the chances of having a left-handed child are 4 in 10 if both parents are left-handed, 2 in 10 if one parent is left-handed, and only 1 in 10 if neither parent is left-handed. Suppose a left-handed child is chosen at random from a population in which 25% of the adults are left-handed. What is the probability that the child's parents are both left-handed?

34. Languages Of the 120 students in a class, 30 speak Chinese, 50 speak Spanish, 75 speak French, 12 speak Spanish and Chinese, 30 speak Spanish and French, and 15 speak Chinese and French. Seven students speak all three languages. A student is chosen at random. What is the probability that he speaks none of these languages?

35. What is the probability that a whole number between 100 and 400 contains the digit 2?

36. Committee Composition PE A committee is composed of w women and m men. If three women and two men are added to the committee, and if one person is selected at random from the enlarged committee, then the probability that a woman is selected can be represented by

(a) $\dfrac{w}{m}$ (b) $\dfrac{w}{w+m}$ (c) $\dfrac{w+3}{m+2}$

(d) $\dfrac{w+3}{w+m+3}$ (e) $\dfrac{w+3}{w+m+5}$

37. Political Poll PE Of a group of people surveyed in a political poll, 60% said they would vote for candidate R. Of those who said they would vote for R, 90% actually voted for R, and of those who did not say they would vote for R, 5% actually voted for R. What percent of the group voted for R?

(a) 56% (b) 59% (c) 62% (d) 65% (e) 74%

38. Coin Tosses When three coins are tossed, what is the probability of at least one tail appearing given that at least one head appeared?

39. Rolling a Die What is the probability of having each of the numbers one through six appear in six consecutive rolls of a die?

40. Balls in an Urn An urn contains 10 red balls and 20 green balls. If four balls are drawn one at a time without replacement, what is the probability that the sequence of colors will be red, green, green, red?

41. Drawing Cards A card is drawn at random from a deck of cards. Then the card is replaced and the deck is thoroughly shuffled. This process is repeated two more times.

(a) What is the probability that all three cards are aces?

(b) What is the probability that at least one of the cards is an ace?

42. March Madness Each March, sixty-four men's college basketball teams compete in the NCAA championship tournament. They are divided into four regions of sixteen teams each. The winners of each region advance to the Final Four. If a fan selects four teams at random, what are the odds against those teams being in the Final Four? *Note*: Of course, the fan will select only one team per region.

43. Matching Socks A drawer contains two red socks and two blue socks. If two socks are drawn randomly from the drawer, what is the probability that the two socks have the same color?

44. Physical Fitness Of 50 fitness buffs surveyed, 15 like bicycling, 20 like jogging, and 5 like bicycling and jogging. What is the probability that a fitness buff selected at random likes only one of the two sports?

45. Tossing Dice Find the odds in favor of getting four different numbers when tossing four dice.

46. Birthdays What is the probability that out of a group of 5 people, exactly two people have the same birthday? *Note*: Assume there are 365 days in a year.

In Exercises 47–49, use a graphing calculator or spreadsheet to calculate the probabilities.

47. Medical Screening A drug company wants to test a drug for a chronic disease. The company wants a sample of 500 people who have the disease. It tests 12,735 people for the disease, which generally affects 5% of the population. The test is known to have a 2% false positive rate and a 4% false negative rate. Six hundred and fifty people test positive for the disease. Based on the test results, how many of the total population actually can be expected to have the disease?

48. Rolling a Die Simulate an experiment in which either you roll a die until you get a 6 or you have rolled the die 15 times. Record the number of times you roll the die until the first 6. Find the relative frequency of each outcome in the set $\{1, 2, 3, \ldots, 15\}$. Perform the experiment at least 20 times.

49. Drawing Cards Simulate an experiment in which you draw 3 cards from a deck of 52 cards, with replacement after each draw. Determine the number of spades in the sample and repeat the experiment 20 times. Find the relative frequency of at least 2 spades in a sample of size 3. What is the theoretical probability of at least 2 spades in a sample of size 3?

Conceptual Exercises

50. Give an example of two events that are mutually exclusive. Give an example of two sets that are not mutually exclusive.

51. Give an example of two independent events.

52. Describe the difference between disjoint events and independent events in your own words.

53. Explain why two mutually exclusive events with nonzero probabilities cannot be independent.

54. Give an example of two events that are mutually exclusive and not independent.

55. Explain why it is intuitively clear that if E and F are independent events, then so are E and F'.

56. What additional information would you need to know in order to compute $\Pr(E \cap F)$ if you already know $\Pr(E)$ and $\Pr(F)$?

CHAPTER TEST

1. **Coins** A box contains a penny, a nickel, a dime, a quarter, and a half dollar. You select two coins at random from the box.
   (a) Construct a sample space for this situation.
   (b) List the elements of the event E in which the total value of the coins you have selected is an even number of cents.

2. Convert the following odds to probabilities.
   (a) 3 to 5   (b) 1,000,000 to 1

3. **Checkers** When Tommy plays checkers against his father, he wins 40% of the time. When he plays against his mother, he wins 30% of the time. What are the odds of him beating his father? losing to his mother?

4. **Candidates for Office** Some of the candidates for president of the computer club at Riverdale High are seniors, and the rest are juniors. Let J be the event in which a junior is elected, and let F be the event in which a female is elected. Describe the following events:
   (a) $J \cap F'$ (b) $(J \cap F)'$ (c) $F' \cup J$

5. **Heads and Tails** Emilio tosses a fair coin five times. What is the probability that he gets at least one head and at least one tail?

6. **Measles Vaccine** Fifteen percent of children attending kindergarten have not had a measles vaccine. In a class of 20 students, what is the probability that at least one has not had a measles vaccine?

7. Suppose E and F are events in a sample space, with $\Pr(E) = \frac{1}{4}$, $\Pr(F') = \frac{3}{8}$, and $\Pr(E' \cap F) = \frac{1}{2}$. Determine the following:
   (a) $\Pr(F)$ (b) $\Pr(E \cup F)$ (c) $\Pr(F|E')$
   (d) Are E and F mutually exclusive?
   (e) Are E and F independent?

8. **Quality Control** Ten of a certain kind of gadget are tested. The probability that any given such gadget is defective is .1. What is the probability that at least one of the 10 gadgets is defective? What is the probability that exactly one of the 10 gadgets is defective?

9. **Cards and Marbles** Wanda has a deck of 52 cards, a box, and an urn. The box contains 5 red marbles and 10 green marbles, while the urn contains 12 red marbles and 8 green marbles. Wanda picks a card at random from the deck. If it is a face card (jack, queen, or king), she then picks a marble from the box. Otherwise, she picks a marble from the urn.
   (a) Determine the probability that she picks a red marble, given that she drew a face card from the deck.
   (b) What is the probability that she ends up with a red marble?
   (c) If E is the event in which Wanda picks a face card and F is the event in which she picks a red marble, are E and F independent? mutually exclusive?
   (d) If Wanda ends up with a green marble, what is the probability that she drew a face card?

10. **Loaded Die** The probability distribution for the result of rolling a loaded die is given in Table 1.

TABLE 1

Outcome	1	2	3	4	5	6
Probability	.15	.20	.10	.25	.25	.05

   (a) Determine the probability that the outcome is an odd number.
   (b) Given that the outcome is odd, what is the probability that the outcome is greater than 4?

11. **Class Rank and Gender** A finite mathematics class of 50 students is composed of freshmen and sophomores according to Table 2. A student from the class is selected at random.

TABLE 2

	Freshmen	Sophomores
Females	12	8
Males	14	16

   (a) What is the probability that the selected student is either female or a sophomore?
   (b) What is the probability that the selected student is male, given that the student is a freshman?

CHAPTER 6 | PROJECT

Two Paradoxes

First Paradox: *Under certain circumstances you have your best chance of winning a tennis tournament if you play most of your games against the best possible opponent.*

Alice and her two sisters, Betty and Carol, are avid tennis players. Betty is the best of the three sisters, and Carol plays at the same level as Alice. Alice defeats Carol 50% of the time but only defeats Betty 40% of the time.

Alice's mother offers to give her $100 if she can win two consecutive games when playing three alternating games against her two sisters. Since the games will alternate, Alice has two possibilities for the sequence of opponents. One possibility is to play the first game against Betty, followed by a game with Carol, and then another game with Betty. We will refer to this sequence as BCB. The other possible sequence is CBC.

1. Make a guess of the best sequence for Alice to choose; the one having the majority of the games against the weaker opponent or the one having the majority of the games against the stronger opponent.
2. Calculate the probability of Alice getting the $100 reward if she chooses the sequence CBC.
3. Calculate the probability of Alice getting the $100 reward if she chooses the sequence BCB.
4. Which sequence should Alice choose?
5. How would you explain to someone who didn't know probability why the sequence you chose is best?

Second Paradox: *The probability of a male applicant being admitted to a graduate school can be higher than the probability for a female applicant even though for each department the probability of a female being admitted is higher.* (This apparent contradiction is known as **Simpson's paradox.**)

To simplify matters, consider a university with two professional graduate programs, medicine and law. Suppose that last year 1000 men and 1000 women applied and the outcome was as shown in Table 1.

TABLE 1

	Men			Women		
	Applied	Accepted	Rejected	Applied	Accepted	Rejected
Law	700	560	140	400	340	60
Medicine	300	40	260	600	160	440

6. What is the probability that a male applicant was accepted to a professional program? female?
7. Which gender does the university appear to be favoring?
8. What is the probability that a male applicant was accepted to law school? female?
9. What is the probability that a male applicant was accepted to medical school? female?
10. Which gender do the individual professional schools appear to be favoring?
11. Without using probability, justify the apparent contradiction between the answers for part 7 and part 10.

THE MATHEMATICS OF FINANCE

This chapter presents several topics in the mathematics of finance, including compound and simple interest, annuities, and amortization. They are presented in the classical way, using methods that are centuries old but that lend themselves to modern computing techniques.

10.1 Interest

When you deposit money into a savings account, the bank pays you a fee for the use of your money. This fee is called **interest** and is determined by the amount deposited, the duration of the deposit, and the interest rate. The amount deposited is called the **principal** or **present value**, and the amount to which the principal grows (after the addition of interest) is called the **future value**, **compound amount**, or **balance**.

The entries in a hypothetical bank statement are shown in Table 1 on the next page. Note the following facts about this statement:

1. The principal is $100.00. The future value after 1 year is $104.06.
2. Interest is being paid four times per year (or, in financial language, *quarterly*).

TABLE 1

Date	Deposits	Withdrawals	Interest	Balance
1/1/08	$100.00			$100.00
4/1/08			$1.00	101.00
7/1/08			1.01	102.01
10/1/08			1.02	103.03
1/1/09			1.03	104.06

3. Each quarter, the amount of the interest is 1% of the previous balance. That is, $1.00 is 1% of $100.00, $1.01 is 1% of $101.00, and so on. Since $4 \times 1\%$ is 4%, we say that the money is earning 4% *annual interest compounded quarterly.*

As in the statement shown in Table 1, interest rates are usually stated as *annual interest rates*, with the interest to be **compounded** (i.e., computed) a certain number of times per year. Some common frequencies for compounding are listed in Table 2. Of special importance is the *interest rate per period*, denoted i, which is calculated by dividing the annual interest rate by the number of interest periods per year.

TABLE 2

Number of interest periods per year	Length of each interest period	Interest compounded
1	One year	Annually
2	Six months	Semiannually
4	Three months	Quarterly
12	One month	Monthly
52	One week	Weekly
365	One day	Daily

For example, in our statement in Table 1, the annual interest rate was 4%, the interest was compounded quarterly, and the interest rate per period was $4\%/4 = 1\%$.

DEFINITION If interest is compounded m times per year and the annual interest rate is r, then the **interest rate per period** is
$$i = \frac{r}{m}.$$

EXAMPLE 1   **Determining interest rate per period**   Determine the interest rate per period for each of the following annual interest rates.

(a) 5% interest compounded semiannually

(b) 6% interest compounded monthly

Solution (a) The annual interest rate is 5% and the number of interest periods is 2. Therefore,
$$i = \frac{5\%}{2} = 2\tfrac{1}{2}\% = 2.5\%.$$

Note: In decimal form, $i = .025$.

(b) The annual interest rate is 6% and the number of interest periods is 12. Therefore,

$$i = \frac{6\%}{12} = \frac{1}{2}\% = .5\%.$$

Now Try Exercise 1   *Note:* In decimal form, $i = .005$.   ∎

Consider a savings account in which the interest rate per period is i. Then the interest earned during a period is i times the previous balance. That is, at the end of an interest period, the new balance, B_{new}, is computed by adding this interest to the previous balance, B_{previous}. Therefore,

$$B_{\text{new}} = 1 \cdot B_{\text{previous}} + i \cdot B_{\text{previous}}$$
$$B_{\text{new}} = (1 + i) \cdot B_{\text{previous}} \qquad (1)$$

Formula (1) says that the balances for successive interest periods are computed by multiplying the previous balance by $(1 + i)$.

EXAMPLE 2   **Computing interest and balances** Compute the balance for the first two interest periods for a deposit of $1000 at 4% interest compounded semiannually.

Solution Here the initial balance is $1000 and $i = 2\% = .02$. Let B_1 be the balance at the end of the first interest period and B_2 the balance at the end of the second interest period. By formula (1),

$$B_1 = (1 + .02)1000 = 1.02 \cdot 1000 = 1020$$

Similarly, applying formula (1) again

$$B_2 = 1.02 \cdot B_1 = 1.02 \cdot 1020 = 1040.40$$

Therefore, the balance is $1020 after the first interest period and $1040.40 after the second interest period.

Now Try Exercises 21(a), (b)   ∎

A simple formula for the balance after any number of interest periods can be derived from formula (1) as follows:

Principal	P
Balance after 1 interest period	$(1 + i)P$
Balance after 2 interest periods	$(1 + i) \cdot (1 + i)P$ or $(1 + i)^2 P$
Balance after 3 interest periods	$(1 + i) \cdot (1 + i)^2 P$ or $(1 + i)^3 P$
Balance after 4 interest periods	$(1 + i)^4 P$
⋮	⋮
Balance after n interest periods	$(1 + i)^n P$.

Denote the future value by the letter F. Then the future value after n interest periods is given by the formula

$$F = (1 + i)^n P, \qquad (2)$$

where i is the interest rate per period and P is the principal or present value of the investment.

EXAMPLE 3   **Computing future values**   Apply formula (2) to the savings account statement discussed at the beginning of this section and calculate the future value after 1 year and after 5 years.

Solution   The principal or present value P is $100. Since the interest rate is 4% compounded quarterly, we have $i = 1\%$, or .01. One year consists of four interest periods, so $n = 4$. Therefore, the future value after 1 year is

$$F = (1+i)^n P = (1+.01)^4 \cdot 100$$
$$= (1.01)^4 \cdot 100$$
$$= \$104.06 \qquad \text{(after rounding to the nearest cent)}$$

Five years consists of $n = 5 \times 4 = 20$ interest periods. Therefore, the future value after 5 years is

Now Try Exercise 5

$$F = (1.01)^{20} \cdot 100 = \$122.02.$$ ■

The Excel spreadsheet in Table 3 shows the effects of interest rates (compounded quarterly) on the future value. The entries in cells B5 and C5 are `=$B$1*(1+A5/4)^20` and `=$B$1*(1+A5/4)^40`, respectively. The remaining entries in the B and C columns were created by dragging fill handles. The dollar signs in `$B$1` prevent references to this location from being changed during this process.

TABLE 3

	A	B	C
1	Principal	$100.00	
2			
3			Future Value
4	Interest Rate	5 Years	10 Years
5	3.0%	$116.12	$134.83
6	3.5%	$119.03	$141.69
7	4.0%	$122.02	$148.89
8	4.5%	$125.08	$156.44
9	5.0%	$128.20	$164.36
10	5.5%	$131.41	$172.68
11	6.0%	$134.69	$181.40
12	6.5%	$138.04	$190.56
13	7.0%	$141.48	$200.16
14	7.5%	$144.99	$210.23
15	8.0%	$148.59	$220.80

The next example is a variation of the previous one.

EXAMPLE 4   **Computing a present value**   How much money must be deposited now in order to have $1000 after 5 years if interest is paid at a 4% annual interest rate compounded quarterly?

Solution As in Example 3, we have $i = .01$ and $n = 20$. However, now we are given F and are asked to solve for P.

$$F = (1+i)^n P$$
$$1000 = (1.01)^{20} P$$
$$P = \frac{1000}{(1.01)^{20}} = 819.54$$

We say that $819.54 is the present value of $1000, 5 years from now, at 4% interest compounded quarterly. The concept of "time value of money" says that at an interest rate of 4% compounded quarterly, $1000 in 5 years is equivalent to $819.54 now.

Now Try Exercise 15 ■

Compound interest problems involve the four variables P, i, n, and F. Given the values of any three of the variables, we can find the value of the fourth. The formula used to find the value of F is

$$F = (1+i)^n P.$$

Solving this formula for P gives

$$P = \frac{F}{(1+i)^n}. \tag{3}$$

EXAMPLE 5

Computing a present value Determine the present value of a $10,000 payment to be received on January 1, 2019, if it is now May 1, 2010, and money can be invested at 6% interest compounded monthly.

Solution Here $F = 10{,}000$, $n = 104$ (the number of months between the two given dates), and $i = \frac{1}{2}\% = .005$. By formula (3),

$$P = \frac{F}{(1+i)^n} = \frac{10{,}000}{(1.005)^{104}} = \$5952.91.$$

Therefore, $5952.91 invested on May 1, 2010, will grow to $10,000 by January 1, 2019.

Now Try Exercise 7 ■

The interest that we have been discussing so far is the most prevalent type of interest and is known as **compound interest**. There is another type of interest, called **simple interest**, which is used in some financial circumstances. Let us now discuss this type of interest.

Interest rates for simple interest are given as an annual interest rate r. Interest is earned *only* on the principal P and the interest is rP for each year. Therefore, the interest earned in n years is nrP. So the future value F after n years is the original amount plus the interest earned. That is,

$$F = P + nrP = 1 \cdot P + nrP = (1 + nr)P. \tag{4}$$

EXAMPLE 6

Computing a balance with simple interest Calculate the future value after 4 years if $1000 is invested at 5% simple interest.

Solution Apply formula (4) with $P = \$1000$, $n = 4$, and $r = 5\%$ or $.05$.

Now Try Exercise 31

$$F = (1 + nr)P = [1 + 4(.05)]1000 = (1.2)1000 = \$1200.$$

■

In Example 6, had the money been invested at 5% compound interest with annual compounding, then the future value would have been $1215.51. Money invested at simple interest is earning interest only on the principal amount. However, with compound interest, after the first interest period, the interest is also earning interest. Thus, if we compare two savings accounts, each earning interest at the same stated annual rate, but with one earning simple interest and the other earning compound interest, the latter will grow at a faster rate.

Effective Rate of Interest The annual rate of interest is also known as the **nominal rate** or the **stated rate**. Its true worth depends on the number of compounding periods. The nominal rate does not help you decide, for instance, whether a savings account paying 3.65% interest compounded quarterly is better than a savings account paying 3.6% interest compounded monthly. A better measure of worth is the *effective rate of interest.*

> **DEFINITION** The **effective rate of interest** is the simple interest rate that yields the same amount of interest after one year as the compounded annual (nominal) rate of interest. The effective rate is also known as the *annual percentage yield* (APY).

The effective rate of interest provides a standardized way of comparing investments. For example, a savings account paying 3.65% interest compounded quarterly has an effective rate of 3.7%, whereas a savings account paying 3.6% compounded monthly has an effective rate of 3.66%. Therefore, the first savings account is better.

Suppose the annual rate of interest r is compounded m times per year. Then with compound interest P dollars will grow to $P(1+i)^m$ in one year, where $i = r/m$. With simple interest r_{eff}, the balance after one year will be $P(1 + r_{\text{eff}})$. Equating the two balances,

$$P(1 + r_{\text{eff}}) = P(1 + i)^m$$
$$1 + r_{\text{eff}} = (1 + i)^m$$
$$r_{\text{eff}} = (1 + i)^m - 1. \tag{5}$$

EXAMPLE 7

Calculating an effective rate Calculate the effective rate of interest for a savings account paying a nominal rate of 3.65% compounded quarterly.

Solution Apply formula (5) with $r = .0365$ and $m = 4$. Then $i = r/m = .0365/4 = .009125$ and

$$r_{\text{eff}} = (1.009125)^4 - 1 \approx .037.$$

Now Try Exercise 47   Therefore, the effective rate is approximately 3.7%. ∎

Let us summarize the key formulas developed so far.

> **Compound Interest**
>
> Future value: $\quad F = (1 + i)^n P$
>
> Present value: $\quad P = \dfrac{F}{(1 + i)^n}$
>
> Effective rate: $\quad r_{\text{eff}} = (1 + i)^m - 1$
>
> where i is the interest rate per period, n is the total number of interest periods, and m is the number of times interest is compounded per year.

Simple Interest

$$\text{Future value:} \quad F \;=\; (1 + nr)P$$

where r is the interest rate and n is the number of years.

INCORPORATING TECHNOLOGY

GC Graphing calculators can easily display successive balances in a savings account. Consider the situation from Table 1, in which \$100 is deposited at 4% interest compounded quarterly. In Figs. 1 and 4 successive balances are displayed in the home screen. In Figs. 2 and 5 successive balances are graphed, and in Figs. 3 and 6 they are displayed in a table.

Figure 1

Figure 2

Figure 3

Figure 4

Figure 5

Figure 6

Displaying successive balances on the home screen   Successive balances can be determined with the relation $B_{\text{new}} = (1 + i)B_{\text{previous}}$. In Figs. 1 and 4, after the principal (**100**) is entered, the last displayed value (**100**) is assigned to **Ans** (on the TI-83/84 Plus) or **ans(1)** (on the TI-89). The instruction **1.01*Ans** (or **1.01*ans(1)**) generates the next balance (**101**) and assigns it to **Ans** (or **ans(1)**). Each subsequent press of ENTER generates another balance.

Graphs with the TI-83/84 Plus and TI-89   In order to obtain the graph in Figs. 2 and 5, $\mathbf{Y_1}$ was set to **1.01^X*100** in the $\mathbf{Y=}$ editor; that is, $(1 + i)^{\text{X}} \cdot P$. Here X, instead of n, is used to represent the number of interest periods. Then the window was set to $[0, 40]$ *by* $[90, 150]$, with an X-scale of 1 and a Y-scale of 10. Then, we pressed GRAPH (on the TI-83/84 Plus) or ◆[GRAPH] (on the TI-89) to display the function, and pressed TRACE (on the TI-83/84 Plus) or F3 (on the TI-89) to obtain the trace cursor. (*Note*: After $\mathbf{Y_1}$ has been defined, values of $\mathbf{Y_1}$ can be displayed on the home screen by entering expressions such as $\mathbf{Y_1(20)}$.)

Tables with the TI-83/84 Plus and TI-89   In order to obtain the tables in Figs. 3 and 6, $\mathbf{Y_1}$ was set to **1.01^X*100** in the $\mathbf{Y=}$ editor. Then 2nd[TBLSET] (on the TI-83/84 Plus) or ◆ [TBLSET] (on the TI-89) was pressed to bring up the TABLE SETUP screen. **TblStart** was set to 0, and Δ**Tbl** was set to 1. Finally, 2nd [TABLE] (on the TI-83/84 Plus) or ◆ [TABLE] (on the TI-89) was pressed to bring up the table.

TVM Solver with the TI-83/84 Plus The details for using this financial calculation tool are presented in Appendix B. In Figs. 7, 8, and 9, TVM Solver is used to solve Examples 3, 4, and 5. *Note:* The values for PV are negative since they represent money paid to the bank. ■

Figure 7. Example 3

Figure 8. Example 4

Figure 9. Example 5

EXAMPLE 8

Determining the amount of time for a balance to exceed a specified amount Consider the situation from Table 1, in which $100 is deposited at 4% interest compounded quarterly. Use a graphing calculator to determine when the balance will exceed $130.

Solution There are four ways to answer this question with a graphing calculator—with the home screen, with a graph, with a table, and with TVM Solver. (*Note:* The first three TI-83/84 Plus screens shown below have TI-89 analogs that can be created in a similar way.)

1. (Home screen) Generate successive balances (while keeping track of the number of times the ENTER key has been pressed) until a balance exceeding 130 is reached. See Fig. 10.

2. (Graph) Set $Y_2 = 130$ and find its intersection with the graph of $Y_1 = 1.01^\wedge X*100$. See Fig. 11.

3. (Table) Scroll down the table for Y_1 until the balance exceeds 130. See Fig. 12.

4. (TVM Solver) See Fig. 13. *Note:* The value for PV is negative since it represents money paid to the bank.

Now Try Exercise 63 In each case we see that the balance will exceed $130 after 27 interest periods. ■

Figure 10

Figure 11

Figure 12

Figure 13

ES The section "Using Excel's Financial Functions" of Appendix C shows how the functions FV, PV, and EFFECT are used to calculate future values, present values, and effective rates of interest.

Practice Problems 10.1

1. Calculate the present value of $1000 to be received 10 years in the future at 6% interest compounded annually.

2. Calculate the future value after 2 years of $1 at 26%

interest compounded weekly.

3. Calculate the future amount of $2000 after 6 months if invested at 6% simple interest.

EXERCISES 10.1

1. Determine i and n for the following situations, where i is the interest rate per period and n is the number of interest periods.

   (a) 12% interest compounded monthly for 2 years

   (b) 8% interest compounded quarterly for 5 years

   (c) 10% interest compounded semiannually for 20 years

2. Determine i and n for the following situations.

   (a) 6% interest compounded annually for 3 years

   (b) 6% interest compounded monthly from January 1, 2005, to July 1, 2009

   (c) 9% interest compounded quarterly from January 1, 2005, to October 1, 2008

3. Determine i, n, P, and F for the following situations.

   (a) $500 invested at 6% interest compounded annually grows to $631.24 in 4 years.

   (b) $800 invested on January 1, 2007, at 6% interest compounded monthly grows to $1455.52 by January 1, 2017.

   (c) $6177.88 is deposited on January 1, 2007. The balance on July 1, 2016, is $9000 and the interest is 4% compounded semiannually.

4. Determine i, n, P, and F for the following situations.

   (a) The amount of money that must be deposited now at 4.5% interest compounded weekly in order to have $7500 in 1 year is $7170.12.

   (b) $3000 deposited at 6% interest compounded monthly will grow to $18,067.73 in 30 years.

   (c) In 1626, Peter Minuit, the first director-general of New Netherlands province, purchased Manhattan Island for trinkets and cloth valued at about $24. Had this money been invested at 8% interest compounded quarterly, it would have amounted to $389,112,397,500,000 by 2010.

5. Calculate the future value of $1000 after 2 years if deposited at 6% interest compounded monthly.

6. Calculate the present value of $10,000 payable in 5 years at 4% interest compounded semiannually.

7. Calculate the present value of $100,000 payable in 25 years at 6% interest compounded monthly.

8. Calculate the future value of $1000 after 1 year if deposited at 7.3% interest compounded daily.

9. Six thousand dollars is deposited in a savings account at 6% interest compounded monthly. Find the balance after 3 years and the amount of interest earned during that time.

10. Two thousand dollars is deposited in a savings account at 4% interest compounded semiannually. Find the balance after 7 years and the amount of interest earned during that time.

11. If $1000 is deposited for five years in a savings account earning 3% interest compounded quarterly, how much interest is earned during the fifth year?

12. If $1000 is deposited for six years in a savings account earning 3.6% interest compounded monthly, how much interest is earned during the sixth year?

13. How much money must you deposit at 4% interest compounded quarterly in order to earn $406.04 interest in one year?

14. How much money must you deposit at 6% interest compounded monthly in order to earn $196.68 interest in three years?

15. (a) How much money would have to be deposited now at 6% interest compounded monthly to accumulate to $4000 in 2 years?

    (b) How much of the $4000 would be interest?

    (c) Prepare a table showing the growth of the account for the first 3 months.

16. (a) How much money would have to be deposited now at 8% interest compounded quarterly to accumulate to $10,000 in 15 years?

    (b) How much of the $10,000 would be interest?

    (c) Prepare a table showing the growth of the account for the first 3 quarters.

17. If you had invested $10,000 on January 1, 2006, at 4% interest compounded quarterly, how much would you have on April 1, 2012?

18. In order to have $10,000 on his 25th birthday, how much would a person just turned 21 have to invest if the money will earn 6% interest compounded monthly?

19. Saving for Retirement Mr. Smith wishes to purchase a $10,000 sailboat upon his retirement in 3 years. He has just won the state lottery and would like to set aside enough cash in a savings account paying 4% interest compounded quarterly to buy the boat upon retirement. How much should he deposit?

20. Savings Account Ms. Jones has just invested $100,000 at 6% interest compounded annually. How much money will she have in 20 years?

21. Consider the following savings account statement:

	Date		
	1/1/09	**2/1/09**	**3/1/09**
Deposit	$1000.00		
Withdrawal			
Interest		$5.00	$5.03
Balance	$1000.00	$1005.00	$1010.03

(a) What annual interest rate is this bank paying?

(b) Give the interest and balance on 4/1/09.

(c) Give the interest and balance on 1/1/11.

22. Consider the following savings account statement:

	Date		
	1/1/08	**7/1/08**	**1/1/09**
Deposit	$10,000.00		
Withdrawal			
Interest		$200.00	$204.00
Balance	$10,000.00	$10,200.00	$10,404.00

(a) Give the interest and balance on 7/1/09.

(b) Give the interest and balance on 1/1/17.

23. Is it more profitable to receive $1000 now or $1700 in 9 years? Assume that money can earn 6% interest compounded annually.

24. Is it more profitable to receive $7000 now or $10,000 in 9 years? Assume that money can earn 4% interest compounded quarterly.

25. Comparing Interest Rates In 1999 the Nasdaq index grew at a rate of 62.2% compounded weekly. Is this rate better or worse than 85% compounded annually?

26. Would you rather earn 8% interest compounded annually or 7.3% interest compounded daily?

27. On January 1, 2006, a deposit was made into a savings account paying interest compounded quarterly. The balance on January 1, 2009 was $10,000 and the balance on April 1, 2009, was $10,100. How large was the deposit?

28. During the 1990s a deposit was made into a savings account paying 4% interest compounded quarterly. On January 1, 2009, the balance was $2020. What was the balance on October 1, 2008?

Exercises 29–42 concern simple interest.

29. Determine r, n, P, and F for each of the following situations.

(a) $500 invested at 4% simple interest grows to $510 in 6 months.

(b) In order to have $550 after 2 years at 5% simple interest, $500 must be deposited.

30. Determine r, n, P, and F for each of the following situations.

(a) At 6% simple interest, $1000 deposited on January 1, 2009, will be worth $1040 on September 1, 2009.

(b) At 4% simple interest, in order to have $3600 in 5 years, $3000 must be deposited now.

31. Calculate the future value after 3 years if $1000 is deposited at 5% simple interest.

32. Calculate the future value after 18 months if $2000 is deposited at 6% simple interest.

33. Find the present value of $3000 in 2 years at 10% simple interest.

34. Find the present value of $2000 in 4 years at 7% simple interest.

35. Determine the (simple) interest rate at which $980 grows to $1000 in 6 months.

36. How many years are required for $1000 to grow to $1210 at 7% simple interest?

37. How many years are required for $500 to grow to $800 at 6% simple interest?

38. At what (simple) interest rate will $1000 grow to $1200 in five years?

39. Determine the amount of time required for money to double at 5% simple interest.

40. Derive the formula for the (simple) interest rate at which P dollars grows to F dollars in n years. That is, express r in terms of P, F, and n.

41. Derive the formula for the present value of F dollars in n years at simple interest rate r.

42. Derive the formula for the number of years required for P dollars to grow to F dollars at simple interest rate r.

43. Suppose a principal of $100 is deposited for 5 years in a savings account at 6% interest compounded semiannually. Which of items (a)–(d) can be used to fill in the blank in the following statement? (*Note:* Before computing, use your intuition to guess the correct answer.)

If the _____ is doubled, then the future value will double.

(a) principal   (b) interest rate

(c) number of interest periods per year

(d) number of years

44. Suppose a principal of $100 is deposited for 5 years in a savings account at 6% simple interest. Which of items (a)–(c) can be used to fill in the blank in the following statement? (*Note*: Before computing, use your intuition to guess the correct answer.)

If the _____ is doubled, then the future value will double.

(a) principal   (b) interest rate

(c) number of years

45. Compute the future value after 1 year for $100 invested at 4% interest compounded quarterly. What simple interest rate will yield the same amount in 1 year?

46. Compute the future value after 1 year for $100 invested at 6% interest compounded monthly. What simple interest rate will yield the same amount in 1 year?

47. Calculate the effective rate for 4% interest compounded semiannually.

48. Calculate the effective rate for 8.45% interest compounded weekly.

49. Calculate the effective rate for 4.4% interest compounded monthly.

50. Calculate the effective rate for 7.95% interest compounded quarterly.

51. Find the nominal rate corresponding to an effective rate of 4.06% if interest is compounded quarterly.

52. Find the nominal rate corresponding to an effective rate of 3% if interest is compounded monthly.

53. If a $1000 investment at compound interest doubles every six years, how long will it take the investment to grow to $8000?

54. If your stock portfolio gained 20% in 2008 and 30% in 2009, then it gained _____ over the two-year period.

(a) 50%   (b) 56%   (c) 60%   (d) 100%

55. If the value of an investment grows at the rate of 4% compounded annually for 10 years, then it grows about _____ over the ten-year period.

(a) 25%   (b) 40%   (c) 44%   (d) 48%

56. True or False An investment growing at the rate of 12% compounded monthly will double (that is increase by 100%) in about 70 months. Therefore, the investment should increase by 50% in about 35 months.

57. Saving for a Gift Clara would like to have $2100 in seven years to give her granddaughter as a twenty-first birthday present. She has $1500 to invest in a seven-year certificate of deposit. What rate of interest compounded annually must the CD earn?

58. Saving for a Purchase Juan would like to have $2300 in three years in order to buy a motorcycle. He has $2000 to invest in a three-year certificate of deposit. What rate of interest compounded annually must the CD earn?

59. Comparing Investments The same amount of money was invested in each of two different investments on January 1, 2007. Investment A increased by 2.5% in 2007, 3% in 2008, and 8.4% in 2009. Investment B increased by the same amount, $r\%$, in each of the three years and was worth the same as investment A at the end of the three-year period. Determine the value of r.

60. If you increase the compound interest rate for an investment by 20%, will the future value increase by 20%?

In Exercises 61–66, use a graphing calculator or spreadsheet to answer the questions.

61. Savings Account One thousand dollars is deposited into a savings account at 6.5% interest compounded annually. What are the balances after 1, 2, and 3 years? How many years are required for the balance to reach $1655? After how many years will the balance exceed $2000?

62. Savings Account Ten thousand dollars is deposited into a savings account at 6% interest compounded monthly. What are the balances after 5, 10, and 15 months? How many months are required for the balance to reach $11,614? After how many months will the balance exceed $13,000?

63. Investment Tom invests $100,000 at 8% interest compounded annually. When will Tom be a millionaire?

64. Savings Account How many years are required for $100 to double if deposited at 6% interest compounded quarterly?

65. Comparing Investments Consider the following two interest options for an investment of $1000: (A) 8% simple interest, (B) 6% interest compounded annually. After how many years will option B outperform option A?

66. Comparing Investments Consider the following two interest options for an investment of $1000: (A) 4% simple interest, (B) 4% interest compounded daily. After how many years will option B outperform option A by $100?

Solutions to Practice Problems 10.1

1. Here we are given the value in the future $F = \$1000$ and are asked to find the present value P. Interest compounded annually has just one interest period per year, so $n = 10 \cdot 1 = 10$ and $i = 6\%/1 = 6\% = .06$. By formula (3),

$$P = \frac{F}{(1+i)^n}$$

$$= \frac{1000}{(1.06)^{10}}$$

$$= \$558.39 \quad \text{(rounding to the nearest cent).}$$

2. Here we are given the present value, $P = 1$, and are asked to find the value F at a future time. Interest compounded weekly has 52 interest periods each year, so $n = 2 \times 52 = 104$ and $i = 26\%/52 = \frac{1}{2}\% = .005$. By formula (2), we have

$$F = (1+i)^n P = 1.005^{10} \cdot 1 = \$1.68.$$

3. In simple interest problems, time should be expressed in terms of years. Since 6 months is $\frac{1}{2}$ of a year, formula (4) gives

$$A = (1 + nr)P = [1 + \tfrac{1}{2}(.06)]2000$$

$$= (1.03)2000$$

$$= \$2060.$$

10.2 Annuities

An **annuity** is a sequence of equal payments made at regular intervals of time. Here are two illustrations.

1. As the proud parent of a newborn daughter, you decide to save for her college education by depositing \$100 at the end of each month into a savings account paying 6% interest compounded monthly. Eighteen years from now, after you make the last of 216 payments, the account will contain \$38,735.32.

2. Having just won the state lottery, you decide not to work for the next 5 years. You want to deposit enough money into the bank so that you can withdraw \$5000 at the end of each month for 60 months. If the bank pays 6% interest compounded monthly, you must deposit \$258,627.80.

The periodic payments in the foregoing financial transactions are called **rent**. The amount of a typical rent payment is denoted by the letter R. Thus, in the preceding examples, we have $R = \$100$ and $R = \$5000$, respectively.

In illustration 1, you make equal payments to a bank in order to generate a large sum of money in the future. This sum, namely \$38,735.32, is called the **future value** of the annuity. Since the amount of money in the savings account is increased each time a payment is made, we refer to this type of annuity as an **increasing annuity**.

In illustration 2, the bank will make equal payments to you in order to pay back the sum of money that you currently deposit. The value of the current deposit, namely \$258,627.80, is called the **present value** of the annuity. Since the amount of money in the savings account is decreased each time a payment is made, we refer to this type of annuity as a **decreasing annuity**.

Increasing Annuities

> **DEFINITION** The **future value of an increasing annuity** of n equal payments is the value of the annuity after the nth payment.

Consider an annuity consisting of n payments of R dollars each deposited into an account paying compound interest at the rate of i per interest period, and that

TABLE 1

Payment	Amount	Number of interest periods on deposit	Future value of payment
1	R	$n-1$	$(1+i)^{n-1}R$
2	R	$n-2$	$(1+i)^{n-2}R$
$\vdots$	$\vdots$	$\vdots$	$\vdots$
$n-2$	R	2	$(1+i)^2 R$
$n-1$	R	1	$(1+i)R$
n	R	0	R

each payment is made at the end of an interest period. Let us derive a formula for the future value of the annuity: that is, a formula for the balance of the account immediately after the last payment.

Each payment accumulates interest for a different number of interest periods, so let us calculate the balance in the account as the sum of n future values, one corresponding to each payment (Table 1). Denote the future value of the annuity by F. Then F is the sum of the numbers in the right-hand column:

$$F = R + (1+i)R + (1+i)^2 R + (1+i)^3 R + \cdots + (1+i)^{n-1}R.$$

A compact expression for F can be obtained by multiplying both sides of this equation by $(1+i)$ and then subtracting the original equation from the new equation.

$$(1+i)F = \quad (1+i)R + (1+i)^2 R + (1+i)^3 R + \cdots + (1+i)^{n-1}R + (1+i)^n R$$
$$\underline{F = R + (1+i)R + (1+i)^2 R + (1+i)^3 R + \cdots + (1+i)^{n-1}R}$$
$$iF = (1+i)^n R - R$$

The last equation can be written $iF = [(1+i)^n - 1] \cdot R$. Dividing both sides by i yields

$$F = \frac{(1+i)^n - 1}{i} \cdot R.$$

We may summarize our calculations as follows.

Suppose that an increasing annuity consists of n payments of R dollars each, deposited at the ends of consecutive interest periods into an account with interest compounded at a rate i per period. Then the future value F of the annuity is given by the formula

$$F = \frac{(1+i)^n - 1}{i} \cdot R. \tag{1}$$

EXAMPLE 1

Calculating the future value of an increasing annuity Calculate the future value of an increasing annuity of $100 per month for 5 years at 6% interest compounded monthly.

Solution Here $R = 100$ and $i = \frac{1}{2}\% = .005$. Since a payment is made at the end of each month for 5 years, there will be $5 \times 12 = 60$ payments. So $n = 60$. Therefore,

Now Try Exercise 3

$$F = \frac{(1+i)^n - 1}{i} \cdot R = \frac{(1.005)^{60} - 1}{.005} \cdot 100 = \$6977.00.$$

We can easily derive a formula that illustrates exactly how the future value of an increasing annuity changes from period to period. Each new balance can be computed from the previous balance with the formula

$$B_{\text{new}} = (1+i)B_{\text{previous}} + R.$$

That is, the new balance equals the growth of the previous balance due to interest, plus the amount paid. So, for instance, if B_1 is the balance after the first payment is made, B_2 is the balance after the second payment is made, and so on, then

$$B_1 = R$$
$$B_2 = (1+i)B_1 + R$$
$$B_3 = (1+i)B_2 + R$$
$$\vdots$$

Successive unpaid balances are computed by multiplying the previous balance by $(1+i)$ and adding R.

> If R is deposited into an increasing annuity at the end of each interest period with interest rate i per period,
>
> $$B_{\text{new}} = (1+i)B_{\text{previous}} + R \qquad (2)$$
>
> can be used to calculate each new balance from the previous balance.

EXAMPLE 2   **Calculating the future value of an increasing annuity**   Consider the annuity of Example 1. Determine the future value after 61 months.

Solution   From Example 1, $i = .005$, the balance after 60 months is \$6977.00, and $R = 100$. Therefore, by (2)

$$[\text{balance after 61 months}] = (1 + .005)[\text{balance after 60 months}] + 100$$
$$= 1.005(6977) + 100 = 7111.89.$$

Therefore, the annuity will have accumulated to \$7111.89 after 61 months.   ∎

Formula (1) can also be used to determine the rent necessary to achieve a certain future value.

EXAMPLE 3   **Determining the rent for an increasing annuity**   Ms. Adams would like to buy a \$300,000 airplane when she retires in 8 years. How much should she deposit at the end of each half-year into an account paying 4% interest compounded semiannually so that she will have enough money to purchase the airplane?

Solution   For this increasing annuity, $n = 16$, $i = 2\% = .02$, and $F = 300,000$. Therefore,

$$F = \frac{(1+i)^n - 1}{i} \cdot R$$

$$300,000 = \frac{(1.02)^{16} - 1}{.02} \cdot R$$

$$300,000 = 18.63928525 \cdot R$$

$$R = \frac{300,000}{18.63928525} = \$16,095.04$$

Now Try Exercise 9   She should deposit \$16,095.04 at the end of each half-year period.   ∎

Decreasing Annuities

> **DEFINITION** The **present value of a decreasing annuity** is the amount of money necessary to finance the sequence of annuity payments. That is, the present value of the annuity is the amount you would need to deposit in order to provide the desired sequence of annuity payments and leave a balance of zero at the end of the term.

Let us find a formula for the present value of the annuity. There are two ways to proceed. On the one hand, the desired present value could be computed as the sum of the present values of the various annuity payments. This computation would make use of the formula for the sum of the first n terms of a geometric progression. However, there is a much "cleaner" derivation that proceeds indirectly to obtain a formula relating the present value P and the rent R.

As before, let us assume that our annuity consists of n payments made at the end of each interest period, with interest compounded at a rate i per interest period.

Situation 1: Suppose that the P dollars were just left in the account and that the annuity payments were not withdrawn. At the end of the n interest periods, there would be $(1+i)^n P$ dollars in the account.

Situation 2: Suppose that the payments are withdrawn but are immediately re-deposited into another account having the same rate of interest. At the end of the n interest periods, there would be $\frac{(1+i)^n - 1}{i} \cdot R$ dollars in the new account.

In both of these situations, P dollars is deposited and it, together with all the interest generated, is earning income at the same interest rate for the same amount of time. Therefore, the final amounts of money in the accounts should be the same. That is,

$$(1+i)^n P = \frac{(1+i)^n - 1}{i} \cdot R$$

$$P = (1+i)^{-n} \cdot \frac{(1+i)^n - 1}{i} \cdot R \quad \text{Multiply both sides by } (1+i)^{-n}.$$

$$= \frac{1 - (1+i)^{-n}}{i} \cdot R \quad \begin{array}{l}\text{Multiply numerator of fraction} \\ \text{by } (1+i)^{-n}.\end{array}$$

> The present value P and the rent R of a decreasing annuity of n payments with interest compounded at a rate i per interest period are related by the formula
>
> $$P = \frac{1 - (1+i)^{-n}}{i} \cdot R.$$

EXAMPLE 4

Determining the present value for a decreasing annuity How much money must you deposit now at 6% interest compounded quarterly in order to be able to withdraw $3000 at the end of each quarter-year for 2 years?

Solution For this decreasing annuity, $R = 3000$, $i = 1.5\% = .015$, and $n = 8$. We are asked to calculate the present value of the sequence of payments.

Now Try Exercise 21

$$P = \frac{1 - (1+i)^{-n}}{i} \cdot R = \frac{1 - 1.015^{-8}}{.015} \cdot 3000 = \$22,457.78 \quad \blacksquare$$

The Excel spreadsheet in Table 2 shows the effect of interest rates (compounded quarterly) on the present value where the duration of the decreasing annuity is two

TABLE 2

	A	B
1	Rent	$3,000.00
2		
3	Interest	Present
4	rate	value
5	3.0%	$23,209.84
6	3.5%	$23,081.91
7	4.0%	$22,955.03
8	4.5%	$22,829.19
9	5.0%	$22,704.37
10	5.5%	$22,580.57
11	6.0%	$22,457.78
12	6.5%	$22,335.97
13	7.0%	$22,215.16
14	7.5%	$22,095.32
15	8.0%	$21,976.44

years. [The entry in cell B5 was set to `=PV(A5/4,8,-$B$1)`. The form of the present value function is `PV(rate,nper,pmt)`. The payment was specified as a negative number since money is being withdrawn from the account. The remainder of the B column was created by selecting the cell B5 and dragging its fill handle. The dollar signs in `$B$1` prevent references to this location from being changed.]

EXAMPLE 5

Determining the rent for a decreasing annuity If you deposit $10,000 into a fund paying 6% interest compounded monthly, how much can you withdraw at the end of each month for 1 year?

Solution For this decreasing annuity, $P = 10,000$, $i = \frac{1}{2}\% = .005$, and $n = 12$. We are asked to calculate the rent for the sequence of payments.

$$P = \frac{1 - (1+i)^{-n}}{i} \cdot R$$

$$10,000 = \frac{1 - (1.005)^{-12}}{.005} \cdot R = 11.61893207 \cdot R$$

Now Try Exercise 5

$$R = \frac{10,000}{11.61893207} = \$860.66$$

REMARK In this section we have considered only annuities with payments made at the end of each interest period. Such annuities are called *ordinary annuities*. Annuities that have payments at the beginning of the interest period are called *annuities due*. Annuities whose payment period is different from the interest period are called *general annuities*.

The two key formulas in this section are:

1. Increasing Annuity: $F = \frac{(1+i)^n - 1}{i} \cdot R$

2. Decreasing Annuity: $P = \dfrac{1 - (1 + i)^{-n}}{i} \cdot R$

The following tips help recall these formulas:

- Both formulas have i in the denominator and R on the right side.
- Since an increasing annuity builds up a future value, formula (1) involves F.
- Since a decreasing annuity depletes a present value, formula (2) involves P.
- Associate *increasing* with *positive* and *decreasing* with *negative*. Formula (1) has a positive exponent and formula (2) has a negative exponent.

COMMENT We have simplified matters by requiring the memorization of only two formulas. However, some people prefer to use four formulas when working with annuities. The two additional formulas are obtained by solving formulas (1) and (2) for R. They are:

3. Increasing Annuity: $R = \dfrac{i}{(1 + i)^n - 1} \cdot F$

4. Decreasing Annuity: $R = \dfrac{i}{1 - (1 + i)^{-n}} \cdot P$ ■

INCORPORATING TECHNOLOGY

GC Graphing calculators can easily display successive balances in an annuity.[1] Consider the situation from Example 1 in which \$100 is deposited at the end of each month at 6% interest compounded monthly. In Figs. 1 and 4 successive balances are displayed in the home screen. In Figs. 2 and 5 successive balances are graphed, and in Figs. 3 and 6 they are displayed in a table.

These figures were obtained with the same processes as Figures 1–6 in Section 10.1. Successive balances were determined with the relation $B_{\text{new}} = (1+i)B_{\text{previous}} + R$. The function to be graphed was specified as $Y_1 = 100(1.005^X - 1)/.005$. The window was set to $[0, 120]$ by $[-4000, 17000]$ with an X-scale of 10 and a Y-scale of 1000. In the TABLE SETUP menu both **TblStart** and Δ**Tbl** were set to 1. In Figs. 7, 8, and 9, TVM Solver is used to solve Examples 1, 3, and 4.   ■

```
100
                     100
1.005*Ans+100
                   200.5
               301.5025
             403.0100125
             505.0250626
```

Figure 1

Figure 2

Figure 3

Figure 4

Figure 5

Figure 6

```
N=60
I%=6
PV=0
PMT=-100
•FV=6977.003051
P/Y=12
C/Y=12
PMT:END BEGIN
```

Figure 7

```
N=16
I%=4
PV=0
•PMT=-16095.037…
FV=300000
P/Y=2
C/Y=2
PMT:END BEGIN
```

Figure 8

```
N=8
I%=6
•PV=-22457.77524
PMT=3000
FV=0
P/Y=4
C/Y=4
PMT:END BEGIN
```

Figure 9

---

[1]We limit our discussion here to increasing annuities. The corresponding analysis for decreasing annuities is similar.

EXAMPLE 6   **Determining the time for a future value to exceed a specified amount**   Consider the situation from Example 1 in which \$100 is deposited monthly at 6% interest compounded monthly. Use a graphing calculator to determine when the balance will exceed \$10,000.

Solution   There are four ways to answer this question with a graphing calculator—with the home screen, with a graph, with a table, and with TVM Solver. (*Note:* The first three TI-83/84 Plus screens shown below have TI-89 analogs that can be created in a similar way.)

1. (Home screen)   Generate successive balances (while keeping track of the number of times the ENTER key has been pressed) until a balance exceeding 10,000 is reached. See Fig. 10.

2. (Graph)   Set Y_2=10000 and find its intersection with the graph of Y_1= 100(1.005^X-1)/.005. See Fig. 11.

3. (Table)   Scroll down the table for Y_1 until the balance exceeds 10,000. See Fig. 12.

4. (TVM Solver) See Fig. 13. *Note:* The value for PV is negative since it represents money paid to the bank.

In each case we see that the balance will exceed \$10,000 after 82 months; that is,

Now Try Exercise 47   after 6 years and 10 months.   ■

Figure 10

Figure 11

Figure 12

Figure 13

ES   The section "Using Excel's Financial Functions" of Appendix C shows how the functions FV, PV, and PMT are used to calculate future values (F), present values (P), and monthly payments (R) for annuities.

Practice Problems 10.2

Decide whether or not each of the following annuities is an ordinary annuity, that is, the type of annuity considered in this section. If so, identify n, i, and R and calculate the present value or the future value, whichever is appropriate.

1. You make a deposit at 9% interest compounded monthly into a fund that pays you \$1 at the end of each month for 5 years.

2. At the end of each week for 2 years you deposit \$10 into a savings account earning 6% interest compounded monthly.

3. At the end of each month for 2 years, you deposit \$10 into a savings account earning 6% interest compounded monthly.

EXERCISES 10.2

1. For each of the following increasing annuities, specify i, n, R, and F.

   (a) If at the end of each month, $50 is deposited into a savings account paying 6% interest compounded monthly, the balance after 10 years will be $8193.97.

   (b) Mr. Smith is saving to buy a $200,000 yacht in the year 2012. Since 2002, he has been depositing $8231.34 at the end of each half-year into a fund paying 4% interest compounded semiannually.

2. For each of the following decreasing annuities, specify i, n, R, and P.

   (a) A retiree deposits $72,582 into a bank paying 6% interest compounded monthly and withdraws $520 at the end of each month for 20 years.

   (b) In order to receive $700 at the end of each quarter-year from 2006 until 2011, Ms. Jones deposited $11,446 into a savings account paying 8% interest compounded quarterly.

3. Calculate the future value of an increasing annuity of $1000 per quarter for 5 years at 6% interest compounded quarterly.

4. Calculate the rent of an increasing annuity at 4% interest compounded semiannually if payments are made every half-year and the future value after 7 years is $10,000.

5. Calculate the rent of a decreasing annuity at 8% interest compounded quarterly with payments made every quarter-year for 7 years and present value $100,000.

6. Calculate the present value of a decreasing annuity of $1000 per year for 10 years at 6% interest compounded annually.

7. **Savings Account** A person deposits $500 into a savings account at the end of every month for 4 years at 6% interest compounded monthly.

   (a) Find the balance at the end of 4 years.

   (b) How much interest will be earned during the 4 years?

   (c) Prepare a table showing the balance and interest for the first three months.

8. **Savings Account** A person deposits $800 into a savings account at the end of every quarter-year for 5 years at 6% interest compounded quarterly.

   (a) Find the balance at the end of 5 years.

   (b) How much interest will be earned during the 5 years?

   (c) Prepare a table showing the balance and interest for the first three quarters.

9. **Saving for a Car** How much must Jim save each month in order to have $12,000 to buy a new car in 3 years if the interest rate is 6% compounded monthly? How much of the $12,000 does Jim actually deposit and how much of it is interest?

10. **Saving to Pay Off a Loan** Valerie needs $5000 3 years from now in order to pay off a loan. How much must she save each quarter for the next 3 years if interest rates are 8% compounded quarterly? How much of the $5000 will be interest?

11. **Comparing Bonus Plans** When Bridget takes a new job, she is offered a $2000 bonus now or the option of an extra $200 each month for the next year. If interest rates are 6% compounded monthly, which choice is better and by how much?

12. **College Allowance** When Michael started college, his father gave him $5000 deposited in a savings account earning 6% interest compounded monthly. Michael withdraws $500 a month starting at the beginning of the second month. Prepare a schedule showing the monthly balance in the account for the first four months.

*A **sinking fund** is an increasing annuity set up by a corporation or government to repay a large debt at some future date. Exercises 13–19 concern such annuities.*

13. **Sinking Fund** A city has a debt of $1,000,000 due in 15 years. How much money must it deposit at the end of each half-year into a sinking fund at 4% interest compounded semi-annually in order to pay off the debt?

14. **Sinking Fund** A corporation wishes to deposit money into a sinking fund at the end of each half-year in order to repay $50 million in bonds in 10 years. It can expect to receive a 12% (compounded semiannually) return on its deposits to the sinking fund. How much should the deposits be?

15. **Sinking Fund** The Federal National Mortgage Association ("Fannie Mae") puts $30 million at the end of each month into a sinking fund paying 12% interest compounded monthly. The sinking fund is to be used to repay debentures that mature 15 years from the creation of the fund. How large is the face amount of the debentures assuming the sinking fund will exactly pay it off?

16. **Sinking Fund** A county has a debt of $12,000,000 due in 10 years. How much money must it deposit at the end of each quarter-year into a sinking fund at 5% interest compounded quarterly in order to pay off the debt?

17. **Saving for an Upgrade** A corporation sets up a sinking fund to replace some aging machinery. It deposits $100,000 into the fund at the end of each month for 10 years. The annuity earns 12% interest compounded monthly. The equipment originally cost $13 million. However, the cost of the equipment is rising 6% each year. Will the annuity be adequate to replace the

equipment? If not, how much additional money is needed?

18. **Saving for a New Warehouse** A corporation sets up a sinking fund to replace an aging warehouse. The cost of the warehouse today would be $8 million. However, the corporation plans to replace the warehouse in 5 years. It estimates that the cost of the warehouse will increase by 10% annually. The sinking fund will earn 12% interest compounded monthly. What should be the monthly payment to the fund?

19. **Saving for a New Headquarters** A corporation decides to set up a sinking fund to raise $5 million in order to erect a new headquarters in 15 years. How much should the corporation deposit into the sinking fund at the end of each quarter if the fund will earn 8% interest compounded quarterly?

20. **Saving for a Bicycle** On January 1, 2008, Tom decided to save for exactly 1 year for a 10-speed bike by depositing $10 at the end of each month into a savings account paying 6% interest compounded monthly. How much did he accumulate?

21. **College Allowance** During Jack's first year at college, his father had been sending him $100 per month for incidental expenses. For the sophomore year, his father decided instead to make a deposit into a savings account on August 1 and have his son withdraw $100 on the first of each month from September 1 to May 1. If the bank pays 6% interest compounded monthly, how much should Jack's father deposit?

22. **Magazine Subscription** Suppose that a magazine subscription costs $45 per year and that you receive a magazine at the end of each month. At an interest rate of 6% compounded monthly, how much are you actually paying for each issue?

23. Is it more profitable to receive $1000 at the end of each month for 10 years or to receive a lump sum of $163,000 at the end of 10 years? Assume that money can earn 6% interest compounded monthly.

24. Is it more profitable to receive a lump sum of $10,000 at the end of 3 years or to receive $750 at the end of each quarter-year for 3 years? Assume that money can earn 8% interest compounded quarterly.

25. **Savings Account** Suppose that you deposited $1000 into a savings account on January 1, 2002, and deposited an additional $100 into the account at the end of each quarter-year. If the bank pays 8% interest compounded quarterly, how much will be in the account on January 1, 2011?

26. **Savings Account** Suppose that you opened a savings account on January 1, 2006, and made a deposit of $100. In 2007 you began depositing $10 into the account at the end of each month. If the bank pays 6% interest compounded monthly, how much money will be in the account on January 1, 2011?

27. **Savings Account** Ms. Jones deposited $100 at the end of each month for 10 years into a savings account earning 6% interest compounded monthly. However, she deposited an additional $1000 at the end of the seventh year. How much money was in the account at the end of the tenth year?

28. **Savings Account** Redo Exercise 27 for the situation where Ms. Jones withdrew $1000 at the end of the seventh year instead of depositing it.

29. **Savings Account** How much money must you deposit into a savings account at the end of each year at 6% interest compounded annually in order to earn $5725.43 interest during a 10-year period?

30. **Savings Account** How much money must you deposit into a savings account at the end of each quarter at 4% interest compounded quarterly in order to earn $403.80 interest during a 5-year period?

31. Suppose you deposit $600 every six months for 5 years into an annuity at 4% interest compounded semiannually. Which of items (a)–(d) can be used to fill in the blank in the following statement? (*Note*: Before computing, use your intuition to guess the correct answer.)

   If the _____ doubles, then the amount accumulated will double.

   (a) rent

   (b) interest rate

   (c) number of interest periods per year

   (d) number of years

32. Suppose you deposit $100,000 into an annuity at 4% interest compounded semiannually and withdraw an equal amount at the end of each interest period so that the account is depleted after 10 years. Which of items (a)–(d) can be used to fill in the blank in the following statement? (*Note*: Before computing, use your intuition to guess the correct answer.)

   If the _____ doubles, then the total amount withdrawn each year will double.

   (a) amount deposited

   (b) interest rate

   (c) number of interest periods per year

   (d) number of years

A **perpetuity** *is similar to a decreasing annuity, except that the payments continue forever. Exercises 33 and 34 concern such annuities.*

33. **Scholarship** A grateful alumnus decides to donate a permanent scholarship of $1200 per year. How much money should be deposited in the bank at 5% interest compounded annually in order to be able to supply the money for the scholarship at the end of each year?

34. Show that to establish a perpetuity paying R dollars at the end of each interest period, it requires a deposit

of R/i dollars, where i is the interest rate per interest period.

A **deferred annuity** *is a type of decreasing annuity whose term is to start at some future date. Exercises 35–38 concern such annuities.*

35. College Fund On his tenth birthday, a boy inherits $10,000, which is to be used for his college education. The money is deposited into a trust fund that will pay him R dollars on his 18th, 19th, 20th, and 21st birthdays. Find R if the money earns 6% interest compounded annually.

36. College Fund Refer to Exercise 35. Find the size of the inheritance that would result in $10,000 per year during the college years (ages 18–21, inclusive).

37. Trust Fund On December 1, 2000, a philanthropist set up a permanent trust fund to buy Christmas presents for needy children. The fund will provide $60,000 each year beginning on December 1, 2010. How much must have been set aside in 2000 if the money earns 6% interest compounded annually?

38. Show that the rent paid by a deferred annuity of n payments that are deferred by m interest periods is given by the formula

$$R = \frac{i(1+i)^{n+m}}{(1+i)^n - 1} \cdot P.$$

39. Municipal Bond A municipal bond pays 4% interest compounded semiannually on its face value of $5000. The interest is paid at the end of every half-year period. Fifteen years from now the face value of $5000 will be returned. The current market interest rate for municipal bonds is 3% compounded semiannually. How much should you pay for the bond?

40. Second Mortgage A businessperson wishes to lend money for a second mortgage on some local real estate. Suppose that the mortgage pays $500 per month for a 5-year period. Suppose that you can invest your money in certificates of deposit paying 6% interest compounded monthly. How much should you offer for the mortgage?

41. Business Note Suppose that a business note for $50,000 carries an interest rate of 18% compounded monthly. Suppose that the business pays only interest for the first 5 years and then repays the loan amount plus interest in equal monthly installments for the next 5 years.

  (a) Calculate the monthly payments during the second 5-year period.

  (b) Assume that the current market interest rate for such loans is 12% compounded monthly. How much should you be willing to pay for such a note?

42. Lottery Payoff A lottery winner is to receive $1000 a month for the next 5 years. How much is this sequence of payments worth today if interest rates are 6% compounded monthly? How is the difference between this amount and the $60,000 paid out beneficial to the agency running the lottery?

43. Formula (2), $B_{\text{new}} = (1+i)B_{\text{previous}} + R$, applies to an increasing annuity. What is the corresponding formula for a decreasing annuity?

44. Lottery Payoff A lottery winner is given two options:

  Option I: Receive a $20 million lump-sum payment

  Option II: Receive 25 equal annual payments totaling $60 million, with the first payment occurring immediately.

If money can earn 6% interest compounded annually, which option is better? *Hint:* With each option, calculate the amount of money earned at the end of 24 years if all the funds are to be deposited into a savings account as soon as they are received.

In Exercises 45–49, use a graphing calculator or spreadsheet to answer the questions.

45. A person deposits $1000 at the end of each year into an annuity earning 5% interest compounded annually. What are the balances (that is, future values) after 2, 3, and 4 years? How many years are required for the balance to reach $30,539? After how many years will the balance exceed $50,000?

46. A person deposits $700 at the end of each quarter-year into an annuity earning 8% interest compounded quarterly. What are the balances (that is, future values) after 1, 2, and 3 quarters? How many quarters are required for the balance to reach $5204? After how many quarters will the balance exceed $10,000?

47. Bicycle Fund Jane has taken a part-time job to save for a $503 racing bike. If she puts $15 each week into a savings account paying 5.2% interest compounded weekly, when will she be able to buy the bike?

48. Home Repairs Fund Bob needs $3228 to have some repairs done on his house. He decides to deposit $100 at the end of each month into an annuity earning 6% interest compounded monthly. When will he be able to do the repairs?

49. Comparing Expense Ratios Mutual funds charge an annual fee, called the *expense ratio*, that usually ranges from about .3% to about 1.5% of the amount of money in the account at the end of the year. For instance, if the expense ratio is .5% and you have $10,000 in the account at the end of the year, then you would be charged $.005 \cdot 10000 = $50 in fees. Suppose that you put $5000 at the beginning of each year into an IRA and that the funds are invested in a mutual fund earning 6% per year, before expenses. How much more will you have at the end of 10 years if the mutual fund has an expense ratio of .3%, as opposed to 1.5%?

Solutions to Practice Problems 10.2

1. An ordinary decreasing annuity with $n = 60$, $i = \frac{3}{4}\% = .0075$, and $R = 1$. You will make a deposit now, in the present, and then withdraw money each month. The amount of this deposit is the present value of the annuity.

$$P = \frac{1 - (1+i)^{-n}}{i} \cdot R$$

$$= \frac{1 - (1.0075)^{-60}}{.0075} \cdot 1$$

$$= \$48.17$$

[*Note*: For this transaction, the future value of the annuity needn't be computed. At the end of 5 years, the fund will have a balance of 0.]

2. Not an ordinary annuity since the payment period (1 week) is different from the interest period (1 month).

3. An ordinary increasing annuity with $n = 24$, $i = .5\% = .005$, and $R = \$10$. There is no money in the account now, in the present. However, in 2 years, in the future, money will have accumulated. So for this annuity, only the future value is of concern to you.

$$F = \frac{(1+i)^n - 1}{i} \cdot R$$

$$= \frac{(1.005)^{24} - 1}{.005} \cdot 10$$

$$= \$254.32$$

10.3 Amortization of Loans

In this section we analyze the mathematics of paying off loans. The loans we shall consider will be repaid in a sequence of equal payments at regular time intervals, with the payment intervals coinciding with the interest periods. The process of paying off such a loan is called **amortization**. In order to obtain a feeling for the amortization process, let us consider a particular case, the amortization of a $563 loan to buy a television set. Suppose that this loan charges interest at a 12% rate with interest compounded monthly and that the monthly payments are $116 for 5 months. The repayment process is summarized in Table 1.

TABLE 1

Payment number	Amount	Interest	Applied to principal	Unpaid balance
1	$116	$5.63	$110.37	$452.63
2	116	4.53	111.47	341.16
3	116	3.41	112.59	228.57
4	116	2.29	113.71	114.85
5	116	1.15	114.85	0.00

Note the following facts about the financial transactions.

1. Payments are made at the end of each month. The payments have been carefully calculated to pay off the debt, with interest, in the specified time interval.

2. Since $i = 1\%$, the interest to be paid each month is 1% of the unpaid balance at the end of the previous month. That is, 5.63 is 1% of 563, 4.53 is 1% of 452.63, and so on.

3. Although we write just one check each month for $116, we regard part of the check as being applied to payment of that month's interest. The remainder, namely $116 - [\text{interest}]$, is regarded as being applied to repayment of the principal amount.

4. The unpaid balance at the end of each month is the previous unpaid balance minus the portion of the payment applied to the principal. A loan can be paid off early by paying just the current unpaid balance.

The four factors that describe the amortization process just described are as follows:

the principal	$563
the interest rate	12% compounded monthly
the term	5 months
the monthly payment	$116

The important fact to recognize is that the sequence of payments in the preceding amortization constitutes a decreasing annuity for the bank, with the person taking out the loan paying the interest. Therefore, the mathematical tools developed in Section 10.2 suffice to analyze the amortization. In particular, we can determine the monthly payment or the principal once the other three factors are specified.

EXAMPLE 1

Calculating values associated with a loan Suppose that a loan has an interest rate of 12% compounded monthly and a term of 5 months.

(a) Given that the principal is $563, calculate the monthly payment.

(b) Given that the monthly payment is $116, calculate the principal.

(c) Given that the monthly payment is $116, calculate the unpaid balance after 3 months.

Solution The sequence of payments constitutes a decreasing annuity with the monthly payments as rent and the principal as the present value. Also, $n = 5$ and $i = 1\% = .01$.

(a) $P = \dfrac{1 - (1 + i)^{-n}}{i} \cdot R$

$563 = \dfrac{1 - (1.01)^{-5}}{.01} \cdot R$

$563 = 4.853431239 \cdot R$

$R = \dfrac{563}{4.853431239} = \$116.00$

(b) $P = \dfrac{1 - (1 + i)^{-n}}{i} \cdot R = \dfrac{1 - 1.01^{-5}}{.01} \cdot 116 = \$563.00$

(c) The unpaid balance is most easily calculated by regarding it as the amount necessary to retire the debt. Therefore, it must be sufficient to generate the sequence of two remaining payments. That is, the unpaid balance is the present value of a decreasing annuity of two payments of $116. So, $n = 2$, $i = .01$, $R = \$116$, and

Now Try Exercises 1 and 3

$$[\text{unpaid balance after 3 months}] = \dfrac{1 - (1.01)^{-2}}{.01} \cdot 116 = \$228.57. \qquad \blacksquare$$

A **mortgage** is a long-term loan used to purchase real estate. The real estate is used as collateral to guarantee the loan.

EXAMPLE 2

Calculating values associated with a mortgage On December 31, 1990, a house was purchased with the buyer taking out a 30-year, $112,475 mortgage at 9% interest, compounded monthly. The mortgage payments are made at the end of each month.

(a) Calculate the amount of the monthly payment.

(b) Calculate the unpaid balance of the loan on December 31, 2016, just after the 312th payment.

(c) How much interest will be paid during the month of January 2017?

(d) How much of the principal will be paid off during the year 2016?

(e) How much interest will be paid during the year 2016?

(f) What is the total amount of interest paid during the 30 years?

Solution (a) Denote the monthly payment by R. Then \$112,475 is the present value of an annuity of $n = 360$ payments, with $i = \frac{3}{4}\% = .0075$. Therefore,

$$P = \frac{1 - (1+i)^{-n}}{i} \cdot R$$

$$112{,}475 = \frac{1 - (1.0075)^{-360}}{.0075} \cdot R = 124.2818657 \cdot R$$

$$R = \frac{112{,}475}{124.2818657} = \$905.00$$

(b) The remaining payments constitute a decreasing annuity of 48 payments. Therefore, the unpaid balance is the present value of that annuity.

$$[\text{unpaid balance}] = \frac{1 - (1+i)^{-n}}{i} \cdot R$$

$$= \frac{1 - (1.0075)^{-48}}{.0075} \cdot 905$$

$$= \$36{,}367.23$$

(c) The interest paid during one month is i, the interest rate per month, times the unpaid balance at the end of the preceding month. Therefore,

$$[\text{interest for January 2017}] = \tfrac{3}{4}\% \text{ of } \$36{,}367.23$$
$$= .0075 \cdot 36{,}367.23$$
$$= \$272.75.$$

(d) Since the portions of the monthly payments applied to repay the principal have the effect of reducing the unpaid balance, this question may be answered by calculating how much the unpaid balance will be reduced during 2016. Reasoning as in part (b), we determine that the unpaid balance on December 31, 2015 (just after the 300th payment), is equal to \$43,596.90. Therefore,

$$[\text{amount of principal repaid in 2016}]$$
$$= [\text{unpaid balance Dec. 31, 2015}] - [\text{unpaid balance Dec. 31, 2016}]$$
$$= \$43{,}596.90 - \$36{,}367.23 = \$7229.67.$$

(e) During the year 2016, the total amount paid is $12 \times 905 = \$10{,}860$. But by part (d), \$7229.67 is applied to repayment of principal, the remainder being applied to interest.

$$[\text{interest in 2016}] = [\text{total amount paid}] - [\text{principal repaid in 2016}]$$
$$= \$10{,}860 - \$7229.67 = \$3630.33$$

(f) The total amount of money paid during the 30 years is

$$360 \cdot 905 = \$325{,}800.$$

Since the principal is \$112,475, the rest of the total amount paid is interest. That is,

Now Try Exercise 5

$$[\text{total amount of interest paid}] = 325{,}800 - 112{,}475 = \$213{,}325.$$ ∎

In the early years of a mortgage, most of each monthly payment is applied to interest. For the mortgage described in Example 2, the interest portion will exceed the principal portion until the twenty-third year. Fig. 1 shows how the monthly payment is apportioned between interest and repayment of principal.

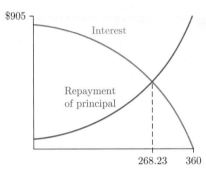

Figure 1

Each new (unpaid) balance can be computed from the previous balance with the formula

$$B_{\text{new}} = (1+i)B_{\text{previous}} - R.$$

That is, the new balance equals the growth of the previous balance due to interest, minus the amount paid. Successive balances are computed by multiplying the previous balance by $(1+i)$ and subtracting R.

If $\$P$ is borrowed at interest rate i per period and $\$R$ is paid back at the end of each interest period, then the formula

$$B_{\text{new}} = (1+i)B_{\text{previous}} - R \tag{1}$$

can be used to calculate each new balance, B_{new}, from the previous balance, B_{previous}.

The Excel spreadsheet in Table 2 on the next page calculates the payment per period and shows the successive balances for the annuity of Example 2. [The entry in cell B4 was set to `=-PMT(B1,B2,B3)`. The form of the payment function is `PMT(rate,nper,pv)`. The value of the payment function is a negative number since the money is paid to the bank. B10 was set to B3 and B11 was set to `=(1+$B$1)*B10-$B$4`. The remainder of the B column was created by selecting the cell B11 and dragging its fill handle. C11 was set to `=$B$1*B10` and D11 was set to `=$B$4-C11`. The remainder of the C and D columns was created by dragging fill handles.]

EXAMPLE 3   **Calculating the unpaid balance on a mortgage** Refer to Example 2. Compute the unpaid balance of the loan on January 31, 2017, just after the 313th payment.

TABLE 2 Amortization table

	A	B	C	D
1	Interest rate	0.75%		
2	Number of periods	360		
3	Principal	$112,475.00		
4	Payment per period	$905.00		
5				
6		**Amortization Table**		
7				
8		Unpaid		Applied to
9	Payment number	balance	Interest	principal
10	0	$112,475.00		
11	1	$112,413.56	$843.56	$61.44
12	2	$112,351.67	$843.10	$61.90
13	3	$112,289.30	$842.64	$62.36
14	4	$112,226.47	$842.17	$62.83
15	5	$112,163.17	$841.70	$63.30
16	6	$112,099.40	$841.22	$63.78
17	7	$112,035.14	$840.75	$64.25
18	8	$111,970.41	$840.26	$64.74
19	9	$111,905.19	$839.78	$65.22
20	10	$111,839.48	$839.29	$65.71
21	11	$111,773.27	$838.80	$66.20
22	12	$111,706.57	$838.30	$66.70

	A	B	C	D
359	349	$9,521.20	$77.61	$827.38
360	350	$8,687.61	$71.41	$833.59
361	351	$7,847.77	$65.16	$839.84
362	352	$7,001.63	$58.86	$846.14
363	353	$6,149.14	$52.51	$852.49
364	354	$5,290.26	$46.12	$858.88
365	355	$4,424.94	$39.68	$865.32
366	356	$3,553.13	$33.19	$871.81
367	357	$2,674.78	$26.65	$878.35
368	358	$1,789.84	$20.06	$884.94
369	359	$898.26	$13.42	$891.58
370	360	$0.00	$6.74	$898.26
371	Payment number	Unpaid	Interest	Applied to
372		balance		principal

Solution By formula (1),

$$B_{\text{Jan}} = (1+i)B_{\text{Dec}} - R = (1.0075) \cdot 36{,}367.23 - 905$$
$$= \$35{,}734.98.$$

Sometimes amortized loans stipulate a **balloon payment** at the end of the term. For instance, you might pay $200 at the end of each quarter-year for 3 years and an additional $1000 at the end of the third year. The $1000 is a balloon payment.

EXAMPLE 4

Determining how much you can afford to borrow How much money can you borrow at 8% interest compounded quarterly if you agree to pay $200 at the end of each quarter-year for 3 years and in addition a balloon payment of $1000 at the end of the third year?

Solution Here you are borrowing in the present and repaying in the future. The amount of the loan will be the present value of *all* the future payments. The future payments consist of an annuity and a lump-sum payment. Let us calculate the present values of each of these separately. Now, $i = 2\% = .02$, $R = 200$, and $n = 12$.

$$[\text{present value of annuity}] = \frac{1 - (1+i)^{-n}}{i} \cdot R$$

$$= \frac{1 - (1.02)^{-12}}{.02} \cdot 200$$

$$= \$2115.07$$

$$[\text{present value of balloon payment}] = \frac{F}{(1+i)^n}$$

$$= \frac{1000}{1.02^{12}}$$

$$= \$788.49$$

Therefore, the amount you can borrow is

Now Try Exercise 11

$$\$2115.07 + \$788.49 = \$2903.56.$$ ∎

INCORPORATING TECHNOLOGY

GC Graphing calculators can easily display successive balances for a loan. Consider the situation from Example 2 in which \$112,475 is borrowed at 9% interest compounded monthly and repaid with 360 monthly payments of \$905. In Figs. 2 and 5, successive balances are displayed in the home screen. In Figs. 3 and 6, successive balances are graphed, and in Figs. 4 and 7 they are displayed as part of an amortization table. (The **Y₂** column gives the interest portion of the monthly payment.)

Figures 2–7 were obtained with the same processes as Figures 1–6 in Section 10.1. Successive balances were determined with the relation

$$B_{\text{new}} = (1+i)B_{\text{previous}} - R.$$

The unpaid balance function to be graphed was specified as

$$\mathtt{Y_1 = 905(1 - 1.0075\,^\wedge\,(X{-}360))/.0075.}$$

The window was set to $[0, 360]$ by $[-15000, 130000]$ with X-scale of 12 and a Y-scale of 10000. In the TABLE SETUP menu **TblStart** was set to **354** on the TI-83/84 Plus and to **356** on the TI-89. The second function was defined as **Y₂=.0075*Y₁(X-1)**; that is, the interest rate times the amount of the previous balance. The up-arrow key can be used to generate earlier balances and interest payments.

TVM Solver with the TI-83/84 Plus In Figs. 8 and 9, TVM Solver is used to solve Examples 2(a) and 2(b). *Note:* The values for PMT are negative since they represent money paid to the bank. ∎

Figure 2

Figure 3

Figure 4

Figure 5

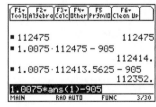

Figure 6

Figure 7

Figure 8. Example 2(a)

Figure 9. Example 2(b)

EXAMPLE 5   **Analyzing the apportionment of mortgage payments** Consider the situation from Example 2 in which $112,475 is borrowed at 9% interest compounded monthly and repaid with 360 monthly payments of $905. When will the repayment of principal portion of the payment surpass the interest portion?

Solution The question can be answered with a table or a graph. (*Note*: The three TI-83/84 Plus screens shown below have TI-89 analogs that can be created in a similar way.)

1. (Table)   As on the previous page, let $Y_1 = 905(1-1.0075^{(X-360)})/.0075$, let $Y_2 = .0075*Y_1(X-1)$, and display the table of Fig. 4. Scroll up the **X** column until an interest greater than half the monthly payment, that is, 452.50 is reached. Set $Y_3 = 905 - Y_2$. Then press ▶ three times to obtain Fig. 10.

2. (Graph)   Let Y_2 and Y_3 be the monthly interest and repayment of principal functions as in part 1. Set the window as in Fig. 11, graph the two functions, and find their point of intersection. See Fig. 12.

X	Y₂	Y₃
268	453.29	451.71
269	449.9	455.1
270	446.49	458.51
271	443.05	461.95
272	439.59	465.41
273	436.1	468.9
274	432.58	472.42

Y₃=451.708727398

Figure 10

```
WINDOW
 Xmin=0
 Xmax=360
 Xscl=12
 Ymin=-250
 Ymax=1000
 Yscl=100
 Xres=1
```

Figure 11

Intersection
X=268.23423 Y=452.5

Figure 12

Now Try Exercise 33

In each case we see that principal repayment will exceed interest after 269 months; that is, after 22 years and 5 months. ∎

ES The section "Using Excel's Financial Functions" of Appendix C shows how the functions IPMT and PPMT are used to calculate the interest and principal reduction portions of a specific payment; that is, the values in column C and D of Table 2. The annuity functions FV, PV, and PMT also apply to mortgages.

Practice Problems 10.3

1. The word "amortization" comes from the French "à mort," meaning "at the point of death." Justify the word.

2. Explain why only present values and not future values arise in amortization problems.

EXERCISES 10.3

1. A loan of $10,000 is to be repaid with monthly payments for 5 years at 6% interest compounded monthly. Calculate the monthly payment.

2. Find the monthly payment on a $100,000, 25-year mortgage at 12% interest compounded monthly.

3. How much money can you borrow at 12% interest compounded semiannually if the loan is to be repaid at half-year intervals for 10 years and you can afford to pay $1000 per half-year?

4. **Car Loan** You buy a car with a down payment of $500 and $100 per month for 3 years. If the interest rate is 9% compounded monthly, how much did the car cost?

5. Consider a $58,331, 30-year mortgage at interest rate 12% compounded monthly with a $600 monthly payment.

   (a) How much interest is paid the first month?

   (b) How much of the first month's payment is applied to paying off the principal?

   (c) What is the unpaid balance after 1 month?

(d) What is the unpaid balance at the end of 25 years?

(e) How much of the principal is repaid during the 26th year?

(f) How much interest is paid during the 301st month?

6. Consider a $21,281.27 loan for 7 years at 8% interest compounded quarterly and a payment of $1000 per quarter-year.

(a) Compute the unpaid balance after 5 years.

(b) How much interest is paid during the fifth year?

(c) How much principal is repaid in the first payment?

(d) What is the total amount of interest paid on the loan?

7. Car Loan Susie takes out a car loan for $8000 for a term of 3 years at 12% interest compounded monthly.

(a) Find her monthly payment.

(b) Find the total amount she pays for the car.

(c) Find the total amount of interest she pays.

(d) Find the amount she still owes after 1 year.

(e) Find the amount she still owes after 2 years.

(f) Find the total interest she pays in year 2.

(g) Prepare an amortization schedule for the first 4 months.

8. Home Financing James buys a house for $370,000. He puts $70,000 down and then finances the rest at 6.3% interest compounded monthly for 25 years.

(a) Find his monthly payment.

(b) Find the total amount he pays for the house.

(c) Find the total amount of interest he pays.

(d) Find the amount he still owes after 23 years.

(e) Find the amount he still owes after 24 years.

(f) Find the total amount of interest he pays in year 24.

(g) Prepare the amortization schedule for the first 3 months.

9. A mortgage at 9% interest compounded monthly with a monthly payment of $1125 has an unpaid balance of $10,000 after 350 months. Find the unpaid balance after 351 months.

10. A loan with a quarterly payment of $1500 has an unpaid balance of $10,000 after 30 quarters and an unpaid balance of $9000 after 31 quarters. If interest is compounded quarterly, find the interest rate.

11. A loan is to be amortized over an 8-year term at 12% interest compounded semiannually, payments of $1000 every 6 months, and a balloon payment of $10,000 at the end of the term. Calculate the amount of the loan.

12. A loan of $105,504.50 is to be amortized over a 5-year term at 12% interest compounded monthly with monthly payments and a $10,000 balloon payment at the end of the term. Calculate the monthly payment.

13. Write out a complete amortization schedule (as in Table 1 at the beginning of this section) for the amortization of a $1000 loan with monthly payments at 12% interest compounded monthly for 4 months.

14. Write out a complete schedule (as in Table 1) for the amortization of a $10,000 loan with payments every 6 months at 12% interest compounded semiannually for 1 year.

15. Mortgage Payments You purchase a $360,000 house, pay $60,000 down, and take out a 30-year mortgage with monthly payments, at an interest rate of 6.3% compounded monthly. How much money will you be paying each month?

16. Terminating a Mortgage In 1998 you purchased a house and took out a 25-year, $50,000 mortgage at 6% interest compounded monthly. In 2008 you sold the house for $150,000. How much money did you have left after you paid the bank the unpaid balance on the mortgage?

17. Cash Flow for a Rental Property You are considering the purchase of a condominium to use as a rental property. You estimate that you can rent the condominium for $1200 per month and that taxes, insurance, and maintenance costs will run about $200 per month. If interest rates are 9% compounded monthly, how large a 25-year mortgage can you assume and still have the rental income cover the monthly expenses?

18. Loan Offers A bank makes the following two loan offers to its credit card customers.

Option I: Pay 0% interest for five months and then 9% interest compounded monthly for the remainder of the duration of the loan.

Option II: Pay 6% interest compounded monthly for the duration of the loan.

With either option there will be a minimum payment of $100 due each month. Suppose you would like to borrow $5500 and pay it back in a year and a half. For which option do you pay the least amount to the bank?

19. Car Loan A car is purchased for $6287.10 with $2000 down and a loan to be repaid at $100 a month for 3 years followed by a balloon payment. If the interest rate is 6% compounded monthly, how large will the balloon payment be?

20. Refinancing a Mortgage A real estate speculator purchases a tract of land for $1 million and assumes a 25-year mortgage at 12% interest compounded monthly.

(a) What is his monthly payment?

(b) Suppose that at the end of 5 years the mortgage is changed to a 10-year term for the remaining balance. What is the new monthly payment?

(c) Suppose that after 5 more years, the mortgage is required to be repaid in full. How much will then be due?

21. Suppose you borrow $10,000 at 4% interest compounded semiannually and pay off the loan in 7 years. Which of items (a)–(d) can be used to fill in the blank in the following statement? (*Note*: Before computing, use your intuition to guess the correct answer.)

If the _____ is doubled, then the total amount paid will double.

(a) amount of the loan

(b) interest rate

(c) number of interest periods per year

(d) term of the loan

22. Suppose you borrow money at 4% interest compounded semiannually and pay off the loan in payments of $1000 per interest period for 5 years. Which of items (a)–(d) can be used to fill in the blank in the following statement? (*Note*: Before computing, use your intuition to guess the correct answer.)

If the _____ is doubled, then the amount that can be borrowed will double.

(a) amount paid per interest period

(b) interest rate

(c) number of interest periods per year

(d) term of the loan

23. Suppose that you make annual payments of $5000 for 20 years into an annuity paying 6% interest compounded annually.

(a) What is the value of the annuity at the end of the 20th year?

(b) Suppose that you elect to have your annuity repaid to you over a 10-year period in annual installments. What is the annual payment you will receive?

(c) Suppose that after you receive payments for 5 years you elect to have the remainder of your annuity paid to you in a lump sum. How much will you receive?

24. Buy Now or Later? According to an article in the *New York Times* on August 9, 2008, economists were predicting that the average interest rate for a 30-year mortgage would increase from 6.7% to 7.1% during the next year and home prices would decline by 9% during that same time period. In August 2008 the Jones family was considering purchasing a $400,000 home. They intended to make a 20% down payment and finance the rest of the cost. What will their monthly payment be if they buy the house in August 2008? A comparable house in August 2009?

25. Comparing Car Loans In August 2008, General Motors was offering the choice of a 0% loan for 36 months, or $1000 cash back on the purchase of a $26,000 Saturn Aura.

(a) If you take the 0% loan offer, how much will your monthly payment be?

(b) If you take the $1000 cash-back offer and can borrow money from your local bank at 6% interest compounded monthly for three years, how much will your monthly payment be?

(c) Which of the two offers is more favorable for you?

26. Comparing Car Loans In August 2008, Toyota was offering the choice of a 0% loan for 48 months, or $2500 cash back on the purchase of a $31,000 4Runner.

(a) If you take the 0% loan offer, how much will your monthly payment be?

(b) If you take the $2500 cash-back offer and can borrow money from your local bank at 6% interest compounded monthly for four years, how much will your monthly payment be?

(c) Which of the two offers is more favorable for you?

27. Repayment of Principal If you take out a 30-year mortgage at 6.8% interest compounded monthly, what percentage of the principal will be paid off after 15 years?

28. Repayment of Principal If you take out a 20-year mortgage at 6.4% interest compounded monthly, what percentage of the principal will be paid off after 10 years?

29. The total interest paid on a 3-year loan at 6% interest compounded monthly is $1,085.16. Determine the monthly payment for the loan.

30. The total interest paid on a 5-year loan at 8% interest compounded quarterly is $2,833.80. Determine the quarterly payment for the loan.

31. Let B_n = balance of a loan after n payments, I_n = the interest portion of the nth payment, and Q_n = the portion of the nth payment applied to the principal. Equation (1) states that $B_n = (1+i)B_{n-1} - R$.

(a) Use the fact that $I_n + Q_n = R$ and $I_n = iB_{n-1}$ to show that

$$B_{n-1} = \frac{R - Q_n}{i}.$$

(b) Use equation (1) and the results that

$$B_{n-1} = \frac{R - Q_n}{i} \quad \text{and} \quad B_n = \frac{R - Q_{n+1}}{i}$$

from part (a) to derive the formula $Q_{n+1} = (1+i)Q_n$.

(c) State in your own words the formula obtained in part (b).

(d) Suppose that for the 10th monthly payment on a loan at 1% interest per month, $100 was applied to the principal. How much of the 11th and 12th payments will be applied to the principal?

32. Let Q_n and I_n be as defined in Exercise 31.

   (a) Use the result in part (b) of Exercise 31 and the facts that $Q_{n+1} = R - I_{n+1}$ and $Q_n = R - I_n$ to show that $I_{n+1} = (1+i)I_n - iR$.

   (b) State in your own words the formula obtained in part (a).

   (c) Suppose that for a loan with a monthly payment of $400 and an interest rate of 1% per month, $100 of the 9th monthly payment goes toward paying off interest. How much of the 10th and 11th payments will be used to pay off interest?

In Exercises 33–40, use a graphing calculator or spreadsheet to answer the questions.

33. Financing a Computer Bill buys a computer for $2188.91 and pays off the loan (at 9% interest compounded monthly) by paying $100 at the end of each month. Determine the balance after 1, 2, and 3 months. After how many months will the loan be paid off?

34. Financing Medical Equipment Alice borrows $20,000 to buy some medical equipment and pays off the loan (at 7% interest compounded annually) by paying $4195.92 at the end of each year. Determine the balance after 1, 3, and 5 years. After how many years will the loan be paid off?

35. A loan of $10,000 at 9% interest compounded monthly is repaid in 80 months with monthly payments of $166.68. How much of the loan will have been paid off after 40 months? When will more than half of the loan have been repaid?

36. A loan of $4000 at 6% interest compounded monthly is repaid in 8 years with monthly payments of $52.57.

After how many months will the loan be one-quarter paid off? One-half? Three-quarters?

37. A 25-year mortgage of $124,188.57 at 8.5% interest compounded monthly has monthly payments of $1000. After how many months will at least 75% of the monthly payment go toward debt reduction?

38. A 30-year mortgage of $118,135.40 at 8.4% interest compounded monthly has monthly payments of $900. After how many months will the amount applied to debt reduction be more than twice the amount applied to interest?

39. Comparing Car Loans In August 2008, General Motors was offering the choice of a 2.9% loan for 36 months, or $2000 cash back on the purchase of a $30,000 Pontiac Grand Prix.

   (a) If you take the 2.9% loan offer, how much will your monthly payment be?

   (b) If you take the $2000 cash-back offer and can borrow money from your local credit union at 7.4% interest compounded monthly for three years, how much will your monthly payment be?

   (c) Which of the two offers is more favorable for you?

40. Comparing Car Loans In August 2008, Ford was offering the choice of a 3.9% loan for 36 months, or $1500 cash back on the purchase of a $21,000 Ford Mustang.

   (a) If you take the 3.9% loan offer, how much will your monthly payment be?

   (b) If you take the $1500 cash-back offer and can borrow money from your local credit union at 8.5% interest compounded monthly for three years, how much will your monthly payment be?

   (c) Which of the two offers is more favorable for you?

Solutions to Practice Problems 10.3

1. A portion of each payment is applied to reducing the debt, and by the end of the term the debt is totally annihilated.

2. The debt is formed when the creditor gives you a lump sum of money now, in the present. The lump sum of money is gradually repaid by you, with interest, thereby generating the decreasing annuity. At the end of the term, in the future, the loan is totally

paid off, so there is no more debt. That is, the future value is always zero!

REMARK You are actually functioning like a savings bank, since you are paying the interest. Think of the creditor as depositing the lump sum with you and then making regular withdrawals until the balance is 0. ∎

10.4 Personal Financial Decisions

You will be faced with several financial decisions shortly after graduating from college. Financial advisers suggest that you open an individual retirement account as soon as you start earning an income. You will probably buy a car and some major appliances with consumer loans. You will consider buying a condominium or a house and will need a mortgage. This section will help you answer the following questions:

- How important is it to open an individual retirement account as soon as possible? What kind of IRA should you open?
- What is the difference between the finance charges on a consumer loan using the add-on method as opposed to the compounding method of Section 10.3?
- How do discount points work and when are they a good choice?
- How do you choose between two mortgages if they have different interest rates and up-front costs?
- What are interest-only and adjustable-rate mortgages, and when are they a good choice?

Individual Retirement Accounts

Money earned in an ordinary savings account is subject to federal, state, and local income taxes. However, a special type of savings account, called an **individual retirement account** (IRA), provides a shelter from these taxes. IRAs are highly touted by financial planners and are available to any individual whose income does not exceed a certain limit. The maximum annual contribution for 2009 is $5000 (but the amount contributed must not exceed the person's earned income). Typically, money in an IRA cannot be withdrawn without penalty until the person reaches $59\frac{1}{2}$ years of age. However, funds may be withdrawn earlier under certain circumstances.

The two main types of IRAs are known as a **traditional IRA** and a **Roth IRA**. Contributions to a traditional IRA are tax deductible, but all withdrawals are taxed. Interest earned is not taxed until it is withdrawn. In contrast, contributions to a Roth IRA are not tax deductible, but withdrawals are not taxed. Therefore, interest earned is never taxed. With a traditional IRA, withdrawals must begin by age $70\frac{1}{2}$. For both types of IRAs, deposits for the year 2009 can be made at any time from January 1, 2009 until April 15, 2010.

EXAMPLE 1

Calculating values associated with a traditional IRA Suppose that for the year 2009 you deposit $5000 of earned income into a traditional IRA, you earn an annual interest rate of 6% compounded annually, and you are in a 30% marginal tax bracket[1] for the duration of the account. We recognize that interest rates and tax brackets are subject to change over a long period of time, but some assumptions must be made in order to evaluate the investment.

(a) How much income tax on earnings will you save for the year 2009?

(b) Assuming no additional deposits are made, how much money will be in the account after 48 years?

(c) Suppose you withdraw all the money in the IRA after 48 years (assuming you are older than $59\frac{1}{2}$). How much will you have left after you pay the taxes on the money?

Solution (a) [income tax saved] = [tax bracket] · [amount]
= .30 · 5000
= 1500

Therefore, $1500 in income taxes will be saved. You will have the full $5000 of earned income to deposit into your traditional IRA.

---

[1] That is, for each additional dollar you earn, you pay an additional $.30 in taxes. Likewise, for each dollar you can deduct, you save $.30 in taxes.

(b) [balance after 48 years] $= P(1+i)^n$
$$= 5000(1.06)^{48} = 81{,}969.36$$

Therefore, after 48 years the balance in the IRA will be \$81,969.36.

(c) Since 30% of the money will be paid in taxes, 70% will be left.

[amount after taxes] $= .70(81{,}969.36) = \$57{,}378.55$ ∎

EXAMPLE 2

Comparing a savings account with a traditional IRA Rework Example 1 with the money going into an ordinary savings account.

Solution (a) None.
$$[\text{earnings after income tax}] = [1 - \text{tax bracket}] \cdot [\text{amount}]$$
$$= \quad .70 \quad \cdot \quad 5000$$
$$= \quad 3500$$

Therefore, \$3500 will be deposited into the savings account.

(b) The interest earned each year will be taxed during that year. Therefore, each year 30% of the interest will be paid in taxes and hence only 70% will be kept. Since 70% of 6% is 4.2%, you will effectively earn just 4.2% interest per year.

[balance after 48 years] $= P(1+i)^n = 3500(1.042)^{48} = \$25{,}218.46$

(c) \$25,218.46, since the interest was taxed in the year it was earned. ∎

Comparing the results from Examples 1 and 2, we see why financial planners encourage people to set up IRAs. The balance upon withdrawal is \$32,160.09 greater with the IRA. The amount of money in the traditional IRA is more than 2.25 times the amount of money in an ordinary savings account.

EXAMPLE 3

Calculating the future value of a Roth IRA Consider the following variation of Example 1. Suppose you earned \$5000, paid your taxes, and then deposited the remainder into a Roth IRA. How much money would you have if you closed out the account after 48 years?

Solution
$$[\text{earnings after income tax}] = [1 - \text{tax bracket}] \cdot [\text{amount}]$$
$$= \quad .70 \quad \cdot \quad 5000$$
$$= \quad \$3500$$

Therefore, \$3500 will be deposited into the Roth IRA.

[balance after 48 years] $= P(1+i)^n = 3500(1.06)^{48} = \$57{,}378.55$

Therefore, after 48 years the balance will be \$57,378.55, the same amount found in part (c) of Example 1. ∎

The result of Example 3 suggests the following general conjecture that is easily verified.

Equivalence of traditional and Roth IRAs With the assumption that your tax bracket does not change, the net earnings upon withdrawal from contributing P dollars into a traditional IRA account is the same amount as would result from paying taxes on the P dollars but then contributing the remaining money into a Roth IRA.

Verification of the Equivalence Conjecture: Suppose P dollars is deposited into a traditional IRA at interest rate r compounded annually for n years. Also, suppose that your marginal tax bracket is k. (In Example 1, $k = .30$.) In general, if taxes are paid on A dollars, then the amount remaining after taxes is

$$A - k \cdot A = A \cdot (1 - k).$$

With a traditional IRA, the future value (or balance) after n years is $[P(1+r)^n]$ and the amount left after taxes are paid is $[P(1+r)^n] \cdot (1 - k)$.

With a Roth IRA, taxes are paid initially on the P dollars and so the amount deposited is $[P \cdot (1 - k)]$. The future value (or balance) after n years is obtained by multiplying the amount deposited by $(1 + r)^n$. That is, the balance is $[P \cdot (1 - k)] \cdot (1 + r)^n$.

Each of the amounts above is the product of the same three numbers; only the order is different. Therefore, the two investments have the same future value. ■

Financial planners not only encourage clients to establish IRAs, but to begin making contributions at an early age. The following example illustrates the advantage of beginning as soon as possible.

EXAMPLE 4

The value of starting an IRA early Earl and Larry each begin full-time jobs in January 2009 and plan to retire in January 2057 after working for 48 years. Assume that any money they deposit into IRAs earns 6% interest compounded annually.

(a) Suppose Earl opens a traditional IRA account immediately and deposits \$5000 into his account at the end of each year for twelve years. After that he makes no further deposits and just lets the money earn interest. How much money will Earl have in his account when he retires in January 2057?

(b) Suppose Larry waits 12 years before opening his traditional IRA and then deposits \$5000 into the account at the end of each year until he retires. How much money will Larry have in his account when he retires in January 2057?

(c) Who paid the most money into his IRA?

(d) Who had the most money in his account upon retirement?

Solution **(a)** Earl's contributions consist of an annuity with $R = 5000$, $i = .06$, and $n = 12$. The future value (or balance) in the account on January 1, 2021 will be

$$F = \frac{(1+i)^n - 1}{i} \cdot R = \frac{(1.06)^{12} - 1}{.06} \cdot 5000 = \$84{,}349.71$$

This money then earns interest compounded annually for 36 years. Using the formula $F = P(1+i)^n$, it grows to

$$84{,}349.71 \cdot (1.06)^{36} = \$687{,}218.34.$$

(b) Larry's contributions consist of an annuity with $R = 5000$, $i = .06$, and $n = 36$. The balance in the account on January 1, 2057 will be

$$F = \frac{(1+i)^n - 1}{i} \cdot R = \frac{(1.06)^{36} - 1}{.06} \cdot 5000 = \$595{,}604.33$$

(c) Larry pays in $36 \cdot 5000 = \$180{,}000$ versus the $12 \cdot 5000 = \$60{,}000$ paid in by Earl. That is, Larry pays in three times as much money as Earl does.

(d) Earl has \$91,614.01 more than Larry. Fig. 1 shows the growths of the accounts. ■

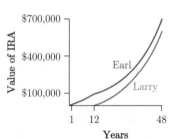

Figure 1

Now Try Exercise 9

Consumer Loans and the Truth-in-Lending Act

Consumer loans are paid off with a sequence of monthly payments in much the same way as mortgages. However, the most widely used method for determining finance charges on consumer loans is the **add-on method**, which results in an understated interest rate. When an add-on method interest rate is stated as r per year, the term of the loan is t years, and the amount of the loan is P, then the total interest to be paid is $P \cdot r \cdot t$. The monthly payment is then determined by dividing the sum of the principal and the interest by the total number of months. For instance, suppose you take out a two-year loan of $1000 at a stated annual interest rate of 6%.

$$[\text{monthly payment}] = (1000 + 1000 \cdot .06 \cdot 2)/(12 \cdot 2)$$
$$= 1000(1.12)/24$$
$$= \$46.67$$

The general formula for the monthly payment R is

$$R = \frac{P(1 + rt)}{12t}.$$

This formula can be solved for r to obtain

$$r = \frac{\frac{12Rt-P}{t}}{P}.$$

Since $12Rt - P$ is the amount of interest paid for the duration of the loan, $\frac{12Rt-P}{t}$ is the amount of interest paid per year and $\frac{\frac{12Rt-P}{t}}{P}$ is the annual percent of the principal that consists of the interest, namely r.

If the loan above were amortized as in Section 10.3, the interest rate would be $i = .06/12 = .005$. The monthly payment would be

$$P = \frac{1 - (1 + i)^{-n}}{i} \cdot R$$

$$1000 = \frac{1 - (1.005)^{-24}}{.005} \cdot R = 22.56286622 \cdot R$$

$$R = \frac{1000}{22.56286622} = \$44.32.$$

This means that the add-on method results in the borrower being charged an additional $46.67 - 44.32 = 2.35$ dollars in interest per month. The problem with the add-on method is that each month the borrower is being charged interest on the entire principal even though after the first month part of the principal has already been repaid.

In 1968, Congress passed the federal Truth-in-Lending Act as a part of the Consumer Protection Act. The law's stated goal is

> to assure a meaningful disclosure of credit terms so that the consumer will be able to compare more readily the various credit terms available . . . .

The Truth-in-Lending Act requires a lender to disclose what is known as the **annual percentage rate** (or **APR**) for any advertised loan. For the loan above, the monthly payment of $46.67 corresponds to an interest rate of 11.134% when the payment is calculated as in Section 10.3. Therefore, the APR is 11.134%.

EXAMPLE 5   **Calculating the monthly payment for a loan with the add-on method**   A one-year loan for $5000 is advertised at 8% using the add-on method. What is the monthly payment?

Solution The interest on the loan is $.08 \cdot (5000) = \$400$. The total amount (principal plus interest) of $5400 is to be paid in 12 monthly payments of $5400/12 = \$450$.   ∎

Now Try Exercise 11

EXAMPLE 6

Determining the interest rate on a consumer loan Suppose a consumer loan of $100,000 for 10 years has an APR of 8% compounded monthly and a monthly payment of $1213.28. What interest rate would be stated with the add-on method?

Solution The total amount paid by the borrower is $120 \cdot 1213.28 = \$145{,}593.60$. Therefore, the interest paid on the loan is $145{,}593.60 - 100{,}000 = \$45{,}593.60$. The interest paid per year is $45{,}593.60/10 = \$4559.36$ which is about 4.56% of $100,000. Therefore, with the add-on method, the interest rate would be given as 4.56%.   ∎

Now Try Exercise 15

The computation of the APR is easily accomplished with a spreadsheet or graphing calculator. For instance, with Excel the APR of 11.134% discussed above is calculated with the RATE function as 12*RATE(24,−46.67,1000,0). This same value is easily obtained on a TI-83/84 Plus calculator with TVM Solver. To determine the APR on an arbitrary graphing calculator, graphically solve the equation $1000 = \frac{1-(1+X)^{-24}}{X} \cdot 46.67$ for X, and then multiply by 12.

Mortgages with Discount Points

Home mortgages have a stated annual interest rate, called the **contract rate**. However, some loans also carry **points** or **discount points**. Each point requires that you pay up-front additional interest equal to 1% of the stated loan amount. For instance, for a $200,000 mortgage with 3 discount points you must pay $6000 immediately. This has the effect of reducing the loan to $194,000, yet requiring the same monthly payment as a $200,000 mortgage having no points.

EXAMPLE 7

Discount points and monthly payments for mortgages Compute the monthly payment for each of the following 30-year mortgages.

Mortgage A: $200,000 at 6% interest compounded monthly, one point

Mortgage B: $198,000 at 6.094% interest compounded monthly, no points

Solution Mortgage A:

$$P = \frac{1-(1+i)^{-n}}{i} \cdot R$$

$$200{,}000 = \frac{1-(1.005)^{-360}}{.005} \cdot R = 166.7916144 \cdot R$$

$$R = \frac{200{,}000}{166.7916144} = \$1199.10$$

Mortgage B:

$$P = \frac{1-(1+i)^{-n}}{i} \cdot R$$

$$198 = \frac{1-\left(1+\left(\frac{.06094}{12}\right)\right)^{-360}}{\left(\frac{.06094}{12}\right)} \cdot R = 165.1235097 \cdot R$$

$$R = \frac{198{,}000}{165.1235097} = \$1199.10$$ ∎

The two monthly payments are the same. With mortgage A, the borrower is essentially borrowing \$198,000 (since \$2000 is paid back to the lender immediately) and then making the same monthly payments as on a \$198,000 loan at 6.094%. The Truth-in-Lending Act requires the lender of mortgage A to specify that the loan has an APR of 6.094%. Purchasing discount points has the effect of changing the APR, which can be calculated by following the steps below.

The following steps calculate the APR for a mortgage loan having a term of n months.

1. Calculate the monthly payment (call it R) on the stated loan amount.

2. Subtract the up-front costs (such as points) from the stated loan amount. Denote the result by P.

3. Find the interest rate that produces the monthly payment R for a loan of P dollars to be repaid in n months.

The interest rate discussed in step 3 can be calculated in Excel with the RATE function as

$$12 * \text{RATE}(n, -R, P, 0).$$

To find the interest rate in step 3 with a TI-83/84 Plus calculator use TVM Solver. On an arbitrary graphing calculator, find the intersection of the graphs of $Y_1 = P$ and $Y_2 = \frac{1-(1+X)^{-n}}{X} \cdot R$, and multiply the X-coordinate by 12.

EXAMPLE 8

Calculating the APR for a mortgage with discount points   Use the three steps just given to calculate the APR for mortgage A of Example 7.

Solution

1. From Example 7, the monthly payment is \$1199.10.

2. $P = 200{,}000 - 2000 = \$198{,}000$ since the up-front costs consist of one discount point.

3. This problem is best solved using technology. The interest rate can be calculated in Excel with the RATE function. The value of

$$12*\text{RATE}(360, -1199.10, 198000, 0)$$

is .06093981. TVM Solver gives the value 6.093981074%. The intersection of the graphs of

$$Y_1 = 198000 \quad \text{and} \quad Y_2 = \frac{1-(1+X)^{-360}}{X} \cdot 1199.10$$

Now Try Exercise 27

occurs at $X = .00507832$. Multiplying by 12 gives an interest rate of .06093984. Therefore, the APR for mortgage A is 6.094%. ∎

The APR allows you to compare loans that are kept for their full terms. However, the typical mortgage is refinanced or terminated after approximately five years; that is, 60 months. Mortgage analysts often rely on the **effective mortgage rate** that takes into account the length of time the loan will be held and the unpaid balance at that time. For the \$200,000 mortgage A discussed in Example 7, the monthly payment is \$1199.10 and we show in Example 9 that the unpaid balance after 60 months is \$186,108.55. With a five-year lifetime, the effective mortgage rate is the interest rate for which a decreasing annuity with a beginning balance of \$198,000 (\$200,000 loan − \$2000 cost of the point) and monthly payment of \$1199.10 will decline to \$186,108.55 after 60 months. A graphing calculator or a spreadsheet can be used to determine that the effective rate of interest for mortgage A is 6.24%. If terminated after 5 years, mortgage A is equivalent to a mortgage of $200,000 at 6.24% interest compounded monthly and having no discount points. That is, with the assumption that mortgage A will be held for only 5 years, the interest rate is effectively 6.24%.

EXAMPLE 9

Calculating values associated with mortgages Consider mortgage A of Example 7. The mortgage had an up-front payment of $2000, an interest rate of 6% compounded monthly, and a monthly payment of $1199.10. Let mortgage C be a 360-month loan of $200,000 at 6.24% compounded monthly with no points.

(a) Find the future value of $2000 after 60 months at 6.24% compounded monthly.

(b) Find the future value of an increasing annuity consisting of 60 monthly payments of $1199.10 with an interest rate of 6.24%.

(c) Find the unpaid balance on mortgage A after 60 months.

(d) Find the monthly payment for mortgage C.

(e) Find the future value of an increasing annuity consisting of 60 monthly payments of the amount found in part (d) with an interest rate of 6.24%.

(f) Find the unpaid balance on mortgage C after 60 months.

(g) Compare the sum of the three amounts found in parts (a), (b), and (c) with the sum of the two amounts found in parts (e) and (f).

Solution (a) Since $.0624/12 = .0052$, the future value of $2000 after 60 months is

$$2000(1.0052)^{60} = \$2730.10.$$

(b) $F = \dfrac{(1+i)^n - 1}{i} \cdot R = \dfrac{(1.0052)^{60} - 1}{.0052} \cdot 1199.10 = \$84{,}179.30$

(c) After 5 years, there are $360 - 60 = 300$ months remaining. The unpaid balance is calculated as the present value of a sequence of 300 payments. Therefore,

$$[\text{unpaid balance after 60 months}] = \dfrac{1 - (1+i)^{-n}}{i} \cdot R$$

$$= \dfrac{1 - 1.005^{-300}}{.005} \cdot 1199.10 = \$186{,}108.55.$$

(d) Let R be the monthly payment for mortgage C. ($P = \$200{,}000$, $n = 360$, and $i = \frac{.0624}{12} = .0052$.)

$$P = \dfrac{1 - (1+i)^{-n}}{i} \cdot R$$

$$200{,}000 = \dfrac{1 - 1.0052^{-360}}{.0052} \cdot R$$

$$200{,}000 = 162.5839228 \cdot R$$

$$R = \dfrac{200{,}000}{162.5839228} = \$1230.13$$

(e) Here we have an increasing annuity with $n = 60$, $i = .0052$, and $R = \$1230.13$.

$$F = \dfrac{(1+i)^n - 1}{i} \cdot R = \dfrac{(1.0052)^{60} - 1}{.0052} \cdot 1230.13 = \$86{,}357.67$$

(f) Mortgage C has $360 - 60 = 300$ months to go. ($R = \$1230.13$, $n = 300$, and $i = .0052$.)

$$[\text{unpaid balance}] = \frac{1 - (1+i)^{-n}}{i} \cdot R$$

$$= \frac{1 - 1.0052^{-300}}{.0052} \cdot 1230.13 = \$186,651.61$$

(g) $[\text{sum of amounts found for mortgage } A] = 2730.10 + 84{,}179.30 + 186{,}108.55$
$$= \$273{,}017.95$$

$[\text{sum of amounts found for mortgage } C] = 86{,}357.67 + 186{,}651.61$
$$= \$273{,}009.28$$

The two sums are very close. This demonstrates the sense in which the two loans are equivalent after 60 months. (The difference of $8.67 is due to round-off error.) ∎

The following steps calculate the effective mortgage rate for a mortgage loan expected to be held for m months.

1. Calculate the monthly payment (call it R) on the stated loan amount.
2. Subtract the up-front costs (such as points) from the stated loan amount. Denote the result by P.
3. Determine the unpaid balance on the stated loan amount after m months. Denote the result by B.
4. Find the interest rate that causes a decreasing annuity with a beginning balance of P dollars and monthly payment R to decline to B dollars after m months.

The interest rate discussed in step 4 can be calculated in Excel with the RATE function as
$$12*\text{RATE}(m, -R, P, -B).$$

To calculate the interest rate with TVM Solver, set $N = m$, $PV = P$, $PMT = -R$, $FV = -B$, $P/Y = 12$ and solve for I%. The interest rate also can be found on a calculator by graphically solving the equation[2]
$$R - iB = (R - iP) \cdot (1+i)^m$$
for i and then multiplying the value of i by 12.

EXAMPLE 10

Calculating effective mortgage rates Use the four steps just given to calculate the effective mortgage rate for mortgage A of Example 7 assuming the mortgage will be held for 5 years.

Solution
1. The monthly payment $R = \$1199.10$ was calculated in Example 7.
2. $P = 200{,}000 - 2000 = 198{,}000$ since the up-front fee consists only of the one discount point.

---
[2]This equation says that the amount of the monthly payment applied to principal in the $(m+1)$st payment is equal to the future value of the amount applied to principal in the first payment. There are several equations that involve m, R, P, and i. We chose this equation since it is one of the simplest.

3. The unpaid balance after 60 months, $B = \$186{,}108.55$, was computed in part (c) of Example 9.

4. This problem is best solved using technology. The interest rate can be calculated in Excel with the RATE function. The value of

$$12*\text{RATE}(60, -1199.10, 198000, -186108.55)$$

Figure 2

is .0624069.

TVM Solver gives an interest rate of 6.240691672% as shown in Fig. 2. With an arbitrary calculator, the interest rate is found by graphically solving

$$1199.10 - X(186108.55) = (1199.10 - X(198000))(1 + X)^{60}$$

for X and then multiplying the answer by 12. The value obtained is .06240696. Therefore, rounded to two decimal places, the effective mortgage rate for mortgage A is 6.24%.   ■

Now Try Exercise 31

NOTE Mortgage analysts have a rule of thumb for calculating the effective mortgage rate for a mortgage with points. For mortgages that will be held for 4 to 6 years, each discount point adds about $\frac{1}{4}\%$ to the stated interest rate. For instance, for the mortgage in Example 10, the rule of thumb predicts that the effective mortgage rate should be $\frac{1}{4}\%$ higher than the stated rate for a mortgage having one discount point. This is very close to the actual increase, .24%. Table 1 extends the rule of thumb to other lifetimes.   ■

TABLE 1	Rule of thumb for the significance of discount points
Lifetime	**Difference between effective mortgage rate and stated interest rate, per discount point**
1 year	1 percentage point
2 years	$\frac{1}{2}$ of a percentage point
3 years	$\frac{1}{3}$ of a percentage point
4 to 6 years	$\frac{1}{4}$ of a percentage point
7 to 9 years	$\frac{1}{6}$ of a percentage point
10 to 12 years	$\frac{1}{7}$ of a percentage point
More than 12 years	$\frac{1}{8}$ of a percentage point

Example 11 shows another way to take the expected lifetime of a loan into account when deciding between two mortgages. If you intend to either sell the house or refinance the loan within a few years, then you should avoid a loan carrying excess points since the large amount of money paid up front will not be recovered. The longer you keep the mortgage, the less expensive points become.

EXAMPLE 11

Using expected lifetime to compare mortgages Suppose a lender gives you a choice between the following two 30-year mortgages of $100,000:

Mortgage A: 6.1% interest compounded monthly, two points, monthly payment of $605.99

Mortgage B: 6.6% interest compounded monthly, no points, monthly payment of $638.66

The best choice of mortgage depends on the length of time you expect to hold the mortgage. Mortgage B is the better choice if you plan to terminate or refinance the mortgage fairly early. Assuming that you can invest money at 3.6% compounded monthly, determine the length of time you must retain the mortgage in order for mortgage A to be the better choice.

Solution The difference in the monthly payments is $638.66 - 605.99 = \$32.67$. Although mortgage A saves \$32.67 per month, it carries two points and therefore requires the payment of an additional \$2000 up front. With mortgage B the \$2000 could be used to generate an income stream of \$32.67 per month for a certain number of months, n, by investing it in an annuity at 3.6% compounded monthly. The value of n is best found with technology.

The number of months, n, can be calculated in Excel with the NPER function. The value of NPER(.003, 32.67, −2000, 0) is approximately 67.74. (*Note*: .003 = .036/12.)

TVM Solver gives a duration of 67.7407041 months as shown in Fig. 3. The number of months, n, also can be found graphically on a calculator by solving

```
■N=67.7407041
 I%=3.6
 PV=-2000
 PMT=32.67
 FV=0
 P/Y=12
 C/Y=12
 PMT:END BEGIN
```

Figure 3

$$P = \frac{1 - (1 + i)^{-n}}{i} \cdot R$$

for n. This equation can be shown to be equivalent to

$$\left(\frac{1}{1 + i}\right)^n = 1 - \frac{iP}{R}.$$

(See Exercise 40 for details.) With the settings $i = .003$, $P = 2000$, and $R = 32.67$, the equation has solution $n = 67.740704$.

Therefore, if you plan to hold the loan for 68 months (about $5\frac{2}{3}$ years) or more, you should choose mortgage A.

Now Try Exercise 53 ∎

Interest-Only and Adjustable-Rate Mortgages

With an **interest-only mortgage**, the monthly payment for a certain number of years (usually five or ten years) consists only of interest payments. That is, there is no amount applied to paying off the principal. At the end of the interest-only period, the monthly payment is determined by the number of months remaining.[3]

EXAMPLE 12   **Calculating monthly payments for an interest-only mortgage** Consider a 30-year mortgage of \$400,000 at 6.6% interest compounded monthly where the loan is interest-only for ten years.

(a) What is the monthly payment during the first ten years?

(b) What is the monthly payment during the last twenty years?

(c) Compare the monthly payment to the monthly payment of \$2554.64 for a conventional 30-year mortgage at 6.6% interest compounded monthly.

Solution Here $P = 400,000$ and $i = \frac{.066}{12} = .0055$.

(a) During the first ten years, the monthly payment is

$$i \cdot P = .0055(400,000) = \$2200.$$

---
[3]We will assume that the interest rate for the second period is the same as the interest rate for the first period. With some interest-only mortgages, the interest rate is reset to conform to prevailing interest rates at that time.

(b) At the beginning of the 11th year, the principal is still $P = 400{,}000$. Since there are $20 \cdot 12 = 240$ months left to pay off the loan, $n = 240$. The value of R is calculated with the formula relating P and R used in Section 10.3.

$$P = \frac{1 - (1 + i)^{-n}}{i} \cdot R$$

$$400{,}000 = \frac{1 - (1.0055)^{-240}}{.0055} \cdot R$$

$$400{,}000 = 133.0721434 \cdot R$$

$$R = \frac{400{,}000}{133.0721434} = 3005.89$$

Therefore, beginning in the 11th year the monthly payment is $3005.89

(c) Since $2554.64 - 2200 = 354.64$, the borrower's payment is $354.64 a month less than a conventional loan for the first ten years. However, since $3005.89 - 2554.64 = 451.25$, the borrower pays an additional $451.25 per month for the last twenty years.

Now Try Exercise 41

Some disadvantages of interest-only mortgages are as follows:

- Interest-only mortgages are riskier for lenders than fixed-rate mortgages and therefore tend to have slightly higher interest rates.
- When the higher monthly payment kicks in, the borrower might have difficulty making the payments.[4]

Some advantages of interest-only mortgages are as follows:

- Borrowers with a modest current income who are reasonably certain that their income will increase in the future can afford to buy a more expensive house.
- In the early years of the mortgage, the savings can be contributed to an IRA that otherwise might not have been affordable.

Another type of mortgage in which monthly payments change is the **adjustable-rate mortgage** (ARM). With an ARM, the interest rate changes periodically as determined by a measure of current interest rates, called an **index**. The most common index in the United States, called the 1-year CMT (constant-maturity Treasury), is based on the yield of 1-year Treasury bills. (During the past ten years, the CMT index has ranged from about 1% to about 6.3%.) The interest rate on the ARM is reset by adding a fixed percent called the **margin** to the index percent. For instance, if the current value of the CMT index is 3% and the margin is 2.7%, then the adjusted interest rate for the mortgage would be 5.7%. The margin usually remains fixed for the duration of the loan.

Of the many types of ARMs, we will consider the so-called 5/1 ARM. With this type of mortgage, the interest rate is fixed for the first five years, and then is readjusted each year depending on the value of an index.

---

[4]The foreclosure crisis of recent years was partially caused by borrowers who expected their house prices to rise. They reasoned that if the mortgage payment was reset to a number that was too much to pay, they would simply sell the house for a profit, repay the loan, and pocket the difference. Or, perhaps they would borrow more based on the new higher value of the home. When house prices actually fell, they faced foreclosure.

Lenders were also at fault. In the 1990s investment bankers developed techniques for packaging mortgages into securities that could be sold to mutual funds and hedge funds. Since there was no perceived risk for the bankers, they lent money to individuals with low credit ratings and questionable ability to repay.

EXAMPLE 13

Calculating values associated with an ARM Consider a $200,000 5/1 ARM that has a 2.7% margin, is based on the CMT index, and has a 30-year maturity. Suppose the interest rate is initially 5.7% and the value of the CMT index is 4.5% five years later when the rate adjusts. Assume that all interest rates use monthly compounding.

(a) Calculate the monthly payment for the first 5 years.

(b) Calculate the unpaid balance at the end of the first 5 years.

(c) Calculate the monthly payment for the 6th year.

Solution (a) $P = \$200,000$, $n = 360$, and $i = .057/12 = .00475$.

The monthly payment for the first 5 years is calculated as follows:

```
N=360
I%=5.7
PV=200000
■PMT=-1160.8008…
FV=0
P/Y=12
C/Y=12
PMT:BEGIN BEGIN
```

$$P = \frac{1 - (1 + i)^{-n}}{i} \cdot R$$

$$200,000 = \frac{1 - (1.00475)^{-360}}{.00475} \cdot R = 172.2948421 \cdot R$$

$$R = \frac{200,000}{172.2948421} = \$1160.80$$

(b) After 5 years, there are $360 - 60 = 300$ months remaining. The unpaid balance is calculated as the present value of a sequence of 300 payments of $1160.80 each.

```
N=300
I%=5.7
PV=185405.1178
PMT=-1160.8
FV=0
P/Y=12
C/Y=12
PMT:BEGIN BEGIN
```

$$[\text{unpaid balance}] = \frac{1 - (1 + i)^{-n}}{i} \cdot R$$

$$= \frac{1 - (1.00475)^{-300}}{.00475} \cdot 1160.80 = \$185,405.12$$

(c) Here $P = \$185,405.12$ and $n = 300$. The annual rate of interest for the 6th year will be $4.5\% + 2.7\% = 7.2\%$. Therefore,

$$i = \frac{.072}{12} = .006$$

```
N=300
I%=7.2
PV=185405.12
■PMT=-1334.1542…
FV=0
P/Y=12
C/Y=12
PMT:BEGIN BEGIN
```

The new monthly payment is calculated as before:

$$P = \frac{1 - (1 + i)^{-n}}{i} \cdot R$$

$$185,405.12 = \frac{1 - (1.006)^{-300}}{.006} \cdot R = 138.9682762 \cdot R$$

$$R = \frac{185,405.12}{138.9682762} = 1334.15$$

Now Try Exercise 43

Therefore, the monthly payment for the 6th year is $1334.15. ■

Caps There are several types of caps that can be specified for ARMs. **Periodic adjustment caps** limit the amount the interest rate can adjust from one adjustment period to the next. **Lifetime caps** limit the interest-rate increase over the lifetime of the loan. **Payment caps** limit the amount the monthly payment may increase from one adjustment to the next. (Periodic adjustment caps and payment caps usually do not apply to the first adjustment.) We will focus on payment caps.

Although payment caps limit the increase to the monthly payment, they can cause a slowdown in the repayment of the principal. The payment cap can even cause the unpaid balance to rise, a phenomenon called **negative amortization**.

EXAMPLE 14

Calculating values associated with an ARM Consider the mortgage discussed in Example 13 and assume that it carries a payment cap of 8%. (That is, the amount of the monthly payment in the 7th year can be at most 8% higher than the monthly payment for the 6th year.) Also, assume that the CMT index is 6.9% at the beginning of the 7th year.

(a) Calculate the unpaid balance of the loan at the beginning of the 7th year, that is, at the beginning of the 73rd month.

(b) Calculate the monthly payment for the 7th year without using the payment cap.

(c) Calculate the monthly payment for the 7th year using the payment cap.

(d) How much interest is due for the 73rd month?

(e) Determine the unpaid balance at the end of the 73rd month.

Solution (a) Here $R = \$1334.15$, $i = .006$, and $n = 288$.

```
N=288
I%=7.2
▪PV=182654.2693
PMT=-1334.15
FV=0
P/Y=12
C/Y=12
PMT:END BEGIN
```

$$[\text{unpaid balance}] = \frac{1-(1+i)^{-n}}{i} \cdot R$$

$$= \frac{1-(1.006)^{-288}}{.006} \cdot 1334.15$$

$$= \$182,654.27$$

(b) Here $P = \$182,654.27$ and $n = 288$. The annual rate of interest for the 7th year will be $6.9\% + 2.7\% = 9.6\%$. Therefore, $i = .096/12 = .008$. The new monthly payment is calculated as before:

```
N=288
I%=9.6
PV=182654.27
▪PMT=-1624.9986...
FV=0
P/Y=12
C/Y=12
PMT:END BEGIN
```

$$P = \frac{1-(1+i)^{-n}}{i} \cdot R$$

$$182,654.27 = \frac{1-(1.008)^{-288}}{.008} \cdot R = 112.4027205 \cdot R$$

$$R = \frac{182,654.27}{112.4027205} = \$1625.00$$

(c) Without the payment cap, the percentage increase in the monthly payment from the 6th year to the 7th year would be

$$\frac{1625.00 - 1334.15}{1334.15} \approx .2180 = 21.8\%$$

Since 21.8% is greater than the payment cap of 8%, the payment cap kicks in to mandate that the monthly payment for the 7th year be

$$1.08 \cdot 1334.15 = \$1440.88$$

(d) The interest due for the 73rd month is

$$.008 \cdot 182,654.27 = \$1461.23$$

(e) The interest due is greater than the monthly payment by

$$1461.23 - 1440.88 = \$20.35$$

Therefore, negative amortization occurs. The $20.35 is added to the previous unpaid balance. The unpaid balance at the end of the 73rd month is

$$182,654.27 + 20.35 = \$182,674.62$$

The increased unpaid balance will be taken into account when the next adjustment of the monthly payment is calculated.

Now Try Exercise 45

A few words of caution about ARMs:

- Usually monthly payments go up when interest rates rise and go down when interest rates fall; but not always.
- Some lenders offer ARMs with an artificially low interest rate, called a *discounted interest rate* or *teaser rate*. Such loans can produce payment shock when the interest rate adjusts.
- If you want to pay off your ARM early to avoid higher monthly payments, you might have to pay a penalty.

Practice Problems 10.4

1. Rework Example 11 under the assumption that the $2000 will not earn any interest.

2. Consider the two loans discussed in Example 7. Calculate the unpaid balance of each loan after 1 month.

3. Which is the better deal for a 30-year mortgage: (a) 6% interest plus three discount points (6.286% APR), or (b) 6.3% interest plus one discount point (6.396% APR)?

EXERCISES 10.4

In Exercises 1 and 2, fill in the blank with the word "free" or "deferred."

1. Interest earned in a traditional IRA is tax _____.

2. Interest earned in a Roth IRA is tax _____.

3. **Traditional IRA** Carlos is 60 years old, is in the 45% marginal tax bracket, and has $300,000 in his traditional IRA. How much money will he have after taxes if he withdraws all the money from the account?

4. **Roth IRA** Rework Exercise 3 for a Roth IRA.

5. **Traditional IRA** If you are 18 years old, deposit $5000 each year into a traditional IRA for 52 years at 6% interest compounded annually, and retire at age 70, how much money will be in the account upon retirement?

6. **Comparing IRAs** Rework Examples 1 and 3 for the case where the marginal tax bracket is 30% when the money is contributed but is only 25% when the balance is withdrawn. Which type of IRA is most advantageous?

7. **Roth IRA** Rework Exercise 5 for a Roth IRA.

8. **Comparing IRAs** Rework Examples 1 and 3 for the case where the marginal tax bracket is 30% when the money is contributed but rises to 35% when the balance is withdrawn. Which type of IRA is most advantageous?

9. **Value of Starting an IRA Early** Redo Example 4 where Earl and Larry are each in a 40% marginal tax bracket, have Roth IRAs, and contribute the remainder of $5000 after taxes are deducted.

10. **Advantage of Prompt IRA Contributions** The contribution into an IRA for a particular year can be made any time from January 1 of that year to April 15 of the following year. Suppose Enid and Lucy both set up traditional IRA accounts on January 1 of 2009 and each contributes $5000 into her account for ten years at 6% interest compounded annually. Assume that Enid makes her contributions as soon as possible and Lucy makes her contributions one year later. Calculate the balances in the two accounts at the time Lucy makes her final contribution.

In Exercises 11–14, use the add-on method to determine the monthly payment.

11. $4000 loan at 10% stated interest rate for one year

12. $6000 loan at 7% stated interest rate for one year

13. $3000 loan at 9% stated interest rate for three years

14. $10,000 loan at 8% stated interest rate for two years

In Exercises 15–18, give the add-on interest rate.

15. A $2000 loan for 1 year at 5% APR with a monthly payment of $171.21

16. A $5000 loan for 1 year at 6% APR with a monthly payment of $430.33

17. A $20,000 loan for 3 years at 6% APR with a monthly payment of $608.44

18. A $10,000 loan for 2 years at 7% APR with a monthly payment of $447.73

19. **Discount Method** Another method used by lenders to determine the monthly payment for a loan is the *discount method*. In this case, the stated interest rate is called the *discount rate* and the formula for determining the total amount paid is

$$[\text{total payment}] = \frac{[\text{loan amount}]}{1 - rt},$$

where r is the discount rate and t is the term of the loan in years. The monthly payment is then $[\text{total payment}]/12t$.

(a) Calculate the monthly payment for a two-year loan of $880 with a discount rate of 6%.

(b) If the add-on method were used instead, would the monthly payment be greater than or less than the amount found in part (a)?

20. True or False For any mortgage with discount points, the APR will be greater than the stated interest rate.

21. True or False For any mortgage that will be terminated before its full term, the effective mortgage rate will be greater than the stated rate.

22. True or False If a mortgage is expected to be held for its entire term, the effective mortgage rate will be the same as the APR.

23. True or False The longer a loan with discount points is expected to be held, the greater its effective mortgage rate.

24. True or False Increasing the discount points for a mortgage increases its APR and its effective mortgage rate.

25. True or False Changing the amount of a loan while keeping the stated interest rate, the term, and the up-front costs the same will have no effect on the APR.

26. True or False Refer to Example 10. If the stated interest rate were 9% instead of 6%, then the effective mortgage rate would be 9.24%. That is, the interest rate would increase by the same amount as before, .24%.

In multiple-choice Exercises 27–30, assume that the loan amount is $250,000 and confirm your answer by calculating monthly payments. (Note: The two monthly payments will not be identical due to round-off error.)

27. The APR for a 25-year mortgage at 9% interest compounded monthly and two discount points is
(a) 8.75%   **(b)** 9.05%   **(c)** 12%   **(d)** 9.25%

28. The APR for a 30-year mortgage at 5.9% interest compounded monthly and one discount point is
(a) 9%   **(b)** 6%   **(c)** 5.7%

29. The APR for a 20-year mortgage at 5.5% interest compounded monthly and four discount points is
(a) 6%   **(b)** 5%   **(c)** 6.5%

30. The APR for a 25-year mortgage at 9% interest compounded monthly and four discount points is
(a) 8.5%   **(b)** 9.5%   **(c)** 11%

In multiple-choice Exercises 31–34, assume that the loan amount is $100,000 and confirm your answer by calculating sums as in Example 9.

31. The effective mortgage rate for a 30-year mortgage at 5.71% interest compounded monthly with 1 discount point that is expected to be kept for 4 years is
(a) 6%   **(b)** 5.54%   **(c)** 6.56%   **(d)** 7%
(*Hint:* For a 5.71%, 30-year mortgage, $R = \$581.03$ and the unpaid balance after 4 years is $94,342.20.)

32. The effective mortgage rate for a 15-year mortgage at 5.481% interest compounded monthly with 3 discount points that is expected to be kept for 10 years is
(a) 5%   **(b)** 6%   **(c)** 6.5%   **(d)** 7%
(*Hint:* For a 5.481%, 15-year mortgage, $R = \$816.08$ and the unpaid balance after 10 years is $42,743.49.)

33. The effective mortgage rate for a 30-year mortgage at 6% interest compounded monthly with 3 discount points that is expected to be kept for 7 years is
(a) 5.5%   **(b)** 6.2%   **(c)** 6.56%   **(d)** 9%

34. The effective mortgage rate for a 30-year mortgage at 9% interest compounded monthly with 2 discount points that is expected to be kept for 7 years is
(a) 9%   **(b)** 8.5%   **(c)** 9.4%   **(d)** 10%

In Exercises 35 and 36, give the two Excel formulas that can be used to obtain the APR and the effective mortgage rate for the mortgage. When calculating the effective mortgage rate, assume the mortgage will be held for 10 years.

35. A 20-year mortgage of $80,000 carrying a stated interest rate of 6% and three points.

36. A 15-year mortgage of $180,000 carrying a stated interest rate of 9% and two points.

In Exercises 37 and 38, give the two equations that can be solved for i with a graphing calculator to obtain the monthly interest rates corresponding to the APR and the effective mortgage rate. Assume that the loans will be held for 5 years.

37. A 15-year mortgage of $120,000 carrying a stated interest rate of 9% and one point.

38. A 20-year mortgage of $150,000 carrying a stated interest rate of 6% and three points.

39. Loan Quandary You decide to buy a $1250 entertainment system for your apartment. The salesman asks you to pay 20% down and is willing to finance the remaining $1000 with a two-year loan having an APR of 5% and a monthly payment of $43.87. (The total of your payments on the loan will be $1052.88.) Suppose you actually have $1000 in your savings account (after the down payment) and can invest it at 4% compounded monthly. You must decide whether or not to take the loan. The salesman tells you that you will come out ahead if you take the loan since $1000 invested at 4% interest compounded monthly grows to $1083.14, which is greater than the total payments on the loan. This doesn't make sense to you since you would be borrowing money at 5% and only earning 4% on the money you invest. What is wrong with the salesman's reasoning? (*Note:* Ignore taxes.)

40. Perform algebraic manipulations on the equation $P = \frac{1-(1+i)^{-n}}{i} \cdot R$ to obtain $\left(\frac{1}{1+i}\right)^n = 1-\left(\frac{iP}{R}\right)$. *Hint:* Multiply the equation by $\frac{i}{R}$, replace $(1+i)^{-n}$ by $\left(\frac{1}{1+i}\right)^n$, and then solve for $\left(\frac{1}{1+i}\right)^n$.

41. Interest-only Mortgage Consider a 15-year mortgage of $200,000 at 6.9% interest compounded monthly where the loan is interest-only for five years. What is the monthly payment during the first five years? last ten years?

42. Interest-only Mortgage Consider a 15-year mortgage of $300,000 at 7.2% interest compounded monthly where the loan is interest-only for five years. What is the monthly payment during the first five years? last ten years?

43. Adjustable-rate Mortgage Consider a 25-year $250,000 5/1 ARM having a 2.5% margin and based on the CMT index. Suppose the interest rate is initially 6% and the value of the CMT index is 4.4% five years later. Assume that all interest rates use monthly compounding.

(a) Calculate the monthly payment for the first 5 years.

(b) Calculate the unpaid balance at the end of the first 5 years.

(c) Calculate the monthly payment for the 6th year.

44. Adjustable-rate Mortgage Consider a 15-year $300,000 5/1 ARM having a 3% margin and based on the CMT index. Suppose the interest rate is initially 6.3% and the value of the CMT index is 3% five years later. Assume that all interest rates use monthly compounding.

(a) Calculate the monthly payment for the first 5 years.

(b) Calculate the unpaid balance at the end of the first 5 years.

(c) Calculate the monthly payment for the 6th year.

45. Adjustable-rate Mortgage Consider the mortgage discussed in Exercise 43 and assume that it carries a payment cap of 7%. Also, assume that the CMT index is 7.7% at the beginning of the 7th year.

(a) Calculate the unpaid balance of the loan at the beginning of the 7th year.

(b) Calculate the monthly payment for the 7th year without using the payment cap.

(c) Calculate the monthly payment for the 7th year using the payment cap.

(d) How much interest is due for the 73rd month?

(e) Determine the unpaid balance at the end of the 73rd month.

46. Adjustable-rate Mortgage Consider Example 14. What is the unpaid balance at the end of the 74th month?

In Exercises 47–56, use a graphing calculator or a spreadsheet to obtain the solution.

47. Find the APR on a $10,000 loan with an add-on method interest rate of 6% compounded monthly for three years.

48. Find the APR on a $15,000 loan with an add-on method interest rate of 8% compounded monthly for two years.

49. Find the APR on a 25-year mortgage of $300,000 carrying a stated interest rate of 6.5% compounded monthly and three points.

50. Find the APR on a 30-year mortgage of $250,000 carrying a stated interest rate of 6% compounded monthly and two points.

51. Find the effective mortgage rate for a 25-year $140,000 mortgage at 6.5% interest compounded monthly with three discount points. Assume that the mortgage will be held for 7 years.

52. Find the effective mortgage rate for a 30-year $250,000 mortgage at 6% interest compounded monthly with two discount points that is expected to be kept for 6 years.

53. Comparing Mortgages Suppose a lender gives you a choice between the following two 25-year mortgages of $175,000:

Mortgage A: 6.3% interest compounded monthly, three points, monthly payment of $1159.84

Mortgage B: 6.5% interest compounded monthly, two points, monthly payment of $1181.61

Assuming that you can invest money at 2.4% compounded monthly, determine the length of time you must retain the mortgage in order for mortgage A to be the better choice.

54. Comparing Mortgages Suppose a lender gives you a choice between the following two 15-year mortgages of $250,000:

Mortgage A: 6.5% interest compounded monthly, one point, monthly payment of $2177.77

Mortgage B: 6.1% interest compounded monthly, two points, monthly payment of $2123.17

Assuming that you can invest money at 3.6% compounded monthly, determine the length of time you must retain the mortgage in order for mortgage B to be the better choice.

55. Comparing Mortgages A lender gives you a choice between the following two 30-year mortgages of $200,000:

Mortgage A: 6.65% interest compounded monthly, one point, monthly payment of $1283.93

Mortgage B: 6.8% interest compounded monthly, no points, monthly payment of $1303.85

Assuming that you can invest money at 4.8% compounded monthly, determine the length of time you must retain the mortgage in order for mortgage A to be the better choice.

56. Comparing Mortgages A lender gives you a choice between the following two 30-year mortgages of $235,000:

Mortgage A: 6.9% interest compounded monthly, one point, monthly payment of $1547.71

Mortgage B: 6.5% interest compounded monthly, three points, monthly payment of $1,485.36

Assuming that you can invest money at 3.3% compounded monthly, determine the length of time you must retain the mortgage in order for mortgage B to be the better choice.

Solutions to Practice Problems 10.4

1. In this case, we merely have to solve $n \cdot (32.67) = 2000$.

$$n = \frac{2000}{32.67} = 61.218$$

Therefore, only take the additional points if you expect to hold onto the loan for more than 61 months (that is, a little more than 5 years).

NOTE This computation is much simpler than the one in Example 11 and can be used to get a rough estimate of the proper number of months. ∎

2. Successive balances can be calculated with the formula $B_{\text{new}} = (1 + i)B_{\text{previous}} - R$. Mortgage A was a $200,000 loan at 6% interest with a monthly payment of $1199.10.

[balance after 1 month]
$$= (1.005) \cdot 200,000 - 1199.10 = \$199,800.90$$

Mortgage B was a $198,000 loan at 6.094% interest with a monthly payment of $1199.10. The monthly interest $i = .06094/12 = .0050783333$.

[balance after 1 month]
$$= (1.0050783333) \cdot 198,000 - 1199.10 = \$197,806.41$$

The balance for mortgage A is $1994.49 higher. The balance will remain higher until the final payment is made.

3. It depends on how long you intend to keep the mortgage. If you expect to hold the mortgage for 30 years, then mortgage A is clearly superior because it has a lower APR. On the other hand, if you expect to terminate the mortgage after two years, then Table 1 on page 508 says that the effective rates are approximately 7.5% $[3 \cdot (\frac{1}{2}\%) + 6\%]$ and 6.8% $[1 \cdot (\frac{1}{2}\%) + 6.3\%]$ respectively, obviously favoring mortgage B.

CHAPTER SUMMARY

1. Money deposited into a *savings account* earns interest at regular time periods. Interest paid on the initial deposit only is called *simple interest*. Interest paid on the current balance (that is, on the initial deposit *and* the accumulated interest) is called *compound interest*.

2. An *increasing (decreasing) annuity* is a sequence of equal deposits (withdrawals) made at the ends of regular time intervals.

3. *Amortization*, a method of retiring a loan (such as a mortgage), consists of a steady stream of equal payments at regular time periods that pays down the loan with interest.

4. The following letters are used with savings accounts, annuities, and loans.

P *principal*, the initial amount of money deposited into a savings account *or* the amount of money borrowed in a loan. P also represents the *present value* of a sum of money to be received in the future; that is, the amount of money needed to generate the future money.

r *annual rate of interest*, interest rate stated by the bank and used to calculate the interest rate per period.

m *number of (compound) interest periods per year*, most commonly 1, 4, or 12.

i the *compound interest rate per period*, calculated as $i = \dfrac{r}{m}$.

n *number of interest periods*.

F *future value*, *compound amount*, or *balance*, value in a savings account or an annuity at some point in the future. For a savings account,

$$F = (1 + i)^n P$$

with compound interest, and $F = (1 + nr)P$ with simple interest.

r_{eff} *effective rate of interest*, the simple interest rate that yields the same amount after one year as the annual rate of interest. $r_{\text{eff}} = (1 + i)^m - 1$.

R rent, periodic deposit into or withdrawal from an annuity *or* periodic payment on a loan.

5. At any time, the *unpaid balance* of a loan is the amount of money needed to retire (that is, pay off) the loan. It is calculated as the present value of all future payments. An additional amount of money paid along with the last periodic payment is called a *balloon payment*.

6. Successive balances can be calculated with the following formulas.

$$B_{new} = (1 + i)B_{previous}$$ savings account with compound interest

$$B_{new} = (1 + i)B_{previous} + R$$ increasing annuity

$$B_{new} = (1 + i)B_{previous} - R$$ loan or decreasing annuity

7. An *individual retirement account* (IRA) is an increasing annuity in which the annual interest earned is either tax free (Roth IRA) or tax-deferred (traditional IRA). Contributions are tax deductible only with a traditional IRA.

8. When finance charges on a consumer loan are calculated with the *add-on method*, the interest paid each month is a fixed percentage of the principal, rather than a fixed percentage of the current balance.

9. For each *discount point* accompanying a mortgage loan, you must pay additional interest up-front equal to 1% of the amount borrowed.

10. The *APR* and the *effective mortgage rate*, which take certain up-front costs into account, are often more useful than the contract interest rate in appraising a loan. Each of them makes use of the reduced loan amount obtained by subtracting the up-front costs from the stated loan amount. The APR is determined by calculating the interest rate corresponding to the reduced loan amount. The effective mortgage rate also takes into account the expected lifetime of the loan and is the interest rate corresponding to an annuity that decreases the reduced loan amount to the balance after the expected lifetime of the loan.

11. With an *interest-only mortgage*, the monthly payments for a certain time period cover only the interest. Subsequent monthly payments completely amortize the loan over the remaining amount of time.

12. With an *adjustable-rate mortgage*, the interest rate is fixed for a specified amount of time and then is reset periodically depending on a floating interest rate determined by an index.

REVIEW OF FUNDAMENTAL CONCEPTS

1. What is meant by *principal*?
2. What is the difference between compound interest and simple interest?
3. What is meant by the *future value* or *balance* in a savings account?
4. How is the interest rate per period determined from annual interest?
5. Explain how compound interest works.
6. Explain how simple interest works.
7. What is meant by the *present value* of a sum of money to be received in the future?
8. Explain the difference between the *nominal* and *effective* rates for compound interest.
9. What is an annuity?
10. What is meant by the *future value* of an annuity? *present value*? *rent*?
11. Describe the two types of annuities discussed in this chapter. In each case, identify the present and future values.
12. Give the formula for computing a new balance from a previous balance for each type of annuity.

13. Give the formula relating F and R in an increasing annuity.
14. Give the formula relating P and R in a decreasing annuity.
15. What are the components of an amortization table of a loan, and how are they calculated?
16. Give the formula for computing a new balance from a previous balance for a loan.
17. What is a balloon payment?
18. Explain how *traditional* and *Roth IRAs* work.
19. How are finance charges on a consumer loan calculated with the *add-on method*?
20. What are *discount points*?
21. How is the APR of a mortgage calculated?
22. How is the effective mortgage rate of a mortgage calculated?
23. What is an interest-only mortgage?
24. What is an adjustable-rate mortgage?

KEY FORMULAS

Simple Interest: $F = (1 + nr)P$, where P is the principal, r is the interest rate, and n is the number of years.

Interest Rate per Period: $i = \dfrac{r}{m}$, where r is the annual interest rate and m is the number of times interest is compounded per year.

Future Value: $F = (1 + i)^n P$, where P is the principal, n is the number of interest periods, and i is the interest rate per period.

Present Value: $P = \dfrac{F}{(1 + i)^n}$, where F is the future value, n is the number of interest periods, and i is the interest rate per period.

Effective Rate of Interest: $r_{\text{eff}} = (1 + i)^m - 1$, where m is the number of interest periods, and i is the interest rate per period.

Increasing Annuity: $F = \dfrac{(1 + i)^n - 1}{i} \cdot R$, where F is the future value, n is the number of interest periods, i is the interest rate per period, and R is the payment made at the end of each period.

Successive Balances in an Increasing Annuity:
$B_{\text{new}} = (1 + i)B_{\text{previous}} + R$

Decreasing Annuity: $P = \dfrac{1 - (1 + i)^{-n}}{i} \cdot R$, where P is the present value, n is the number of interest periods, i is the interest rate per period, and R is the payment made at the end of each period.

Successive Balances in a Decreasing Annuity:
$B_{\text{new}} = (1 + i)B_{\text{previous}} - R$.

SUPPLEMENTARY EXERCISES

1. (PE) If $100 earns 6% interest compounded annually, the future value after 10 years is
   (a) $(100.06)^{10}$ (b) $100 + 10(1.06)$ (c) $100(1.6)^{10}$
   (d) $100(1.06)^{10}$ (e) $100 + (0.06)^{10}$

2. **Saving for Retirement** Mr. West wishes to purchase a condominium for $240,000 cash upon his retirement 10 years from now. How much should he deposit at the end of each month into an annuity paying 6% interest compounded monthly in order to accumulate the required savings?

3. **Mortgage Considerations** The income of a typical family in a certain city is currently $39,200 per year. Family finance experts recommend that mortgage payments not exceed 25% of a family's income. Assuming a current mortgage interest rate of 9% compounded monthly for a 30-year mortgage with monthly payments, how large a mortgage can the typical family in that city afford?

4. Calculate the future value of $50 after a year if deposited at 7.3% compounded daily.

5. Which is a better investment: 10% compounded annually or 9% compounded daily?

6. **Bond Fund** Ms. Smith deposits $200 per month into a bond fund yielding 6% interest compounded monthly. How much are her holdings worth after 5 years?

7. **Nonstandard Mortgage** A real estate investor takes out a $200,000 mortgage subject to the following terms: For the first 5 years, the payments will be the same as the monthly payments on a 15-year mortgage at 12% interest compounded monthly. The unpaid balance will then be payable in full.
   (a) What are the monthly payments for the first 5 years?

(b) What balance will be owed after 5 years?

8. **College Expenses** College expenses at a private college currently average $24,000 per year. It is estimated that these expenses are increasing at the rate of $\frac{1}{2}$% per month. What is the estimated cost of a year of college 10 years from now?

9. What is the present value of $50,000 in 10 years at 6% interest compounded monthly?

10. An investment will pay $10,000 in 2 years and then $5000 one year later. If the current market interest rate is 6% compounded monthly, what should a rational person be willing to pay for the investment?

11. **Car Loan** A woman purchases a car for $12,000. She pays $3,000 as a down payment and finances the remaining amount at 6% interest compounded monthly for 4 years. What is her monthly car payment?

12. **Nonstandard Loan** A businessman buys a $100,000 piece of manufacturing equipment on the following terms: Interest will be charged at a rate of 4% compounded semiannually, but no payments will be made until 2 years after purchase. Starting at that time, equal semiannual payments will be made for 5 years. Determine the semiannual payment.

13. **Retirement Account** A retired person has set aside a fund of $105,003.50 for his retirement. This fund is in a bank account paying 6% interest compounded monthly. How much can he draw out of the account at the end of each month so that there is a balance of $30,000 at the end of 15 years? (*Hint*: First compute the present value of the $30,000.)

14. **Balloon Payment** A business loan of $509,289.22 is to be paid off in monthly payments for 10 years with

a \$100,000 balloon payment at the end of the 10th year. The interest rate on the loan is 12% compounded monthly. Calculate the monthly payment.

15. **Savings Plan** Ms. Jones saves \$100 per month for 30 years at 6% interest compounded monthly. How much are her accumulated savings worth?

16. **Second Mortgage** An apartment building is currently generating an income of \$2000 per month. Its owners are considering a 10-year second mortgage at 12% interest compounded monthly in order to pay for repairs. How large a second mortgage can the income of the apartment house support?

17. **Comparing Investments** Investment A generates \$1000 at the end of each year for 10 years. Investment B generates \$5000 at the end of the fifth year and \$5000 at the end of the tenth year. Assume a market rate of interest of 6% compounded annually. Which is the better investment?

18. **Bond Value** A 5-year bond has a face value of \$1000 and is currently selling for \$800. The bond pays \$5 interest at the end of each month and, in addition, will repay the \$1000 face value at the end of the fifth year. The market rate of interest is currently 9% compounded monthly. Is the bond a bargain? Why or why not?

19. **Effective Rate** Calculate the effective rate for 10% interest compounded semiannually.

20. **Effective Rate** Calculate the effective rate for 18% interest compounded monthly.

21. **Annuities with Extra Deposit** A person makes an initial deposit of \$10,000 into a savings account and then deposits \$1000 at the end of each quarter-year for 15 years. If the interest rate is 8% compounded quarterly, how much money will be in the account after 15 years?

22. **Car Loan** A \$10,000 car loan at 6% interest compounded monthly is to be repaid with 36 equal monthly payments. Write out an amortization schedule for the first 6 months of the loan.

23. **Savings Plan** A person pays \$200 at the end of each month for 10 years into a fund paying 1% interest per month compounded monthly. At the end of the 10th year, the payments cease, but the balance continues to earn interest. What is the value of the fund at the end of the 20th year?

24. A savings fund currently contains \$300,000. It is decided to pay out this amount with 6% interest compounded monthly over a 5-year period. What are the monthly payments?

25. What is the monthly payment on a \$150,000, 30-year mortgage at 9% interest?

26. **Traditional IRA** Elisa, age 60, is currently in the 30% tax bracket and has \$30,000 in a traditional IRA that earns 6% interest compounded annually. She anticipates being in the 35% tax bracket five years from now.

(a) How much money will Elisa have after paying taxes if she withdraws her money now?

(b) How much will Elisa have after paying taxes if she waits five years and then withdraws the money from the account?

27. **Roth IRA** Rework Exercise 26 for a Roth IRA.

28. **Consumer Loan** A consumer loan of \$5000 for 2 years has an APR of 9% compounded monthly and a monthly payment of \$228.42. What interest rate would be stated with the add-on method?

29. **Comparing Loans** Spike is considering purchasing a new computer and has decided to take one of two consumer loans:

Consumer Loan A: 1 year, \$3000, 10% APR, monthly payment of \$263.75

Consumer Loan B: 1 year, \$3000, 6% add-on interest

Which loan should Spike take, and why?

30. Consider a 15-year mortgage of \$90,000 at 6% interest compounded monthly with two discount points and a monthly payment of \$759.47. The APR for the mortgage is obtained by solving $P = \frac{1-(1+i)^{-n}}{i} \cdot R$ for i and then multiplying by 12. What are the values of P, n, and R?

31. Consider a 20-year mortgage of \$100,000 at 6% interest compounded monthly with three discount points and a monthly payment of \$716.43. Assume that the loan is expected to be held for six years at which time the unpaid balance is \$81,298.32. The effective mortgage is obtained in Excel by evaluating $12*\text{RATE}(m, -R, P, -B)$. What are the values of m, R, P, and B?

32. **Comparing Mortgages** Suppose a lender gives you a choice between the following two 25-year mortgages of \$200,000:

Mortgage A: 6.5% interest compounded monthly, two points, monthly payment of \$1350.41

Mortgage B: 7% interest compounded monthly, one point, monthly payment of \$1413.56

Assume that you can invest money at 3.5% compounded monthly. The length of time you must retain the mortgage in order for mortgage A to be the better choice is obtained in Excel by evaluating $\text{NPER}(i, R, -P)$. What are the values of i, R, and P?

33. A 20-year mortgage of \$250,000 at 5.75% interest compounded monthly and two discount points has a monthly payment of \$1755.21. Show that the APR for this mortgage is 6%.

34. A 30-year mortgage of \$100,000 at 5.5% interest compounded monthly and three discount points has a monthly payment of \$567.79. Assume that the loan is expected to be terminated after eight years at which

time the unpaid balance will be $86,837.98. Show that the effective mortgage rate is 6%.

35. **Interest-only Mortgage** Consider a 25-year mortgage of $380,000 at 6.9% interest compounded monthly where the loan is interest-only for ten years. What is the monthly payment during the first ten years? Last fifteen years?

36. **Adjustable-rate Mortgage** Consider a 25-year $220,000 5/1 ARM having a 2.8% margin and based on the CMT index. Suppose the value of the CMT index is 3.5% when the loan is initiated and is 4.55% five years later. Assume that all interest rates use monthly compounding.

 (a) Calculate the monthly payment for the first 5 years.

 (b) Calculate the unpaid balance at the end of the first 5 years.

 (c) Calculate the monthly payment for the 6th year.

Conceptual Exercises

37. If interest is compounded semiannually, will the effective rate be higher or lower than the nominal rate?

38. If you decrease the interest rate for an investment by 10%, will the future value decrease by 10%?

39. Consider a decreasing annuity. If the amount withdrawn each month increases by 5%, will the duration decrease by 5%? Give an example to justify your answer.

40. If you increase the number of months in which to pay off a loan, will you increase or decrease the monthly payment? The total amount of interest paid? Give an example to justify your answers.

41. Give an intuitive explanation why successive payments for a mortgage contribute steadily more towards repayment of the principal.

CHAPTER TEST

1. If $500 is deposited into an account earning 6.5% simple interest, what is the balance in the account after 9 months?

2. Calculate the present value of $5000 payable in 3 years at 4% simple interest.

3. A principal of $1025 is deposited into an account paying 5% interest compounded quarterly for 3 years. What is the future value? How much interest is earned?

4. What is the present value of $25,000 payable in 10 years at 8% interest compounded monthly?

5. Victoria is planning for her retirement by depositing $250 at the end of each month into an annuity paying 6% interest compounded monthly. How much money will have accumulated in 15 years?

6. Find the present value of a decreasing annuity that pays $500 per month for 4 years if the money earns 6% interest compounded monthly.

7. **Increasing Annuity** Calculate the rent of an increasing annuity at 4% interest compounded semiannually if payments are made every 6 months and the future value after 5 years is $12,000.

8. **Decreasing Annuity** Calculate the rent of a decreasing annuity at 9% interest compounded monthly with payments made every month for 10 years and present value $200,000.

9. **Annuity with Extra Deposit** Graham opens an account with $300 and then deposits an additional $50 at the end of each month. What is the balance after 4 years if the money earns 6% interest compounded monthly?

10. **Loan Balance** After making the fifth semiannual payment of $350 on a loan, Wanda's unpaid balance is $2499.93. If the interest rate is 3% compounded semiannually, what will Wanda's unpaid balance be after she makes her sixth payment?

11. **Car Loan** Nigel takes out a 5-year car loan for $8000 at 9% interest compounded monthly.

 (a) What is his monthly payment?

 (b) How much interest is paid the first month?

 (c) What is the unpaid balance after the first month?

 (d) After 4 years, Nigel wishes to retire the loan by making a single payment. How much does he owe?

12. **Nonstandard Mortgage** If you make a $45,000 down payment on a house and take out a 25-year mortgage with quarterly payments of $3500 at 6% interest compounded quarterly, what was the price of the house?

13. **Advantage of Starting an IRA Early** Enid and Lucy each begin full-time jobs in January 2009 and plan to retire in January 2049, after working for 40 years. Assume that any money that they deposit into IRAs earns 6% interest compounded annually.

 (a) Suppose Enid opens a traditional IRA account immediately and deposits $5000 into her account at the end of each year for 11 years. How much money will Enid have in her account when she retires in January 2049?

 (b) Suppose Lucy waits 11 years before opening her traditional IRA and then deposits $5000 into the account at the end of each year until she retires. How much money will Lucy have in her account when she retires in January 2049?

14. A three-year loan for $4000 is advertised at 10% using the add-on method. What is the monthly payment?

15. A 15-year mortgage of $250,000 at 8.829% interest compounded monthly and one discount point has a monthly payment of $2510.31. Show that the APR for this mortgage is 9%.

16. A 30-year mortgage carries two points, is expected to be terminated after 5 years, and has an effective mortgage rate of 6.3%.

   (a) If the expected termination time is increased to 6 years, will the effective mortgage rate increase or decrease?

   (b) If the number of points is increased to three, will the effective mortgage rate increase or decrease?

17. Under what circumstances will the effective mortgage rate and the APR for a mortgage be the same?

18. **Interest-only Mortgage** Consider a 30-year mortgage of $500,000 at 7.8% interest compounded monthly where the loan is interest-only for ten years. What is the monthly payment during the first ten years? Last twenty years?

CHAPTER 10 | PROJECT

Two Items of Interest

Item 1: Successive Interest Computations

1. Suppose a \$100,000 investment grows 3% during the first year and 4% during the second year. By what percent will it have grown after the two-year period? (*Note*: The answer is not 7%.)

2. Rework Exercise 1 for the case where the investment earns 4% during the first year and 3% during the second year. Is the answer to Exercise 2 greater than, less than, or equal to the answer to Exercise 1?

3. Consider an annuity in which \$100,000 is invested and \$10,000 is withdrawn at the end of each year. Suppose the interest rate is 3% during the first year and 4% during the second year. What is the balance at the end of the second year?

4. Rework Exercise 3 where the interest rate is 4% during the first year and 3% during the second year. Is the balance at the end of the second year greater than, less than, or equal to the answer to Exercise 3? Explain why your answer to this question makes sense.

5. Show that if an investment of P dollars declines by 4% during a year, the balance at the end of the year is $P \cdot (1 - .04)$; that is, $P \cdot (.96)$.

6. Show that if an investment of P dollars declines by r% during a year, the balance at the end of the year is $P \cdot (1 - r/100)$. We say that the investment earned $(-r)$%.

7. Show that if an investment of P dollars earns r% one year and s% the following year, then the balance after the two-year period is $P(1+r/100)(1+s/100)$. Conclude that the order of the two numbers r and s does not affect the balance after two years. (*Note*: The numbers r and s can be positive or negative.)

8. Which of the following two statements is true?

   (a) Suppose an investment of P dollars earns 4% one year and loses 4% the next year. Then the value of the investment at the end of the two-year period will be P dollars.

   (b) Suppose investment A earns 4% one year and then loses 3% the next year, and investment B loses 3% one year and then gains 4% the next year. Then the balances of the two investments will be the same after the two-year period.

Item 2: Rule of 72

9. Show that if \$1000 is invested at 8% interest compounded annually, then it will double in about 9 years. (*Note*: $9 = 72/8$.)

10. Show that if \$1000 is invested for 6 years, then it will approximately double in that time if it appreciates at 12% per year. (*Note*: $12 = 72/6$.)

Rule of 72   If money is invested at r% interest compounded annually, then it will double in about $72/r$ years. Alternately, if money is invested for n years, then it will double during that time if it appreciates by about $72/n$% per year.

11. Conclude from the Rule of 72 that for an interest rate of r%, then $(1+r/100)^{72/r} \approx 2$. Also, conclude that for a number of years, n, $(1 + .72/n)^n \approx 2$.

We needn't restrict ourselves to doubling. For instance, the *Rule of 114* says that if money is invested at $r\%$ interest, then it will triple in about $114/r$ years. Table 1 gives the numbers associated with several different multiples. Let's denote the number associated with m by N_m. That is, $N_2 = 72$ and $N_3 = 114$.

TABLE 1

m	Number associated with increasing m-fold
2	72
3	114
4	144
5	167
6	186

12. Notice that $N_6 = N_2 + N_3$. Explain why this makes sense.

13. Explain why $N_{n \cdot p} = N_n + N_p$ for any positive numbers n and p.

14. Find N_{10} and then use that number to estimate the amount of time required for your money to increase tenfold if invested at 8% interest compounded annually. Check your answer by raising (1.08) to that power.

15. Use the values of N_2 and N_3 to find $N_{1.5}$, the number associated with money increasing by one-half. Estimate the amount of time required for $1000 to grow to $1500 when invested at 7% interest compounded annually.

DIFFERENCE EQUATIONS AND MATHEMATICAL MODELS

In this chapter we discuss a number of topics from the mathematics of finance—compound interest, mortgages, and annuities. As we shall see, all such financial transactions can be described by a single type of equation, called a *difference equation*. Furthermore, the same type of difference equation can be used to model many other phenomena, such as the spread of information, radioactive decay, and population growth, to mention a few.

11.1 Introduction to Difference Equations I

To understand what difference equations are and how they arise, consider two examples concerning financial transactions in a savings account.

EXAMPLE 1 **Balance equation** Suppose that a savings account initially contains \$40 and earns 6% interest, compounded annually. Determine a formula that describes how to compute each year's balance from the previous year's balance.

Solution The balances in the account for the first few years can be given as in the following chart, where y_0 is the initial balance (balance after zero years), y_1 is the balance after one year, and so on.

Year	Balance	Interest for year
0	$y_0 = \$40$	$(.06)40 = \$2.40$
1	$y_1 = 42.40$	$(.06)42.40 = \$2.54$
2	$y_2 = 44.94$	$(.06)44.94 = \$2.70$
3	$y_3 = 47.64$	

Once the balance is known for the beginning of a particular year, the balance at the beginning of the next year is computed as follows:

[balance at beginning of next year] = [balance at beginning of previous year]
+ [interest on balance for previous year].

That is,

$$y_1 = y_0 + .06y_0$$
$$y_2 = y_1 + .06y_1$$
$$y_3 = y_2 + .06y_2.$$

(Notice that since $2 = 3 - 1$, the last equation is $y_3 = y_{3-1} + .06y_{3-1}$.) In general, if y_n is the balance after n years, then y_{n-1} is the balance at the end of the preceding year, so

$$y_n = y_{n-1} + .06y_{n-1} \quad \text{for} \quad n = 1, 2, 3, \ldots.$$

This equation can be simplified:

$$y_n = y_{n-1} + .06y_{n-1} = 1 \cdot y_{n-1} + .06y_{n-1} = (1 + .06)y_{n-1} = 1.06y_{n-1}. \quad (1)$$

In other words, the balance after n years is 1.06 times the balance after $n - 1$ years. This formula describes how the balance is computed in successive years. For instance, using this formula, we can compute y_4. Indeed, setting $n = 4$ and using the value of y_3 from the preceding chart,

$$y_4 = 1.06y_{4-1} = 1.06y_3 = 1.06(47.64) = \$50.50.$$

In a similar way we can compute all of the year-end balances, one after another, by using formula (1). ∎

EXAMPLE 2

Balance equation Suppose that a savings account contains $40 and earns 6% interest, compounded annually. At the end of each year a $3 withdrawal is made. Determine a formula that describes how to compute each year's balance from the previous year's balance.

Solution As in Example 1, we compute the first few balances in a straightforward way and organize the data in a chart.

Balance	+ Interest for year	− Withdrawal
$y_0 = \$40$	$(.06)40 = \$2.40$	$3
$y_1 = 39.40$	$(.06)39.40 = \$2.36$	3
$y_2 = 38.76$		

Reasoning as in Example 1, let y_n be the balance after n years. Then, by analyzing the calculations of the preceding chart, we see that

$$y_n = y_{n-1} + .06y_{n-1} - 3$$
[new balance] = [previous balance] + [interest on previous balance] − [withdrawal]

or

$$y_n = 1.06y_{n-1} - 3. \tag{2}$$

This formula allows us to compute the values of y_n successively. For example, the preceding chart gives $y_2 = 38.76$. Therefore, from equation (2) with $n = 3$,

$$y_3 = (1.06)y_2 - 3 = (1.06)(38.76) - 3 = 38.09. \qquad\blacksquare$$

Equations of the form (1) and (2) are examples of what are called *difference equations*.

> **DEFINITION** A **difference equation** is an equation of the form
>
> $$y_n = ay_{n-1} + b,$$
>
> where a and b are specific numbers.

Figure 1

For example, for the difference equation (1) we have $a = 1.06$ and $b = 0$. For the difference equation (2) we have $a = 1.06$ and $b = -3$. A difference equation gives a procedure for calculating the term y_n from the preceding term y_{n-1}, thereby allowing one to compute all the terms—provided, of course, that a place to start is given. For this purpose one is usually given a specific value for y_0. Such a value is called an **initial value**. In both of the previous examples the initial value was 40.

Whenever we are given a difference equation, our goal is to determine as much information as possible about the terms y_0, y_1, y_2, and so on. To this end there are three things we can do:

Figure 2

1. *Generate the first few terms.* This is useful in giving us a feeling for how successive terms are generated.

2. *Graph the terms.* The terms that have been generated can be graphed by plotting the points $(0, y_0)$, $(1, y_1)$, $(2, y_2)$, and so on. Corresponding to the term y_n, we plot the point (n, y_n). The resulting graph (Fig. 1) depicts how the terms increase or decrease as n increases. In Figs. 2 and 3 we have drawn the graphs corresponding to the difference equations of Examples 1 and 2.

3. *Solve the difference equation.* By a *solution* of a difference equation we mean a general formula from which we can directly calculate any terms without first having to calculate all of the terms preceding it. One can always write down a solution using the values of a, b, and y_0. Assume for now that $a \neq 1$. Then a solution of $y_n = ay_{n-1} + b$ is given by

Figure 3

$$y_n = \frac{b}{1-a} + \left(y_0 - \frac{b}{1-a}\right)a^n, \qquad a \neq 1. \tag{3}$$

(This formula will be derived in Section 11.2.)

EXAMPLE 3

Solving a difference equation Solve the difference equation $y_n = 1.06y_{n-1}$, $y_0 = 40$.

Solution Here $a = 1.06$, $b = 0$, $y_0 = 40$. So $b/(1-a) = 0$, and from equation (3),

$$y_n = 0 + (40 - 0)(1.06)^n$$
$$y_n = 40(1.06)^n. \qquad\blacksquare$$

EXAMPLE 4

Solving a difference equation Solve the difference equation $y_n = 1.06y_{n-1} - 3$, $y_0 = 40$. Determine y_{21}.

Solution Here $a = 1.06$, $b = -3$, $y_0 = 40$. So $b/(1-a) = -3/(1 - 1.06) = -3/-.06 = 50$. Therefore,

$$y_n = 50 + (40 - 50)(1.06)^n$$
$$y_n = 50 - 10(1.06)^n.$$

In particular,

$$y_{21} = 50 - 10(1.06)^{21}.$$

Since $(1.06)^{21} \approx 3.4$,

$$y_{21} \approx 50 - 10(3.4) = 50 - 34 = 16.$$

So, after 21 years, the bank account of Example 2 will contain about $16. [If we did not have the solution $y_n = 50 - 10(1.06)^n$, we would need to perform 21 successive calculations in order to determine y_{21}.] ■

In the next two examples we apply our entire three-step procedure to analyze some specific difference equations.

EXAMPLE 5

Analyzing a difference equation Apply the three-step procedure to study the difference equation $y_n = .2y_{n-1} + 4.8$, $y_0 = 1$.

Solution First we compute a few terms:

$$y_0 = 1$$
$$y_1 = .2(1) + 4.8 = 5$$
$$y_2 = .2(5) + 4.8 = 5.8$$
$$y_3 = .2(5.8) + 4.8 = 5.96$$
$$y_4 = .2(5.96) + 4.8 = 5.992.$$

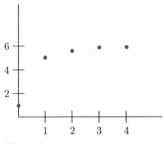

Figure 4

Next, we graph these terms (Fig. 4). That is, we plot $(0, 1)$, $(1, 5)$, $(2, 5.8)$, $(3, 5.96)$, $(4, 5.992)$. Note that the values of y_n increase. Finally, we solve the difference equation. Here $a = .2$, $b = 4.8$, $y_0 = 1$. Thus,

$$\frac{b}{1-a} = \frac{4.8}{1 - .2} = \frac{4.8}{.8} = 6$$

Now Try Exercise 7

$$y_n = 6 + (1 - 6)(.2)^n = 6 - 5(.2)^n. \qquad ■$$

EXAMPLE 6

Analyzing a difference equation Apply the three-step procedure to study the difference equation $y_n = -.8y_{n-1} + 9$, $y_0 = 10$.

Solution The first few terms are

$$y_0 = 10$$
$$y_1 = -.8(10) + 9 = -8 + 9 = 1$$
$$y_2 = -.8(1) + 9 = -.8 + 9 = 8.2$$
$$y_3 = -.8(8.2) + 9 = 2.44$$
$$y_4 = -.8(2.44) + 9 = 7.048.$$

The graph in Fig. 5 corresponds to these terms. Notice that in this case the points oscillate up and down. To solve the difference equation, note that

$$\frac{b}{1-a} = \frac{9}{1-(-.8)} = \frac{9}{1.8} = 5.$$

Thus

Now Try Exercise 11

$$y_n = 5 + (10 - 5)(-.8)^n = 5 + 5(-.8)^n.$$ ∎

Figure 5

Difference equations can be used to describe many real-life situations. The solution of a particular difference equation in such instances yields a mathematical model of the situation. For example, consider the banking problem of Example 2. We described the activity in the account by a difference equation, where y_n represents the amount of money in the account after n years. Solving the difference equation, we found that

$$y_n = 50 - 10(1.06)^n.$$

And this formula gives a mathematical model of the bank account.

Here is another example of a mathematical model derived using difference equations.

EXAMPLE 7

Population modeling Suppose that the population of a certain country is currently 6 million. The growth of this population attributable to an excess of births over deaths is 2% per year. Further, the country is experiencing immigration at the rate of 40,000 people per year.

(a) Find a mathematical model for the population of the country.

(b) What will be the population of the country after 35 years?

Solution (a) Let y_n denote the population (in millions) of the country after n years. Then $y_0 = 6$. The growth of the population in year n due to an excess of births over deaths is $.02y_{n-1}$. There are $.04$ (million) immigrants each year. Therefore,

$$y_n = y_{n-1} + .02y_{n-1} + .04 = 1.02y_{n-1} + .04.$$

So the terms satisfy the difference equation

$$y_n = 1.02y_{n-1} + .04, \qquad y_0 = 6.$$

Here

$$\frac{b}{1-a} = \frac{.04}{1 - 1.02} = \frac{.04}{-.02} = -2$$

$$y_n = -2 + (6 - (-2))(1.02)^n \qquad \text{or}$$

$$y_n = -2 + 8(1.02)^n.$$

This last formula is our desired mathematical model for the population.

(b) To determine the population after 35 years, merely compute y_{35}:

$$y_{35} = -2 + 8(1.02)^{35} \approx -2 + 8(2) = 14,$$

Now Try Exercise 19

since $(1.02)^{35} \approx 2$. So the population after 35 years will be about 14 million. ∎

INCORPORATING TECHNOLOGY

GC Graphing calculators can easily generate successive terms of a difference equation. Consider the difference equation $y_n = .2y_{n-1} + 4.8$, $y_0 = 1$ of Example 5. In Figs. 6 and 9 on the next page successive terms are displayed in the home screen. In Figs. 7 and 10 successive terms are graphed, and in Figs. 8 and 11 they are displayed in a table.

Figure 6

Figure 7. Trace cursor after being moved several times.

Figure 8

Figure 9

Figure 10

Figure 11

Displaying successive terms on the home screen In Figs. 6 and 9, after the initial value (1) is entered, the last displayed value (1) is assigned to **Ans** (on the TI-83/84 Plus) or **ans(1)** (on the TI-89). The instruction **.2*Ans+4.8** (or **.2*ans(1)+4.8** on the TI-89) generates the next term (5) and assigns it to **Ans** (or **ans(1)**). Each subsequent press of ENTER generates another term.

Graphs with the TI-83/84 Plus and TI-89 In order to obtain the graphs in Figs. 7 and 10 the calculator must be set to sequence mode. This is accomplished by pressing MODE and selecting **Seq** on the fourth line of the TI-83/84 Plus, or setting **Graph** to **SEQUENCE** on the TI-89. In the **Y=** editor, difference equations are defined with letters such as **u**, **v**, **u1**, and **u2** instead of y. In the **Y=** editor of the TI-83/84 Plus, set n**Min** $= 0$, set **u(n)=.2u(n-1)+4.8**, and set **u(nMin)** $= \{1\}$. (n**Min** is the minimum value of n, always 0 for our purposes.) In the **Y=** editor of the TI-89, set **u1 = .2*u1(n-1)+4.8**, and set **ui1=1**. (**ui1** is the initial value of the difference equation.) (*Note*: After u or u1 has been defined, values of u(n) or u1(n) can be displayed on the home screen by entering expressions such as **u(5)** or **u1(5)**.)

The familiar items in the WINDOW screen, **Xmin**, **Xmax**, **Xscl**, **Ymin**, **Ymax**, and **Yscl** have the same meanings as with graphs of functions. Points will be evaluated for values of n from **nMin** to **nMax**, and points will be plotted starting at **PlotStart**. When **PlotStart** is set to 1, graphing begins at y_0. When **PlotStep** is set to 1, no points are skipped. In Figs. 7 and 10, the settings were $[-.1, 6]$ *by* $[-2, 8]$ (on the TI-83/84 Plus) and $[-1, 7]$ *by* $[-1, 7]$ (on the TI-89), **nMin** $= 0$, **nMax** $= 6$, and **PlotStart** $=$ **PlotStep** $= 1$.

We pressed GRAPH (on the TI-83/84 Plus) or ◆ [GRAPH] (on the TI-89) to display the graphs of the difference equations. You can press TRACE (on the TI-83/84 Plus) or F3 (on the TI-89) to obtain a trace cursor. Each time you press the right-arrow key, the trace cursor will move to the next point and its coordinates will be displayed.

Tables with the TI-83/84 Plus and TI-89 In order to obtain the tables in Figs. 8 and 11, the setting in the **Y=** editor is the same as for graphs. Then 2nd [TBLSET] (on the TI-83/84 Plus) or ◆ [TblSet] (on the TI-89) was pressed to bring up the TABLE SETUP screen. **TblStart** was set to 0, and Δ**Tbl** was set to 1. Finally,

2nd [TABLE] (on the TI-83/84 Plus) or ◆ [TABLE] (on the TI-89) was pressed to bring up the table. You can use the down-arrow key to generate further terms. ∎

ES The table and graph in Fig. 12 are easily created in an Excel spreadsheet. The following steps create the second column of the table:

1. To enter the numbers 0 through 6 in the first column, enter **0** into cell A2, enter **1** into cell A3, select the two cells, and drag the fill handle down to A8.
2. Type **1** into cell B2 and press Enter.
3. Type **=.2*B2+4.8** into cell B3 and press Enter.
4. Click on cell B3 and drag its fill handle down to B8.

To create the graph, carry out the following steps:

1. Select the range A2:B8.
2. (Excel 2007) On the **Insert** tab, in the **Charts** group, click on **Scatter**. (Excel 97-2003) Click the **Chart Wizard** button (holds a picture of a histogram) on the toolbar, and click on **XY (Scatter)** in the **Chart type** list box.
3. (Excel 2007) Click on **Scatter with only Markers** in the gallery that opens. *Note*: You can rest the mouse on any chart type to see its name. (Excel 97-2003) Click on the **Finish** button.
4. Click on the legend located to the right of the graph and press the **Del** key.

	A	B
1	n	y_n
2	0	1
3	1	5
4	2	5.8
5	3	5.96
6	4	5.992
7	5	5.9984
8	6	5.99968
9		
10		

Figure 12. Excel table and graph for $y_n = .2y_{n-1} + 4.8$.

Practice Problems 11.1

1. Consider the difference equation $y_n = -2y_{n-1} + 21$, $y_0 = 7.5$.
   (a) Generate y_0, y_1, y_2, y_3, and y_4 from the difference equation.
   (b) Graph these first few terms.
   (c) Solve the difference equation.

2. Use the solution in Problem 1(c) to obtain the terms y_0, y_1, and y_2.

EXERCISES 11.1

For each of the difference equations in Exercises 1–6, identify a and b and compute $b/(1 - a)$.

1. $y_n = 4y_{n-1} - 6$
2. $y_n = -3y_{n-1} + 16$
3. $y_n = -\frac{1}{2}y_{n-1}$
4. $y_n = \frac{1}{3}y_{n-1} + 4$
5. $y_n = -\frac{2}{3}y_{n-1} + 15$
6. $y_n = .5y_{n-1} - 4$

In Exercises 7–14, (a) generate y_0, y_1, y_2, y_3, y_4 from the difference equation. (b) Graph these first few terms. (c) Solve the difference equation.

7. $y_n = \frac{1}{2}y_{n-1} - 1$, $y_0 = 10$

8. $y_n = .5y_{n-1} + 5$, $y_0 = 2$

9. $y_n = 2y_{n-1} - 3$, $y_0 = 3.5$

10. $y_n = 5y_{n-1} - 32$, $y_0 = 8$

11. $y_n = -.4y_{n-1} + 7$, $y_0 = 17.5$

12. $y_n = -2y_{n-1}$, $y_0 = \frac{1}{2}$

13. $y_n = 2y_{n-1} - 16$, $y_0 = 15$

14. $y_n = 2y_{n-1} + 3$, $y_0 = -2$

15. The solution to $y_n = .2y_{n-1} + 4.8$, $y_0 = 1$ is $y_n = 6 - 5(.2)^n$. Use the solution to compute y_0, y_1, y_2, y_3, y_4.

16. The solution to $y_n = -.8y_{n-1} + 9$, $y_0 = 10$ is $y_n = 5 + 5(-.8)^n$. Use the solution to compute y_0, y_1, y_2.

17. **Account Balance** One thousand dollars is deposited into a savings account paying 5% interest compounded annually. Let y_n be the amount after n years. What is the difference equation showing how to compute y_n from y_{n-1}?

18. **Population Decline** The population of a certain country is currently 70 million but is declining at the rate of 1% each year. Let y_n be the population after n years. Find a difference equation showing how to compute y_n from y_{n-1}.

19. **Population Decline** The population of a certain country is currently 70 million but is declining at the rate of 1% each year due to an excess of deaths over births. In addition, the country is losing one million people each year due to emigration. Let y_n be the population after n years. Find a difference equation satisfied by y_n.

20. **Account Balance** One thousand dollars is deposited into an account paying 5% interest compounded annually. At the end of each year $100 is added to the account. Let y_n be the amount in the account after n years. Find a difference equation satisfied by y_n.

21. Consider the difference equation $y_n = y_{n-1} + 2$, $y_0 = 1$.

    (a) Generate y_0, y_1, y_2, y_3, y_4.

    (b) What is special about the graph?

    (c) Why cannot formula (3) be used to obtain the solution?

22. Rework Exercise 21 for $y_n = y_{n-1} - 2$, $y_0 = 10$.

23. **Loan Balance** Suppose that you take a consumer loan for $55 at 20% annual interest and pay off $36 at the end of each year for two years. Compute the balance on the loan immediately after you make the first payment (i.e., the amount you would pay if you wanted to settle the account at the beginning of the second year).

24. **Loan Balance** Refer to Exercise 23. Set up the difference equation for y_n, the balance after n years.

25. **Savings Plan** Ferdinand knows that he will need to replace his home office equipment someday. He deposits $800 into a savings account paying 4% interest compounded annually. At the end of each year he deposits $250 into the account. Let y_n be the amount in the account after n years.

    (a) Find a difference equation satisfied by y_n.

    (b) Solve the difference equation.

    (c) How much money will he have in the account after 7 years?

26. **Loan Balance** Anne takes out a $317 loan at 10% annual interest. She pays off $100 at the end of each year for 4 years. Compute the balance on the loan immediately after she makes the first payment. Compute the balance after the second payment.

27. **Automobile Depreciation** A rule of thumb states that cars in personal use depreciate by 15% each year. Suppose a new car is purchased for $20,000. Let y_n be the value of the car after n years.

    (a) Find a difference equation satisfied by y_n.

    (b) Solve the difference equation.

    (c) How much will the car be worth after 5 years?

Exercises 28–34 require the use of a graphing calculator or spreadsheet.

In these exercises,

(a) Generate a table displaying the values of y_0 to y_6.

(b) Graph the first 24 terms of the difference equation.

(c) Use the table or graph to answer the questions.

28. $y_n = 1.2y_{n-1} - 2$, $y_0 = 12.5$. What is y_{11}? For what value of n does y_n first exceed 100?

29. $y_n = 1.05y_{n-1} - 7.8$, $y_0 = 102.67$. What is y_{14} (rounded to two decimal places)? For what value of n does $y_n = 0$ (rounded to two decimal places)?

30. $y_n = .8y_{n-1} + .6$, $y_0 = 10$. What is y_{12}? For what values of n is y_n within .1 units of 3?

31. $y_n = -.85y_{n-1} + 11.1$, $y_0 = 4$. What is y_{12}? For what values of n is y_n within .1 units of 6?

32. $y_n = -1.05y_{n-1} + 1.5$, $y_0 = 10$. What is y_{14}? For what value of n is y_n approximately 23.037?

33. $y_n = .75y_{n-1} + 1.25$, $y_0 = 2$. What is y_{10}? For what values of n is y_n within .01 units of 5?

34. $y_n = -y_{n-1} + .2$, $y_0 = 1$. What special behavior do the terms exhibit?

Solutions to Practice Problems 11.1

1. (a) $y_0 = 7.5.$

$y_1 = -2(7.5) + 21 = -15 + 21 = 6.$

$y_2 = -2(6) + 21 = -12 + 21 = 9.$

$y_3 = -2(9) + 21 = -18 + 21 = 3.$

$y_4 = -2(3) + 21 = -6 + 21 = 15.$

(b) We graph the points $(0, 7.5)$, $(1, 6)$, $(2, 9)$, $(3, 3)$, $(4, 15)$ in Fig. 13. (In order to accommodate the points, we use a different scale for each axis.)

Figure 13

(c) $y_n = \dfrac{b}{1-a} + \left(y_0 - \dfrac{b}{1-a}\right)a^n.$

Since $a = -2$ and $b = 21$,

$$\frac{b}{1-a} = \frac{21}{1-(-2)} = \frac{21}{3} = 7.$$

$$y_n = 7 + (7.5 - 7)(-2)^n = 7 + \tfrac{1}{2}(-2)^n.$$

2. $y_n = 7 + \tfrac{1}{2}(-2)^n.$

$y_0 = 7 + \tfrac{1}{2}(-2)^0 = 7 + \tfrac{1}{2} = 7.5.$

(Here we have used the fact that any number to the zeroth power is 1.)

$y_1 = 7 + \tfrac{1}{2}(-2)^1 = 7 + \tfrac{1}{2}(-2) = 7 - 1 = 6.$

$y_2 = 7 + \tfrac{1}{2}(-2)^2 = 7 + \tfrac{1}{2}(4) = 7 + 2 = 9.$

11.2 Introduction to Difference Equations II

The main result of Section 11.1 is the following:

> The difference equation $y_n = ay_{n-1} + b$, with $a \neq 1$, has solution
>
> $$y_n = \frac{b}{1-a} + \left(y_0 - \frac{b}{1-a}\right)a^n. \tag{1}$$

When $a = 1$, the difference equation $y_n = a \cdot y_{n-1} + b$ is $y_n = 1 \cdot y_{n-1} + b$ or just $y_n = y_{n-1} + b$. In this case the solution is given by a formula different from (1):

> The difference equation $y_n = y_{n-1} + b$ has the solution
>
> $$y_n = y_0 + bn. \tag{2}$$

EXAMPLE 1   **Solving a difference equation of the form $y_n = y_{n-1} + b$**

(a) Solve the difference equation $y_n = y_{n-1} + 2$, $y_0 = 3$.

(b) Find y_{100}.

Solution   **(a)** Since $a = 1$, the solution is given by (2). Here $b = 2$, $y_0 = 3$. Therefore,

$$y_n = 3 + 2n.$$

(b) $y_{100} = 3 + 2(100) = 203.$

Now Try Exercise 1   *Note:* Without (2), determining y_{100} would require 100 computations. ∎

Both (1) and (2) are derived at the end of this section. Before deriving them, however, let us see what they tell us about simple interest, compound interest, and consumer loans.

Simple Interest Suppose that a certain amount of money is deposited in a savings account. If interest is paid only on the initial deposit (and not on accumulated interest), then the interest is called **simple interest**. For example, if $40 is deposited at 6% simple interest, then each year the account earns .06(40), or $2.40. So the bank balance accumulates as follows:

Year	Amount	Interest
0	$40.00	$2.40
1	42.40	2.40
2	44.80	2.40
3	47.20	

EXAMPLE 2

Modeling simple interest

(a) Find a formula for y_n, the amount in the aforementioned account at the end of n years.

(b) Find the amount at the end of 10 years.

Solution (a) Let y_n = the amount at the end of n years. So $y_0 = 40$. Moreover,

[amount at end of n years] = [amount at end of $n - 1$ years] + [interest].
$$y_n \qquad = \qquad y_{n-1} \qquad + \quad 2.40.$$

This difference equation has $a = 1$, $b = 2.40$, so from formula (2),

$$y_n = y_0 + bn = 40 + (2.40)n.$$

This is the desired formula.

Now Try Exercise 7 (b) $y_{10} = 40 + (2.40)10 = 40 + 24.00 = \$64.$ ∎

Compound Interest When interest is calculated on the current amount in the account (instead of on the amount initially deposited), the interest is called **compound interest**. The interest discussed in Section 11.1 was compound, being computed on the balance at the end of each year. Such interest is called *annual* compound interest. Often interest is compounded more than once a year. For example, an interest rate might be stated as 6% compounded *semiannually*. This means that interest is computed every 6 months, with 3% given for each 6-month period. At the end of each such period the interest is added to the balance, which is then used to compute the interest for the next 6-month period. Similarly, 6% *interest compounded quarterly* means .06/4 or .015 interest four times a year. And 6% interest compounded six times a year means .06/6 or .01 interest each interest period of 2 months. Or, in general, if 6% interest is compounded k times a year, then .06/k interest is earned k times a year. This illustrates the following general definition:

DEFINITION If interest is at a yearly rate r and is compounded k times per year, then the **interest rate per period** (denoted i) is $i = r/k$.

EXAMPLE 3

Modeling compound interest Suppose that the interest rate is 6% compounded monthly. Find a formula for the amount after n months.

Solution Here $r = .06$, $k = 12$, so that the monthly interest rate is $i = .005$. Let y_n denote the amount after n months. Then, reasoning as in Section 11.1,

$$y_n = y_{n-1} + .005y_{n-1} = 1.005y_{n-1}.$$

The solution of this difference equation is obtained as follows:

Now Try Exercise 3

$$\frac{b}{1-a} = 0 \qquad y_n = 0 + (y_0 - 0)(1.005)^n = y_0(1.005)^n.$$

EXAMPLE 4

Modeling simple and compound interest Suppose that interest is computed at the rate i per interest period. Find a general formula for the balance y_n after n interest periods under (a) simple interest, (b) compound interest.

Solution (a) With simple interest, the interest each period is just i times the initial amount—that is, $i \cdot y_0$. Therefore,

$$y_n = y_{n-1} + iy_0.$$

Apply (2) with $b = iy_0$. Then

$$y_n = y_0 + (iy_0)n.$$

(b) With compound interest, the interest each period is i times the current balance, or $i \cdot y_n$. Therefore,

$$y_n = y_{n-1} + iy_{n-1} = (1+i)y_{n-1}.$$

Here $b/(1-a) = 0$, so that

$$y_n = 0 + (y_0 - 0)(1+i)^n = y_0(1+i)^n.$$

Summarizing,

If y_0 dollars is deposited at interest rate i per period, then the amount after n interest periods is

Simple interest: $y_n = y_0 + (iy_0)n$ (3)

Compound interest: $y_n = y_0(1+i)^n.$ (4)

EXAMPLE 5

Account balance How much money will you have after seven years if you deposit $500 at 4% interest compounded quarterly?

Solution Apply formula (4). Here a period is a quarter, or 3 months. In 7 years there are $7 \cdot 4 = 28$ periods. The interest rate per period is

$$i = \frac{.04}{4} = .01.$$

The amount after 28 periods is

Now Try Exercise 9

$$y_{28} = 500(1.01)^{28} = \$660.65.$$

Consumer Loans It is common for people to buy cars or appliances "on time." Basically, they are borrowing money from the dealer and repaying it (with interest) with several equal payments until the loan is paid off. Each time period, part of the payment goes toward paying the interest and part goes toward reducing the balance of the loan. A consumer loan used to purchase a house is called a **mortgage**.

EXAMPLE 6

Loan balance Suppose that a consumer loan of $2400 carries an interest rate of 12% compounded annually and a yearly payment of $1000.

(a) Write down a difference equation for y_n, the balance owed after n years.

(b) Compute the balances after 1, 2, and 3 years.

Solution **(a)** At the end of each year the new balance is computed as follows:

$$[\text{new balance}] = [\text{previous balance}] + [\text{interest}] - [\text{payment}].$$

Since the interest is compound, it is computed on the previous balance:

$$y_n = y_{n-1} + .12y_{n-1} - 1000.$$

Thus

$$y_n = 1.12y_{n-1} - 1000, \qquad y_0 = 2400$$

is the desired difference equation.

(b) $y_1 = 1.12y_0 - 1000 = (1.12)(2400) - 1000 = \$1688$

$y_2 = 1.12y_1 - 1000 = (1.12)(1688) - 1000 = 890.56$

$y_3 = 1.12y_2 - 1000 = (1.12)(891) - 1000 \approx 0.$

Now Try Exercise 17

Although savings accounts using simple interest are practically unheard of, consumer loans are often computed using simple interest. Under simple interest, interest is paid on the entire amount of the initial loan, not just on the outstanding balance.

EXAMPLE 7   **Loan balance**   Rework Example 6, except assume that the interest is now simple.

Solution **(a)** As before,

$$[\text{new balance}] = [\text{previous balance}] + [\text{interest}] - [\text{payment}].$$

Now, however, since the interest is simple, it is computed on the original loan y_0. So

$$y_n = y_{n-1} + .12y_0 - 1000, \qquad y_0 = 2400.$$

(b) $y_1 = y_0 + .12y_0 - 1000 = \$1688$

$y_2 = y_1 + .12y_0 - 1000 = 976$

$y_3 = y_2 + .12y_0 - 1000 = 264.$

REMARK Note that after three years the loan of Example 7 is not yet paid off, whereas the loan of Example 6 is. Therefore, the loan at 12% simple interest is more expensive than the one at 12% compound interest. Actually, a 12% simple interest loan might be comparable to a 16% compound interest loan. At one time it was a common practice to advertise loans in terms of simple interest to make the interest rate seem cheaper. But the Federal Truth-in-Lending Act now requires that all loans be stated in terms of their equivalent compound interest rate.

Verification of Formula (1)   From the difference equation $y_n = ay_{n-1} + b$ we get

$$y_1 = ay_0 + b$$

$$y_2 = ay_1 + b = a(ay_0 + b) + b$$

$$= a^2y_0 + ab + b$$

$$y_3 = ay_2 + b = a(a^2y_0 + ab + b) + b$$

$$= a^3y_0 + a^2b + ab + b$$

$$y_4 = ay_3 + b = a(a^3y_0 + a^2b + ab + b) + b$$

$$= a^4y_0 + a^3b + a^2b + ab + b.$$

The pattern that clearly develops is

$$y_n = a^n y_0 + a^{n-1}b + a^{n-2}b + \cdots + a^2 b + ab + b. \tag{5}$$

Multiply both sides of (5) by a and then subtract the new equation from (5). Notice that many terms drop out.

$$
\begin{aligned}
y_n &= \quad a^n y_0 + \qquad\quad a^{n-1}b + a^{n-2}b + \cdots + a^2 b + ab + b \\
ay_n &= a^{n+1}y_0 + a^n b + a^{n-1}b + a^{n-2}b + \cdots + a^2 b + ab \\
\hline
y_n - ay_n &= a^n y_0 - a^{n+1}y_0 - a^n b + b
\end{aligned}
$$

The last equation can be written

$$(1-a)y_n = (1-a)a^n y_0 - ba^n + b.$$

Now, divide both sides of the equation by $(1-a)$. [*Note*: Since $a \neq 1$, $1 - a \neq 0$.]

$$
\begin{aligned}
y_n &= y_0 a^n - \frac{b}{1-a} \cdot a^n + \frac{b}{1-a} \\
&= \frac{b}{1-a} + \left(y_0 - \frac{b}{1-a} \right) a^n,
\end{aligned}
$$

which is formula (1). ∎

Verification of Formula (2)   Formula (1) gives the solution of the difference equation $y_n = ay_{n-1} + b$ in the case $a \neq 1$. The preceding reasoning also gives the solution in case $a = 1$—namely equation (5) holds for any value of a. In particular, for $a = 1$ equation (5) reads

$$
\begin{aligned}
y_n &= a^n y_0 + a^{n-1}b + a^{n-2}b + \cdots + a^2 b + ab + b \\
&= 1^n y_0 + 1^{n-1}b + 1^{n-2}b + \cdots + 1^2 b + 1b + b \\
&= y_0 + b + b + \cdots + b + b + b \\
&= y_0 + bn.
\end{aligned}
$$

Thus we have derived formula (2). ∎

Practice Problems 11.2

1. Solve the following difference equations.
   (a) $y_n = -.2y_{n-1} + 24$, $y_0 = 25$
   (b) $y_n = y_{n-1} - 3$, $y_0 = 7$
2. **Land Value** In 1626, Peter Minuit, the first director-general of New Netherlands Province, purchased Manhattan Island for trinkets and cloth valued at about \$24. Suppose that this money had been invested at 7% interest compounded quarterly. How much would it have been worth by the U.S. bicentennial year, 1976?

EXERCISES 11.2

1. Solve the difference equation $y_n = y_{n-1} + 5$, $y_0 = 1$.
2. Solve the difference equation $y_n = y_{n-1} - 2$, $y_0 = 50$.

In Exercises 3–8, find an expression for the amount of money in the bank after five years when the initial deposit is \$80 and the annual interest rate is as given.

3. 9% compounded monthly
4. 4% simple interest
5. 100% compounded daily
6. 8% compounded quarterly
7. 7% simple interest
8. 12% compounded semiannually
9. Determine the amount of money accumulated after one year when \$1 is deposited at 40% interest compounded
   (a) annually   (b) semiannually   (c) quarterly.

10. Find the general formula for the amount of money accumulated after t years when A dollars is invested at annual interest rate r compounded k times per year.

11. For the difference equation $y_n = 2y_{n-1} - 10$, generate y_0, y_1, y_2, y_3, y_4 and describe the graph corresponding to the initial condition:
    (a) $y_0 = 10$ (b) $y_0 = 11$ (c) $y_0 = 9$

12. For the difference equation $y_n = \frac{1}{2}y_{n-1} + 5$, generate y_0, y_1, y_2, y_3, y_4 and describe the graph corresponding to the initial condition:
    (a) $y_0 = 10$ (b) $y_0 = 18$ (c) $y_0 = 2$

In Exercises 13–16, solve the difference equation and, by inspection, determine the long-run behavior of the terms (i.e., the behavior of the terms as n gets large).

13. $y_n = .4y_{n-1} + 3$, $y_0 = 7$

14. $y_n = 3y_{n-1} - 12$, $y_0 = 10$

15. $y_n = -5y_{n-1}$, $y_0 = 2$

16. $y_n = -.7y_{n-1} + 3.4$, $y_0 = 3$

17. **Mortgage Balance** A bank loan of $250,525 at 6.6% interest compounded monthly is made in order to buy a house and is paid off at the rate of $1600 per month for 30 years. (Such a loan is called a *mortgage*.) The balance at any time is the amount still owed on the loan, that is, the amount that would have to be paid out to repay the loan all at once at that time. Find the difference equation for y_n, the balance after n months.

18. **Mortgage Balance** Refer to Exercise 17. Express in mathematical notation the fact that the loan is paid off after 30 years.

19. **Depreciation Modeling** A house is purchased for $50,000 and depreciated over a 25-year period. Let y_n be the (undepreciated) value of the house after n years. Determine and solve the difference equation for y_n, assuming straight-line depreciation (i.e., each year the house depreciates by $\frac{1}{25}$ of its original value).

20. **Depreciation Modeling** Refer to Exercise 19. Determine and solve the difference equation for y_n, assuming the double-declining balance method of depreciation (i.e., each year the house depreciates by $\frac{2}{25}$ of its value at the beginning of that year).

21. **Population Growth PE** If a population of 500 bacteria doubles in size every 5 minutes, approximately how many minutes will it take for the population to grow to 500,000?
    (a) 45   (b) 50   (c) 55   (d) 60   (e) 65

22. **Savings Account PE** The balance in a savings account doubles every 12 years. Approximately how many years will it take for the balance to grow from $100 to $25,000?
    (a) 60   (b) 72   (c) 84   (d) 96   (e) 108

23. **Investment Value PE** By how much does the value of an investment increase in 2 weeks if it grows at the rate of $50 per day?

(a) $100   (b) $640   (c) $700
(d) $1000   (e) $1400

24. **Population Growth PE** A city's population grows at the rate of one person every 20 minutes. By how many people does the population grow in 6 hours?
    (a) 18   (b) 20   (c) 60   (d) 120   (e) 180

25. **Population Growth PE** A population doubles every year for 5 years. If the size of the population after the 5 years is 100,000, what was the population at the end of the second year?
    (a) 7500   (b) 10,000   (c) 12,500
    (d) 25,000   (e) 50,000

26. **Investment Value PE** The value of an investment doubles every month for 8 months. After the eighth month, the investment was worth $400,000. What was the investment worth after the fourth month?
    (a) $25,000   (b) $50,000   (c) $75,000
    (d) $100,000   (e) $200,000

27. **Bacteria Growth PE** If a culture of 10^5 bacteria doubles in size every 15 minutes, how many bacteria are present after 1 hour?
    (a) $10^4(10^5)$ (b) $(10^5)^4$ (c) $2^4(10^5)$
    (d) $2(10^5)$ (e) $4(10^5)$

28. **Population Growth PE** A population of 10^7 doubles in size every 6 months. How big is the population after 8 years?
    (a) $(10^7)^{16}$ (b) $10^{16}(10^7)$ (c) $16(10^7)$
    (d) $2(10^7)$ (e) $2^{16}(10^7)$

Exercises 29–35 require the use of a graphing calculator or spreadsheet.
In these exercises, answer the questions by generating a table or graph of an appropriate difference equation.

29. One thousand dollars is deposited into a savings account at 6% interest compounded quarterly. Determine the balance after 3 years. When will the balance reach $1659? How many quarters are required for the initial deposit to double?

30. Redo Exercise 29 for simple interest of 1.5% per quarter-year.

31. **Account Balance** Two hundred dollars is deposited into a savings account at simple interest of 4.5% annually. Determine the balance after 5 years. When will the balance reach or exceed $308? How many years are required for the initial deposit to double?

32. **Account Balance** Redo Exercise 31 for compound interest of 4.5% compounded annually.

33. **Credit Card Debt** Roberto has a $2000 debt on a credit card charging 18% interest compounded monthly. If he makes a $105 payment at the end of each month (and has no new charges), how many months will it take for his debt to be less than $105?

34. Consider the difference equation $y_n = -.9y_{n-1} + 19$, $y_0 = 5$. What value do the terms approach as n gets large?

35. Consider the difference equation $y_n = .85y_{n-1} + 9$, $y_0 = 5$. What value do the terms approach as n gets large?

Solutions to Practice Problems 11.2

1. **(a)** Since $a = -.2 \neq 1$, use formula (1).

$$\frac{b}{1-a} = \frac{24}{1-(-.2)} = \frac{24}{1.2} = \frac{240}{12} = 20$$

$$y_n = 20 + (25 - 20)(-.2)^n = 20 + 5(-.2)^n$$

(b) Since $a = 1$, use formula (2).

$$y_n = 7 + (-3)n = 7 - 3n$$

2. Since interest is compounded quarterly, the interest per period is $.07/4 = .0175$. Three hundred and fifty years consists of $4(350) = 1400$ interest periods. Therefore, by (4), the amount accumulated is

$$y_{1400} = 24(1.0175)^{1400}.$$

(This amount is approximately \$850 billion, which is more than Manhattan Island was worth in 1976.)

11.3 Graphing Difference Equations

In this section we introduce a method for sketching the graph of the difference equation $y_n = ay_{n-1} + b$ (with initial value y_0) directly from the three numbers a, b, and y_0. As we shall see, the graphs arising from difference equations can be described completely by two characteristics—vertical direction and long-run behavior. To begin we introduce some vocabulary to describe graphs.

The **vertical direction** of a graph refers to the up-and-down motion of successive terms. A graph **increases** if it rises when read from left to right—that is, if the terms get successively larger. A graph **decreases** if it falls when read from left to right—that is, if the terms get successively smaller. Figure 1 shows the graphs of two difference equations. Both graphs increase. Figure 2 shows two examples of decreasing graphs. A graph that is either increasing or decreasing is called **monotonic**. That is, a graph is monotonic if it always heads in one direction—up or down.

Figure 1. Increasing graphs.

Figure 2. Decreasing graphs.

Figure 3. Oscillating graphs.

Figure 4. Constant graph.

The extreme opposite of a monotonic graph is one that changes its direction with every term. Such a graph is called **oscillating**. Figure 3 shows two examples of oscillating graphs. A difference equation having an oscillating graph has terms y_n that alternately increase and decrease.

In addition to the monotonic and oscillating graphs, there are the **constant** graphs, which always remain at the same height. That is, all the terms y_n are the same. A constant graph is illustrated in Fig. 4.

One of the main results of this section is that the graph of a difference equation $y_n = ay_{n-1} + b$ is always either monotonic, oscillating, or constant. This threefold classification gives us all the possibilities for the vertical direction of the graph.

Long-run behavior refers to the eventual behavior of the graph. Most graphs of difference equations exhibit one of two types of long-run behavior. Some approach a horizontal line and are said to be **asymptotic** to the line. Some go indefinitely high or indefinitely low and are said to be **unbounded**. These phenomena are illustrated in Figs. 5 and 6.

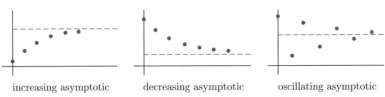

Figure 5. Asymptotic graphs.   increasing asymptotic   decreasing asymptotic   oscillating asymptotic

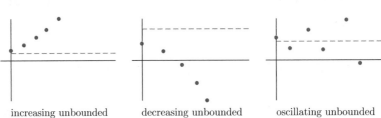

Figure 6. Unbounded graphs.   increasing unbounded   decreasing unbounded   oscillating unbounded

The dashed horizontal lines in Figs. 5 and 6 each have the equation $y = b/(1-a)$. Note that in Fig. 5 the terms move steadily closer to the dashed line and in Fig. 6 they move steadily farther away from the dashed line. In the first case we say that the terms are **attracted** to the dashed line and in the second case we say that they are **repelled** by it.

Constant Graphs   The general formula for the nth term of a difference equation where $a \neq 1$ is

$$y_n = \frac{b}{1-a} + \left(y_0 - \frac{b}{1-a} \right) a^n.$$

It is clear that as n varies so does a^n, and this makes y_n vary with n—unless, of course, the coefficient of a^n is 0, in which case the graph is constant. Thus we have the following result:

> The graph of $y_n = ay_{n-1} + b$ ($a \neq 1$) is constant if $y_0 - b/(1-a) = 0$; that is, if $y_0 = b/(1-a)$.

Thus, when the graph starts out on the line $y = b/(1-a)$, it stays on the line.

EXAMPLE 1

Graphing a difference equation   Sketch the graph of the difference equation $y_n = 2y_{n-1} - 1$, $y_0 = 1$.

Solution First compute $b/(1-a)$:

$$\frac{b}{1-a} = \frac{-1}{1-2} = 1.$$

But $y_0 = 1$. So $b/(1-a)$ and y_0 are the same and the graph is constant, always equal to 1 (Fig. 7).

Now Try Exercise 17 ■

Throughout this section assume that $a \neq \pm 1$. Then the graph of a given difference equation either is constant or is one of the types shown in Figs. 5 and 6. We can determine the nature of the graph by looking at the coefficients a and b and the initial value y_0. We have seen how constant graphs are handled. Thus, assume that we are dealing with a nonconstant graph—that is, the graph of a difference equation for which a^n actually affects the formula for y_n. Monotonic graphs may be differentiated from oscillating graphs by the following test.

$y_n = 2y_{n-1} - 1, \; y_0 = 1$

Figure 7

> **Test 1**   If $a > 0$, then the graph of $y_n = ay_{n-1} + b$ is monotonic.
>
>   If $a < 0$, then the graph is oscillating.

The next two examples provide a convincing argument for Test 1.

EXAMPLE 2   **Vertical direction of a difference equation**   Discuss the vertical direction of the graph of $y_n = -.8y_{n-1} + 9$, $y_0 = 50$.

Solution   The formula for y_n yields

$$y_n = 5 + 45(-.8)^n.$$

$y_n = -.8y_{n-1} + 9, \; y_0 = 50$

Figure 8

Note that the term $(-.8)^n$ is alternately positive and negative, since any negative number to an even power is positive and any negative number to an odd power is negative. Therefore, the expression $45(-.8)^n$ is alternately positive and negative. So $y_n = 5 + 45(-.8)^n$ is computed by alternately adding and subtracting something from 5. Thus y_n oscillates around 5. In this example $a = -.8$ (a negative number), so that the behavior just observed is consistent with that predicted by Test 1. The graph is sketched in Fig. 8. Note that in this case 5 is just $b/(1-a)$, so the graph oscillates about the line $y = b/(1-a)$. ∎

The reasoning of Example 2 works whenever $a < 0$. The oscillation of a^n from positive to negative and back forces the term

$$\left(y_0 - \frac{b}{1-a} \right) a^n$$

to swing back and forth from positive to negative. So the value of

$$y_n = \frac{b}{1-a} + \left(y_0 - \frac{b}{1-a} \right) a^n$$

swings above and below $b/(1-a)$. In other words, the graph oscillates about the line $y = b/(1-a)$.

EXAMPLE 3   **Vertical direction of a difference equation**   Discuss the vertical direction of the graph of $y_n = .8y_{n-1} + 9$, $y_0 = 50$.

Solution   In this case $b/(1-a) = 45$, and the formula for y_n gives

$$y_n = 45 + 5(.8)^n.$$

$y_n = .8y_{n-1} + 9, \; y_0 = 50$

Figure 9

The expression $5(.8)^n$ is always positive. As n gets larger, $5(.8)^n$ gets smaller, so that y_n decreases to 45. That is, the graph is steadily decreasing to $y = 45$ (Fig. 9). Here $a = .8 > 0$, so Test 1 correctly predicts that the graph is monotonic. ∎

Using the following result, it is possible to determine whether a graph is asymptotic or unbounded.

> ***Test 2***   If $|a| < 1$, then the graph of $y_n = ay_{n-1} + b$ is asymptotic to the line $y = b/(1-a)$. If $|a| > 1$, then the graph is unbounded and moves away from the line $y = b/(1-a)$.

Let us examine some difference equations in light of Test 2.

EXAMPLE 4   **Vertical direction and long-run behavior of a difference equation**   Discuss the graphs of the difference equation $y_n = .2y_{n-1} + 4.8$, with $y_0 = 1$ and with $y_0 = 11$.

Solution   The graphs are shown in Fig. 10. Since $a = .2$, which has absolute value less than 1, Test 2 correctly predicts that each graph is asymptotic to the line $y = b/(1-a) = 4.8/(1-.2) = 6$. When the initial value is less than 6, the graph increases and moves toward the line $y = 6$. When the initial value is greater than 6, the graph decreases toward the line $y = 6$. In each case the graph is *attracted* to the line $y = 6$.   ■

Figure 10 $y_0 = 1$ $y_0 = 11$

EXAMPLE 5   **Applying Test 2**   Apply Test 2 to the difference equation $y_n = -.8y_{n-1} + 9$, $y_0 = 50$.

Solution $|a| = |-.8| = .8 < 1$. So by Test 2 the graph is asymptotic to the line $y = b/(1-a) = 5$. This agrees with the graph as drawn in Fig. 8 on the previous page.   ■

EXAMPLE 6   **Vertical direction and long-run behavior of a difference equation**   Discuss the graphs of $y_n = 1.4y_{n-1} - 8$, with $y_0 > 20$ and with $y_0 < 20$.

Solution   The graphs are shown in Fig. 11. Since $a = 1.4 > 0$, Test 1 predicts that the graphs are monotonic. Since $|a| = |1.4| = 1.4 > 1$, Test 2 predicts that the graphs are unbounded. Here

$$\frac{b}{1-a} = \frac{-8}{1-(1.4)} = \frac{-8}{-.4} = 20.$$

Both graphs move away from the line $y = 20$ as if being *repelled* by a force.   ■

Figure 11

EXAMPLE 7   **Vertical direction and long-run behavior of a difference equation**   Discuss the graph of the difference equation $y_n = -2y_{n-1} + 60$, where $y_0 > 20$.

Solution A graph is drawn in Fig. 12. Since $a = -2 < 0$, Test 1 predicts that the graph is oscillating. Since $|a| = |-2| = 2 > 1$, Test 2 predicts that the graph is unbounded. Here

Figure 12

$$\frac{b}{1-a} = \frac{60}{1-(-2)} = \frac{60}{3} = 20.$$

Notice that successive points move farther away from $y = 20$; that is, they are repelled by the line. ∎

Verification of Test 2 The key to verifying Test 2 is to make the following two observations:

1. If $|a| < 1$, then the powers a, a^2, a^3, a^4, ... become successively smaller and approach 0. For example, if $a = .4$, then this sequence of powers is

$$.4, .16, .064, .0256, \ldots .$$

2. If $|a| > 1$, then the powers $a, a^2, a^3, a^4, \ldots$ become unbounded; that is, they become arbitrarily large. For example, if $a = 3$, then this sequence is $3, 9, 27, 81, \ldots .$

To verify Test 2, look at the formula for y_n:

$$y_n = \frac{b}{1-a} + \boxed{\left(y_0 - \frac{b}{1-a}\right) a^n}.$$

If $|a| < 1$, then the powers of a get smaller and smaller; so the boxed term approaches 0. That is, y_n approaches $b/(1-a)$ and the graph is asymptotic to $y = b/(1-a)$. If $|a| > 1$, the powers of a are unbounded, so that the boxed term becomes arbitrarily large in magnitude. Thus y_n is unbounded, and so is the graph. ∎

In the case where $|a| < 1$, the graphs (whether oscillating or monotonic) are *attracted* steadily to the line $y = b/(1-a)$. In the case where $|a| > 1$, the graphs are *repelled* by the line $y = b/(1-a)$. Thinking of graphs as being attracted or repelled helps us in making a rough sketch.

Figure 13

Sign of a:	$\begin{cases} \text{Positive} \\ \text{Negative} \end{cases}$	Monotonic Oscillating
Size of a:	$\begin{cases} \lvert a\rvert < 1 \\ \lvert a\rvert > 1 \end{cases}$	Attract Repel

Figure 13 shows some of the graphs already examined with the appropriate descriptive words labeling the line $y = b/(1-a)$.

Based on Tests 1 and 2 and the discussion of constant graphs, we can state a procedure for making a rough sketch of a graph without solving or generating terms.

To sketch the graph of $y_n = a\,y_{n-1} + b$, $a \neq 0, \pm 1$:

1. Draw the line $y = b/(1-a)$ as a dashed line.

2. Plot y_0. If y_0 is on the line $y = b/(1-a)$, the graph is constant and the procedure terminates.

3. If a is positive, write MONO, since the graph is then monotonic. If a is negative, write OSC, since the graph is then oscillating.

4. If $|a| < 1$, write ATTRACT, since the graph is attracted to the line $y = b/(1 - a)$. If $|a| > 1$, write REPEL, since the graph is repelled from the line.

5. Use all the information to sketch the graph.

EXAMPLE 8   **Graphing a difference equation** Sketch the graph of $y_n = .6y_{n-1} + 8$, $y_0 = 50$.

Solution 1. $\dfrac{b}{1-a} = \dfrac{8}{1 - (.6)} = \dfrac{8}{.4} = 20$. So draw the line $y = 20$.

2. $y_0 = 50$, which is not on the line $y = 20$. So the graph is not constant.

3. $a = .6$, which is positive. Write MONO above the dashed line.

4. $|a| = |.6| = .6 < 1$. Write ATTRACT below the dashed line.

5. The preceding information tells us to start at 50 and move monotonically toward the line $y = 20$.

Now Try Exercise 17

EXAMPLE 9   **Graphing a difference equation** Sketch the graph of $y_n = -1.5y_{n-1} + 5$, $y_0 = 2.6$.

Solution 1. $\dfrac{b}{1-a} = \dfrac{5}{1 - (-1.5)} = \dfrac{5}{2.5} = 2$. So draw the line $y = 2$.

2. $y_0 = 2.6$, which is not on the line $y = 2$. So the graph is not constant.

3. $a = -1.5$, which is negative. Write OSC above the dashed line.

4. $|a| = |-1.5| = 1.5 > 1$. Write REPEL below the dashed line.

5. The preceding information says that the graph begins at 2.6, oscillates about, and is steadily repelled by the line $y = 2$.

Now Try Exercise 19

The preceding procedure does not give an exact graph, but it shows the nature of the graph. This is exactly what is needed in many applications.

EXAMPLE 10   **Using a mortgage balance equation**   Suppose that the yearly interest rate on a mortgage is 9% compounded monthly and that you can afford to make payments of $300 per month. How much can you afford to borrow?

Solution   Let $i =$ the monthly interest rate, $R =$ the monthly payment, and $y_n =$ the balance after n months. Recall that $y_0 =$ the initial amount of the loan. Then the balance after n months equals the balance after $n - 1$ months plus the interest on that balance minus the monthly payment. That is,

$$y_n = y_{n-1} + iy_{n-1} - R = (1+i)y_{n-1} - R.$$

In this particular example, $i = .09/12 = .0075$ and $R = 300$, so the difference equation reads

$$y_n = 1.0075y_{n-1} - 300.$$

Apply our graph-sketching technique to this difference equation. Here

$$\frac{b}{1-a} = \frac{-300}{1 - (1.0075)} = \frac{-300}{-.0075} = 40{,}000.$$

Since $a = 1.0075$ is positive and $|a| = 1.0075 > 1$, the words MONO and REPEL describe the graphs.

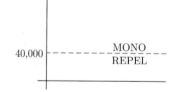

Let us see what happens for various initial values. If $y_0 > 40{,}000$, the balance increases indefinitely.

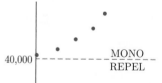

If $y_0 = 40{,}000$, the balance will always be 40,000.

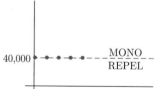

If $y_0 < 40{,}000$, the balance decreases steadily and eventually reaches 0, at which time the mortgage is paid off.

Therefore, the loan must be less than $40,000 in order for it to be paid off eventually.

Now Try Exercise 25

Practice Problems 11.3

1. **Parachuting** A parachutist opens her parachute after reaching a speed of 100 feet per second. Suppose that y_n, the speed n seconds after opening the parachute, satisfies $y_n = .1y_{n-1} + 14.4$. Sketch the graph of y_n.

2. Rework Problem 1 if the parachute opens when the speed is 10 feet per second.

3. **Retirement Fund** Upon retirement, a person deposits a certain amount of money into the bank at 6% interest compounded monthly and withdraws $100 at the end of each month.

   (a) Set up the difference equation for y_n, the amount in the bank after n months.

   (b) How large must the initial deposit be so that the money will never run out?

EXERCISES 11.3

Each of the graphs in Fig. 14 comes from a difference equation of the form $y_n = ay_{n-1} + b$. In Exercises 1–8, list all graphs that have the stated property.

1. Monotonic   2. Increasing

3. Unbounded   4. Constant

5. Repelled from $y = b/(1-a)$

6. Decreasing   7. $|a| < 1$ 8. $a < 0$

In Exercises 9–14, sketch a graph having the given characteristics.

9. $y_0 = 4$, monotonic, repelled from $y = 2$

10. $y_0 = 5$, monotonic, attracted to $y = -3$

11. $y_0 = 2$, oscillating, attracted to $y = 6$

12. $y_0 = 7$, monotonic, repelled from $y = 10$

13. $y_0 = -2$, monotonic, attracted to $y = 5$

14. $y_0 = 1$, oscillating, repelled from $y = 2$

In Exercises 15–20, make a rough sketch of the graph of the difference equation without generating terms or solving the difference equation.

15. $y_n = 3y_{n-1} + 4$, $y_0 = 0$

16. $y_n = .3y_{n-1} + 3.5$, $y_0 = 2$

17. $y_n = .5y_{n-1} + 3$, $y_0 = 6$

18. $y_n = 4y_{n-1} - 18$, $y_0 = 5$

19. $y_n = -2y_{n-1} + 12$, $y_0 = 5$

20. $y_n = -.6y_{n-1} + 6.4$, $y_0 = 1$

21. **Spread of Information** A particular news item was broadcast regularly on radio and TV. Let y_n be the number of people who had heard the news within n hours after broadcasting began. Sketch the graph of y_n, assuming that it satisfies the difference equation $y_n = .7y_{n-1} + 3000$, $y_0 = 0$.

22. **Radioactive Decay** The radioactive element strontium 90 emits particles and slowly decays. Let y_n be the amount left after n years. Then y_n satisfies the difference equation $y_n = .98y_{n-1}$. Sketch the graph of y_n if initially there are 10 milligrams of strontium 90.

23. **Price Equation** Laws of supply and demand cause the price of oats to fluctuate from year to year. Suppose that the current price is $1.72 per bushel and that the price n years from now, p_n, satisfies the difference equation $p_n = -.6p_{n-1} + 1.6$. (Prices are assumed to have been adjusted for inflation.) Sketch the graph of p_n.

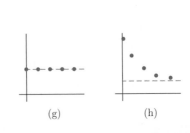

(a)   (b)   (c)   (d)

(e)   (f)   (g)   (h)

Figure 14

24. Population Growth Under ideal conditions a bacteria population satisfies the difference equation $y_n = 1.4y_{n-1}$, $y_0 = 1$, where y_n is the size of the population (in millions) after n hours. Sketch a graph that shows the growth of the population.

25. Mortgage Planning Suppose that the interest rate on a mortgage is 9% compounded monthly. If you can afford to pay \$450 per month, how much money can you borrow?

26. Mortgage Planning A municipal government can take out a long-term construction loan at 8% interest compounded quarterly. Assuming that it can pay back \$100,000 per quarter, how much money can it borrow?

27. Savings Account Withdrawals A person makes an initial deposit into a savings account paying 6% interest compounded annually. He plans to withdraw \$120 at the end of each year.

   (a) Find the difference equation for y_n, the amount after n years.

   (b) How large must y_0 be such that the money will not run out?

28. Savings Account Withdrawals Casimir makes an initial deposit into a savings fund paying 4% compounded quarterly for his teenage daughter, Julie. She plans to withdraw \$200 at the end of each quarter to buy some new clothes.

   (a) Find the difference equation for y_n, the amount in the account after n quarters.

   (b) How large must the initial deposit be so that Julie will not run out of money?

29. Mortgage Planning Gabriella is looking to take out a loan at 10% interest compounded semiannually for her greenhouse and flower business. If she can make a \$1500 payment at the end of each half-year, how much can she afford to borrow?

30. Loan Payments Suppose that a loan of \$10,000 is to be repaid at \$120 per month and that the annual interest rate is 12% compounded monthly. Then the interest for the first month is $.01 \cdot (10,000)$, or \$100. The \$120 paid at the end of the first month can be thought of as paying the \$100 interest and paying \$20 toward the reduction of the loan. Therefore, the balance after 1 month is $\$10,000 - \$20 = \$9980$. How much of the \$120 paid at the end of the second month goes for interest and how much is used to reduce the loan? What is the balance after 2 months?

Exercises 31–36 require the use of a graphing calculator or spreadsheet.

In these exercises, find a difference equation with the given properties. Then confirm your answer by graphing the difference equation.

31. The terms begin at 1 and monotonically approach 8.

32. The terms begin at 9 and monotonically approach 4.

33. The terms begin at 1 and monotonically increase without bound.

34. The terms begin at 12, oscillate, and approach 6.

35. The terms begin at 5, oscillate, and are unbounded.

36. The terms begin at 50 and monotonically decrease without bound.

Solutions to Practice Problems 11.3

1. $\dfrac{b}{1-a} = \dfrac{14.4}{1-(.1)} = \dfrac{14.4}{.9} = \dfrac{144}{9} = 16.$ $y_0 = 100$, which is greater than $b/(1-a)$. Since $a = .1$ is positive, the terms y_n are monotonic. Since $|a| = .1 < 1$, the terms are attracted to the line $y = 16$. Now, plot $y_0 = 100$, draw the line $y = 16$, and write in the words MONO and ATTRACT [Fig. 15(a)]. Since the terms are attracted to the line monotonically they must move downward and asymptotically approach the line [Fig. 15(b)]. (Notice that the terminal speed, 16 feet per second, does not depend on the speed of the parachutist when the parachute is opened.)

2. Everything is the same as before except that now $y_0 < 16$. The speed increases to a terminal speed of 16 feet per second.

(a)

(b)

Figure 15

(Continued)

3. (a) $i = .06/12 = .005$

$$y_n = y_{n-1} + (\text{interest}) - (\text{withdrawal})$$
$$= y_{n-1} + .005y_{n-1} - 100$$
$$= (1.005)y_{n-1} - 100$$

(b) $\dfrac{b}{1-a} = \dfrac{-100}{1-(1.005)} = \dfrac{-100}{-.005} = 20{,}000.$ Since $a = 1.005 > 0$, the graph is monotonic. Since $|a| = 1.005 > 1$, the graph is repelled from the line $y = 20{,}000$.

If $y_0 < 20{,}000$, the amount of money in the account decreases and eventually runs out.

If $y_0 = 20{,}000$, the amount of money in the account stays constant at 20,000.

If $y_0 > 20{,}000$, the amount of money in the account grows steadily and is unbounded.

Answer: $y_0 \geq 20{,}000$.

11.4 Mathematics of Personal Finance

In this section we apply the theory of difference equations to the study of mortgages and annuities.

Mortgages   Most families take out bank loans to pay for a new house. Such a loan, called a mortgage, is used to purchase the house and then is repaid with interest in monthly installments over a number of years, usually 25 or 30. The monthly payments are computed so that after exactly the correct length of time the unpaid balance[1] is 0 and the loan is thereby paid off.

Mortgages can be described by difference equations, as follows. Let y_n be the unpaid balance on the mortgage after n months. In particular, y_0 is the initial amount borrowed. Let i denote the monthly interest rate and R the monthly mortgage payment. Then

$$\begin{bmatrix} \text{balance after} \\ n \text{ months} \end{bmatrix} = \begin{bmatrix} \text{balance after} \\ n - 1 \text{ months} \end{bmatrix} + \begin{bmatrix} \text{interest for} \\ \text{month} \end{bmatrix} - \begin{bmatrix} \text{payment} \end{bmatrix}$$

$$y_n \qquad = \qquad y_{n-1} \qquad + \qquad iy_{n-1} \qquad - \qquad R$$

$$y_n = (1+i)y_{n-1} - R. \tag{1}$$

EXAMPLE 1

Finding the amount of a mortgage   Suppose that you can afford to pay \$1100 per month and the yearly interest rate is 6.6% compounded monthly. Exactly how much can you borrow if the mortgage is to be paid off in 30 years?

Solution   The monthly interest rate is $.066/12 = .0055$, so equation (1) becomes in this case

$$y_n = 1.0055y_{n-1} - 1100.$$

Further, we are given that the mortgage runs for 30 years, or 360 months. Thus

$$y_{360} = 0. \tag{2}$$

---

[1] The balance after n months is the amount that would have to be paid at that time in order to retire the debt.

Our problem is to determine y_0, the amount of the loan. From our general theory we first compute $b/(1-a)$:

$$\frac{b}{1-a} = \frac{-1100}{1-(1.0055)} = 200{,}000.$$

The formula for y_{360} is then given by

$$y_{360} = \frac{b}{1-a} + \left(y_0 - \frac{b}{1-a}\right)a^{360}$$

$$= 200{,}000 + (y_0 - 200{,}000)(1.0055)^{360}$$

$$= 200{,}000 + (y_0 - 200{,}000)(7.203556648)$$

However, by equation (2), $y_{360} = 0$, so that

$$0 = 200{,}000 + (y_0 - 200{,}000)(7.203556648) = 7.203556648 y_0 - 1{,}240{,}711.33$$

$$y_0 = \frac{1{,}240{,}711.33}{7.203556648} = 172{,}235.94.$$

Thus, the initial amount, that is, the amount that can be borrowed, is $172,235.94.

Now Try Exercise 5

■

Table 1 shows the status of the mortgage after selected payments. After the first payment of $1100 is made, the balance of the loan is $y_1 = \$172{,}083.24$. This payment consists of $947.30 interest and $152.70 repayment of the loan. In the early months almost all of the monthly payment goes toward interest. With each passing month, however, the amount of interest declines and the amount applied to reducing the debt increases.

TABLE 1

Payment Number	1	2	120	240	348	360
Balance on loan	$172,083.24	$171,929.70	$146,379.36	$96,442.63	$12,739.97	$0.00
Interest	947.30	946.46	806.70	533.55	75.70	6.02
Reduction of debt	152.70	153.54	293.30	566.45	1,024.30	1,093.98

EXAMPLE 2

Determining mortgage payments Suppose that we have a 30-year mortgage for $140,000 at 7.5% interest, compounded monthly. Find the monthly payment.

Solution Here the monthly interest rate i is just $.075/12 = .00625$ and $y_0 = 140{,}000$. Since the mortgage is for 30 years, we have

$$y_{360} = 0.$$

The difference equation for the mortgage is

$$y_n = 1.00625 y_{n-1} - R \qquad y_0 = 140{,}000.$$

Now

$$\frac{b}{1-a} = \frac{-R}{1-1.00625} = \frac{R}{.00625} = 160R.$$

The formula for y_n is

$$y_n = 160R + (140{,}000 - 160R)(1.00625)^n$$

Thus

$$0 = y_{360} = 160R + (140{,}000 - 160R)(1.00625)^{360}.$$

To complete the problem, solve this equation for R.   Using $(1.00625)^{360} = 9.421533905$,

$$160R + (140{,}000 - 160R)(9.421533905) = 0$$
$$1347.445425R = 1{,}319{,}014.747$$

Now Try Exercise 11
$$R = \$978.90. \qquad \blacksquare$$

Annuities   The term "annuity" has several meanings. For our purposes an annuity is a bank account into which equal sums are deposited at regular intervals, either weekly, monthly, quarterly, or annually. The money draws interest and accumulates for a certain number of years, after which it becomes available to the investor. Annuities are often used to save for a child's college education or to generate funds for retirement.

The growth of money in an annuity can be described by a difference equation. Let $y_n = $ [the amount of money in the annuity after n time periods], $i = $ [the interest rate per time period], $D = $ [the deposit per time period]. Then $y_0 = $ [the amount after 0 time periods] $= 0.$[2] Moreover,

$$
\begin{aligned}
y_n &= \text{[previous amount]} + \text{[interest]} + \text{[deposit]} \\
&= \quad y_{n-1} \quad\quad + \quad iy_{n-1} \quad + \quad D \\
&= (1+i)y_{n-1} + D.
\end{aligned}
$$

This last equation is the difference equation of the annuity.

EXAMPLE 3

Finding the future balance of an annuity   Suppose that $20 is deposited into an annuity at the end of every quarter-year and that interest is earned at the annual rate of 8%, compounded quarterly. How much money is in the annuity after 10 years?

Solution   Since 10 years $= 40$ quarters, the problem is to compute y_{40}. Now $D = 20$ and $i = .08/4 = .02$. So the difference equation reads

$$y_n = 1.02y_{n-1} + 20.$$

In this case

$$\frac{b}{1-a} = \frac{20}{1-1.02} = -1000.$$

Thus
$$y_n = -1000 + [0 - (-1000)](1.02)^n = -1000 + 1000(1.02)^n.$$

In particular, setting $n = 40$,

$$y_{40} = -1000 + 1000(1.02)^{40}.$$

Using $(1.02)^{40} = 2.208039664$,

$$y_{40} = -1000 + 1000(2.208039664) = -1000 + 2208.039664 = 1208.039664.$$

Now Try Exercise 7   Thus after 10 years the account contains $1208.04. $\blacksquare$

EXAMPLE 4

Determining the periodic deposit with an annuity   How much money must be deposited at the end of each quarter into an annuity at 8% interest compounded quarterly in order to have $10,000 after 15 years?

---

[2]One model for the situation $y_0 = 0$ is a payroll savings plan, where a person signs up at time zero and has the first deduction made at the end of the next pay period.

Solution Here D is unknown. But $i = .02$. Also, 15 years = 60 quarters, so that $y_{60} = 10,000$. The difference equation in this case reads

$$y_n = 1.02y_{n-1} + D, \qquad y_0 = 0.$$

Then

$$\frac{b}{1-a} = \frac{D}{1-1.02} = \frac{D}{-.02} = -50D$$

and

$$y_n = -50D + (0 - (-50D))(1.02)^n$$
$$= -50D + 50D(1.02)^n.$$

Set $n = 60$. Then

$$y_{60} = -50D + 50D(1.02)^{60}.$$

However, from the statement of the problem, $y_{60} = 10,000$. Thus we have the equation

$$10,000 = -50D + 50D(1.02)^{60}$$

to be solved for D. But $(1.02)^{60} = 3.281030788$, so that

$$-50D + 50(3.281030788)D = 10,000$$
$$-50D + 164.0515394D = 10,000$$
$$114.0515394D = 10,000$$

Now Try Exercise 9

$$D = \frac{10,000}{114.0515394} = \$87.68.$$ ■

INCORPORATING TECHNOLOGY

GC A complete table similar to Table 1 is called an *amortization table* and is easily created with a graphing calculator. Consider a mortgage with difference equation $y_n = 1.0075y_{n-1} - 300$, $y_0 = 37{,}284.56$. Let v_n be the interest portion of the nth payment. Then $v_n = .0075y_{n-1}$ for $n = 1, 2, 3, \ldots$. These two difference equations are entered into the **Y=** editor as follows.

TI-83/84 Plus	TI-89
nMin = 0	u1=1.0075*u1(n-1)-300
u(n)=1.0075u(n-1)-300	ui1=37284.56
u(nMin)=37284.56	u2=.0075*u1(n-1)
v(n)=.0075u(n-1)	ui2=0
v(nMin)=0	

To create the tables in Figs. 1 and 2, press [2nd] [TBLSET] (on the TI-83/84 Plus) or [♦] [TblSet] (on the TI-89) to bring up the TABLE SETUP screen. **TblStart** and Δ**Tbl** should be set to 1. Then, pressing [2nd] [TABLE] (on the TI-83/84 Plus) or [♦] [TABLE] (on the TI-89) brings up the table. You can use the down-arrow key to generate further balances and interest payments. ■

n	u(n)	v(n)
1	37264.1	279.63
2	37244	279.48
3	37223	279.33
4	37202	279.17
5	37181	279.02
6	37160	278.86
7	37139	278.7

u(n)=37264.1942

Figure 1

Figure 2

ES Figure 3 contains an amortization table similar to the ones in Figs. 1 and 2 but shown in an Excel spreadsheet. To obtain the numbers in the B column, **37284.56** was entered into B2, **=1.0075*B2−300** was entered into B3, and B3 was selected and its fill handle dragged down to cell B9. To obtain the numbers in the C column, **=0.0075*B2** was entered into C3, and C3 was selected and its fill handle dragged down to cell C9. *Note*: The cells in the B and C columns were formatted to show two decimal places.

	A	B	C
1		**Balance**	**Interest**
2	0	37284.56	
3	1	37264.19	279.63
4	2	37243.68	279.48
5	3	37223.00	279.33
6	4	37202.18	279.17
7	5	37181.19	279.02
8	6	37160.05	278.86
9	7	37138.75	278.70

Figure 3

Practice Problems 11.4

1. **Savings Account** Suppose that you deposit $650,000 into a bank account paying 5% interest compounded annually and you withdraw $50,000 at the end of each year. Find a difference equation for y_n, the amount in the account after n years.

2. Refer to Problem 1. How much money will be in the account after 20 years?

3. Refer to Problem 1. Assume that the money is tax-free and that you could earn 5% interest compounded annually. Would you rather have $650,000 now or $50,000 a year for 20 years?

EXERCISES 11.4

In Exercises 1–4, give the difference equation for y_n, the amount (or balance) after n interest periods.

1. A mortgage loan of $32,500 at 9% interest compounded monthly and having monthly payments of $261.50.

2. A bank deposit of $1000 at 6% interest compounded semiannually.

3. An annuity for which $4000 is deposited into an account at 6% interest compounded quarterly and $200 is added to the account at the end of each quarter.

4. A bank account into which $20,000 is deposited at 6% interest compounded monthly and $100 is withdrawn at the end of each month.

5. How much money can you borrow at 12% interest compounded monthly if the loan is to be paid off in monthly installments for 10 years and you can afford to pay $660 per month?

6. Find the monthly payment on a $38,000, 25-year mortgage at 12% interest compounded monthly.

7. Find the amount accumulated after 20 years if, at the end of each year, $300 is deposited into an account

paying 6% interest compounded annually.

8. How much money would you have to put into an account initially at 8% interest compounded quarterly in order to have $6000 after 14 years?

9. How much money would you have to deposit at the end of each month into an annuity paying 6% interest compounded monthly in order to have $6000 after 12 years?

10. How much money would you have to put into a bank account paying 6% interest compounded monthly in order to be able to withdraw $150 each month for 30 years?

11. **Car Loan** In order to buy a used car, a person borrows $4000 from the bank at 12% interest compounded monthly. The loan is to be paid off in 3 years with equal monthly payments. What will the monthly payments be?

12. How much money would you have to deposit at the end of each month into an annuity paying 6% interest compounded monthly in order to have $1620 after 4 years?

Exercises 13–16 require the use of a graphing calculator or a spreadsheet.

In these exercises, use a table or graph of an appropriate difference equation to answer the questions.

13. **Corporate Loan** The ABC Corporation borrows $45 million (at 8% interest compounded annually) to buy a shopping center. The loan is repaid with annual payments of $4 million per year. Determine the balance after 10 years. After how many years will the loan be paid off?

14. **Merchandise Financing** John buys a stereo system for $605.54 and pays for it with monthly payments of $90. The interest rate is 12% compounded monthly. Determine the amount still owed after 4 months. After how

many months will the loan be repaid?

15. A person deposits $100 at the end of each month into an annuity earning 6% interest compounded monthly. What are the balances (that is, future values) after 5, 10, and 15 months? How many months are required for the balance to reach $3228? After how many months will the balance exceed $4000?

16. **Savings Plan** Alice embarks on a savings routine. She decides to deposit $75 at the end of every three months into a savings account paying 6% interest compounded quarterly. How much money will she have accumulated after 5 years? When will she have accumulated $2474? After how many quarters will her savings exceed $4000?

Solutions to Practice Problems 11.4

1. $$\begin{bmatrix}\text{amount after}\\ n \text{ years}\end{bmatrix} = \begin{bmatrix}\text{amount after}\\ n-1 \text{ years}\end{bmatrix} + \begin{bmatrix}\text{interest for}\\ n\text{th year}\end{bmatrix}$$

$$- \begin{bmatrix}\text{withdrawal at}\\ \text{end of year}\end{bmatrix}$$

$$y_n = y_{n-1} + .05 y_{n-1} - 50,000 = (1.05)y_{n-1} - 50,000$$

$$y_0 = 650,000$$

2. Solve the difference equation and set $n = 20$.

$$\frac{b}{1-a} = \frac{-50,000}{1-(1.05)} = \frac{-50,000}{-.05} = 1,000,000$$

$$y_n = 1,000,000 + (650,000 - 1,000,000)(1.05)^n$$

$$= 1,000,000 - 350,000(1.05)^n$$

$$y_{20} = 1,000,000 - 350,000(2.653297705)$$

$$= 71,345.80$$

3. $650,000. According to Problem 2, this money could be deposited into the bank. You could take out $50,000 per year and still have $71,345.80 left over after 20 years.

11.5 Modeling with Difference Equations

In this section we show how difference equations may be used to build mathematical models of a number of phenomena. Since the difference equation describing a situation contains as much data as the formula for y_n, we shall regard the difference equation itself as a mathematical model. We demonstrate in this section that the difference equation and a sketch of its graph can often be of more use than an explicit solution.

The concept of proportionality will be needed to develop some of these models.

Proportionality To say that two quantities are proportional is the same as saying that one quantity is equal to a constant times the other quantity. For instance, in a state having a 4% sales tax, the sales tax on an item is proportional to the price of the item, since

$$[\text{sales tax}] = .04[\text{price}].$$

Here, the constant of proportionality is .04. In general, for two proportional quantities we have

$$[\text{first quantity}] = k[\text{second quantity}],$$

where k is some fixed constant of proportionality. Note that if both quantities are positive and if the first quantity is known always to be smaller than the second, then k is a positive number less than 1; that is, $0 < k < 1$.

EXAMPLE 1

Radioactive decay   Certain forms of natural elements, such as uranium 238, strontium 90, and carbon 14, are radioactive. That is, they decay, or dissipate, over a period of time. Physicists have found that this process of decay obeys the following law: Each year the amount that decays is proportional to the amount present at the start of the year. Construct a mathematical model describing radioactive decay.

Solution   Let y_n = the amount left after n years. The physical law states that

$$[\text{amount that decays in year } n] = k \cdot y_{n-1},$$

where $k \cdot y_{n-1}$ represents a constant of proportionality times the amount present at the start of that year. Therefore,

$$y_n \quad = \quad y_{n-1} \quad - \quad k \cdot y_{n-1}$$

$$\begin{bmatrix} \text{amount after} \\ \text{year } n \end{bmatrix} = \begin{bmatrix} \text{amount after} \\ \text{year } n-1 \end{bmatrix} - \begin{bmatrix} \text{amount that decays} \\ \text{in year } n \end{bmatrix}$$

or

$$y_n = (1-k)y_{n-1},$$

where k is a constant between 0 and 1. This difference equation is the mathematical model for radioactive decay. ∎

EXAMPLE 2

Radioactive decay   Experiment shows that for cobalt 60 (a radioactive form of cobalt used in cancer therapy) the decay constant k is given by $k = .12$.

(a) Write the difference equation for y_n in this case.

(b) Sketch the graph of the difference equation.

Solution (a)   Setting $k = .12$ in the result of Example 1, we get

$$y_n = (1-.12)y_{n-1} \quad \text{or} \quad y_n = .88y_{n-1}.$$

(b)   Since .88 is positive and less than 1, the graph is monotonic and attracted to the line $y = b/(1-a) = 0/(1-.88) = 0$. The graph is sketched in Fig. 1. ∎

Now Try Exercise 3

Figure 1

EXAMPLE 3

Growth of a bacteria culture   A bacteria culture grows in such a way that each hour the increase in the number of bacteria in the culture is proportional to the total number present at the beginning of the hour. Sketch a graph depicting the growth of the culture.

Solution   Let y_n = the number of bacteria present after n hours. Then the increase from the previous hour is ky_{n-1}, where k is a positive constant of proportionality. Therefore,

$$y_n \quad = \quad y_{n-1} \quad + \quad ky_{n-1}$$

$$\begin{bmatrix} \text{number after} \\ n \text{ hours} \end{bmatrix} = \begin{bmatrix} \text{number after} \\ n-1 \text{ hours} \end{bmatrix} + \begin{bmatrix} \text{increase during} \\ n\text{th hour} \end{bmatrix}$$

or

$$y_n = (1 + k)y_{n-1}.$$

This last equation gives a mathematical model of the growth of the culture. Since $a = 1 + k > 0$ and $|a| > 1$, the graph is monotonic and repelled from $b/(1 - a) = 0$. Thus the graph is as drawn in Fig. 2. ■

Figure 2

MONO
REPEL

EXAMPLE 4

Spread of information Suppose that at 8 A.M. on a Saturday the local radio and TV stations in a town start broadcasting a certain piece of news. The number of people learning the news each hour is proportional to the number who had not yet heard it by the end of the preceding hour.

(a) Write a difference equation describing the spread of the news through the population of the town.

(b) Sketch the graph of this difference equation for the case where the constant of proportionality is .3 and the population of the town is 50,000.

Solution The example states that two quantities are proportional. The first quantity is the number of people learning the news each hour and the second is the number who have not yet heard it by the end of the preceding hour.

(a) Let y_n = the number of people who have heard the news after n hours. The terms $y_0, y_1, y_2, \ldots$ are increasing.

Let P = the total population of the town. Then the number of people who have not yet heard the news after $n-1$ hours is $P - y_{n-1}$. Thus the assumption can be stated in the mathematical form

$$y_n \qquad = \qquad y_{n-1} \qquad + \qquad k(P - y_{n-1})$$

$$\begin{bmatrix} \text{number who know} \\ \text{after } n \text{ hours} \end{bmatrix} = \begin{bmatrix} \text{number who know} \\ \text{after } n - 1 \text{ hours} \end{bmatrix} + \begin{bmatrix} \text{number who learn} \\ \text{during } n\text{th hour} \end{bmatrix},$$

where k is a constant of proportionality. The constant k tells how fast the news is traveling. It measures the percentage of the uninformed population that hears the news each hour. It is clear that $0 < k < 1$.

(b) For part (b) we assume that $k = .3$ and that the town has a population of 50,000. Further, we measure the number of people in thousands. Then $P = 50$ and the mathematical model of the spread of the news is

$$y_n = y_{n-1} + .3(50 - y_{n-1}) = y_{n-1} + 15 - .3y_{n-1} = .7y_{n-1} + 15.$$

Suppose that initially no one had heard the news, so that

$$y_0 = 0.$$

Now we may sketch the graph:

$$\frac{b}{1 - a} = \frac{15}{1 - .7} = \frac{15}{.3} = 50.$$

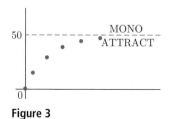

Figure 3

MONO
ATTRACT

50

Since $a = .7$, the graph is monotonic and attracted to the line $y = 50$ (Fig. 3).

Note that the number of people who hear the news increases and approaches the population of the entire town. The increases between consecutive terms are large at first and then become smaller. This coincides with the intuitive impression that the news spreads rapidly at first and then progressively slower.

Now Try Exercise 5 ■

EXAMPLE 5

Supply and demand This year's level of production and price for most agricultural products greatly affect the level of production and price next year. Suppose that the current crop of soybeans in a certain country is 80 million bushels. Let q_n denote the quantity[3] of soybeans grown n years from now, and let p_n denote the market price in n years. Suppose experience has shown that q_n and p_n are related by the following equations:

$$p_n = 20 - .1q_n \qquad q_n = 5p_{n-1} - 10.$$

Draw a graph depicting the changes in production from year to year.

Solution What we seek is the graph of a difference equation for q_n.

$$q_n = 5p_{n-1} - 10 = 5(20 - .1q_{n-1}) - 10 = 100 - .5q_{n-1} - 10 = -.5q_{n-1} + 90$$

This is a difference equation for q_n with

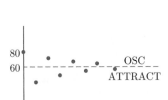

$$a = -.5 \qquad b = 90 \qquad \frac{b}{1-a} = \frac{90}{1-(-.5)} = 60.$$

Since a is negative, the graph is oscillating. Since $|a| = .5 < 1$, the graph is attracted to the line $y = b/(1-a) = 60$. The initial condition is $q_0 = 80$. So the graph is as drawn in Fig. 4. Note that the graph oscillates and approaches 60. That is, the crop size fluctuates from year to year and eventually gets close to 60 million bushels.

Figure 4

Now Try Exercise 13 ■

Practice Problems 11.5

1. **Glucose Infusion** Glucose is being given to a patient intravenously at the rate of 100 milligrams per minute. Let y_n be the amount of glucose in the bloodstream after n minutes, measured in milligrams. Suppose that each minute the body takes from the bloodstream 2% of the amount of glucose present at the beginning of that minute. Find a difference equation for y_n and sketch its graph. (*Hint:* Each minute the amount of glucose in the bloodstream is increased by

the intravenous infusion and decreased by the absorption into the body.)

2. **Light at Ocean Depths** Sunlight is absorbed by water and so, as one descends into the ocean, the intensity of light diminishes. Suppose that at each depth, going down one more meter causes a 20% decrease in the intensity of the sunlight. Find a difference equation for y_n, the intensity of the light at a depth of n meters, and sketch its graph.

EXERCISES 11.5

1. **Population Dynamics** In a certain country with current population 100 million, each year the number of births is 3% and the number of deaths 1% of the population at the beginning of the year. Find the difference equation for y_n, the population after n years. Sketch its graph.

2. **Population Dynamics** A small city with current popula-

tion 50,000 is experiencing an emigration of 600 people each year. Assuming that each year the increase in population due to natural causes is 1% of the population at the start of that year, find the difference equation for y_n, the population after n years. Sketch its graph.

---

[3]q_n in terms of millions of bushels, p_n in terms of dollars per bushel.

3. **Drug Absorption** After a certain drug is injected, each hour the amount removed from the bloodstream by the body is 25% of the amount in the bloodstream at the beginning of the hour. Find the difference equation for y_n, the amount in the bloodstream after n hours, and sketch the graph.

4. **Elevation and Atmospheric Pressure** The atmospheric pressure at sea level is 14.7 pounds per square inch. Suppose that at any elevation an increase of 1 mile results in a decrease of 20% of the atmospheric pressure at that elevation. Find the difference equation for y_n, the atmospheric pressure at elevation n miles, and sketch its graph.

5. **Spread of Information** A sociological study[4] was made to examine the process by which doctors decide to adopt a new drug. Certain doctors who had little interaction with other physicians were called "isolated." Out of 100 isolated doctors, each month the number who adopted the new drug that month was 8% of those who had not yet adopted the drug at the beginning of the month. Find a difference equation for y_n, the number of isolated physicians using the drug after n months, and sketch its graph.

6. **Solution Concentration** A cell is put into a fluid containing an 8 milligram/liter concentration of a solute. (This concentration stays constant throughout.) Initially, the concentration of the solute in the cell is 3 milligrams/liter. The solute passes through the cell membrane at such a rate that each minute the increase in concentration in the cell is 40% of the difference between the outside concentration and the inside concentration. Find the difference equation for y_n, the concentration of the solute in the cell after n minutes, and sketch its graph.

7. **Learning Curve** Psychologists have found that in certain learning situations in which there is a maximum amount that can be learned, the additional amount learned each minute is proportional to the amount yet to be learned at the beginning of that minute. Let 12 units of information be the maximum amount that can be learned and let the constant of proportionality be 30%. Find a difference equation for y_n, the amount learned after n minutes, and sketch its graph.

8. **Genetics** Consider two genes A and a in a population, where A is a dominant gene and a is a recessive gene controlling the same genetic trait. (That is, A and a belong to the same locus.) Suppose that initially 80% of the genes are A and 20% are a. Suppose that in each generation .003% of genes A mutate to gene a. Find a difference equation for y_n, the percentage of genes a after n generations, and sketch its graph. [*Note*: The percentage of genes $A = 100 -$ (the percentage of genes a).]

9. **Account Balance** Thirty thousand dollars is deposited in a savings account paying 5% interest compounded annually, and $1000 is withdrawn from the account at the end of each year. Find the difference equation for y_n, the amount in the account after n years, and sketch its graph.

10. **Account Balance** Rework Exercise 9 where $15,000 is deposited initially.

11. **Thermodynamics** When a cold object is placed in a warm room, each minute its increase in temperature is proportional to the difference between the room temperature and the temperature of the object at the beginning of the minute. Suppose that the room temperature is $70°F$, the initial temperature of the object is $40°F$, and the constant of proportionality is 20%. Find the difference equation for y_n, the temperature of the object after n minutes, and sketch its graph.

12. **Electricity Usage** Suppose that the annual amount of electricity used in the United States will increase at a rate of 1.8% each year and that this year 3.2 trillion kilowatt-hours are being used. Find a difference equation for y_n, the number of kilowatt-hours to be used during the year that is n years from now, and sketch its graph.

13. **Supply and Demand** Suppose that in Example 5 the current price of soybeans is $4.54 per bushel. Find the difference equation for p_n and sketch its graph.

14. **Drug Absorption** The popular sleep-aid drug Zaleplon has a half-life of one hour. That is, the amount of the drug present in the body is halved each hour. If 10 mg of Zaleplon is taken at bedtime, what is the difference equation for the amount of the drug present in the body after n hours? How much will be eliminated after 8 hours?

15. **Drug Absorption** The anti-inflammatory drug Advil® has a half-life of 2 hours. That is, the amount of the drug present in the body is halved every two hours. After 4 hours _____ of the drug will remain in the body.
    (a) 0%   **(b)** 25%   **(c)** 66%   **(d)** 33%

Exercises 16–18 require the use of a graphing calculator or spreadsheet.

In these exercises, answer the questions by generating successive terms of the appropriate difference equation.

16. **Thermodynamics** A steel rod of temperature $600°$ is immersed in a large vat of water at temperature $75°$. Each minute its decrease in temperature is proportional to the difference between the water temperature and the temperature of the rod at the beginning of the minute, where the constant of proportionality is .3. What is the temperature after 2 seconds? When will the temperature drop below $80°$?

---

[4]James S. Coleman, Elihu Katz, and Herbert Menzel, "The Diffusion of an Innovation Among Physicians," *Sociometry*, 20, 1957, pp. 253–270.

17. **Population Dynamics** The birth rate in a certain city is 3.5% per year and the death rate is 2% per year. Also, there is a net movement of population out of the city at a steady rate of 300 people per year. The population in 2009 was 5 million. Estimate the 2014 population. When will the population exceed 6 million? When will the population have doubled to 10 million?

18. **Spread of Information** Consider the sociological study of Exercise 5. Out of a group of *nonisolated* doctors, let y_n be the percent who adopted the new drug after n months. Then y_n satisfies the difference equation

$$y_n = .0025y_{n-1}(500 - y_{n-1}), \quad y_0 = 3.$$

That is, initially 3% were using the drug. What percent were using the drug after 1 year? When were over half of the doctors using the drug? When were over 99% using the drug?

19. **Caffeine Absorption** After caffeine is absorbed into the body, 13% is eliminated from the body each hour. Assume a person drinks an 8-oz cup of brewed coffee containing 130 mg of caffeine, and the caffeine is absorbed immediately into the body. Find the difference equation for y_n, the amount of caffeine in the body after n hours. Solve the difference equation. After how many hours will 65 mg (one-half the original amount) remain in the body? How much caffeine will be in the body 24 hours after the person drank the coffee?

20. **Caffeine Absorption** Refer to Exercise 19. Suppose the person drinks a cup of coffee at 7 A.M. and then drinks a cup of coffee at the end of each hour until 7 A.M. the next day. Find the difference equation for y_n, the amount of caffeine in the body after n hours. Solve the difference equation. How much caffeine will be in the body at the end of the 24 hours?

Solutions to Practice Problems 11.5

1. The amount of glucose in the blood is affected by two factors. It is being increased by the steady infusion of glucose; each minute the amount is increased by 100 milligrams. On the other hand, the amount is being decreased each minute by $.02y_{n-1}$. Therefore,

$$
\begin{array}{ccc}
y_n & = & y_{n-1} \\
\begin{bmatrix} \text{amount after} \\ n \text{ minutes} \end{bmatrix} & = & \begin{bmatrix} \text{amount after} \\ n-1 \text{ minutes} \end{bmatrix} \\
+ & 100 & - & .02y_{n-1} \\
+ & \begin{bmatrix} \text{increase due} \\ \text{to infusion} \end{bmatrix} & - & \begin{bmatrix} \text{amount taken} \\ \text{by the body} \end{bmatrix}
\end{array}
$$

or

$$y_n = .98y_{n-1} + 100.$$

To sketch the graph, first compute $b/(1-a)$.

$$\frac{b}{1-a} = \frac{100}{1-.98} = \frac{100}{.02} = 5000.$$

The amount of glucose in the blood rises and approaches 5000 milligrams (Fig. 5).

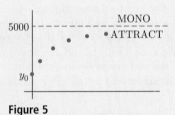

Figure 5

2. The change in intensity in going from depth $n-1$ meters to n meters is 20% of the intensity at $n-1$ meters. Therefore,

$$
\begin{array}{ccccc}
y_n & = & y_{n-1} & - & .20y_{n-1} \\
\begin{bmatrix} \text{intensity at} \\ n \text{ meters} \end{bmatrix} & = & \begin{bmatrix} \text{intensity at} \\ n-1 \text{ meters} \end{bmatrix} & - & \begin{bmatrix} \text{change in} \\ \text{intensity} \end{bmatrix}
\end{array}
$$

$$y_n = .8y_{n-1}.$$

Thus $b/(1-a) = 0$, and the graph is as shown in Fig. 6.

Figure 6

CHAPTER SUMMARY

1. A *difference equation* of the form $y_n = ay_{n-1} + b$, where a, b, and y_0 are specified, determines a sequence of numbers in which each of the numbers (that is, $y_1, y_2, \ldots$) is obtained from the preceding number by multiplying the preceding number by a and adding b. The first number in the sequence, y_0, is called the *initial value*.

2. The graph of a difference equation is obtained by graphing the points $(0, y_0), (1, y_1), (2, y_2), \ldots$.

3. The value of the nth term of a difference equation $y_n = ay_{n-1} + b$ (y_0 given) can be obtained directly (that is, without generating the preceding terms) with one of the following formulas:

$$y_n = \frac{b}{1-a} + \left(y_0 - \frac{b}{1-a}\right) a^n \quad (a \neq 1)$$

$$y_n = y_0 + bn \quad (a = 1).$$

4. Money deposited in a savings account is called the *principal*. The amount of money earned by the deposit is determined by the type of interest (*simple* or *compound*), the yearly rate of interest, and, for compound interest, the number of times interest is compounded annually. Suppose P dollars is deposited at yearly interest rate r. With simple interest, the balance after n years, y_n, satisfies the difference equation

$$y_n = y_{n-1} + rP, \quad y_0 = P.$$

With interest compounded k times per year, the *interest rate per period* is $i = r/k$ and the balance after n years, y_n, satisfies the difference equation

$$y_n = (1+i)y_{n-1}, \quad y_0 = P.$$

5. Terminology has been developed to describe the behavior of graphs of difference equations.

increasing	rises when read from left to right
decreasing	falls when read from left to right
monotonic	either increasing or decreasing
oscillating	changes its direction from rising to falling with every term
constant	always has the same value, y_0
attracted	moves closer and closer to the line $y = b/(1-a)$
repelled	moves farther and farther away from the line $y = b/(1-a)$ without bound

6. The five-step procedure for sketching the graph of a difference equation appears on pages 543–544.

7. A *mortgage* is a loan that is paid off in equal payments. The sequence of successive balances (that is, amounts still owed) satisfies a difference equation of the form

$$y_n = (1+i)y_{n-1} - R,$$

where i is the interest rate per period and R is the payment per period.

8. An *annuity* is a sequence of equal deposits into a savings account. The sequence of successive balances satisfies a difference equation of the form

$$y_n = (1+i)y_{n-1} + D,$$

where i is the interest rate per period and D is the payment per period.

REVIEW OF FUNDAMENTAL CONCEPTS

1. Explain how a sequence of numbers is generated by a difference equation of the form $y_n = ay_{n-1} + b$.

2. What is meant by an initial value for the difference equation in Question 1?

3. How do you obtain the graph of the difference equation in Question 1?

4. Give the formula that is the solution of the difference equation $y_n = ay_{n-1} + b$ with $a \neq 1$ and then with $a = 1$.

5. Explain how both simple interest and compound interest work.

6. What does it mean for a graph to be increasing? decreasing? monotonic? oscillating? constant?

7. Describe the possible long-run behaviors of the graph of the difference equation $y_n = ay_{n-1} + b$, $a \neq 1$.

8. Give the five-step procedure for sketching the graph of $y_n = ay_{n-1} + b$, $a \neq 1$.

9. What is a mortgage, and how are its successive balances calculated?

10. What is an annuity, and how are its successive balances calculated?

KEY FORMULAS

The solution of the difference equation $y_n = ay_{n-1} + b$ with y_0 given is

$$y_n = \frac{b}{1-a} + \left(y_0 - \frac{b}{1-a}\right)a^n, \quad \text{if } a \neq 1$$

$$y_n = y_0 + bn, \quad \text{if } a = 1.$$

With P dollars invested at simple interest rate r, the balance after n years, y_n, satisfies the difference equation $y_n = y_{n-1} + rP$, $y_0 = P$.

With P dollars invested at compound interest with periodic interest rate i, the balance after n interest periods, y_n, satisfies the difference equation $y_n = (1+i)y_{n-1}$, $y_0 = P$.

The balance y_n after the nth payment on a mortgage at periodic interest rate i and periodic payment R satisfies the difference equation $y_n = (1+i)y_{n-1} - R$.

The balance y_n after the nth deposit of D dollars into an annuity earning periodic interest rate i satisfies the difference equation $y_n = (1+i)y_{n-1} + D$.

SUPPLEMENTARY EXERCISES

1. Consider the difference equation $y_n = -3y_{n-1} + 8$, $y_0 = 1$.
   (a) Generate y_1, y_2, y_3 from the difference equation.
   (b) Solve the difference equation.
   (c) Use the solution in part (b) to obtain y_4.

2. Consider the difference equation $y_n = y_{n-1} - \frac{3}{2}$, $y_0 = 10$.
   (a) Generate y_1, y_2, y_3 from the difference equation.
   (b) Solve the difference equation.
   (c) Use the solution in part (b) to obtain y_6.

3. **Account Balance** How much money would you have to put into a savings account initially at 3.05% interest compounded quarterly in order to have $2474 after 7 years?

4. **Account Balance** How much money would you have in the bank after 2 years if you deposited $1000 at 5.2% interest compounded weekly?

5. Make a rough sketch of the graph of the difference equation $y_n = -\frac{1}{3}y_{n-1} + 8$, $y_0 = 10$, without generating terms.

6. Make a rough sketch of the graph of the difference equation $y_n = 1.5y_{n-1} - 2$, $y_0 = 5$, without generating terms.

7. **Population Dynamics** The population of a certain city is currently 120,000. The growth rate of the population due to more births than deaths is 3% per year. Furthermore, each year 600 people move out of the city. Let y_n be the population after n years.
   (a) Find the difference equation for the population growth.
   (b) What will be the population after 20 years?

8. **Mortgage** The monthly payment on a $35,000, 30-year mortgage at 12% interest compounded monthly is $360.

Let y_n be the unpaid balance of the mortgage after n months.
   (a) Give the difference equation expressing y_n in terms of y_{n-1}. Also, give y_0.
   (b) What is the unpaid balance after 7 years?

9. **Annuity** How much money must be deposited at the end of each week into an annuity at 5.2% (= .052) interest compounded weekly in order to have $40,000 after 21 years?

10. **Mortgage Payments** Find the monthly payment on a $33,100, 20-year mortgage at 6% interest compounded monthly.

11. **Loan** How much money can you borrow at 8% interest compounded annually if the loan is to be paid off in yearly installments for 18 years and you can afford to pay $2400 per year?

12. **Alumnus Gift** A college alumnus pledges to give his alma mater $50 at the end of each month for 4 years. If the college puts the money in a savings account earning 6% interest compounded monthly, how much money will be in the account at the end of 4 years?

13. **Political Campaign** An unknown candidate for governor in a state having 1,000,000 voters mounts an extensive media campaign. Each day, 10% of the voters who do not yet know about him become aware of his candidacy. Let y_n be the number of voters who are aware of his candidacy after n days. Find a difference equation for y_n, and sketch its graph.

14. **State Legislature** Suppose that 100 people were just elected to a certain state legislature and that after each term 8% of those still remaining from this original group will either retire or not be reelected. Let y_n be the number of legislators from the original group of 100 who are still serving after n terms. Find a difference equation for y_n, and sketch its graph.

CHAPTER TEST

1. Consider the difference equation $y_n = \frac{1}{2}y_{n-1} + 3$, $y_0 = -2$.
   (a) Determine y_1, y_2, y_3.
   (b) Solve the difference equation.
   (c) Use the solution in part (b) to determine y_4.

2. Consider the difference equation $y_n = y_{n-1} + 50$, $y_0 = 60$.
   (a) Determine y_1, y_2, y_3.
   (b) Solve the difference equation.
   (c) Use the solution in part (b) to determine y_4.

3. Make a rough sketch of the graph of each difference equation without generating terms or solving the difference equation.
   (a) $y_n = .6y_{n-1} + 20$, $y_0 = 10$
   (b) $y_n = -1.25y_{n-1} + 9$, $y_0 = 2$

4. **Chlorine Concentration** Ideally, the concentration of chlorine in a swimming pool should be between 1 and 2 parts per million (ppm). Due to the sun and bacteria, about 20% of the chlorine dissipates each day. Suppose that initially a swimming pool has a concentration of 1 ppm. How much chlorine, in ppm, should be added to the pool at the end of each day so that the concentration will approach 1.5 ppm as the days progress?

5. **Bank Loan** Brittany takes out a loan from a bank and repays it in quarterly payments. The balance after n quarters, y_n, satisfies the difference equation $y_n = 1.02y_{n-1} - 3000$, $y_0 = 31,726$.
   (a) How much money did Brittany borrow?
   (b) What was the yearly rate of interest?
   (c) How much did Brittany pay each quarter?
   (d) What will the balance of the loan be after the first quarterly payment?

6. **Loan Status** The following table shows partial data for the initial status of a 2-year loan with monthly payments.

Payment Number	1	2	3
Balance	A	$8,888.01	B
Interest	$100	$96.31	$92.58
Reduction of debt	$354.15	$357.84	C

   (a) What is the monthly payment?
   (b) What is the yearly rate of interest?
   (c) Find A, B, and C.

7. **Mortgage** I plan to take out a 25-year mortgage at 9% interest compounded monthly. If I am able to pay $1000 per month, how much can I borrow?

8. **Annuity** Suppose that $500 is deposited into an annuity at the end of each year and that interest is 6% compounded annually. Let y_n be the balance at the end of n years.
   (a) Give the difference equation for y_n. (Include the initial value.)
   (b) How much money will be in the annuity after 17 years?

9. **Annuity** How much money would you have to deposit at the end of each month into an annuity paying 6% interest compounded monthly in order to have $20,000 after 10 years?

10. **Drug Absorption** Patients with certain heart problems are often treated with digitoxin, a derivative of the digitalis plant. The rate at which a person's body eliminates digitoxin is proportional to the amount of digitoxin present. Each day about 10% of any given amount of the drug will be eliminated. Suppose that a dose of .05 milligram is given daily to a patient. Find the difference equation for y_n, the amount in the bloodstream after n doses, and describe the graph.

CHAPTER 11 | PROJECT

Connections to Markov Processes

This chapter project uses difference equations to find the stable distribution for a Markov process and gain insights into the rate with which distribution matrices approach the stable distribution.

1. Show that any 2×2 stochastic matrix can be written in the form

$$A = \begin{bmatrix} 1-s & r \\ s & 1-r \end{bmatrix},$$

where r and s are numbers between 0 and 1.

In this discussion, we will make the assumption that r and s are not both zero and are not both one. Denote the successive distribution matrices associated with matrix A as

$$\begin{bmatrix} x_0 \\ y_0 \end{bmatrix}, \quad \begin{bmatrix} x_1 \\ y_1 \end{bmatrix}, \quad \begin{bmatrix} x_2 \\ y_2 \end{bmatrix}, \dots,$$

where

$$\begin{bmatrix} x_n \\ y_n \end{bmatrix} = A \cdot \begin{bmatrix} x_{n-1} \\ y_{n-1} \end{bmatrix} \quad \text{for } n = 1, 2, 3, \dots.$$

2. Show that $x_n = [1 - (r+s)]x_{n-1} + r$ and $y_n = [1 - (r+s)]y_{n-1} + s$. (*Hint*: Use the fact that $x_{n-1} + y_{n-1} = 1$.)

3. Show that the values of x_n approach $\dfrac{r}{r+s}$ as n gets large.

4. Show that the values of y_n approach $\dfrac{s}{r+s}$ as n gets large.

5. Express the stable distribution for A in terms of r and s.

6. Apply the result in part 5 to the 2×2 matrix in Example 1 of Section 8.2 to obtain the stable distribution for the working women Markov process.

7. Use the result in part 2 to solve for $\begin{bmatrix} x_n \\ y_n \end{bmatrix}$. That is, obtain an explicit formula for each entry that does not depend directly on A or on the preceding terms in the sequence other than the initial terms x_0 and y_0.

8. Explain why successive distribution matrices approach the stable distribution rapidly when $r + s$ is close to 1.

9. When will successive distributions oscillate about the stable distribution as they approach it?

APPENDICES

APPENDIX A
Areas Under the Standard Normal Curve

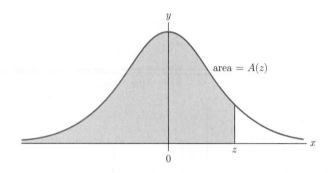

TABLE 1	Areas under the standard normal curve								
z	$A(z)$	z	$A(z)$	z	$A(z)$	z	$A(z)$	z	$A(z)$
−3.50	.0002	−2.00	.0228	−.50	.3085	1.00	.8413	2.45	.9929
−3.45	.0003	−1.95	.0256	−.45	.3264	1.05	.8531	2.50	.9938
−3.40	.0003	−1.90	.0287	−.40	.3446	1.10	.8643	2.55	.9946
−3.35	.0004	−1.85	.0322	−.35	.3632	1.15	.8749	2.60	.9953
−3.30	.0005	−1.80	.0359	−.30	.3821	1.20	.8849	2.65	.9960
−3.25	.0006	−1.75	.0401	−.25	.4013	1.25	.8944	2.70	.9965
−3.20	.0007	−1.70	.0446	−.20	.4207	1.2813	.9000	2.75	.9970
−3.15	.0008	−1.65	.0495	−.15	.4404	1.30	.9032	2.80	.9974
−3.10	.0010	−1.60	.0548	−.10	.4602	1.35	.9115	2.85	.9978
−3.05	.0011	−1.55	.0606	−.05	.4801	1.40	.9192	2.90	.9981
−3.00	.0013	−1.50	.0668	.00	.5000	1.45	.9265	2.95	.9984
−2.95	.0016	−1.45	.0735	.05	.5199	1.50	.9332	3.00	.9987
−2.90	.0019	−1.40	.0808	.10	.5398	1.55	.9394	3.05	.9989
−2.85	.0022	−1.35	.0885	.15	.5596	1.60	.9452	3.10	.9990
−2.80	.0026	−1.30	.0968	.20	.5793	1.65	.9505	3.15	.9992
−2.75	.0030	−1.25	.1056	.25	.5987	1.70	.9554	3.20	.9993
−2.70	.0035	−1.20	.1151	.30	.6179	1.75	.9599	3.25	.9994
−2.65	.0040	−1.15	.1251	.35	.6368	1.80	.9641	3.30	.9995
−2.60	.0047	−1.10	.1357	.40	.6554	1.85	.9678	3.35	.9996
−2.55	.0054	−1.05	.1469	.45	.6736	1.90	.9713	3.40	.9997
−2.50	.0062	−1.00	.1587	.50	.6915	1.95	.9744	3.45	.9997
−2.45	.0071	−.95	.1711	.55	.7088	2.00	.9772	3.50	.9998
−2.40	.0082	−.90	.1841	.60	.7257	2.05	.9798		
−2.35	.0094	−.85	.1977	.65	.7422	2.10	.9821		
−2.30	.0107	−.80	.2119	.70	.7580	2.15	.9842		
−2.25	.0122	−.75	.2266	.75	.7734	2.20	.9861		
−2.20	.0139	−.70	.2420	.80	.7881	2.25	.9878		
−2.15	.0158	−.65	.2578	.85	.8023	2.30	.9893		
−2.10	.0179	−.60	.2743	.90	.8159	2.35	.9906		
−2.05	.0202	−.55	.2912	.95	.8289	2.40	.9918		

APPENDIX B
Using the TI-83/84 Plus Graphing Calculators

Functions

Functions are graphed in a rectangular window like the one shown in Fig. 1. The numbers on the x-axis range from **Xmin** to **Xmax**, and the numbers on the y-axis range from **Ymin** to **Ymax**. The distances between tick marks are **Xscl** and **Yscl** on the x- and y-axes, respectively. To specify these quantities, press WINDOW and type in the values of the six variables. Figure 2 gives the settings associated with the window in Fig. 4. The axis ranges corresponding to this setting are often denoted by $[-4, 4]$ by $[-5, 8]$. (*Note*: To enter a negative number, use the (−) key on the bottom row of the calculator.)

Figure 1. Typical window

Figure 2. Settings for Fig. 4

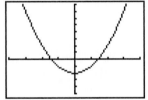

Figure 3. Function declarations

To specify functions, press the Y= key and type expressions next to the function names $Y_1, Y_2, \ldots$. (*Note*: To erase an expression, use the arrow keys to move the cursor anywhere on the expression, and press CLEAR.) In the screen of Fig. 3, called the "**Y=** editor," several functions have been specified. The expressions were produced with the following keystrokes:

Y_1: X,T,θ,n x^2 − 2

Y_2: 2 X,T,θ,n (Notice that a multiplication sign is not needed.)

Y_3: 2nd [√] 1 + X,T,θ,n)

Y_4: (−) 1 ÷ ((1 − X,T,θ,n))

Y_5: 2 ^ X,T,θ,n (^ is the symbol for exponentiation.)

Y_6: 5 VARS ▶ 1 3   (The standard method for entering a function.)

Notice that in Fig. 3 the equal sign in Y_1 is highlighted, whereas the other equal signs are not

highlighted. This highlighting can be toggled by moving the cursor to an equal sign and pressing ENTER. Functions with highlighted equal signs are said to be *selected*. Pressing the GRAPH key instructs the calculator to graph all selected functions. (*Note*: The words **Plot1 Plot2 Plot3** on the first row are used for statistical plots. The backslash symbol preceding each function is used to specify one of seven possible styles for the graph of the function.)

Press GRAPH to obtain Fig. 4. Then press TRACE and press ▶, the right-arrow, 29 times to obtain Fig. 5. Each time a right- or left-arrow key is pressed, the trace cursor moves along the curve and the coordinates of the trace cursor are displayed.

Figure 4

Figure 5

To approximate the function value for a specific value of x, move the trace cursor as close as possible to the value of x and read the y-coordinate of the point. For a more precise function value, press 2nd [CALC] 1, type in a value for **X** (such as 2.5), and press ENTER. See Fig. 6. Alternately, you can just enter 2.5 without first pressing 2nd [CALC] 1.

Figure 6

Figure 7

A point where the graph crosses the x-axis is called an *x-intercept*. The coordinates of an x-intercept can be approximated by tracing. The x-coordinate of an x-intercept of the function Y_1 is called a *zero* of Y_1 or a *root* of the equation $Y_1 = 0$. Figure 4 shows that Y_1 has a zero between 1 and 2 and the value of the zero is about 1.5. For a precise value of the zero, press 2nd [CALC] 2 and answer the questions. See Fig. 7. Reply to "**Left Bound?**" by moving the trace cursor to a point whose x-coordinate is less than the root and pressing ENTER. Reply to "**Right Bound?**" by moving the trace cursor to a point whose x-coordinate is greater than the root and pressing ENTER. See Fig. 8. Reply to **"Guess?"** by moving the trace cursor near the x-intercept and pressing ENTER. Figure 9 shows the resulting display. An alternate way to find a zero of a function is to reply to the questions by entering appropriate numbers. For instance, after pressing 2nd [CALC] **2**, respond to **"Left Bound?"** by typing in the number 1 and pressing ENTER, respond to **"Right Bound?"** by typing in the number 2 and pressing ENTER, and respond to **"Guess?"** by typing in the number 1.5 and pressing ENTER. The final screen will be identical to Fig. 9.

Figure 8   **Figure 9**

So far, all operations were carried out while looking at the graph of a function. These same operations also can be carried out in the home screen, which is invoked by pressing 2nd [QUIT]. For instance, the function **Y₁** can be evaluated at 4 by entering $Y_1(4)$ and pressing ENTER.

Return to the **Y=** editor by pressing Y= and then select **Y₂** so that now both **Y₁** and **Y₂** are selected. Press GRAPH to obtain the graphs of the two functions. Press TRACE and then press the right-arrow key several times. Now press the down-arrow key several times. Each time the down-arrow key is pressed, the trace cursor moves from one curve to the other. The identity of the function containing the cursor is given in the upper left part of the screen. Move the cursor as close as possible to the point of intersection of the two curves to approximate the coordinates of the intersection point. For more precise values, press 2nd [CALC] **5** and answer the questions. Reply to **"First curve?"** by moving the trace cursor to one of the curves and pressing ENTER. Reply to **"Second curve?"** by moving the trace cursor to the other curve and pressing ENTER. Reply to **"Guess?"** by either moving the trace cursor near the point of intersection or typing in a number close to the x-coordinate of the point and pressing ENTER. Figure 10 shows the resulting display.

Figure 10

Tables

When you press 2nd [TABLE], a table of function values is displayed with a column for each selected function. (If more than two functions are selected, you must press the right-arrow key to see the third and later functions.) Prior to invoking a table, you should press 2nd [TBLSET] to specify certain properties of the table. See Fig. 11. The values for **X** will begin with the setting of **TblStart** and increase by the setting of **ΔTbl**. For our purposes, the settings for **Indpnt** and **Depend** should always be **Auto**. After you press 2nd [TABLE] to display the table (see Fig. 12), you can use the up- and down-arrow keys to generate further values.

Figure 11   **Figure 12**

Matrices

The TI-83/84 Plus can store up to 10 matrices referred to as $[A], [B], [C], \ldots$. Pressing 2nd [MATRX] or 2nd [MATRIX] produces the screen in Fig. 13 with the three menus **NAMES**, **MATH**, and **EDIT**. The **NAMES** menu is used to display the name of a matrix on the home screen, the **MATH** menu is used to perform certain operations on a single matrix, and the **EDIT** menu is used to define a new matrix or alter an existing matrix.

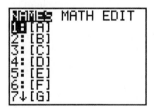

Figure 13

To create a new matrix   Press 2nd [MATRX] ◄ to call up the **MATRIX EDIT** menu, and then press a number corresponding to one of the unused matrix names to obtain a matrix-entry screen. Type in the number of rows, press ENTER, type in the number of columns, and press ENTER to specify the size of the matrix. Then type in the first entry of the matrix, press ENTER, type in the next entry of the matrix, press ENTER, and so on until all entries have been entered. See Fig. 14 on the next page.

Figure 14

To alter an existing matrix Press $\boxed{2\text{nd}}$ [MATRX] $\boxed{\blacktriangleleft}$ to call up the matrix **EDIT** menu, and then press a number corresponding to the name of the matrix to be altered. Move the cursor to any entry you want to change, type in the new number, and press $\boxed{\text{ENTER}}$. You can change as many entries as you like, even the number of rows and columns.

To delete a matrix Press $\boxed{2\text{nd}}$ [MEM] **2 5** to obtain a list of all matrices that have been created. Use the down-arrow key to select the desired matrix, and then press $\boxed{\text{ENTER}}$ $\boxed{\text{DEL}}$ **2**.

To display the name of a matrix on the home screen Press $\boxed{2\text{nd}}$ [MATRX] to obtain a list of all matrix names. Use the down-arrow key to select the desired matrix, and then press $\boxed{\text{ENTER}}$. Alternately, from the matrix **NAMES** menu, type the number associated with the matrix.

Lists

A list can be thought of as a sequence or an ordered set of up to 999 numbers. Although lists can have custom names, we will use the built-in names $L_1, L_2, \ldots, L_6$ that are found above the numeric keys. To display L_1 on the home screen, press $\boxed{2\text{nd}}$ [L_1]. The elements of list L_1 can be referred to as $L_1(1), L_1(2), L_1(3), \ldots$. A set of numbers can be placed into a list by enclosing them with set braces and storing them in the list. However, often the stat list editor provides the best way to place numbers into lists and to view lists.

To invoke the stat list editor, press $\boxed{\text{STAT}}$ **1**. Initially, the stat list editor has columns labeled L_1, L_2, and L_3. See Fig. 15. Three more columns for lists are off the screen.

L1	L2	L3	1
▓▓▓▓▓▓	------	------	
L1(1)=			

Figure 15

To place a number into a list in the stat list editor Move the cursor to the dashed line, type in the number, and press either the down-arrow key or the $\boxed{\text{ENTER}}$ key.

To remove a number from a list in the stat list editor Move the cursor to the number and press $\boxed{\text{DEL}}$.

To delete all numbers in a list from the stat list editor Move the cursor to the list name at the top of the screen and press $\boxed{\text{CLEAR}}$ $\boxed{\text{ENTER}}$.

To create a scatterplot of a set of points whose x-coordinates are in L_1 and whose y-coordinates are in L_2 Press $\boxed{2\text{nd}}$ [STAT PLOT] **1**, create the screen in Fig. 16, and press $\boxed{\text{GRAPH}}$. (*Note*: Check that the window settings are adequate for displaying the points.)

Figure 16

Histograms

The following steps display a frequency histogram with rectangles centered above the integers $a, a + 1, \ldots, b$.

- Press $\boxed{\text{STAT}}$ **1** to invoke the list editing screen shown in Fig. 15.
- Enter each number from a to b having nonzero frequency in the L_1 column and its associated frequency to its right in the L_2 column. Or, ignore the L_2 column and place each number (repeated according to its frequency) in the L_1 column.
- Press $\boxed{2\text{nd}}$ [STAT PLOT] **1** to invoke a screen similar to Fig. 16.
- Select "On" in the second line, the histogram icon in the Type line, and L_1 in the Xlist line. If you ignored the L_2 column in the second step, place 1 in the Freq line; otherwise, place L_2 in the Freq line.
- Press $\boxed{\text{WINDOW}}$ to invoke the window screen in Fig. 2.
- Set Xmin $= a - .5$, Xmax $= b + .5$, Xscl $= 1$, Ymin $\approx -.3*$(greatest frequency), Ymax $\approx 1.2*$(greatest frequency), Yscl $\approx .1*$(greatest frequency). *Note*: These Y settings allow ample space for the display of values while tracing.
- Press $\boxed{\text{GRAPH}}$ to view the histogram.
- To view the height of a rectangle, press $\boxed{\text{TRACE}}$ and use the arrow keys to move the cursor to the top center of the rectangle. The values of *min*, *max*, and *n* will be the x-coordinate of the left side of the rectangle, the x-coordinate of the right side of the rectangle, and the height of the rectangle, respectively.

A relative frequency histogram can be displayed by placing the relative frequencies in the L_2 column of the list editor. If so, the *greatest relative frequency* should be used in place of the *greatest frequency* when setting the values of Ymin, Ymax, and Yscl.

TVM Solver

TVM stands for "Time Value of Money." TVM Solver is a powerful calculating tool than can compute the values discussed in Chapter 10, "The Mathematics of Finance." Compound interest problems, annuities, and mortgages involve five numbers: duration, interest rate, periodic payment (0 for compound interest problems), present value, and future value. Once four of the five numbers are known, TVM Solver can be used to calculate the fifth number. The TVM Solver screen, shown in Fig. 17, is invoked by pressing APPS ENTER ENTER.

Figure 17

Figure 18

The eight lines of TVM Solver hold the following information:

N: The duration in terms of interest periods.

I%: The annual interest rate given as a percent; such as 6 or 4.5. In Chapter 10 its value would be $100r$.

PV: The present value. It is the principal of a compound interest problem, and the loan amount of a mortgage. It has the value 0 for an increasing annuity.

PMT: The periodic payment. It is the rent of an annuity or mortgage, and has value 0 in a compound interest problem.

FV: The future value. It is the balance in a compound interest problem and an annuity. It has the value 0 for a mortgage.

P/Y: The number of payments per year. For our purposes, it is the same as C/Y.

C/Y: The number of times interest is compounded per year. That is, 1, 2, 4, 12, 52, or 365.

PMT: When payments are paid—the *end* or *beginning* of each interest period. For our purposes, it will always be set to END.

Note: Amounts paid to the bank, such as the principal in a compound interest problem or the rent of a mortgage, are given as negative numbers.

To use TVM Solver.

- Enter all information except for one of the top five values, the value to be calculated.
- Move the cursor to the line containing the value to be calculated.
- Press ALPHA [SOLVE]. (*Note*: The green word SOLVE is located above the ENTER key.) A small square will appear to the left of the line and the calculated value will appear in the line.

Fig. 18 shows that the interest rate required for a deposit of $100 to double to $200 in 10 years with interest compounded quarterly is almost 7%. (The value entered for PV is negative since it represents money paid to the bank.)

Finance Functions

In addition to containing TVM Solver, the finance menu contains several functions. The two functions most valuable to us, Eff and Nom, calculate effective and nominal interest rates. (To display one of these functions on the home screen, press APPS ENTER, scroll to the function, and press ENTER.) If interest rate r compounded m times per year is a nominal rate, then $r_{\text{eff}} = \texttt{Eff}(100r, m)/100$. For instance, the effective rate .037 found in Example 7 of Section 10.1 can be calculated as $\texttt{Eff(3.65,4)}/100$.

Similarly, the value of $\texttt{Nom}(100r_{\text{eff}}, m)/100$ is the corresponding nominal rate. For instance, the value of $\texttt{Nom(3.7,4)}/100$ is approximately 3.65%. *Note*: The values for effective and nominal rates calculated with Eff and Nom will differ slightly from those calculated in Section 10.1 due to rounding errors.

APPENDIX C
Spreadsheet Fundamentals

Figure 1.   Upper-left corner of a Microsoft Excel spreadsheet.

Cell

A *cell* is a small rectangle located at the intersection of a column and a row. Its *address* or *reference* (also known as its *relative address* or *relative reference*) consists of its column letter followed by its row number. When you click on a cell, its border thickens and its address is displayed in the Name box. Such a cell is said to be *selected* or *active*. After you type text, a number, or a formula into an active cell and press the Enter key, the text, number, or the value of the formula is displayed in the cell. The exact information you typed (known as the *content* of the cell) is displayed in the Formula bar whenever you reselect the cell.

Range

A *range of cells* or *range* is a rectangular array of more than one cell. The *address* or *reference* of a range consists of the address of the cell in the upper-left corner of the range, a colon (:), and then the address of the cell in the lower-right corner. To *select* a range, hold down the left mouse button while you drag the cursor from the upper-left cell to the lower-right cell. You can fill a range by entering information into each cell individually. However, often you fill an entire range with a single formula. If so, you should press Ctrl+Shift+Enter (instead of just Enter) after typing in the formula. Such a formula, called a *range formula* or an *array formula*, is automatically displayed in the Formula bar surrounded by braces.

Moving a Cell or Range

You can move a selected cell or range by dragging its border, or by pressing Ctrl+X, clicking on the new location, and pressing Ctrl+V. If the content of the original cell or range uses relative addresses, these addresses automatically change to reflect the new position of the cell or range. (You can prevent an address from changing by preceding its column letter and row number with dollar signs. Such an address is called an *absolute address*.)

Naming a Cell or Range

As an alternative to identifying cells or ranges with addresses, you can give a *name* to a cell or range. To specify a name, select the cell or range, click on the Name box, type in the name, and press the Enter key. (*Note:* The name will not be registered if you forget to press the Enter key.) Names can contain up to 255 characters (no spaces), must begin with a letter or underscore character, and cannot look like addresses. Deleting the contents of a cell or range does not delete its name. To delete a name with Excel 2007, click Name Manager in the Defined Names group on the Formulas tab, click on the name that you want to change in the Name Manager dialog box, press the Delete key, and then click OK to confirm the deletion. To delete a name in Excel 97-2003, click on Name in the Insert menu, click on Define, click on the name in the list of names that appears, click the Delete button, and click the OK button.

Entering a Formula

Formulas are what make a spreadsheet a spreadsheet. To specify that the entry typed into a selected cell or range is a formula, you first type an equal sign (=). The equal sign is followed by a expression containing numbers, addresses, names, functions, and operators such as +, −, *, /, and ^ (exponentiation).

Copying a Formula

Select the cell or range whose content is the original formula. There are two methods to copy the formula. (*Note*: With both methods, all relative addresses will be altered appropriately.)

First method: Press Ctrl+C, select the location(s) to hold the copy or copies, and press Ctrl+V.

Second method: Hover the mouse pointer over the cell's fill handle until the pointer becomes a crosshair (+). Drag the pointer vertically or horizontally along the cells that are to hold the copy or copies.

Installing Add-Ins

Two Excel tools that we use in this book are called *Solver* and *Data Analysis*. Solver is used to find solutions to systems of linear equations and to linear programming problems. Data Analysis is used to analyze data. To see if these tools have been installed with Excel 2007, look in the Analysis group on the Data tab. If they are not present, click the round Microsoft Office button, click Excel Options, click Add-Ins, select Excel Add-ins in the Manager box, click Go, select Analysis ToolPak and Solver Add-in in the Add-ins window, and click OK. To see if these tools have been installed with Excel 97-2003, click the Tools button on the menu bar and see if the tools are listed. If not, click on Add-Ins in the Tools menu, check the boxes next to Analysis ToolPak and Solver, and then click on the OK button. In some cases, they will not become available until you exit Excel and reinvoke it. Also, you might be instructed to insert your Microsoft Office DVD and run the setup routine to install them.

Entering a Formula by Pointing

Instead of typing the address of a cell into a formula manually, just click on the cell. A dotted rectangle will surround the cell, the cell's name or address will appear in the formula, and the word *Point* will appear in the status bar below the spreadsheet. To enter the address of a range, click on the upper-left cell of the range and drag the mouse cursor to the lower-right cell of the range. A dotted line will surround the range. When you release the mouse, the range's name or address will appear in the formula.

Converting Formulas to Values

Sometimes the formulas that were used to fill a cell or range are no longer needed. To replace their contents with the formulas' values, select the cell or range, and press Ctrl+C. With Excel 2007, click Paste in the Clipboard group on the Home tab, and then click Paste Values. With Excel 97-2003, click on *Paste Special* in the Edit menu, click on the Values circle, and click on the OK button.

Summing a Column or Row of Numbers

Click on the top number in the column or row, drag the mouse pointer to one or more cells beyond the column or row of numbers, and click on *AutoSum*. (In Excel 2007, "Σ AutoSum" is found in the Editing group on the Home tab. In Excel 97-2003, the AutoSum button (Σ) is located in the Standard toolbar.) The contents of the last cell will be a formula containing the SUM function and the value of the cell will be the sum of the numbers in the column or row.

Simulating a Random Sample from a Probability Distribution

The following steps use Excel's Data Analysis tool to create a random sample from a discrete probability distribution. The sample numbers will be displayed in a range of m rows and n columns.

- Place the probability table in the first two columns of the spreadsheet. That is, column A should contain the possible outcomes (which must be numeric) and column B should contain the associated probabilities.
- Click on Data Analysis. (With Excel 2007, Data Analysis is in the Analysis group on the Data tab. With Excel 97-2003, Data Analysis is in the Tools menu.)
- Double-click on Random Number Generation in the Data Analysis dropdown list.
- Enter the number of columns (n) of random numbers into the "Number of Variables" box.
- Enter the number of random numbers (m) that you would like to generate in each column into the Number of Random Numbers box.
- Select "Discrete" as the Distribution.
- Place the address of the range containing the probability distribution in the "Value and Probability Input Range" box. This can be accomplished by placing the cursor in the box, clearing the box if necessary, dragging the mouse pointer from cell A1 to the lower-right corner of the probability table, and releasing the mouse button.
- Click on the Output Range circle, and enter the address of an $m \times n$ array of cells.
- Click on the OK button to generate the desired random sample.

Creating a Frequency Distribution Table and Histogram for the Random Sample Generated Above

The following steps use Excel's Data Analysis tool to create a frequency distribution and optionally a histogram for a range of cells containing the random numbers generated above.

- Click on Data Analysis.

- Double-click on Histogram in the Data Analysis list.
- Place into the Input Range box the address of the range of cells containing the random sample.
- Place into the Bin Range box the address of the range of possible outcomes; that is, the first column of the probability table.
- Click the Output Range circle and key in the address of any cell to the right of the cells already filled.
- If you would like also to display a histogram, click the small rectangle to the left of Chart Output.
- Click the OK button to see the frequency distribution table and possibly the histogram. (*Note*: The word More and the number 0 appear in the last row of the table and in the histogram. To delete them, select the row, click the right mouse button, click Delete, select "Shift cells up", and click OK.)

Using Goal Seek to Solve an Equation Having One Unknown

Suppose the contents of cell B1 contains a formula whose value depends on the value of A1, and you know the value you would like B1 to have. Then the *Goal Seek* tool can be used to determine the value of A1 that will produce the sought-after value in B1. For example, you can use Goal Seek to find the interest rate (compounded annually) for which $100 will grow to $146 after 11 years. Enter `=100*(1+A1)^11` into cell B1 and click on the Goal Seek tool. (In Excel 2007, you locate Goal Seek by clicking on What-If Analysis in the Data Tools group on the Data tab. In Excel 97-2003, Goal Seek is in the Tools menu.) A Goal Seek window will appear. Fill in the window as shown in Fig. 2, and then click the OK button. The

solution, $\approx .0035$ (that is, 3.50%), will appear in cell A1 of the spreadsheet. *Note*: Using the Goal Seek tool is sometimes referred to as *backsolving*.

Figure 2

Using the Insert Function Dialog Box

To invoke the Insert Function dialog box, click on the Insert Function button located next to the Formula bar. The dialog box allows you to display the more than 300 available functions and descriptions of their arguments and what they do. When you select a function and click on OK (or double-click on the function), a Function Arguments dialog box appears to help you specify the arguments of the function. You can fill in each argument box by typing or pointing. To assist you when using the pointing method, you can click on the icon at the right side of an argument box to temporarily collapse the dialog box and thereby make more of the spreadsheet visible. After you have filled the boxes for all the arguments, press OK (or the Enter key) to fill a single cell with the value of the function, or press Ctrl+Shift+Enter to fill a range of cells.

Using Excel's Financial Functions

The five most important financial functions for our purposes are shown in Table 1.

The values of these functions and their parameters are signed according to their flows. Money received by you is given a positive value, and money paid by you is given a negative value. For instance, the values of savings account deposits and loan payments are negative, and the values of savings account withdrawals and loan amounts are positive. Table 2 shows how to use these functions to solve some examples from the text.

Table 3 contains some other useful financial functions. Example 5 of Section 10.3 can be solved by keying

$$=\text{IPMT}(0.75\%,A1,360,112475,0)$$
$$-\text{PPMT}(0.75\%,A1,360,112475,0)$$

into B1 and using Goal Seek to set cell B1 to the value 0 by changing cell A1.

TABLE 1		
Function	**Used to calculate**	**Function and required arguments**
FV	future value	FV(rate, nper, pmt, pv)
PV	present value	PV(rate, nper, pmt, fv)
PMT	periodic payment	PMT(rate, nper, pv, fv)
NPER	number of interest periods	NPER(rate, pmt, pv, fv)
EFFECT	effective rate of interest	EFFECT(nominal_rate, nper)

TABLE 2		
Section	**Example**	**Function and required arguments**
10.1	3	FV(1%, 4, 0, −100)
10.1	5	PV(0.5%, 104, 0, 10000)
10.1	7	EFFECT(3.65%, 4)
10.2	1	FV(0.5%, 60, −100, 0)
10.2	3	PMT(2%, 16, 0, 300000)
10.2	4	PV(1.5%, 8, 3000, 0)
10.2	5	PMT(0.5%, 12, −10000, 0)
10.2	6	NPER(0.5%, −100, 0, 10000)
10.3	2(a)	PMT(0.75%, 360, 112475, 0)
10.3	4	PV(2%, 12, 200, 1000)

TABLE 3		
Function	**Used to calculate**	**Function and required arguments**
RATE	interest rate per period	RATE(nper, pmt, pv, fv)
IPMT	interest portion of loan payment number *per*	IPMT(rate, per, nper, pv, fv)
PPMT	principal reduction portion of loan payment number *per*	PPMT(rate, per, nper, pv, fv)
NOMINAL	nominal rate of interest	NOMINAL(effective_rate, nper)

APPENDIX D
Using the TI-89 Graphing Calculator

Functions

Functions are graphed in rectangular windows like the one shown in Fig. 1. The numbers on the x-axis range from **xmin** to **xmax**, and the numbers on the y-axis range from **ymin** to **ymax**. The distance between the tick marks are **xscl** and **yscl** on the x- and y-axes, respectively. To specify these quantities, press $\blacklozenge$ [WINDOW] and type in the values of these variables. Figure 2 shows the settings associated with the windows in Figs. 1 and 4. The axis ranges associated with this setting are often written $[-4, 4]$ by $[-5, 8]$. (*Note*: To enter a negative number you must use the $\boxed{(-)}$ key on the bottom row of the calculator.)

Figure 1. Typical window

Figure 2. Settings for Figs. 1 and 4

Figure 3. Function declarations

To input functions, press $\blacklozenge$ [Y=] and type expressions next to the function names **y1**, **y2**, ... (*Note*: To erase an expression, use the arrow keys to move to that function and press $\boxed{\text{CLEAR}}$ or $\boxed{\leftarrow}$. To edit an expression once it has been entered, use the arrow keys to highlight the expression and press $\boxed{\text{F3}}$.) In the screen of Fig. 3, called the "**Y=** editor", several functions have been specified. The expressions were input with the following keystrokes:

y1: $\boxed{\text{X}}$ $\boxed{\frown}$ **2** $\boxed{-}$ **2** ($\frown$ is the symbol for exponentiation.)

y2: **2** $\boxed{\text{X}}$ (Notice that a multiplication symbol is not necessary.)

y3: $\boxed{\text{2ND}}$ $\boxed{\sqrt{}}$ **1** $\boxed{+}$ $\boxed{\text{X}}$ $\boxed{)}$

y4: $\boxed{(-)}$ **1** $\boxed{\div}$ $\boxed{((}$ **1** $\boxed{+}$ $\boxed{\text{X}}$ $\boxed{)}$

y5: **5** $\boxed{\text{Y}}$ **3** $\boxed{((}$ $\boxed{\text{X}}$ $\boxed{)}$

Notice that in Fig. 3 there is a check mark in front of **y1** while the other functions do not have check marks in front of them. The check mark can be toggled with the $\boxed{\text{F4}}$ button. Functions with a check mark are said to be

selected. Pressing $\blacklozenge$ [GRAPH] instructs the calculator to graph all selected functions. *Note*: Arrowing up from **y1** shows **Plot1**, **Plot2**, (up to **Plot9**) which are used for statistical plots. There are eight possible styles for the graph of a function found in the STYLE menu accessed by $\boxed{\text{2ND}}$ [F6].

Press $\blacklozenge$ [GRAPH] to obtain Fig. 4. Then press $\boxed{\text{F3}}$ to trace and press $\boxed{\blacktriangleright}$, the right arrow, 49 times to obtain Fig. 5. Each time a right- or left-arrow key is pressed, the trace cursor moves along the curve and the coordinates of the trace cursor are displayed below the graph.

Figure 4

Figure 5

To approximate the function value for a specific value of x, move the cursor as close as possible to the value of x and read the y-coordinate of the point. For a more precise function value, there are two options. While using the trace cursor, input the value of x and press $\boxed{\text{ENTER}}$. Alternatively, press $\boxed{\text{F5}}$, for the Math menu, then **1**, then type in the value of x (such as 2.5), and press $\boxed{\text{ENTER}}$. See Fig. 6.

Figure 6

Figure 7

A point where the graph crosses the x-axis is called an x-*intercept*. Tracing can approximate the coordinates of an x-intercept. The x-coordinate of an x-intercept of the function **y1** is called a *zero* of **y1** or a *root* of the equation **y1=0**. Figure 4 shows that **y1** has a zero between 1 and 2 and the value is about 1.5. For a more precise value of the zero, press $\boxed{\text{F5}}$ **2** and answer the questions. See Fig. 7. Reply to "**Lower Bound?**" by either moving the trace cursor to a point whose x-coordinate is less than the root and pressing $\boxed{\text{ENTER}}$ or by simply typing in a value for the x-coordinate which is less than the root (say 1) and pressing $\boxed{\text{ENTER}}$. See Fig. 8. Reply to "**Upper Bound?**" by either moving the trace cursor to a point whose x-coordinate is greater than the root and pressing $\boxed{\text{ENTER}}$ or by simply typing in a value for the x-coordinate which is greater than the root (say 2) and pressing ENTER. Figure 9 shows the resulting display.

Figure 8   **Figure 9**

Many operations can be carried out using the home screen, which is invoked by pressing HOME. For instance, the function **y1** can be evaluated at -2 by entering **y1(-2)** and pressing ENTER.

Return to the **Y=** editor by pressing ◆[Y=] and then select **y2** so that both **y1** and **y2** are selected. Press ◆ [GRAPH] to obtain the graphs of both functions. Press F3 to trace and then press the right-arrow key several times. Now press the down-arrow key several times. Notice that each time the down-arrow key is pressed, the trace cursor moves from one curve to the other. The identity of the function containing the cursor is indicated in the upper right hand part of the screen. Move the cursor as close as possible to the point of intersection to approximate the coordinates of the point of intersection. For more precise values, press F5 **5** and answer the questions. Reply to "**1st Curve?**" by moving the trace cursor to one of the curves and pressing ENTER. Reply to "**2nd Curve?**" by moving the trace cursor to the other curve and pressing ENTER. Reply to "**Lower Bound?**" by either moving the trace cursor to the left of the point of intersection or typing in a number less than the x-coordinate of the point and pressing ENTER. Reply to "**Upper Bound?**" by either moving the trace cursor to the right of the point of intersection or typing in a number greater than the x-coordinate of the point and pressing ENTER. Figure 10 shows the resulting display.

Figure 10

Tables

When ◆ [TABLE] is pressed, a table of function values is displayed showing a column for each selected function. (If more than three functions are selected, use the right-arrow key to see the fourth and later functions.) Prior to invoking a table, press ◆ [TBLSET] to specify certain properties of the table. See Fig. 11. The values for **x** will

begin with the setting of **tblStart** and increase by the setting of **Δtbl**. For our purposes, the setting for **Graph <-> Table** should be **OFF** and the setting for **Independent** should be **AUTO**. After the table is displayed by pressing ◆ [TABLE] (see Fig. 12), use the up- and down-arrow keys to generate further values.

Figure 11   **Figure 12**

Matrices

Although matrices can be created directly on the home screen, it is usually better to use the Data/Matrix Editor

To create a new matrix   Press APPS, move the cursor to Data/Matrix Editor, and press ENTER followed by **3** to open a **New** matrix. Press ▶ **2** to set the **Type** to **Matrix**. Suppose we want to input a 2×3 matrix. Arrow down to **Variable** and type in a name for the matrix (say **a**). Next input the **Row dimension** (2) and the **Col dimension** (3). See Fig. 13. Then press ENTER twice to obtain the matrix-entry screen. Finally, type in the first entry of the matrix, press ENTER, type in the next entry of the matrix, press ENTER, and so on until all entries have been entered. See Fig. 14.

Figure 13   **Figure 14**

To alter an existing matrix   Press APPS, move the cursor to Data/Matrix Editor, and press ENTER followed by **2** to **Open** an existing matrix. Press ▶ **2** to set the **Type** to **Matrix**. Arrow down to **Variable** and press ▶ to view a list of all saved matrices. Use the down-arrow key to select the matrix you wish to change and press ENTER. Press ENTER again to obtain the matrix-entry screen. Use the arrow keys to highlight the entry to be altered, type the new value, and press ENTER. Change as many entries as needed. If an extra row or column needs to be added, press 2ND [F6] **1**, and then press **2** to insert a new row above the current row or press **3** to insert a new column to the left of the current column. If a row or column needs to be deleted, press 2ND [F6] **2**, and then press **2** to remove the current row or press **3** to remove the current column. The matrix can also be directly resized by pressing 2ND [F6] **6** and then inputting the new row and column dimensions.

To delete a matrix   Press 2ND [Var-Link] to view a list of all variables that have been saved including matrices. Use the down-arrow key to highlight the matrix to be deleted, and then press ←. A screen appears asking for confirmation; press ENTER to delete. If there are multiple matrices to be deleted, highlight each matrix in turn and press F4 each time, then press ←. The confirmation screen will appear; press ENTER to delete.

To display the name of a matrix on the home screen To display a matrix on the home screen, simply type its name on the entry line and press ENTER. Alternately, press 2ND [Var-Link] to view a list of all variables that have been saved including matrices. Use the down-arrow key to highlight the matrix to be displayed, press ENTER to place the matrix name on the entry line, and press ENTER again to see the matrix displayed on the home screen.

To carry out elementary row operations   The three elementary row operations are carried out with the following commands from the MATH/Matrix/Row ops menu.

Interchange *rowA* and *rowB* of *matrix*

   `rowSwap(matrix, rowA, rowB)`

Multiply *rowA* by *value*

   `mRow(value, matrix, rowA)`

Add *value·rowA* to *rowB*

   `mRowAdd(value, matrix, rowA, rowB)`

When one of these commands is carried out, the resulting matrix is displayed but the stored matrix is not changed. Therefore, when a sequence of commands is executed to carry out the Gauss–Jordan elimination method, each command should be followed with STO ▶ *matrix* to change the stored matrix. For instance, if in Example 5 of Section 2.1 the original matrix is named *a*, then the first three row operations are carried out with

   `mRow(1/3,a,1)` STO ▶ a
   `mRowAdd(-4,a,1,2)` STO ▶ a
   `mRowAdd(2,a,1,3)` STO ▶ a

Lists

A list can be thought of as a sequence or an ordered set of up to 999 numbers. There are two basic ways to create a list. In the home screen, a set of numbers can be placed into a list by enclosing the numbers with braces and storing in a variable. See Fig. 15. Lists can also be created in the Data/Matrix Editor by pressing APPS, selecting the Data/Matrix editor, and pressing ENTER followed by **3** to open a new **List**. Press ▶ **3** to set the **Type** to **List**.

Then type in a name for the **Variable**. Press ENTER twice to open the list editor. Type the numbers into the first column that is labeled **c1**. (*Note*: There are 99 columns available.) See Fig. 16.

Figure 15   **Figure 16**

To place a number into a list in the list editor   Type in the number, and press either an arrow key or the ENTER key.

To remove a number from a list in the list editor Move the cursor to the number and press ←.

To remove all numbers in a list in the list editor Move the cursor to the column, then press 2ND [F6] **5** to clear the entire column.

To create a scatter plot of a set of points whose *x*-coordinates are in c1 and whose *y*-coordinates are in c2   First note that when a second column is added, the variable type automatically changes from **List** to **Data**. From the list/data editor press F2 F1 to see Fig. 17. Change the **Plot Type** to **Scatter**, and change the **Mark** to **Dot** (or **Box** or **Cross** or **Plus** or **Square**). Set **x** to **c1** and **y** to **c2**. Leave **Use Freq and Categories?** set to **NO**. See Fig. 18. Press ENTER to save the plot definitions. To view the scatter plot, first set the window to the appropriate ranges and then press ◆ [GRAPH] or type F2 **9** (ZoomData) to have the calculator automatically set the ranges to the data values and graph the scatter plot. (*Note*: Make sure all functions have been deselected before you graph the scatter plot.)

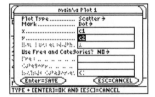

Figure 17   **Figure 18**

Histograms

The following steps display a frequency histogram with rectangles centered above the integers $a, a+1, \ldots, b$.

• Press APPS, move the cursor to Data/Matrix Editor, and press ENTER followed by **3** to open a **New** data screen. Then type in a name for the variable. Press ENTER twice to open a data editing screen similar to that in Fig. 16.

- Enter each number from a to b having nonzero frequency in the **c1** column and its associated frequency to its right in the **c2** column. Or, ignore the **c2** column and place each number (repeated according to its frequency) in the **c1** column.
- Press $\boxed{\text{F2}}$ $\boxed{\text{F1}}$ to invoke a screen similar to Fig. 17. Or, press $\boxed{\blacklozenge}$ [Y=], select **Plot1**, and press $\boxed{\text{F3}}$ to invoke a screen similar to Fig. 17. (*Note*: Make sure to uncheck any other functions defined in the **Y=** editor.)
- Press $\boxed{\blacktriangleright}$ 4 to set the **Plot Type** to **Histogram**. Set **x** to **c1**, set **Hist. Bucket Width** to 1. If the frequencies are in **c2**, set **Use Freq and Categories?** to **YES** by pressing $\boxed{\blacktriangleright}$ 2 and then type **c2** in the **Freq** box. If only **c1** is used, leave **Use Freq and Categories?** set to **NO**. Press $\boxed{\text{ENTER}}$ to save the plot definitions.
- Press $\boxed{\blacklozenge}$ [WINDOW] to invoke a window screen similar to Fig. 2.
- Set **xmin** $= a - .5$, **xmax** $= b + .5$, **xscl** $= 1$, **ymin** $\approx -.3*$(greatest frequency), **ymax** $\approx 1.2*$(greatest frequency), **yscl** $\approx .1*$(greatest frequency). (*Note*: These y settings will allow ample space for the display of values while tracing.)
- Press $\boxed{\blacklozenge}$ [GRAPH] to display the histogram.
- To view the height of each rectangle, press $\boxed{\text{F3}}$ and use the arrow keys to move the cursor to the top center of the rectangles. The value of **min** is the x-coordinate of the left edge of the rectangle, the value of **max** is the x-coordinate of the right edge of the rectangle, and the value of n is the height of the rectangle.

A relative frequency histogram can be displayed by placing the relative frequencies in the **c2** column of the data editor. If so, the *greatest relative frequency* should be used in place of the *greatest frequency* when setting **ymin**, **ymax**, and **yscl**.

Least-Squares Line

The following steps find the straight line that minimizes the least-squares error for the points $(1, 4)$, $(2, 5)$, and $(3, 8)$.

- Use $\boxed{\text{APPS}}$ to display the Data/Matrix editor.
- Press **3** to display a New dialog box.
- Press $\boxed{\blacktriangledown}$ $\boxed{\blacktriangledown}$ and give a name to the variable, such as **dat**.
- Press $\boxed{\text{ENTER}}$ twice to display a spreadsheet.
- Enter the three x-values (1, 2, and 3) into the first column.

- Enter the three y-values (4, 5, and 8) into the second column.
- Press $\boxed{\text{F5}}$ to invoke a Calculate dialog box.
- Set **Calculation Type** to **LinReg**; that is, press **5**.
- Set **x** to **c1**, and set **y** to **c2**.
- Set **Store RegEQ** to **y1(x)**.
- Press $\boxed{\text{ENTER}}$ to invoke a STAT VARS window displaying $\mathbf{y = a \cdot x + b}$, $\mathbf{a = 2}$, $\mathbf{b = 1.666667}$, $\mathbf{corr = .960769}$, $\mathbf{R^2 = .923077}$. (*Note*: $\frac{5}{3} \approx 1.666667$.) The expression $\mathbf{2 \cdot x + 1.6666666666667}$ will be assigned to $\mathbf{y1(x)}$ in the **Y=** editor.)
- Press $\boxed{\text{ENTER}}$ or $\boxed{\text{ESC}}$ to return to the spreadsheet.
- Press $\boxed{\text{F2}}$ to invoke the Plot window.
- Press $\boxed{\text{F1}}$ to invoke the dialog box for setting Plot1.
- Set **Plot Type** to **Scatter**, set **Mark** to **Box**, set **x** to **c1**, set **y** to **c2**, and then press $\boxed{\text{ENTER}}$.
- Press $\boxed{\blacklozenge}$ $\boxed{\text{F2}}$ and set the window to $[-4, 4]$ *by* $[-4, 9]$.
- Press $\boxed{\blacklozenge}$ $\boxed{\text{F3}}$ to produce the graph. (*Note*: The point plotting feature can be suspended by going to the **Y=** window, moving the cursor to Plot1 and pressing $\boxed{\text{F4}}$. Pressing $\boxed{\text{F5}}$ instead, clears the value assigned to Plot1.)

Statistics

The following steps find the mean and standard deviation for a sample.

- Invoke the Data/Matrix editor from the APPS menu.
- Select **3** to set up a new data variable dialog box.
- Set **Type** to **Data**, and give the variable a name such as **s**.
- Press $\boxed{\text{ENTER}}$ twice to invoke a spreadsheet.
- Place the numbers from the left column of the frequency table in the **c1** column and the frequency figures in the **c2** column.
- Press $\boxed{\text{F5}}$ to bring up the Calculate dialog box.
- Set **Calculation Type** to **OneVar**, set **x** to **c1**, set **Use Freq and Categories** to **YES**, and set **Freq** to **c2**.
- Press $\boxed{\text{ENTER}}$ twice to bring up a STAT VARS window. The sample mean and the sample standard deviation appear denoted by $\overline{\text{x}}$ and **Sx**. *Note*: The population standard deviation, σ_X, can be displayed on the home screen. From the home screen, press $\boxed{\text{2ND}}$ [CHAR] **1**, arrow down to σ, press $\boxed{\text{ENTER}}$, press $\boxed{\text{X}}$, and press $\boxed{\text{ENTER}}$.

ANSWERS

CHAPTER 1

Exercises 1.1, page 7

1., 3., 5.

7.

9. e   **11.** Yes   **13.** No   **15.** $m = 5, b = 8$
17. $m = 0, b = 3$ **19.** $y = -2x + 3$
21. $x = \frac{5}{3}$ **23.** $(2, 0), (0, 8)$ **25.** $(7, 0)$, none

27.

29.

31.

33.

35. a, b, c, e   **37. (a)** L_3 **(b)** L_1 **(c)** L_2 **41. (a)**

39. (a) Water at a temperature of $72°F$ was placed in the kettle.   **(b)** $162°F$
(c) $4\frac{2}{3}$ minutes, or 4 minutes, 40 seconds

(b) In 1960, 2.5 trillion cigarettes were sold.
(c) 1980
(d) 7 trillion

43. (a)

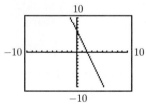

(b) In 1997 the yearly insurance rate for a small car was $678.
(c) $858   **(d)** The year 2012
45. (a) In 2000, 10% of college freshmen smoked.   **(b)** 6.3%   **(c)** 2007
47. $y = -1.5x + .9$ **49.** $y = 0$ **51.** $y = b$ **53.** $2x - y = -3$
55. $1 \cdot x + 0 \cdot y = -3$ **57.** $2x + 3y = -15$ **61.** $y = x - 9$
63. $y = x + 7$ **65.** $y = x + 2$ **67.** $y = x + 9$

69. (a)

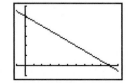

(b) 0
(c) $(2, 0), (0, 6)$

71. (a)

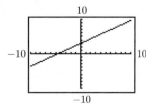

(b) $\frac{13}{3}$
(c) $(-4.5, 0), (0, 3)$

73. $[-10, 110]$ by $[-10, 60]$

Exercises 1.2, page 16

1. False   **3.** True   **5.** $x \geq 4$ **7.** $x \geq 3$ **9.** $y \leq -2x + 5$ **11.** $y \geq 15x - 18$ **13.** $x \geq -\frac{3}{4}$ **15.** Yes   **17.** No
19. Yes   **21.** Yes   **23.**   **25.**   **27.**

29.   **31.**   **33.**   **35.**

37.   **39.**   **41.**   **43.**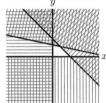

45. Yes   **47.** No   **49.** Below   **61.**
51. Above
53. $\begin{cases} y \geq 2x - 1 \\ y \leq 2x \end{cases}$
55. d   **57.** e
59. (a) $(6, 2.5)$ **(b)** Above

Exercises 1.3, page 22

1. $(2, 3)$ **3.** $(2, 1)$ **5.** $(12, 3)$ **17.**   **19.**   **21.**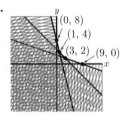
7. Yes   **9.** $x = \frac{10}{3}, y = \frac{1}{3}$
11. $x = -\frac{7}{9}, y = -\frac{22}{9}$
13. $A = (3, 4), B = (6, 2)$
15. $A = (0, 0), B = (2, 4),$
$C = \left(5, \frac{11}{2}\right), D = (5, 0)$

23. (a) \$2.00   **(b)** \$.05 or less   **25.** 29,500 units; \$3.00   **27.** 180; \$13.60   **29.** $(18, 63)$; Both plans cost 63
cents for 18 minute calls.   **31.** d   **33.** $(1.69, 3.38)$ **35.** $(1, 1)$

37. (a)   **(b)** $(2, 1)$ **(c)**   **(d)** Yes

Exercises 1.4, page 30

1. $\frac{2}{3}$ **5.** $m = \frac{5}{4}$ **7.** $m = \frac{4}{5}$ **9.** Undefined   **11.**   **13.**

3. 5

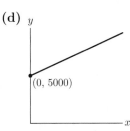

15. $y = -2x + 7$ **17.** $y = -2x + 4$ **19.** $y = \frac{1}{4}x + \frac{3}{2}$ **21.** $y = -x$ **23.** $y = 3$ **25.** $(0, 3)$ **27.** Each unit sold yields a commission of \$5. In addition, she receives \$60 per week base pay.

29. (a) $(0, 1200)$; at \$1200 no one will buy the item.
(b) $(400, 0)$; even if the item is given away, only 400 will be taken.
(c) -3; to sell an additional item, the price must be reduced by \$3.
(d) \$150   **(e)** 300 items

(f)

31. (a) $y = 90x + 5000$ **(d)**
(b) \$5000   **(c)** \$90

33. (a) \$30,000   **(b)** 60 coats
(c) $(0, 0)$; if no coats are sold, there is no revenue.
(d) 100; each additional coat yields an additional \$100 in revenue.

35. (a)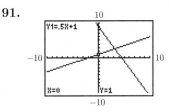

(b) 17,600 gallons
(c) 12,000 gallons
(d) $(0, 30,000)$; the tank holds 30,000 gallons.
(e) $(75, 0)$; the tank is empty after 75 days.

37. (a) $y = .1x + 220$ **(b)** \$420   **(c)** \$3200
39. $y = 3x - 1$ **41.** $y = x + 1$ **43.** $y = -7x + 35$
45. $y = 4$ **47.** $y = \frac{1}{2}x$ **49.** $y = -2x$ **51.** $5; 1; -1$
53. $-\frac{5}{4}; -\frac{3}{2}; -\frac{3}{4}$ **55. (a)** (C)   **(b)** (B)   **(c)** (D)
(d) (A)   **57.** $y = x + 1$ **59.** $y = 5$ **61.** $y = -\frac{2}{3}x$
63. $F = \frac{9}{5}C + 32$ **65.** $y = \frac{2837}{11}x + 2848$; \$4137.55
67. $y = -\frac{1}{2}x + 25$; 21 mpg   **69.** 341,001
71. $y = .1x + 1.9$; \$2.6 million   **73.** $y \geq 4x + 3$

75. $\begin{cases} y \leq -\frac{1}{2}x + 4 \\ y \leq -x + 5 \\ y \geq x - 3 \\ x \geq 0, y \geq 0 \end{cases}$ **77.** $k = 9$ **91.** 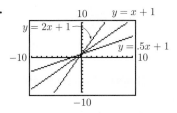   **93.**
79. $a = -.05$
83. c   **85.** e
87. c   **89.** d

Exercises 1.5, page 41

1. 4   **3.** 6.70   **5.** $m = -1.4, b = 8.5$ **7.** $y = 4.5x - 3$ **9.** $y = -2x + 11.5$ **11. (a)** $y = .338x + 21.6$
(b) About 393   **13. (a)** $y = .419x + 17.1$ **(b)** About 26.7%   **(c)** 2011 (or late 2010)
15. (a) $y = .153x + 73.5$ **(b)** 78.09   **(c)** 81.15   **(d)** 87.27 This is an example of a fit that is not capable of extrapolating beyond the given data.   **17. (a)** $y = .048x + 2.89$ **(b)** \$3.18   **(c)** 2013   **19.** $y = -.5x + 6.5$

Chapter 1: Supplementary Exercises, page 46

1. $x = 0$ **2.**

$(2, -1)$

3. $\left(2, -\frac{4}{5}\right)$ **6.**

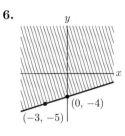

$(-3, -5)$ $(0, -4)$

4. $\frac{3}{4}$

5. $y = -\frac{1}{2}x + 5$

7. Yes   **8.** $(3, 5)$ **9.** $y = \frac{1}{5}x + 13$

10. 10   **11.** $(5, 0)$

12.

$(0, 6)$

13. $(7, 10)$ **14.**

15. $(0, 7)$

16. The rate is \$35 per hour plus a flat fee of \$20.   **17.** No   **18.** $y = \frac{2}{3}x - 2$ **19.** d

20. $y \le \frac{2}{3}x + \frac{3}{2}$ **21.** $y \ge 2.4x - 5.8$

22. $x = -.3,\ y = .4$ **23.** $y = -\frac{2}{5}x + \frac{7}{5}$

24. $x \ge \frac{6}{5}$

25. $m = -2$;
y-intercept: $(0, 8)$;
x-intercept: $(4, 0)$;

$(0, 8)$ $(4, 0)$

26. No

28. (a) (C) **(b)** (A) **(c)** (B) **(d)** (D)

29. (a) L_3 **(b)** L_1 **(c)** L_2 **30.** $\begin{cases} y \le -\frac{7}{8}x + 5 \\ y \ge \frac{8}{7}x - \frac{43}{14} \\ x \ge 0, y \ge 0 \end{cases}$; $\left(\frac{43}{16}, 0\right)$

31. 300 units; \$2

32. $(0, 0), (10, 0), (9, 5), (6, 7), (0, 4)$

33. (a) In 2000, 8.8% of entering college freshmen intended to eventually obtain a degree in a medical field.   **(b)** 9.6%   **(c)** 2004

34. (a) $y = 10x - 6000$ **(c)**
(b) x-intercept: $(600, 0)$,
y-intercept: $(0, -6000)$

$(600, 0)$ $(0, -6000)$

35. (a) A: $y = .1x + 50$,
B: $y = .2x + 40$
(b) B   **(c)** A
(d) 100 miles
36. (a) $y = .031x + .69$
(b) 2000

37.

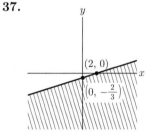

$(2, 0)$ $\left(0, -\frac{2}{3}\right)$

38. \$5000   **39.** $\begin{cases} y \le \frac{5}{4}x + 5 \\ y \le -\frac{2}{5}x + 2 \\ y \ge \frac{3}{5}x - 3 \\ y \ge -\frac{5}{2}x - 5 \end{cases}$ **40.** $\begin{cases} y \le -\frac{2}{3}x + 2 \\ y \ge -3 \\ x \ge -2 \\ x \le 4 \end{cases}$ **41.** $y = 14{,}800x + 417{,}000$; 505,800   **42.** 106,286

43. 18.1%   **44. (a)** $y = 1.06x + 1.71$ **(b)** 71.2   **(c)** 91.0   **45. (a)** $y = .18x + 3.06$ **(b)** 4.68%   **(c)** 2013

46. (a) $y = .152x - 3.063$ **(b)** About 21   **(c)** About 165 grams   **47.** Up   **48.** Counterclockwise   **51.** No; no

Chapter 1: Chapter Test, page 49

1.

$(1, 3)$

2. 5

3. $y = -2x + 1$

4. $(6, 1)$

6.

$(0, 8)$ $(8, 0)$

7. $y = 2x - \frac{71}{11}$
8. $(16, 0); (25, 0); (13, 36); (2, 14)$
9. Less than \$2500; greater than \$2500
10. (a) $y = .033x + .819$ **(b)** \$0.98
(c) 2012

CHAPTER 2

Exercises 2.1, page 60

1. $\xrightarrow{2R_1}$ $\begin{cases} x - 6y = 4 \\ 5x + 4y = 1 \end{cases}$ **3.** $\xrightarrow{R_2 + 5R_1}$ $\begin{cases} x + 2y = 3 \\ 14y = 16 \end{cases}$ **5.** $\xrightarrow{R_3 + (-4)R_1}$ $\begin{cases} x - 2y + z = 0 \\ y - 2z = 4 \\ 9y - z = 5 \end{cases}$

7. $\xrightarrow{R_1 + \frac{1}{2}R_2}$ $\begin{bmatrix} 1 & 0 & | & 5 \\ 0 & 1 & | & 4 \end{bmatrix}$ **9.** $\begin{bmatrix} -3 & 4 & | & -2 \\ 1 & -7 & | & 8 \end{bmatrix}$ **11.** $\begin{bmatrix} 1 & 13 & -2 & | & 0 \\ 2 & 0 & -1 & | & 3 \\ 0 & 1 & 0 & | & 5 \end{bmatrix}$ **13.** $\begin{cases} -2y = 3 \\ x + 7y = -4 \end{cases}$

15. $\begin{cases} 3x + 2y = -3 \\ y - 6z = 4 \\ -5x - y + 7z = 0 \end{cases}$ **17.** Multiply the second row of the matrix by $\frac{1}{3}$.   **19.** Change the first row of the

matrix by adding to it 3 times the second row.   **21.** Interchange rows 2 and 3.   **23.** $\begin{bmatrix} 1 & 2 & | & 0 \\ 0 & 10 & | & 5 \end{bmatrix}$

25. $\begin{bmatrix} 1 & 2 & | & 3 \\ 3 & -2 & | & 0 \end{bmatrix}$ **27.** $\begin{bmatrix} 1 & 3 & | & -5 \\ 0 & 1 & | & 7 \end{bmatrix}$ **29.** $R_2 + 2R_1$ **31.** $R_1 + (-2)R_2$ **33.** $R_1 \leftrightarrow R_2$ or $R_1 \leftrightarrow R_3$

35. $R_1 + (-3)R_3$ **37.** $x = -1, y = 1$ **39.** $x = -\frac{8}{7}, y = -\frac{9}{7}, z = -\frac{3}{7}$ **41.** $x = -1, y = 1$ **43.** $x = 1, y = 2,$
$z = -1$ **45.** $x = -2.5, y = 15$ **47.** $x = 1, y = -6, z = 2$ **49.** $x = -1, y = -2, z = 5$ **51.** b   **53.** d   **55.** 150
short sleeve, 200 long sleeve   **57.** 262 adults, 88 children   **59.** $x = \$25,000, y = \$50,000, z = \$25,000$ **61.** $23\frac{1}{3}$
pounds of first type, 85 pounds of second type, $201\frac{2}{3}$ pounds of third type   **67.** $x = 1, y = -6, z = 2$

Exercises 2.2, page 69

1. $\begin{bmatrix} 1 & -2 & 3 \\ 0 & 13 & -8 \end{bmatrix}$ **3.** $\begin{bmatrix} 9 & -1 & 0 & -7 \\ -\frac{1}{2} & \frac{1}{2} & 1 & 3 \\ 5 & -1 & 0 & -3 \end{bmatrix}$ **5.** $\begin{bmatrix} 1 & \frac{3}{2} \\ 0 & -9 \\ 0 & \frac{7}{2} \end{bmatrix}$ **7.** $\begin{bmatrix} 4 & 3 & 0 \\ 1 & 1 & 0 \\ \frac{1}{6} & \frac{1}{2} & 1 \end{bmatrix}$ **9.** $y = $ any value, $x = 3 + 2y$

11. $x = 1, y = 2$ **13.** No solution   **15.** $z = $ any value, $x = -6 - z, y = 5$ **17.** No solution   **19.** $z = $ any value,
$w = $ any value, $x = 2z + w, y = 5 - 3w$ **21.** $x = 5, y = 7$ **23.** Possible answers: $z = 0, x = -13, y = 9; z = 1,$
$x = -8, y = 6; z = 2, x = -3, y = 3$ **25.** Possible answers: $y = 0, x = 23, z = 5; y = 1, x = 16, z = 5; y = 2,$
$x = 9, z = 5$ **27.** $x = $ food 1, $y = $ food 2, $z = $ food 3; $z = $ any amount, $x = 300 - z, y = 100 - z$ $(0 \le z \le 100)$
29. 6 floral squares, the other 90 any mix of solid green and solid blue   **31.** $x = \pm1, y = \pm2, z = \pm3$ **33.** No
solution if $k \ne -12$. Infinitely many if $k = -12$.   **35.** b   **37.** One; $x = 7, y = 3$ **39.** No solution

Exercises 2.3, page 81

1. 2×3 **3.** 1×3, row matrix   **5.** 2×2, square matrix   **7.** $-4; 0$ **9.** $i = 1, j = 3$ **11.** $\begin{bmatrix} 9 & 3 \\ 7 & -1 \end{bmatrix}$

13. $\begin{bmatrix} 1 & 3 \\ 1 & 2 \\ 4 & -2 \end{bmatrix}$ **15.** $\begin{bmatrix} 11 \end{bmatrix}$ **17.** $\begin{bmatrix} 10 \end{bmatrix}$ **19.** Yes; 3×5 **21.** No   **23.** Yes; 3×1 **25.** $\begin{bmatrix} 6 & 17 \\ 6 & 10 \end{bmatrix}$ **27.** $\begin{bmatrix} 21 \\ -4 \\ 8 \end{bmatrix}$

29. $\begin{bmatrix} 5 & 6 \\ 7 & 8 \end{bmatrix}$ **31.** $\begin{bmatrix} .48 & .39 \\ .52 & .61 \end{bmatrix}$ **33.** $\begin{bmatrix} 25 & 17 & 2 \\ 3 & -1 & 2 \\ 1 & 1 & 4 \end{bmatrix}$ **35.** $\begin{cases} 2x + 3y = 6 \\ 4x + 5y = 7 \end{cases}$ **37.** $\begin{cases} x + 2y + 3z = 10 \\ 4x + 5y + 6z = 11 \\ 7x + 8y + 9z = 12 \end{cases}$

39. $\begin{bmatrix} 3 & 2 \\ 7 & -1 \end{bmatrix} \begin{bmatrix} x \\ y \end{bmatrix} = \begin{bmatrix} -1 \\ 2 \end{bmatrix}$ **41.** $\begin{bmatrix} 1 & -2 & 3 \\ 0 & 1 & 1 \\ 0 & 0 & 1 \end{bmatrix} \begin{bmatrix} x \\ y \\ z \end{bmatrix} = \begin{bmatrix} 5 \\ 6 \\ 2 \end{bmatrix}$ **47. (a)** $\begin{bmatrix} 340 \\ 265 \end{bmatrix}$ **(b)** Mike's clothes cost $340;

Don's clothes cost $265.   **49. (a)** $\begin{bmatrix} 2282.50 & 2322.50 & 3550.50 \end{bmatrix}$, total cost for the plain, milk chocolate-covered,

and dark chocolate-covered items   **(b)** $\begin{bmatrix} 3138.00 \\ 3337.50 \\ 6772.50 \end{bmatrix}$, total revenue from peanuts, raisins, and espresso beans

51. (a) I: 2.75, II: 2, III: 1.3   **(b)** A: 74, B: 112, C: 128, D: 64, F: 22   **53.** 10,100 voting Democratic, 7900 voting Republican   **55.** Carpenters: $1000, bricklayers: $1050, plumbers: $600   **57. (a)** $[162 \quad 150 \quad 143]$, number of units of each nutrient consumed at breakfast   **(b)** $[186 \quad 200 \quad 239]$, number of units of each nutrient consumed at lunch   **(c)** $[288 \quad 300 \quad 344]$, number of units of each nutrient consumed at dinner   **(d)** $[5 \quad 8]$, total number of ounces of each food that Mikey eats during a day   **(e)** $[636 \quad 650 \quad 726]$, number of units of each nutrient consumed per day   **59. (a)** $\begin{bmatrix} 720 \\ 646 \end{bmatrix}$ **(b)** $720

61. (a) $T = \begin{bmatrix} 30 & 45 \\ 30 & 50 \\ 15 & 10 \end{bmatrix}$ $\begin{matrix} \text{Preparation} \\ \text{Baking} \\ \text{Finishing} \end{matrix}$ with columns Boston cream pie, Carrot cake

(b) $S = \begin{bmatrix} 20 \\ 8 \end{bmatrix} \begin{matrix} \text{Boston cream pie} \\ \text{Carrot cake} \end{matrix}$; $TS = \begin{bmatrix} 960 \\ 1000 \\ 380 \end{bmatrix} \begin{matrix} \text{Preparation} \\ \text{Baking} \\ \text{Finishing} \end{matrix}$ **(c)** Total baking time: 1000 minutes or 16 2/3 hours; total finishing time: 380 minutes or 6 1/3 hours

63. (a) $T = \begin{bmatrix} 2 & 3 & 2 \\ 1.5 & 2 & 1 \end{bmatrix} \begin{matrix} \text{Huge One} \\ \text{Regular Joe} \end{matrix}$ with columns Cutting, Sewing, Finishing   **(b)** $S = \begin{bmatrix} 32 \\ 24 \end{bmatrix} \begin{matrix} \text{Huge One} \\ \text{Regular Joe} \end{matrix}$

(c) $A = \begin{bmatrix} 27 & 56 \end{bmatrix}$ with columns Huge One, Regular Joe; $AT = \begin{bmatrix} 138 & 193 & 110 \end{bmatrix}$ with columns Cutting, Sewing, Finishing; $AS = [2208]$ **(d)** 193 hours

(e) $2208   **67.** $\begin{bmatrix} 3 & -2 & 1 \\ -5 & 6 & 7 \end{bmatrix}$ **69.** 4×4 **71.** $[7998 \quad 56,685 \quad 96,158] \begin{bmatrix} 15.1 \\ 15.2 \\ 12.6 \end{bmatrix}$

73. $\begin{bmatrix} 27.9 & 130.6 & -69.88 \\ 106.75 & -149.44 & 26.1 \\ -47.5 & 336.2 & -18.7 \end{bmatrix}$ **75.** $\begin{bmatrix} -69.14 & 147.9 & -43.26 \\ 158.05 & -3.69 & 33.46 \\ -176.1 & 259.5 & 59.3 \end{bmatrix}$ **77.** $\begin{bmatrix} 160.16 & -26.7 & 4 \\ 2.7 & 150.85 & -53 \\ 187.4 & -35.5 & 48.6 \end{bmatrix}$

79. They match.

Exercises 2.4, page 94

1. $x = 2$, $y = 0$ **3.** $\begin{bmatrix} 1 & -2 \\ -3 & 7 \end{bmatrix}$ **5.** $\begin{bmatrix} 1 & -1 \\ -\frac{5}{2} & 3 \end{bmatrix}$ **7.** $\begin{bmatrix} 1.6 & -.4 \\ -.6 & 1.4 \end{bmatrix}$ **9.** $[\frac{1}{3}]$ **11.** $x = 4$, $y = -\frac{1}{2}$ **13.** $x = 32$, $y = -6$ **15. (a)** $\begin{bmatrix} .8 & .3 \\ .2 & .7 \end{bmatrix} \begin{bmatrix} x \\ y \end{bmatrix} = \begin{bmatrix} m \\ s \end{bmatrix}$ **(b)** $\begin{bmatrix} x \\ y \end{bmatrix} = \begin{bmatrix} 1.4 & -.6 \\ -.4 & 1.6 \end{bmatrix} \begin{bmatrix} m \\ s \end{bmatrix}$ **(c)** 110,000 married; 40,000 single   **(d)** 130,000 married; 20,000 single   **17. (a)** $\begin{bmatrix} .7 & .1 \\ .3 & .9 \end{bmatrix} \begin{bmatrix} x \\ y \end{bmatrix} = \begin{bmatrix} u \\ v \end{bmatrix}$ **(b)** $\begin{bmatrix} x \\ y \end{bmatrix} = \begin{bmatrix} \frac{3}{2} & -\frac{1}{6} \\ -\frac{1}{2} & \frac{7}{6} \end{bmatrix} \begin{bmatrix} u \\ v \end{bmatrix}$ **(c)** 8500; 4500   **19.** $x = 9$, $y = -2$, $z = -2$ **21.** $x = 1$, $y = 5$, $z = -4$, $w = 9$ **25. (a)** $\begin{bmatrix} 1 & 2 \\ .9 & 0 \end{bmatrix} \begin{bmatrix} x \\ y \end{bmatrix} = \begin{bmatrix} a \\ b \end{bmatrix}$ **(b)** After 1 year: 1,170,000 in group I and 405,000 in group II. After 2 years: 1,980,000 in group I and 1,053,000 in group II.   **(c)** 700,000 in group I and 55,000 in group II.   **29.** One possible answer is $\begin{bmatrix} 1 & 1 \\ 1 & 1 \end{bmatrix} \begin{bmatrix} x \\ y \end{bmatrix} = \begin{bmatrix} 2 \\ 3 \end{bmatrix}$.

31. $\begin{bmatrix} -\frac{10}{73} & \frac{75}{292} \\ \frac{25}{73} & -\frac{5}{292} \end{bmatrix}$ **33.** $\begin{bmatrix} \frac{1020}{8887} & \frac{2910}{8887} & -\frac{500}{8887} \\ \frac{3050}{8887} & \frac{860}{8887} & \frac{1990}{8887} \\ \frac{125}{8887} & \frac{618}{8887} & \frac{810}{8887} \end{bmatrix}$ **35.** $x = -\frac{4}{5}$, $y = \frac{28}{5}$, $z = 5$ **37.** $x = 0$, $y = 2$, $z = 0$, $w = 2$

39. Displays ERR:SINGULAR MAT.

Exercises 2.5, page 101

1. $\begin{bmatrix} -2 & 3 \\ 5 & -7 \end{bmatrix}$ **3.** $\begin{bmatrix} \frac{7}{2} & \frac{3}{2} \\ -2 & -1 \end{bmatrix}$ **5.** No inverse **7.** $\begin{bmatrix} -1 & 2 & -4 \\ 1 & -1 & 3 \\ 0 & 0 & 1 \end{bmatrix}$ **9.** No inverse **11.** $\begin{bmatrix} -5 & 6 & 0 & 0 \\ 1 & -1 & 0 & 0 \\ 0 & 0 & -\frac{1}{46} & \frac{1}{46} \\ 0 & 0 & \frac{25}{46} & -\frac{1}{23} \end{bmatrix}$

13. $x = 2, y = -3, z = 2$ **15.** $x = 4, y = -4, z = 3, w = -1$ **17.** $\begin{bmatrix} -3 & 7 \\ 1 & -2 \end{bmatrix}$ **19.** $\begin{bmatrix} -3 & 5 \\ 10 & -16 \end{bmatrix}$

Exercises 2.6, page 107

1. 20 cents **3.** Energy sector **5.** Coal: $8.84 billion, steel: $3.725 billion, electricity: $9.895 billion

7. Computers: $354 million, semiconductors: $172 million **11. (a)** $A = \begin{matrix} & T & E \\ \begin{bmatrix} .25 & .30 \\ .20 & .15 \end{bmatrix} & \begin{matrix} T \\ E \end{matrix} \end{matrix}$

(b) $\begin{bmatrix} 1.47 & .52 \\ .35 & 1.30 \end{bmatrix}$ **(c)** Transportation: $8.91 billion, energy: $5.65 billion. **13.** Plastics: $955,000, industrial equipment: $590,000 **15.** Manufacturing: $398 million, transportation: $313 million, agriculture: $452 million **19.** $\begin{bmatrix} 10.25 \\ 13.82 \\ 8.65 \end{bmatrix}$

Chapter 2: Supplementary Exercises, page 110

1. $\begin{bmatrix} 1 & -2 & \frac{1}{3} \\ 0 & 8 & \frac{16}{3} \end{bmatrix}$ **2.** $\begin{bmatrix} 1 & 0 & 1 \\ 2 & 1 & 0 \\ -12 & 0 & 7 \end{bmatrix}$ **3.** $x = 4, y = 5$ **4.** $x = 50, y = 2, z = -12$ **5.** $x = -1, y = \frac{2}{3}, z = \frac{1}{3}$

6. No solution **7.** $z = $ any value, $x = 1 - 3z, y = 4z, w = 5$ **8.** $x = 7, y = 3$ **9.** $\begin{bmatrix} 5 \\ 3 \\ 7 \end{bmatrix}$ **10.** $\begin{bmatrix} 6 & 17 \\ 12 & 26 \end{bmatrix}$

11. $x = -2, y = 3$ **12. (a)** $x = 13, y = 23, z = 19$ **(b)** $x = -4, y = 13, z = 14$ **13.** $\begin{bmatrix} -1 & 3 \\ \frac{1}{2} & -1 \end{bmatrix}$

14. $\begin{bmatrix} 5 & -1 & -1 \\ -3 & 1 & 0 \\ -1 & 0 & 1 \end{bmatrix}$ **15.** Corn: 500 acres; Wheat: 0 acres; Soybeans: 500 acres **16. (a)** $\begin{bmatrix} 5455 \\ 5275 \end{bmatrix}$; total

month's costs for each store **(b)** $\begin{bmatrix} 6600 \\ 6360 \end{bmatrix}$; total month's revenue for each store **(c)** $\begin{bmatrix} 35 \\ 15 \\ 40 \end{bmatrix}$; profit for each

piece of equipment **(d)** $\begin{bmatrix} 1145 \\ 1085 \end{bmatrix}$; total month's profit for each store **17. (a)** $\begin{bmatrix} 10,100 & 8230 & 4670 \end{bmatrix}$; total amount invested in bonds, stocks, and the conservative fixed income fund, respectively **(b)** $\begin{bmatrix} 522.40 & 1807.30 \end{bmatrix}$; total returns on the investments for one year and five years, respectively **(c)** $8230 is the total amount invested in stocks. **(d)** $522.40 is the total return after one year.

18. (a) $\begin{bmatrix} 238 \\ 246 \\ 233 \\ 236 \end{bmatrix}$; total amount earned by each person for the week **(b)** Most: Quinn; least: Tamia

(c) Quinn and Zack each earn $239. **(d)** 30 hours **19.** 4 apples, 9 bananas, 5 oranges **20. (a)** A: 9400, 8980; B: 7300, 7510 **(b)** A: 10,857, 12,082; B: 6571, 5959 **21.** Industry I: 20; industry II: 20 **22.** a **23. (a)** True **(b)** False **(c)** True **25.** No

Chapter 2: Chapter Test, page 112

1. $x = 2$, $y = 4$, $z = -5$ **2. (a)** $x = 4$, $y = -3$, $z = 6$ **(b)** $x = 2$, $y = 3$, $z = 5$ **(c)** No solution
(d) $z =$ any value; $x = z + 2$, $y = -2z + 2$ **(e)** $y =$ any value; $x = -2y$, $z = 0$ **3.** $w = 1$, $z = 2$, $x = 3$, $y = 5$
4. (1) $z = 0$, $y = 6$, $x = 9$; **(2)** $z = 1$, $y = 2$, $x = 15$; **(3)** $z = -1$, $y = 10$, $x = 3$ **5.** Not defined; $\begin{bmatrix} 2 & 2 & 2 \\ 2 & 3 & 2 \end{bmatrix}$;

$\begin{bmatrix} -2 & 3 \\ -2 & 4 \end{bmatrix}$; not defined; $\begin{bmatrix} -1 & 0 & -1 \\ -1 & 1 & 1 \\ 1 & 0 & 1 \end{bmatrix}$ **6. (a)** $.5x + y + z = m$; $3x + 2.5y + 2z = v$; $4x + 3y + 2z = p$

(b) $\begin{bmatrix} .5 & 1 & 1 \\ 3 & 2.5 & 2 \\ 4 & 3 & 2 \end{bmatrix} \cdot \begin{bmatrix} x \\ y \\ z \end{bmatrix} = \begin{bmatrix} m \\ v \\ p \end{bmatrix}$ **(c)** 550 hours molding time, 1450 hours oven time, 1700 hours painting time

7. $\begin{bmatrix} \frac{1}{2} & -\frac{1}{2} & \frac{1}{2} \\ \frac{1}{2} & -\frac{1}{2} & -\frac{1}{2} \\ -\frac{1}{2} & \frac{3}{2} & \frac{1}{2} \end{bmatrix}$ **8.** 400 students   **9.** Wood: \$1.98, steel: \$7.39, coal: \$3.87

CHAPTER 3

Exercises 3.1, page 121

1. Yes   **3.** No   **5. (a)**

	A	**B**	**Truck capacity**
Volume	4 cubic feet	3 cubic feet	300 cubic feet
Weight	100 pounds	200 pounds	10,000 pounds
Earnings	\$13	\$9	

(b) $4x + 3y \leq 300$; $100x + 200y \leq 10{,}000$
(c) $y \leq 2x, x \geq 0, y \geq 0$
(d) $13x + 9y$

(e)

7. (a)

	Essay questions	**Short-answer questions**	**Available**
Time to answer	10 minutes	2 minutes	90 minutes
Quantity	10	50	
Required	3	10	
Worth	20 points	5 points	

(b) $10x + 2y \leq 90$ **(c)** $x \geq 3, x \leq 10, y \geq 10, y \leq 50$ **(d)** $20x + 5y$

(e)

9. (a)

	Alfalfa	**Corn**	**Requirements**
Protein	.13 pound	.065 pound	4550 pounds
TDN	.48 pound	.96 pound	26,880 pounds
Vitamin A	2.16 IUs	0 IUs	43,200 IUs
Cost/lb	\$0.01	\$0.016	

(b) $.13x + .065y \geq 4550$;
    $.48x + .96y \geq 26{,}880$;
    $2.16x \geq 43{,}200$; $y \geq 0$

(c)

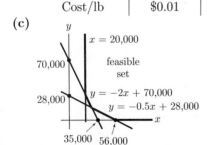

(d) $.01x + .016y$

Exercises 3.2, page 130

1. $(20, 0)$ **3.** $(6, 0)$ **5.** $(0, 5)$ **7.** $(3, 3)$ **9.** $(0, 7)$ **11.** $(2, 1)$ **13.** Ship 75 crates of cargo A and no crates of cargo B. **15.** Answer 3 essay questions and 30 short-answer questions. **17.** The minimum cost of $504 is achieved by buying 28,000 pounds of alfalfa and 14,000 pounds of corn. **19.** Make 16 chairs and no sofas. **21.** The minimum value is 30 and occurs at $(2, 6)$. **23.** The maximum value is 49 and occurs at $(2, 9)$. **25.** The maximum value is 6600 and occurs at $(12, 36)$. **27.** The minimum value is 40 and occurs at $(4, 3)$. **29.** Produce 9 hockey games and 8 soccer games each day. **31.** Supply 6 tubes of food A and 6 tubes of food B. **33.** Make 400 cans of Fruit Delight and 500 cans of Heavenly Punch. **35.** The farmer should plant $83\frac{1}{3}$ acres of oats and $16\frac{2}{3}$ acres of corn to make a profit of $6933.33. **37.** (b) The farmer should plant 78 acres of oats and 22 acres of corn to make a profit of $7040. Yes, it provides more profit. **39.** Produce 49 regular bags and 14 deluxe bags. **41.** The feasible set contains no points. **43.** The maximum value is 84 and occurs at $(12, 0)$.

Exercises 3.3, page 143

1. (a) $y = -\frac{3}{2}x + \frac{c}{14}$ (b) Up (c) B **3.** Possible answer: $5x + y$ **5.** Possible answer: $2x + y$ **7.** Possible answer: $x + 5y$ **9.** Possible answer: $2x + 3y$ **11.** C **13.** D **15.** D **17.** C **19.** $\frac{1}{4} \leq k \leq 3$ **21.** Feed 1 can of brand A and 3 cans of brand B. **23.** Mr. Jones should invest $2000 in low-risk stocks, $3000 in medium-risk stocks, and $4000 in high-risk stocks. **25.** Let (a, b) correspond to a cars shipped from Baltimore to Philadelphia, b cars shipped from Baltimore to Trenton, $4 - a$ cars shipped from NY to Philadelphia, and $7 - b$ cars shipped from NY to Trenton. Then the minimum cost of $990 is achieved at $(0, 5)$, $(4, 1)$, or anywhere on the line segment connecting these two points. **27.** Produce 90,000 gallons of gasoline, 5000 gallons of jet fuel, and 5000 gallons of diesel fuel. **29.** Buy 9 high-capacity trucks and 21 low-capacity trucks. **31.** Ship 400 pounds of coffee from Seattle to Salt Lake City and 350 pounds from San José to Reno. **33.** Create 22 of Kit I, 10 of Kit II, and 12 of Kit III. **35.** rice: $[9.33, 42]$; soybeans: $[7, 31.5]$

Chapter 3: Supplementary Exercises, page 146

1. Use 10 type A planes and 3 type B planes. **2.** Use 2 ounces of wheat germ and 1 ounce of enriched oat flour. **3.** Produce 9 hardtops and 16 sports cars. **4.** Make 500 boxes of mixture A and 200 boxes of mixture B. **5.** Publish 60 elementary books, 8 intermediate books, and 4 advanced books. **6.** Transport 80 computers from Rochester and 45 computers from Queens. **7.** Transport no computers from warehouse A to outlet I, 200 computers from warehouse A to outlet II, 200 computers from warehouse B to outlet I, and 100 computers from warehouse B to outlet II. **8.** Invest $2000 in the CD, $0 in mutual funds, and $8000 in stocks. **9.** Yes; No **10.** Yes; No

Chapter 3: Chapter Test, page 147

1. Step 1: Translate the problem into mathematical language. Identify variables and write the inequalities and objective function.
Step 2: Graph the feasible set.
Step 3: Determine the vertices of the feasible set.
Step 4: Evaluate the objective function at each vertex. Determine the optimal point.

2. (a) Minimize $70x + 90y$ subject to $\begin{cases} 20x + 30y \geq 300 \\ 10x + 20y \geq 200 \\ x \geq 0, y \geq 0 \end{cases}$

(b) Maximize $.07x + .06y + .045z$ subject to $\begin{cases} y \geq 150,000 \\ z \leq 200,000 \\ x + y + z \leq 500,000 \\ x \geq .5y \\ x \geq 0, y \geq 0, z \geq 0 \end{cases}$

3. (a)

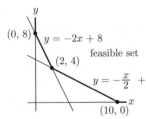

(b) No   **4.** $(0, 10)$; $(7, 5)$; $(9, 3)$; $(9, 0)$; $(0, 0)$

5. (a) $x = 10$, $y = 0$ **(b)** $x = 3$, $y = 6$

6. (a) $y = -\frac{8}{5}x + 640$ **(b)** $y = -\frac{8}{5}x + \frac{c}{5}$ **(c)** down   **(d)** E

7. C

8. 8 bears and 6 wreaths

FEASIBLE SETS FOR CHAPTER 3

Exercises 3.2

21.

23.

25.

27.

29.

31.

33.

35.

37.

39.

Exercises 3.3

21.

23.

25.

27.

29.

31.

33.

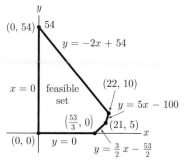

Chapter 3: Supplementary Exercises

1.

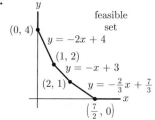

2.

feasible
set

3.

4.

5.

6.

7.

8.

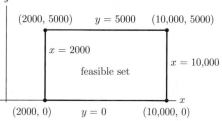

CHAPTER 4

Exercises 4.1, page 159

1. $\begin{cases} 20x + 30y + u \qquad\quad = 3500 \\ 50x + 10y \qquad + v \quad\;\; = 5000 \\ -8x - 13y \qquad\qquad + M \;\; = 0 \end{cases}$ Maximize M given $x \geq 0,\, y \geq 0,\, u \geq 0,\, v \geq 0.$

3. $\begin{cases} x + y + z + u & = 100 \\ 3x + z + v & = 200 \\ 5x + 10y + w & = 100 \\ -x - 2y + 3z + M & = 0 \end{cases}$ Maximize M given $x \ge 0$, $y \ge 0$, $z \ge 0$, $u \ge 0$, $v \ge 0$, $w \ge 0$.

5. $\begin{cases} 4x + 6y - 7z + u & = 16 \\ 3x + 2y + v & = 11 \\ 9y + 3z + w & = 21 \\ -3x - 5y - 12z + M & = 0 \end{cases}$ Maximize M given $x \ge 0$, $y \ge 0$, $z \ge 0$, $u \ge 0$, $v \ge 0$, $w \ge 0$.

7. (a)
$\begin{array}{ccccccc|c}
x & y & t & u & v & w & M & \\
3 & 2 & 1 & 0 & 0 & 0 & 0 & 10 \\
1 & 0 & 0 & 1 & 0 & 0 & 0 & 15 \\
0 & 1 & 0 & 0 & 1 & 0 & 0 & 3 \\
1 & 1 & 0 & 0 & 0 & 1 & 0 & 5 \\
-1 & -15 & 0 & 0 & 0 & 0 & 1 & 0
\end{array}$
   (b) $x = 0$, $y = 0$, $t = 10$, $u = 15$, $v = 3$, $w = 5$, $M = 0$

9. (a)
$\begin{array}{cccccc|c}
x & y & u & v & w & M & \\
1 & 3 & 1 & 0 & 0 & 0 & 24 \\
0 & 1 & 0 & 1 & 0 & 0 & 5 \\
1 & 7 & 0 & 0 & 1 & 0 & 10 \\
-2 & -1 & 0 & 0 & 0 & 1 & 50
\end{array}$
   (b) $x = 0$, $y = 0$, $u = 24$, $v = 5$, $w = 10$, $M = 50$

11. $x = 15$, $y = 0$, $u = 10$, $v = 0$, $M = 20$ **13.** $x = 10$, $y = 0$, $z = 15$, $u = 23$, $v = 0$, $w = 0$, $M = -11$

15. (a)
$\begin{array}{ccccc|c}
x & y & u & v & M & \\
1 & \frac{3}{2} & \frac{1}{2} & 0 & 0 & 6 \\
0 & -\frac{1}{2} & -\frac{1}{2} & 1 & 0 & 4 \\
0 & -5 & 5 & 0 & 1 & 60
\end{array}$
$x = 6$, $y = 0$, $u = 0$, $v = 4$, $M = 60$

(b)
$\begin{array}{ccccc|c}
x & y & u & v & M & \\
\frac{2}{3} & 1 & \frac{1}{3} & 0 & 0 & 4 \\
\frac{1}{3} & 0 & -\frac{1}{3} & 1 & 0 & 6 \\
\frac{10}{3} & 0 & \frac{20}{3} & 0 & 1 & 80
\end{array}$
$x = 0$, $y = 4$, $u = 0$, $v = 6$, $M = 80$

(c)
$\begin{array}{ccccc|c}
x & y & u & v & M & \\
0 & 1 & 1 & -2 & 0 & -8 \\
1 & 1 & 0 & 1 & 0 & 10 \\
0 & -10 & 0 & 10 & 1 & 100
\end{array}$
$x = 10$, $y = 0$, $u = -8$, $v = 0$, $M = 100$

(d)
$\begin{array}{ccccc|c}
x & y & u & v & M & \\
-1 & 0 & 1 & -3 & 0 & -18 \\
1 & 1 & 0 & 1 & 0 & 10 \\
10 & 0 & 0 & 20 & 1 & 200
\end{array}$
$x = 0$, $y = 10$, $u = -18$, $v = 0$, $M = 200$

17. d   **19. (a)** Group I: x, y; Group II: u, v, M **(b)** (i) feasible; I: y, u; II: x, v, M (ii) feasible; I: x, u; II: y, v, M (iii) not feasible; I: y, v; II: x, u, M (iv) not feasible; I; x, v; II: u, y, M **(c)** Operation (i)

Exercises 4.2, page 169

1. (a) 3   **(b)**
$\begin{array}{c}
 \\
u \\
y \\
M
\end{array}
\begin{array}{ccccc|c}
x & y & u & v & M & \\
\frac{16}{3} & 0 & 1 & -\frac{2}{3} & 0 & 6 \\
\frac{1}{3} & 1 & 0 & \frac{1}{3} & 0 & 2 \\
0 & 0 & 0 & 4 & 1 & 24
\end{array}$
   (c) $x = 0$, $y = 2$, $u = 6$, $v = 0$; $M = 24$

3. (a) 10   **(b)**
$\begin{array}{c}
 \\
u \\
y \\
M
\end{array}
\begin{array}{ccccc|c}
x & y & u & v & M & \\
-13 & 0 & 1 & -\frac{6}{5} & 0 & 6 \\
\frac{3}{2} & 1 & 0 & \frac{1}{10} & 0 & \frac{1}{2} \\
7 & 0 & 0 & \frac{1}{5} & 1 & 1
\end{array}$
   (c) $x = 0$, $y = \frac{1}{2}$, $u = 6$, $v = 0$, $M = 1$

5. $x = 0$, $y = 5$; $M = 15$ **7.** $x = 12$, $y = 20$; $M = 88$ **9.** $x = 0$, $y = \frac{19}{3}$, $z = 5$; $M = 44$ **11.** $x = 0$, $y = 30$; $M = 90$ **13.** $x = 50$, $y = 100$; $M = 1300$ **15.** 24 basketballs, 224 footballs **17.** 98 chairs, 4 sofas, 21 tables **19.** 11 hours bicycling, 4 hours swimming, 15 hours jogging; 3 pounds **21.** 65 type A restaurants and 5 type C restaurants **23.** 100 bags of mix B and 25 bags of mix C **25.** $x = 100$, $y = 50$; $M = 45,000$ **27.** $x = \frac{8}{5}$, $y = \frac{3}{5}$; $M = 10$ **29.** $x = 5$, $y = 0$, $z = 0$; $M = 80$

Exercises 4.3, page 178

1. $x = \frac{3}{5}$, $y = \frac{22}{5}$; 156 **3.** $x = \frac{5}{2}$, $y = \frac{1}{2}$; 8 **5.** $x = 3$, $y = 5$; 59 **7.** $x = 5$, $y = 4$; 38 **9.** 1 serving of food A, 3 servings of food B **11.** Stock 100 of brand A, 50 of brand B, and 450 of brand C. **13.** Supply all computers from Chicago at a cost of \$8800. **15.** $x = 1$, $y = 1$; $M = -1$

Exercises 4.4, page 187

1. $x = 4$, $y = 22$; profit $= \$122$ **3.** $x = 25$, $y = 25$; cost $= \$250$ **5.** $-400 \le h \le \frac{400}{3}$ **7.** $\begin{bmatrix} 9 & 1 & 1 \\ 4 & 8 & -3 \end{bmatrix}$

9. $\begin{bmatrix} 7 \\ 6 \\ 5 \\ 1 \end{bmatrix}$ **11.** Yes **13.** Minimize $\begin{bmatrix} 7 & 5 & 4 \end{bmatrix} \begin{bmatrix} x \\ y \\ z \end{bmatrix}$ subject to the constraints $\begin{bmatrix} 3 & 8 & 9 \\ 1 & 2 & 5 \\ 4 & 1 & 7 \end{bmatrix} \begin{bmatrix} x \\ y \\ z \end{bmatrix} \ge \begin{bmatrix} 75 \\ 80 \\ 67 \end{bmatrix}$ and

$\begin{bmatrix} x \\ y \\ z \end{bmatrix} \ge \begin{bmatrix} 0 \\ 0 \\ 0 \end{bmatrix}$. **15.** Maximize $\begin{bmatrix} 3 & 5 \end{bmatrix} \begin{bmatrix} x \\ y \end{bmatrix}$ subject to the constraints $\begin{bmatrix} 3 & 6 \\ 7 & 5 \\ 4 & 3 \end{bmatrix} \begin{bmatrix} x \\ y \end{bmatrix} \le \begin{bmatrix} 90 \\ 138 \\ 120 \end{bmatrix}$ and $\begin{bmatrix} x \\ y \end{bmatrix} \ge \begin{bmatrix} 0 \\ 0 \end{bmatrix}$.

17. Minimize $2x + 3y$ subject to the constraints $\begin{cases} 7x + 4y \ge 33 \\ 5x + 8y \ge 44 \\ x + 3y \ge 55 \\ x \ge 0,\ y \ge 0 \end{cases}$ **19.** -2; $[25, 55]$

Exercises 4.5, page 198

1. Minimize $80u + 76v$ subject to the constraints $\begin{cases} 5u + 3v \ge 4 \\ u + 2v \ge 2 \\ u \ge 0, v \ge 0 \end{cases}$ **3.** Maximize $u + 2v + w$ subject to the

constraints $\begin{cases} u - v + 2w \le 10 \\ 2u + v + 3w \le 12 \\ u \ge 0,\ v \ge 0,\ w \ge 0 \end{cases}$ **5.** Maximize $-7u + 10v$ subject to the constraints $\begin{cases} -2u + 8v \le 3 \\ 4u + v \le 5 \\ 6u + 9v \le 1 \\ u \ge 0,\ v \ge 0 \end{cases}$

7. $x = 12$, $y = 20$, $M = 88$; $u = \frac{2}{7}$, $v = \frac{6}{7}$, $M = 88$ **9.** $x = 0$, $y = 2$, $M = 24$; $u = 0$, $v = 12$, $w = 0$, $M = 24$

11. Maximize $3u + 5v$ subject to the constraints $\begin{cases} u + 2v \le 3 \\ u \le 1 \\ u \ge 0,\ v \ge 0 \end{cases}$ $x = \frac{5}{2}$, $y = \frac{1}{2}$, minimum $= 8$; $u = 1$, $v = 1$,

maximum $= 8$ **13.** Minimize $6u + 9v + 12w$ subject to the constraints $\begin{cases} u + 3v \ge 10 \\ -2u + w \ge 12 \\ v + 3w \ge 10 \\ u \ge 0,\ v \ge 0,\ w \ge 0 \end{cases}$

$x = 3$, $y = 12$, $z = 0$, maximum $= 174$; $u = 0$, $v = \frac{10}{3}$, $w = 12$, minimum $= 174$ **15.** Suppose we can hire workers out at a profit of u dollars per hour, sell the steel at a profit of v dollars per unit, and sell the wood at a profit of w dollars per unit. To find the minimum profit at which that should be done, minimize

$90u + 138v + 120w$ subject to the constraints $\begin{cases} 3u + 7v + 4w \geq 3 \\ 6u + 5v + 3w \geq 5 \\ u \geq 0,\ v \geq 0,\ w \geq 0. \end{cases}$ **17.** Suppose we can buy anthracite at u

dollars per ton, ordinary coal at v dollars per ton, and bituminous coal at w dollars per ton. To find the maximum cost at which this should be done, maximize $80u + 60v + 75w$ subject to the constraints

$\begin{cases} 4u + 4v + 7w \leq 150 \\ 10u + 5v + 5w \leq 200 \\ u \geq 0,\ v \geq 0,\ w \geq 0 \ . \end{cases}$ **19.** \$3.63   **21.** $x = 2$, $y = 1$, maximum $= 74$

Chapter 4: Supplementary Exercises, page 200

1. $x = 2$, $y = 3$, max. $= 18$ **2.** $x = 0$, $y = 7$, max. $= 35$ **3.** $x = 4$, $y = 5$, max. $= 23$ **4.** $x = 2$, $y = 4$, max. $= 34$ **5.** $x = 5$, $y = 1$, min. $= 6$ **6.** $x = 0$, $y = 6$, min. $= 12$ **7.** $x = 4$, $y = 1$, min. $= 110$ **8.** $x = 4$, $y = 3$, min. $= 41$ **9.** $x = 1$, $y = 6$, $z = 8$, max. $= 884$ **10.** $x = 60$, $y = 8$, $z = 20$, $w = 0$, max. $= 312$

11. Minimize $14u + 9v + 24w$ subject to the constraints $\begin{cases} u + v + 3w \geq 2 \\ 2u + v + 2w \geq 3 \\ u \geq 0,\ v \geq 0,\ w \geq 0 \end{cases}$ **12.** Maximize $8u + 5v + 7w$

subject to the constraints $\begin{cases} u + v + 2w \leq 20 \\ 4u + v + \ w \leq 30 \\ u \geq 0,\ v \geq 0,\ w \geq 0 \end{cases}$ **13.** Primal: $x = 4$, $y = 5$, max. $= 23$; Dual: $u = 1$, $v = 1$,

$w = 0$, min. $= 23$ **14.** Primal: $x = 4$, $y = 1$, min. $= 110$; Dual: $u = \frac{10}{3}$, $v = \frac{50}{3}$, $w = 0$, max. $= 110$

15. $A = \begin{bmatrix} 1 & 2 \\ 1 & 1 \\ 3 & 2 \end{bmatrix}$, $B = \begin{bmatrix} 14 \\ 9 \\ 24 \end{bmatrix}$, $C = \begin{bmatrix} 2 & 3 \end{bmatrix}$, $X = \begin{bmatrix} x \\ y \end{bmatrix}$ Primal: Maximize CX subject to $AX \leq B$, $X \geq \mathbf{0}$.

Dual: $U = \begin{bmatrix} u \\ v \\ w \end{bmatrix}$ Minimize $B^T U$ subject to $A^T U \geq C^T$, $U \geq \mathbf{0}$.   **16.** $A = \begin{bmatrix} 1 & 4 \\ 1 & 1 \\ 2 & 1 \end{bmatrix}$, $B = \begin{bmatrix} 8 \\ 5 \\ 7 \end{bmatrix}$, $C = \begin{bmatrix} 20 & 30 \end{bmatrix}$,

$X = \begin{bmatrix} x \\ y \end{bmatrix}$ Primal: Minimize CX subject to $AX \geq B$, $X \geq \mathbf{0}$. Dual: $U = \begin{bmatrix} u \\ v \\ w \end{bmatrix}$ Maximize $B^T U$ subject to

$A^T U \leq C^T$, $U \geq \mathbf{0}$.   **17. (a)** 30 attack sticks, 40 defense sticks   **(b)** \$22   **18.** \$210

Chapter 4: Chapter Test, page 201

1.

	x	y	z	u	v	w	M	
	1	1	-2	1	0	0	0	10
	2	-1	3	0	1	0	0	18
	1	3	1	0	0	1	0	21
	-2	-1	3	0	0	0	1	0

2. $x = 35$, $y = 0$, $z = 30$, $u = 0$, $v = 0$, $w = 42$, $M = 560$ Dual:

$x = 0$, $y = 14$, $z = 0$, $u = 0$, $v = \frac{7}{2}$, $w = 0$, $M = 560$ **3.** Maximize $3x - 4y$ subject to $\begin{cases} 6x + 7y \leq 120 \\ 15x + 5y \leq 195 \ ; \\ x \geq 0,\ y \geq 0 \end{cases}$

$x = 13$, $y = 0$, $u = 42$, $v = 0$, $M = 39$ **4.** $x = 2$, $y = 4$, $u = 0$, $v = 4$, $w = 0$, $M = 44$.   **5.** Maximize $6u + 3v$

subject to $\begin{cases} u + 2v \leq 3 \\ u - \ v \leq 2 \\ u \geq 0,\ v \geq 0 \end{cases}$ **6. (a)** Maximize $\begin{bmatrix} .50 & .35 \end{bmatrix} \begin{bmatrix} x \\ y \end{bmatrix}$ subject to the constraints $\begin{bmatrix} 2 & 1 \\ 2 & 3 \end{bmatrix} \begin{bmatrix} x \\ y \end{bmatrix} \leq \begin{bmatrix} 6000 \\ 9600 \end{bmatrix}$ and

$\begin{bmatrix} x \\ y \end{bmatrix} \geq \begin{bmatrix} 0 \\ 0 \end{bmatrix}$.   **(b)** Minimize $\begin{bmatrix} 6000 & 9600 \end{bmatrix} \begin{bmatrix} u \\ v \end{bmatrix}$ subject to the constraints $\begin{bmatrix} 2 & 2 \\ 1 & 3 \end{bmatrix} \begin{bmatrix} u \\ v \end{bmatrix} \geq \begin{bmatrix} .50 \\ .35 \end{bmatrix}$ and $\begin{bmatrix} u \\ v \end{bmatrix} \geq \begin{bmatrix} 0 \\ 0 \end{bmatrix}$.

(c) Minimize $6000u + 9600v$ subject to the constraints $\begin{cases} 2u + 2v \geq .50 \\ u + 3v \geq .35 \\ u \geq 0, \ v \geq 0 \end{cases}$ where u is a measure of the value of a pound of paper and v is a measure of the value of a minute of labor. **(d)** The dual gives the minimum acceptable profit that can be achieved by selling the paper and hiring out the workers.

CHAPTER 5

Exercises 5.1, page 210

1. (a) $\{5, 6, 7\}$ **(b)** $\{1, 2, 3, 4, 5, 7\}$ **(c)** $\{1, 3\}$ **(d)** $\{5, 7\}$ **3. (a)** $\{a, b, c, d, e, f\}$ **(b)** $\{c\}$ **(c)** $\varnothing$
5. $\varnothing, \{1\}, \{2\}, \{1, 2\}$ **7. (a)** {all male college students who like football} **(b)** {all female college students}
(c) {all female college students who don't like football} **(d)** {all male college students or all college students who like football} **9. (a)** $S = \{1983, 1984, 1987, 1999, 2003, 2006\}$
(b) $T = \{1980, 1983, 1985, 1989, 1991, 1995, 1996, 1997, 1998, 1999, 2003\}$ **(c)** $S \cap T = \{1983, 1999, 2003\}$
(d) $S \cup T = \{1980, 1983, 1984, 1985, 1987, 1989, 1991, 1995, 1996, 1997, 1998, 1999, 2003, 2006\}$
(e) $S' \cap T = \{1980, 1985, 1989, 1991, 1995, 1996, 1997, 1998\}$ **(f)** $S \cap T' = \{1984, 1987, 2006\}$ **11.** From 1980 to 2007, during only three years did the Standard and Poor's Index increase by 2% or more during the first five days and not increase by 16% or more for that year. **13. (a)** $\{d, f\}$ **(b)** $\{a, b, c, e, f\}$ **(c)** $\varnothing$ **(d)** $\{a, c\}$
(e) $\{e\}$ **(f)** $\{a, c, e, f\}$ **(g)** $\{a, b, c, e\}$ **(h)** $\{a, c\}$ **(i)** $\{d\}$ **15.** S **17.** U **19.** $\varnothing$ **21.** $L \cup T$
23. $L \cap P$ **25.** $P \cap L \cap T$ **27.** S' **29.** $S \cup A \cup D$ **31.** $(A \cap S)' \cap D$ **33.** {male students at Mount College}
35. {people who are both teachers and students at Mount College} **37.** {males or students at Mount College}
39. {females at Mount College} **41.** S' **43.** $(V \cup C) \cap S'$ **45.** $(V \cup C)'$ **47. (a)** $\{B, C, D, E\}$
(b) $\{C, D, E, F\}$ **(c)** $\{A, D, E, F\}$ **(d)** $\{A, C, D, E, F\}$ **(e)** $\{A, F\}$ **(f)** $\{D, E\}$ **49.** Possible answer: $\{2\}$ **51.** $S \subseteq T$ **53.** True **55.** True **57.** False **59.** True

Exercises 5.2, page 217

1. 7 **3.** 0 **5.** 11
7. $S \subseteq T$ **9.** 19 million
11. 10 **13.** 452

39. $S' \cup T'$ **41.** $S \cap T'$ **43.** U **45.** S'
47. $R \cap T$ **49.** $R' \cap S \cap T$ **51.** $T \cup (R \cap S')$
53. $(R \cap S \cap T) \cup (R' \cap S' \cap T')$

55. People who are not illegal aliens or everyone over the age of 18 who is employed **57.** Everyone over the age of 18 who is unemployed **59.** Noncitizens or legal aliens who are unemployed

Exercises 5.3, page 222

1. 11 **3.** 46 **5.** 11 **11.**
7. 75 **9.** 30

23. 25 **25.** 4, 2, 1
27. 28 **29.** 12

31. (a)   **(b)** 2   **33.** 190   **35.** 180   **37.** 210   **39.** d   **41.** 450   **43.** 3750   **45.** 30   **47.** 4
(c) 5   **49.** 40   **51.** 27   **53.** 20   **55.** 90   **57.** 6   **59.** 140   **61.** 30   **63.** 35   **65.** 3

Exercises 5.4, page 228

1. 15   **3.** 676   **5.** 380   **7.** 20   **9.** 120   **11.** 64   **13.** 6840   **15.** 870   **17.** 24   **19.** 32   **21.** 360,000
23. (a) 2401   **(b)** 840   **(c)** 343   **(d)** 240   **25. (a)** 362,880   **(b)** 40,320   **(c)** 720   **27.** 256   **29.** 729
31. 168   **33.** 175,760,000   **35.** 160   **37.** 145   **39.** 972   **41.** 1,048,576   **43.** 16   **45.** d   **47.** 24   **49.** 7755
51. 33   **53.** 324   **55.** 1512   **57.** 999,999,999   **59.** 16   **61.** 48   **63.** 48; 1152   **65.** 900

Exercises 5.5, page 235

1. 12   **3.** 120   **5.** 120   **7.** 5   **9.** 7   **11.** n **13.** 1   **15.** $\dfrac{n(n-1)}{2}$ **17.** 720   **19.** 72   **21.** 24   **23.** 36
25. 2730   **27.** 210   **29.** 210   **31.** 120   **33.** 28   **35.** 30,240   **37.** 252   **39.** 38,955,840   **41.** 161,700; 35
43. 15,600   **45.** 75,287,520   **47.** 2,598,960   **49.** 1287   **51.** 1140   **53.** 120   **55.** 70   **57.** Yes; Moe: 36; Joe: 35
59. 479,001,600   **61.** 14,400   **63.** 840   **65.** 10,080   **67.** 120   **69.** 379,236   **71.** 96,875   **73.** 10   **75.** 680
77. b   **79.** 56   **81.** semester system   **83. (a)** 1,221,759   **(b)** 3,921,225   **(c)** first lottery   **(d)** second
lottery

Exercises 5.6, page 242

1. (a) 64   **(b)** 20   **(c)** 22   **(d)** 57   **3.** 126   **5. (a)** 120   **(b)** 56   **(c)** 64   **7.** $\approx 7.14 \cdot 10^{44}$ **9.** 60
11. 67,800,320   **13.** 80   **15.** 3,527,160   **17.** 3528   **19.** 225,225   **21.** 165,765,600   **23.** 210   **25.** 30,240
27. 870,912,000   **29.** 24   **31.** 24   **33.** 3744   **35.** 3050   **37.** 369   **39.** 1500   **41.** 3,628,800   **43.** 64   **45.** 16
47. 262,495   **49.** .264%   **51.** Four aces

Exercises 5.7, page 248

1. 15   **3.** 8   **5.** 153   **7.** 1   **9.** 1   **11.** n **13.** 1   **15.** $n!$ **17.** 64   **19.** $x^{10}, 10x^9y, 45x^8y^2$ **21.** $105x^2y^{13}$,
$15xy^{14}, y^{15}$ **23.** $184{,}756x^{10}y^{10}$ **25.** 330   **27.** 64   **29.** 16   **31.** 32   **33.** 255   **35.** 196,608   **37.** 120   **39.** 16
41. 247   **43.** 4096   **47.** 3696   **49.** $2835x^3$ **51.** 32,767

Exercises 5.8, page 253

1. 20   **3.** 180   **5.** 210   **7.** 34,650   **9.** 166,320   **11.** 1,401,400   **13.** 2,858,856   **15.** 99,768,240
17. 2,546,168,625   **19.** 488,864,376   **21.** 12   **23.** 135,135   **25.** 126   **27.** 115,166,175,166,136,334,240

Chapter 5: Supplementary Exercises, page 256

1. $\varnothing, \{a\}, \{b\}, \{a,b\}$ **2.**   **3.** 120   **5.**   **6.** $x^{12}, 12x^{11}y, 66x^{10}y^2$ **7.** 840
4. 240   **8.** 15   **9.** 35   **10.** 13,860   **11.** 0
12. 136   **13.** 6   **14.** 49   **15.** 47
16. 11   **17.** 46   **18.** 58   **19.** 22   **20.** 23   **21.** 126   **22.** 2^{40} **23.** 550   **24.** 480   **25.** 20   **26.** 450,000
27. 8,100,000,000   **28.** 146,813,779,479,510   **29.** 390,625; 325,089   **30.** 792   **31.** $C(100,14)$ **32.** 27,500
33. 59,049   **34.** $C(60,10)$ **35.** 9,765,625   **36.** 85,766,121   **37.** 210   **38.** 66,512,160   **39.** 14!   **40.** $\dfrac{1}{5!} \cdot \dfrac{100!}{(20!)^5}$
41. $\dfrac{80}{99} \cdot \dfrac{1}{5!} \cdot \dfrac{100!}{(20!)^5}$ **42.** 135   **43.** $C(n,2) - n$ or $\dfrac{n(n-3)}{2}$ **44.** 48   **45.** 34,560   **46.** 95,040   **47.** 5148
48. 648   **49.** 243   **50.** 4512   **51.** 12,696   **52.** 6   **53.** 72   **54.** 12   **55.** 45; 35   **56.** Second teacher   **57.** 4200
58. 5   **59.** 5040   **60. (a)** 14,520   **(b)** 25,344   **61.** 29   **62.** 70   **63.** 36,504   **64.** 12   **65.** 16,360,143,800
66. (a) 224,640,000   **(b)** There are 20 times as many plates in (a).

Chapter 5: Chapter Test, page 259

1. (a) 24   **(b)** 210   **(c)** 153   **(d)** 1   **(e)** 30   **2. (a)** True   **(b)** True   **(c)** False   **3. (a)** {a, e}   **(b)** Ø
4. $C \cap E$ represents the set of certified public accountants who are self-employed. $C \cup E'$ represents the set of people who are either certified public accountants or are not self-employed.

5.

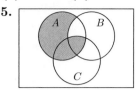

6. 10   **7.** 5   **8.** 60
9. (a) 2,209,413,024   **(b)** 210
10. 210   **11.** 144   **12.** 136,800
13. 792   **14.** 128   **15.** 2520

CHAPTER 6

Exercises 6.2, page 270

1. (a) {RS, RT, RU, RV, ST, SU, SV, TU, TV, UV}   **(b)** {RS, RT, RU, RV}   **(c)** {TU, TV, UV}
3. (a) {HH, HT, TH, TT}   **(b)** {HH, HT}   **5. (a)** {(I, red), (I, white), (II, red), (II, white)}
(b) {(I, red), (I, white)}   **7. (a)** $S = $ {All positive numbers of minutes}   **(b)** "More than 5 minutes but less than 8 minutes," Ø, "5 minutes or less," "8 minutes or more," "5 minutes or less," "Less than 4 minutes," S
9. (a) {(Fr, Lib), (Fr, Con), (So, Lib), (So, Con), (Jr, Lib), (Jr, Con), (Sr, Lib), (Sr, Con)}   **(b)** {(Fr, Con), (So, Con), (Jr, Con), (Sr, Con)}   **(c)** {(Jr, Lib)}   **(d)** {(So, Lib), (Jr, Lib), (Sr, Lib)}   **11. (a)** No
(b) Yes   **13.** Ø, {a}, {b}, {c}, {a, b}, {a, c}, {b, c}, S   **15.** Yes   **17. (a)** {0, 1, 2, 3, 4, 5, 6, 7, 8, 9, 10}   **(b)** {6, 7, 8, 9, 10}   **19. (a)** No   **(b)** Yes   **(c)** Yes   **21.** The set of integers from 0 to 8   **23.** (7, 4); 81
25. {2, 6, 9, 10}; 1.7%   **27.** {Colonel Mustard, Miss Scarlet, Professor Plum, Mrs. White, Mr. Green, Mrs. Peacock} **(a)** 324   **(b)** "The murder occurred in the library with a gun."   **(c)** "Either the murder occurred in the library or it was done with a gun."

Exercises 6.3, page 281

1. (a) $\frac{46,277}{774,746}$ **(b)** $\frac{48,132}{774,746}$ **(c)** $\frac{726,614}{774,746}$ **3. (a)** $\frac{5}{36}$ **(b)** $\frac{1}{6}$ **5.** $\frac{1}{19}$ **7. (a)** $\frac{1}{6}$ **(b)** 1 to 5   **9. (a)** .7
(b) .7   **11. (a)** $\frac{10}{11}$ **(b)** $\frac{1}{3}$ **(c)** $\frac{4}{9}$ **13.** 9 to 91   **15.** $\frac{11}{18}; \frac{7}{18}$ **17. (a)** .7   **(b)** .2   **19.** .9   **21.** .6
23. (a) .7   **25.**

Number of Colleges Applied to	Probability
1	.17
2	.12
3	.14
4	.16
5 to 20	.41

(b) 7000

27. (a) .15, .55, .20, .10   **(b)** .30
29. (a) Some categories are left out—people who use a computer for both school and work, for example.   **(b)** .83   **31.** 41 to 9

33. (a) $\frac{3}{8}, \frac{1}{4}, \frac{2}{5}, \frac{1}{5}$ **(b)** $\frac{49}{40}$, which is greater than 1   **(c)** Bookies have to make a living. The payoffs are a little lower than they should be; thus allowing the bookie to make a profit.   **35.** 1   **37.** 0

Exercises 6.4, page 288

1. (a) $\frac{1}{9}$ **(b)** $\frac{2}{9}$ **3. (a)** $\frac{7}{13}$ **(b)** $\frac{6}{13}$ **(c)** $\frac{4}{13}$ **(d)** $\frac{9}{13}$ **5. (a)** $\frac{2}{429}$ **(b)** $\frac{7}{429}$ **(c)** $\frac{427}{429}$ **7.** $\frac{11}{12}$ **9.** $\frac{5}{6}$
11. $\frac{16}{17}$ **13.** $\frac{5}{7106}$ **15.** $\frac{47}{250}$ **17.** $\frac{13}{49}$ **19. (a)** .25   **(b)** .75   **(c)** .8   **21.** 0   **23.** $\frac{1}{11}$ **25.** $\frac{2}{5}$ **27. (a)** $\frac{15}{28}$
(b) $\frac{15}{56}$ **(c)** $\frac{9}{56}$ **(d)** $\frac{9}{14}$ **29.** $\frac{5}{6}$ **31.** $\frac{5}{16}$ **33.** $\frac{1}{1,919,190}$ **35.** .90055   **37.** .066   **39. (a)** .119   **(b)** .152
41. .625   **43. (a)** 1 to 146,107,961   **(b)** $\frac{1}{146,107,962}$ **45.** $\frac{5}{7}$ **47.** $\frac{8815}{499422} \approx$ .01765   **49.** $\frac{12}{25}$ **51.** .729
53. (a) .00144   **(b)** .0211   **55. (a)** .1054   **(b)** .2155   **57.** 13   **59. (a)** 4   **(b)** .2139   **61.** 27   **63.** 6

Exercises 6.5, page 299

1. $\frac{1}{3}, \frac{1}{5}$ **3.** $\frac{4}{7}$ **5.** No   **7. (a)** .36   **(b)** .81   **9.** .7967   **11.** $\frac{3}{4}, \frac{1}{2}$ **13. (a)** .4   **(b)** .6   **(c)** .75   **15.** $\frac{1}{4}$
17. .94   **19.** No   **21.** .009975   **23.** .2401   **27.** .4, .24, .36   **31. (a)** $\frac{1}{10}$ **(b)** 100 per 1000   **(c)** $\frac{1}{20}$
33. (a) .28   **(b)** .07   **(c)** .6065   **35. (a)** .16   **(b)** .64   **(c)** .36   **(d)** .42   **(e)** .64   **(f)** .31

37. (a) .2686 **(b)** .4239 **(c)** .5749 **(d)** .0297 **39. (a)** .40 **(b)** .56 **(c)** .18 **(d)** .70 **(e)** .45 **(f)** .67 **41. (a)** .7599 **(b)** .0642 **(c)** .7348 **45.** $\frac{10}{143}$; $\frac{25}{286}$ **47.** $\frac{1}{6}$; $\frac{1}{3}$ **49.** .0986 **51.** $\frac{1}{1717}$ **53.** Yes **55.** $\frac{1}{16}$ **57. (a)** $1000p$ **(b)** $1000p - 499,500p^2$ **59.** .24; .24; Toss the coin twice. If HT comes up, let the home team kick off. If TH comes up, let the visiting team kick off. If HH or TT comes up, repeat the coin toss until one of each face occurs. **61.** No **63.** Not independent **65. (a)** 3.69×10^{-6} **(b)** 6.16×10^{-7} **(c)** a

Exercises 6.6, page 309

1. **3.** **5.** .08 **11.**

7. .295
9. $\frac{7}{12}$

$\frac{1201}{5525} \approx .22$ **13.** .14 **15.** $\frac{25}{27}$ **17.** .86 **19.** $\frac{4}{7}$ **21. (a)** .60 **(b)** .75 **23.** $1 - (.9999)^n$ **25.** Same shape; probability of winning card game is greater. **27. (a)** $\frac{1}{4}$; $\frac{3}{4}$ **(b)** .7 **29.** $\frac{6}{11}$ **31.** .999996 **33.** $\frac{25}{26}$ **35.** $\frac{3}{8}$ **37.** .66 **39. (a)** .99 **(b)** .0180 Oliver is almost certain to win each game. However, he is almost certain to lose the 400-game match. **41.** .92

Exercises 6.7, page 315

1. $\frac{8}{53}$ **3.** $\frac{3}{7}$ **5.** .075 **7.** $\frac{8}{9}$ **9. (a)** .1325 **(b)** $\frac{12}{53} \approx .23$ **11.** $\frac{5}{103} \approx .049$ **13. (a)** .01 **(b)** $\frac{33}{34} \approx .971$ **15.** $\frac{31}{37} \approx .838$ **17. (a)** $\frac{1}{4}$ **(b)** $\frac{13}{17} \approx .765$ **(c)** .130 **19. (a)** $\frac{5}{9}$ **(b)** 11%

Chapter 6: Supplementary Exercises, page 325

1. $\frac{31}{32}$ **2.** No **3.** $\frac{4}{9}$ **4.** $\frac{1}{12}$ **5.** $\frac{2}{5}$ **6.** $\frac{2}{11}$ **7.** $\frac{1}{5}$ **8.** $\frac{1}{5}$ **9.** .4667 **10.** .3333 **11.** $\frac{7}{15}$ **12. (a)** $\frac{1}{10}$ **(b)** $\frac{2}{5}$ **13. (a)** $\frac{2}{15}$ **(b)** $\frac{1}{3}$ **14. (a)** $\left(\frac{1}{36}\right)^3$ **(b)** $\left(\frac{1}{10}\right)^4$ **(c)** $\frac{167}{500}$ **(d)** $\left(\frac{13}{18}\right)^3\left(\frac{1}{2}\right)^4$ **15. (a)** $\frac{1}{12}$ **(b)** $\frac{1}{2}$ **16.** $\frac{7}{12}$ **17.** $\frac{1}{21}$ **18.** $\frac{2}{3}$ **19.** No **20.** $\frac{2}{3}$ **21.** $\frac{1}{3}$ **22.** $\frac{19}{49}$ **23.** $\frac{1}{6}$ **24.** $\frac{1}{21}$ **25.** $\frac{2}{3}$ **26.** Switch **27.** $\frac{13}{25}$ **28.** 13 to 37 **29.** $\frac{1}{120,960}$ **30.** $\frac{1}{6}$ **31.** $\frac{5}{16}$ **32.** $\frac{1}{3}$ **33.** $\frac{4}{25}$ **34.** $\frac{1}{8}$ **35.** $\frac{138}{301}$ **36.** e **37.** a **38.** $\frac{6}{7}$ **39.** $\frac{5}{324}$ **40.** $\frac{95}{1827}$ **41. (a)** $\frac{1}{2197}$ **(b)** $\frac{469}{2197}$ **42.** 65,535 to 1 **43.** $\frac{1}{3}$ **44.** .5 **45.** 5 to 13 **46.** .02695 **47.** 421 **49.** Theoretical probability: $\frac{5}{32}$

Chapter 6: Chapter Test, page 328

1. (a) $S = \{\text{PN, PD, PQ, PH, ND, NQ, NH, DQ, DH, QH}\}$ **(b)** $E = \{\text{PN, PQ, NQ, DH}\}$ **2. (a)** $\frac{3}{8}$ **(b)** $\frac{1,000,000}{1,000,001}$ **3. (a)** 2 to 3 **(b)** 7 to 3 **4. (a)** A male junior is elected. **(b)** A female junior is not elected. **(c)** A male or a junior is elected. **5.** $\frac{15}{16}$ **6.** .9612 **7. (a)** $\frac{5}{8}$ **(b)** $\frac{3}{4}$ **(c)** $\frac{2}{3}$ **(d)** No **(e)** No **8.** .6513; .3874 **9. (a)** $\frac{1}{3}$ **(b)** $\frac{7}{13}$ **(c)** No; No **(d)** $\frac{1}{3}$ **10. (a)** .50 **(b)** .50 **11. (a)** $\frac{18}{25}$ **(b)** $\frac{7}{13}$

CHAPTER 7

Exercises 7.1, page 337

1. **3.** **5.** **7.** b

9.

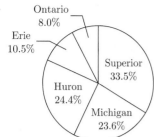

Ontario 8.0%
Erie 10.5%
Superior 33.5%
Huron 24.4%
Michigan 23.6%

11. .602 **13.**

15. c

17.

2 5 7 10 15

19.

10 13 17 21 24
interquartile range = 8

21.

20 28 42 52.5 56
interquartile range = 24.5

23. (A)–(c), (B)–(d), (C)–(a), (D)–(b)

25. (a) min = 200, Q_1 = 400, Q_2 = 600, Q_3 = 700, max = 800   **(b)** 25%   **(c)** 25%
(d) 50%   **(e)** 75%

27.

.200 .229 .2835 .317 .350

.091 .175 .270 .325 .359

Exercises 7.2, page 347

1.

Grade	Relative frequency
0	.08
1	.12
2	.40
3	.24
4	.16

3.

Number of calls during minute	Relative frequency
20	.05
21	.05
22	0
23	.10
24	.30
25	.20
26	0
27	.15
28	.10
29	.05

5.

Number of heads	Probability
0	$\frac{1}{8}$
1	$\frac{3}{8}$
2	$\frac{3}{8}$
3	$\frac{1}{8}$

7.

Number of red balls	Probability
0	$\frac{4}{35}$
1	$\frac{18}{35}$
2	$\frac{12}{35}$
3	$\frac{1}{35}$

9.

Number of red balls	Player's earnings	Probability
2	$5	$\frac{1}{15}$
1	$1	$\frac{8}{15}$
0	–$1	$\frac{6}{15}$

11. .6   **13.**

k	$\Pr(X^2 = k)$
0	.1
1	.2
4	.3
9	.2
16	.2

15.

k	$\Pr(X - 1 = k)$
-1	.1
0	.2
1	.3
2	.2
3	.2

17.

k	$\Pr(\frac{1}{5}Y = k)$
1	.3
2	.4
3	.1
4	.1
5	.1

19.

k	$\Pr((X + 1)^2 = k)$
1	.1
4	.2
9	.3
16	.2
25	.2

21.

Grade	Relative frequency	
	9 AM class	10 AM class
F	.17	.16
D	.25	.23
C	.33	.15
B	.17	.21
A	.08	.25

The 9 A.M. class has the distribution centered on the C grade with relatively few A's. The 10 A.M. class has a large percentage of A's and D's with fewer C's.

23. 80%   **25.**

(a) 25%

(b) 60%

(c)

(d) ≈ 25

27. (a) 59

(b) 5%

(c) 54

(d) 35%

(e) ≈ 54

29. (a) $\Pr(U = 4) = \frac{1}{15}$

(b) $\frac{2}{3}$ **(c)** $\frac{14}{15}$ **(d)** $\frac{1}{3}$

(e)

Exercises 7.3, page 354

1. $\frac{25}{216}$

3. $\frac{3}{64}$

5. .3174

7. .1488

9. .8507

11. .2007

13. .2618

15.

k	$\Pr(X = k)$
0	.0168
1	.0896
2	.2090
3	.2787
4	.2322
5	.1239
6	.0413
7	.0079
8	.0007

17. d **19.** .5583 **21.** .0820

23. $\frac{20}{27}$ **25.** 9 **27.** .20736

29. (a) .375 **(b)** .5

(c) .125 **31.** a **33.** .5

35. .102

37. (a) .2898 **(b)** 21 games

39. (a) .0003976 **(b)** .02624

41. (a) .0290

(b)

k	$\Pr(X = k)$
0	.0105
1	.0524
2	.1258
3	.1929
4	.2122
5	.1782
6	.1188

(c) .0047

43. 178

Exercises 7.4, page 364

1. 2.35   **3. (a)** 2.9   **(b)**

Grade	Relative Frequency
4	.3
3	.4
2	.2
1	.1

(c) 2.9

5. $\bar{x}_A = 1.5$, $\bar{x}_B = 1.6$; Group A had fewer cavities.

7.

Earnings	Probability
−$1	$\frac{37}{38}$
$35	$\frac{1}{38}$

$E(X) \approx -5.26\cent$

9.

Earnings	Probability
−50¢	$\frac{1}{3}$
0¢	$\frac{4}{15}$
50¢	$\frac{1}{5}$
$1	$\frac{2}{15}$
$1.50	$\frac{1}{15}$

$E(X) \approx 16.67\cent$

11. $1000   **13.** 4.47   **15.** 10   **17.** Three free throws
19. Many possible answers   **21.** 58.5°   **23.** d   **25.** b
27. c   **29.** d   **31.** b   **33.** a   **35.** a

Exercises 7.5, page 373

1. 1.4   **3.** B   **5. (a)** $\mu_A = 15$, $\sigma_A^2 = 160$, $\mu_B = 13$, $\sigma_B^2 = 141$ **(b)** A   **(c)** B   **7. (a)** $\mu_A = 103$, $\sigma_A^2 = 4.6$, $\mu_B = 104$, $\sigma_B^2 = 3.4$ **(b)** B   **(c)** B   **9.** 6, ≈ 1.732 **11.** 3, ≈ 1.719 **13. (a)** $\geq .75$ **(b)** $\geq .89$ **(c)** $\geq .31$
15. ≥ 4688 **17.** 8   **19. (a)** $\mu = 7$, $\sigma^2 = \frac{35}{6}$ **(b)** $\frac{5}{6}$ **(c)** $\geq \frac{19}{54}$ **21.** 2   **25.** $\mu = 50{,}334.75$, $\sigma \approx 2364.08$
27. $\mu = 4.72$, $\sigma \approx 1.40$

Exercises 7.6, page 387

1. .8944   **3.** .4013   **5.** .2417   **7.** .6170   **9.** 1.75   **11.** .75   **13.** ≈ 1.28 **15.** $\mu = 6$, $\sigma = 2$ **17.** $\mu = 9$, $\sigma = 1$
19. $-\frac{8}{3}$ **21.** a   **23.** .9772   **25.** .6247   **27.** .9544   **29.** .5   **31.** .0002   **33.** .9876   **35.** .0122   **37. (a)** 616
(b) Between 396 and 644   **(c)** 674   **39.** 19,750 miles   **41. (a)** 5.35 ounces   **(b)** 4.76 ounces   **43.** The
normal curve is translated to the right.   **45.** .2358

Exercises 7.7, page 393

1. (a) .1974   **(b)** .7888   **(c)** .9878   **3.** .0062   **5.** .2743   **7.** .0013   **9.** .6368   **11.** .1056   **13.** 2, .1469
15. .7498   **17.** .61   **19.** Exact: .2356; normal approximation: .2358   **21.** Exact: .0812; normal approximation: .0813

Chapter 7: Supplementary Exercises, page 397

1.

2.

interquartile range = 9

3. (a)

k	$\Pr(X = k)$
0	$\frac{8}{27}$
1	$\frac{12}{27}$
2	$\frac{6}{27}$
3	$\frac{1}{27}$

(b) $\mu = 1$, $\sigma^2 = \frac{2}{3}$

4. .2266 **5.** .2857 **6.** .2646
7. $\geq \frac{8}{9}$ **8.** $\mu = 4.8$, $\sigma^2 = 19.76$
9. 10.56%

10.

k	$\Pr(X = k)$
0	$\frac{1}{70}$
1	$\frac{16}{70}$
2	$\frac{36}{70}$
3	$\frac{16}{70}$
4	$\frac{1}{70}$

$\mu = 2$, $\sigma^2 = \frac{4}{7}$

11. .0122 **12.** .84 **13.** 22.5 **14.** $-.75$
15. (a) 1.39%   **(b)** 124.75
16. 52; choose true for all the questions.
21. Yes **22.** Yes

Chapter 7: Chapter Test, page 398

1. .58 **2.**

20   26   30   37   42

interquartile range $= 11$

3. (a)

Number of Heads, k	$\Pr(X = k)$
0	.25
1	.50
2	.25

(b)

k	$\Pr(2X + 5 = k)$
5	.25
7	.50
9	.25

4. (a) .296 **(b)** .619 **(c)** 2 **5.** .4, 3.24, 1.8 **6.** Lucy; $\approx$ 11 cents per roll **7. (a)** .8413 **(b)** .9878
(c) .7162 **8. (a)** .1587 **(b)** .7745 **(c)** 99 mg/100 ml, 113 mg/100 ml **9. (a)** .3983 **(b)** .0118; .0092;
difference is .0026 **(c)** .9962; .9878; difference is .0084

CHAPTER 8

Exercises 8.1, page 409

1. Yes **3.** No **5.** Yes **7.**
$\begin{array}{cc} & \text{A} \quad \text{B} \\ \begin{array}{c} \text{A} \\ \text{B} \end{array} & \begin{bmatrix} .3 & .5 \\ .7 & .5 \end{bmatrix} \end{array}$
9.
$\begin{array}{cccc} & \text{A} & \text{B} & \text{C} \\ \begin{array}{c} \text{A} \\ \text{B} \\ \text{C} \end{array} & \begin{bmatrix} \frac{1}{3} & \frac{2}{9} & \frac{1}{3} \\ \frac{1}{3} & \frac{4}{9} & \frac{1}{6} \\ \frac{1}{3} & \frac{1}{3} & \frac{1}{2} \end{bmatrix} \end{array}$
11.
$\begin{array}{cccc} & \text{A} & \text{B} & \text{C} \\ \begin{array}{c} \text{A} \\ \text{B} \\ \text{C} \end{array} & \begin{bmatrix} .4 & .2 & 0 \\ .5 & 0 & 0 \\ .1 & .8 & 1 \end{bmatrix} \end{array}$

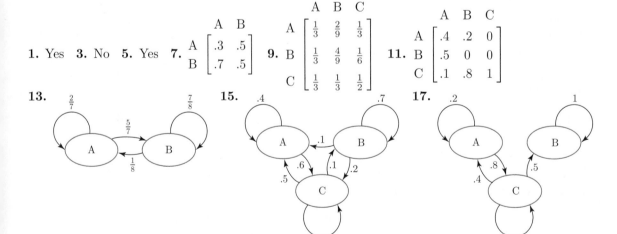

13. **15.** **17.**

19. 53.5%, 56.75% **21.** 40% will be in zone I, 40% will be in zone II, and 20% will be in zone III.

23. (a)
$\begin{array}{cc} & \text{S} \quad \text{O} \\ \begin{array}{c} \text{S} \\ \text{O} \end{array} & \begin{bmatrix} .992 & .007 \\ .008 & .993 \end{bmatrix} \end{array}$
(b) 36.17%, 36.33% **25. (a)**
$\begin{array}{cc} & \text{L} \quad \text{R} \\ \begin{array}{c} \text{L} \\ \text{R} \end{array} & \begin{bmatrix} .9 & .7 \\ .1 & .3 \end{bmatrix} \end{array}$
(b) $\begin{bmatrix} .88 & .84 \\ .12 & .16 \end{bmatrix}$ **(c)** $\begin{bmatrix} .8 \\ .2 \end{bmatrix}_1$, $\begin{bmatrix} .86 \\ .14 \end{bmatrix}_2$
(d) 87.5% **27. (a)** 4% **(b)** 96% of the freshmen who held middle-of-the-road political views continued to
hold those views as sophomores.

(c)

(d) 43.88%; 44.68% **29. (a)**

$$\begin{array}{cc} & \begin{array}{ccc} U & S & R \end{array} \\ \begin{array}{c} U \\ S \\ R \end{array} & \begin{bmatrix} .86 & .05 & .03 \\ .08 & .86 & .05 \\ .06 & .09 & .92 \end{bmatrix} \end{array}$$

(b) 11.4%

31. (a)
$$\begin{array}{c} \\ V \\ C \end{array} \begin{array}{cc} V & C \end{array} \begin{bmatrix} .128 & .663 \\ .872 & .337 \end{bmatrix}$$
(b) .59452 **33.** $\begin{bmatrix} .44 \\ .56 \end{bmatrix}_3$, $\begin{bmatrix} .44 \\ .56 \end{bmatrix}_4$

35. All powers are $\begin{bmatrix} \frac{1}{3} & \frac{1}{3} \\ \frac{2}{3} & \frac{2}{3} \end{bmatrix}$.

37. $\begin{bmatrix} .1 & .3 \\ .9 & .7 \end{bmatrix}$; $\begin{bmatrix} .28 & .24 \\ .72 & .76 \end{bmatrix}$; $\begin{bmatrix} .24 & .25 \\ .76 & .75 \end{bmatrix}$; $\begin{bmatrix} .25 & .25 \\ .75 & .75 \end{bmatrix}$; $\begin{bmatrix} .25 & .25 \\ .75 & .75 \end{bmatrix}$ **39.** No **41. (a)** $\begin{bmatrix} .35 \\ .65 \end{bmatrix}$; $\begin{bmatrix} .425 \\ .575 \end{bmatrix}$; $\begin{bmatrix} .3875 \\ .6125 \end{bmatrix}$;

$\begin{bmatrix} .40625 \\ .59375 \end{bmatrix}$ **43.** $\begin{bmatrix} .4 \\ .6 \end{bmatrix}$ **45.** $\begin{bmatrix} .4 & .4 \\ .6 & .6 \end{bmatrix}$

Exercises 8.2, page 420

1. Yes **3.** Yes **5.** Yes **7.** $\begin{bmatrix} \frac{1}{6} \\ \frac{5}{6} \end{bmatrix}$ **9.** $\begin{bmatrix} .6 \\ .4 \end{bmatrix}$ **11.** $\begin{bmatrix} \frac{5}{14} \\ \frac{3}{7} \\ \frac{3}{14} \end{bmatrix}$ **13.** 87.5% **15.** 20% **17.** 40%

19. (a)
$$\begin{array}{c} \\ A \\ B \\ C \end{array} \begin{array}{ccc} A & B & C \end{array} \begin{bmatrix} .7 & .1 & .1 \\ .2 & .8 & .3 \\ .1 & .1 & .6 \end{bmatrix}$$
(b) 34%; 30.4% **(c)** $\frac{1}{4}$ at location A, $\frac{11}{20}$ at location B, $\frac{1}{5}$ at location C **21.** 25%

23. $\begin{bmatrix} .5 \\ .5 \end{bmatrix}$ is a stable distribution for the matrix $A = \begin{bmatrix} 0 & 1 \\ 1 & 0 \end{bmatrix}$ because $.5 + .5 = 1$ and $\begin{bmatrix} 0 & 1 \\ 1 & 0 \end{bmatrix}\begin{bmatrix} .5 \\ .5 \end{bmatrix} = \begin{bmatrix} .5 \\ .5 \end{bmatrix}$. However, given an arbitrary initial distribution $\begin{bmatrix} \quad \\ \quad \end{bmatrix}_0 \neq \begin{bmatrix} .5 \\ .5 \end{bmatrix}$, $A^n \begin{bmatrix} \quad \\ \quad \end{bmatrix}_0$ will not approach $\begin{bmatrix} .5 \\ .5 \end{bmatrix}$ as n gets large, so the existence of a stable distribution for A does not contradict the main premise of this section. **25.** $\begin{bmatrix} .7 & .7 \\ .3 & .3 \end{bmatrix}$; $\begin{bmatrix} .7 \\ .3 \end{bmatrix}$

27. $\begin{bmatrix} \frac{8}{35} & \frac{8}{35} & \frac{8}{35} \\ \frac{3}{7} & \frac{3}{7} & \frac{3}{7} \\ \frac{12}{35} & \frac{12}{35} & \frac{12}{35} \end{bmatrix}$; $\begin{bmatrix} \frac{8}{35} \\ \frac{3}{7} \\ \frac{12}{35} \end{bmatrix}$

Exercises 8.3, page 430

1. Yes **3.** No **5.** No **7.** Yes **9.**
$$\begin{array}{c} \\ B \\ A \\ C \end{array} \begin{array}{ccc} B & A & C \end{array} \begin{bmatrix} 1 & .3 & .4 \\ 0 & .2 & .5 \\ 0 & .5 & .1 \end{bmatrix}$$
11.
$$\begin{array}{c} \\ D \\ A \\ B \\ C \end{array} \begin{array}{cccc} D & A & B & C \end{array} \begin{bmatrix} 1 & .4 & 0 & .1 \\ 0 & .1 & 1 & .6 \\ 0 & .2 & 0 & .1 \\ 0 & .3 & 0 & .2 \end{bmatrix}$$
13. $R = [.5]$; $S = \begin{bmatrix} .3 \\ .2 \end{bmatrix}$;

$F = [2]$; $\begin{bmatrix} 1 & 0 & .6 \\ 0 & 1 & .4 \\ 0 & 0 & 0 \end{bmatrix}$ **15.** $R = \begin{bmatrix} .3 & .6 \\ .1 & .2 \end{bmatrix}$; $S = \begin{bmatrix} .1 & 0 \\ .5 & .2 \end{bmatrix}$; $F = \begin{bmatrix} 1.6 & 1.2 \\ .2 & 1.4 \end{bmatrix}$; $\begin{bmatrix} 1 & 0 & .16 & .12 \\ 0 & 1 & .84 & .88 \\ 0 & 0 & 0 & 0 \\ 0 & 0 & 0 & 0 \end{bmatrix}$ **17.** $R = \begin{bmatrix} .5 & 0 \\ .1 & .6 \end{bmatrix}$;

$$S = \begin{bmatrix} .1 & .2 \\ .3 & 0 \\ 0 & .2 \end{bmatrix}; \quad F = \begin{bmatrix} 2 & 0 \\ .5 & 2.5 \end{bmatrix}; \quad \begin{bmatrix} 1 & 0 & 0 & | & .3 & .5 \\ 0 & 1 & 0 & | & .6 & 0 \\ 0 & 0 & 1 & | & .1 & .5 \\ \hline 0 & 0 & 0 & | & 0 & 0 \\ 0 & 0 & 0 & | & 0 & 0 \end{bmatrix}$$

19. If the gambler begins with \$2, he should have \$1 for an expected number of .79 plays.

21. (a)

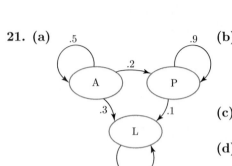

(b)
$$\begin{array}{c} \\ L \\ A \\ P \end{array} \begin{array}{ccc} L & A & P \\ \begin{bmatrix} 1 & | & .3 & .1 \\ 0 & | & .5 & 0 \\ 0 & | & .2 & .9 \end{bmatrix} \end{array}$$

(c)
$$\begin{array}{c} \\ L \\ A \\ P \end{array} \begin{array}{ccc} L & A & P \\ \begin{bmatrix} 1 & | & 1 & 1 \\ 0 & | & 0 & 0 \\ 0 & | & 0 & 0 \end{bmatrix} \end{array}$$

(d) 6

23. (a)

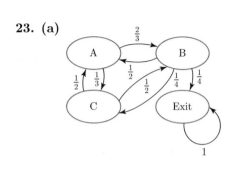

(b)
$$\begin{array}{c} \\ E \\ A \\ B \\ C \end{array} \begin{array}{cccc} E & A & B & C \\ \begin{bmatrix} 1 & 0 & \frac{1}{4} & 0 \\ 0 & 0 & \frac{1}{2} & \frac{1}{2} \\ 0 & \frac{2}{3} & 0 & \frac{1}{2} \\ 0 & \frac{1}{3} & \frac{1}{4} & 0 \end{bmatrix} \end{array}$$

(c)
$$\begin{array}{c} \\ E \\ A \\ B \\ C \end{array} \begin{array}{cccc} E & A & B & C \\ \begin{bmatrix} 1 & 1 & 1 & 1 \\ 0 & 0 & 0 & 0 \\ 0 & 0 & 0 & 0 \\ 0 & 0 & 0 & 0 \end{bmatrix} \end{array}$$

(d) 10.6 minutes

25. (a)
$$\begin{array}{c} \\ D \\ G \\ F \\ S \end{array} \begin{array}{cccc} D & G & F & S \\ \begin{bmatrix} 1 & 0 & | & .2 & .1 \\ 0 & 1 & | & 0 & .9 \\ 0 & 0 & | & 0 & 0 \\ 0 & 0 & | & .8 & 0 \end{bmatrix} \end{array}$$

(b)
$$\begin{array}{c} \\ D \\ G \\ F \\ S \end{array} \begin{array}{cccc} D & G & F & S \\ \begin{bmatrix} 1 & 0 & | & .28 & .1 \\ 0 & 1 & | & .72 & .9 \\ 0 & 0 & | & 0 & 0 \\ 0 & 0 & | & 0 & 0 \end{bmatrix} \end{array}$$

(c) .72　**(d)** 1.8 years　**27. (a)** $\frac{13}{14}$; $\frac{11}{14}$　**(b)** $\frac{20}{7}$ months　**(c)** \$5786; \$1214

29. (a) $\frac{3}{4}$; $\frac{1}{2}$; $\frac{1}{4}$　**(b)** 4　**31.** $\frac{50}{81}$; $5\frac{1}{2}$

Chapter 8: Supplementary Exercises, page 434

1. Stochastic, neither　**2.** Stochastic, regular　**3.** Stochastic, regular　**4.** Stochastic, absorbing　**5.** Not stochastic　**6.** Stochastic, absorbing　**7.** $\begin{bmatrix} \frac{5}{9} \\ \frac{4}{9} \end{bmatrix}$　**8.** $\begin{bmatrix} 1 & 0 & 0 & | & \frac{1}{2} & \frac{1}{2} \\ 0 & 1 & 0 & | & \frac{1}{4} & \frac{1}{8} \\ 0 & 0 & 1 & | & \frac{1}{4} & \frac{3}{8} \\ \hline 0 & 0 & 0 & | & 0 & 0 \\ 0 & 0 & 0 & | & 0 & 0 \end{bmatrix}$　**9. (a)**
$$\begin{array}{c} \\ H \\ M \\ L \end{array} \begin{array}{ccc} H & M & L \\ \begin{bmatrix} .5 & .4 & .3 \\ .4 & .3 & .5 \\ .1 & .3 & .2 \end{bmatrix} \end{array};$$
(b) 38%

(c) $\frac{19}{97}$　**10. (a)**
$$\begin{array}{c} \\ P \\ N \end{array} \begin{array}{cc} P & N \\ \begin{bmatrix} .8 & .3 \\ .2 & .7 \end{bmatrix} \end{array}$$
(b) 30%　**(c)** 60%　**11.** $\begin{bmatrix} 1 & 0 & | & \frac{11}{12} & 1 & \frac{1}{2} \\ 0 & 1 & | & \frac{1}{12} & 0 & \frac{1}{2} \\ \hline 0 & 0 & | & 0 & 0 & 0 \\ 0 & 0 & | & 0 & 0 & 0 \\ 0 & 0 & | & 0 & 0 & 0 \end{bmatrix}$　**12. (a)**
$$\begin{array}{c} \\ I \\ II \\ III \\ IV \end{array} \begin{array}{cccc} I & II & III & IV \\ \begin{bmatrix} 1 & 0 & | & 0 & \frac{1}{4} \\ 0 & 1 & | & \frac{1}{3} & \frac{1}{4} \\ \hline 0 & 0 & | & 0 & \frac{1}{2} \\ 0 & 0 & | & \frac{2}{3} & 0 \end{bmatrix} \end{array}$$

(b) $\frac{5}{12}$　**(c)** $\frac{5}{8}$　**(d)** $2\frac{1}{2}$ minutes　**13.** c　**14.** 58.5%　**15. (a)** If the traffic is Moderate on a particular day, then for the next day the probability of Light is .2, the probability of Moderate is .75, and the probability of

Heavy is .05.　　**(b)** About 37.0%, Light; 47.8%, Moderate; 15.2%, Heavy　　**(c)** About 3 days　　**16.** State G:

≈ 1.48 months; state S: ≈ 1.83 months.　　**17. (a)** $\begin{bmatrix} \frac{122}{1683} \\ \frac{23}{99} \\ \frac{4}{9} \\ \frac{422}{1683} \end{bmatrix}$; In the long run, the probability of having 1, 2, 3, or 4

units of water in the reservoir at any given time will be $\frac{122}{1683}$, $\frac{23}{99}$, $\frac{4}{9}$, or $\frac{422}{1683}$, respectively.　　**(b)** About \$6881

Chapter 8: Chapter Test, page 436

1. (a) stochastic　　**(b)** not stochastic　　**(c)** not stochastic　　**(d)** stochastic　　**2. (a)** not regular　　**(b)** regular

(c) regular　　**3.** b　　**4.** $\begin{bmatrix} \frac{3}{7} \\ \frac{4}{7} \end{bmatrix}$; $\begin{bmatrix} \frac{3}{7} & \frac{3}{7} \\ \frac{4}{7} & \frac{4}{7} \end{bmatrix}$　　**5. (a)** $\begin{bmatrix} .70 & .60 \\ .30 & .40 \end{bmatrix}$　　**(b)** $\begin{bmatrix} .50 \\ .50 \end{bmatrix}$　　**(c)** 66.5%

(d) $\begin{bmatrix} .70 & .60 \\ .30 & .40 \end{bmatrix} \begin{bmatrix} \frac{2}{3} \\ \frac{1}{3} \end{bmatrix} = \begin{bmatrix} \frac{2}{3} \\ \frac{1}{3} \end{bmatrix}$　　**6. (a)** absorbing　　**(b)** not absorbing　　**(c)** absorbing

7. (a)
$$\begin{array}{c} \\ \text{PC} \\ \text{Apple} \\ \text{None} \end{array} \begin{array}{ccc} \text{PC} & \text{Apple} & \text{None} \\ \left[\begin{array}{ccc} 1 & 0 & .3 \\ 0 & 1 & .1 \\ 0 & 0 & .6 \end{array}\right. \end{array}$$
(b) $\begin{bmatrix} 1 & 0 & \frac{3}{4} \\ 0 & 1 & \frac{1}{4} \\ \hline 0 & 0 & 0 \end{bmatrix}$　　**(c)** 25%　　**(d)** 2.5 years

CHAPTER 9

Exercises 9.1, page 445

1. R: row 2; C: column 1　　**3.** R: row 2; C: column 1　　**5.** R: row 1; C: column 1　　**7. (a)** row 1, column 2

(b) 0　　**9.** $\begin{array}{c} \\ H \\ T \end{array} \begin{array}{cc} H & T \\ \left[\begin{array}{cc} 2 & -1 \\ -1 & -4 \end{array}\right] \end{array}$; strictly determined; R shows heads, C shows tails

11. $\begin{array}{c} \\ F \\ A \\ N \end{array} \begin{array}{ccc} F & A & N \\ \left[\begin{array}{ccc} 8000 & -1000 & 1000 \\ -7000 & 4000 & -2000 \\ 3000 & 3000 & 2000 \end{array}\right] \end{array}$; strictly determined; both should be neutral　　**13.** $\begin{array}{c} 5 \\ 10 \end{array} \begin{array}{ccc} 6 & 7 & 8 \\ \left[\begin{array}{ccc} 1 & -5 & -5 \\ -6 & 3 & 2 \end{array}\right] \end{array}$; not

strictly determined

Exercises 9.2, page 451

1. (a) 0　　**(b)** 1　　**(c)** -1.12　　**(d)** .5 [b is most advantageous to R]　　**3.** \$29,200　　**5.** 0　　**7.** No, no saddle

point, yes, $\begin{bmatrix} \frac{11}{16} \\ \frac{5}{16} \end{bmatrix}$　　**9.** No, no saddle point, yes, $\begin{bmatrix} \frac{1}{30} \\ \frac{29}{30} \end{bmatrix}$　　**11.** Yes, Renée row 1, Carlos column 1; value $= 1$; no

Exercises 9.3, page 461

1. Minimize $y_1 + y_2$ subject to $\begin{cases} y_1 + 4y_2 \geq 1 \\ 6y_1 + 3y_2 \geq 1 \\ y_1 \geq 0,\ y_2 \geq 0 \end{cases}$　　**3.** $\begin{bmatrix} \frac{1}{2} & \frac{1}{2} \end{bmatrix}$; $\begin{bmatrix} \frac{1}{4} \\ \frac{3}{4} \end{bmatrix}$　　**5.** $\begin{bmatrix} \frac{1}{2} & \frac{1}{2} \end{bmatrix}$; $\begin{bmatrix} \frac{5}{9} \\ \frac{4}{9} \end{bmatrix}$　　**7.** $\begin{bmatrix} \frac{2}{5} & \frac{3}{5} \end{bmatrix}$; $\begin{bmatrix} \frac{3}{5} \\ \frac{2}{5} \end{bmatrix}$

9. $\begin{bmatrix} \frac{7}{13} & \frac{6}{13} \end{bmatrix}$　　**11.** $\begin{bmatrix} \frac{1}{5} \\ \frac{4}{5} \end{bmatrix}$　　**13.** No, Carlos: $\begin{bmatrix} \frac{1}{3} \\ \frac{2}{3} \end{bmatrix}$, Renée: $\begin{bmatrix} \frac{1}{3} \\ \frac{2}{3} \end{bmatrix}$, $v = -\frac{1}{3}$　　**15. (a)** $\begin{bmatrix} \frac{8}{17} & \frac{9}{17} \end{bmatrix}$　　**(b)** $\begin{bmatrix} \frac{8}{17} \\ \frac{9}{17} \end{bmatrix}$

(c) about \$2765   **17.** $\begin{bmatrix} \frac{5}{8} & \frac{3}{8} & 0 \end{bmatrix}$; $\begin{bmatrix} \frac{1}{2} \\ \frac{1}{2} \end{bmatrix}$

Chapter 9: Supplementary Exercises, page 464

1. Strictly determined; R 3, C 3; 2   **2.** Not strictly determined   **3.** Not strictly determined   **4.** Strictly determined; R 1, C 2; 1   **5.** 7   **6.** 2   **7.** 1.4   **8.** -1.3 **9.** $\begin{bmatrix} \frac{4}{11} & \frac{7}{11} \end{bmatrix}$; $\begin{bmatrix} \frac{6}{11} \\ \frac{5}{11} \end{bmatrix}$ **10.** $\begin{bmatrix} \frac{8}{17} & \frac{9}{17} \end{bmatrix}$; $\begin{bmatrix} \frac{10}{17} \\ \frac{7}{17} \end{bmatrix}$ **11.** $\begin{bmatrix} 0 & 1 \end{bmatrix}$

12. $\begin{bmatrix} \frac{1}{4} \\ \frac{3}{4} \end{bmatrix}$ **13. (a)** Carol should play the two $\frac{9}{14}$ of the time and the six $\frac{5}{14}$ of the time. Ruth should play the

two $\frac{5}{14}$ of the time and the six $\frac{9}{14}$ of the time.   **(b)** Ruth   **14. (a)**

$$\begin{array}{c} \\ A \\ B \\ C \end{array} \begin{array}{ccc} S & A & W \\ \begin{bmatrix} 3000 & 2000 & 1000 \\ 6000 & 2000 & -3000 \\ 15{,}000 & 1000 & -10{,}000 \end{bmatrix} \end{array}$$

(b) Buy stock A   **15.** Consider the optimal strategies using the maxima/minima technique.   **16.** $h < 4$

Chapter 9: Chapter Test, page 465

1. (a) A move R_1 by R and C_3 by C results in a payoff of 6 to R.   **(b)** A move R_3 by R and C_2 by C results in a payoff of 10 to C.   **(c)** No   **3. (a)** row 3, column 2, value $= 2$ **(b)** row 1, column 1, value $= 0$

4.
$$\begin{array}{c} \\ 1 \\ 2 \\ 3 \\ 4 \\ 5 \end{array} \begin{array}{ccccc} 1 & 2 & 3 & 4 & 5 \\ \begin{bmatrix} -1 & -1 & -1 & -1 & -1 \\ 2 & -2 & -2 & -2 & -2 \\ 3 & 3 & -3 & -3 & -3 \\ 4 & 4 & 4 & -4 & -4 \\ 5 & 5 & 5 & 5 & -5 \end{bmatrix} \end{array}$$
; Yes; -1; C **5. (a)** On average, C gains .16 every time the game is played.

(b) $C = \begin{bmatrix} .4 \\ .1 \\ .5 \end{bmatrix}$ **6. (a)** $C = \begin{bmatrix} \frac{3}{5} \\ \frac{2}{5} \end{bmatrix}$; $R = \begin{bmatrix} \frac{9}{10} & \frac{1}{10} \end{bmatrix}$ **(b)** C

CHAPTER 10

Exercises 10.1, page 477

1. (a) $i = .01, n = 24$ **(b)** $i = .02, n = 20$ **(c)** $i = .05, n = 40$ **3. (a)** $i = .06, n = 4, P = \$500,$ $F = \$631.24$ **(b)** $i = .005, n = 120, P = \$800, F = \$1455.52$ **(c)** $i = .02, n = 19, P = \$6177.88, F = \$9000$ **5.** \$1127.16   **7.** \$22,396.57   **9.** \$7180.08; \$1180.08   **11.** \$34.19   **13.** \$10,000   **15. (a)** \$3548.74   **(b)** \$451.26

(c)

Month	Interest	Balance
0		\$3548.74
1	\$17.74	\$3566.48
2	\$17.83	\$3584.31
3	\$17.92	\$3602.23

17. \$12,824.32   **19.** \$8874.49   **21. (a)** 6%   **(b)** \$5.05; \$1015.08   **(c)** \$5.61; \$1127.16   **23.** \$1700 in 9 years   **25.** Better   **27.** \$8874.49   **29. (a)** $r = .04, n = \frac{1}{2}, P = \$500, F = \$510$ **(b)** $r = .05, n = 2,$ $P = \$500, F = \$550$ **31.** \$1150   **33.** \$2500   **35.** 4.08%   **37.** 10   **39.** 20 years   **41.** $P = \dfrac{F}{1 + nr}$ **43.** a   **45.** \$104.06; 4.06%   **47.** 4.04%   **49.** 4.49%   **51.** 4%   **53.** 18 yrs.   **55.** d   **57.** $\approx 4.9\%$ **59.** 4.6   **61.** \$1065; \$1134.23; \$1207.95; 8; 12   **63.** 30 years   **65.** 11

Exercises 10.2, page 487

1. (a) $i = .005, n = 120, R = \$50, F = \$8193.97$ **(b)** $i = .02, n = 20, R = \$8231.34, F = \$200,000$

3. $23,123.67 **5.** $4698.97 **7. (a)** $27,048.92 **(b)** $3048.92 **(c)**

Month	Interest	Balance
1		500
2	2.50	1002.50
3	5.01	1507.51

9. $305.06; $10,982.16, $1017.84 **11.** $200 each month; $343.75 **13.** $24,649.92 **15.** $2.5 billion **17.** No; $277,151.11 **19.** $43,839.83 **21.** $877.91 **23.** $1000 at the end of each month **25.** $7239.32 **27.** $17,584.62 **29.** $1800 **31.** a **33.** $24,000 **35.** $4339.35 **37.** $591,898.46 **39.** $5600.40 **41. (a)** $1269.67 **(b)** $65,134.88 **43.** $B_{\text{new}} = (1+i)B_{\text{previous}} - R$ **45.** $2050, $3152.50, $4310.13; 19; 26 **47.** After 33 weeks **49.** $4734.59

Exercises 10.3, page 496

1. $193.33 **3.** $11,469.92 **5. (a)** $583.31 **(b)** $16.69 **(c)** $58,314.31 **(d)** $26,973.02 **(e)** $4188.65 **(f)** $269.73 **7. (a)** $265.71 **(b)** $9565.56 **(c)** $1565.56 **(d)** $5644.58 **(e)** $2990.59 **(f)** $534.53

(g)

Payment number	Amount	Interest	Applied to principal	Unpaid balance
1	$265.71	$80.00	$185.71	$7814.29
2	265.71	78.14	187.57	7626.72
3	265.71	76.27	189.44	7437.28
4	265.71	74.37	191.34	7245.94

9. $8950 **11.** $14,042.36

13.

Payment number	Amount	Interest	Applied to principal	Unpaid balance
1	$256.28	$10.00	$246.28	$753.72
2	256.28	7.54	248.74	504.98
3	256.28	5.05	251.23	253.74
4	256.28	2.54	253.74	0.00

15. $1856.92 **17.** $119,161.62 **19.** $1196.68 **21.** a **23. (a)** $183,927.96 **(b)** $24,989.92 **(c)** $105,266.63 **25. (a)** $722.22 **(b)** $760.55 **(c)** a **27.** 26.56% **29.** $346.81 **31. (d)** $101, $102.01 **33.** $2105.33, $2021.12, $1936.28, 24 months **35.** $4258.21; after 46 months **37.** 261 **39. (a)** $871.11 **(b)** $869.69 **(c)** b

Exercises 10.4, page 513

1. deferred **3.** $165,000 **5.** $1,641,407.11 **7.** $1,641,407.11 **9. (a)** $412,330.96 **(b)** $357,362.60 **(c)** Larry **(d)** Earl **11.** $366.67 **13.** $105.83 **15.** 2.73% **17.** 3.17% **19. (a)** $41.67 **(b)** $41.07; the monthly payment is less. **21.** False **23.** False **25.** False **27.** d **29.** a **31.** a **33.** c **35.** 12*RATE(240, -573.14, 77600, 0); 12*RATE(120, -573.14, 77600, -51624.70)
37. $(((1+i)^{180} - 1)/(i(1+i)^{180})) \cdot 1217.12 = 118800; 1217.12 - i \cdot 96081.51 = (1217.12 - i \cdot 118800)(1+i)^{60}$
39. The salesman should compare the present value of the loan payments with the $1000. **41.** $1150; $2311.87 **43. (a)** $1610.75 **(b)** $224,829.73 **(c)** $1729.63 **45. (a)** $219,418.04 **(b)** $2181.80 **(c)** $1850.70 **(d)** $1865.05 **(e)** $219,432.39 **47.** 11.08% **49.** 6.83% **51.** 7.08% **53.** 87.72 months **55.** 128.63 months

Chapter 10: Supplementary Exercises, page 518

1. (d) **2.** $1464.49 **3.** $101,497 **4.** $53.79 **5.** 10% compounded annually **6.** $13,954.01 **7. (a)** $2400.34 **(b)** $167,304.95 **8.** $43,665.52 **9.** $27,481.64 **10.** $13,050.08 **11.** $211.37 **12.** $12,050.34 **13.** $782.92 **14.** $6872.11 **15.** $100,451.50 **16.** $139,401.04 **17.** Investment A **18.** Yes, it is a bargain since the present value is $879.57. **19.** 10.25% **20.** 19.56% **21.** $146,861.85

22.

Payment number	Amount	Interest	Applied to principal	Unpaid balance
1	$304.22	$50.00	$254.22	$9745.78
2	304.22	48.73	255.49	9490.29
3	304.22	47.45	256.77	9233.52
4	304.22	46.17	258.05	8975.47
5	304.22	44.88	259.34	8716.13
6	304.22	43.58	260.64	8455.49

23. $151,843.34 **24.** $5799.84 **25.** $1206.93
26. (a) $21,000 **(b)** $26,095.40
27. (a) $30,000 **(b)** $40,146.77 **28.** 4.82%
29. Consumer Loan A, The monthly payment for loan B is $265.00. **30.** $P = 88,200,$
$n = 180, R = 759.47$ **31.** $P = 97,000, m = 72,$
$R = 716.43; B = 81,298.32$ **32.** $i = .035/12,$
$R = 63.15, P = 2000$ **35.** $2185; $3394.34

36. (a) $1458.08 **(b)** $198,690.34 **(c)** $1582.46 **37.** Higher **38.** No **39.** No **40.** Decrease; increase

Chapter 10: Chapter Test, page 520

1. $524.38 **2.** $4464.29 **3.** $1189.77; $164.77 **4.** $11,263.09 **5.** $72,704.68 **6.** $21,290.16 **7.** $1095.92
8. $2533.52 **9.** $3086.04 **10.** $2187.43 **11. (a)** $166.07 **(b)** $60 **(c)** $7893.93 **(d)** $1899.00
12. $225,686.46 **13. (a)** $405,610.82 **(b)** $368,198.99 **14.** $144.44 **16. (a)** It will decrease because the cost of the points will be spread over a longer period of time. **(b)** Increasing the number of points will increase the effective cost of the loan, therefore, increasing its interest rate. **17.** If there are no points, or the mortgage is not terminated early. **18.** $3250; $4120.18

CHAPTER 11

Exercises 11.1, page 531

1. 4, −6; 2 **3.** $-\frac{1}{2}, 0; 0$ **5.** $-\frac{2}{3}, 15; 9$

7. (a) 10, 4, 1, $-\frac{1}{2}, -\frac{5}{4}$ **(b)** **(c)** $y_n = -2 + 12\left(\frac{1}{2}\right)^n$

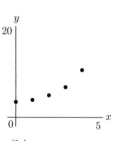

9. (a) 3.5, 4, 5, 7, 11 **(b)** **(c)** $y_n = 3 + (.5)2^n$

11. (a) 17.5, 0, 7, 4.2, 5.32 **(b)** **(c)** $y_n = 5 + 12.5(-.4)^n$

13. (a) 15, 14, 12, 8, 0   **(b)**

(c) $y_n = 16 - 2^n$ **15.** 1, 5, 5.8, 5.96, 5.992

17. $y_n = 1.05y_{n-1}, y_0 = 1000$

19. $y_n = .99y_{n-1} - 1{,}000{,}000,\ y_0 = 70{,}000{,}000$

21. (a) 1, 3, 5, 7, 9   **(b)** The points lie on a straight line.   **(c)** $a = 1$, so the denominator of $\frac{b}{1-a}$ is zero.   **23.** \$30

25. (a) $y_n = 1.04y_{n-1} + 250;\ y_0 = 800$ **(b)** $y_n = -6250 + 7050(1.04)^n$ **(c)** about \$3027.32

27. (a) $y_n = .85y_{n-1},\ y_0 = 20{,}000$ **(b)** $y_n = 20{,}000(.85)^n$ **(c)** \$8,874.11

29. (a)

   (b)

   (c) 50.41; 22   **31. (a)**

(b)

   (c) 5.715516; $n \geq 19$ **33. (a)**

   (b)

(c) 4.831059; $n \geq 20$

Exercises 11.2, page 537

1. $y_n = 1 + 5n$ **3.** $80(1.0075)^{60}$ **5.** $80\left(1 + \frac{1}{365}\right)^{1825}$ **7.** 108   **9. (a)** \$1.40   **(b)** \$1.44   **(c)** \$1.46

11. (a) 10, 10, 10, 10, 10; points lie on a horizontal line   **(b)** 11, 12, 14, 18, 26; points curve upward   **(c)** 9, 8, 6, 2, -6; points curve downward   **13.** $y_n = 5 + 2(.4)^n$; y_n approaches 5   **15.** $y_n = 2(-5)^n$; y_n gets arbitrarily large, alternating between being positive and negative.   **17.** $y_n = 1.0055y_{n-1} - 1600,\ y_0 = 250{,}525$

19. $y_n = y_{n-1} - 2000,\ y_0 = 50{,}000;\ y_n = 50{,}000 - 2000n$ **21.** b   **23.** c   **25.** c   **27.** c   **29.** \$1195.62; $8\frac{1}{2}$ years; 47   **31.** \$245; 12 years; 23   **33.** 22   **35.** 60

Exercises 11.3, page 546

1. a, b, d, f, h

3. b, d, e, f

5. b, d, e, f

7. a, c, h, possibly g

9. Possible answer:

11. Possible answer:

13. Possible answer:

15.

17.

19.

21.

23.

25. less than \$60,000   **27. (a)** $y_n = 1.06y_{n-1} - 120$ **(b)** at least \$2000
29. less than \$30,000   **31.** Possible answer: $y_n = .5y_{n-1} + 4$, $y_0 = 1$
33. Possible answer: $y_n = 2y_{n-1}$, $y_0 = 1$
35. Possible answer: $y_n = -2y_{n-1}$, $y_0 = 5$

Exercises 11.4, page 552

1. $y_n = 1.0075y_{n-1} - 261.50$, $y_0 = 32,500$ **3.** $y_n = 1.015y_{n-1} + 200$, $y_0 = 4000$ **5.** \$46,002.34   **7.** \$11,035.68
9. \$28.55   **11.** \$132.86   **13.** \$39.205 million; 30   **15.** \$505.03; \$1022.80; \$1553.65; 30; 37

Exercises 11.5, page 556

1. $y_n = 1.02y_{n-1}$, $y_0 = 100$ million   **3.** $y_n = .75y_{n-1}$

5. $y_n = .92y_{n-1} + 8$, $y_0 = 0$

7. $y_n = .7y_{n-1} + 3.6$, $y_0 = 0$

9. $y_n = 1.05y_{n-1} - 1000$, $y_0 = 30,000$

11. $y_n = .8y_{n-1} + 14$, $y_0 = 40$

13. $p_n = -.5p_{n-1} + 21$, $p_0 = 4.54$ **15.** b   **17.** 5.38 million; 2022; 2056   **19.** $y_n = .87y_{n-1}$, $y_0 = 130$;

$y_n = 130(.87)^n$; 5 hours; 4.6 mg

Chapter 11: Supplementary Exercises, page 560

1. (a) 5; −7; 29   **(b)** $y_n = 2 - (-3)^n$ **(c)** −79   **2. (a)** $\frac{17}{2}$; 7; $\frac{11}{2}$ **(b)** $y_n = 10 - \frac{3}{2}n$ **(c)** 1   **3.** \$2000.00
4. \$1109.54   **5.**   **6.**

7. (a) $y_n = 1.03y_{n-1} - 600$, $y_0 = 120,000$
(b) 200,611   **8. (a)** $y_n = 1.01y_{n-1} - 360$,
$y_0 = 35,000$ **(b)** \$33,693.28   **9.** \$20.22
10. \$237.14   **11.** \$22,492.53   **12.** \$2,704.89

13. $y_n = .9y_{n-1} + 100,000, y_0 = 0$ **14.** $y_n = .92y_{n-1}, y_0 = 100$

Chapter 11: Chapter Test, page 561

1. (a) 2, 4, 5   **(b)** $y_n = 6 - 8\left(\frac{1}{2}\right)^n$ **(c)** 5.5   **2. (a)** 110, 160, 210   **(b)** $y_n = 60 + 50n$ **(c)** 260
3. (a)   **(b)**   **4.** .3 ppm   **5. (a)** \$31,726   **(b)** 8%
(c) \$3000   **(d)** \$29,360.52
6. (a) \$454.15   **(b)** 12.5%
(c) \$9,245.85; \$8,526.44; \$361.57
7. \$119,161.62
8. (a) $y_n = 1.06y_{n-1} + 500; y_0 = 0$
(b) \$14,106.44   **9.** \$122.04

10. $y_n = .9y_{n-1} + .05; y_0 = 0$. The graph begins at the origin, increases monotonically, and approaches the line $y = .5$.

CHAPTER 12

Exercises 12.1, page 567

1. Statement   **3.** Statement   **5.** Not a statement   **7.** Not a statement   **9.** Statement   **11.** Not a statement
13. Not a statement   **15.** Statement   **17.** p: The Phelps Library is in New York.
q: The Phelps Library is in Dallas.
$p \vee q$
19. p: The Smithsonian Museum of Natural History has displays of rocks.
q: The Smithsonian Museum of Natural History has displays of bugs.
$p \wedge q$
21. p: Amtrak trains go to Chicago.
q: Amtrak trains go to Cincinnati.
$\sim p \wedge \sim q$ or $\sim(p \vee q)$
23. (a) Ozone is opaque to ultraviolet light, and life on earth requires ozone.   **(b)** Ozone is not opaque to ultraviolet light, or life on earth requires ozone.   **(c)** Ozone is not opaque to ultraviolet light, or life on earth does not require ozone.   **(d)** It is not the case that life on earth does not require ozone.   **25. (a)** $p \vee q$
(b) $p \wedge \sim q$ **(c)** $q \wedge \sim p$ **(d)** $\sim p \wedge \sim q$

Exercises 12.2, page 575

5.

p	q	$p \wedge \sim q$
T	T	**F** F
T	F	**T** T
F	T	**F** F
F	F	**F** T

7.

p	q	$(p \vee \sim q)$	$\vee$	$\sim p$
T	T	T F	**T**	F
T	F	T T	**T**	F
F	T	F F	**T**	T
F	F	T T	**T**	T

9.

p	q	$\sim$	$((p \vee q)$	$\wedge$	$(p \wedge q))$
T	T	**F**	T	T	T
T	F	**T**	T	F	F
F	T	**T**	T	F	F
F	F	**T**	F	F	F

11.

p	q	p ⊕ (~p ∨ q)
T	T	T**F** F T T
T	F	T**T** F F F
F	T	F**T** T T T
F	F	F**T** T T F

13.

p	q	r	(p ∧ ~r) ∨ q
T	T	T	T
T	T	F	T
T	F	T	F
T	F	F	T
F	T	T	T
F	T	F	T
F	F	T	F
F	F	F	F

15.

p	q	r	~[(p ∧ r) ∨ q]
T	T	T	F
T	T	F	F
T	F	T	F
T	F	F	T
F	T	T	F
F	T	F	F
F	F	T	T
F	F	F	T

17.

p	p ∨ ~p
T	T
F	T

19.

p	q	r	p ⊕ (q ∨ r)
T	T	T	F
T	T	F	F
T	F	T	F
T	F	F	T
F	T	T	T
F	T	F	T
F	F	T	T
F	F	F	F

21.

p	q	r	(p ∨ q) ∧ (p ∨ r)
T	T	T	T
T	T	F	T
T	F	T	T
T	F	F	T
F	T	T	T
F	T	F	F
F	F	T	F
F	F	F	F

23.

p	q	(p ∨ q) ∧ ~(p ∨ q)
T	T	F
T	F	F
F	T	F
F	F	F

25.

p	q	r	~(p ∨ q) ∧ r
T	T	T	F
T	T	F	F
T	F	T	F
T	F	F	F
F	T	T	F
F	T	F	F
F	F	T	T
F	F	F	F

27.

p	q	r	~p ∨ (q ∧ r)
T	T	T	T
T	T	F	F
T	F	T	F
T	F	F	F
F	T	T	T
F	T	F	T
F	F	T	T
F	F	F	T

29. They are identical.   **31.** They are identical.   **33.** (p ∧ q) ∨ r is T and p ∧ (q ∨ r) is F when p is F and r is T. Otherwise, the tables are identical.   **35. (a)**

p	p|p
T	F
F	T

(b)

p	q	(p|p)|(q|q)
T	T	T
T	F	T
F	T	T
F	F	F

(c)

p	q	(p|q)|(p|q)
T	T	T
T	F	F
F	T	F
F	F	F

(d)

p	q	p|((p|q)|q)
T	T	F
T	F	F
F	T	T
F	F	T

37. (a) T   **(b)** F   **(c)** T   **(d)** F   **(e)** F   **(f)** F   **39. (a)** F   **(b)** F   **(c)** F

(d) F   **41.**   **43.**   **45.** 0   **47. (a)** T   **(b)** T   **49. (a)** T   **(b)** F

51.

Exercises 12.3, page 582

1.

p	q	$p \to \sim q$
T	T	F
T	F	T
F	T	T
F	F	T

3.

p	q	$(p \oplus q) \to q$
T	T	T
T	F	F
F	T	T
F	F	T

5.

p	q	r	$(\sim p \wedge q) \to r$
T	T	T	T
T	T	F	T
T	F	T	T
T	F	F	T
F	T	T	T
F	T	F	F
F	F	T	T
F	F	F	T

7.

p	q	$(p \to q) \leftrightarrow (\sim p \vee q)$
T	T	T
T	F	T
F	T	T
F	F	T

9.

p	q	r	$(p \to q) \to r$
T	T	T	T
T	T	F	F
T	F	T	T
T	F	F	T
F	T	T	T
F	T	F	F
F	F	T	T
F	F	F	F

11.

p	q	r	$\sim(p \vee q) \to (\sim p \wedge r)$
T	T	T	T
T	T	F	T
T	F	T	T
T	F	F	T
F	T	T	T
F	T	F	T
F	F	T	T
F	F	F	F

13.

p	q	$(p \vee q) \leftrightarrow (p \wedge q)$
T	T	T
T	F	F
F	T	F
F	F	T

15.

p	q	r	$[p \wedge (q \vee r)] \leftrightarrow [(p \wedge q) \vee (p \wedge r)]$
T	T	T	T
T	T	F	T
T	F	T	T
T	F	F	T
F	T	T	T
F	T	F	T
F	F	T	T
F	F	F	T

17. $((\sim p) \wedge (\sim q)) \to ((\sim p) \wedge q)$ **19.** $(((\sim p) \wedge (\sim q)) \vee r) \to ((\sim q) \wedge r)$ **21.** T **23.** T **25.** T **27.** F **29.** T
31. $p \leftrightarrow q$ **33.** $q \to p$; hyp: q; con: p **35.** $q \to p$; hyp: q; con: p **37.** $\sim p \to \sim q$; hyp: $\sim p$; con: $\sim q$
39. $\sim p \to \sim q$; hyp: $\sim p$; con: $\sim q$; TRUE **41.** $\sim q \to \sim p$; hyp: $\sim q$; con: $\sim p$; TRUE **43. (a)** hyp: A person is
healthy. con: The person lives a long life. **(b)** hyp: The train stops at the station. con: A passenger requests
the stop. **(c)** hyp: The azalea grows. con: The azalea is exposed to sunlight. **(d)** hyp: I will go to the
store. con: Jane goes to the store. **45. (a)** If City Sanitation collects the garbage, then the mayor calls.
(b) The price of beans goes down if there is no drought. **(c)** Goldfish swim in Lake Erie if Lake Erie is fresh
water. **(d)** Tap water is not salted if it boils slowly. **47. (a)** 4 **(b)** 4 **(c)** 4 **(d)** 4 **(e)** 6 **(f)** 6
49. (a) 7 **(b)** 7 **(c)** 0 **(d)** 7 **(e)** 0 **(f)** 0 **51. (a)** 6 **(b)** -12 **(c)** 0 **(d)** 0 **(e)** 28 **(f)** 0
53. (a) 3 **(b)** 3 **(c)** -37 **(d)** -7 **(e)** 43 **(f)** -7

Exercises 12.4, page 590

5. (d) $p|(q|q)$ **(e)** $\sim(p \wedge q)$ **7.**

p	q	c	$(p \to q) \leftrightarrow [(p \wedge \sim q) \to c]$
T	T	F	T
T	F	F	T
F	T	F	T
F	F	F	T

9. False

11. $\sim[\sim(p \vee q) \vee \sim(\sim p \vee \sim q)]$ **13.** $\sim(p \vee q) \vee (q \wedge \sim r)$ **15.** $(p \wedge \sim q) \vee (p \vee \sim r)$ **17. (a)** Arizona does not
border California, or Arizona does not border Nevada. **(b)** There are no tickets available, and the agency
cannot get tickets. **(c)** The killer's hat was neither white nor gray. **19.** $\sim p \wedge q \wedge \sim r$ **21. (a)** Jeremy does
not take 12 credits and Jeremy does not take 15 credits this semester. **(b)** Sandra did not receive a gift from

Sally or Sandra did not receive a gift from Sacha.   **23. (a)** "The Old Man and the Sea" was written by Ernest Hemingway or "The Old Man and the Sea" was written by Jack London. "The Old Man and the Sea" was not written by Ernest Hemingway and not written by Jack London.   **(b)** "H. M. S. Pinafore" was written by Gilbert and "H. M. S. Pinafore" was written by Sullivan. "H. M. S. Pinafore" was not written by Gilbert or not written by Sullivan.   **25. (a)** I have a ticket to the theater, and I did not spend a lot of money. **(b)** Basketball is played on an indoor court, and the players do not wear sneakers.   **(c)** The stock market is going up, and interest rates are not going down.   **(d)** Humans have enough water, and humans are not staying healthy.   **27. (a)** If the number of odd numbers in a sum is even, then the sum is even. (T)   **(b)** If K is next to W, then the computer keyboard is not standard. (T)   **29. (a)** Contrapositive: If a bird is not a hummingbird, then it is not small. (F) Converse: If a bird is a hummingbird, then it is small. (T) **(b)** Contrapositive: If two nonvertical lines are not parallel, they do not have the same slope. (T) Converse: If two nonvertical lines are parallel, they have the same slope. (T)   **(c)** Contrapositive: If we are not in France, then we are not in Paris. (T) Converse: If we are in France, we must be in Paris. (F)   **(d)** Contrapositive: If you can legally make a U-turn, then the road is not one-way. (T) Converse: If you cannot legally make a U-turn, then the road is one-way. (F)   **31.** Ask either guard, "If I asked you whether your door was the door to freedom, would you say yes?"   **33.**

p	q	r	$(p \to q)$	$\wedge$	$(q \to r)$	$\implies$	$(p \to r)$
T	T	T	T	T	T	**T**	T
T	T	F	T	F	F	**T**	F
T	F	T	F	F	T	**T**	T
T	F	F	F	F	T	**T**	F
F	T	T	T	T	T	**T**	T
F	T	F	T	F	F	**T**	T
F	F	T	T	T	T	**T**	T
F	F	F	T	T	T	**T**	T

Exercises 12.5, page 597

1. $m = $ "Sue goes to the movies."
$r = $ "Sue reads."

1. $m \vee r$	hyp.
2. $\sim m$	hyp.
3. r	disj. syll. (1, 2)

3. $a = $ "My allowance comes this week."
$p = $ "I pay the rent."
$b = $ "My bank account will be in the black."
$e = $ "I will be evicted."

1. $(a \wedge p) \to b$	hyp.
2. $\sim p \to e$	hyp.
3. $\sim e \wedge a$	hyp.
4. $\sim e$	subtr. (3)
5. p	mod. tollens (2, 4)
6. a	subtr. (3)
7. b	mod. ponens (5, 6, 1)

5. $p = $ "The price of oil increases."
$a = $ "The OPEC countries are in agreement."
$d = $ "There is a U.N. debate."

1. $p \to a$	hyp.
2. $\sim d \to p$	hyp.
3. $\sim a$	hyp.
4. $\sim p$	mod. tollens (1, 3)
5. d	mod. tollens (2, 4)

7. $g = $ "The germ is present."
$r = $ "The rash is present."
$f = $ "The fever is present."

1. $g \to (r \wedge f)$	hyp.
2. f	hyp.
3. $\sim r$	hyp.
4. $\sim r \vee \sim f$	addition (3)
5. $\sim (r \wedge f)$	De Morgan (4)
6. $\sim g$	mod. tollens (1, 5)

9. $c =$ "The material is cotton."
$r =$ "The material is rayon."
$d =$ "The material can be made into a dress."

1.	$(c \lor r) \to d$	hyp.
2.	$\sim d$	hyp.
3.	$\sim (c \lor r)$	mod. tollens (1, 2)
4.	$\sim c \land \sim r$	De Morgan (3)
5.	$\sim r$	subtraction (4)

11. Invalid   **13.** Valid   **15.** Valid   **17.** Invalid   **19.** Invalid

21. $s =$ "Sam goes to the store."
$m =$ "Sam needs milk."
$H_1 = s \to m$
$H_2 = \sim m$
$C = \sim s$

1.	s	$\sim C$
2.	$s \to m$	H_1
3.	m	$\sim H_2$; mod. ponens (1, 2)

23. $n =$ "The newspaper reports the crime."
$t =$ "Television reports the crime."
$s =$ "The crime is serious."
$k =$ "A person is killed."
$H_1 = (n \land t) \to s$
$H_2 = k \to n$
$H_3 = k$
$H_4 = t$
$C = s$

1.	$\sim s$	$\sim C$
2.	$(n \land t) \to s$	H_1
3.	$\sim (n \land t)$	mod. tollens (1, 2)
4.	$\sim n \lor \sim t$	De Morgan (3)
5.	t	H_4
6.	$\sim n$	disj. syllogism (4, 5)
7.	$k \to n$	H_2
8.	$\sim k$	$\sim H_3$; mod. tollens (6, 7)

25. $j =$ "Jimmy finds his keys."
$h =$ "He does his homework."

Direct proof

1.	$\sim j \to h$	H_1
2.	$\sim h$	H_2
3.	j	mod. tollens (1, 2)

Indirect proof

1.	$\sim j$	$\sim C$
2.	$\sim j \to h$	H_1
3.	h	mod. ponens (1, 2)
4.	$\sim h$	H_2

$\left. \right\}$ contradiction

27. $m =$ "Marissa goes to the movies."
$k =$ "Marissa is in a knitting class."
$i =$ "Marissa is idle."

1.	$\sim m \to \sim i$	H_1
2.	$\sim k \to i$	H_2
3.	$\sim k$	H_3
4.	i	mod. ponens (2, 3)
5.	m	mod. tollens (1, 4)

Exercises 12.6, page 605

1. (a) F   (b) T   (c) T   (d) T   (e) F   **3.** (a) $\forall x \, p(x)$ (b) $\sim [\forall x \, p(x)]$ (c) $\forall x \sim p(x)$ (d) (c) implies (b)   **5.** $\forall x \sim p(x)$, or $\sim [\exists x \, p(x)]$. This is FALSE. Abby meant to say, "Not all men cheat on their wives."   **7.** (a) $\forall x \, p(x)$ (b) $\exists x \sim p(x)$ (c) $\exists x \, p(x)$ (d) $\sim [\forall x \, p(x)]$ (e) $\forall x \sim p(x)$ (f) $\sim [\exists x \, p(x)]$ (g) (b) and (d); (e) and (f)   **9.** (a) T   (b) F   **11.** (a) T   (b) F   (c) T   (d) F   (e) F   (f) T (g) F   (h) T   **13.** (a) Not every dog has his day.   (b) No men fight wars.   (c) Some mothers are unmarried.   (d) There exists a pot without a cover.   (e) All children have pets.   (f) Every month has 30 days.   **15.** (a) "The sum of any two nonnegative integers is greater than 12." FALSE: let $x = 1$, $y = 2$. "There exist two nonnegative integers whose sum is not greater than 12."   (b) "For any nonnegative integer, there is another nonnegative integer that, added to the first, makes a sum greater than 12." TRUE.   (c) "There is a nonnegative integer that, added to any other nonnegative integer, makes a sum greater than 12." TRUE. (d) "There are two nonnegative integers the sum of which is greater than 12." TRUE.   **17.** (a) FALSE: let $x = 2, y = 3$.   (b) TRUE: for any x, let $y = x$.   (c) TRUE: let $x = 1$.   (d) FALSE: no y is divisible by every x.   (e) TRUE: for any y, let $x = y$.   (f) TRUE: any x divides itself.   **19.** (a) $\forall x [x \geq 8 \to x \leq 10]$ (b) No; consider $x = 11$.   **21.** $S = \{2, 4, 6, 8\}, T = \{1, 2, 3, 4, 6, 8\}$. So $\forall x [x \in S \to x \in T]$.

23. The solutions to $(x-8)(x-3)=0$ are 8 and 3. The solutions to $x^2 = 9$ are -3 and 3. Therefore, $S = T = \{3\}$. So, $\forall x(x \in S \leftrightarrow x \in T)$.

Exercises 12.7, page 610

1. $(p \vee q) \wedge (p \vee \sim q)$ **3.** $((p \wedge q) \wedge \sim r) \wedge (\sim q \vee r)$ **5.** p ___ ; 1

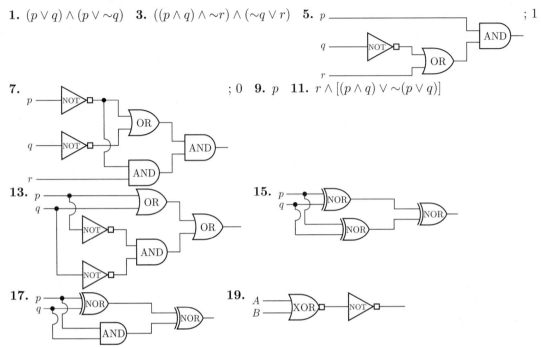

7.

; 0   **9.** p **11.** $r \wedge [(p \wedge q) \vee \sim (p \vee q)]$

13.

15.

17.

19.

Chapter 12: Supplementary Exercises, page 614

1. (a) Statement   **(b)** Not a statement   **(c)** Statement   **(d)** Not a statement   **(e)** Statement   **2. (a)** If two lines are perpendicular, then their slopes are negative reciprocals of each other.   **(b)** If goldfish can live in a fishbowl, then the water is aerated.   **(c)** If it rains, then Jane uses her umbrella.   **(d)** If Sally gives Morris a treat, then he ate all his food.   **3. (a)** Contrapositive: If the Yankees are not playing in Yankee Stadium, then they are not in New York City; Converse: If the Yankees are playing in Yankee Stadium, then they are in New York City.   **(b)** Contrapositive: If the earthquake is not considered major, then the Richter scale does not indicate the quake is a 7; Converse: If the earthquake is considered major, then the Richter scale indicates the quake is a 7.   **(c)** Contrapositive: If the coat is not warm, then it is not made of fur; Converse: If the coat is warm, then it is made of fur.   **(d)** Contrapositive: If Jane is not in Moscow, then she is not in Russia; Converse: If Jane is in Moscow, then she is in Russia.   **4. (a)** Two triangles are similar but their sides are unequal.   **(b)** For every real number $x, x^2 \neq 5$.   **(c)** There exists a positive integer n such that n is even and n^2 is not even.   **(d)** For every real number $x, x^2 + 4 \neq 0$.   **5. (a)** Tautology   **(b)** Tautology   **(c)** Not a tautology   **(d)** Not a tautology   **6. (a)**

p	q	r	$p \to (\sim q \vee r)$
T	T	T	T
T	T	F	F
T	F	T	T
T	F	F	T
F	T	T	T
F	T	F	T
F	F	T	T
F	F	F	T

(b)

p	q	r	$p \wedge (q \leftrightarrow (r \wedge p))$
T	T	T	T
T	T	F	F
T	F	T	F
T	F	F	T
F	T	T	F
F	T	F	F
F	F	T	F
F	F	F	F

7. (a) True   **(b)** False   **8. (a)** True   **(b)** False   **9. (a)** False   **(b)** True   **10. (a)** 17   **(b)** 100
(c) 100   **(d)** 100   **11. (a)** 50   **(b)** -25 **(c)** -15 **(d)** 10   **12. (a)** Cannot be determined   **(b)** TRUE

(c) TRUE   (d) Cannot be determined   (e) Cannot be determined   **13. (a)** Cannot be determined
(b) Cannot be determined   **(c)** TRUE   **14. (a)** TRUE   **(b)** FALSE   **(c)** TRUE   **15. (a)** Cannot be
determined   **(b)** Cannot be determined   **(c)** TRUE

16. t = "Taxes go up."
s = "I sell the house."
m = "I move to India."

1. $t \to (s \wedge m)$ hyp.
2. $\sim m$ hyp.
3. $\sim s \vee \sim m$ addition (2)
4. $\sim (s \wedge m)$ De Morgan (3)
5. $\sim t$ mod. tollens (1, 4)

17. m = "I study mathematics."
b = "I study business."
p = "I can write poetry."

1. $m \wedge b$ hyp.
2. $b \to (\sim p \vee \sim m)$ hyp.
3. b subtraction (1)
4. $\sim p \vee \sim m$ mod. ponens (2, 3)
5. m subtraction (1)
6. $\sim p$ disj. syllogism (4, 5)

18. d = "I shop for a dress."
h = "I wear high heels."
s = "I have a sore foot."

1. $d \to h$ hyp.
2. $s \to \sim h$ hyp.
3. d hyp.
4. h mod. ponens (1, 3)
5. $\sim s$ mod. tollens (2, 4)

19. a = "Asters grow in the garden."
d = "Dahlias grow in the garden."
s = "It is spring."

1. $a \vee d$ hyp.
2. $s \to \sim a$ hyp.
3. s hyp.
4. $\sim a$ mod. ponens (2, 3)
5. d disj. syllogism (1, 4)

20. t = "The professor gives a test."
h = "Nancy studies hard."
d = "Nancy has a date."
s = "Nancy takes a shower."
$H_1 = t \to h$
$H_2 = d \to s$
$H_3 = \sim t \to \sim s$
$H_4 = d$
$C = h$

1. $\sim h$ $\sim C$
2. $t \to h$ H_1
3. $\sim t$ mod. tollens (1, 2)
4. $\sim t \to \sim s$ H_3
5. $\sim s$ mod. ponens (3, 4)
6. $d \to s$ H_2
7. $\sim d$ $\sim H_4$; mod tollens (5, 6)

21.   ; 0

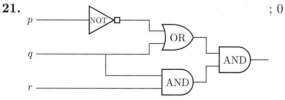

22. $p \wedge \sim q \wedge r$ **23.** $(p \text{ NOR } q) \text{ NOR } (p \text{ AND } q)$

24.

25. *p*

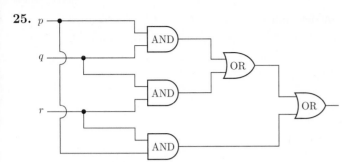

Chapter 12: Chapter Test, page 615

1.

p	*q*	$(p \wedge \sim q) \to q$
T	T	T
T	F	F
F	T	T
F	F	T

2. (a) Statement   **(b)** Not a Statement   **(c)** Statement   **(d)** Statement
(e) Not a Statement   **3.** If the coach does not buy Bob ice cream, then Bob did not hit a triple or a home run.
4. Every integer is either even or greater than 8.   **5.** False; True   **6. (a)** Neither   **(b)** Tautology
(c) Contradiction   **7. (a)** True   **(b)** False   **(c)** True   **(d)** False   **8.** The argument is valid.
9. (a) Every English dictionary contains the word "Internet."   **(b)** There is a student at the university who
does not listen to jazz.   **(c)** There is a floor at which the elevator does not stop.   **10. (a)** $p \to q$
(b) $q \to p$ **(c)** $p \to q$ **(d)** $p \to q$ **(e)** $q \to p$ **11. (a)** -19 **(b)** 0   **(c)** 180   **(d)** 0   **12. (a)** False
(b) True   **13.** *p*   **14.**   ; 0

INDEX

Index of Applications